I0031687

INDO-CHINA

Prepared by the British Naval Intelligence Division of the Admiralty during World War II and released in 1943, this handbook is now an important geographical and historical reference work, documenting the region's environment and natural resources as they were before the developments of recent decades, and describing traditional culture, infrastructure, administration and the extent of foreign influence as it then was. It covers the areas of the present-day countries of Cambodia, Vietnam and Laos. Unrivalled in the scope and the quality of information current at the time of first publication, this volume is an essential foundation for all researchers and students interested in the history and background to the contemporary dynamics of the region.

GEOGRAPHICAL HANDBOOK SERIES

IRAQ AND THE PERSIAN GULF • *Naval Intelligence Division*

WESTERN ARABIA AND THE RED SEA • *Naval Intelligence Division*

INDO-CHINA • *Naval Intelligence Division*

INDO-CHINA

NAVAL INTELLIGENCE DIVISION

Routledge
Taylor & Francis Group

LONDON AND NEW YORK

First published 2006 by Kegan Paul International

2 Park Square, Milton Park, Abingdon, Oxon OX14 4RN
711 Third Avenue, New York, NY 10017, USA

Routledge is an imprint of the Taylor & Francis Group, an informa business

First issued in paperback 2016

Copyright © Kegan Paul, 2006

Transferred to Digital Printing 2010

All rights reserved. No part of this book may be reprinted or reproduced or
utilised in any form or by any electronic, mechanical, or other means, now
known or hereafter invented, including photocopying and recording, or in any
information storage or retrieval system, without permission in writing from
the publishers.

Notice:
Product or corporate names may be trademarks or registered trademarks, and
are used only for identification and explanation without intent to infringe.

British Library Cataloguing in Publication Data
A catalogue record for this book is available from the British Library

ISBN 13: 978-0-7103-1027-9 (hbk)
ISBN 13: 978-1-138-97261-2 (pbk)

Publisher's Note
The publisher has gone to great lengths to ensure the quality of this reprint
but points out that some imperfections in the original copies may be
apparent. The publisher has made every effort to contact original copyright
holders and would welcome correspondence from those they have been
unable to trace.

PREFACE

IN 1915 a Geographical Section was formed in the Naval Intelligence Division of the Admiralty to write Geographical Handbooks on various parts of the world. The purpose of these handbooks was to supply, by scientific research and skilled arrangement, material for the discussion of naval, military, and political problems, as distinct from the examination of the problems themselves. Many distinguished collaborators assisted in their production, and by the end of 1918 upwards of fifty volumes had been produced in Handbook and Manual form, as well as numerous short-term geographical reports. The demand for these books increased rapidly with each new issue, and they acquired a high reputation for accuracy and impartiality. They are now to be found in Service Establishments and Embassies throughout the world, and in the early years after the last war were much used by the League of Nations.

The old Handbooks have been extensively used in the present war, and experience has disclosed both their value and their limitations. On the one hand they have proved, beyond all question, how greatly the work of the fighting services and of Government Departments is facilitated if countries of strategic or political importance are covered by handbooks which deal, in a convenient and easily digested form, with their geography, ethnology, administration, and resources. On the other hand, it has become apparent that something more is needed to meet present-day requirements. The old series does not cover many of the countries closely affected by the present war (e.g. Germany, France, Poland, Spain, Portugal, to name only a few); its books are somewhat uneven in quality, and they are inadequately equipped with maps, diagrams, and photographic illustrations.

The present series of Handbooks, while owing its inspiration largely to the former series, is in no sense an attempt to revise or re-edit that series. It is an entirely new set of books, produced in the Naval Intelligence Division by trained geographers drawn largely from the Universities, and working at sub-centres established at Oxford and Cambridge, and is printed by the Oxford and Cambridge University Presses. The books follow, in general, a uniform scheme, though minor modifications will be found in particular cases; and they are illustrated by numerous maps and photographs.

The purpose of the books is primarily naval. They are designed first to provide, for the use of Commanding Officers, information in a comprehensive and convenient form about countries which they may be called upon to visit, not only in war but in peace-time; secondly, to maintain the high standard of education in the Navy and, by supplying officers with material for lectures to naval personnel ashore and afloat, to ensure for all ranks that visits to a new country shall be both interesting and profitable.

Their contents are, however, by no means confined to matters of purely naval interest. For many purposes (e.g. history, administration, resources, communications, etc.) countries must necessarily be treated as a whole, and no attempt is made to limit their treatment exclusively to coastal zones. It is hoped therefore that the Army, the Royal Air Force, and other Government Departments (many of whom have given great assistance in the production of the series) will find these Handbooks even more valuable than their predecessors proved to be both during and after the last war.

J. H. GODFREY
Director of Naval Intelligence
1942

The foregoing preface has appeared from the beginning of this series of Geographical Handbooks. It describes so effectively their origin and purpose that I have decided to retain it in its original form.

This volume has been prepared for the Naval Intelligence Division at the Cambridge sub-centre (General Editor, Dr H. C. Darby). It has been edited and mainly written by Mr J. C. Stuttard, with contributions from Dr Raymond Firth, Mr T. G. Tutin, Dr Charles Wilcocks, the British Museum (Natural History) and the Research Department of the Foreign Office. The maps and diagrams have been drawn by Miss Margaret Alexander, Mr A. O. Cole, Miss K. S. A. Froggatt and Mrs Gwen Raverat.

E. G. N. RUSHBROOKE
Director of Naval Intelligence

December 1943

CONTENTS

LIST OF MAPS AND DIAGRAMS

LIST OF PLATES

Chapter I

GEOLOGY AND PHYSICAL FEATURES

Introduction: Structure and Geology: Deltas of Tonkin and North Annam: Highlands of East Tonkin: Mountains and Plateaux between the Fleuve Rouge and the Mekong: Chaîne Annamitique, and Coastal Plains of Annam: Plain of the lower Mekong: Mountains of Western Cambodia: Bibliographical Note

INTRODUCTION

The territories known collectively as Indo-China form part of the French empire and comprise the colony of Cochin-China, the protectorates of Annam, Tonkin, Cambodia and Laos and the leased territory of Kwang Chow Wan*. They cover some 740,000 sq. km. or 286,000 sq. miles, that is, more than one-third larger than France and over three times the size of Great Britain. The country lies between the parallels 8° 30′ and 23° 20′ N and the meridians 109° 30′ and 100° 10′ E. It is about 1,600 km. in length from north to south and varies from 200 to 800 km. in width from east to west. It is bounded by China on the north and by Siam and Burma on the west, while its shores are washed by the waters of the Gulf of Tonkin, the South China Sea and the Gulf of Siam (Fig. 1).

Indo-China may be described in the broadest terms as consisting of the Fleuve Rouge basin, the Chaîne Annamitique and the basin of the Mekong. The lowlands, where population is most dense and civilization most advanced, contrast sharply with the sparsely populated and little developed mountains and plateaux which surround them. There is a great diversity in the physical characteristics of these upland areas. The north of Tonkin is a mountainous region of high peaks and ridges with deep gorges carved by the Fleuve Rouge and its tributaries. The highlands of Laos and Annam are made up of a series of plateaux, among which may be mentioned the plateaux of Tran Ninh, Darlac and Lang Bian. In the south-west, the little known and thickly forested Monts des Cardamomes rise steeply from the Gulf of Siam and extend eastwards to overlook the great flood plain of the Mekong.

The Fleuve Rouge (Red River) and Mekong are the two main rivers of Indo-China. They differ greatly in length, and the alinement

---

* For an account of the leased territory of Kwang Chow Wan see Appendix X.

of the one is far less variable than that of the other. The Fleuve Rouge is 1,170 km. in length from its source in Yunnan to the Gulf of Tonkin. It enters Indo-China at Lao Kay and has a north-west–south-east direction in common with the main structural lines. About 200 km. below Lao Kay it is swollen by two important waterways, the sources of which are in China: on the left bank the Rivière Claire

Fig. 1. The location of Indo-China in Asia

and on the right bank the Rivière Noire, both navigable for steam launches in their lower reaches. The Fleuve Rouge carries enormous quantities of material in suspension; this material is deposited in its delta which covers an area of over 15,000 sq. km.

The Mekong is one of the great rivers of Asia, with a total length of 4,400 km. or nearly four times that of the Fleuve Rouge. In northern Laos, the river describes two sharp bends, abandoning a south-western for an eastern course. The south-western course is followed not only by several reaches of the Mekong, but also by the upper tributaries of the Menam. As the watersheds dividing these two streams have a low altitude, it is postulated that the Mekong and Menam were in early Tertiary times one major river draining into the Gulf of Siam, and that subsequent earth movements brought about a change in course by initiating river capture on a large scale. The present-day course of the Mekong has thus resulted from a union of several waterways which were at one time independent. The river has never been an important routeway, for numerous rapids impede navigation. Rapids occur frequently in the upper reaches above Vientiane, but for 500 km. below this town the Mekong flows unhindered by physical obstacles. More rapids occur between Savannakhet and Kratie. Below these rapids the Mekong meanders slowly across its flood-plain and delta, entering the China Sea through five mouths.

STRUCTURE AND GEOLOGY

The geological history of Indo-China is not accurately known and the following should be regarded as a tentative account of the probable structural evolution. The whole structure is grouped around a resistant crystalline massif of early Palaeozoic age forming the central and southern parts of the Chaîne Annamitique (Fig. 2); the rocky coast of south Annam would seem to be due to fracturing of this massif. The south China massif acted as another area of resistance. Differential movement as between these two massifs led to folding in the intermediate area at various periods in geological time. Early Carboniferous folding probably affected the whole area encircling the rigid blocks, but its influence is most clear in north Annam which has remained stable since this period. Intrusive igneous activity accompanied the initiation of these folds. West of the central massif the early structural history is not at all certain. The disturbances in Carboniferous times seem to have engendered a narrow belt of folded ranges stretching from northern Laos to Cambodia. Between these western folds and the central massif there extended a large basin corresponding at the present day to the Mekong valley. Marine transgressions in Permian, Triassic, and early Cretaceous times led to widespread deposition of sandstone in this basin and in parts of Tonkin.

During the Tertiary period another disturbance took place, and the northern part of the Chaîne Annamitique acted as a resistant massif against which were folded the mountains of Tonkin and Laos.

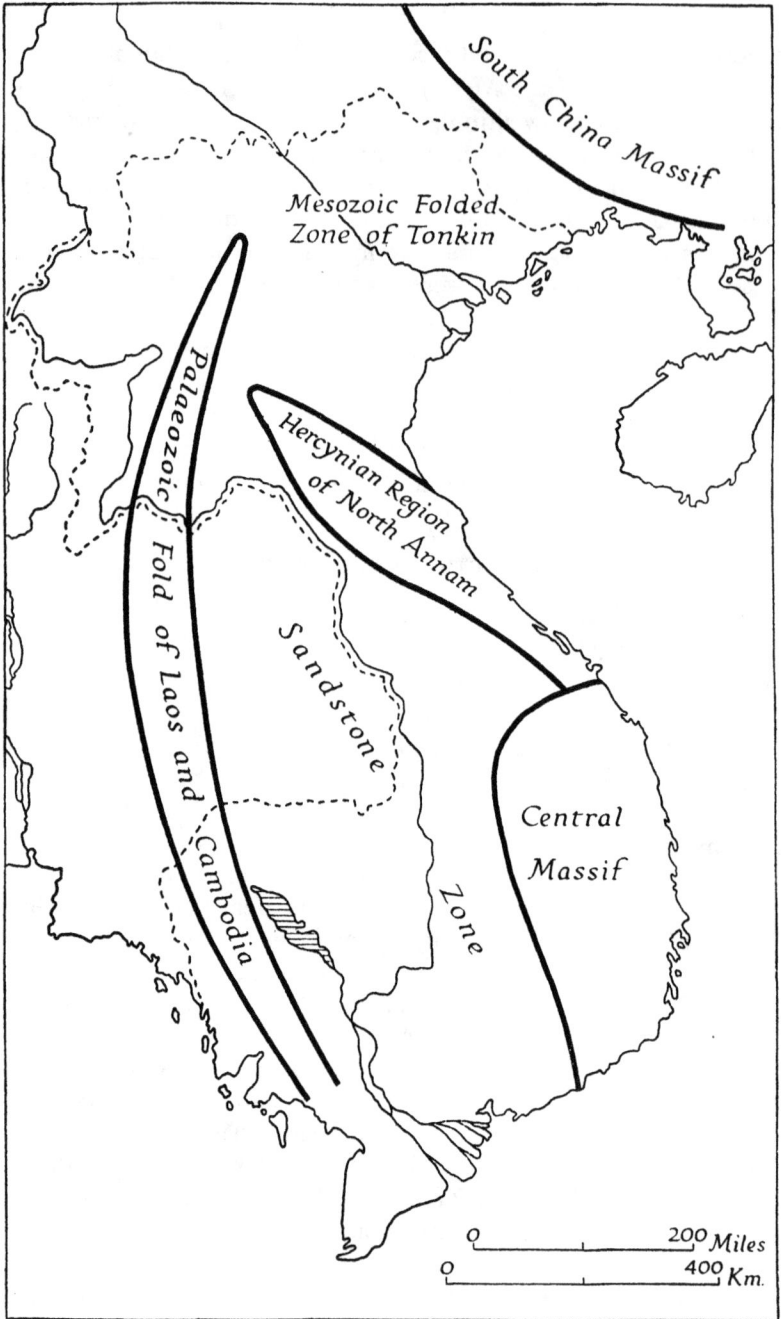

Fig. 2. Structure

Source: F. Blondel, 'Etat des nos connaissances en 1929 sur la géologie de l'Indochine française', *Bulletin Service géologique de l'Indochine*, vol. XVIII, Supplement,
16 pp. folding map (Hanoi, 1929).

The north-west–south-east trend of the massif induced a similar trend in the folded ranges of Tonkin; the Monts des Cardamomes and the Mekong also follow this trend. On the other hand, the alinement in northern Laos is north-east–south-west, the same direction as the Patkai hills of Burma. The relationship between these ranges and the Indo-Burman mountain system has not yet been properly determined. In more recent times, continental uplift and faulting have resulted in the river gorges of Tonkin and in the steep-sided plateaux of Annam. These latest tectonic changes were accompanied by extensive outpourings of basalt, particularly in the southern part of the Chaîne Annamitique. Finally, at the present day the rise of shore level is bringing about an increase in the land area.

The varied geological make-up of Indo-China gives rise to several different types of scenery (Figs. 3 and 4). The great alluvial lowlands are an important and characteristic feature; they comprise vast level expanses, generally fertile and well cultivated. In the mountainous interior crystalline rocks such as granite, gneiss, and rhyolite, cover an extensive area and form the highest and most rugged summits in the whole country. Limestone provides a third and most distinctive type of scenery. The limestone surfaces are extremely dissected, whether at a high elevation as in parts of the northern Chaîne Annamitique, or at sea level as in the Baie d'Along. In the limestone plateau regions, caves, underground streams and small natural basins (*poljes* and *dolines*) are common. The large areas underlain by sandstone and basalt have a very different scenery from the crystalline and limestone regions. Broad, often monotonously level plateaux take the place of serrated mountain peaks and drainage is on the surface rather than underground.

On the basis of the main structural and relief elements, Indo-China may be divided into the following regions (Fig. 5): (1) deltas of Tonkin, and north Annam; (2) highlands of east Tonkin; (3) mountains and plateaux between the Fleuve Rouge and Mekong; (4) Chaîne Annamitique and coastal plains of Annam; (5) plain of the lower Mekong; (6) mountains of west Cambodia. Each of these regions will be described in detail.

DELTAS OF TONKIN AND NORTH ANNAM (Fig. 8)

The deltas of Tonkin and north Annam which extend over a vast area from Ha Tinh to Quang Yen, occupy ancient gulfs of the sea. River alluvium and slight emergence of the land have built up this

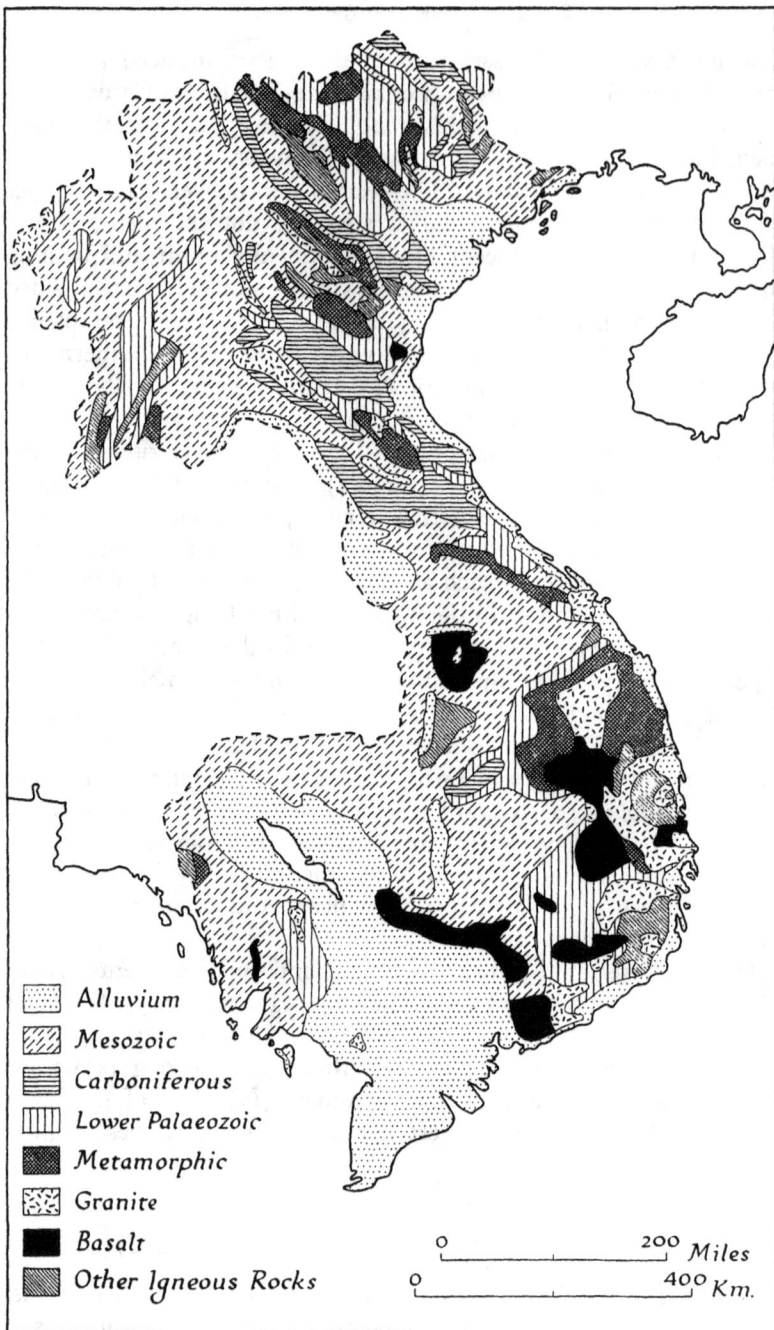

Fig. 3. Geology
Source: *Atlas de l'Indochine*, plate 11 (Hanoi, 1928).

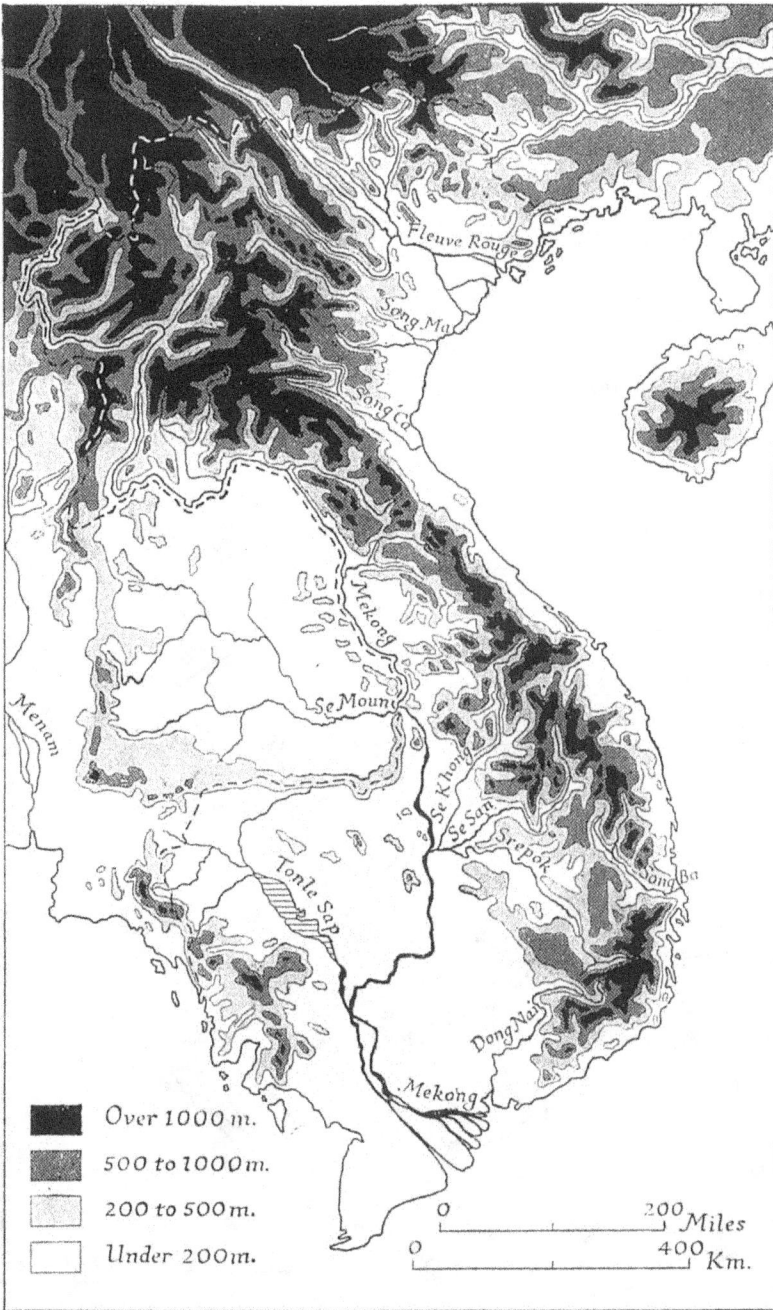

Fig. 4. Relief and drainage
Source: *Atlas de l'Indochine*, plate 12 (Hanoi, 1928).

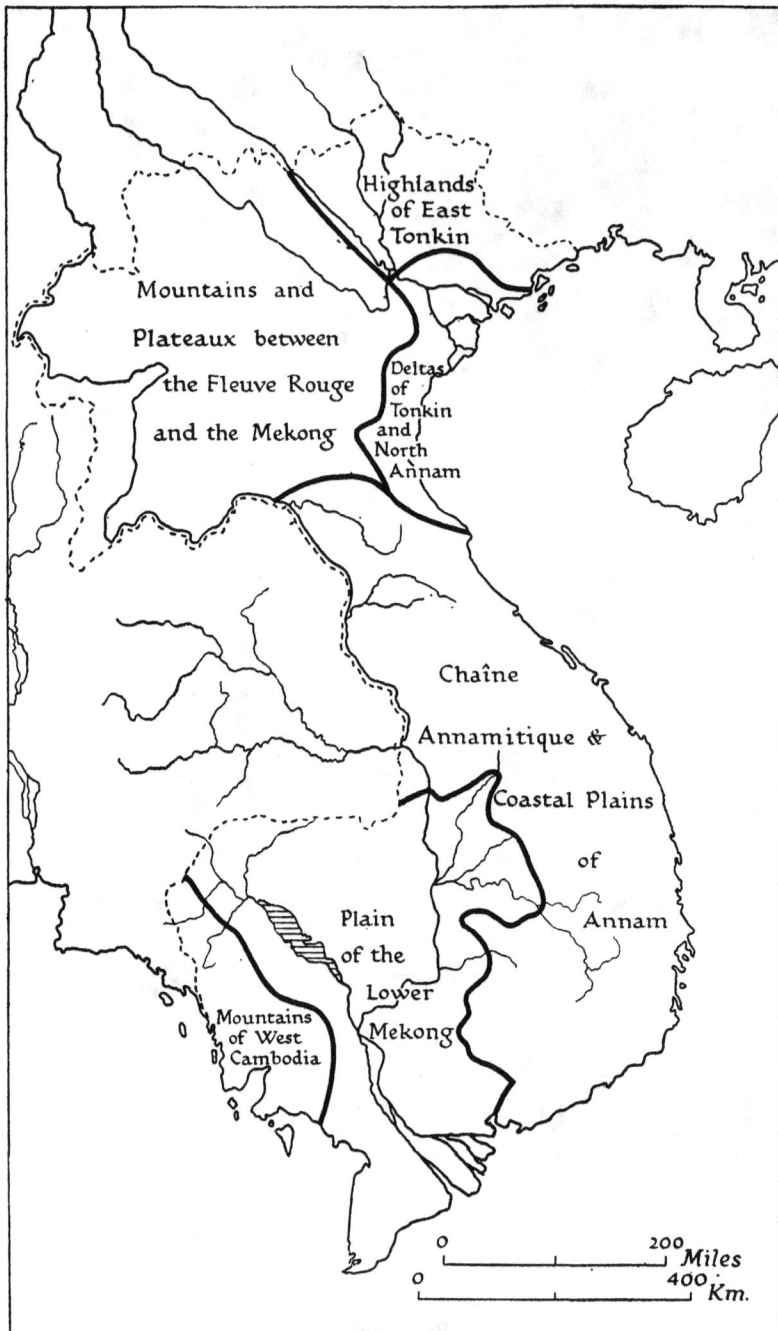

Fig. 5. Physical regions

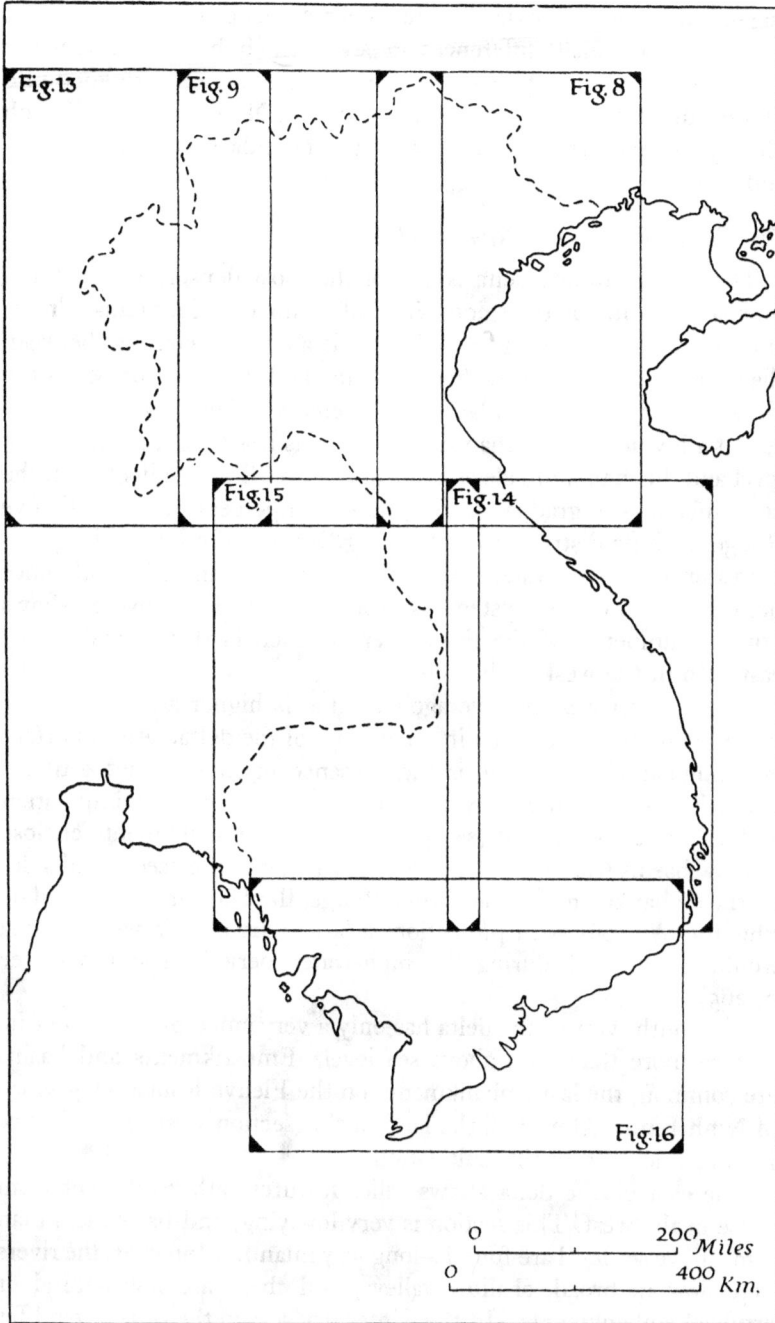

Fig. 6. Key to physical regional maps (Figs. 8, 9, 13-16)

region. Extreme flatness is the chief characteristic of the relief. There are, however, small differences in level which have an important influence upon cultivation and settlement. The region is divided into two by the range of limestone hills between Ninh Binh and Thanh Hoa, along the crest of which runs the boundary between Tonkin and Annam.

The Fleuve Rouge (Red River) Delta

The Fleuve Rouge delta is one of the most densely peopled and intensively cultivated regions in Indo-China. Mountains almost entirely surround the region and there is a striking contrast between the rugged character of the highland ring and the even surface of the alluvial plains. The boundary of the delta is defined by the limit of recent alluvium. More than half this area is less than 3 m. above sea level and the maximum elevation is only 15 m. The gradient from the coast inland is so gradual as to be almost imperceptible. The Fleuve Rouge, with its distributaries the Song Day and the Lach Giang, has a greater volume of water than the Song Thai Binh. This difference between the two river systems is brought out in Fig. 7 which shows how the influence of the tides extends much farther inland in the east than in the west of the delta.

In the north-west the average elevation is higher and the surface generally more broken than in other parts of the delta. An important and singular characteristic is the presence of natural and artificial embankments (bourrelets) which provide security from inundation and so attract settlement (see p. 241). These embankments enclose shallow basins (casiers): the basin of Ha Dong is enclosed on all sides by the embankments of the Fleuve Rouge, the Day, and the Canal de Phu Ly. Without such protection, a large part of this western area would be flooded during the high-water period in summer (see p. 265).

The south-west of the delta has only a very small proportion of its surface more than 1 m. above sea level. Embankments and basins are common, the last embankments on the Fleuve Rouge lying south of Ninh Binh. Almost all the land in this section west of the Fleuve Rouge is devoted to rice cultivation.

The east of the delta shows relief features rather different from those in the west. This section is very lowlying, and basins less than 1 m. above sea level are found a long way inland. Moreover, the rivers here flow in broad, shallow valleys, and there are few natural or artificial embankments. In the winter dry season the tides extend far up the rivers and at this period a large area is also subject to brackish water (Fig. 7).

The coastal region is occupied by lines of ancient sand dunes and expanses of recent marine deposits. The sand dunes increase in number from north to south of the delta.

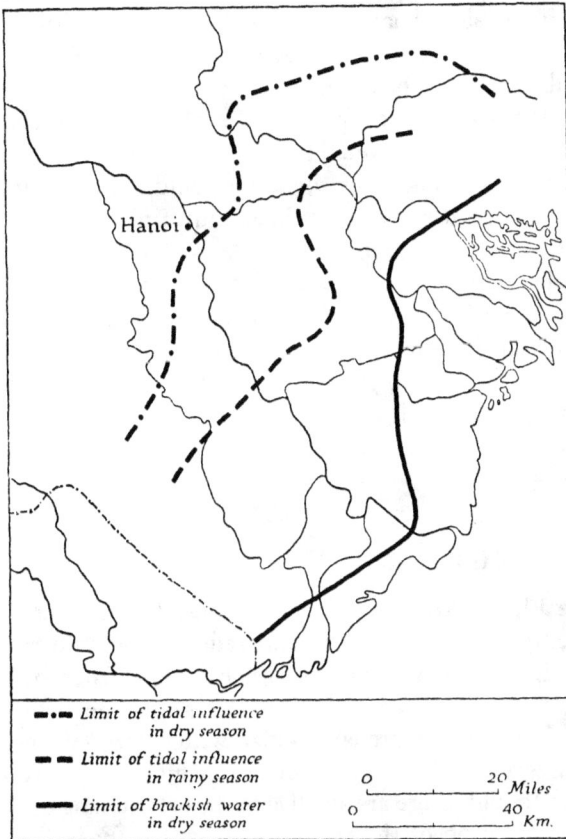

Fig. 7. Influence of tides in the Tonkin delta
Source: P. Gourou, *Les Paysans du Delta tonkinois*, p. 78 (Paris, 1936).

The Song Ma, Song Chu and Song Ca Deltas

The Song Ma, Song Chu, and Song Ca coastal lowlands have relief features very similar to those of the Fleuve Rouge. Wide, level stretches of alluvium predominate with small undulations scarcely perceptible to the eye; varied crop cultivation provides contrasting tones of green on this monotonous surface. Near Vinh and Ha Tinh small steep-sided hills rise to over 200 m. in height and appear as prominent landmarks in the surrounding plain. The total area of these lowlands from the frontier of Tonkin to the Porte d'Annam is 6,750 sq. km. A low broken range of basaltic hills separates the Song Ma and Song Chu deltas from that of the Song Ca.

The plains of north Annam comprise three zones which are different in size and physical character. The hinterland, sloping gradually towards the coast, varies in altitude from 3 or 4 m. to 8 or 10 m. and is principally made up of light, sandy, permeable soils. Farther east lies a very low zone of heavy clays; the plains near Thanh Hoa are less than 1 m. above sea-level. These two zones are not wholly distinct from one another; sometimes the higher land is broken in places by basins, and sometimes the rivers have built up alluvial banks which introduce a certain variety in the lower land. The Song Ma is bordered by a double series of embankments along the whole of its lower course from near Phu Quang to the sea. Embankments of this kind are exceptional in Annam. They emphasize the similarity with conditions in the Fleuve Rouge delta and the physical differences between the plains north and south of the Porte d'Annam. A third and final zone includes the broad sandy dunes alined parallel with the coast.

HIGHLANDS OF EAST TONKIN (Fig. 8)

East of the Fleuve Rouge up to the Chinese frontier lies a region of extreme complexity in structure and relief. Mountain ranges composed principally of igneous rocks rise above low plateaux and valleys developed on less resistant calcareous or sandstone beds. Many of the mountain ranges are arcuate in plan with a north-west–south-east trend, seen very clearly in the depression which runs from Cao Bang to the sea. Although there are small areas near Ha Giang over 2,000 m., the average elevation of the region is not great. East Tonkin is the most densely populated mountainous region in Indo-China.

The river system of east Tonkin is as varied as its relief. Rivers run either in accordance with the mountain arcs or with a north-west–south-east alinement. The Rivière Claire, south of the Ha Giang, and the upper reaches of the Song Cau, are representative of the first trend; while the Fleuve Rouge and Song Ki Cong are examples of the second trend. In south-east Tonkin a north-north-east–south-south-west relief trend has developed and the Song Luc Nam follows this alinement over the greater part of its course. Recent elevation

Fig. 8. Tonkin and northern Annam
Source: *Atlas de l'Indochine*, plates 30, 31, 33, 34, 36 and 37 (Hanoi, 1928).

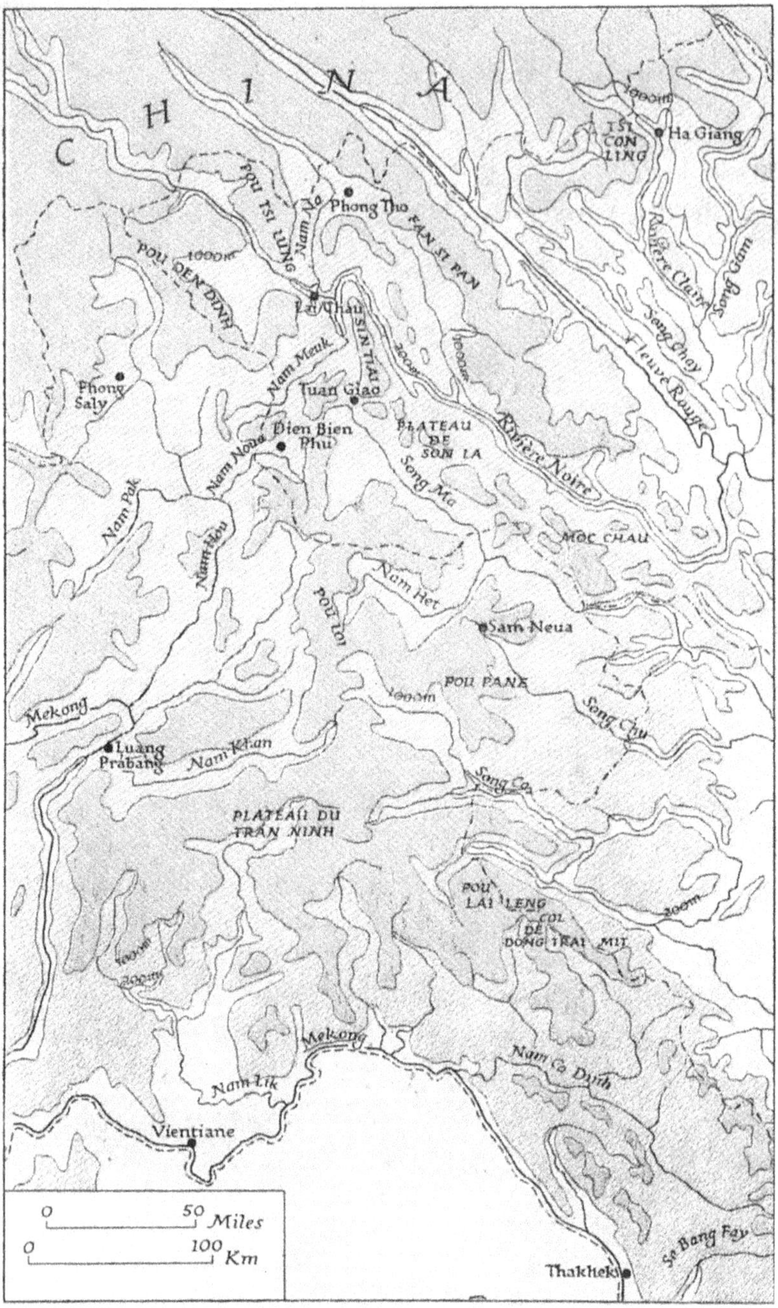

Fig. 9. Northern Laos and western Tonkin
Source: *Atlas de l'Indochine*, plates 30, 32, 33 and 36 (Hanoi, 1928).

has caused rejuvenation of the drainage, and many rivers flow in deep, narrow gorges parallel to or across the main structural lines.

Hills and Valleys of South-East Tonkin

The relatively low altitude, broken topography, and ease of access from China has made this region important as a *pays de passage* for both immigrant and invader. The upland zone near the coast is disposed in a series of arcs, and this characteristic would be even more apparent but for the alluvium which conceals the main structural lines. One of these arcs is broken by the north-west–south-east

Fig. 10. Country north of Lang Son (drawn from a photograph)

axis of the Song Tien Yen. Another arc mainly convex to the south follows the Dong Trieu range, the coast east of Quang Yen, and the numerous rocky islands offshore.

From Thai Nguyen eastwards to the Song Ki Cong valley extends a lowland belt developed principally on sandstones or slates of Mesozoic age. The lowland lacks variety and its aspect has been made even more monotonous by extensive deforestation. Near Lang Son is the Tertiary basin of Loc Binh, whose level floor contrasts with the undulating character of the rest of the lowland.

The undulating lowland belt is bordered to the north by another upland zone which has great variety in relief. The Tam Dao range, formed of rhyolite, is a dominating feature of the landscape between the

Rivière Claire and the Song Cau valleys. Other igneous rocks, especially granite and gabbro, give rise to peaks or narrow ridges. The country east of the Song Cau is very different, for here calcareous plateaux, of which that known as Bac Son is the largest, take the place of rugged mountain chains. Several broad pockets of schist break the surface of these plateaux.

Mountains of North-East Tonkin

The highland chains of north-east Tonkin are a prolongation of the Yunnan plateau. Rugged peaks contrast with level plateaux, fertile depressions and deeply entrenched valleys. A common structural feature is the north-west–south-east alinement of both the rivers and the mountain chains (Plates 1, 2).

The main watershed of the region, which separates the rivers flowing to the Si Kiang from those flowing to the Fleuve Rouge, includes several massifs differing greatly in relief and rock character. Close to the Chinese frontier rises the Binh Lang massif, a calcareous plateau, very sparsely peopled and difficult of access. Several rocky summits, for the most part wooded, reach a height of over 1,500 m. (Plate 2), while solution basins and caves are a common feature. Farther south Pia Ouac (1,930 m.), a granite peak clothed with dense forest, stands out clearly from the bare Nui Tong Tinh plateau formed of gneiss and limestone. Access to Pia Ouac is not difficult, and prospectors have long been attracted by the tin resources of the region. Finally, there are the limestone massifs of Kun Hi, and Coc Xo, each bordered to the east and west by great depressions. Kun Hi is wholly uninhabited and practically inaccessible; no roads or pathways exist and the ravine bottoms are covered with a tangled undergrowth.

East of the main watershed the land descends over a series of plateaux and basins to the upper Si Kiang valley. The Song Bac Giang which rises on the Kun Hi massif flows over a smooth undulating sandstone plateau to join the Song Ki Cong north of Lang Son. Bamboo covers a large part of the plateau surface and gives it a rather monotonous appearance. In the north, near the Chinese frontier, is the desolate calcareous massif of Lu Khu, almost wholly treeless except on its borders (Plate 2). There are few roads or villages. East of Cao Bang, a sandstone plateau separates two severely dissected limestone areas.

West of the main watershed lies a narrow depression, composed of schists, deeply entrenched by the Song Cau, and by the headstreams

Plate 1. The valley of the Song Ki Cong at Lang Son

View looking westwards down the Song Ki Cong valley with rhyolitic hills fringing the Bac Son massif in the background. The river bends to the north behind the low jagged limestone hills in the middle distance. Lang Son lies on the left bank of the river near the point where it is crossed by the bridge carrying the railway from Hanoi to Na Cham. The main road is the Route Coloniale no. 1.

Plate 2. Country near Nguyen Binh, west of Cao Bang

The river is a tributary of the Song Bang Giang which flows towards the Si Kiang. In the background on the left there are densely forested limestone hills. On the right is a motor road leading to the tin mines of Tinh Tuc. The valley is largely occupied by terraced rice fields.

of the Song Gam. Granite peaks overlook the depression to the west. Between these granite ranges and the middle Song Chay extends a vast limestone massif; access to the forested central region south-west of Ha Giang is especially difficult. The bare and rugged crystalline massifs immediately south of the Chinese frontier between the Rivière Claire and the Song Chay have a very different aspect. Tsi Con Ling (2,431 m.) is the highest mountain in north-east Tonkin.

MOUNTAINS AND PLATEAUX BETWEEN THE FLEUVE ROUGE AND THE MEKONG (Figs. 9, 13)

This region includes the extensive mountainous area between the Fleuve Rouge and the Mekong. The average elevation is greater than in east Tonkin. Two trends dominate the relief; the one has a north-west–south-east direction, predominant in the mountains and valleys of the east; and the other runs north-east–south-west, a trend well developed in the upper Mekong basin. With a few exceptions, the rivers flow along deep, narrow valleys cut in crystalline rocks, limestone, or sandstone. The whole mountainous region is generally infertile, little cultivated and sparsely peopled, and is in great contrast with the region east of the Fleuve Rouge. The Pou Den Dinh-Pou Loi watershed between the Fleuve Rouge and Mekong separates areas of great variety in structure and relief.

Fleuve Rouge to Pou Den Dinh-Pou Loi watershed (west Tonkin)

The land drained by the Rivière Noire, Song Ma, Song Chu and Song Ca is made up of ranges differing greatly in their rock character. Immediately west of the Fleuve Rouge rises the crystalline Fan Si Pan - Sa Phin range which extends for nearly 300 km. and culminates in the Fan Si Pan peak (3,142 m. c. 10,000 ft.), the highest point in Indo-China. Over the greater part of this chain there is a much steeper slope on the west than the east.

Between the Rivière Noire valley and the Nam Na - Song Ma depression lies another mountainous area with the same alinement as the Fan Si Pan range but geologically very different. This second mountainous area comprises a number of calcareous plateaux forming a more or less continuous narrow band from Phong Tho to Thanh Hoa. The limestone massifs near Phong Tho and Lai Chau have been greatly denuded and low isolated peaks are a common feature; the Sin Tiai limestone massif is almost inaccessible, except in the south where it slopes to the Tuan Giao depression. South-east of this depression lies the Plateau de Son La, of greater extent and more fertile than the other massifs. Moreover, its average elevation is only about 600 m., while the others exceed 1,000 m. The calcareous plateaux are continued farther south by the Moc Chau massif and by the line of hills dividing Annam from Tonkin (Fig. 12).

A well-developed depression followed by the Nam Na, Nam Meuk and Song Ma runs parallel with the north-west–south-east trending limestone massifs. This area is for the most part difficult to cross, since the rivers flow in deep canyons cut in Triassic and crystalline

Fig. 11. The valley of the Rivière Noire near Lai Chau
(drawn from a photograph)

rocks. Between the Nam Na depression and the Rivière Noire rises the isolated granite massif of Pou Tsi Lung (3,076 m.).

The Pou Den Dinh-Pou Loi range is a divide between streams flowing east to the Gulf of Tonkin and west to the Mekong (Fig. 9). Pou Den Dinh massif (1,867 m.) is formed principally of sandstone, for the most part unforested but covered with a dense undergrowth. A plain occupied by the upper Nam Meuk and Nam Noua cuts transversely across the main watershed and facilitates communication between Lai Chau and Luang Prabang. This is the only large plain in the whole mountainous area between the Fleuve Rouge and the Mekong. Farther south, the massifs west of the Nam Na-Song Ma depression broaden considerably and include several parallel ranges

Fig. 12. Rugged limestone hills to the west of the Tonkin delta

The hills rise abruptly from the flat lowland of the delta and are covered with forest to their summits. In the left foreground there is a coffee plantation and large modern farm buildings.

Source: P. Gourou, *Les Paysans du Delta tonkinois*, plate 5 (Paris, 1936).

formed mainly of granite. Near Sam Neua is the granite summit of Pou Pane (2,079 m.) overlooking the Nam Het and Song Chu gorges; while the main watershed comprises a line of mountains dominated by Pou Loi (2,257 m.), a granite dome which may be clearly seen as far away as Sam Neua or Luang Prabang.

Pou Den Dinh-Pou Loi Watershed to the Mekong (north Laos)

West of the Pou Den Dinh-Pou Loi divide both mountains and rivers in general change in alinement from north-west–south-east to north-east–south-west. The Mekong above Ban Houei Sai and below Luang Prabang and the Nam Hou south-west of Dien Bien Phu exhibit this trend. Physically, northern Laos differs in other ways from western Tonkin. Instead of long narrow mountain ranges there are for the most part broad plateaux and plains of Mesozoic sandstone overlying older rocks; the latter outcrop as high limestone precipices in the Nam Hou valley (Fig. 13).

The country north of Luang Prabang is divided by the Nam Hou into two very different sections. To the east lies a rugged mountainous region with deeply entrenched river valleys, poor in soil and sparsely inhabited. The Nam Noua valley offers a fairly easy route to Dien Bien Phu and Lai Chau. West of the Nam Hou, while there are several minor elevations, broad fertile plains constitute the characteristic relief feature. Near Phong Saly are several small plains, while close to the Mekong lie the extensive plains around Muong Sing and Vien Pou Kha.

South-east of Luang Prabang and overlooking the Nam Khan valley extends the Plateau du Tran Ninh. It is composed of sandstone and averages 1,000 to 1,200 m. in elevation. The level nature of this plateau contrasts with the high mountain ranges on its periphery, where many summits reach over 2,000 m. Pou Lai Leng (2,711 m.) is a prominent landmark between the Song Ca and the Mekong valleys. South of this peak there is a rapid descent to the Col de Dong Trai Mit which separates the mountains and plateaux of the north from the Chaîne Annamitique.

Chaîne Annamitique and Coastal Plains of Annam (Fig. 14)

This vast region embraces the whole area over 100 m. in altitude lying east of the Mekong between the Col de Dong Trai Mit and Cap Saint Jacques. It also includes the small coastal plains of Annam which vary greatly in character and which are separated from each other by long spurs reaching to the sea from the interior highlands.

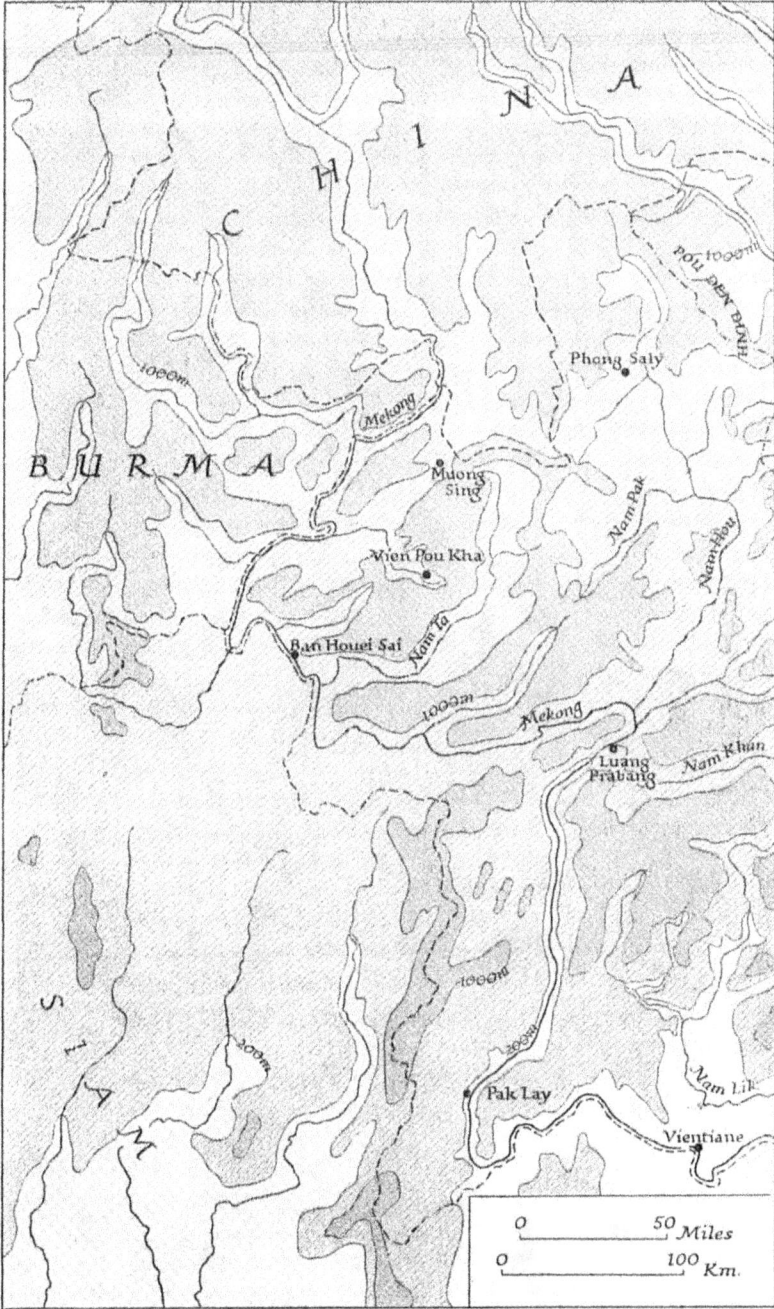

Fig. 13. North-western Laos and adjacent countries
Source: *Atlas de l'Indochine*, plates 30–33 and 36 (Hanoi, 1928).

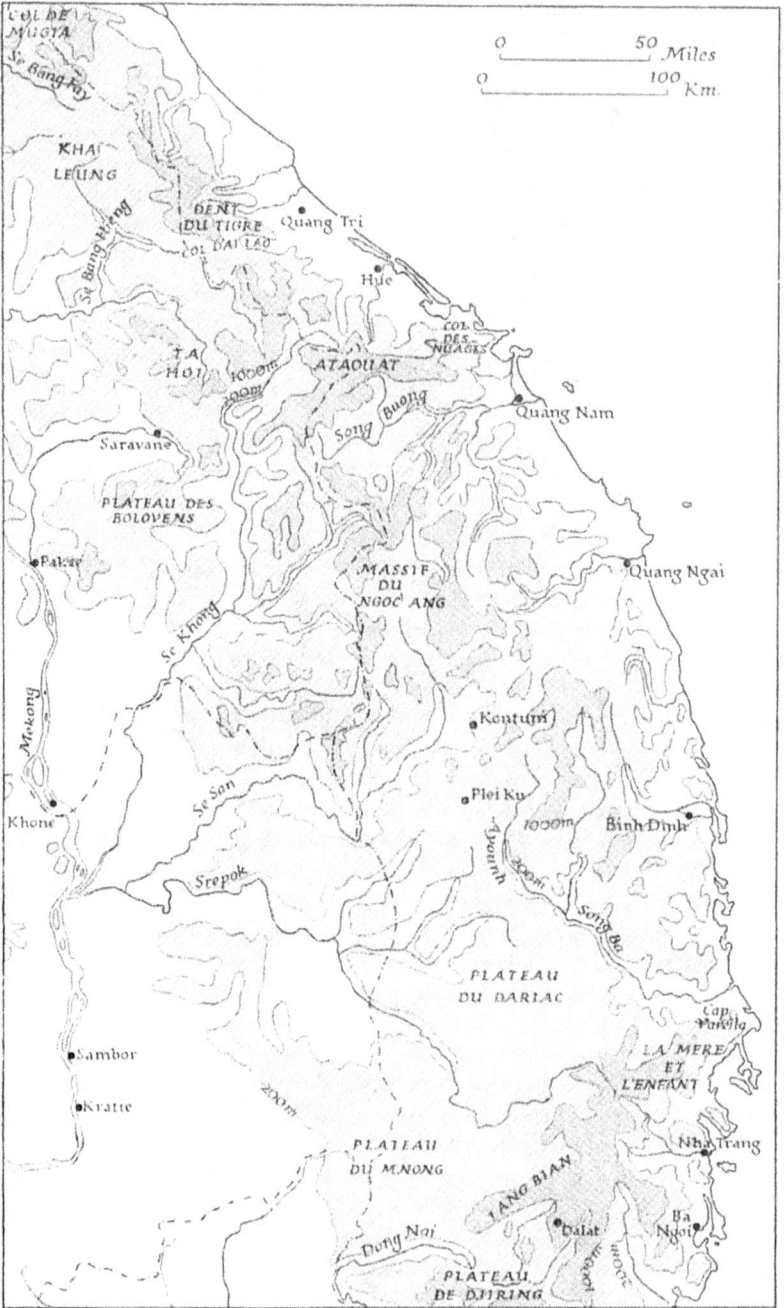

Fig. 14. Annam, southern Laos and eastern Cambodia
Source: *Atlas de l'Indochine*, plates 36, 37, 39, 40, 42 and 43 (Hanoi, 1928).

The Chaîne Annamitique is not strictly speaking a mountain chain, but a series of eroded plateaux dominated by high isolated peaks. These plateaux present a much steeper slope to the east than to the west. Geologically, the region comprises two different features: in the north from Tran Ninh to the Song Buong valley near Tourane is a folded chain of early Carboniferous age, while south of Tourane lies a very ancient crystalline massif with extensive lava flows emitted after severe fracturing of the land surface during late Tertiary times. The rivers of this region vary greatly in length, in water flow and in the character of their valleys. Streams flowing to the Mekong such as the Se Bang Hieng, Se Khong, and Se San, are much longer than those entering the China Sea. In the whole section from the Porte d'Annam to Cap Saint Jacques only the Song Buong and Song Ba attain a great length; and even these are small when compared with Se Khong or Se San. The western rivers have broader valleys and a slighter gradient than those in the east. On the other hand, the upper Se Bang Fay and Se Khong have cut narrow gorges in the limestone and sandstone plateaux. Deeply entrenched valleys are not so common a feature as in northern Laos and Tonkin.

From the point of view of relief, the region may be divided into three main areas: (1) Plateau du Tran Ninh to Col d'Ai Lao; (2) Col d'Ai Lao to Plateau du Darlac; (3) Massif of south Annam.

Plateau du Tran Ninh to Col d'Ai Lao

The mountainous area south-east of the Plateau du Tran Ninh is narrow, with some parts less than 100 km. in width. As few sections reach a great height and as there are many low passes the region is easy to cross. North of the Col de Mu Gia, the broad Nam Ca Dinh valley developed in Liassic sandstone, lies between a granite and a limestone massif. A steep escarpment marks the junction of the valley sandstone with the rocks of the periphery. South of the Col de Mugia, the limestone massif extends across the whole chain here entrenched by the upper Se Bang Fay. Near Ai Lao, the granitic Dent du Tigre (1,701 m.) is a prominent landmark. The Col d'Ai Lao is a level basaltic zone providing an easy route from the Mekong to the coast of Annam near Quang Tri.

Two broad sandstone plateaux, known respectively as Kha Leung and Ta Hoi, lie west of the principal mountain chain and are separated by an escarpment from the alluvial plains of Savannakhet and Saravane. The grassland of these plateaux contrasts strikingly with the thickly forested mountain ranges.

2-2

Between the foot of the Chaîne Annamitique and the sea, from the Porte d'Annam to the Col des Nuages, extends a long narrow plain, well watered and densely peopled. The plain comprises ancient alluvial terraces, modern alluvial flats, lagoons and sand dunes.

Col d'Ai Lao to Plateau du Darlac

This large area, 450 km. in length and averaging 250 km. in breadth, has very varied relief features. Rugged crystalline massifs, densely forested and almost inaccessible, contrast with relatively lowlying sandstone country and with broad, level expanses of basalt. There is similar variety in the coastal section where wide alluvial plains alternate with lowlands of extreme narrowness.

South of the Col d'Ai Lao the little known Massif de l'Ataouat, formed of granite and gneiss, rises to a height of over 2,000 m. (Fig. 14). It has a very steep slope overlooking the coastal plain and is separated from the larger crystalline Massif du Ngoc Ang by a gently folded plateau. Although easier to cross than the massifs to the north and south, this plateau does not offer as good a route as parts of the northern Chaîne Annamitique. No col is lower than 1,400 m.

The Massif du Ngoc Ang has the greatest extent of crystalline rocks in the whole of Indo-China. The mica-schists and gneiss form rounded hills which never exceed 2,000 m. in altitude; the granites give rise to a more rugged relief and form the highest summits (Ngoc Ang, 2,598 m.). Outpourings of lava accompanied the block faulting of Tertiary times, and basaltic plateaux to-day in part flank the massif on its southern and western slopes. The country around Plei Ku presents a typical volcanic aspect with well-preserved cones and crater lakes.

The chief basaltic region in the west is the Plateau des Bolovens, separated from the Chaîne Annamitique by the broad Se Khong valley. A number of sandstone peaks, the remnants of a former plateau, stand above the general level; basalt fills the valleys between these peaks and, except on the east, there is a very gentle slope to the surrounding plains. The plateau is predominantly grassland; certain areas are liable to become marshy during the wet season.

Between the crystalline massifs of the Kontum region and those of south Annam there is a relatively lowlying area, generally well cultivated and easy to cross. South of Plei Ku a low plateau only 500 m. above sea level, drained by the Ayounh (a tributary of the Song Ba) on the east and by the Srepok on the west, provides a good

Plate 3. Plateau country near Dalat

The huts belong to a Moi village in this sparsely settled region.

Plate 4. The Jougah Falls near Dalat

route from the coast to the Mekong valley. The plateau is separated from the coastal plains by the mountains of Binh Dinh, whose north-south direction obliges the Song Ba to make a large detour towards the south. From the valley of the Song Ba the land rises gradually to the Plateau du Darlac which is developed mainly on basalt and has an average elevation of about 800 m.

South and south-west of the Plateau du Darlac extends a broad depression covered with marshes and lakes fed by the Srepok. The level countryside and the plentiful supply of water make this area suitable for irrigated rice cultivation.

From the Col des Nuages to Cap Varella, the Chaîne Annamitique presents a steep front towards the sea. The plains of Quang Nam, Quang Ngai, and Binh Dinh, are over 1,000 sq. km. in area and reach a greater distance inland than the corresponding plains farther north. Alluvial deposits, sand dunes, and lagoons are a characteristic feature. Spurs from the interior massifs separate these lowlands from one another, and in some sections the coastal plain is almost entirely absent (Fig. 14).

Massif of South Annam

The southern section of the Chaîne Annamitique comprises a number of plateaux for the most part made up of granite, rhyolite and basalt. The plateaux of Mnong and Djiring, separated by the Dong Nai valley, are composed of sandstones overlain in some parts by basalt. Mnong is an almost level plateau with shallow valleys; Djiring has a tabular appearance and only a few isolated hills stand above the general surface. East of these two plateaux igneous rocks predominate. The country around Dalat is made up of schists and metamorphosed sandstones forming an undulating surface (Plate 3). Farther north, rugged mountains take the place of monotonous plateaux. The granitic and rhyolitic mountains of Lang Bian (2,000 m.) overlook the Dalat plateau, and Chu Yang Sin (2,405 m.) is the highest point of south Annam. This mountain range has a northward extension in the Mère et l'Enfant massif (2,050 m.) which reaches the sea at Cap Varella.

The coastal lowlands bordering the Chaîne Annamitique south from Cap Varella are generally very narrow and relatively infertile. The plains of Nha Trang and Ba Ngoi are encumbered with dunes and alluvial terraces. South of Cap Padaran, where the coast changes in general direction from north–south to north-east–south-west, the plains widen, attaining 10–15 km. near Phan Thiet, but these plains are infertile, for thousands of hectares are covered with ancient alluvium and with the largest sand dunes in the whole country.

PLAIN OF THE LOWER MEKONG (Figs. 15, 16)

The plain of the Mekong below Pakse is almost completely level except in those few parts where low rounded hills break the surface. Modern alluvium and ancient alluvial terraces constitute the greater part of the area.

Lowland east of the Tonle Sap Alluvial Plain

This section has a more varied relief than the rest of the region. Alluvial deposits are restricted to a narrow zone bordering the Mekong. Almost horizontal beds of Triassic clay cover a large part of the surface, while sandstone strata of the same age give rise to small upland areas near Khone. South of Kratie, where a belt of basalt runs east-west across the country, the ground becomes slightly undulating; the Mekong cuts through this belt in a series of rapids. The Mekong has a much braided course in this region, and, apart from the rapids near Kratie, there are further obstacles to navigation at Sambor and Khone (see p. 442).

The Tonle Sap Alluvial Plain

The lake of Tonle Sap is the dominating feature in the lowland west of the Mekong. It was originally an arm of the sea and has been in its present condition for a relatively short geological period. In Quaternary times the Mekong entered the sea east of Phnom Penh. Under the influence of a recent rise in shore level the Mekong extended its course southwards, preventing the movement of tidal waters into Tonle Sap. The passage from sea gulf to inland lake was so gradual that many marine species are still found here having become adapted to the changed conditions.

The water level in Tonle Sap is closely dependent on the regime of the Mekong. At low water, from November to June, the lake drains into the Mekong; but at high water, from June to October, the direction of flow is reversed, owing to the great height of the river at this season.

At low water, Tonle Sap covers 2,700 sq. km., measuring 160 km. in length and 35 km. at its widest point. There are three parts to the lake: Grand Lac, Petit Lac and Veal Phoc (Plain of Mud). Both the Grand Lac and Petit Lac have a maximum depth of 2 m. These two

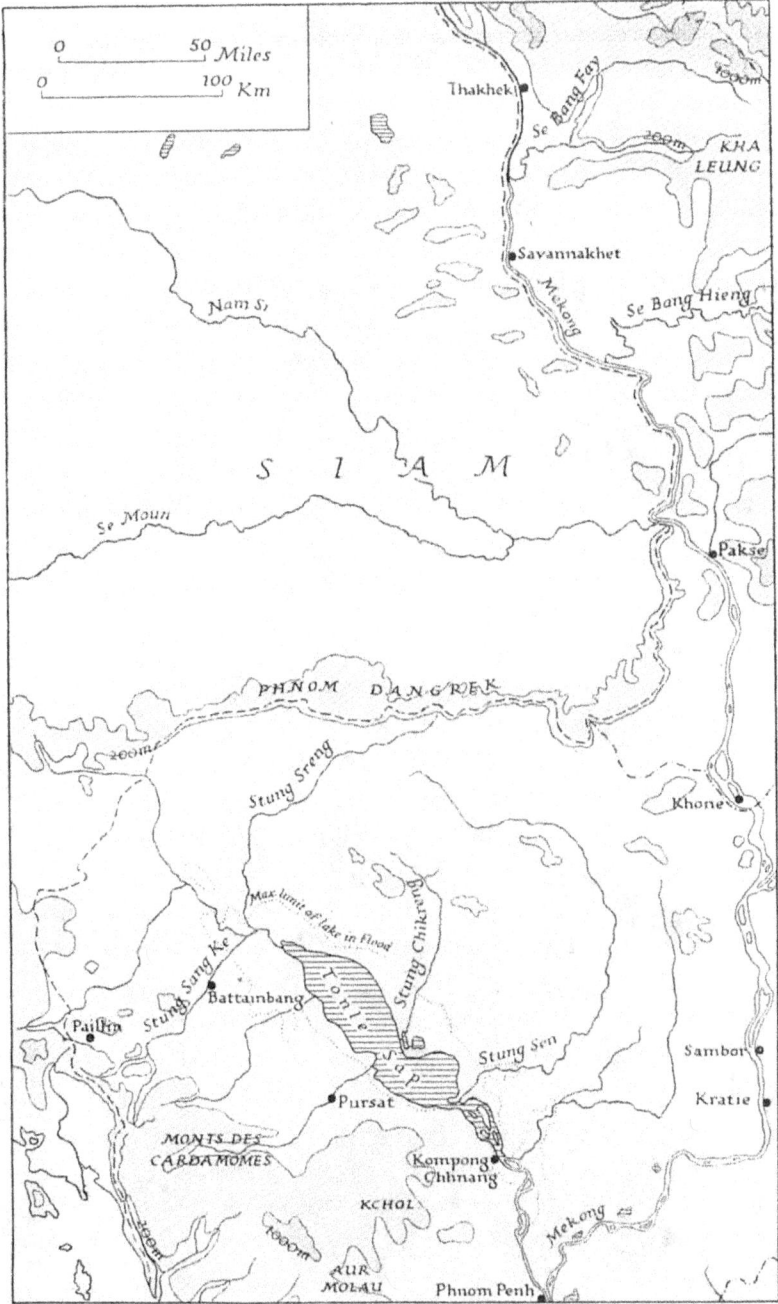

Fig. 15. Southern Laos and Cambodia
Source: *Atlas de l'Indochine*, plates 36, 39 and 42 (Hanoi, 1928).

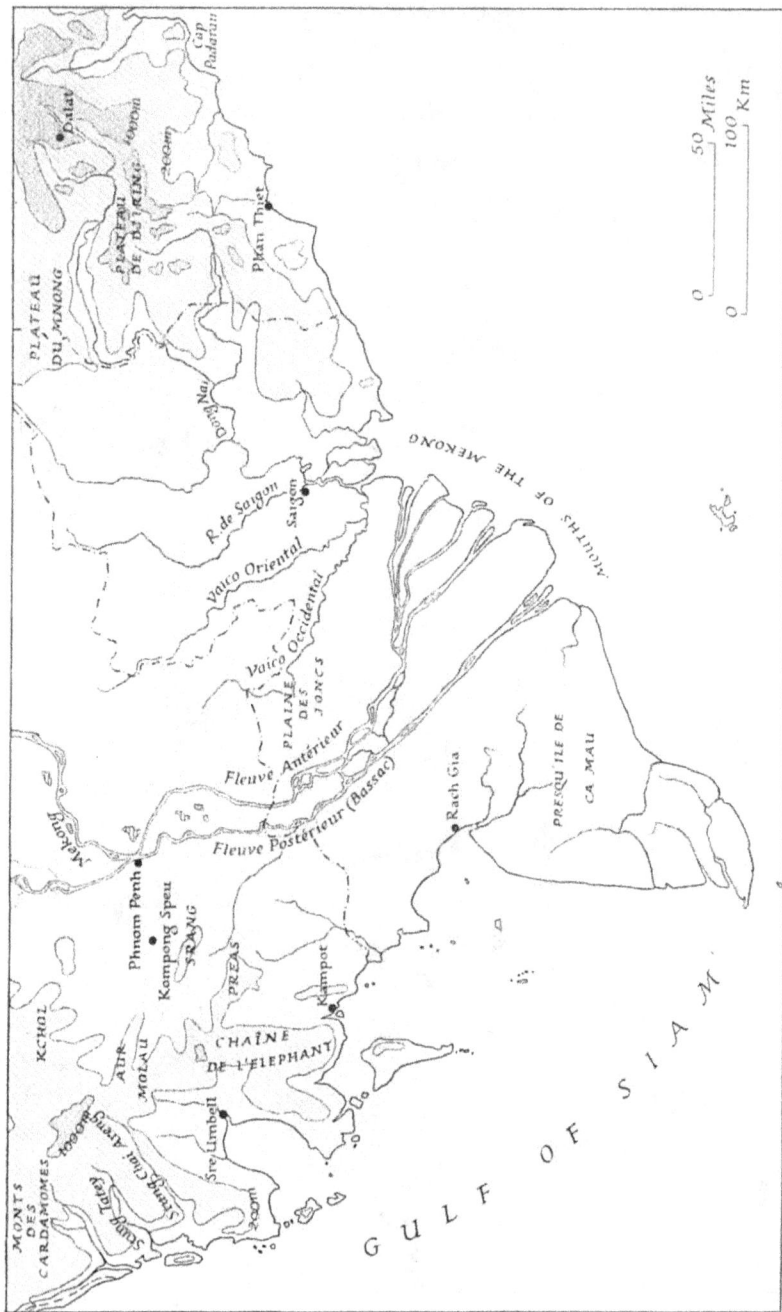

Fig. 16. Cochin-China

Source: *Atlas de l'Indochine*, plates 42, 43, 45 and 46 (Hanoi, 1928).

parts are connected by a very shallow channel called by Cambodians 'Tigers' Feet crossing', since tigers are supposed to cross the lake at this point. Several rivers are building deltas, thus rapidly reducing the width of the channel; Veal Phoc is essentially a mud flat composed of material brought down by the Stung Sen.

In the period of high water, the lake floods the adjacent plains and increases its area to 10,000 sq. km. It becomes over 300 km. in length and in some places 100 km. wide. At some points the depth of water on the flood plain is as much as 14 m.

The Mekong Delta

The delta of the Mekong may be said to begin at Phnom Penh where the river bifurcates into two branches, the Fleuve Antérieur and Fleuve Postérieur (Fig. 16). East of the Mekong extends the less fertile delta of the Vaico, Saigon and Dong Nai rivers. The whole area is a monotonous plain, and few parts are more than 3 m. above sea level. The fertile delta soil consists of a very coherent river mud, interrupted here and there by long, narrow deposits of sand. The land is intensively cultivated and supports a dense population, except in the Plaine des Joncs and the Presqu'île de Ca Mau.

MOUNTAINS OF WESTERN CAMBODIA (Figs. 15, 16)

The mountains of western Cambodia hold an isolated and commanding position between the Mekong lowland and the Gulf of Siam. They comprise a densely forested compact mass of plateaux and mountains with an average altitude of about 1,000 m., and although relatively close to centres of dense population they remain very little known. The region is composed primarily of Mesozoic sandstone with expanses of crystalline and calcareous rock in the north and east. The rivers are short, and in their upper courses flow in deeply entrenched valleys. From the point of view of relief two broad zones are distinguishable: (1) a low, broken plateau zone rising immediately to the south-west of the Tonle Sap alluvial plain; (2) a high plateau zone, including the Monts des Cardamomes and the Chaîne de l'Eléphant.

The Low Plateau Zone

This zone is characterized by an undulating plateau surface with several scattered eminences, generally tabular in form (*buttes*) standing above the general level. It extends from Kampot on the coast to slightly north of Kompong Speu, where it is interrupted by the massif of Kchol only to be continued again beyond this massif in the provinces of Pursat and Battambang. Between Kampot and Kompong Speu there are a large number of low hills which vary greatly in rock composition. Near the coast east of Kampot steep-sided limestone and crystalline hills, with orchards on their lower slopes, rise prominently above the level alluvial plain, intensively cultivated for rice and densely peopled. Farther inland towards Kompong Speu limestone no longer appears, granite and quartzite predominating in the rugged massif of Preas and Triassic sandstone in the Srang massif.

North of Kompong Speu the land first slopes almost imperceptibly towards Phnom Penh, but the continuity of this low plateau zone is then broken by the high massif of Kchol (see p. 25). The characteristic features of a gently inclined plateau surface with isolated tabular hills again appear around Pursat and Battambang. Although Mesozoic sandstone predominates, crystalline rocks and limestone figure in the landscape west of Battambang.

On the western side of this region facing the Gulf of Siam, the low plateau zone is little developed. In some sections tabular sandstone hills stand above the narrow coastal plain, but the high plateau zone for the most part reaches almost to the sea along the whole length of this coastline.

The High Plateau Zone

This zone covers a large area in western Cambodia, extending over 250 km. from Kampot to Paillin and almost 200 km. across in the latitude of Kompong Chhnang. There are four main upland areas, separated from each other by cols or depressions: the Chaîne de l'Eléphant, the Monts des Cardamomes, and the massifs of Aur Molau and Kchol. With the exception of the latter, sandstone of Mesozoic age is everywhere predominant. The Chaîne de l'Eléphant which lies north-west of Kampot has very steep slopes on every side and falls to the sea in an almost vertical face, 1,000 m. in height. Northwards beyond the track leading from Sre Umbell to Kompong Speu is the Aur Molau massif, also bounded by steep slopes, but more dissected than the Chaîne de l'Eléphant. Both the Chaîne de l'Eléphant and the Aur Molau massifs are densely forested and difficult of access.

North-west of the Aur Molau massif is a complex mountain region with rocky summits, deeply entrenched valleys and precipitous slopes on almost every side. Several summits reach over 1,400 m., the highest being the peak of Sankos (1,744 m.). Along the upper courses of the Stung Tatey and Stung Chai Areng several small pockets of basalt overlie the sandstone. The greater part of the Monts des Cardamomes is covered by an almost impenetrable forest.

To the east of the Monts des Cardamomes, and separated from them by a narrow depression, stands the isolated granitic massif of Kchol. This massif rises steeply above the alluvial plain of Tonle Sap and is a prominent landmark from both Kompong Chhnang and Phnom Penh.

BIBLIOGRAPHICAL NOTE

(1) Since 1912 the *Service géographique de l'Indochine* has published a number of *Mémoires* and *Bulletins* which deal in detail with the geology of a large part of the country. The most recent syntheses are F. Blondel, 'Etat des nos connaissances en 1929 sur la géologie de l'Indochine française', *Bulletin Service géologique de l'Indochine*, vol. XVIII, 16 pp. (Hanoi, 1929), and J. Fromaget, 'Observations et reflexions sur la géologie stratigraphique et structurale de l'Indochine', *Bulletin de la Société géologique de France*, 5th ser. vol. IV, pp. 101–64 (Paris, 1934).

(2) A full treatment of the physical features of the country is given in Commandant Dussault, 'Structure et géographie physique', *Inventaire général de l'Indochine*, Société de Géographie de Hanoi (Hanoi, 1926). Shorter surveys are found in P. Gourou, *L'Utilisation du Sol en Indochine française*, pp. 17–72 (Paris, 1940), in Georges Maspero, *Un Empire Colonial français: l'Indochine*, vol. I, pp. 4–18 (Paris, 1929), and in J. Sion, 'Asie des Moussons', *Géographie Universelle*, vol. IX, pp. 417–53 (Paris, 1929). There is a good account of the limestone areas of Indo-China in L. Cuisinier, 'Régions calcaires de l'Indochine', *Annales de Géographie*, vol. XXXVIII, pp. 266–73 (Paris, 1929).

(3) The following works deal with the physical geography of particular regions: E. Chassigneux, 'La Région de Hai Ninh', *La Géographie*, vol. XLVI, pp. 33–68 (Paris, 1926). This article gives a detailed description of the geology and relief of the frontier region near Mon Cay in Tonkin. V. Delahaye, *La Plaine des Joncs et sa mise en valeur* (Rennes, 1928). An account of the lowlying and thinly peopled plain to the north of the Mekong delta. Le Nulzec, 'Le Plateau des Cardamomes cambodgiens', *La Géographie*, vol. XLVI, pp. 305–43 (Paris, 1926). A good account of the little known mountain region in western Cambodia. H. Maître, *Les Régions Moi du Sud-Indochinois*, 3 vols. (Paris, 1909–12). The classic work on the Moi peoples and their environment. C. Robequain, *Le Thanh Hoa: Etude géographique d'une Province annamite*, 2 vols. (Paris, 1929). Contains a full description of the physical characteristics of the delta region of the Song Ma in north Annam.

(4) A valuable series of photographs illustrating many aspects of the geography of Indo-China will be found in vols XXIV and XXV of *France, Métropole et Colonies*, edited by A. Demangeon, A. Cholley and C. Robequain (Paris, 1934). The photographs are accompanied by explanatory text.

Chapter II

COASTS

GENERAL FEATURES

The coastline of Indo-China is bordered by the Gulf of Tonkin, the South China Sea and the Gulf of Siam. It shows great variety of relief form. Rocky islands fringe the shore in north-east Tonkin, while mountains fall sharply to sea level in central Annam and west Cambodia. Several deep-water bays provide first class anchorages for the largest vessels. A large part of the coastline, however, is low-lying, with shallow lagoons and sand dunes as in north Annam, or with alluvial flats as in the delta regions of the Fleuve Rouge and the Mekong. Shifting sand bars at the mouths of many rivers frequently restrict penetration inland. Lighthouses mark the entrance channels to the principal ports and indicate the position of the more prominent headlands, such as Cap Varella and Cap Padaran.

On the basis of relief features, the coastline of Indo-China may conveniently be divided into nine sections. Along the Gulf of Tonkin littoral, there is first the stretch from Mon Cay to Quang Yen followed to the south-west by the Fleuve Rouge delta and by the delta coast of north Annam. Bordering the South China Sea are five sections: from the Porte d'Annam to Cap Batangan, from this point south to Cap Varella, followed by the rugged stretch between this headland and Cap Padaran, then a short strip to Cap Saint Jacques and lastly the delta of the Mekong. The coast of Cambodia forms the ninth and final section.

MON CAY TO QUANG YEN (Fig. 18)

Between the Chinese frontier and the Fleuve Rouge delta forest-covered hills fall to a shore fringed by a large number of islands, varying greatly in size and form. This section of coast provides many secure anchorages, with depths of 5–10 fm. (9·1–18·2 m.), especially in the

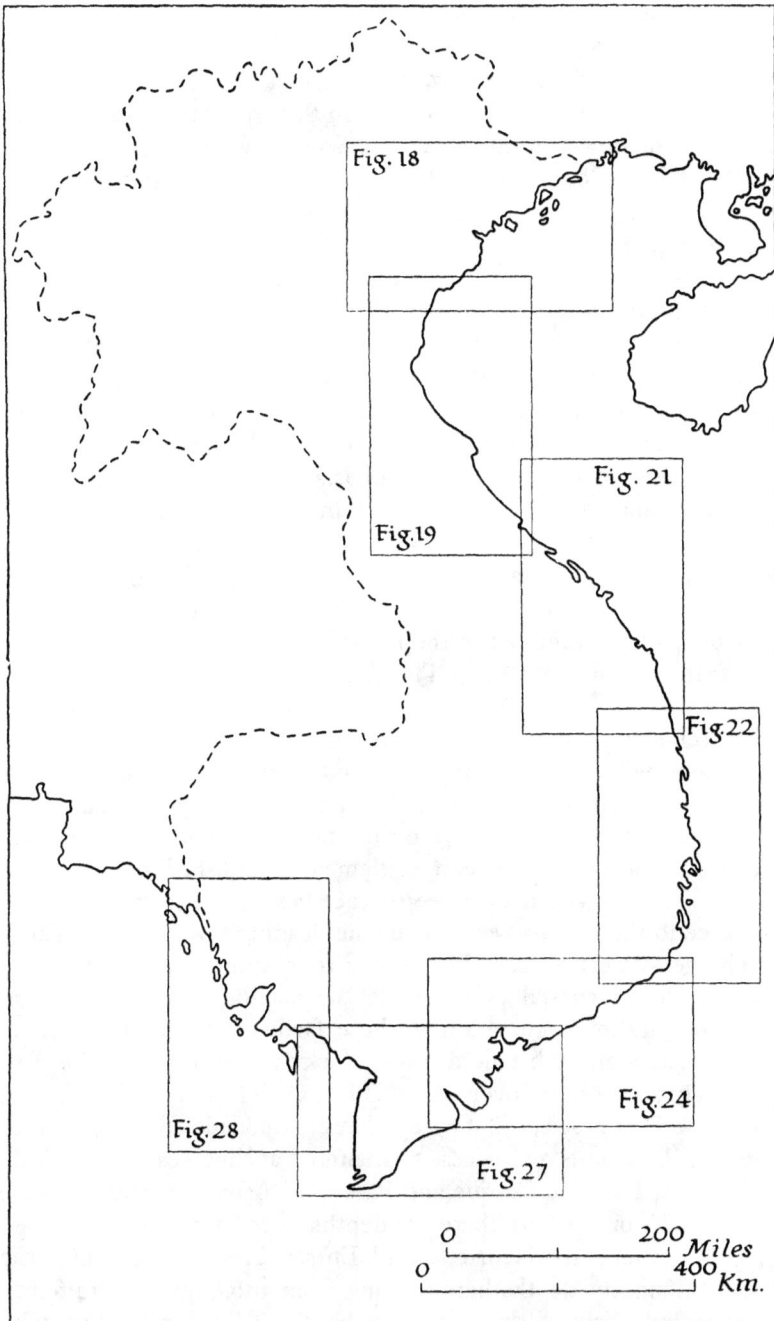

Fig. 17. Key to coastal maps (Figs. 18, 19, 21, 22, 24, 27, 28)

Baie d'Along and the Baie de Fai Tsi Long. The anchorages, which
are the only ones available for large vessels along the Tonkin littoral,
lie in relatively undisturbed waters, the rocky islands and islets on
their seaward side sheltering them from the typhoon in late summer
and from the powerful north-east monsoon in winter. There are few
landing places along this coast, as impenetrable mangrove swamps
occur in most parts where the shore is lowlying.

The stretch of coast from Mon Cay to Cam Pha is characterized
by a coastal plain of variable width and broken by low, rounded,
sandstone hills with the islands of Kersaint, Château Renaud, Grand
Singe, Deux Chaînes and Kebao lying offshore. These islands trend
north-east to south-west and are formed mainly of sandstone; they
rise steeply from the sea to over 150 m., and in places to over 400 m.
Farther out to sea are the Ile Madeleine, Ile de la Table, and Kao Tao
group. Between the inner group of islands and the mainland is a
narrow channel, 2–8 km. wide, with calm water at all seasons, owing
to its well-sheltered position. Extensive mangrove swamps and mud
banks border the coastal plain. Near Mon Cay, the Song Ca Long
has deposited alluvium and built up a delta the shape of which is
controlled by the sand bar of the Ile de Traco. With the exception of
the Song Ca Long and Song Tien Yen, the rivers are small, but all
have turbulent courses as they emerge from the hills. The town of
Tien Yen stands in a forested valley at the junction of the river of
that name with the Song Pho Ca, and about 8 km. above Pointe
Pagode from which point channels branch to Port Wallut and Cam
Pha. Port Wallut (see p. 399), on the northern shores of the Ile de
Kebao, is the only important settlement established on the inner
group of islands; Cam Pha (see p. 398) lies on the mainland at the
entrance to the narrow western channel leading towards Tien Yen.

The coast west of Cam Pha trends roughly east-west and has a
very restricted coastal plain, while the islands offshore are more
numerous and more rugged than those farther east. In the Baie de
Fai Tsi Long and the Baie d'Along, rocky limestone islets rise precipitously to heights of over 150 m. (Plate 5). The larger islands, such
as Rousse, Dao Trao and Cat Ba, are densely wooded. Several channels
between the islands give access to sheltered anchorages: the Passe de
la Mouche, Passe du Casque and Passe de l'Aspic lead into the Baie
de Fai Tsi Long, where there are depths of from 7 to 12 fm. (12·8–
21·9 m.); the Passe Henriette and Entrée Profonde lead into the
Baie d'Along, the depths here ranging from 5 to 8 fm. (9·1–14·6 m.).
The central parts of the two main bays are little encumbered by

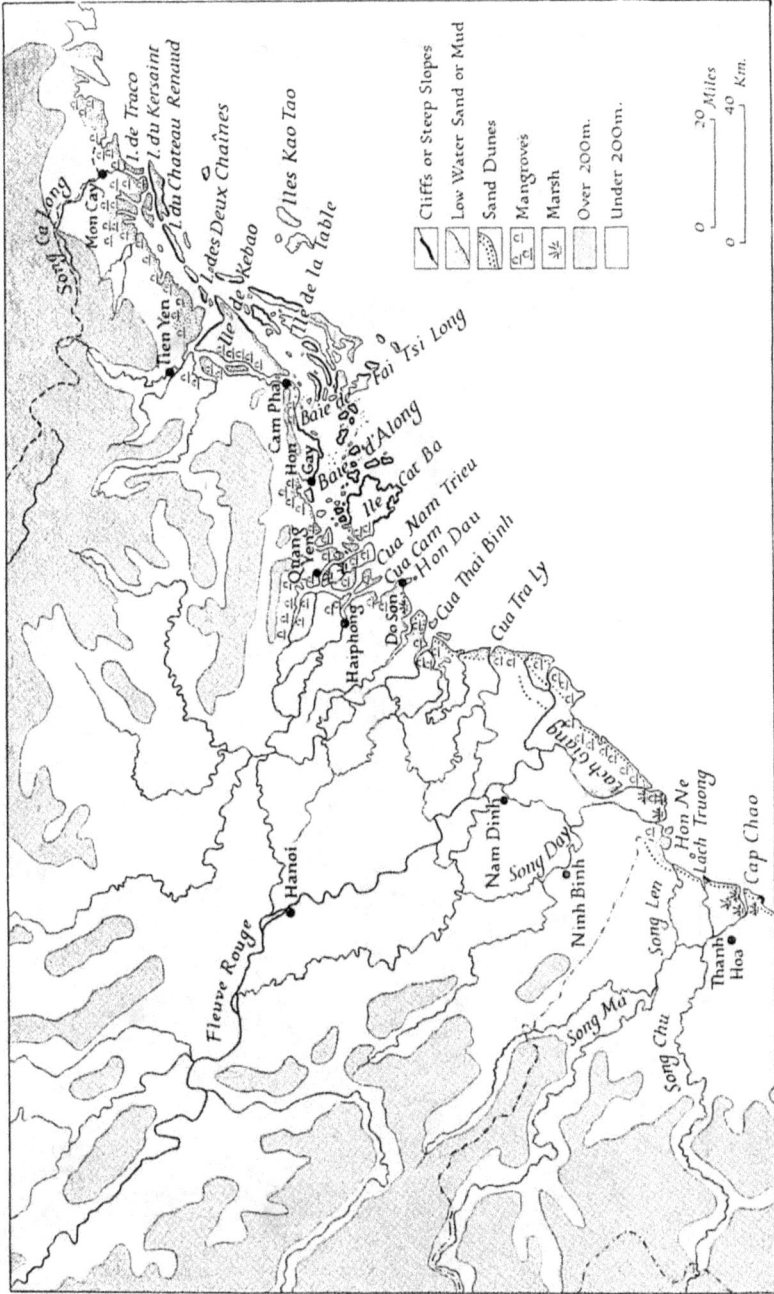

Fig. 18. Coastal features: Tonkin

Source: Carte de l'Indochine, 1:500,000; sheet no. 5 (1938).

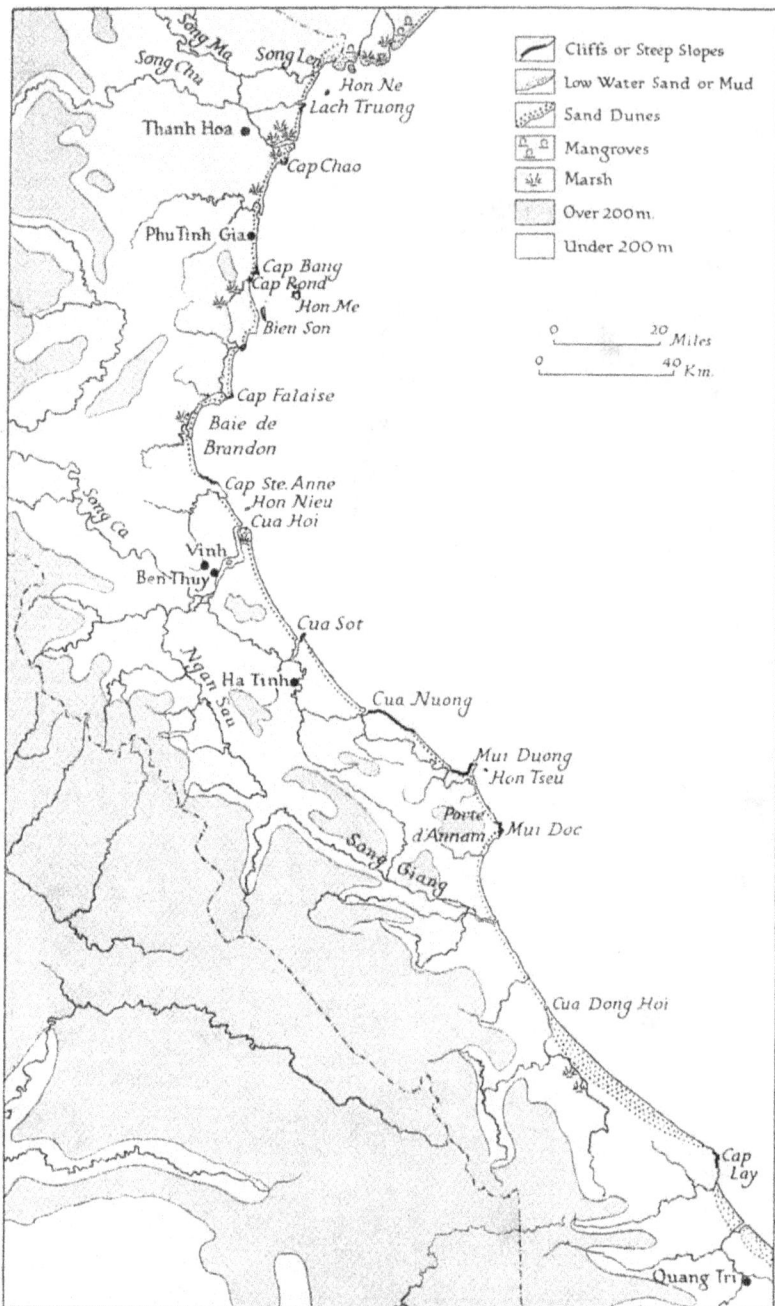

Cliffs or Steep Slopes
Low Water Sand or Mud
Sand Dunes
Mangroves
Marsh
Over 200 m.
Under 200 m

Song Ma
Song Chu
Song Lo
Hon Ne
Lach Truong
Thanh Hoa
Cap Chao
Phu Tinh Gia
Cap Baug
Cap Rond
Hon Me
Bien Son
Cap Falaise
Baie de Brandon
Cap Ste. Anne
Hon Nieu
Cua Hoi
Song Ca
Vinh
Ben Thuy
Cua Sot
Ngan Sau
Ha Tinh
Cua Nuong
Mui Duong
Hon Tseu
Porte d'Annam
Mui Doc
Song Giang
Cua Dong Hoi
Cap Lay
Quang Tri

0   20 Miles
0   40 Km.

Fig. 19. Coastal features: northern Annam
Source: Carte de l'Indochine, 1 : 500,000; sheets 8 (1929) and 11 (1931).

islands, but between them lies a stretch of water, dotted with rocky islets, extending to within half a kilometre of the mainland. This middle stretch has greater depths than either of the bays, and the Chenal d'Hamelin, which passes through it, is the principal approach to the port of Hon Gay (see p. 389). Along the coast of the mainland hills fall sharply to the sea; but 1 km. west of Hon Gay a narrow break (Cua Luc) gives entrance by sea to the small bay known as Port Courbet. Near Quang Yen, the Song Binh Huong and other streams have built up a delta for the most part overgrown by man-groves. Except at Hon Gay, where there are several coal wharves, few landing places are available on this coast.

Communications

An electric railway, about 8 km. in length, connects Cam Pha with the neighbouring coal mines; and a steam railway, 11 km. in length, runs from Hon Gay to the coal mines of Ha Tou. Both lines are of metre gauge.

A road connects Mon Cay and Quang Yen by way of Tien Yen, Cam Pha and Hon Gay. Another metalled road runs inland from Tien Yen to Lang Son near the Chinese frontier.

FLEUVE ROUGE (RED RIVER) DELTA (Fig. 18)

The coastline of the Fleuve Rouge delta comprises recent marine deposits, sand dunes and alluvium. There are few good anchorages. The Cua Nam Trieu forms part of the main approach channel to Haiphong, the second port in Indo-China (see p. 380). Dinh Vu island, a swampy stretch of land overgrown with mangroves, lies between the Cua Nam Trieu and the Cua Cam, on which Haiphong stands, a canal, 1 km. in length, linking the two waterways. Near Do Son, south of the Cua Cam estuary, the general flatness is relieved by rounded hills, reaching in places to over 100 m., while a narrow peninsula, with undulating relief, juts out to sea for nearly 6 km. Vessels may anchor off Hon Dau which lies 2 km. south-east of this peninsula; there is a lighthouse and semaphore station on the island.

The Fleuve Rouge and its tributaries, the Tra Ly, the Lach Giang and the Day, which enter the sea south of the Do Son penin-sula, have mouths seldom more than half a kilometre wide, though the volume of water carried is much greater than in the streams farther north (see p. 10). Low sand dunes and vast expanses of sea mud, backed by rice fields, protected from flooding by artificial embankments, figure largely in the central and southern stretches of the delta coastline. The dunes run parallel with the shore, north-south from the Song Thai Binh to the mouth of the Fleuve Rouge and north-east, south-west in the remaining section to the mouth of the Song Day. The southerly coastline of the delta is progressing seawards at the rate of about 100 m. a year, the rivers here carrying a large body of alluvium, while much other material is carried southwards by currents.

Communications

No railway reaches to the coast; the nearest railway connexions are at Haiphong, Nam Dinh and Ninh Binh, from 10 to 40 km. inland. Several good metalled roads from Do Son, Quat Lam and Van Ly, link up with the road network in other parts of the delta.

FLEUVE ROUGE (RED RIVER) DELTA TO PORTE D'ANNAM (Fig. 19)

This section of coast is bordered by an almost continuous line of dunes broken only in a few places by cliffs and by the estuaries of the Song Len, Song Ma and Song Ca. The coast lies athwart the path of the north-east monsoon which blows strongly during the winter months and hinders the movement of shipping at this period. There are few sheltered anchorages. Most of the rivers have sand bars at their mouths, and only vessels of shallow draught can enter them.

Between the Tonkin-Annam frontier and the Song Len estuary sand dunes bear NNW-SSE, parallel with the coast, and extend in long lines separated by narrow depressions, though the actual shoreline comprises low banks made up of mud carried from the Fleuve Rouge delta by an offshore current. Considerable areas of the mud flats are overgrown with mangroves. Near the frontier and about 3 km. inland broken limestone hills, which rise precipitously to heights of over 100 m., form a prominent landmark. The Song Len, 7 km. to the south, has a winding course with a narrow mouth encumbered by shifting sand and mud. Hon Ne, which lies a short distance offshore, provides a sheltered anchorage in depths of about $3\frac{3}{4}$ fm. (6·9 m.). Another anchorage is available in the Lach Truong estuary, 10 km. from the Song Len. A low range of hills marks the entrance to the Lach Truong, and southwards from there, in the Song Ma delta region, gently sloping beaches backed by low dunes predominate. The Song Ma is one of the longest rivers of north Indo-China, and like the Fleuve Rouge, it has a variable regime with maximum flow at the end of the summer; the entrance to the river is obstructed by a bar with depths over it of less than 1 fm. (<2 m.). Thanh Hoa, a provincial capital, lies about 15 km. above the mouth of the Song Ma.

Irregularity of shore form characterizes the coastal stretch between the Song Ma and Song Ca deltas. About 5 km. south-south-west of the mouth of the Song Ma lies the small granite peninsula of Sam Son, with Cap Chao, 45 m. in height, at its eastern end (Fig. 20). This

Fig. 20. Cap Chao

This granite headland, 45 m. in height, is a prominent feature south of the Song Ma delta.

Source: Georges Maspero, *Un Empire Colonial français: l'Indochine*, vol. II, p. 250 (Paris, 1930).

cape has sandy beaches on either side of it, which are used as landing places for local craft. For nearly 30 km. south of Cap Chao the coast has a regular outline with dunes extending inland for 1 or 2 km. The coastal plain behind the dunes is thickly peopled and intensively cultivated. Near Phu Tinh Gia the plain narrows to less than 10 km., and the zone of sand ridges along the shore thins out appreciably. A range of hills, from 300 to 600 m. high, approaches to within 5 km. of the shore, the chief summits being Nui Tu Vi (559 m.), a conical-

shaped peak, Nui Kak (500 m.), and Nui Bom (326 m.). Two headlands, Cap Bang (91 m.) and Cap Rond (92 m.), break the smoothness
of the coast a short distance south of Phu Tinh Gia, and close to these
headlands are several rocky islets, notably Bien Son (169 m.), on
which there is a lighthouse, Hon Me (234 m.) and Hon Dot (109 m.).
Vessels may anchor in depths of from 4 to 4½ fm. (7·3–8·2 m.) off the
south-western side of Hon Me. A little south of Cap Bang lies the
Baie de Brandon, and from here the coastline of the Gulf of Tonkin,
which has trended in a general NNE-SSW direction for several hundreds
of kilometres, bears NNW-SSE. The bay, which is entered between Cap
Falaise (169 m.) and Cap Ste Anne, affords little shelter; there is,
however, a good anchorage for vessels of shallow draught in the
Lach Quen estuary in the lee of the former headland. A gently
inclined sandy beach runs round the head of the bay, while several
small coves backed by hills indent its south-western shores.

In the Song Ca (Cua Hoi) delta region and in the neighbourhood of
Ha Tinh the coast is once again predominantly regular in outline.
Parallel series of sand dunes fringe the shore and, unlike those in the
Thanh Hoa region, the dunes here have few settlements on them.
The Song Ca has a bar at its mouth, composed of hard sand and
liable to frequent change; in 1930, a channel was dredged through the
bar, when at high water ships drawing 5·2 m. (17 ft.) could ascend
20 km. upstream to the small port of Ben Thuy (see p. 393). Several
islets lie in the approaches to the mouth of the river: Hon Matt
(217 m.) provides a sheltered anchorage off its south-western shores
in a depth of 11 fm. (20·1 m.). Hon Nieu (132 m.) also provides an
anchorage protected from north-easterly winds in a depth of about
4¼ fm. (8 m.). South-east of the Song Ca, a number of conical-
shaped summits overlook the coast; Nui Ong, lying about 4 km.
inland, is the highest peak with an elevation of 710 m. The hills are
terminated by the Cua Sot estuary, while southward of the estuary
is the conspicuous promontory of Mui Sot. This headland rises
steeply to a height of 87 m. and is connected with the coast by a
narrow, low, sandy isthmus; Ru Sot (387 m.) stands about 1 km.
inland from the isthmus. Ha Tinh, the capital of the province of
that name, is situated in a well-watered plain 10 km. south of Ru
Sot. The plain narrows close to the Cua Nuong estuary, and from
here southwards there are high and precipitous cliffs with sandy
beaches between them. Mui Duong, a rocky promontory, 174 m.
high, is the most conspicuous of these cliffs; two islets offshore, Hon
Tseu (144 m.) and Hon Shim (33 m.), have good anchorages in

Plate 5. Baie d'Along

The coastal waters are studded with numerous rocky limestone islets, some of which rise precipitously to a height of over 150 m. The larger ones are inhabited by troupes of monkeys.

Plate 6. Coast near the mouth of the Huong Giang

View looking westward over the lagoons into which the Huong Giang (left background) flows before entering the sea by the gap between the two sandspits, seen near the centre of the photograph. Hue lies about 12 km. up the river.

Plate 7. The Montagnes de Marbre south of Tourane

These limestone hills are probably of Devonian age and rise abruptly from the alluvial plain. They have numerous caves, some of which contain Buddhist shrines. The hills are almost entirely surrounded by flooded rice fields.

depths of about 6 fm. (11 m.). A sandy beach, backed by dunes, follows south of Mui Duong, but after 12 km. a high spur from the Chaîne Annamitique reaches the coast in several rocky capes, the most prominent of which is Mui Doc, 236 m. in elevation; the Porte d'Annam is the subsidiary spur joining this cape to the main range.

Communications

A single-track, metre-gauge, railway, part of the Trans-Indo-Chinese line from Hanoi to Saigon, runs along the coastal plain only a short distance from the shore as far as Vinh, but beyond here turns inland up the Ngan Sau valley, approaching the coast again south of the Porte d'Annam. A short branch line connects Vinh and the port of Ben Thuy.

Several good roads connect the shoreline with the Route Coloniale no. 1 which runs through the whole coastal region. Other routes following the Song Ma and Song Ca valleys give access to the interior plateaux.

PORTE D'ANNAM TO CAP BATANGAN (Figs. 19, 21)

The coastal stretch between the Porte d'Annam and Cap Batangan, a distance of nearly 500 km., continues the predominant NNW-SSE trend and also resembles the section previously described with its long lines of sand dunes. On the other hand, the coastal plain is generally narrower than in the Thanh Hoa, Vinh and Ha Tinh regions. Although many streams have turbulent courses and often carry a large body of water, none is comparable in length to the Song Ma or the Song Ca. The bay and port of Tourane is the most frequently used anchorage. Long stretches of the coast, however, possess no anchorages, and strong winds at times make approach from the sea difficult.

For about 250 km. from the Porte d'Annam to the Lagune de Cau Hai, south of Hue, the shore curves smoothly south-south-east, and except for the low promontory of Cap Lay, comprises sandy beaches backed by dunes. The entrance to the Song Giang, a considerable stream which rises on the slopes of the Col de Mu Gia, provides an anchorage in a depth of 6 fm. (11 m.), but there is a bar off the mouth which should not be crossed without local knowledge. Another good anchorage is available off Cua Dong Hoi, but owing to the exposed position it cannot be used during the period of the north-east monsoon. South of Dong Hoi, the zone of sand dunes behind the coast increases in width from 1 or 2 km. to as much as 7 km., while they often attain an altitude of 30 m. Between the sandy littoral and the steep-sided hills lies a fertile strip of lowland built by alluvium from a large number of relatively small streams. This lowland is densely peopled and has extensive areas under rice. Cap Lay, formed of granite and 30 m. in elevation, is the only conspicuous feature along the coast; its forest covering contrasts markedly with the absence of vegetation on the sand dunes to the north and south. The dune coast continues southward of Cap Lay, and close to the mouth of the Huong Giang there is an inner and outer belt separated by shallow lagoons, varying in width from 1 to 4 km. (Plate 6). Vessels drawing 1·5 m. (5 ft.) may ascend the Huong Giang to Hue, the capital of Annam, in late summer. At the southerly extreme of the Lagune de l'Est another lagoon, the Lagune de Cau Hai, about 15 km. from east to west and about 6 km. from north to south, terminates the great belt of sand dunes which have been so prominent a feature of the coast all the way from the Porte d'Annam.

South of the Lagune de Cau Hai as far as Tourane, the coast becomes rugged and irregular in outline as spurs from the Chaîne Annamitique fall sharply to the sea. Cap Chon May overlooks a semicircular bay where there is an anchorage in a depth of 7 fm. (12·8 m.), with good holding ground, though it becomes dangerous to shipping and hardly tenable in the period of the north-east monsoon. An upland area with two main summits, Nui Vinh Fong (473 m.) and Dong Nhut (585 m.), lies immediately behind the bay on its south-western side. After a short stretch of sandy beaches, covered with brushwood, the coast again takes on a rugged appearance. The high spur of the Col des Nuages, which has several summits over 1000 m. elevation, juts far out to sea on the north-western side of the Baie de Tourane. The bay is entered between this spur and the rocky Presqu'île de Tien Sha (600 m.), joined to the mainland by a low isthmus. Vessels of shallow draught can find a sheltered anchorage south-east of the Ilôt de l'Observatoire, a small islet linked by an embankment of the Presqu'île de Tien Sha; a deeper, though more exposed anchorage lies west or south-west of this islet. The north-western shores of the Baie de Tourane are generally steep and bordered by rocks lying close offshore, but the head of the bay is low, with a broad sandy beach (Plate 8). The port of Tourane, which lies at the mouth of the Song Cam Le, is accessible to ships with a draught of about 3·7 m. (12 ft.).

The stretch of coast from Tourane to Cap Batangan for the most

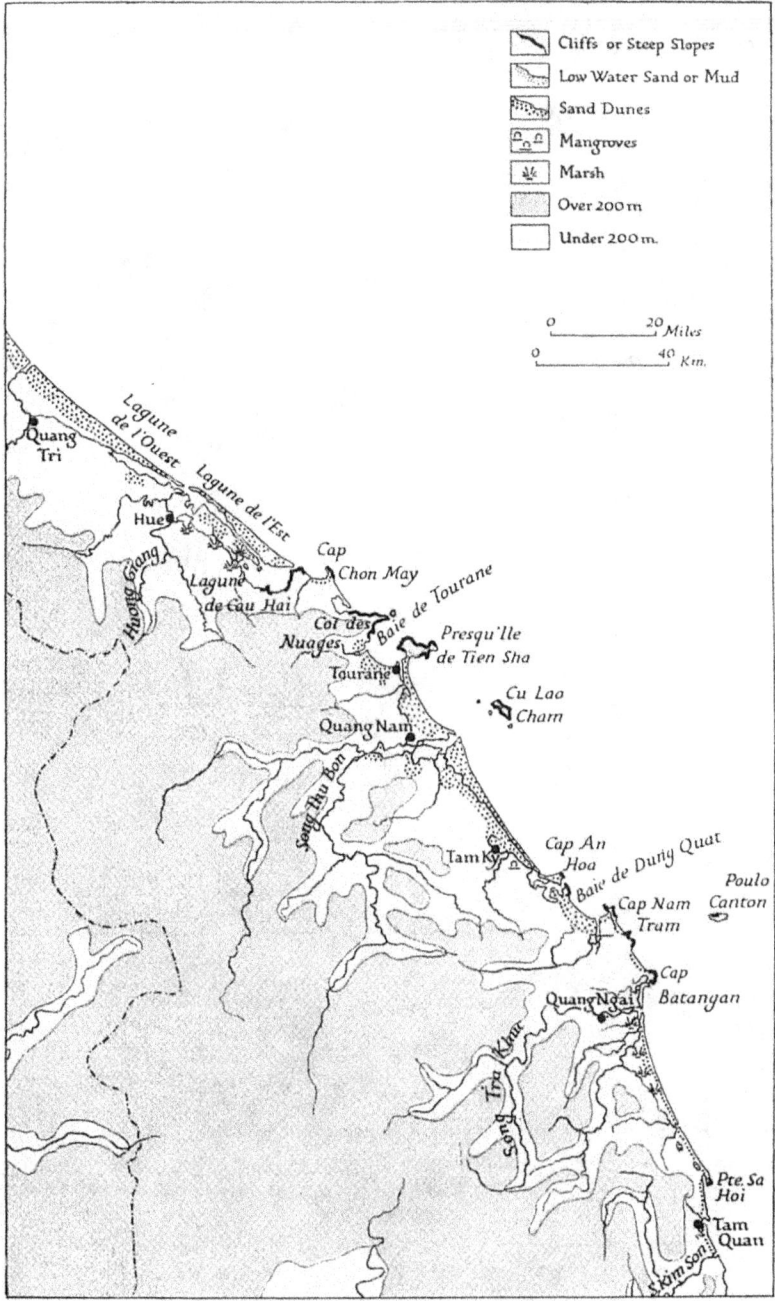

Key (legend):
- Cliffs or Steep Slopes
- Low Water Sand or Mud
- Sand Dunes
- Mangroves
- Marsh
- Over 200 m.
- Under 200 m.

0 — 20 Miles
0 — 40 Km.

Quang Tri

Lagune de l'Ouest
Lagune de l'Est

Hue

Huong Giang

Lagune de Cau Hai

Cap Chon May

Baie de Tourane

Col des Nuages

Presqu'île de Tien Sha

Tourane

Quang Nam

Cu Lao Cham

Song Thu Bon

Tam Ky

Cap An Hoa

Baie de Dung Quat

Poulo Canton

Cap Nam Tram

Cap Batangan

Quang Ngai

Song Tra Khuc

Pte. Sa Hoi

Tam Quan

Kim Son

Fig. 21. Coastal features: central Annam
Source: Carte de l'Indochine, 1 : 500,000; sheets 11 and 12 (1931) and 15 (1927).

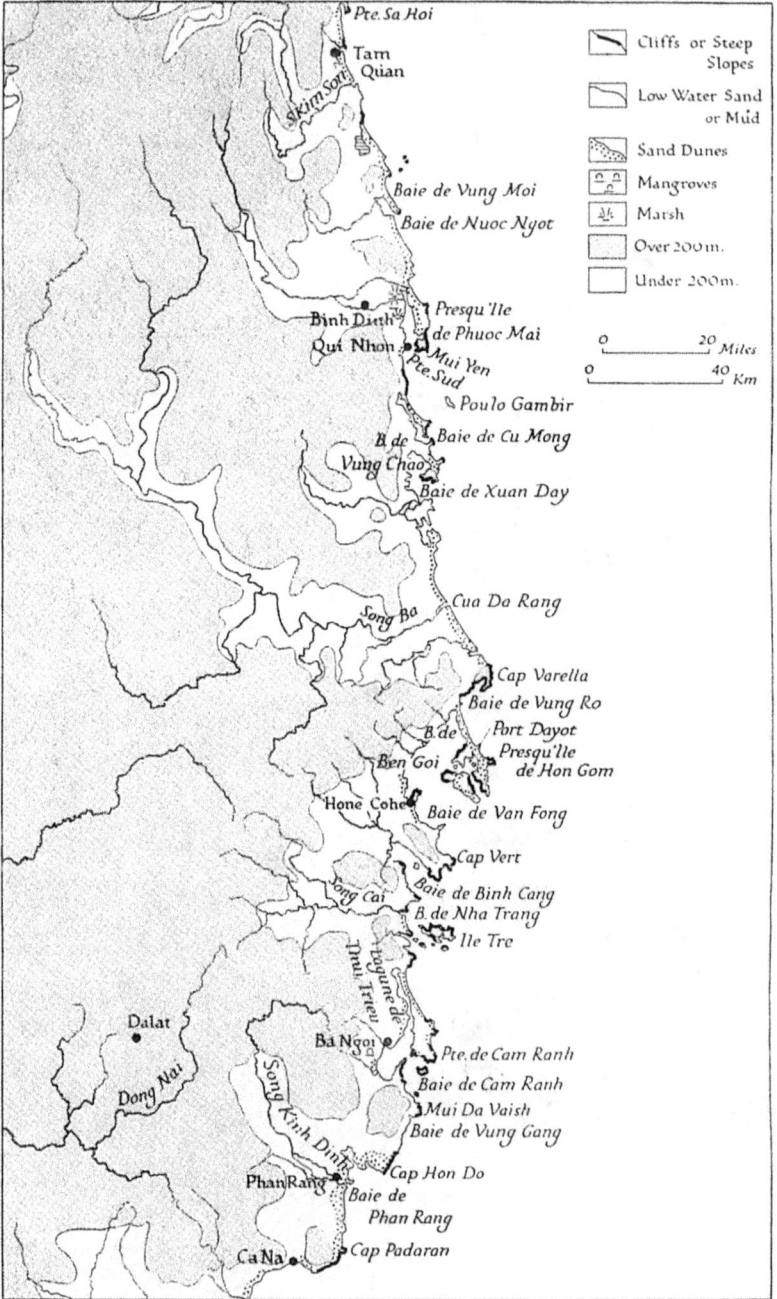

Fig. 22. Coastal features: southern Annam
Source: Carte de l'Indochine, 1 : 500,000; sheets 15 and 18 (1927).

part comprises long lines of sandy beaches, with shallow lagoons on their landward side. South of the Song Cam Le the coastal plain broadens to more than 20 km.; near Quang Nam several rocky hills, the Montagnes de Marbre, form prominent landmarks (Plate 7). The plain is watered by numerous streams which carry a heavy volume of water, particularly after the period of maximum rainfall in late summer. Inland waterways link the Baie de Tourane with the Song Thu Bon which follows more than one channel while crossing the coastal plain, but enters the sea by a single mouth, the Cua Dai. A group of islands lies about 15 km. off the entrance to the river; the largest island, Cu Lao Cham (517 m.), provides a sheltered anchorage on its south-western side in depths of from 4 to 4½ fm. (7·3–8·2 m.). For over 50 km. southwards from Cua Dai no break occurs in the line of sand dunes; as in the coastal region near Hue, there is a narrow outer belt of dunes forming the actual shoreline separated from the much broader inner belt by a lagoon-like water-way. Near Tam Ky, the zone of dunes becomes broken up by numerous small streams into isolated sandy stretches, while the width of the coastal plain here narrows considerably, steep-sided hills rising abruptly to over 200 m. and, farther inland, to over 1,000 m. (Nui Chua, 1,362 m.). From the coastal plain, Cap An Hoa or Pointe Happoix (41 m.) appears like a rocky island, though it is in fact the northern extremity of a lowlying peninsula which borders the Baie de Dung Quat. This bay has sandy shores, except close to Cap An Hoa and to the two headlands, Pointe Intérieure and Cap Nam Tram, marking the approach from the south-east. The mouth of the Song Tra Bon lies at the head of the bay; at high water, vessels drawing 1·8 m. (6 ft.) can anchor off the eastern bank about 1 km. within the entrance to the river. During the north-east monsoon the Baie de Dung Quat presents no sheltered anchorages, but at other times vessels may anchor south-westwards of the Pointe Intérieure in depths of from 3 to 9 fm. (5·5–16·5 m.). Between Cap Nam Tram and Cap Batangan lie three small bays, each of which have depths of less than 5 fm. (9·1 m.). About 25 km. offshore is the island group of Poulo Canton, consisting of Cu Lao Re (179·5 m.) and Cu Lao Bo Bai (33 m.), both surrounded by a reef. Cap Batangan, 34 m. high, is fringed by a reef, and rocks lie offshore for a distance of over 1 km.

Communications

The Trans-Indo-Chinese railway runs along the coastal plain on the landward side of the sand dunes, except in the mountainous region between Hue and Tourane, where it passes through several tunnels under the Col des Nuages.

Long stretches of the sand dunes which fringe the coast are crossed only by narrow, winding tracks, but good roads lead from Cua Viet to Quang Tri, Thuan An to Hue, Cua Dai to Quang Nam, and Son Tra to Xuan Yen. The coastal plain is traversed throughout its length by the Route Coloniale no. 1, a well-metalled road suitable for motor traffic. Two roads allow penetration of the interior mountains: the one from Quang Tri leading via the Col d'Ai Lao to Savannakhet, the other from Tam Ky to Kontum. A network of roads serves the densely populated plains, particularly around Hue, Tourane, and Tam Ky.

CAP BATANGAN TO CAP VARELLA (Figs. 21, 22)

The coast in this section, which follows an alinement almost due north-south, is made up partly of low sandhills with a narrow, well-watered plain adjoining, and partly of sheltered bays backed by high mountains. The Song Ba, the longest river of central and southern Annam, enters the sea along this stretch of coast. There are many fine anchorages available for large ships in the bays south of Binh Dinh; landing places exist in certain of these bays. The small port of Qui Nhon lies at the entrance to the bay of the same name.

For over 120 km. southwards from Cap Batangan to the Presqu'île de Phuoc Mai the coast is predominantly regular in outline and comprises sandy beaches with a belt of dunes extending an average distance of 1 km. inland. Some of the sandhills reach a height of more than 50 m. Quang Ngai, a provincial capital and market town, lies 10 km. from the sea in the centre of the coastal plain, on the right bank of the Song Tra Khuc. The coastal plain narrows farther south to less than 5 km. in width, and three small lakes or lagoons have formed behind the sandhills close to Pointe Sa Hoi (92 m.). Sand-spits almost enclose the mouths of the Song Tam Quan and Song Kim Son, both of which provide anchorages offshore in depths of 7–8 fm. (12·8–14·6 m.). A chain of mountains, over 600 m. in height, rises sharply from the Song Kim Son, but after only 7 km. the coast again becomes low and sandy, except for the rocky projections overlooking the bays of Vung Moi and Nuoc Ngot. A group of rocky islets lies off the northern shores of the Baie de Vung Moi, and during the south-west monsoon there is a good anchorage for vessels in depths of about 8 fm. (14·6 m.). The mountains which fringe the

Plate 8. Baie de Tourane

The town of Tourane lies at the head of the bay on the left bank of the estuary of the Song Cam Le. In the background are the mountains of the Col des Nuages.

Plate 9. Entrance to the Baie de Qui Nhon

View looking south-south-west towards the open sea. Qui Nhon lies at the base of the sand spit in the middle distance; the Presqu'île de Phuoc Mai is in the foreground.

Plate 10. Baie de Nha Trang

The Song Cai, on which the town of Nha Trang lies, enters the head of the bay.

coast near the Baie de Nuoc Ngot continue south with only one short break to the Presqu'île de Phuoc Mai.

The Presqu'île de Phuoc Mai is the northernmost part of a rugged stretch of coastline which includes the four sheltered bays of Qui Nhon, Cu Mong, Xuan Day and Vung Chao. The Baie de Qui Nhon is bounded on the east by the mountains of Phuoc Mai and on the west by the cultivated plains surrounding Binh Dinh. It has a narrow entrance between the rocky headland of Pointe Sud and the Pointe de Gia, the termination of a sandspit on which stands the town and port of Qui Nhon (Plate 9). A bar obstructs the entrance, but a channel has been dredged through it to a depth of $2\frac{3}{4}$ fm. (5 m.), and immediately within the bar vessels may find secure anchorage in a small area in depths of from 5 to 12 fm. (9·1–21·9 m.). The rest of the bay is shallow.

The Baie de Cu Mong, which lies about 20 km. south of Qui Nhon, is entered from the sea between two low headlands set about 2 km. apart. Small vessels can anchor south-south-west of the entrance in a depth of $2\frac{3}{4}$ fm. (5 m.). Poulo Gambir, whose lighthouse guides shipping to the port of Qui Nhon, lies about 8 km. offshore.

A rocky peninsula, about 5 km. in width, separates the Baie de Cu Mong from the two large inlets of Vung Chao and Xuan Day. This peninsula has several small indentations on its eastern side, and above these shores hills rise sharply to over 200 m. elevation. There are high cliffs at the headland known as Mui No O. Vung Chao, one of the most sheltered bays on the coast of Indo-China, is approached through the Baie de Xuan Day. Steep cliffs, about 70 m. in height, mark the broad entrance to the latter, within which there are depths of from 6 to 8 fm. (11–14·6 m.). During the north-east monsoon, the anchorages here are less secure than those in the Baie de Vung Chao, where, however, the depths seldom exceed 4 fm. (7·3 m.). The coastal plain along the western shore of the two bays is very restricted in area, while spurs divide it into a number of separate sections. Song Cau, a provincial capital and small market town, stands where the river of the same name enters the Baie de Vung Chao.

Between the Baie de Xuan Day and Cap Varella the shoreline becomes more regular with sandy beaches backed by sandhills, while the bordering mountains gradually recede, giving place to a broad coastal plain around the mouth of the Song Ba (Cua Da Rang). This river has a width of about 3 km. near where it enters the sea, though the actual mouth is less than $\frac{1}{2}$ km. wide owing to the growth of two sandspits. South of the Cua Da Rang, the low sandy plain, here overgrown by trees, is abruptly terminated by a high spur which reaches the sea in the prominent granitic headland of Cap Varella. This headland consists of steep cliffs rising to four rocky peaks, each over 300 m. in elevation (Fig. 23).

Fig. 23. Cap Varella

This headland, the most easterly point of Indo-China, lies about 100 km. north of the Baie de Cam Ranh and about the same distance south of the port of Qui Nhon. The stretch of water in the centre background is the sheltered Baie de Vung Ro. The Route Coloniale no. 1 is seen following the slopes of the hills in the left background.
Source: photograph.

Communications

From Quang Ngai to Tam Quan the Trans-Indo-Chinese line runs close to the coast on the inner side of the sand dunes, but beyond here it follows a course from 20 to 30 km. inland, approaching the coast again north of the Cua Da Rang. The railway passes through a long tunnel under the mountain range of which Cap Varella is the eastern extremity. The port of Qui Nhon is connected by a branch line with the main railway.

The Route Coloniale no. 1 follows a course similar to that of the railway. Near Qui Nhon it divides into two sections, the one following close to the railway, the other keeping near to the coast. Other roads run inland from Quang Ngai to Kontum (Route Coloniale no. 14), and from Binh Dinh to Plei Ku (Route Coloniale no. 19).

CAP VARELLA TO CAP PADARAN (Fig. 22)

South of Cap Varella lies the most rugged and broken section of the Indo-Chinese coastline. Granitic peninsulas, bounded by cliffs and with rocky islands offshore, enclose deep-water inlets with small, marshy plains at their heads, while above the strips of lowland rise high and forested mountains. Ben Goi, Nha Trang, Cam Ranh and Phan Rang bays form the principal inlets, within which are many secure anchorages suitable for the largest class of ship. Owing to the nature of the relief, landings can only be made at a few places; railway and road run close to the coast.

Three out of the four rocky peaks forming Cap Varella lie on a peninsula, rather less than 2 km. across, which borders the Baie de Vung Ro on its eastern side. This bay has depths of from 8 to 10 fm. (14·6–18·2 m.) and is one of the safest anchorages along the coast of Annam. Ten kilometres to the south the Presqu'île de Hon Gom, enclosing the two bays of Van Fong and Ben Goi, juts out to sea in a NNW-SSE direction, its mountainous southern extremity being joined to the mainland by a low sandy isthmus. Hon Lon lies off the western shores of the peninsula and overlooks the sheltered inlet of Port Dayot, where vessels may find safe anchorage at all times of the year in depths of 8–12 fm. (14·6–22 m.). The Baie de Van Fong, which leads into the Baie de Ben Goi, is approached between Hon Lon and Mui Ban Than (Cap Vert); a more sheltered approach to Ben Goi is through the Lach Cua Be and Port Dayot channels. Both bays provide anchorages in depths varying from 6 to 12 fm. (11–22 m.); the shallow bight of Hone Cohe in the Baie de Ben Goi gives shelter for small vessels (see p. 400). A number of fishing villages are situated along the shores of the mainland. Behind the narrow coastal plain, the range of La Mère et l'Enfant (2,050 m.) is a high and conspicuous feature, though the mountains frequently become obscured by cloud.

The Baie de Binh Cang and the Baie de Nha Trang, the next large inlets along the coast, are entered between Mui Hon Thi (Pointe Sèche), a little south of Cap Vert, and Ile Tre which consists of three wooded summits (400–600 m.) connected by low isthmuses. Mui Ke Ga, a headland with steep cliffs over 30 m. in elevation, separates the two bays. The Baie de Binh Cang is over 15 km. in length and from 5 to 7 km. in width, but the stretch above the group of forested islets, half-way from its entrance, is very shallow. Below the islets, depths increase from 1½ to 9 fm. (2·7–16·5 m.) near the entrance and vessels can find safe anchorage here during both monsoons. The Baie de Nha Trang has deeper water, but is more exposed than Binh Cang. Its western shores consist mainly of a sandy beach on which landings can easily be made. The Song Cai enters the head of the bay, and at its mouth, which is obstructed by a bar, lies the town of Nha Trang. Inland from here the Song Cai has cut a broad valley through mountains exceeding 600 m. in height (Plate 10).

The coast southwards from the Baie de Nha Trang is rugged for a few kilometres, with Mui Dong Ba as the most prominent feature, but beyond here it becomes lowlying with sandhills backed by the Lagune de Thui Trieu. This lagoon and the marshland above it drains into the Baie de Cam Ranh.

The Baie de Cam Ranh is one of the finest natural harbours in Indo-China, offering secure and sheltered anchorages throughout the year to all classes of ships (see p. 395). It consists of an outer and inner reach, both having deep water and good holding ground. Two conspicuous headlands, the Pointe de Cam Ranh and Mui Da Vaish or Faux Cap Varella (419 m.), mark the entrance to the outer section, within which there are several rocky islands such as Ile Tagne, Hon Shut, and the Ile de la Prise. The best anchorages are found in the waters north of Ile Tagne in depths from 8 to 11 fm. (14·6–20·1 m.). Le Goulet, a channel about 1 km. wide and bordered by two capes, Mui Hon Lan and Mui Sept, which form the northern extreme of the mountain ranges bordering the outer bay, gives access to the sheltered inner harbour of Cam Ranh. Good holding ground exists in all parts of the bay, but the most frequently used anchorage lies northwards of Mui Hon Lan, in depths of about 8 fm. (14·6 m.). The bay becomes very shallow near the mouth of the Lagune de Thui Trieu, reference to which has already been made. A narrow coastal plain, watered by numerous small streams and in places overgrown by mangroves, fringes the inner harbour. Ba Ngoi is a small port on its western shores (see p. 395).

South of Mui Da Vaish or Faux Cap Varella the coast is irregular and mountains rise steeply inland to over 800 m. The Baie de Vung Gang, immediately south of this headland, has deep water (15 fm.) close offshore and provides a good anchorage. In this rocky stretch, the coast trends NNE-SSW, but after about 20 km. it bears almost due east-west along the north side of the Baie de Phan Rang. This bay, which is entered between Cap Hon Do and the mouth of the Song Kinh Dinh, has good holding ground, and safe anchorage can be

Fig. 24. Coastal features: southern Annam and eastern Cochin-China

Source: Carte de l'Indochine, 1 : 500,000; sheets 17 and 20 (1929).

obtained in a depth of $3\frac{3}{4}$ fm. (6·9 m.). Rocks lie close offshore around the greater part of the bay, while a sand bar obstructs the entrance to the Song Kinh Dinh. The town and port of Phan Rang (see p. 397) is situated on this river about 5 km. above its mouth, and a number of other settlements lie in the surrounding coastal plain. From the head of the Baie de Phan Rang, the coast runs in a north-south direction for over 20 km. to the prominent headland of Cap Padaran, its cliffs rising sharply to a height of 150 m.

Communications

After tunnelling through the mountain range west of Cap Varella, the Trans-Indo-Chinese railway passes along the shores of the Baie de Ben Goi and close to the shores of the Baie de Nha Trang. It then turns inland joining the coast again at Ba Ngoi, but from here south to Cap Padaran it keeps more than 10 km. inland. A branch line connects Tourcham with the hill station of Dalat.

The Route Coloniale no. 1 runs close to and parallel with the railway along the greater part of the coast. The road follows the western shores of the Baie de Cam Ranh and the Lagune de Thui Trieu to the north of it. Other roads run inland from the head of the Baie de Binh Cang to Ban Me Thuot on the Plateau du Darlac (Route Coloniale no. 21) and from Phan Rang to Dalat (Route Coloniale no. 11).

CAP PADARAN TO CAP SAINT JACQUES (Fig. 24)

This section of coast, which trends NE-SW, has two distinct stretches, comprising broad bays and rocky headlands as far as the Pointe de Ke Ga, whilst beyond here the shore is more regular in outline. Both monsoons blow parallel with the shore, and the adjoining coastal plain has a lower rainfall than any part of Indo-China. There are few deep anchorages, and those in shallow waters sometimes have insecure holding ground. Landings can be made at certain places along the coast.

Near Cap Padaran mountains rise abruptly from the sea, and the Baie de Padaran, a broad stretch of water with anchorages in depths of from 5 to 7 fm. (9·1–12·8 m.), lies between their south-western extremity and Pointe Lagan (Fig. 25). Reefs and sand or mud banks fringe its shore in several places, while hills restrict the coastal plain to a narrow strip, except near the village of Vinh Hao and north of Ca Na, where there is a low gap leading to Phan Rang. The Baie de

Phan Ri, the next large indentation along the coast, is bounded by Pointe Lagan and Pointe Guio; at its head vessels can anchor close to the mouth of the Song Luy in depths of 4–5 fm. (7·3–9·1 m.), and also off a rocky point east of Phan Ri in depths of about 2 fm. (3·6 m.). Sea fishing is here an important activity. The shores are

Fig. 25. Coast near Ca Na south of Phan Rang (drawn from a photograph)

Fig. 26. Cap Saint Jacques (drawn from a photograph)

The three granite hills overlooking the Baie de Ganh Rai (seen in the background) mark the seaward approach to the port of Saigon.

wooded east of Phan Ri, but treeless west of this town, where an isolated upland area, separated from the Chaîne Annamitique by the broad Song Luy valley, borders the coast. From Pointe Guio to the Pointe de Ke Ga, 70 km. to the south-west, there are first three small indentations backed by forested hills, then the large Baie de Phan Thiet. Shallow water, less than 3 fm. (5·5 m.) in depth, stands offshore for a distance of nearly 3 km. in the north-east of the bay, but the depths increase westwards, and off the town of Phan Thiet there is an anchorage in 4½ fm. (8·2 m.).

The stretch of coast westwards from the Baie de Phan Thiet is distinguished by the size of its sand dunes which extend some distance inland. These dunes frequently reach a height of 25–50 m., though some exceed 80 m.; they stand out prominently in the forested coastal plain. Cap Ba Kiem is the only prominent feature along the coast between the Pointe de Ke Ga and Cap Tiwan. The isolated range of mountains reaching to the sea at Cap Tiwan separates the dune coastline of south Annam from the alluvial shores of the Mekong delta. A shallow bay lies between this promontory and the triple-peaked headland of Cap Saint Jacques, which rises like an island overlooking the Baie de Ganh Rai (Fig. 26).

Communications

The Trans-Indo-Chinese railway runs close to the shores of the Baie de Padaran, then turns inland along the Song Luy valley and keeps at a distance of between 20 and 50 km. from the coast all the way to Saigon. A short branch railway connects the town of Phan Thiet with the main line.

The Route Coloniale No. 1 follows a similar course to that of the railway. Phan Thiet lies at the junction of this highway with the metalled road to Djiring. Another well-metalled route (Route Coloniale no. 15) leads from Cap Saint Jacques to Baria and Saigon. Secondary roads run inland from Phan Ri, Phan Thiet, Lagi, Pointe Tram, and the shores on both sides of Cap Tiwan.

MEKONG DELTA (Figs. 24, 27)

The coast in this section comprises river alluvium and sea mud with occasional expanses of sand along the shore. Three stretches of coast may be recognized: the delta of the Rivière de Saigon and the Dong Nai, the Mekong delta, and the Presqu'île de Ca Mau. Except in the approaches to the port of Saigon, no good anchorages exist, and owing to sand bars at their mouths few of the rivers are navigable to other than small vessels.

The delta of the Rivière de Saigon and the Dong Nai is entered between Cap Saint Jacques and the lowlying Pointe de Mirador, about 30 km. to the west-south-west. Saigon, the largest port in Indo-China, lies on the right bank of the Rivière de Saigon, 80 km. above its mouth (see p. 373). The main approach channel, which has a minimum depth of 5·8 m. (19 ft.), passes near to the high cliffs of Cap Saint Jacques, then turns north-westwards through the Baie de Ganh Rai to enter the Rivière de Saigon and follows its winding course upstream all the way to the port. Sluggish streams, tributary to the main stream, break up the lower delta region into numerous islands, for the most part overgrown by mangroves. The Song Soirap, which receives the waters of the Vaico Occidental about 12 km. above its mouth, can be used by small boats of shallow draught.

South-westwards of the Song Soirap lies the Mekong delta coast which, unlike the previous stretch, has a relatively small area under mangrove and a high proportion of land under cultivation. Moreover, the five distributaries of the main stream follow a much less tortuous course than those in the delta farther north. The Fleuve Antérieur, the easterly and principal arm of the Mekong, after dividing near Vinh Long into several branches, enters the sea by four mouths. Cua Tieu, the north-easternmost mouth, has depths of about 2·4 m. (8 ft.) over its bar and is used by vessels proceeding to the small port of My Tho, 40 km. upstream (see p. 407). The Fleuve Postérieur (Bassac) debouches into the sea in a single mouth, about 20 km. broad. The shores of the delta and the long narrow islands which encumber the lower reaches of the rivers frequently change in form, owing to constant deposition of sediment by fluvial or marine action. The island group of Poulo Condore lying about 100 km. from the mouth of the Fleuve Antérieur and in the track of vessels approaching Saigon, provides several good anchorages.

The Presqu'île de Ca Mau, which forms the southern extremity of Indo-China, is a vast lowlying plain with extensive areas covered by dense forest or mangrove swamp. Unlike the other two stretches of delta coast, no large river mouths break the smoothness of its shoreline. Offshore currents deposit material carried from the mouth of the Mekong, and in the south-west the coast is extending out to sea at the rate of 60–80 m. a year. From the mouth of the Fleuve Postérieur, the coast runs in a general north-east, south-west direction to the Pointe de Ca Mau, then turns sharply northwards to the Baie de Rach Gia, where it bears NW-SE in alinement. Two small rocky bluffs (Les Mamelles), 30 m. high, about 50 km. north of the Pointe de Ca Mau, are the only prominent features along the coast. The island group of Poulo Dama, off the western shores of the peninsula, provides an anchorage in depths of 5–7 fm. (9·1–12·8 m.). From the town of Rach Gia, situated on the bay of the same name, vessels drawing 1·8 m.

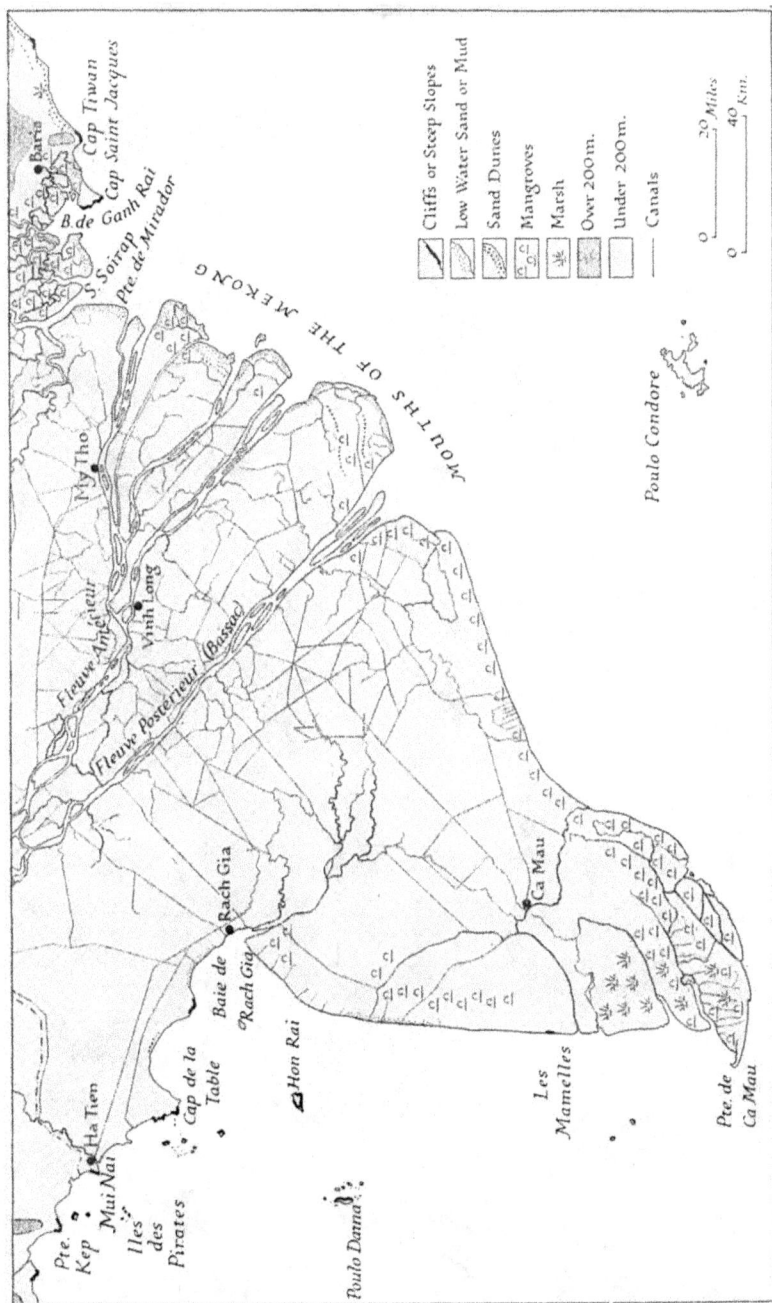

Fig. 27. Coastal features: Cochin-China

Source: Carte de l'Indochine, 1 : 500,000; sheets 17 and 20 (1929).

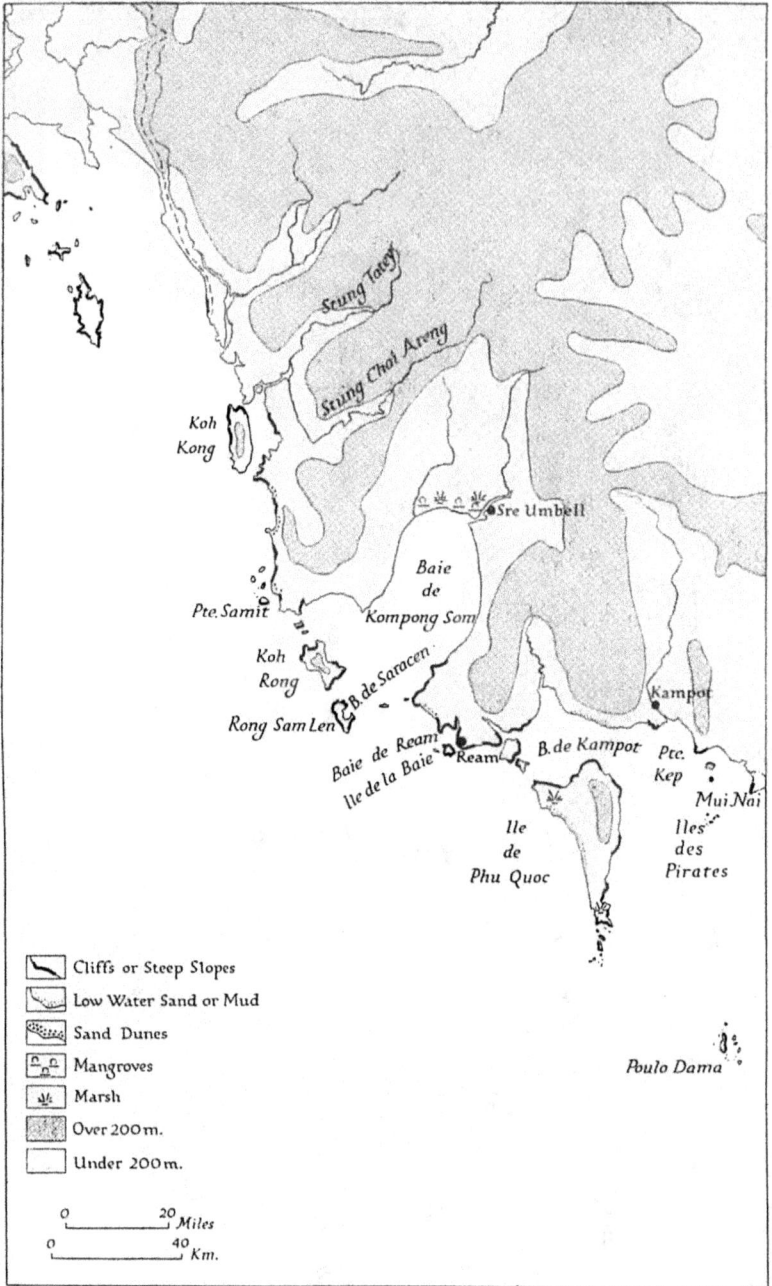

Fig. 28. Coastal features: Cambodia
Source: Carte de l'Indochine, 1 : 500,000; sheets 16, 17 and 20 (1929).

(6 ft.) can reach the Mekong by inland waterways. Cap de la Table
(184 m.), with several small rocky islands offshore, forms a prominent
landmark between Rach Gia and the alluvial plains around Ha Tien.

Communications

No railway runs inland from the coast. My Tho, on the Mekong
south-west of Saigon, is the terminus of the Trans-Indo-Chinese line.

A network of good roads serves the Mekong delta region, while
Rach Gia and Ha Tien also have road connexions with the interior.
In the frequently flooded coastal stretches of the Presqu'île de Ca
Mau there are very few roads, and the chief means of communication
is by water. The many navigable canals throughout the delta region
are widely used for travelling from place to place.

COAST OF CAMBODIA (Fig. 28)

With its rugged headlands and sheltered bays the coastline from Ha
Tien to the Siamese frontier resembles that between Cap Batangan
and Cap Padaran. The forested Chaîne de l'Eléphant and Monts des
Cardamomes, which rise steeply above the narrow coastal plain, lie
directly in the path of the south-west monsoon and receive the
heaviest rainfall in Indo-China. A number of sheltered anchorages
are available within the bays and close to several of the islands.
Except for the Baie de Kampot and Baie de Ream, the coast possesses
few landing places and has generally poor land communications.

Between Mui Nai overlooking the town of Ha Tien, and Pointe Kep,
20 km. north-westwards, lies a shallow bight, with the Ile du Pic and
the Iles des Pirates a short distance offshore. Vessels drawing 4 m.
(13 ft.) can anchor in the mouth of the Ha Tien river, while there are
also anchorages in depths of 3 fm. (5·5 m.) east of Hon Tre Lon
(Grand Pirate) and south of the Ile du Pic. Pointe Kep, a conspicuous headland rising to nearly 300 m. in height only about 1 km.
from the shore, forms the eastern border of the Baie de Kampot.
The approach to this bay from the Gulf of Siam is made through
channels to the east and west of Phu Quoc, a large rocky island, about
50 km. in length, with mountains bordering its northern, eastern and
southern shores. The deeper western channel, used by large vessels,
suffers from exposure to the south-west monsoon. Sheltered anchorages are found within the bay, 2 km. south of Cap Bumbi, in
depths of 3¾ fm. (6·9 m.). Near Kampot, the Chaîne de l'Eléphant
falls sharply to the sea.

North-westwards of the deep-water channel leading to Kampot lies the Baie de Ream, with several islands marking its entrance and a sandy beach backed by steep-sided hills at its head. Vessels of less than 4·6 m. (15 ft.) draught can enter the bay and anchor off the north-eastern extreme of the Ile de la Baie in a depth of about 3 fm. (5·5 m.). A little farther along the coast from Ream is the Baie de Kompong Som, one of the largest single indentations on the Indo-Chinese littoral, extending inland for nearly 80 km. and with a width of about 40 km. A group of rocky islands, including Rong Sam Len (229·5 m.), and Koh Rong (319 m.), lie in the entrance to the bay. There is a good anchorage in the Baie de Saracen, on the eastern side of Rong Sam Len, and also in sheltered waters off the north-eastern side of Koh Rong; the bay itself shallows rapidly inland and is exposed to the south-west monsoon. The northern shores are for the most part lowlying with extensive areas under mangrove. Beyond Pointe Samit, which bounds the Baie de Kompong Som on the north-west, the coast has many small irregularities, rocky headlands alternating with sandy bays. Where the swiftly flowing Stung Tatey enters the sea, Koh Kong, a table-topped island, 456 m. high at its northern end, lies close offshore. The channel between Koh Kong and the mainland offers a sheltered anchorage. Thirty kilometres north of this channel is the boundary between Indo-China and Siam.

Communications

There is no railway along or near the coast in this region. Ha Tien, Kampot, Ream and Sre Umbell, at the head of the Baie de Kompong Som, are connected by a lightly metalled road; from Kampot, the Route Coloniale no. 17 gives access to Phnom Penh. Only narrow, winding tracks penetrate the Monts des Cardamomes and the Chaîne de l'Eléphant.

BIBLIOGRAPHICAL NOTE

(1) The British *Admiralty Pilot* (*China Sea*, vol. 1, London, 1938) and the French *Instructions Nautiques: Mer de Chine*, vol. 1 (Paris, 1933) provide detailed descriptions of the coast and coastal waters.

(2) A general account of the coastline is given in R. Castex, *Les Rivages indochinois* (Paris, 1904) and in P. Gourou, *L'Utilisation du Sol en Indochine française*, pp. 49–65 (Paris, 1940). The coastal features of part of Tonkin are described in E. Chassigneux, 'La Région de Hai Ninh', *La Géographie*, vol. XLVI, pp. 33–68 (Paris, 1926), and in P. Gourou, *Les Paysans du Delta tonkinois*, pp. 35–42 (Paris, 1936). Another work which contains a good account of a short section of the coastline is C. Robequain, *Le Thanh Hoa: Etude géographique d'une Province annamite*, vol. II, pp. 255–75 (Paris, 1929).

(3) Relevant material will also be found elsewhere in this handbook in the chapters on ports, roads, railways and waterways.

Chapter III

CLIMATE

Introduction: Pressure and Winds: Typhoons: Temperature: Precipitation:
Humidity: Visibility: Cloudiness: Bibliographical Note

INTRODUCTION

Indo-China has a tropical monsoon climate, analogous in many ways
to that of Peninsular India or Burma. The regular seasonal alternation
of wind, with northerly winds in winter and southerly winds in
summer, controls almost every aspect of weather conditions. Important modifications in the general nature of the climate are imposed
by the great differences in latitude and by the marked variety in relief.

The country is well served with meteorological stations. The
Central Observatory lies at Phu Lien situated on an isolated hill,
115 m. above sea level, about 10 km. to the south of Haiphong. There
are three types of stations recording meteorological data:

(*a*) Meteorological stations, sending information on weather
conditions to the Central Observatory.

(*b*) Climatological stations which generally supply data to the
agricultural and health services.

(*c*) Pluviometric stations, simple observation posts recording only
the amount of rainfall.

The meteorological and climatological stations are shown in
Fig. 29.

PRESSURE AND WINDS

Pressure conditions in Indo-China are controlled by changing
barometric distributions over Asia and over the seas which surround
the continent to the south and east. In winter, Asia is the seat of
a well-developed high pressure with its centre near Lake Baikal and
winds (north-east monsoon) blow outwards from the land mass to
the low-pressure region in equatorial latitudes. On the other hand,
in summer, pressure is low over central Asia and this causes a reversal
of wind direction from north-east to south-west. In general, the
seasonal variations of pressure are far more extreme in the north
than in the south of Indo-China (Fig. 30).

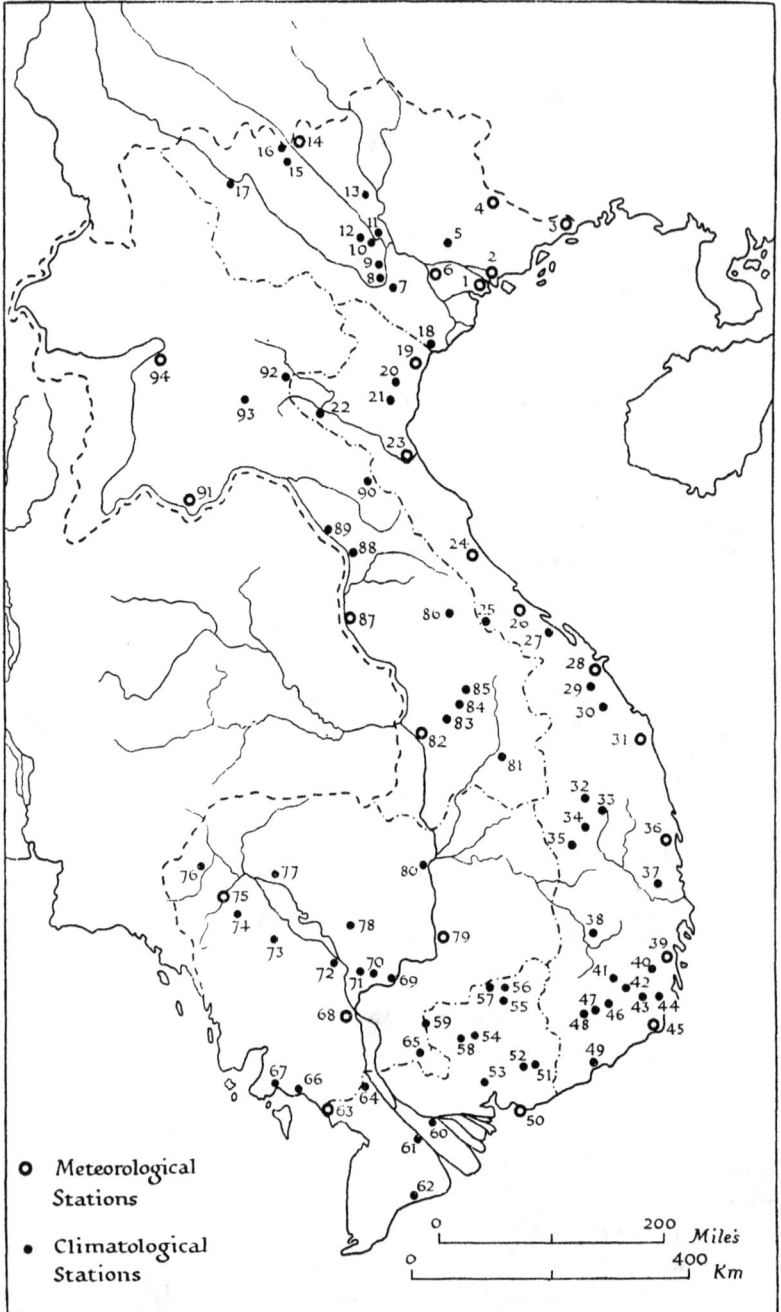

Fig. 29. Meteorological and climatological stations.
For key to numbers see p. 49

Source: E. Bruzon and P. Carton, *Le Climat de l'Indochine et les Typhons de la Mer de Chine*, following p. 21 (Hanoi, 1930).

List of Meteorological and Climatological Stations shown on Fig. 29

1. Phu Lien	48. Djiring
2. Haiphong	49. Phan Thiet
3. Mon Cay	50. Cap Saint Jacques
4. Lang Son	51. Gia Ray
5. Phu Lang Thuong	52. Xuan Loc
6. Hanoi	53. Saigon
7. Phu Mon	54. Bong Trang
8. Da Chong	55. Thuan Loi
9. La Pho	56. Phu Rieng
10. Phu Ho	57. Bak Kir
11. Phu Tho	58. Ben Cat
12. Thanh Ba	59. Dau Tieng
13. Tuyen Quang	60. Vinh Long
14. Lao Kay	61. Can Tho
15. Chapa	62. Bac Lieu
16. Ta Phing	63. Ha Tien
17. Lai Chau	64. Tan Chau
18. Phat Diem	65. Soai Rieng
19. Thanh Hoa	66. Kampot
20. Nhu Xuan	67. Val d'Emeraude
21. Cao Trai	68. Phnom Penh
22. Cua Rao	69. Kompong Cham
23. Vinh	70. Sdeung Chey
24. Dong Hoi	71. Stung Khya
25. Khe Sanh	72. Kompong Chhnang
26. Quang Tri	73. Pursat
27. Hue	74. Muong Russey
28. Tien Sha	75. Battambang
29. Bana	76. Toul Samrong
30. Duc Phu	77. Siem Reap
31. Quang Ngai	78. Kompong Thom
32. Kontum	79. Kratie
33. Dak Doa	80. Stung Treng
34. Plei Ku	81. Attopeu
35. Iapuch	82. Pakse
36. Qui Nhon	83. Paksong
37. Thach Ban	84. Tha Teng
38. Ban Me Thuot	85. Saravane
39. Nha Trang	86. Tchepone
40. Hon Ba	87. Savannakhet
41. Dalat	88. Thakhek
42. Petit Lang Bian	89. Boneng
43. Diom	90. Nape
44. Lang Hanh	91. Vientiane
45. Cap Padaran	92. Nong Het
46. Arbre Broye	93. Xieng Khouang
47. Lien Harah	94. Luang Prabang

Winter Monsoon (mid-September to March)

The monsoon first appears as early as mid-September in north Tonkin, following the development of a high-pressure system over Kwangsi and Yunnan; but south of lat. 20° N it is not well established

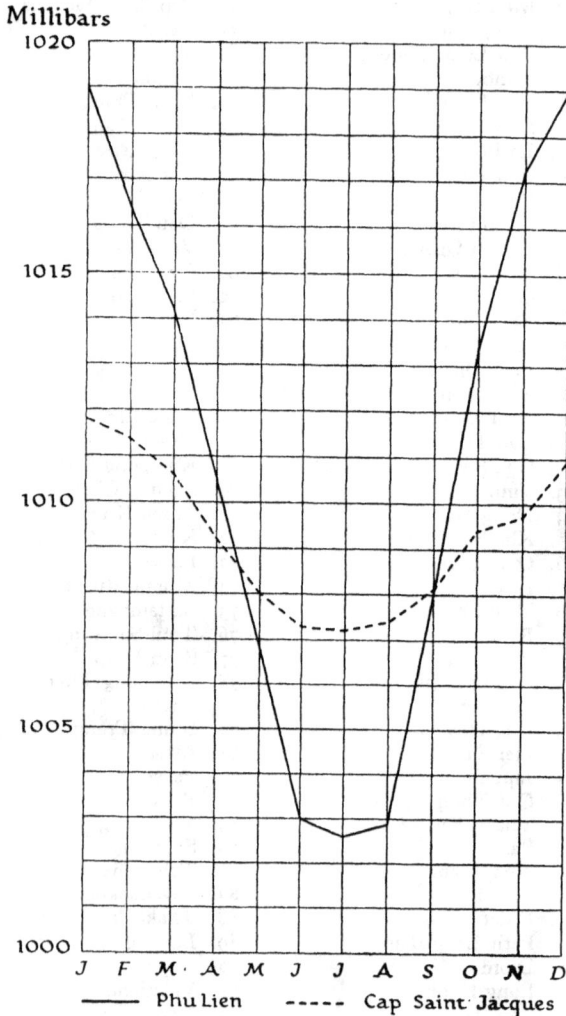

Fig. 30. Annual atmospheric pressure changes at Phu Lien (Tonkin) and Cap Saint Jacques (Cochin-China)

The graphs show the mean monthly values over the period 1907–27 for Phu Lien and 1907–19 for Cap Saint Jacques.

Source: E. Bruzon and P. Carton, *Le Climat de l'Indochine et les Typhons de la Mer de Chine*, facing p. 40 (Hanoi, 1930).

until the first week of October and in lat. 10° N not until the third
week (Fig. 33). There is great variety in the direction of the monsoon.
It is generally a north wind in Tonkin and north-east in north Annam,
Laos and Cambodia; but along the coasts of south Annam and
Cochin-China it blows parallel to the shore (Fig. 34). Where high
land drops sharply to the sea offshore winds frequently occur; and
this tendency sometimes brings about a local reversal in the direction
of the monsoon.

The force of the north-east monsoon is not constant. It blows in
successive pulsations of varying strength, sometimes exceeding force 7
on the Beaufort scale, whilst at other times falling below force 4. The
frequency of strong winds decreases from north to south.

Summer Monsoon (June to September)

After the two transitional months of April and May, when winds
are variable, the summer regime becomes established in early June
(Figs. 31, 32). The summer monsoon in Indo-China does not
'burst' with extreme violence like its counterpart in Peninsular
India. Indeed, it sets in with less suddenness and force than is characteristic of the commencement of the winter monsoon. Throughout
June, July and August a low-pressure system is stabilized over south
Indo-China and there is a regular in-blowing wind from the south-
west or south. In central Laos, north Annam and Tonkin slow-
moving shallow depressions, passing west-east across the country,
introduce variable conditions of pressure and wind.

The direction of the summer monsoon is south-east in Tonkin,
south-west in Laos, Cambodia and Cochin-China. Along the coast
south of Tourane it blows from the south-east as far as Cap Padaran,
but from the south-west between Cap Padaran and Cap Saint
Jacques (Fig. 34). The summer monsoon in this region seldom
exceeds force 5 on the Beaufort scale, except at times in the coastal
lowlands of Tonkin and Cochin-China.

Diurnal Variation of Pressure

Over the whole of Indo-China there is a double oscillation of
pressure during the twenty-four hours. The barogram shows a
minimum at 0400 hr., a high maximum at 1000 hr., a second minimum
at 1600 hr. and a lower maximum from 2000 to 2400 hr. The ampli-
tude, which is usually from 2 to 4 mb., decreases with increasing
latitude.

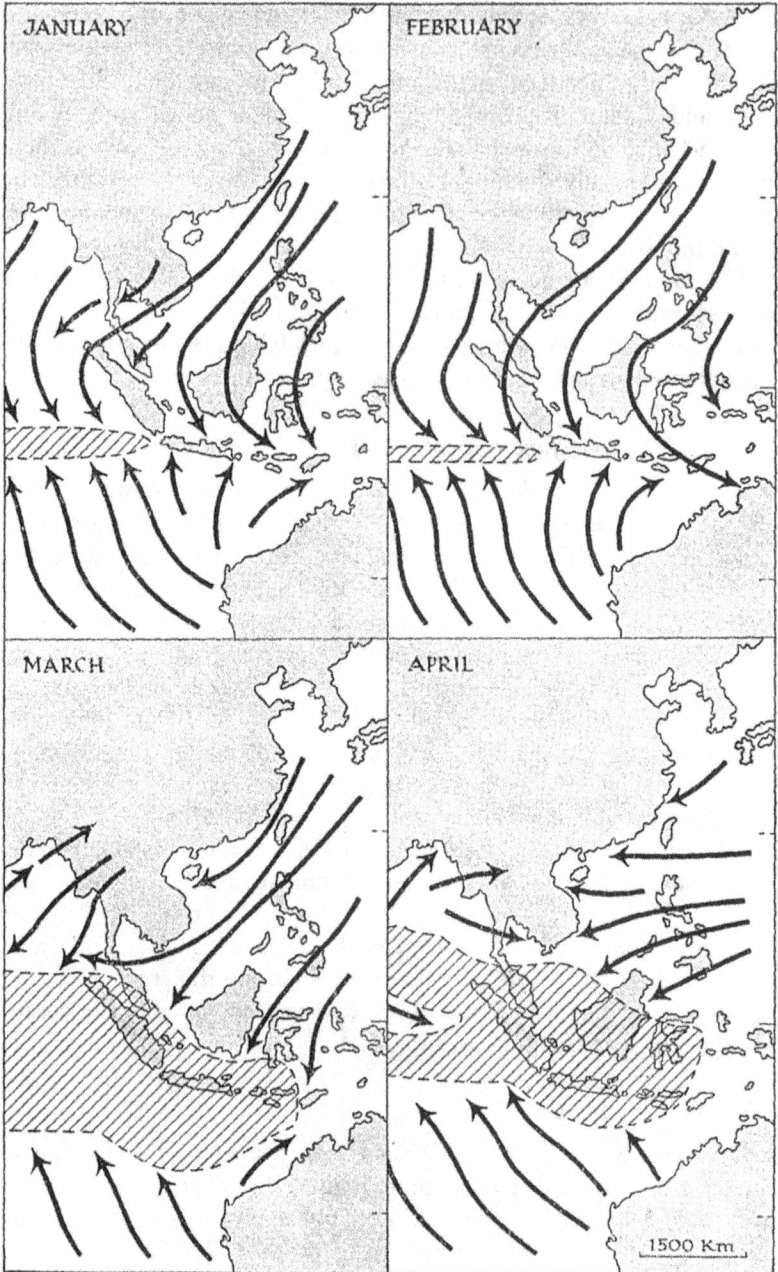

Fig. 31. Winds in south-east Asia: January to April
The area with oblique shading has light variable winds.

Source: A. Grimes, 'The Journey of Fa Hsien from Ceylon to Canton', *Journal of the Malayan Branch of the Royal Asiatic Society*, vol. XIX, part 1 (Singapore, 1941).

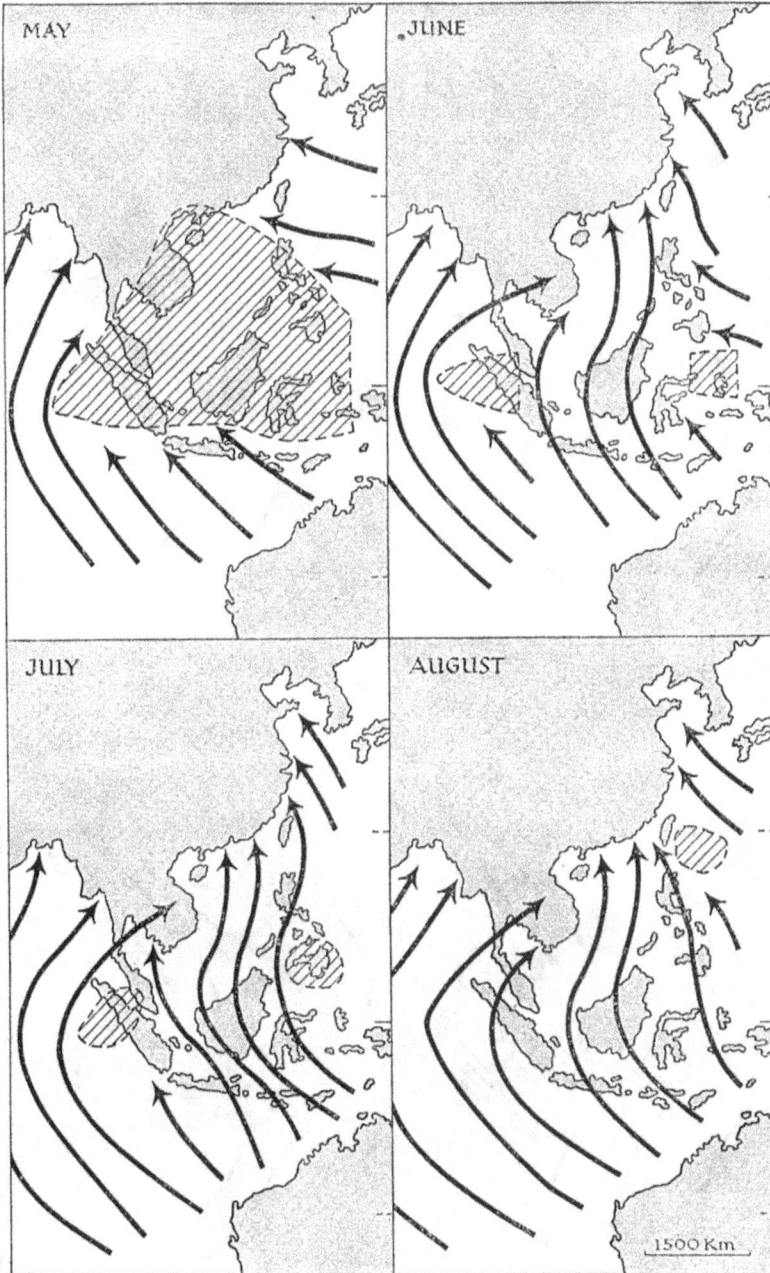

Fig. 32. Winds in south-east Asia: May to August

The area with oblique shading has light variable winds.

Source: A. Grimes, 'The Journey of Fa Hsien from Ceylon to Canton', *Journal of the Malayan Branch of the Royal Asiatic Society*, vol. XIX, part 1 (Singapore, 1941).

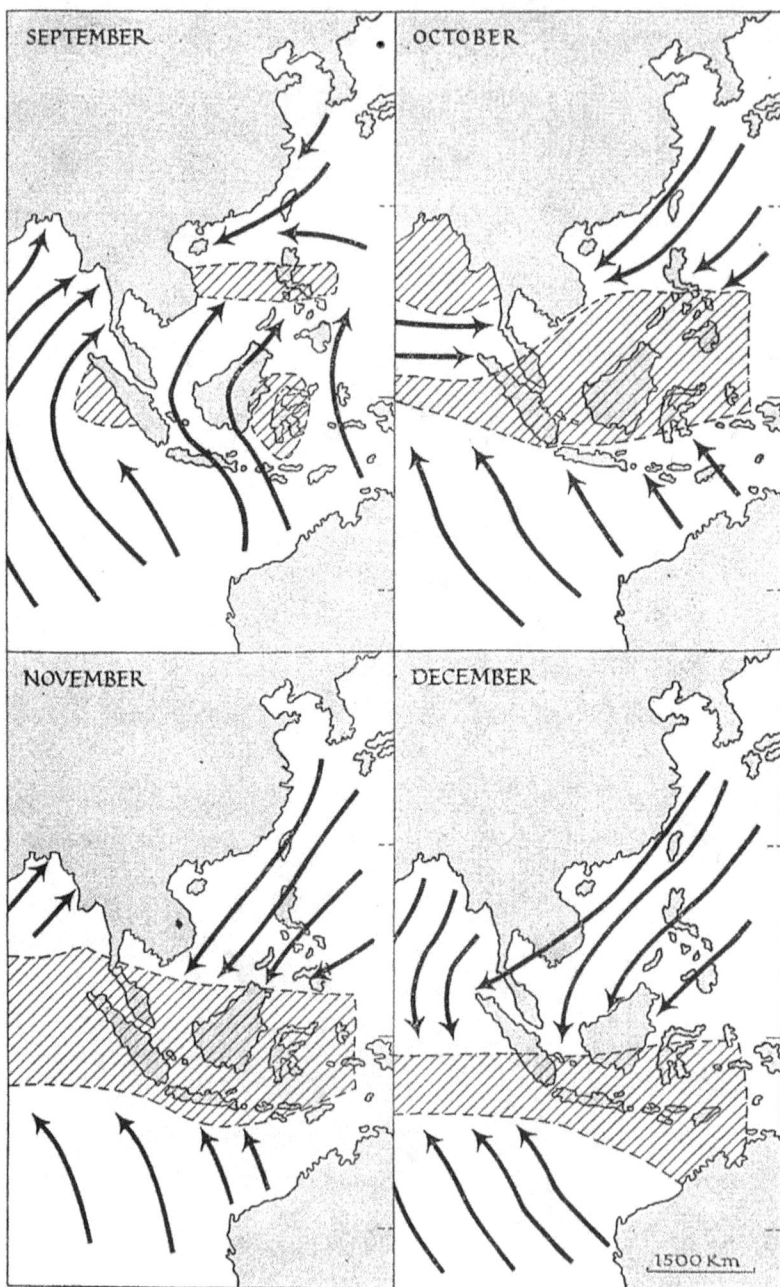

Fig. 33. Winds in south-east Asia; September to December
The area with oblique shading has light variable winds.
Source: A. Grimes, 'The Journey of Fa Hsien from Ceylon to Canton', *Journal of the Malayan Branch of the Royal Asiatic Society*, vol. XIX, part 1 (Singapore, 1941).

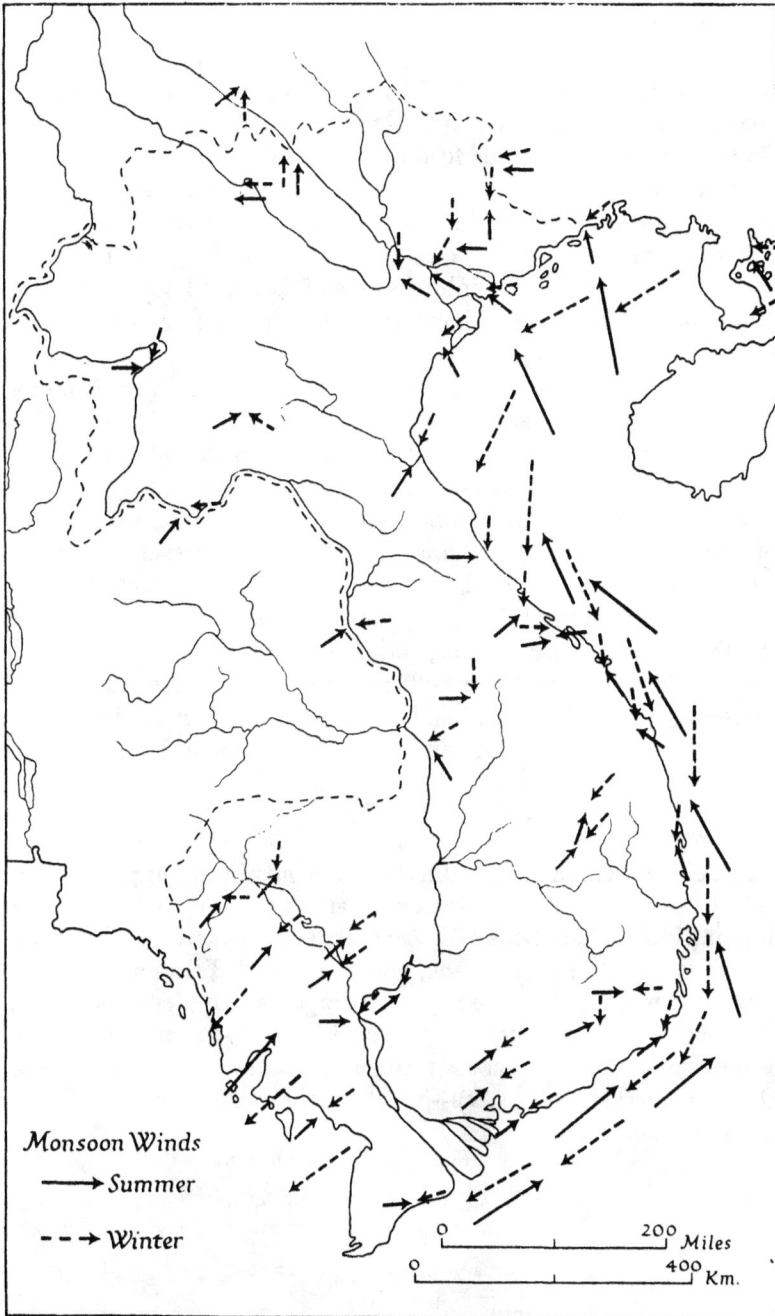

Fig. 34. Monsoon winds

Source: E. Bruzon and P. Carton, *Le Climat de l'Indochine et les Typhons de la Mer de Chine*, facing p. 32 (Hanoi, 1930).

Local Winds

The high plateaux of Annam and Laos (Tran Ninh, Kontum, Darlac, Lang Bian) are marked by local winds which differ in their excessive aridity from the general character of the monsoon. During the summer months, winds forming part of the south-west monsoon descend the steep eastern slopes of the plateaux and pass across the coastal plains near Ha Tinh, Tourane, Binh Dinh and Nha Trang. These 'Winds of Laos', as they are often called, constitute the dominant winds at Binh Dinh in July and August. They are hot and dry, sometimes blowing with extreme violence and provoking intense evaporation (see p. 71).

At all periods of the year, land and sea breezes are a common occurrence, especially along the coasts of Annam and Cochin-China. They originate from the differential heating of land and sea. The sea breeze usually first begins to be felt at 1000 hr., reaching a maximum force in the early afternoon and dying away at sunset, while in the late evening it is replaced by a land breeze which persists until about sunrise. The effect of land and sea breezes is most noticeable in coastal plains protected from the prevailing wind by the configuration of the land. In these regions, local breezes may become the pre-dominating wind and have sufficient force to reverse the general monsoon current. The land and sea breezes occur more frequently during the summer monsoon and the transitional months than during the winter monsoon.

Winds in the Upper Air

Little information is available on the winds in the upper air over Indo-China. The following account is largely based on details given in the Air Ministry handbook *Weather in the China Seas and in the western part of the North Pacific Ocean*, vol. II, pp. 146–8 (London, 1937).

During winter, the height of the upper winds depends on the changing thickness of the north-east monsoon current. The table below shows the probable average thickness of the north-east monsoon current (lat. 20° N)—based on observations at Hong Kong and Phu Lien.

Month	Height (m.)
October	3,000
November	2,400
December	2,000
January	1,800
February	1,500
March	1,500
April	1,200

Source: *Weather in the China Seas and in the western part of the North Pacific Ocean*, vol. II, p. 147 (London, 1937).

The upper winds between 2,500 and 3,500 m. are easterly, but above this height they veer or back and tend to become westerly. The line of division between these two winds increases in height with decreasing latitude, and south of lat. 15° N easterly winds probably blow up to at least 6,000 m. In the layer between the monsoon current and the upper westerlies the winds are generally very light; their velocity, however, increases rapidly as soon as a westerly component appears in the wind direction.

In the transitional month of May upper westerlies still prevail at heights above 1,500 m., but the velocity no longer increases rapidly with increasing heights. During the summer monsoon period, June to September, the average height reached by the prevailing south-westerly monsoon is probably not less than 1,800 m., while the easterly upper current prevails above 3,000 m. In late September and early October, before the final setting in of winter monsoon conditions, the wind at any height up to 2,500 m. is for the most part little different from that at the surface with regard both to direction and velocity. Easterly winds predominate at heights between 4,000 and 9,000 m.

TYPHOONS

Typhoons are well-marked low-pressure systems which, although generally restricted in size and variable in frequency, have an important influence upon the climate of Indo-China and the China Sea. Tropical cyclones of this kind not only very often cause extensive material damage, but also bring heavy rainfall particularly to the coast of central Annam. While the majority of typhoons originate between the parallels of 5 and 20° N and the meridians of 130 and 150° E some form near the Paracel Islands (long. 112° E) in the South China Sea. Typhoons are believed to result in part from widespread convection of very hot moist air and in part from a disturbance of the normal balance between two opposing currents of air.

Over the period 1918–29 Indo-China and the South China Sea experienced ninety-eight typhoons with a monthly distribution as follows:

Jan.	2	May	4	Sept.	11
Feb.	0	June	6	Oct.	15
Mar.	0	July	22	Nov.	15
Apr.	0	Aug.	17	Dec.	6

Source: E. Bruzon and P. Carton, *Le Climat de l'Indochine et les Typhons de la Mer de Chine*, following p. 274 (Hanoi, 1930).

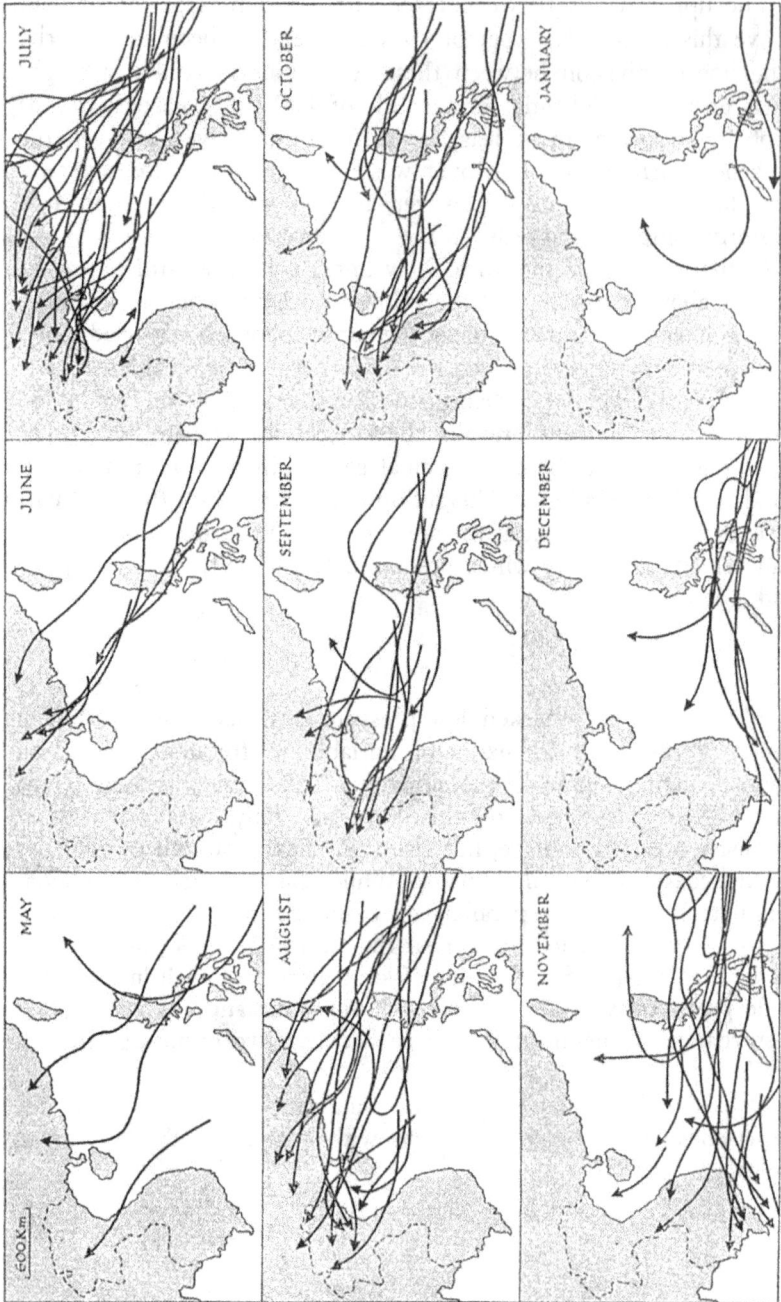

Fig. 35. Typhoon tracks in Indo-China and the South China Sea (1918-29)

Source: E. Bruzon and P. Carton, *Le Climat de l'Indochine et les Typhons de la Mer de Chine*, following p. 274 (Hanoi, 1930).

This table shows clearly the predominance of typhoons in the period from July to November. The mean track of typhoons moves northwards from February to the middle of August and then moves south until January. The few cyclones which form close to the Philippine Islands in January, February, March and April all fill up before reaching the coast of Indo-China. Typhoons in May and June are still infrequent, and July is the earliest month in which they can be confidently expected. During July, August and September the danger area on the coast of Indo-China lies north of the 15th parallel, but in October and November the tracks move rapidly south over Annam and Cochin-China to below latitude 10° s (Fig. 35).

The passage of a typhoon is marked by rapid changes in atmospheric pressure. A slow fall on the barograph trace first occurs when the centre is between 800 and 200 km. distant; then as the centre approaches to within 150 km. there is a more distinct fall; and finally, pressure reaches a minimum when the typhoon passes near or overhead. In the rear of the typhoon pressure rises as rapidly as it fell in advance of the storm.

The surface winds at a particular point in the track of a typhoon vary greatly in direction and velocity. On the coast of central Annam a typhoon is heralded by onshore winds blowing from the north or north-west, and these increase in force as the storm approaches the land (see p. 61). The average wind strength reaches force 6 about 250 km. from the centre, increasing to force 10 at 80 km. and force 12 at 50 km. The mean wind velocity to be expected is about 70–80 knots. In the 'eye' or centre of the typhoon light variable breezes or squalls alternate with complete calms. Winds again become violent as the rear of the typhoon passes overhead (Fig. 36).

Cirriform and fractocumulus clouds generally appear in advance of a typhoon. Fractocumulus or 'scud' as they are sometimes called, are dark, ragged clouds which drift just above the horizon becoming more numerous and coalescing as the typhoon approaches. About 150 km. from the centre dark nimbus clouds form and torrential rain sets in. In the 'eye' of the storm the sky clears and rain ceases to fall. Nimbostratus clouds, accompanied by heavy rain, again develop in the rear of the typhoon. As the typhoon recedes nimbostratus break up into fractocumulus and cirrus clouds.

The following description of the typhoon which passed over Nha Trang and Hon Ba in 1926 clearly indicates the principal characteristics of this kind of storm:

'The typhoon first appeared about the 2nd November bearing

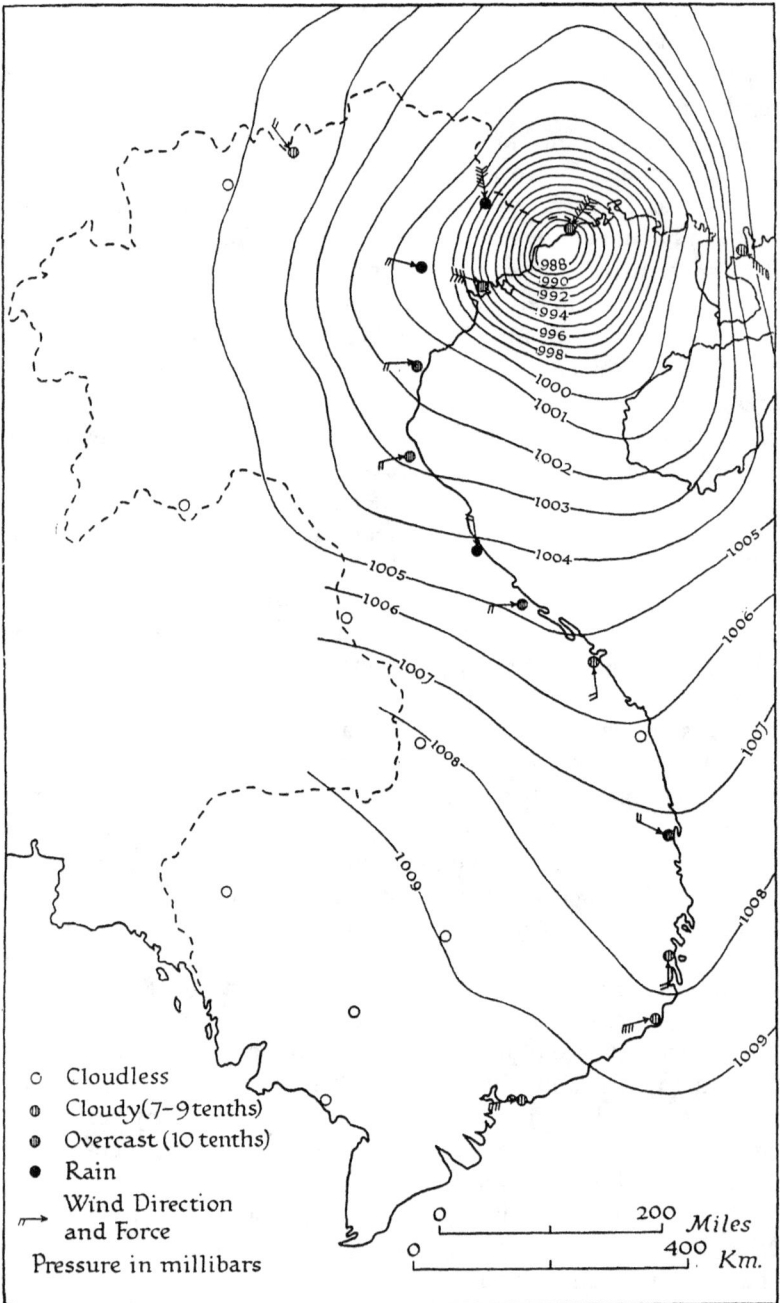

Fig. 36. Synoptic chart of a typhoon, 10.00 hr. 25 August 1924
Source: E. Bruzon and P. Carton, *Le Climat de l'Indochine et les Typhons de la Mer de Chine*, facing p. 278 (Hanoi, 1930).

west-north-west from the island of Yap and by the 3rd was 700 km. east of Manila. On the night of 5–6 November it crossed the Philippines to the south of Manila. Over the China Sea, under the influence of the Chinese high-pressure system, its course changed from west to west-south-west. The typhoon struck the coast of Annam on November 7th. At Nha Trang about 1600 hours on this day the wind began to blow violently from the west-north-west. During the night its violence increased and its course changed successively to north-west, north, and north-north-east. Pressure reached a minimum at Hon Ba, on the plateau, two hours after the

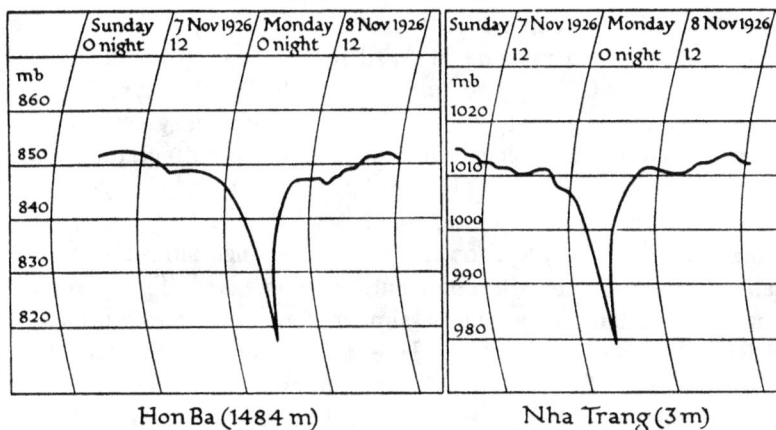

Hon Ba (1484 m)   Nha Trang (3 m)

Fig. 37. Barograph of a typhoon, at Hon Ba and Nha Trang, 7–8 November 1926
Source: E. Bruzon and P. Carton, Le Climat de l'Indochine et les Typhons de la Mer de Chine, following p. 278 (Hanoi, 1930).

lowest reading at Nha Trang. Considerable damage was done to the forest surrounding Hon Ba, many trees being uprooted or broken and in some places entire groves destroyed. The typhoon brought torrential rain to the whole Annam coast from Faifoo to Cap Padaran'* (Fig. 37).

TEMPERATURE

Indo-China lies entirely within the tropics and the whole country, except in some mountainous areas, experiences high temperatures throughout the year. At Hanoi, in the north, the coldest month (January) has a mean temperature of 63° F. (17·2° C.); the mean

* See E. Bruzon and P. Carton, Le Climat de l'Indochine et les Typhons de la Mer de Chine, p. 302 (Hanoi, 1930).

annual temperature here is 74° F. (23·6° C.), which differs by only
a few degrees from the corresponding figures for Hue (77° F.,
25° C.) and Saigon (81·5° F., 27·6° C.). Differences in latitude and
the effect of relief have imposed two temperature regimes, the regime
of Saigon and the regime of Hanoi.

The 'regime of Saigon' extends along the coast of Annam to
Nha Trang or Qui Nhon and west of the mountains as far north
as Luang Prabang. The annual range of temperature of Saigon is
small (6·2° F., 3·7° C.); the hottest month is April (85° F., 29·7° C.)
and the coldest month, December (78·8° F., 26° C.) (Fig. 38). The
chief distinguishing characteristic, however, is the existence of two
maxima and minima, a typical feature of the equatorial climate.
Saigon has its two maxima in April (85° F., 29·7° C.) and August
(81·5° F., 27·5° C.), its two minima in July (81° F., 27·2° C.) and
December (78·8° F., 26° C.). Diurnal variation is greater in the
hottest than in the coldest month. The daily temperature range
averages 21–27° F. (12–15° C.) in April and 18–19° F. (10–11° C.)
in December. In both cases, there is a steep rise of temperature
from 0600 hr. (min.) to 1400 hr. (max.), and then almost as rapid a
fall during the late afternoon and evening. Nha Trang, on the
coast of Annam, experiences similar temperature conditions to
Saigon, but farther north at Hue this regime is no longer in
evidence (Fig. 38). West of the main mountain divide the double
maxima and minima is met at Luang Prabang, only a few degrees
south of the latitude of Hanoi. However, in its high annual range
of temperature Luang Prabang more closely resembles the 'regime
of Hanoi'.

The 'regime of Hanoi' covers Tonkin and north Annam. Annual
temperature range at Hanoi is greater than at Saigon, averaging
22° F. (12° C.); June (84·5° F., 29·2° C.) is the hottest month and
January (62·6° F., 17° C.) the coldest (Fig. 38). A single maximum
and minimum temperature characterizes this regime; the double
maximum and minimum has entirely disappeared. Sharp diurnal
changes in temperature are experienced over the whole of northern
Indo-China. The greatest daily range occurs in winter, the reverse
of what happens in the 'regime of Saigon'. In January, the temperature may fall as much as 32° F. (18° C.) in under 10 hr.; in
June the daily temperature differences are small and approximate
to the range experienced at Saigon during the winter.

On the mountains and plateaux of the Chaîne Annamitique temperatures are much lower than in the plains to the east and west.

Dalat, at a height of 1,500 m. on the Plateau du Lang Bian, has a mean annual temperature of 14° F. (7·8° C.) less than Nha Trang which lies at sea level in almost the same latitude. Farther

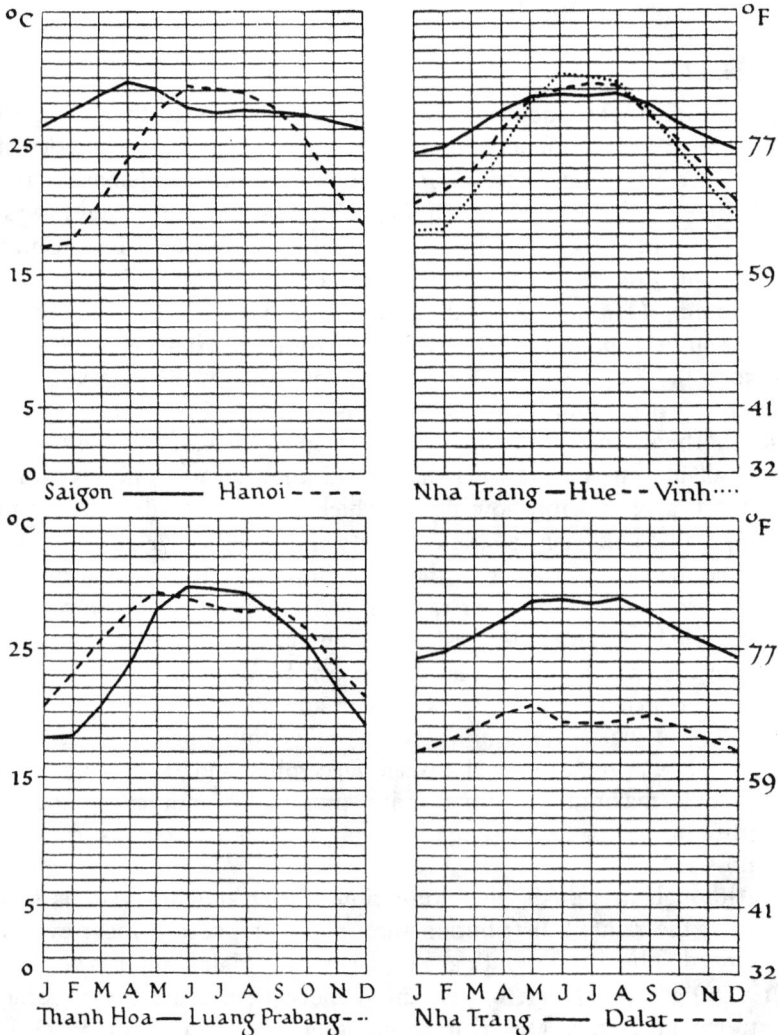

Fig. 38. Annual temperature curves for selected stations

Based on monthly means for the periods 1907–29 for Hanoi, Saigon, Thanh Hoa, Vinh and Nha Trang; 1912–29 for Luang Prabang; 1907–8 and 1915–29 for Hue; 1918, 1921–6 and 1928–9 for Dalat.

Source: E. Bruzon and P. Carton, *Le Climat de l'Indochine et les Typhons de la Mer de Chine*, pp. 229–54 (Hanoi, 1930).

north, the mean annual temperature at Xeing Khouang on the Plateau du Tran Ninh (1,200 m.) is 67° F. (19·2° C.) compared with 77° F. (25·3° C.) at Luang Prabang.

PRECIPITATION

Rainfall

Like all tropical monsoon countries, Indo-China for the most part receives a heavy annual rainfall (Fig. 39). Relief has an important influence upon its distribution. The Monts des Cardamomes and Chaîne de l'Eléphant, which lie in the path of the south-west monsoon, have the highest yearly rainfall in the whole of Indo-China (Fig. 40). Rainfall at Val d'Emeraude in Kampot province is 5,340 mm. (214 in.). Annual rainfall is also very great in the central and southern parts of the Chaîne Annamitique (Hon Ba, 3,748 mm. (150 in.)). The plains of the lower Mekong and Fleuve Rouge are relatively dry areas, but the driest region is the strip of lowland along the south Annam coast from Phan Thiet to Cap Padaran. The mean annual rainfall at Cap Padaran for the period 1907–29 was only 757 mm. (30 in.), a remarkably low figure which may be ascribed partly to the parallel alinement of the coast and the monsoon (Figs. 34, 40).

The monsoonal regime is the most important factor determining the seasonal distribution of rainfall. As a general rule summer, or the period of the south-west monsoon, is the wettest season and winter, when the north-east monsoon blows, the driest season (Figs. 41–43). Saigon receives a mean annual rainfall of 2,022 mm. (81 in.), of which 1,908 mm. (76 in.) falls from April to December and only 114 mm. (4 in.) between December and April (Fig. 40). A double maximum in June and September is another significant feature in the rainfall regime of Saigon, as of other stations in south Indo-China.

Although in Tonkin the alternation of wet and dry seasons still occurs, the rainfall distribution throughout the year is more evenly balanced. The driest month at Phu Lien, near Haiphong, has 30 mm. (1·5 in.) in December, or ten times more than the corresponding extreme at Saigon. Out of an annual total of 1,767 mm. (71 in.) this station receives 220 mm. (9 in.) from December to April (cf. data given for Saigon above and see Fig. 40). The greater part of the winter precipitation comes in the form of drizzle (the *crachin*), which is economically beneficial since it allows a rice harvest during the 'dry' season.

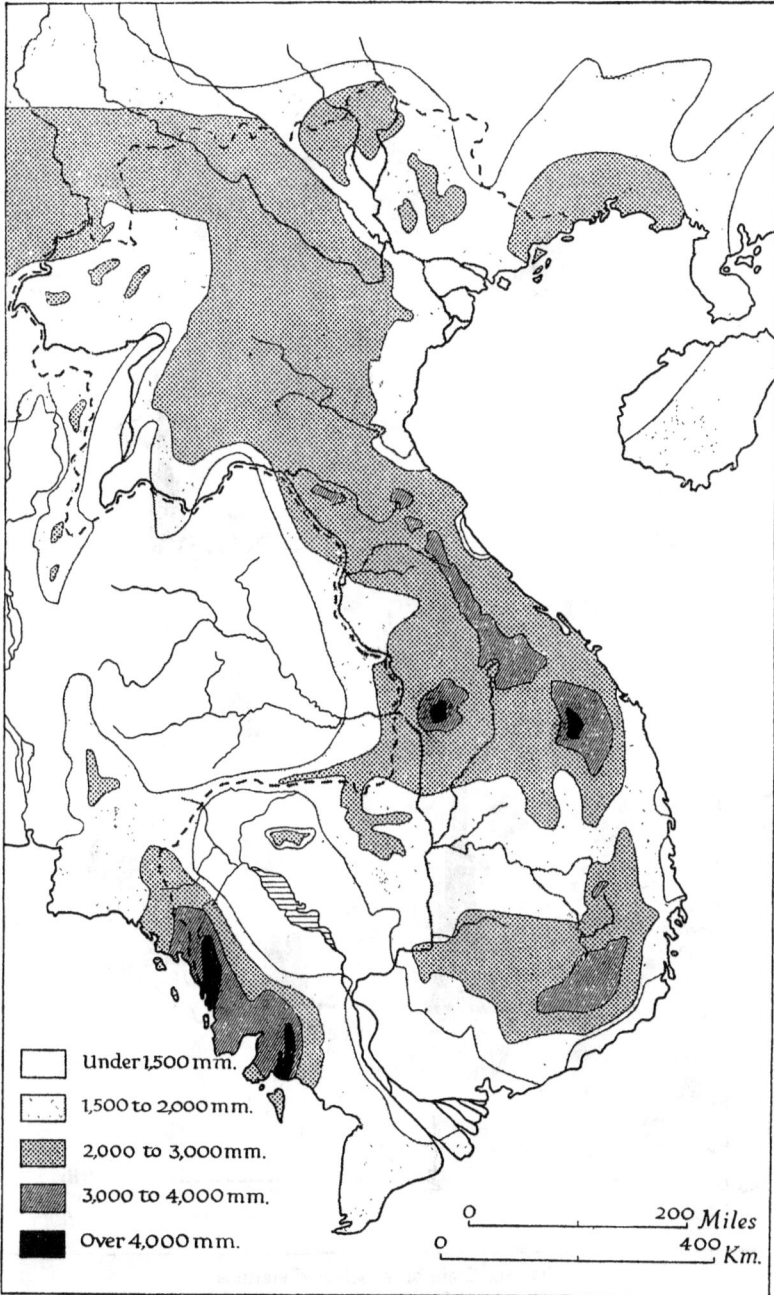

	Under 1,500 mm.
	1,500 to 2,000 mm.
	2,000 to 3,000 mm.
	3,000 to 4,000 mm.
	Over 4,000 mm.

Fig. 39. Mean annual rainfall

Source: P. Gourou, *L'Utilisation du Sol en Indochine Française*, p. 79 (Paris, 1940).

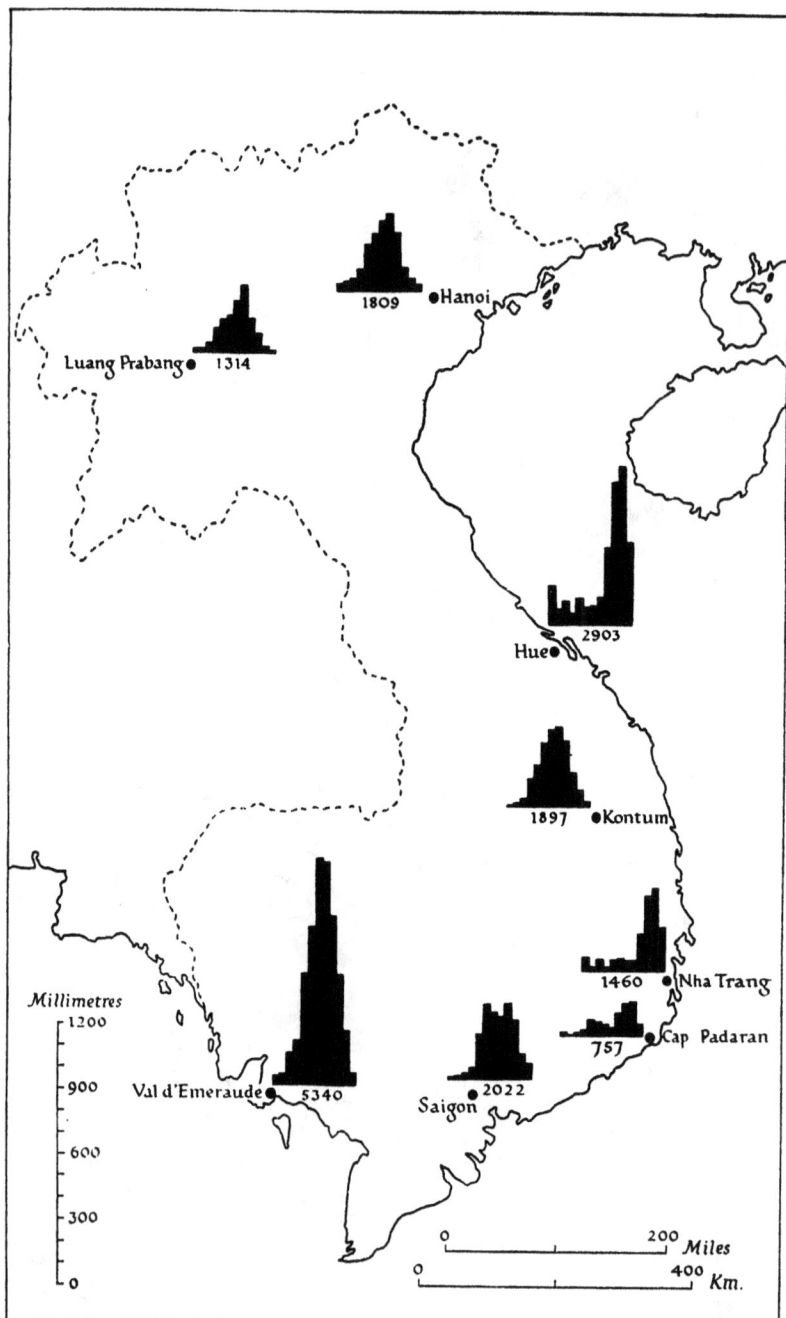

Fig. 40. Rainfall at selected stations

Based on monthly means for the period 1907–29 for Hanoi, Nha Trang, Cap Padaran and Saigon; 1912–29 for Hue; 1917–29 for Kontum; 1922–9 for Val d'Emeraude; 1907–8 and 1910–29 for Luang Prabang.

Source: E. Bruzon and P. Carton, *Le Climat de l'Indochine et les Typhons de la Mer de Chine*, pp. 80–159 (Hanoi, 1930).

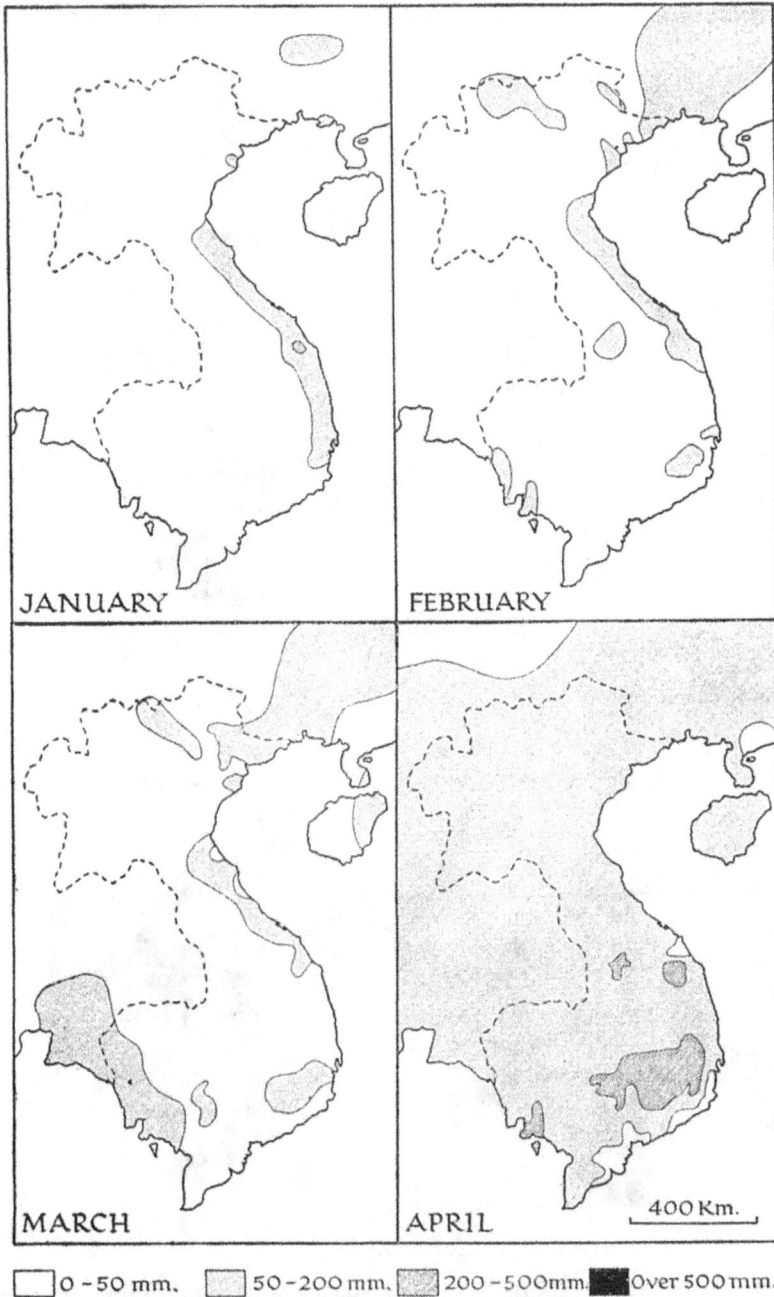

Fig. 41. Mean monthly rainfall, 1907–29, January to April

Source: E. Bruzon and P. Carton, *Le Climat de l'Indochine et les Typhons de la Mer de Chine*, following p. 77 (Hanoi, 1930).

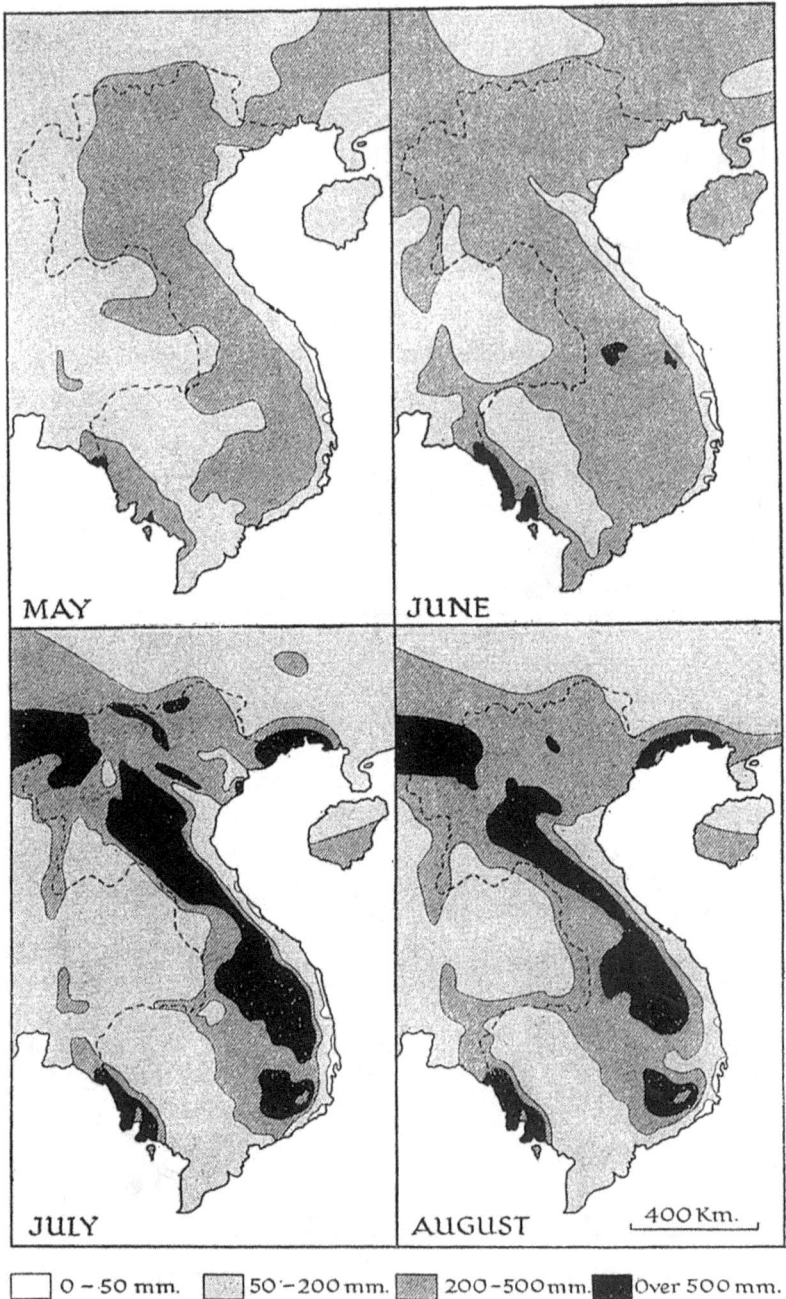

Fig. 42. Mean monthly rainfall, 1907–29, May to August

Source: E. Bruzon and P. Carton, *Le Climat de l'Indochine et les Typhons de la Mer de Chine*, following p. 77 (Hanoi, 1930).

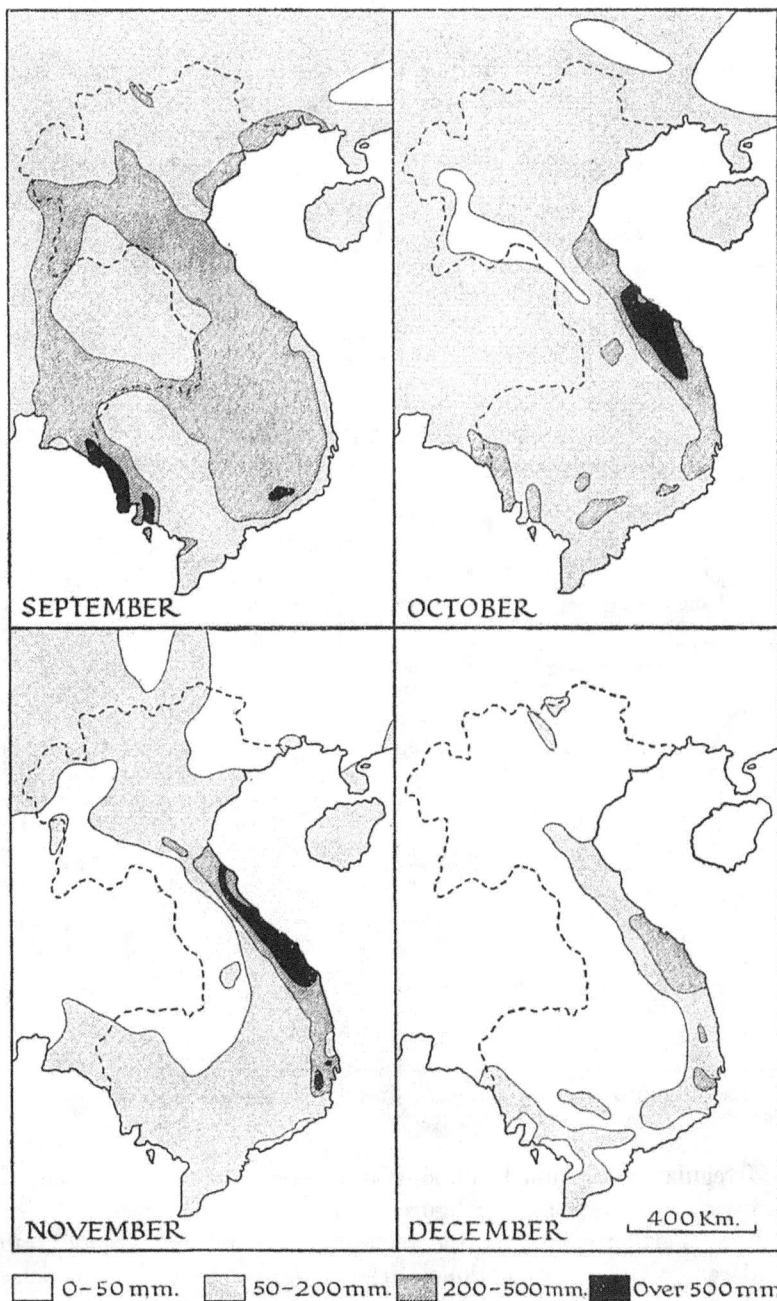

Fig. 43. Mean monthly rainfall, 1907–29, September to December

Source: E. Bruzon and P. Carton, *Le Climat de l'Indochine et les Typhons de la Mer de Chine*, following p. 77 (Hanoi, 1930).

Central Annam has a very different rainfall regime from other parts of the country, the wettest period occurring from September to January rather than during the summer. At Hue, 2,260 mm. (91 in.) falls in these months and only 643 mm. (26 in.) in the rest of the year (Fig. 40). The winter rainfall maximum is due in part to the onshore north-east monsoon winds, but it should be noted that the highest fall occurs two or three months before the climax period of the monsoon (January). This anomaly may be ascribed to the frequency of typhoons in October and November (Fig. 35).

Variability of rainfall from year to year is a common feature of the climate of Indo-China. The following figures for several scattered stations clearly illustrate this tendency:

Annual Rainfall, 1907–29 (mm.)

Station	Mean	Absolute max.	Absolute min.
Tonkin			
Mon Cay	2,853	4,119	1,733
Lang Son	1,439	2,029	756
Chapa	2,847	3,497	2,184
Hanoi	1,809	2,741	1,275
Phu Lang Thuong	1,503	2,064	1,012
Phu Lien	1,768	2,587	1,357
Annam			
Thanh Hoa	1,751	2,778	1,153
Vinh	1,788	2,671	987
Dong Hoi	1,982	2,603	1,531
Hue	2,903	4,269	1,880
Quang Ngai	2,262	3,505	961
Qui Nhon	1,627	3,081	856
Nha Trang	1,460	2,245	739
Padaran	757	1,186	409
Cochin-China			
Saigon	2,022	2,718	1,571
My Tho	1,404	1,932	971
Cambodia			
Phnom Penh	1,432	2,310	969
Val d'Emeraude	5,340	6,259	4,293
Laos			
Luang Prabang	1,314	1,879	510

Source: E. Bruzon and P. Carton, *Le Climat de l'Indochine et les Typhons de la Mer de Chine*, pp. 82–159 (Hanoi, 1930).

Irregularity of annual rainfall is most severe in north and central Annam, as shown by the figures for Hue, Quang Ngai and Qui Nhon. Farther south, in the region of low rainfall around Cap Padaran, years of exceptional dryness (*c.* 400 mm., 16 in.) cause widespread desiccation.

The above figures should be considered in relation to the evaporation if their full value is to be appreciated. This varies from 500 mm. (12·5 in.) to over 1,100 mm. (27·5 in.) in the year. Seasonal evaporation is conditioned by relative humidity, cloudiness, and winds. At Phu Lien in Tonkin evaporation is feeblest in the *crachin* period (February, March, April), when humidity and cloudiness are high and wind strength slight. The greatest evaporation occurs in the dry winter months (October, November, December), though it is also high in June and July, the period of maximum temperature and wind strength. In central Annam, winds have an important desiccating influence, particularly the warm, dry 'Winds of Laos' which during the summer sweep through passes in the Chaîne Annamitique.

The problem of insufficient rainfall is very complex and cannot be understood solely by a study of annual variability in rainfall and in evaporation. A year with a normal rainfall may be economically disastrous if one or two months record figures below the average. At Vinh, for example, while the early rice harvest month (December) receives on the average 79 mm. (1·9 in.) of rain, in 1915 the fall was only 2 mm. (0·05 in.). The second rice harvest at Vinh takes place in July-August when 130 mm. (5 in.) to 160 mm. (6 in.) usually falls, but in 1927 the figure was only 27 mm. (1 in.) during this period and in 1908 as low as 5 mm. (0·2 in.). Regions of irregular annual rainfall are particularly susceptible to this monthly irregularity.

Excessive rainfall is just as prevalent and no less harmful than the opposite extreme. Floods frequently destroy the harvest and cause widespread damage to household property, roads and railways. During the passage of a typhoon on 21–22 September 1927, 604 mm. (15·1 in.) fell at Phu Lien in 26 hr. Other exceptionally high figures of daily rainfall are indicated in the following table:

	mm.	Date
Tonkin		
Ile de Kebao	630	22 September 1927
Thanh Ba	462	12 August 1907
Chapa	350	6 May 1920
Hanoi	277	30 September 1916
Annam		
Dong Hoi	341	20 October 1912
Tien Sha	489	10 November 1912
Quang Ngai	490	19 October 1926
Qui Nhon	309	12 November 1924
Hon Ba	278	18 February 1920
Cambodia		
Kaskong	502	3 August 1923
Val d'Emeraude	458	1 July 1925

Source: E. Bruzon and P. Carton, *Le Climat de l'Indochine et les Typhons de la Mer de Chine*, pp. 160–61 (Hanoi, 1930).

Torrential rain of this kind, which may bring to one area several hundred millimetres of rain in a single day, spells economic ruin to many thousands of peasants.

Snow

Snow is seldom seen in Indo-China, and has been recorded only in the extreme north of Tonkin at heights above 1,500 m. and even here the depth is generally quite small. The figures below give the number of days in which snow fell at Chapa (22° 30' N and 1,640 m. altitude) from 1916 to 1930.

Snow Days

1916	1	1921	0	1926	0
1917	1	1922	2	1927	0
1918	0	1923	2	1928	0
1919	0	1924	0	1929	1
1920	0	1925	1	1930	0
				(January to June)	

Source: E. Bruzon and P. Carton, *Le Climat de l'Indochine et les Typhons de la Mer de Chine*, p. 170 (Hanoi, 1930).

The rarity of snow may be ascribed not only to the low latitude, but also to the coincidence of the temperature minimum with the dry season.

Hail

Precipitation in the form of hail occurs rather more frequently than snow. Like snow, it seldom falls outside the mountainous region of Tonkin, except when accompanying thunderstorms. Frequency of hail at Chapa is shown in the following table:

Hail Days

1918	5	1923	1	1927	0
1919	1	1924	4	1928	0
1920	3	1925	1	1929	2
1921	4	1926	5	1930	4
1922	10			(January to June)	

Source: E. Bruzon and P. Carton, *Le Climat de l'Indochine et les Typhons de la Mer de Chine*, p. 171 (Hanoi, 1930).

The hail associated with thunderstorms sometimes brings stones of great size.

Thunderstorms

Thunderstorms are common in Indo-China. The Central Observatory at Phu Lien has determined the average number of storm days (period 1907-29) for the Fleuve Rouge delta.

Storm Days

Jan.	1	May	22	Sept.	21
Feb.	1	June	25	Oct.	8
Mar.	3	July	28	Nov.	2
Apr.	10	Aug.	28	Dec.	—

Total, 149

Source: E. Bruzon and P. Carton, *Le Climat de l'Indochine et les Typhons de la Mer de Chine*, p. 222 (Hanoi, 1930).

The storms are thus almost entirely restricted to the summer or period of maximum rainfall and temperature. Over Annam the frequency of thunderstorms is rather less than farther north. Observations at Hue show that the maximum daily frequency in any one month is 9 (in May), and of the remaining months none have more than an average of 5 days with thunder. No information is available concerning storms in the other parts of the country, but they are probably fairly frequent throughout the south-west monsoon season. Thunderstorms occur more often in the afternoon than in any other period of the day.

HUMIDITY

Relative humidity maintains a high level at all seasons throughout the greater part of Indo-China. In the south and along the east coast humidity is highest during the rainy season—June to October, in Cochin-China and Cambodia, October to January in Annam. On the other hand, while relative humidity in Tonkin also reaches a maximum in the summer period of maximum precipitation it is almost equally high from February to April at the time of the *crachin* (Fig. 44). If a daily rather than monthly average is taken then the *crachin* period has a higher relative humidity than any other time of the year.

The mountain regions of Indo-China have a more variable relative humidity than the lowlands. Abundant rainfall from the winter monsoon, accompanied by very heavy masses of clouds, frequently leads to a relative humidity of 100%: at Hon Ba (1,484 m.) in January 1928 the hygrometer registered this level for 16 days in succession. By contrast, there is an extremely low humidity at the end of the winter season: in March and April, Hon Ba has a humidity as low as 10%. On the high plateaux exposed to both the north-east and south-west monsoons relative humidity is generally speaking very much lower. Dalat (1,500 m.) has a mean annual humidity of 70%

compared with 90% for Hon Ba, only a few kilometres to the north-east. The mountain areas of Tonkin and Laos have on the average a higher humidity than the surrounding plains.

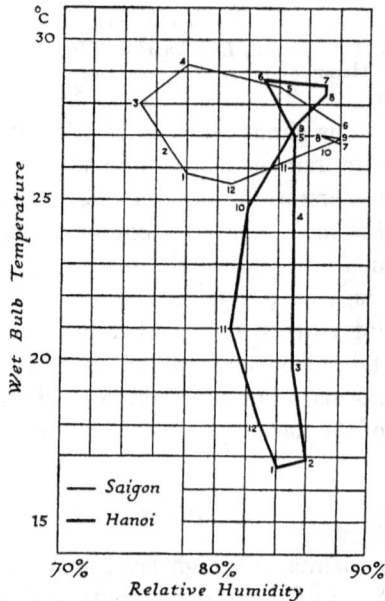

Fig. 44. Climograph for Saigon and Hanoi

This shows wet bulb temperatures, relative humidity and the relations between them for each month of the year. The figures by the curves indicate the months of the year.

Source: E. Bruzon and P. Carton, *Le Climat de l'Indochine et les Typhons de la Mer de Chine*, facing p. 202 (Hanoi, 1930).

VISIBILITY

Visibility is very poor over Tonkin during the drizzly or *crachin* period from February to April. At this time fog or mist usually occurs on about 10–15 days per month. During the rest of the year the monthly average is much lower, perhaps 2 or 3 days. Farther south, there is no corresponding extended foggy period such as exists in Tonkin. However, central Annam has poor visibility in the first few weeks of the north-east monsoon season (October) and from January to April when the Asiatic winter high pressure is weakening. In south Annam and Cochin-China fog is uncommon at any period of the year.

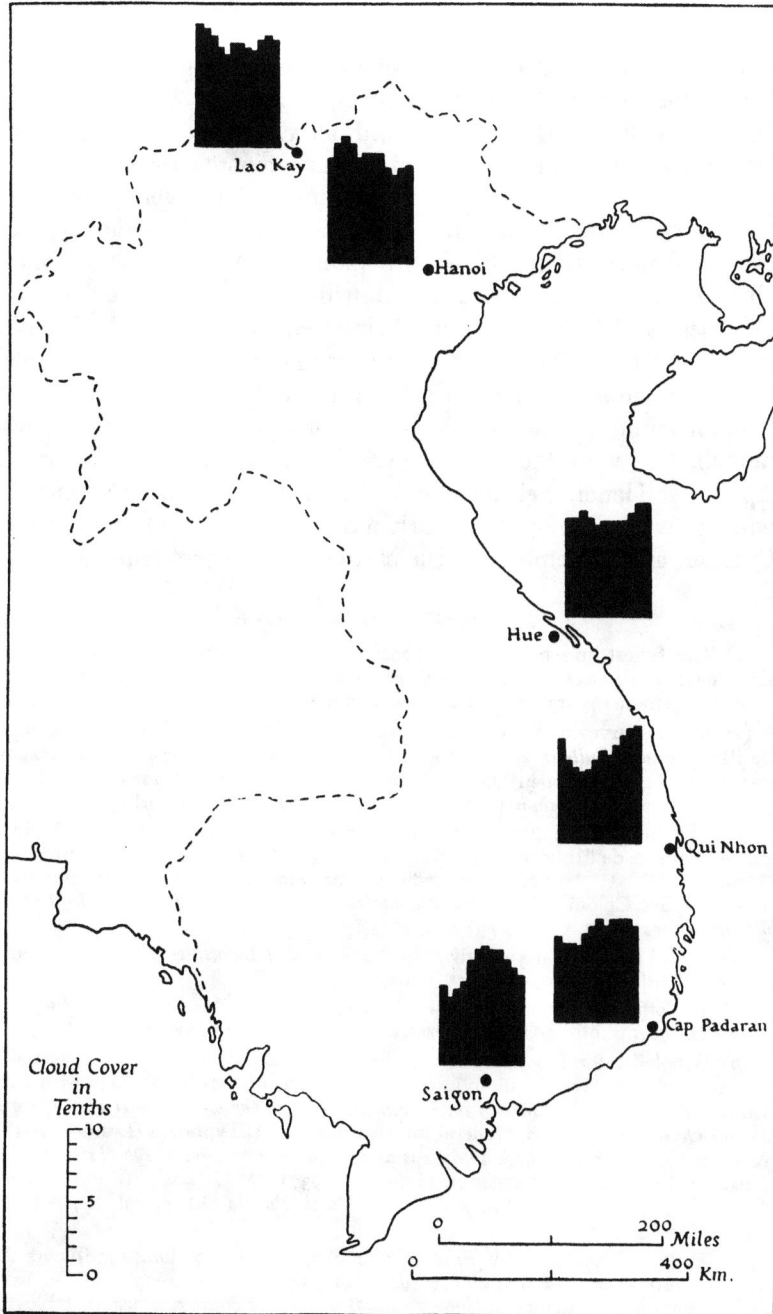

Fig. 45. Cloudiness. Monthly means for selected stations

Source: E. Bruzon and P. Carton, *Le Climat de l'Indochine et les Typhons de la Mer de Chine*, p. 220 (Hanoi, 1930).

CLOUDINESS

Over the greater part of Indo-China cloudiness is generally highest during the period of maximum precipitation. At Saigon, May to October is the cloudiest period, with an average of between seven-tenths and eight-tenths of cloud in each month; the dry season, January to April, is the least cloudy and has an average monthly cloud amount of between five-tenths and six-tenths (Fig. 45). In central Annam (Qui Nhon) the rainfall maxima in November, December, and January coincide with the greatest cloud-cover, densities as high as eight-tenths being frequently recorded (Fig. 45). March, April and May are the clearest months in this region, when the cloud amount averages six-tenths. In Tonkin, on the other hand, maximum cloudiness coincides not with the season of heaviest rainfall, but with the drizzly period (*crachin*) from February to April. At Hanoi, February and March are the cloudiest months with an average amount of nearly nine-tenths (Fig. 45). September, October, and November are the clearest months (six-tenths).

BIBLIOGRAPHICAL NOTE

(1) The fullest and most comprehensive work is E. Bruzon and P. Carton, *Le Climat de l'Indochine et les Typhons de la Mer de Chine* (Hanoi, 1930). It contains many maps and much statistical material.

(2) A brief survey of the climatic conditions is given in P. Carton, 'Le Climat de l'Indochine', *Bulletin économique de l'Indochine*, vol. XXXI, pp. 71–110 (Hanoi, 1928) and in W. Köppen and R. Geiger, *Handbuch der Klimatologie*, vol. IV, part R, C. Braak, *Klimakunde von Hinterindien und Insulindien* (Berlin, 1931).

(3) The following papers deal with special aspects: G. Le Cadet, 'Régime pluviométrique de l'Indochine', *Bulletin économique de l'Indochine*, vol. XX, pp. 1–51 (Hanoi, 1917). H. Hubert, 'Les mouvements généraux de l'air atmosphérique au-dessus des Colonies françaises', *Annales de Physique du Globe de la France d'Outre-Mer*, vol. II, pp. 1–27 (Paris, 1935).

(4) Useful rainfall maps are given in the *Atlas de l'Indochine* (Hanoi, 1928) and in the *Atlas des Colonies françaises* (Paris, 1934).

(5) The official French sources of information are the *Annales* and the *Bulletins pluviométriques* published by the *Service météorologique de l'Indochine*.

(6) Detailed information about the climate and the weather of the coasts and adjoining seas is given in the following publications of the British Meteorological Office: M.O. 404a, *Weather in the China Seas and in the western part of the North Pacific Ocean*, vol. I, part 1, General information, part 2, Typhoons (London, 1938). M.O. 404b, *Weather in the China Seas and in the western part of the North Pacific Ocean*, vol. II, Local information (London, 1937). M.O. 404c, *Weather in the China Seas and in the western part of the North Pacific Ocean*, vol. III, Aids to forecasting (London, 1938).

(7) The British *Admiralty Pilot* (China Sea, vol. I, London, 1938) and the French *Instructions Nautiques: Mer de Chine*, vol. I (Paris, 1933) include brief descriptions of weather conditions along the coast and provide useful tables of data, especially on air temperatures, rain and winds.

Chapter IV

VEGETATION

Introduction: Tropical Rain Forest: Monsoon Forest: Pine Forest: Mangroves:
Savanna: Other Vegetation Types: Bibliographical Note

INTRODUCTION

Indo-China in its primeval state was probably entirely covered with
dense forest. About one-seventh of the area of the country has been
cleared, and the forests so extensively modified as to produce savanna
or parkland in another three-sevenths. The remainder, amounting to
about 300,000 sq. km., is still covered with dense forest though, as
will be explained later, the larger part of this is of secondary origin.
Only about 5% of Great Britain is covered with forest (including
open woodland and coppice under this heading), while the comparable figure for Indo-China is between 70 and 80%. The following
table, based on an evaluation made in 1925, gives the forest area in
each state and the percentage of the total area of each state which is
covered by forest.

State	Forest area sq. km.	Percentage of forest area in each state
Annam	60,000	40·8
Cambodia	40,000	22·1
Cochin-China	18,000	27·7
Laos	160,000	64·9
Tonkin	35,000	30·2
Total	313,000	

Source: P. Gourou, *L'Utilisation du Sol en Indochine française*, p. 359 (Paris, 1940).

As is general in wet tropical countries, a large proportion of the
plant species consists of trees and shrubs and at least 50% of the
entire flora is made up in this way; the majority of these are trees.
In contrast with this, not more than about 4% of British plants are
woody and only about 1% are trees. The number of species which
occur in Indo-China is not known with any certainty, but is probably
ten to twenty times the number in Great Britain.

Several distinct kinds of forest occur, the chief of which are tropical
rain forest, monsoon forest, pine forest and mangroves. The general

distribution of these types is shown in Fig. 46. In each of these kinds of forest primary and secondary types may be recognized. A primary forest is one which is unaltered by man, while a secondary one results from clearing or partially clearing the primary forest by felling or burning and allowing the seedlings which spring up to grow into trees. If agricultural land (including pasture) is no longer cultivated, secondary forest will develop.

TROPICAL RAIN FOREST

Tropical rain forest occurs in regions with a rainfall of more than 2,000 mm. (80 in.) per annum, where the rain is fairly evenly distributed throughout the year. In Indo-China it occupies the plains and lower slopes of the mountains up to about 700 m. but local variations in the vegetation are caused by soil. A well-drained light soil may bear monsoon forest even though the rainfall is 2,000 mm. or more, while evergreen forest may occur in regions with less than 2,000 mm. of rain a year if drainage is impeded by a hard impervious 'pan' in the subsoil.

In most tropical forests one species seldom forms more than a very small percentage of the total number of trees, whereas in temperate woodlands, for example, in Great Britain, one kind of tree is usually more common than any other in a given area. Some of the tree species found in rain forests of Indo-China are confined to particular types of soil, while others are found only in the north or south, though the general appearance of the forest is not much affected by these changes. The most distinct type of rain forest is found in the seasonally inundated region which occupies an area of about 7,000 sq. km. round Tonle Sap. Few species are able to survive the periodical flooding, one of the commonest being a tree called *Hydnocarpus* from the fruits of which Chaulmoogra oil, used in the treatment of leprosy, is obtained. Tall forest trees with winged fruits (Fig. 47), belonging to the family *Dipterocarpaceae*, are of frequent occurrence and are specially characteristic of the Indo-Malayan forests, not being found elsewhere in the world. They are known to the natives as *dau*. The family *Leguminosae*, to which the familiar peas and beans belong, contributes many trees to these forests, one of the chief among them being *trac* (*Dalbergia cochinchinensis*) with smooth, grey, fibrous bark and very slender pods. Palms are thinly scattered in the rain forest, but not many of them reach a large size. One of the most important ones is the climbing rotan whose stems

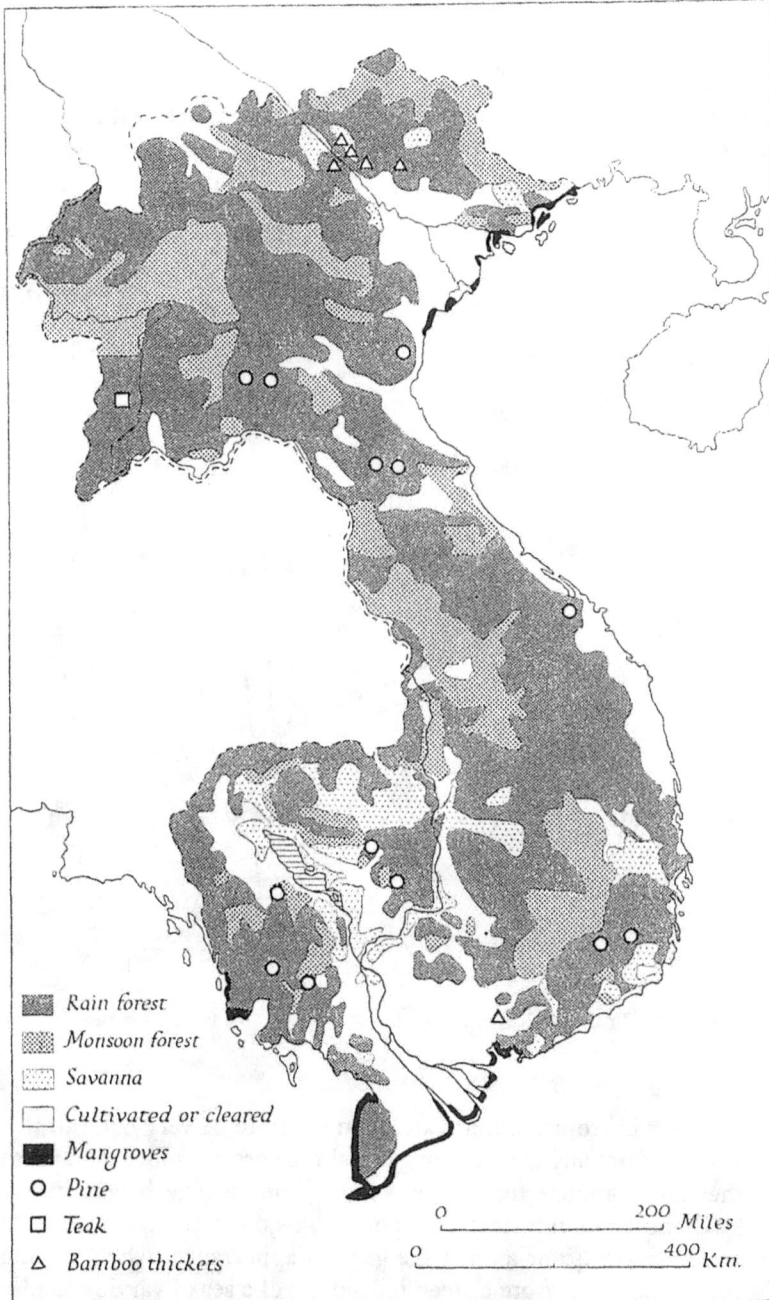

Rain forest
Monsoon forest
Savanna
Cultivated or cleared
Mangroves
O Pine
□ Teak
△ Bamboo thickets

0   200 Miles
0   400 Km.

Fig. 46. Distribution of vegetation types
Source: P. Maurand, 'L'Indochine forestière', *Bulletin économique de l'Indochine*, vol. XLI, folding map (Hanoi, 1938).

grow to a great length and yield the rattan cane of commerce. In parts of Annam pure stands of a palm (*Corypha Lecomtei*) occur in the forest.

The rain forests, especially in the south, often swarm with leeches, particularly during and after rain (see p. 468).

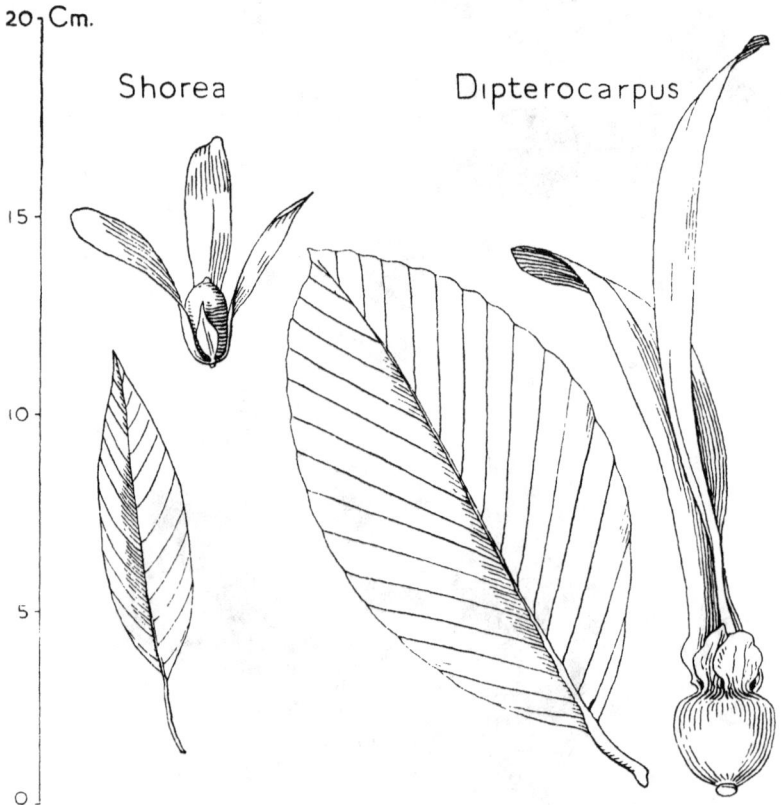

Fig. 47. Fruit and leaves of two forest trees (drawn from specimens)

Primary Rain Forest

The trees in tropical forests are often stated to be very tall, but this is only exceptionally true and in general they are not taller than those of the more familiar temperate woods. The average height in the Indo-Chinese rain forests is 25–30 m. (*c.* 75–90 ft.), though occasional trees may reach 40 or 45 m.; the general appearance, when looking down on this forest from a steep hill side, is of a sea of varying shades of green with the scattered crowns of the taller trees standing clear above it. The heights given here, especially those of the taller trees, may need modification when fuller information is available.

In addition to the outstanding trees and the large trees whose crowns form a more or less continuous canopy, there are smaller trees which, when mature, reach a height of 15 to 20 m. and below this again there is usually a fair abundance of seedlings and saplings of various ages and sizes. Fig. 48 shows the structure of a typical rain forest. A plan of construction similar in essentials to this can be seen in an English wood, though there are usually fewer layers. The chief

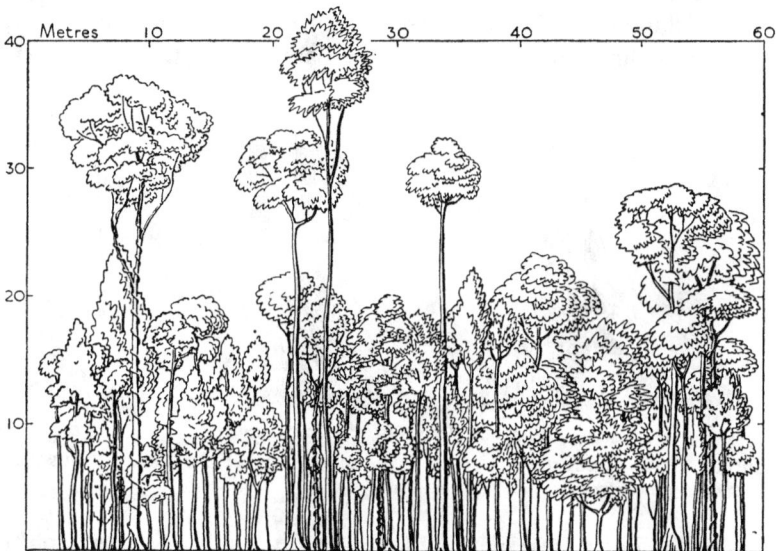

Fig. 48. Profile of rain forest

Mature trees only are shown, the undergrowth having been omitted for the sake of clarity. The strip of forest represented is 7·6 m. wide.

Source: P. W. Richards, 'Ecological observations on the rain forest of Mount Dulit, Sarawak', *Journal of Ecology*, vol. XXIV, p. 10 (London, 1936).

differences are due to the much greater suitability of the tropical climate for tree growth, which results in the shading out of herbaceous plants on the ground and the striking abundance of tree seedlings.

Orchids and many other herbaceous plants grow upon the branches and twigs of the trees, where they can get sufficient light. They are not in danger of drying up, since the humidity is high and the rainfall abundant. Such plants do not draw any food from the trees they grow upon and are known as epiphytes to distinguish them from parasites which actually draw their food supplies from the plant or animal to which they attach themselves. A certain number of bushes and small trees adopt the epiphytic way of life in the rain forest and may send out long roots which grow right down into the soil; these shrubs sometimes kill their host by shading. Woody climbing plants, known as lianes or lianas, are not uncommon and represent another method by which the light problem is solved by plants incapable of producing a tall and massive stem.

Primary rain forest may usually be penetrated with little difficulty. The crowns of the larger trees are most often completely hidden by the smaller trees and saplings, and the trunks are all that can be seen when walking in the forest. These differ from one another in colour, in the smoothness or roughness of the bark, and in the presence or

Fig. 49. Types of tree buttresses

Source: F. W. Foxworthy, 'Commercial timber trees of the Malay Peninsula', *Malayan Forest Records*, No. 3 (Singapore, 1927).

absence of buttresses; with practice, many kinds of trees can be recognized by these features. Buttresses (Fig. 49) are enlargements of the lower part of the trunk; they may be thin and plank-like or much thicker and rounded. They spread out from the trunk from about 50 cm. to 7 m. above the ground and so much increase the labour of felling a tree that it is customary to erect a platform to enable the tree to be cut through above the point at which the buttresses arise.

Owing to the widespread effects of shifting cultivation, primary rain forest in Indo-China is now confined to remote or inaccessible regions, such as the Monts des Cardamomes in Cambodia. In the neighbourhood of Savannakhet, there is a superb forest of this kind which can only be reached by sampan in the rainy season and has not been interfered with by man because it has the reputation of being peopled by evil spirits.

Secondary Rain Forest

Secondary rain forest, which develops when newly cleared forest land is left uncultivated, covers a very large area in Indo-China. The trees are mostly small and very close together, which makes this kind of forest much less easily penetrable than the primary forest just described. The more valuable hardwoods are generally slow growing and, since they cannot compete with the rapid growth of the soft-wooded trees, they are consequently scarce or absent in secondary forest. Another conspicuous feature of the secondary forests is the local abundance of lianes and herbaceous climbers. These form tangled thickets, more or less impenetrable without the aid of a cutlass or machete.

MONSOON FOREST

This type of forest occurs mainly in regions with a rainfall of between 1,500 mm. and 2,000 mm. per annum and with a dry season of several months' duration. It is usually far more open and easier to walk through than rain forest, though in places there are dense, spiny, impenetrable thickets; the trees shed their leaves completely in the dry season instead of being evergreen. Epiphytes and lianes are scarce or absent. Fires are frequent, sometimes occurring annually in the dry season and these drastically reduce the number of species, as only those which are fire-resistant can survive. Tree seedlings and saplings are rare, except where fires are prevented. As a very large proportion of this forest is considerably modified by the fires, almost all of it should therefore be considered as secondary forest. The trees mostly belong to the family *Dipterocarpaceae* and are called *ca chac* in Annam, *phchec* in Cambodia and *chich* in Laos. Teak (*Tectona grandis*), a fine tree with remarkably large leaves, is rare in the monsoon forests of Indo-China, though a small area of it is known on the crystalline rocks near Pak Lay in Laos. Since teak can stand repeated fires without serious injury, it tends to increase at the expense of less fire-resistant species. *Tranh* (*Imperata cylindrica*), known as *lalang* or *alang-alang* in Malaya, makes up a large part of the under-growth. It is a tall, coarse grass, called by the French 'herbe à paillote', and when young provides fair grazing, though its principal use is for thatch.

When a cleared area of monsoon forest is abandoned after a few crops have been cultivated, the ground is colonized first by various herbs which are rapidly succeeded by a dense growth of bamboos and wild bananas. These bamboo areas are particularly common in Tonkin as is indicated in Fig. 46. It must be borne in mind that a bamboo thicket may become secondary forest in a few years, since the shade and protection from drying provided by the dense growth makes the habitat particularly suitable for the germination of tree seeds.

In the dry season the trees of the monsoon forest are bare and the broad leaves of the dipterocarps cover the ground with a brown carpet; the *tranh* goes yellow as it dries and the spiny bamboos which border the rivers rattle as they knock against each other in the wind. The whole forest takes on a yellowish or reddish brown colour. The leafless trees blossom about a month before the end of the dry season; the flowers of some of them are strongly scented, while others appear as if on fire, being covered with beautiful, large bright red flowers.

When the rains begin, leaves appear with extraordinary rapidity, the young shoots of *tranh* spring up, and all the forest becomes bright green.

An abundance of animals makes this forest a remarkably good hunting ground. Hares, wild boar, deer, gaur (a kind of wild bull), tigers and elephants occur in the more open parts and monkeys are found particularly in the forest fringing the rivers.

Pine Forest

Pine forests differ conspicuously from the forests so far described in usually consisting of pines with little or no mixture of other species. They occur mainly on the mountains at altitudes of more than 700 m., though they are also found locally at lower altitudes near the coast. They cover altogether several hundred thousand hectares. Two main kinds of pine can be easily recognized: *Pinus Merkusii* with the needles in groups of two, like the familiar Scots pine, and *Pinus Khasya* with the needles in groups of three.

The pine forests are frequently very open and are, like the monsoon forest, liable to periodic fires which keep down the undergrowth and prevent the growth of young trees. In some places on the mountains the pines are mixed with, or replaced by, forests of broad-leaved trees in which oaks and trees related to the temperate magnolias are found. Other conifers of less familiar types occur, sometimes abundantly, in certain of the mountain regions.

MANGROVES

Mangroves, a general term covering a considerable variety of trees and shrubs which are found only on muddy sea shores and in the lower parts of estuaries, occupy an area of about 458,500 ha. in Indo-China. They can grow in slimy mud down to high water neap tides and usually form a fairly narrow belt which, however, is very difficult and unpleasant to penetrate. The swamps can best be approached from the land, where the mud is seldom more than knee deep; on the seaward side, they can only be reached in small flat-bottomed boats or on a kind of sledge. The bare mud between the trees swarms with brightly coloured crabs.

The mangroves fall into two main groups: those with 'stilt roots' which grow out from the branches and help to support the tree in the half liquid mud in which it lives, and those with a wide spreading root-system mainly below the surface of the mud, but with 'knees' sticking up into the air. These projecting portions are believed to give the roots the air they need, which they cannot get from the completely waterlogged soil. The other curious feature of this group of plants is that in some of them the seeds start to grow while still attached to the tree so that a stout and heavy root is produced. When the seed falls it lands with the root downwards, and the weight is sufficient to drive the root into the soft mud so that the seed is not washed away at high tide and is in the right position for growing into a tree.

Although all the mangroves have one or other of the characteristics described above, they belong to many different families; that is to say, they differ widely from each other in the structure of the flower or fruit. Duoc (*Rhizophora conjugata*), which frequently reaches a height of 20 m., is the finest of all the mangrove species in Indo-China.

The marshy zone to landward of the mangrove swamps of Cochin-China and Cambodia is frequently covered by a dense forest in which tram (*Melaleuca leucadendron*) is almost the only tree. It grows to a height of 15–20 m. and has a slender trunk with the bark peeling off in very thin brown papery sheets.

SAVANNA

Savanna vegetation in Indo-China is found in regions naturally suited to monsoon forest which have been so considerably modified by cultivation and by fires as to produce grassland or parkland. It also occurs in areas of poor soil unfavourable to dense forest. *Tranh*, to which reference has been made, is the principal herbaceous constituent of the savanna. The commonest of the shrubs is *sim* (*Rhodomyrtus tomentosa*), which grows to a height of about 2 m. and has large pink flowers recalling those of the peach; these are succeeded by purple fruits which are somewhat acid when ripe and have a flavour resembling both the guava and the gooseberry. *Alnus nepalensis*, related to the English alder, occurs particularly in the savannas of the north.

OTHER VEGETATION TYPES

In places where there are fairly stable dunes a thin forest of small trees, many with narrow leathery leaves, occurs. On shifting dunes, *Casuarina*, known locally as 'Filaos' and in Australia as 'Beefwood' or 'She Oak', has been extensively planted and has grown very well, stabilizing the sand and producing woods of considerable commercial value. *Casuarina* may easily be recognized as it has slender green branches and is apparently leafless, though the rings of small, brownish scales, which can be seen when the twigs are carefully examined, are actually very small leaves.

The name of heaths or moors ('landes') is given to certain areas on the borders of the plains of Annam and Tonkin where there is a poor, dry, lateritic soil supporting a vegetation which recalls the appearance of European heaths. A scented shrub belonging to the myrtle family (*Boeckia frutescens*) is specially abundant and is known locally as 'Bruyère'.

BIBLIOGRAPHICAL NOTE

(1) A good brief account of the vegetation is given in P. Gourou, *L'Utilisation du Sol en Indochine française*, ch. 13 passim (Paris, 1940). The forests of the country, forest management and the principal products and soil degeneration are fully described in P. Maurand, 'L'Indochine forestière', *Bulletin économique de l'Indochine*, vol. XLI, pp. 801–29, 975–1061, 1350–74 (Hanoi, 1938). A general account of the forests and detailed descriptions of the trees and timbers, with keys for their identification, is also given in Henri Lecomte, *Les Bois de l'Indochine* (Paris, 1925).

(2) The classic systematic account of the flora is H. M. Lecomte, *Flore générale de l'Indochine*, 5 vols. (Paris, 1907–31).

(3) An excellent illustrated account of mangrove forests, closely resembling those in Indo-China, is J. G. Watson, *Mangrove Forests of the Malay Peninsula* (Singapore, 1928). Keys for the identification of the species are given and there is much interesting general information.

Chapter V

FAUNA

INTRODUCTION

Zoologists divide the land areas of the world into six major faunal regions, each comprising a number of sub-regions. The Indo-Chinese sub-region of the 'Oriental' major region is a large triangular area extending from the eastern Himalayas (Darjeeling district) to Hong Kong in the north and to the isthmus of Kra in the south. The fauna of this area has a certain uniformity of type. A large number of its species are common to the whole region, and, in the higher units of classification, the genera and sometimes even the families are peculiar to it. In this chapter, however, only that part of the sub-region known as French Indo-China is considered, and the term Indo-China when used refers to that area.

The physical conditions of the country have an important influence on its fauna. The southern part is essentially tropical in character. The northern part, with a more temperate climate and more definite seasonal changes, has, in addition to its tropical fauna, a number of species of Chinese origin which have invaded the country from the north. A further distinction can be made between a lowland and a mountain fauna; comparatively few of the species which are found in the coastal lowlands also occur in the mountainous interior and vice versa.

As late as the middle of the nineteenth century, the country was still almost unknown from a zoological point of view. Until the French occupation, political conditions were such that only diplomatic envoys and missionaries had access to the interior, and no collections of any significance were brought back to Europe. Within the last thirty years, French, British and American naturalists have visited most of the country, and all the commoner species are now represented in museum collections. Whilst it is probable that nearly all the vertebrates have been discovered, very little information is available about the life histories, biology, numbers and distribution of any species except those which have been of commercial interest.

In the invertebrates an immense field of research still remains untouched.

In this chapter a brief general survey of the major faunal groups is attempted, but only the most common or interesting species are mentioned by name. English names are given whenever good ones are available, but a number of Latin names are inevitable.

MAMMALS

Much remains to be discovered about the smaller species, especially rodents, shrews and bats, but the larger game animals are now well known.

Primates

Great apes are unknown in Indo-China, but the gibbons, langurs and macaques, popularly known as monkeys, are well represented. The common monkey of the islands and coastal areas is the Crab-eating Macaque, a powerful animal with a brown coat and a long tail. Gibbons are plentiful wherever there are large stretches of jungle, and their loud wailing notes are frequently heard at sunrise and sunset. With their long arms they are able to swing from tree to tree with great facility. The Grey-headed Langur is found on Ile Cat Ba in the Gulf of Tonkin; it has the curious and unmonkey-like habit of taking refuge in holes in the ground when alarmed. The Douc Langur, unique among monkeys for its brilliant coat of many colours, is often seen in the tropical rain forests of the Col des Nuages, travelling in troupes of from thirty to fifty. A still more curiously coloured species is Delacour's Langur, which is black except for its white rump and white circles round its eyes. Two species of lemur are found only in dense jungle and are strictly nocturnal in their habits.

Carnivores

The tiger and the leopard are found wherever there are large tracts of jungle. They are particularly abundant on the Plateau du Lang Bian and in the northern part of Laos. Of the smaller cats, the Clouded Leopard, the Leopard Cat and the Fishing Cat are the best known. There are also at least nine different species of Civets (*Viveridae*), some of which are widely distributed. The Crab-eating Mongoose occurs throughout the country.

Two species of weasel are known, four of badger and four of otter. One of the otters is almost indistinguishable from its English

relative. It is numerous in the coastal districts and is equally at
home in fresh water and in the sea.

The Wild Dog has been recorded in several widely separated
localities; there is an interesting form on the Ile de Phu Quoc, off the
coast of Cambodia, with a broad strip of hair, turned the wrong way,
extending the whole length of its back from the head to the base of
the tail.

The Malay or Honey Bear occurs throughout the forests of the
country; the Himalayan Black Bear has been shot in the north and
in central Annam.

Insectivores

Shrews of many species are common and widely distributed, but
on account of their small size and secretive habits they are not often
seen. A mole, nearly allied to the British mole, has been found in
the hilly districts of the north.

Bats

Some forty species of bats are known from Indo-China, and many
more will doubtless be found. The largest and most conspicuous are
the fruit bats. They sleep by day in trees, and live in colonies that
may contain many thousands. When certain fruits are in season they
often cause great damage in the orchards.

Rodents

There are some thirty species of squirrels in the country. Several
varieties of the small Striped Squirrel are common in the cultivated
areas and do much damage to the crops. The beautiful Yellow-handed
Squirrel abounds in the forests of the Col des Nuages and the Giant
Squirrel is common in the north. The flying squirrels, of which there
are at least six species, prefer open forest, sleeping by day in holes in
the trees and issuing as night falls to seek their food. They are, of
course, not able to fly in the way that birds can, but by means of the
broad membrane extending between the fore and the hind limbs they
are capable of gliding a distance of 20 m. (70 ft.) or more.

Rats, mice and voles are abundant throughout the country, but
many of the species have a very local distribution. The largest,
Edwards's Giant Rat, and the smallest, the tiny Harvest Mouse, both
occur at Chapa in the mountains of Tonkin. Bamboo rats, as their
name implies, inhabit the bamboo forests. They resemble giant voles,
and their presence in the district can always be detected by the large
heaps of earth like mole hills which they cast up.

Two species of porcupine are found in the north. Hares are found in parkland, particularly in the central and southern parts of the country. There are no rabbits in Indo-China.

Ungulates

The Indian Elephant occurs on the plateaux of south Annam, near Vinh in north Annam, and in the forests near Siem Reap in Cambodia; the herds are gradually diminishing in size. Before the French occupation of the country, elephant hunting was an annual sport of the kings of Cambodia, the animals being driven into large stockades erected for the purpose. A few Rhinoceros have been shot in the valley of the Mekong, but they are now becoming very rare.

The Sambur and the Brow-antlered Deer are the best known species of deer, and their flesh is sold locally in the markets for food. The smaller Barking Deer and the Hog Deer are almost as numerous. The tiny Mouse Deer, a timid helpless creature no bigger than a hare, is common in the forests of the south. Its flesh is excellent eating. The Serow, a heavily built animal with short, curved horns, is found wherever there are bare, rocky hills.

The Gaur, the Bantang, and the Buffalo are the only species of wild oxen in the country. The Gaur, which grows to a height of almost 2 m., has a huge head, a dark brown coat and white or yellow limbs below the knees and hocks. The Bantang, almost equal in height to the Gaur, has a chestnut coat with white or grey spots on the limbs. It is found locally in thick jungle, and is dangerous. Buffaloes occur in the wild state, and large numbers are domesticated for use in the rice fields and as transport animals.

The Wild Boar is plentiful locally in more or less open country. It often does great damage to the crops and is shot whenever opportunity occurs.

Edentates

The Pangolin or Scaly Anteater, a curious and primitive creature, covered with large scales and able to roll itself into a ball like a hedgehog, is not uncommon. Its skin is often to be seen on sale in the shops.

BIG-GAME HUNTING

Indo-China offers hunting equal in standard to that of India or parts of Africa. Among the best hunting grounds are the plateaux of Lang Bian and Darlac. The chief game animals are elephants, tigers, leopards, Gaur and Bantang, several species of deer, and wild boars. In suitable country all are fairly plentiful. The French residents indulge in much shooting, especially of deer, from motor cars. The most popular method is to travel quietly by night along the roads that pass through jungle country, spotting the animals with the headlights. The tiger and leopard are shot from ambush, with the help of a decoy; wild oxen are usually stalked.

Lang Bian is the most accessible of the recognized hunting grounds, being easily reached from the coast by road or rail, or from Saigon by road. Big-game hunting on this plateau is regulated by a law of 1917; the region is divided into three districts known as preserved, protected and free. In the preserved district shooting is prohibited except to holders of special licences; these are available for three months and only one is issued to the same person in a year. A licence entitles the holder to shoot a very limited number of animals. Shooting of most big game is prohibited at all times in the protected district, although certain small animals may be shot between 15 September and 15 March. In the free district, male game may be shot at any season, though a licence, valid for one month, is necessary for Gaur. The cost of a licence in the preserved district was about 200 piastres.

BIRDS

The main characteristics of the bird fauna of Indo-China are now known, but, as in the case of the mammals, most of the investigations made have had to depend on museum collections rather than on field observations. While, therefore, it is now possible to name almost any bird seen without much difficulty and to give a broad indication of its distribution, extremely little is known about the habits and biology of any species. Only a few representative birds can be mentioned here under the heading of each order represented.

Cormorants, Gannets and Pelicans (Steganopodes)

The Common and Lesser Cormorants frequent the inland waters, where the Darter or Snake Bird is also found. This last named is so called because of its habit of swimming submerged with only its long snake-like neck above water. Rosy and Spotted Pelicans abound on the inland waters of the south. Out at sea Red-fronted Gannets or Boobies dive for fish.

Herons, Egrets, Ibises and Storks (Ciconiiformes)

Among the herons are the Common Grey Heron, the Purple Heron and the Lesser Egret, a pure white bird with black legs. The Reef Heron, a dimorphic species, either white or black, frequents the shores. The Cattle Egret is plentiful in the fields, often perching on the backs of Water Buffaloes to search for ticks. Two species of Pond Heron frequent the small pools, their brown colour blending well with the surroundings, but on taking flight are conspicuous by their white wings. Night Herons, with grey backs and black heads, roost in colonies in the trees during the day and become active at dusk. The most interesting of the Ibises found in the country is the Giant Ibis, a large bronze-brown bird with a bare head. It occurs locally in flocks and is found only in Siam and Indo-China.

Storks are often seen on marshy ground. The commonest species are the White-necked, the Painted and the Open-billed.

Ducks and Geese (Anseriformes)

Widgeon and Common Teal visit the country in great numbers in winter and afford excellent sport. The two common breeding ducks are the Tree Duck and the Cotton Teal. The Grey Lag Goose is found in the north in the cool season.

Waders, Gulls and Terns (Charadriiformes)

Many of the wading birds are well-known European species. They winter or pass through on migration. Fantail and Pintail Snipe abound in the rice fields and are shot in thousands. The Jack Snipe is rare. An occasional Woodcock may be met with, and the Painted Snipe is an abundant resident. It is an interesting bird with beautiful painted plumage; its build is clumsy and its flight heavy and rail-like. The female is polyandrous and leaves the care of the young to her various mates. This bird is often shot because it is an easy target, but its flesh is poor for eating.

The Lesser Ringed Plover is a resident; the Siberian Golden Plover is a common winter visitor. There are two other resident plovers, namely, the Spur-winged Plover and the Red-wattled Lapwing. The first has a sharp spur on the bend of the wing; the other is a noisy creature and is most easily identified by its cry of 'did-'e-do-it'.

The Black-headed Gull is an abundant winter visitor, and various terns, the largest being the Great Crested Tern and the smallest the

Lesser Tern; both are found on the coast. On the rivers, the small Whiskered Tern, grey above and black below, is often seen.

Cranes, Bustards, Rails and Waterhens (Gruiformes)

Cranes, particularly the Sarus Crane, a tall grey bird with orange-red head and neck, may be seen on the open plains. In Cochin-China there is a colony of the Bengal Florican, a bustard otherwise resident in Assam. Two species of Lily Trotter or Jacana, the Bronze-winged and the Pheasant-tailed, haunt the ponds and lakes. Both have greatly enlarged toes and claws which enable them to walk with ease over the floating leaves of water-lilies and other aquatic plants. Rails of several species are common, but they are seldom seen. The White-breasted Water Hen is as familiar as the British Moorhen, which also occurs in the country; the beautiful and striking Purple Moorhen is abundant locally.

Game Birds (Galliformes)

Indo-China is famous for game birds, the largest of which is the Burmese Pea-fowl with its neck and breast of a metallic blue-green colour. A smaller bird is the Argus Pheasant which lives in deep forest and is seldom seen by Europeans. It cries like a peacock and is believed by the Japanese to be the mythical phoenix. Several varieties of Peacock-Pheasant, grey birds with fan-like tails marked with purple 'eyes', inhabit the forests, and no less than six varieties of the Silver Pheasant live in the mountainous districts. The Fire-backed Pheasant, which has little fear of man, is common in the rain forests of the Col des Nuages; it is grey and deep blue with a splash of yellow and crimson on the back and crimson cheeks surmounted by a tuft of blue feathers on the head, a wonderful combination of colour. The Red Jungle Fowl is common everywhere, frequenting the fringes of the forests. In the north are several varieties of the Common Pheasant; and Tree Partridges, as large as the Common Partridge, inhabit the hills. The most abundant game bird is the Chinese Francolin. The Grey Quail visits Indo-China in winter, and in some parts the Little Bustard Quail is found. This bird is not a true quail but a hemipode; the male performs the duties of the female in hatching and rearing the young.

Pigeons and Doves (Columbiformes)

Green Fruit Pigeons, all of varying shades of green, are abundant. In the south the large Imperial Pigeon is found, and flocks of Spotted Doves may often be seen.

Birds of Prey (*Falconiformes*)

Of the three species of vultures, the Pondicherry or Black Vulture and the White-backed Vulture are common in the south. Many birds-of-prey are migrants from the north, namely the Peregrine, Merlin, Kestrel, Sparrow-hawk and the Marsh and Pied Harriers. The last two may often be seen quartering the ground in search of food. There are many eagles, but they are difficult to identify. Brahminy Kites, with white heads and brown backs, haunt the river banks and harbours, feeding on fish and frogs. Over the towns and villages Black Kites circle on the look out for garbage. The Osprey is common. The smallest members of the family are the Pigmy Falcons, which are black and white in colour and no larger than starlings. They feed on insects.

Owls (*Strigiformes*)

Owls are seldom seen although they are abundant throughout the country. They range in size from the large Eagle Owl to the Pigmy Owlet, no bigger than a British Song Thrush. The Barn Owl, which is found all over the world, is not rare.

Cuckoos (*Cuculiformes*)

The Indian Cuckoo, like the English Cuckoo, but with a different note, is a migrant, and the Ko-el, so called from its insistent call of 'ko-el, ko-el', is abundant. The Ground Cuckoo, the largest member of the family, is a grey bird with a blue head, and is known only from Indo-China.

Parrots (*Psittaciformes*)

The Alexandrine Parrot, the male of which has a rose-coloured ring on the neck, is common in the south, while the Red-breasted Parrot, with a grey head, is found everywhere. The little Indian Loriquet, not more than 15 cm. (6 in.) long, lives in flocks.

Woodpeckers (*Piciformes*)

Many of the Woodpeckers are brightly coloured. The Yellow-naped Woodpecker and the black and white Pigmy Woodpecker are the most widely distributed. The Rufus Woodpecker, a dark brown bird with darker bars, is of special interest. It feeds on termites and ants and makes its nests in those of the tree ant. The Wryneck is widely distributed in winter.

The most familiar of the Barbets is the Coppersmith, so called because of its monotonous 'tonk tonk', like the sound of a smith beating copper. The large Green Barbet is a devourer of fruit and is a familiar sight in gardens.

Nightjars (*Caprimulgiformes*)

The Nightjar, owing to its nocturnal feeding habits, is seldom seen. It resembles the European bird. A near relative, the Frogmouth, has similar habits. These birds nest on trees, fixing their little cups of down on to the top of boughs. They are difficult to see when at rest during the day on tree stumps, logs, or branches which they closely resemble on account of their mingled lichen-grey and brown plumage and upright posture. Seated motionless in such surroundings, and in such an attitude as they adopt, they provide a wonderful example of natural camouflage.

Swifts (*Apodiformes*)

Palm Swifts stick their nests to the underside of the leaves of the *Borassus* palm and are found wherever it grows. The giant of the family is the Needle-tailed Swift, which has a wing span of 50 cm. and is reputed to fly at 130 km.p.h., which is faster than any other bird known. The Brown Swift breeds in caves along the coast of Cambodia. Their nests, collected under government control, form the well-known 'bird's nest' soup. Some of the Swallows are resident; others are visitors in the cold weather. One variety resembles the European Swallow, but has a chestnut instead of a white throat. The Daurian Swallow, with a chestnut rump and streaked underparts, is equally abundant.

Kingfishers, Hornbills and Hoopoes (*Coraciiformes*)

Many species of Kingfishers haunt the rivers. They range in size from the Common Kingfisher to the Stork-billed Kingfisher, a large greenish blue bird with a brown head. Unlike the other members of its family, the White-breasted Kingfisher feeds on insects, lizards, etc., and frequents gardens away from water.

The Pied is the most abundant of the Hornbills, but the Great Indian Hornbill, a large black and white bird, over 120 cm. long, with a huge bill surmounted by a casque, is not rare. They feed in flocks, prefer the tallest trees of the forest, and when in flight make a loud, droning noise with their wings. Hornbills breed in holes in trees. When the hen begins to incubate, the cock plasters up the entrance with mud, leaving only a small hole through which the hen receives the food he brings. This he casts up enfolded in the lining of the gizzard.

A Hoopoe, very like the European bird, is abundant in cultivated country.

Passerine Birds (*Passeriformes*)

The family of Flycatchers has many representatives, some of which are of great beauty. The Paradise Flycatcher, either brown or white with a long tail, is common in gardens. A common garden bird is the black and white Magpie Robin; it has the habits of a robin, but is rather larger in size and different in colour. It is represented in the forests by the Shama, well known as a songster. Most of the thrushes are migrants. None of them is found near habitations except the Blue Thrush, which is often seen perched on buildings.

All the Warblers are small and difficult to identify; many are migratory. A common bird in cultivated areas is the Tailor Bird with a green back and brown head; it builds its nest inside two or three leaves, which it stitches together for the purpose. The Wren Warbler, a small brown bird, has a similar habit but uses only one leaf.

The Babblers, a group of noisy birds, have many representatives including the Scimitar Babbler, which has a curved red and yellow bill and brown plumage. The members of the family vary in size; one of the largest is the Hwamei, common in China but found also in Tonkin. It is in great demand as a cage bird. Another bird much sought after is the Pekin Robin; it is green in colour with a red bill and orange breast. Most beautiful of all is the Mesia, with its black head and patches of deep crimson on the chest, wings and base of the tail.

The most familiar of the Bulbuls is the Red-vented, a noisy brown bird with a red patch under its tail. It frequents gardens like the Red-whiskered Bulbul, which has a patch of crimson on each white cheek.

The commonest of the Drongos is the King Crow, a black bird with a long tail. It is fond of perching on points of vantage and is very pugnacious. The Jungle Crow, similar to the Carrion Crow of Europe, and a species of Magpie are both widely distributed, particularly in coastal districts.

The Chinese Tit, very like our Great Tit, and the Crow Tit, allied to our Bearded Tit, are both found in the north. The Sunbirds include many beautiful species which are often mistaken for Humming Birds, a group found only in the Americas. The Purple Sunbird is a regular visitor to gardens.

The Wagtails, Pipits and Larks are migratory; they resemble the well-known species found in Europe.

There are two groups of Weaver Birds. One group breeds in colonies and constructs large retort-shaped nests; the other is less sociable and makes round nests about the size of a football.

Two kinds of Starling are plentiful in cultivated country. The Indian Crackle lives in the forests; it is a heavily built black bird, with a red bill and yellow wattles, and is a popular cage bird on account of its ability to talk.

REPTILES

Crocodiles

Two species of crocodile inhabit the southern part of the country. The Estuarine Crocodile (*Crocodilus porosus*) is found at the mouths of muddy rivers and canals near the sea and is common in the delta of the Mekong. It takes freely to salt water, but does not ascend the rivers above tidal limits. It grows to a length of 5 or 6 m., will attack man, and is responsible for a number of deaths every year. The Siamese Crocodile (*C. siamensis*) inhabits the rivers above the tidal limits and is abundant in fresh-water swamps. It does not exceed 3·5 m. in length and feeds upon fishes and crustaceans. It is abundant in the swamps of Cambodia and is said to be plentiful in a small lake at Tak Lak on the Plateau du Lang Bian at an altitude of 1,500 m.

Tortoises and Turtles

Three species of marine turtle inhabit the coastal waters of Indo-China, namely, the Green or Edible Turtle (*Chelonia mydas*), the Hawksbill Turtle (*Eretmechelys imbricata*) and the Loggerhead (*Caretta caretta*). The Green Turtle, so called on account of the green colour of its fat, is the source of all genuine turtle soup; the horny shell of the Hawksbill forms the 'tortoise' shell of commerce; the Loggerhead has no commercial value, but its eggs are eaten. All three species breed on the small sandy islands off the coast of Cambodia, and the eggs, which are about as large as table-tennis balls, are collected under government control and sold in the markets. Their flavour is not appreciated by Europeans.

Indo-China is rich in fresh-water tortoises; no less than eighteen species are found in the country. Some are restricted to the south,

others, entrants from China, are found only in Tonkin. They inhabit
ponds, marshes and canals, and feed upon molluscs and crustacea.
The three common species in the lowlands of the south are the
Amboyna Pond Tortoise (*Cuora amboinensis*), the Black Pond Tortoise (*Siebenrockiella crassicollis*) and *Damonia subtrijuga*. The commonest species in Tonkin is the Chinese Terrapin (*Ocadia sinensis*).
The true land tortoises (*Testudo*) are found in the hilly country and
are nowhere common. The Mud Turtles or Soft-Shelled Turtles
differ from all others in having the shell covered with skin instead
of horny plates. One species, *Trionyx cartilagineus*, is found throughout the country.

Lizards

About sixty species of lizards have so far been recorded from the
country, and more will no doubt be found. Geckos are common
everywhere. The House Geckos (*Hemidactylus*, *Gehyra* and *Gecko*
species), although found on trees in the country, prefer human habitations, and it is seldom that a house is found without one or more of
these little creatures. By means of the adhesive pads to their digits
they can ascend smooth vertical surfaces; the gecko that runs up the
walls of rooms, crosses the ceiling and falls with a flop on the table,
is either *Hemidactylus frenatus* or *Gehyra mutilata*. They feed on
insects. Flying lizards (*Draco*) are common in the wooded districts,
but being entirely arboreal in their habits are seldom seen. The
Changeable Lizard (*Calotes versicolor*) and the Moustached Lizard
(*C. mystaceus*) are common on the shrubs and bushes in the south.
The former is often, but erroneously, called the chameleon on account
of its ability to change colour. True chameleons are found only in
India and Africa. The male of *C. versicolor* in the breeding season—
February to May—assumes a vivid scarlet colour, that of *C. mystaceus*
a rich blue.

In sandy country, particularly in districts near the sea, an interesting lizard, *Leiolepis belliana*, occurs. It lives in colonies, burrowing
into the soil; each family has its own hole. It is a handsome creature,
the back being covered with red or yellow spots and stripes. Its flesh
is eaten by the country people. Skinks, which are small, brown lizards
with highly polished scales, abound in all gardens and open country.
They live on the ground. The Water Monitor (*Varanus salvator*), the
largest lizard of Asia, attaining a length of 3 m. or more, is common
in the estuaries and can often be seen searching the mud flats for
food at low tide.

Snakes

Snakes are plentiful throughout Indo-China, but unless looked for are not often seen. It is possible to live for months in the country and not see one. Most of the species are nocturnal in their habits, and during the day time hide in holes in the ground or under fallen logs or in thick herbage. Snakes in the tropics do not bask in the sun as they do in colder latitudes. The vast majority of the species met with are harmless, but native opinion on this point must not always be taken as reliable.

Harmless Snakes. The Reticulated Python (*Python reticulatus*) is not uncommon in the south, and is found very often in warehouses and huts, even in thickly populated districts. It is the largest snake known, and although individuals of 9 m. in length have been recorded, it is seldom that specimens of more than 5 or 6 m. in length are met with to-day. They feed on small mammals and birds, and when living in and about human habitations appear to prefer cats to any other kind of diet. The Indian Python (*P. molurus*) occurs only in the north. It does not exceed 3·5 m. in length but is a much bulkier creature than the Reticulated Python.

The Sunbeam Snake (*Xenopeltis unicolor*) and the Pipe Snake (*Cylindrophis rufus*) inhabit the lowland country of the south and are common in the neighbourhood of towns and villages. The Sunbeam Snake is deep purplish black and highly irridescent. The Pipe Snake has an extremely short stumpy tail which it curls over its back when disturbed, showing the red colour underneath.

Grass snakes or Keelbacks (*Natrix*) are represented by some thirty species. The two commonest, found generally in rice fields, are the Chequered Keelback (*N. piscator*) and the Red-neck (*N. subminiata*). They feed on frogs and fish and are fond of water. The Common Rat Snake (*Ptyas mucosus*), which grows to a length of 2·5 m., has diurnal habits and is abundant in the lowlands. In spite of its name it feeds chiefly on toads.

The Whip Snakes (*Dryophis*) and Bronze-backs (*Ahaetulla*) represent the arboreal snakes. All are of slender form and can move with amazing speed through the bushes and trees in which they live. Most of the Bronze-backs are brilliantly coloured. The two commonest species, often seen in gardens, are *Dryophis nasutus* and *Ahaetulla ahaetulla*. The Golden Tree Snake (*Chrysopelea ornata*) frequently enters houses. It is a very good climber and can ascend walls and tree trunks with ease, taking advantage of every projection and irregularity to maintain its hold.

7-2

The fresh-water snakes (*Homalopsinae*) are represented by ten species. They inhabit ponds and slow-flowing rivers, usually within tidal limits.

Poisonous Snakes. The mortality caused by snake bite in Indo-China when compared with that in India, where many thousands of people are said to be killed annually, is infinitesimal. The only species that are of real danger to man are the two cobras. The Common Cobra (*Naja naja*) occurs everywhere except in thick jungle. It varies in colour from dark brown to almost black, but olivaceous or greenish individuals are sometimes met with. The well-known spectacle-mark on the hood, typical of the Indian form, is never seen in Indo-China; the variety found there has a mark like a monocle, or quite often no mark at all. A fully grown Cobra is about 1·5 m. in length. The King Cobra or Hamadryad is a much rarer snake. It lives in open jungle country. It is the largest poisonous snake known and has been recorded 5·5 m. in length. Those individuals that have been known to attack human beings are usually females guarding their eggs.

There are two species of Krait, namely, the Banded Krait (*Bungarus fasciatus*) and *B. magnimaculata*. Their poison is fatal to large animals, but there is no record of man having been bitten by them. The Coral snakes (*Callophis*) are also represented by two species and like the Kraits do not attack man.

Sea snakes (*Hydrophiidae*) abound in the coastal waters of the south; along the rocky coast of Annam they are seldom seen. At the river mouths they are caught by fishermen in their nets in hundreds, and on calm days they may be seen basking on the surface of the water in great numbers. They can be distinguished from all land snakes by the vertically flattened tail and the absence of ventral shields. In the water they are active and graceful swimmers, but on land are quite helpless. Twelve species have been recorded from Indo-Chinese waters; all of them are extremely poisonous.

The Pit Vipers, so called because they have a deep pit in the side of the face between the eye and the nostril, are represented by *Ancistrodon* (one species) and *Trimeresurus* (six species). The former has terrestrial habits and is found only in the south, generally in dry country near the sea; the latter are arboreal. *T. albolabris*, which is vivid green in colour, with a bright red or orange stripe along the flank, is not uncommon in gardens and plantations. Its bite, as with all the known species of the genus, produces pain and swelling, but is not fatal to man.

Russell's Viper (*Vipera russelli*) is found in the north, but is never abundant as it is in Burma.

AMPHIBIANS

With the exception of one species of newt, the tailed amphibians are not represented in Indo-China. Frogs and toads (*Rana* and *Bufo* species) occur everywhere and are most in evidence during the summer monsoon. The Bull Frog (*Kaloula pulchra*), common in many coastal areas in the south, buries itself underground during the dry weather, but as soon as the first rain falls, it emerges to breed, and its deep and mournful croak, when the full chorus is in voice, can be heard a long way off.

Two of the largest species of frogs found in the country are *Rana tigrina* and *R. cancrivora*. Both are carnivorous in habit and have been known to eat small mammals. They are fairly common in the fields in coastal areas and are the only amphibians that are eaten by the country people. As with the Edible Frog in France, only the hind legs are eaten.

The Tree frogs (*Rhacophorus*) are abundant. One species (*R. leucomystax*) enters houses and is often found in the bath room. Its breeding habits are interesting, the eggs being laid in a large ball of froth beaten up by the creature's hind legs and suspended or attached just above the water. As the tadpoles hatch out they wriggle themselves free and drop into the water and continue their development in the usual way.

FISHES

The fishes of Indo-China form an important part of the diet of the people, especially in the villages where pork is scarce. They are eaten fresh, dried and salted, or prepared as pastes and sauces to flavour rice. As might be expected, all those species which enter into the diet of the people have distinctive names. An excellent means of getting to know the common fish of any district is by a visit to the local fish market.

In the lower reaches of the Mekong and other rivers, and in lagoons near the coast, brackish water fishes predominate; the true freshwater fauna is found only farther inland. In coastal areas sharks, dogfish and rays of many kinds occur; some rays extend their range into the lake of Tonle Sap, notably *Dasybatus uarnak*, a Sting Ray. The flesh of both sharks and rays is cut into strips, salted and dried in the sun. Much of it is exported. The shark fins become the well-known Chinese delicacy. The Saw fish (*Pristis*) is not uncommon near the coast and may attain a length of 6 m.

At some seasons other fish predominate in the nets, such as the *Sciaenidae* or Drums, Perch-like fishes that produce loud noises or grunts by means of a muscular apparatus connected with the air bladder; the *Polynemidae* or Thread-fins that have five or more thread-like rays at the lower part of the pectoral fin; fishes of the mackerel family (*Scombridae*); herring-like fishes (*Clupeidae*); cat fishes of the genus *Arius*. A coastal and brackish water Perch-like fish, *Lates calcarifer*, grows to a length of 2 m. and weighs 60 kg.; it is much esteemed as food. It is fattened in enclosures in a lagoon near Hue. One of the most conspicuous fishes of the mud flats in the coastal districts is the Mud Skipper (*Periophthalmus*), which has large protruding eyes and pectoral fins adapted for walking. It lives literally at the water's edge, moving up and down on the mud with the rise and fall of the tide. An alarmed Mud Skipper generally seeks safety on land rather than taking to the water as one would expect. Among the *Clupeidae* the species of Shad deserve mention. They are coastal fishes that enter fresh water to spawn. They are sold in the markets in Saigon from July to November and at Phnom Penh and Vinh Long later. By February they are migrating again to the sea to feed, having become thin and worthless as human food after spawning. The Archer Fish (*Toxotes*) is a brackish water Perch-like fish, extending into fresh water. It is famed for the accuracy of its aim in shooting insects with a jet of water from its mouth.

Among the true fresh-water fishes perhaps the most remarkable are the labyrinthic fishes which include the Climbing Perch (*Anabas*) and the Snake Head (*Ophicephalus*). Both these fishes have in addition to the gills an accessory apparatus enabling them to breathe air. In *Anabas* this is the famous labyrinthic organ above the gills; *Ophicephalus* has a pair of pharyngeal pouches which serve the same purpose. This is a great asset to the vendor of fish who can keep his wares not merely fresh, but alive. To the labyrinthic fishes also belong the Gourami (*Osphronemus*) and the Fighting fish (*Betta*), a gorgeously coloured little creature that provides the well-known sport of Siam and Malaya.

The snake-like Spiny Eel (*Mastacembelus*), which lurks in quiet water and preys on other fishes, is also characteristic of these waters. It is easily recognized by its tapering snout ending in three tentacles, two of which are tubular nostrils.

Apart from the species mentioned above, the bulk of the fresh-water fish fauna belongs to the *Cyrinoidea* (Carp-like fishes) and the *Siluroidea* (Cat fishes); both groups include numerous species.

INVERTEBRATES

Insects

The insects form by far the largest class among the invertebrates. The predominating Orders of the country are the *Lepidoptera* (Butterflies and Moths), *Hymenoptera* (Ants, Bees and Wasps), *Isoptera* (Termites or White Ants), *Coleoptera* (Beetles), *Diptera* (Flies and Mosquitoes), *Orthoptera* (Crickets, Grasshoppers and Stick Insects) and *Odonata* (Dragonflies), all of which are represented by enormous numbers of species.

Of all these Orders the butterflies are the best known. About 900 species have now been recorded from the country. Many species in the north are peculiar to that region, being found nowhere else. The Swallow-tails (*Papilionidae*) include some of the most striking species, such as the genus *Ornithoptera*, large black butterflies with patches of translucent gold on the hind wings. The *Pieridae* are another con-spicuous family, several species of which form migratory swarms at times. One of the commonest genera is *Terias*, small yellow butter-flies with black-bordered wings. Members of the genus *Euploea* (family *Danaidae*) are also conspicuous with their glossy blue-black wings. The largest butterfly found in the country is *Stichophthalmus*; it has a wing span of 90–100 mm. ($3\frac{1}{2}$–4 in.).

One of the most interesting studies is the seasonal variation which many species undergo, according to whether they hatch out in the wet or in the dry season. It affects both the colour and the shape of the wings. Some have 'eye-spots', and these are larger, blacker and richer in colour in the wet season, smaller and paler in the dry. Others change only in the tone of their coloration, being darker in the wings. The shape of the wing may be affected by the growth of 'tails' and by the development of a dark line on the under side of the wings connecting the 'tails'. When the insect is at rest with the wings folded, it bears a striking resemblance to a dead leaf, the lower 'tail' forming the stalk and the dark line the mid-rib of the leaf. As they rest in the foliage or on the floor of the forest it is almost impossible to distinguish them from their surroundings.

The Moths, owing to their nocturnal habits and to the fact that the Order contains a large number of minute species, commonly called the *Microlepidoptera*, are much less well known. But it may be stated roughly that in the number of their species they exceed the butterflies by at least 15 to 1. The largest species of all is the Atlas Moth (*Attacus*), which may have a wing span of 300 mm. It is not uncommon in the south where it often flies into houses. The Hawk Moths (*Sphingidae*) include many beautiful species; in the richness of their colours they rival the butterflies. An interesting sub-family is the *Chalcosiinae* which has members that bear a close resemblance to certain butterflies of the genus *Delias* with which they often fly in company.

Ants, nearly a hundred species of which are known from Indo-China, are amongst the most prominent of the *Hymenoptera*. One of the largest and commonest is *Sima rufonigra*, sometimes called the Kringer, a black and red species that builds a nest in trees or bushes, sticking the leaves together with a gummy secretion. When these are disturbed they issue forth in myriads and their stings can be most unpleasant. At the beginning of the rainy season 'flying ants' (*Dorylus* species) often invade the houses in huge numbers at night, attracted by lights inside. They are the males that have been driven out of the nests by the workers.

Solitary Wasps, so called because they live alone and not in colonies, abound everywhere. They prey upon spiders, caterpillars and other insects, paralyzing but not killing their victims, and storing them in prepared nests as food for their own grubs. The species of *Odynerus* enters houses and builds mud cells in the keyholes of drawers or in holes or cracks in timber. The Spider-wasps of the family *Pompilidae* prey upon spiders, and having overcome them drag them to pre-viously prepared burrows, where they lay their eggs. The Digger Wasps—the largest and most conspicuous species belonging to the genus *Chlorion*—feed on grasshoppers. The genus *Vespa* includes some of the largest wasps or hornets. They live in colonies and build large nests in trees or attached to overhanging rocks. The large and showy blue-backed bees of the genus *Xylocopa* burrow into wood and provision the nest with a paste—bee bread—made of honey and pollen. There are also many species of Honey Bee.

Here and there in the monsoon forests may be seen the tall earth mounds made by termites or white ants. These are not *Hymenoptera* like the other ants, but form a distinct group of their own, the *Isoptera*. Like the true ants they have types of individuals specialized for the purposes of reproduction, labour and defence. The winged sexual forms of several colonies swarm at the same time, and out of countless numbers a few individuals escape the attacks of birds, alight and cast their wings. A single pair forms a new colony by making a small burrow. The first young are mostly workers which are tended by their parents, and when mature, take over the nursing of the young. The queen becomes enormous and helpless, and is fed by the workers; she is said to lay up to a million eggs a year. The nests vary considerably in type. The great mounds that attract attention are made of earth cemented together with the saliva of the ter-mites. Some species are very destructive of timber buildings, paper, etc.

All the main families of beetles (*Coleoptera*) are represented in Indo-China. There are the Stag-beetles (*Lucanidae*), Tiger beetles (*Cicindelidae*), Chafers (*Scarabaeidae*), which include both the Dung-beetles and Goliath-beetles, Water-beetles (*Dytiscidae*) and Whirli-gig beetles (*Gyrinidae*), Carrion beetles (*Silphidae*), Lady-birds (*Coccinellidae*), Pill-beetles (*Byrrhidae*), Glow-worms and Fireflies (*Malacodermidae*), Blister-beetles (*Cantharidae*), Leaf-beetles *Chryso-melidae*), Longicorn-beetles (*Cerambycidae*) and the *Staphylinidae*, represented in England by the Devil's Coach-horse. Each family has an enormous number of species. Only a small proportion of the total number that occur in the country is so far known, but some idea of the magnitude of the task that awaits future naturalists can be gained from our knowledge of the beetles of India, which is now fairly complete. In the *Fauna of British India*, thirteen volumes are devoted to them and five or six more still remain to be written. The total number of species described so far is nearly 6,000.

Indo-China is particularly rich in Stag-beetles, Chafers and Longi-corns. Some spend their adult life among flowers, others in rotting wood. The Chafers, noteworthy for their beautiful colours, mostly greens of varying hues, fly by day, but the majority of beetles are nocturnal. Blister-beetles are not uncommon in the hill country. Fireflies of several species are common along the river banks, and at night their rhythmical pulsations of light among the bushes or low trees where they swarm is a very beautiful sight.

Of the many species of flies (*Diptera*), only those that directly con-cern man as carriers of disease need be mentioned. The mosquitoes which carry malaria (*Anopheles*), as well as other kinds (*Culex*) which do not carry it, abound everywhere except in the hills; they are seldom found above an altitude of 1,200 m. For further informa-tion about malaria-carrying mosquitoes see pp. 110–14. Sandflies (*Phlebotomus*) are common in the plains and can cause great annoyance at night, because, on account of their small size, they can penetrate the meshes of the ordinary mosquito net.

The *Orthoptera* include many large and striking forms of long-horned grasshoppers (*Tettigonidae*), crickets (*Gryllidae*), cockroaches (*Blattidae*), and especially of stick-insects (*Phasmidae*). In the tropical forest most of these are inactive in the daytime and are seldom seen, on account of their cryptic coloration. With the onset of darkness they begin to move, and their strident notes—as if produced by a variety of musical instruments—can be heard on all sides. When a number are congregated together, the noise can be almost deafening. A migratory locust (*Locusta migratoria*) visits Tonkin and can cause great damage to crops.

Dragonflies (*Odonata*) are abundant in the lowlands; some of them are exceptionally large and brilliantly coloured.

Arachnids (Spiders, Scorpions, Mites and Ticks)

Spiders are classified according to their web-spinning habits: the wanderers and hunters that spin little, and the sedentary forms that spin much. Several hundred species are known from Indo-China, and it is certain that many more will be discovered. A large black hairy spider (*Selenocosmia*) inhabits the open country of the south. It lives in burrows in the ground and is powerful enough to attack and kill small mammals and birds. It is the only species in the country that can be considered dangerous to man, but its bite is not fatal.

Three species of scorpions are common in the country districts, a large black or dark green one (*Palamnacus indicus*) and two smaller brown or yellowish species (*Chaerilus*). The sting of *Palamnacus indicus* can cause great pain and swelling which may last for several days.

False scorpions (*Pseudoscorpiones*), smallish, scorpion-like creatures armed with claws but without jointed tail or sting, are common in all gardens. They are quite harmless.

The *Pedipalpi*, sometimes called whip-scorpions, although not all of them have whips (= tails), are found mostly in caves. On account of their enormous palps or claws they are much feared by men, but having no sting are really harmless.

Mites and ticks abound, and the more the ordinary man sees of them the less he wants to know about them. One of the commonest ticks, *Rhipicephalus* sp. is the despair of all dog-owners, attaching itself to the soft skin between the toes and inside the ears of the animal, where it cannot be reached. An almost daily hunt is required if the dog is to be kept free of them. For further information about ticks, see p. 469.

The King Crab (*Limulus*), though it looks like a crab, belongs to this group. It is common on the coast of Cambodia, and may be identified by its long spine-like tail. It is caught in the breeding season for the sake of its eggs, which are considered a great delicacy. In appearance they are like salmon caviare, but their flavour, unfortunately, is entirely different.

Myriapods (*Centipedes and Millipedes*)

A large centipede (*Scolopendra*), reaching a length of 20 cm., is often found in the warehouses at ports. It can give a very painful bite.

Crustaceans

Crabs abound everywhere, in the sea, on the seashore, in the fields and even on the mountain tops. All crabs are edible, but not many are worth eating. The swimming crabs (*Portunidae*), the largest and most succulent of the species, so called because their hindmost pair of legs are modified for swimming, are caught at sea and are brought into the markets for sale. The crayfish, closely related to the European langouste, is common in coastal areas. Several species of Fiddler Crab (*Gelasimus*) inhabit the mud flats of brackish water. The male is armed with one enormous claw, the other being vestigial. In some coastal districts various brackish and fresh-water crabs (*Potamonidae*) do damage to the rice crops by burrowing into and undermining the embankments that hold the water in the fields. The true fresh-water crabs are found chiefly in mountain streams. They have an abbreviated larval development and breed in the mountains.

Annelids (*Leeches and Worms*)

The only members of this group that attract the attention of the ordinary traveller are the leeches. These live in forests and swamps, and lurk on leaves and branches waiting until a suitable mammalian prey presents itself. They are a cause of acute discomfort to man (see p. 468).

BIBLIOGRAPHICAL NOTE

(1) The most comprehensive report on the mammals, which includes information about all the specimens in the British Museum and the Paris Museum, as well as those in America, is by Wilfred H. Osgood: 'Mammals of the Kelly-Roosevelts and Delacour Asiatic Expeditions', *Field Museum of Natural History*, Publication

No. 312, Zoological Series, vol. XVIII, no. 10, pp. 193–339 (Chicago, 1932). This work, however, is mainly systematic and contains little about habits; the only other sources, apart from the original descriptions of new species, are the numerous scattered references in the narratives of travellers and naturalists. Big-game hunting is discussed in detail by J. Bordeneuve: *Les Grandes Chasses en Indochine* (Saigon, 1925). Further information about hunting will be found in Achille Murat's 'La Chasse' in *Un Empire Colonial français: l'Indochine*, by Georges Maspero, vol. II, pp. 267–73 (Paris, 1930); and in L. Murat's *La Chasse en Indochine* (Paris, 1915). Hunting regulations are summarized in Sylvain Levi's *Indochine*. Exposition Coloniale Internationale, Paris, 1931, vol. I, pp. 98–101 (Paris, 1931), and also by Pierre Bouvard and F. Millet in *La Chasse au Lang Bian, Nouveau Guide Illustré* (Bergerac, France, 1920) (in French and English).

(2) The only general work on the birds, including a very full bibliography, is by J. Delacour and P. Jabouille: *Les Oiseaux de l'Indochine française*, 4 vols. (Paris: Exposition Coloniale Internationale, 1931).

(3) The reptiles of French Indo-China are included in the 'Fauna of British India' series by Malcolm Smith. Vol. I, Crocodiles and Chelonians. Vol. II, Lizards. Vol. III, Snakes (in the press).

(4) The best work on the fresh-water fishes, with a full bibliography, is by P. Chevey and F. le Poulain: *La Pêche dans les eaux douces du Cambodge* (Saigon, 1940). Another important work is P. Chabanaud's 'Inventaire de la faune ichtyologique des Pêches de l'Indochine', *Bulletin économique de l'Indochine*, vol. XXVII, pp. 561–81, (Hanoi, 1924).

(5) There is no comprehensive work dealing with the invertebrates, but a series of papers by R. de Vitalis de Salvaza may be mentioned: *Faune entomologique de l'Indochine*, Fasc. 1–5, 1921; Fasc. 6, 1923; Fasc. 7–8, 1924 (Saigon: l'Institut Scientifique de l'Indochine). An interesting account of white ants is to be found in Jean Bathellier's 'Contributions à l'étude, systématique et biologique des Termites de l'Indochine, vol. I, pp. 125–365 in *Faune des Colonies françaises*, edited by A. Gruvel (Paris, 1927).

[It has not been possible to consult an important publication, *La Faune de l'Indochine*, apparently issued in a number of separate parts by the Société de Géographie, Hanoi, *c.* 1927.]

Chapter VI

MEDICAL SERVICES AND HEALTH CONDITIONS

Medical Organization: Insect-borne Diseases: Intestinal Diseases: Other Diseases: Nutrition: Infantile Mortality: Water Supplies: Hints on the Preservation of Health: Bibliographical Note

MEDICAL ORGANIZATION

The head of the medical services of Indo-China is the Inspector-General of Public Health, under whose direction are the Provincial Health Officers and their subordinate staffs. In general, except in some of the larger centres, there is no separation into Medical Officers concerned only with curative medicine, and Health Officers concerned only with sanitation. Since the native expects any doctor to treat any disease, the policy adopted by the French has been to make medical officers responsible for the purely public health aspects of medical work in addition to hospital practice.

There are about 110 European medical men, not including the teaching staff of the medical school of Hanoi, and 240 native medical practitioners, principally Annamites, who have received their training locally. Subordinate staff comprises hospital assistants, dispensers, nurses and midwives. There are over 450 medical institutions, including European and native hospitals, infectious diseases hospitals, maternity institutions, dispensaries and leper asylums. In addition to work in stationary institutions, monthly tours of rural areas are conducted, not so much to give treatment to all the sick as to detect the cases and to direct them to the treatment centres. Preventive duties include vaccination against smallpox and cholera, anti-malarial measures, treatment of venereal disease and the spread of medical knowledge. Medical education is also conducted in schools, emphasis being laid on mothercraft and domestic economy.

Higher medical education is well organized. Native doctors are trained at the Hanoi medical school where the course occupies four years, some of the students passing after graduation to medical schools in Paris. Nurses and midwives are trained at Cho Lon, dispensers at Hanoi. Two Pasteur institutes have been established, one at Saigon and one, concerned largely with veterinary medicine, at Nha Trang.

These institutes provide vaccines for several diseases; there are, in addition, vaccine institutes and public health laboratories at Hanoi, Hue and Phnom Penh.

Haiphong, Tourane, Saigon and Phnom-Penh have quarantine stations where all the usual arrangements are made to inspect immigrants and to hold them in quarantine if suspected of infective disease. Clayton apparatus for the fumigation of ships and river craft is available at several places. The public health service, however, includes not only these stationary institutions, but also mobile units which are employed in connexion with matters of general hygiene, sanitation and vaccination. Health organization in Laos is still very imperfect, but in recent years there has been a development in the use of aircraft for public health purposes. To cope with the migration of Annamite labour into Laos, from the point of view of the introduction of infective disease, several observation posts have been established on the labour routes.

INSECT-BORNE DISEASES

Malaria

This disease, which causes more sickness than any other in the world, is particularly prevalent in tropical countries. Over the greater part of Indo-China every indigenous native probably suffers from it not once only, but many times during life. In 1937 malaria accounted for one-fifth of all hospital cases—from 15·7 % in Tonkin to 28 % in Laos—and in medical institutions it is responsible for more deaths than any other disease, except cholera.

Malaria is most prevalent in the foot-hills and mountainous districts and least prevalent (though still present) in the great deltas of the Mekong and Fleuve Rouge. The distribution of malaria in Indo-China thus provides a good illustration of the fact that lowlying swampy ground is not always the most dangerous in this respect (Fig. 50). The explanation of this fact is to be found in the biological habits of the mosquitoes which carry the disease from man to man; as animals are not susceptible to human malaria, there is no question of an animal reservoir of the disease. Malaria is carried by mosquitoes of the genus *Anopheles*, of which there are many species. Only a minority of these species, however, carry the disease, and of this number but a few are found in Indo-China. For mosquito breeding water is essential; but all mosquitoes will not breed in all waters. Some species of *Anopheles* prefer swamp water, others cannot breed

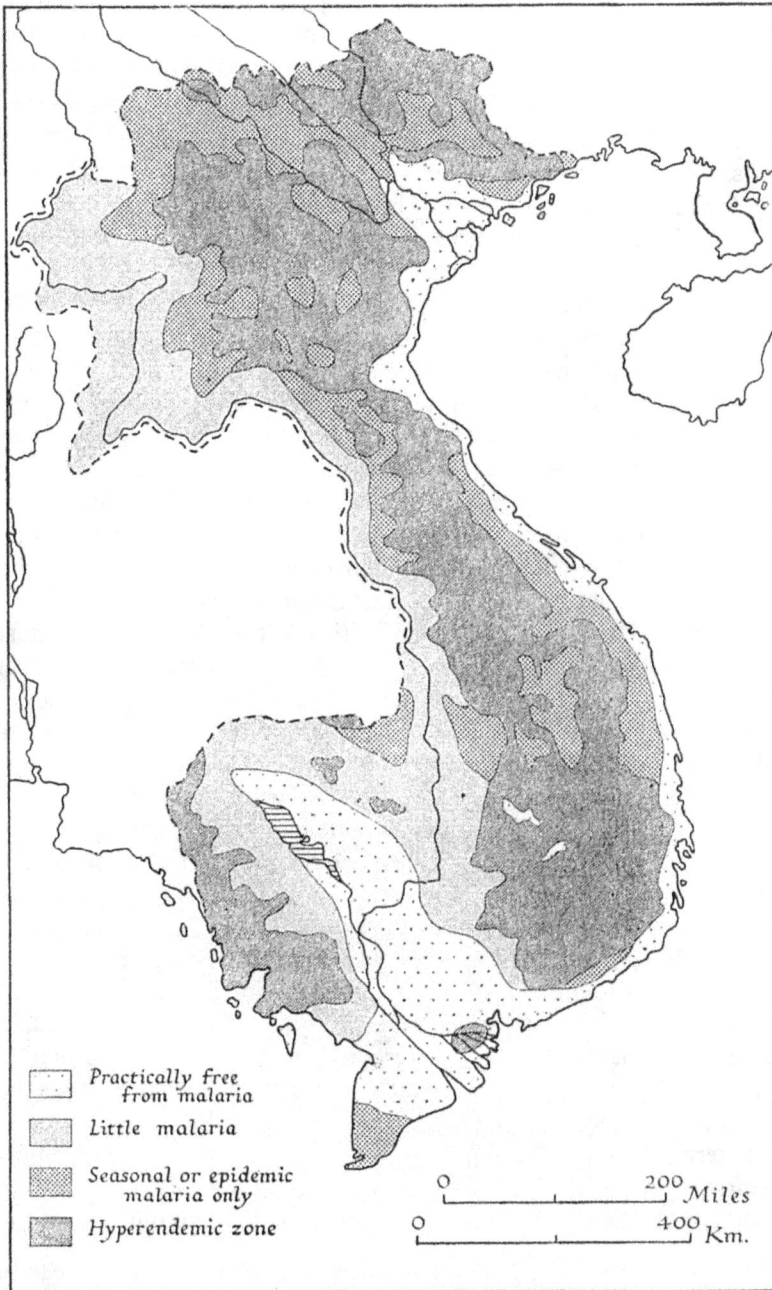

Fig. 50. Distribution of malaria

Source: League of Nations Health Organization. *Intergovernmental Conference of Far Eastern Countries on Rural Hygiene.* Preparatory Papers: Report of French Indo-China, Fig. 25 (Geneva, 1937).

unless the water is brackish, others demand the small backwaters of mountain streams open to the sun, others must have shade and relatively cool water. Further, the adult *Anopheles* mosquitoes vary in their feeding habits: some prefer human blood, and these are therefore the most dangerous; others will seek out animals, and for this reason are less likely themselves to be infected even if for any reason driven to attack man. Thus, in the Fleuve Rouge lowlands round Hanoi are found *A. vagus* and *A. hyrcanus* var. *sinensis*, both of which breed in swamps, irrigation canals or rice fields, but which are strongly attracted to animals; malaria is not very prevalent in this region. The same holds good of the delta of the Mekong near Saigon. In the hills and foot-hills, however, breeding conditions in the streams, especially in the dry season, are favourable to *A. minimus*, *A. jeyporiensis* and *A. maculatus*, all of which are attracted to man and all of which are dangerous vectors of malaria.* These facts more than others provide the explanation of the distribution of malaria.

The control of malaria is largely the control of *Anopheles* mosquito breeding, and entails the destruction of collections of water, or an alteration of conditions in water, calculated to make it unsuitable for the larvae. The habits and potentialities of the vector species must be closely investigated before measures are undertaken to control them. This work requires minute and careful study which should take into account the seasonal climatic conditions and the variations of these from year to year.

Malaria is not a single disease; there are several well-differentiated types, of which two are common and one more rare. These types vary not only in the appearance and behaviour of the causative organism, which is injected into the blood by the infected mosquito, but also in the severity of the fevers they provoke. The benign tertian form, found in the tropical, sub-tropical and temperate zones of the world, does not lead to any considerable mortality, in spite of the fact that it causes high fever and leads to relapses after long periods of time. The sub-tertian (or malignant tertian) variety, a much more lethal infection, causes widespread infant and even adult mortality and is the precursor of the grave condition known as blackwater fever. This sub-tertian malaria is essentially a tropical variety and occurs abundantly in Indo-China. The less common quartan malaria is relatively mild and its distribution patchy. These types have no uniform distri-

---

* This is not a complete list of the *Anopheles* of Indo-China. In addition *A. aconitus*, *A. tesselatus*, *A. barbirostris*, *A. philippinensis* and others are found, but they are of less importance.

bution in Indo-China; the reason for this is not clear, but the fact is of considerable importance. Thus, for instance, in the delta of the Fleuve Rouge and the lowlying land around Saigon, benign tertian malaria is the type most commonly found, though sub-tertian may occur in seasonal epidemics. Sub-tertian malaria is predominant in the highlands of Indo-China. Its sequel, blackwater fever, is seen especially in the mountains of Annam and Tonkin.

The effect of sub-tertian malaria on the population inhabiting these highly infected regions may be devastating. The children become infected in early infancy, and in the absence of quinine or other specific treatment there is a high infant mortality. Even if the infants escape death they pass through long periods of ill health, with recurring bouts of fever and consequent emaciation. This emaciated condition is often superficially concealed by the protuberance of the abdomen, caused by the enormous enlargement of the spleen due to the disease. In districts where the malaria is transmitted throughout the year, immunity may be acquired during childhood and youth, and adult life passed in a state of chronic infection which, however, is compatible with good health. If the disease is transmitted seasonally, owing to the seasonal increase of mosquito breeding due to climatic conditions, the immunity acquired may to some extent be lost in the periods of non-transmission. As a result the natives in adult life suffer from the disease year after year, and may be liable to blackwater fever. This peculiarity in the natural history of malaria is of very great importance in industry. There have been considerable movements of native labourers from areas where malaria is not common into districts of high incidence, and the result has been a high degree of disease with consequent loss of time and lowering of production. Moreover, where measures have not been taken to ensure adequate treatment, a high death-rate has occurred. In recent years the protection and treatment of these labourers has been placed upon a sound and wise footing, thanks largely to the researches carried out in Malaya by Sir Malcolm Watson. In his work he found that the control of and diminution in malaria in estate labourers has led to a marked decline in the incidence of diseases of quite different nature. Whereas at one time the natives feared to migrate to malarious districts, this fear is now very considerably reduced.

The measures taken include the siting of labour and other camps away from mosquito-breeding places and the elimination of breeding by drainage, by the clearing and periodic flushing of streams, by regulation of shade, by the covering of water with oil or with the

arsenical preparation Paris green. Further, with anti-malarial drugs
the French authorities in Indo-China also claim highly successful
results. It is most important for these matters to be borne in mind if
there is any question of movement of population or of troops.

Although the importance of malaria is perhaps most obviously
demonstrated through its effect on the health and efficiency of estate
labourers, there can be little doubt that its baleful influence is actually
most severe on the village populations whose health is not so directly
related to industrial output. It is the function of government to
improve the health of all classes, but so far there has been little prospect
of eradicating malaria in the rural communities. The prevention of
mosquito breeding demands intelligence, understanding and meticu-
lous care, qualities which may be obtained on estates under the close
supervision of Europeans, but to expect native communities to under-
stand and to carry out the necessary measures is at present impossible.
It is equally impossible to issue the relevant drugs in quantity sufficient to exert a preventive action, and even if it were possible, the
results achieved by drug prophylaxis alone have time after time been
proved to be inadequate. The outlook for these natives would therefore appear to be as gloomy, in this respect, as ever, but this is perhaps
too pessimistic a view. Small doses of quinine or atebrin given to
children in the acute stages of malaria will avert death without
actually eradicating the disease. If the doses are not too large the
process of immunization will continue, and this treatment, therefore,
may be expected to reduce infant mortality without rendering adole-
scents and adults more susceptible. Such treatments may be obtained
at the numerous small dispensaries scattered throughout the country,
and should be encouraged. The effect of quinine is so dramatic that
natives soon recognize its value. A second factor which influences
the course and severity of malaria is the state of nutrition (see
p. 124), and one effect of a general improvement in diet may be
a reduction in malaria. Malaria tends to retreat before efficient agriculture, so that the two ends may be achieved by the one process.

Dengue

This is a mosquito-borne disease of little intrinsic importance which
should, however, be borne in mind by medical men in Indo-China.
The vector is the mosquito *Aëdes aegypti*, which breeds in domestic
water; it is elsewhere the carrier of yellow fever. If this disease
were introduced into Indo-China it would probably spread widely.
With the development of air travel, infected mosquitoes or persons in

the incubation (and infective) stage of the disease may be transported from Africa to India and the Far East to initiate epidemics in those countries, and for this reason the authorities should be vigilant to prevent such a disaster. The measures in force in India and other countries are well known to health authorities; to be effective the whole-hearted support of the administrative services is necessary.

Plague

There are said to be three permanent foci of plague in Indo-China, at Cho Lon, Phnom Penh and in Kwang Chow Wan (Che Kam and Tang Hai) respectively. The first is small, the other two of greater importance; all are in the Chinese communities of the places concerned. Plague has also from time to time been introduced from abroad, from Canton and Hong Kong, and has spread from one part of the country to another.

Plague is essentially a disease of rodents, particularly of rats, and is conveyed to man by infected rat fleas which leave dead animals and attack man. It is therefore closely associated with grain stores and with ships and ports. The most dangerous rat is the black rat, *Rattus rattus*, because it frequents human habitations, and the most efficient flea vector is *Xenopsylla cheopis*. The common form of the disease is bubonic, in which the flea infects a limb, at the root of which form the characteristic glandular swellings or buboes, but outbreaks of the fatal pneumonic form have been recorded from the island of Kassutin in the Mekong, and from Vinh Long in Cochin-China.

Plague has occurred in all parts of the country, the places particularly mentioned being Tourane, Haiphong, Lang Son, Bac Ninh and Hon Gay. In 1914 there were 2,054 cases with 1,587 deaths, but in recent years the incidence has been less and it is not now regarded as a serious problem, though its reintroduction from abroad is clearly always possible. Anti-plague vaccination has been performed on a considerable scale and anti-rat measures have been taken in the permanent foci.

Typhus

Three forms of typhus are found in Indo-China. The classical, epidemic, louse-borne type has been seen repeatedly in Tonkin. This form is found only in man and is transmitted from man to man by the human louse, which does not live on other animals. It is therefore a disease associated with crowded conditions, since under these the lice can most easily pass from person to person, and with poverty, since it is among the poor that lice are most commonly found. Movements of refugees may provide conditions suitable for an outbreak, but, in fact, large epidemics have not been recorded. The second form is conveyed to man by rat fleas. It has been found in the rats of Saigon, Hanoi, Nam Dinh and Tuyen Quang, and in man repeatedly in Cochin-China and Annam. The third, mite-borne, type is probably identical with the scrub typhus of Malaya and the mite fever of Sumatra. It has been reported from Cochin-China, especially in European prospectors, from Annam, where it is frequent in the Moi, and from Cambodia, where twenty cases were recorded in plantation labourers in 1937. It is transmitted to man by larval mites found in scrub or bush country.

With the exception of the louse-borne type, none of these diseases is likely to break out in epidemic form, but they should all be remembered as possible diagnoses in cases of fever.

Relapsing Fever

This disease has not been seen in epidemic proportions for many years. In the early part of the century, however, epidemics did occur, but treatment with salvarsan brought them under control. In Indo-China this disease is conveyed by lice, which are very common under conditions of over-population and poverty.

INTESTINAL DISEASES

Cholera

Cholera has appeared in epidemic form in Indo-China many times since the beginning of the century, but French medical writers claim that it has usually been introduced from other countries and that it is not merely a question of an endemic disease flaring up periodically to epidemic proportions. The epidemics are regarded as probably largely due to carriers. Thus in 1926 cholera was introduced from India by way of Siam, producing the terrible epidemic which affected the whole of the Far East. In 1937 the influx of refugees from China led to another serious outbreak, during which 12,715 cases were recognized and 9,246 deaths occurred. This epidemic first affected Tonkin, and then spread to Annam, and in both these territories was characterized by the wideness of its extent rather than the intensity of its incidence in any one area. Contamination of rural water supplies has probably played an important part in the spread of the disease. The 1912 famine in Cambodia not only created a refugee movement, but reduced the available water supplies; the small wells were heavily used and soon became grossly contaminated with the result that cholera spread rapidly. The habits of the natives also have a direct bearing on the spread of cholera. For instance, it is quite customary for bodies to be buried at any convenient spot, and they may be found in shallow graves in the immediate vicinity of wells. In Indo-China human excreta are largely used as a fertilizer, and the danger of contamination of vegetables by this means is evident. The handling of faeces in this way undoubtedly plays an important part in the spread of cholera, typhoid and dysentery.

In the face of epidemics sanitary measures are taken where possible, but the problem is one of great difficulty. The French authorities have relied largely on enormous campaigns of anti-cholera inoculation, and the majority of writers report favourably on this measure. Adequate control, however, can only be achieved by the slow process of control of water supplies and the education of the inhabitants in sanitation and personal cleanliness.

Typhoid Group of Fevers

Of these true typhoid is the most common, and a considerable number of cases are reported each year from all parts; in 1937 there were records of 1,279 cases. In Cochin-China it is seen especially in Saigon and the provinces of Gia Dinh, Ben Tre, Soc Trang and My Tho, where it is usually of a rather benign type. In Tonkin the incidence appears to be rising; cases occur in Europeans through the consumption of oysters, and in natives from the eating of vegetables grown near Hanoi in fields fertilized with manure of human faeces. Native races are ignorant of the fact that many diseases may be acquired through faecal contamination of food and water, and indeed their everyday observation of animals must rather lead them to regard excreta as harmless. Whether the problem may best be met by medical education of the people, or by the creation of a standard of good taste by an appeal to the aesthetic sense is a matter for speculation; an approach from both directions is probably necessary. That the matter is of some urgency can hardly be denied. It is not enough to warn the natives against the faeces of persons actually ill, since typhoid bacilli are frequently passed by convalescents and by healthy carriers, while the same is probably true, though to a smaller extent, of the organism of cholera.

Dysentery

Cases of amoebic dysentery have been reported for many years in large numbers, but the numbers confirmed by laboratory examination are but a fraction of those diagnosed on clinical grounds. In 1937 the figures were: Cochin-China 34,667, Annam 25,523, Cambodia 19,866, Tonkin 9,633, Laos 6,159. These figures are very high, and it may be that diagnosis is not always accurate. Liver abscess, a known sequela of amoebic dysentery, is becoming more rare, possibly because of the now fairly common specific treatment of the dysentery with emetine. Amoebic dysentery occurs often in the Fleuve Rouge delta, but is much more rare in the mountains.

A considerable number of cases of bacillary dysentery have been reported in Tonkin, but there can be little doubt that many more are not diagnosed. This disease causes a high proportion of infant deaths in the tropics.

These diseases are spread by the contamination of food and water with human faecal material, either directly or through the medium of house flies. The remarks on the spread of typhoid apply equally to the dysenteries.

OTHER DISEASES

Helminthic Diseases. Under this heading are included all diseases due to worms, whether in the intestinal tract or the blood or the internal organs. One of the most important is *hookworm* infection, in which the adult worms inhabit the small intestine and suck blood from the bowel wall. This infection is caused by the embryos of the worms, which hatch in moist, shaded soil from eggs passed in the faeces, penetrating the human skin and reaching, by a circuitous route, the intestine, where the adults live. Preventive measures must be based on the knowledge of this process. Constant loss of blood in heavy infections leads to severe anaemia, and even in moderate infections causes loss of strength and energy enough to predispose to other diseases and to reduce efficiency for work.

The embryos cannot travel more than a few feet in soil, and to become infected, therefore, it is necessary for a person to come into contact with soil very close to a place which has been contaminated by human faeces. Direct sunlight and dry soil are inimical to the embryos, which flourish best in warm climates in the shade of bushes or trees, spots often chosen by natives for defaecation. Prevention, therefore, entails the construction of suitable latrines and the education of the natives in their use, since it has been shown in practice that treatment alone is not enough to eradicate the infection in native communities. Hookworm disease is one of the great tropical problems, and its eradication is far more difficult than this brief account can indicate.

In Indo-China the distribution of the infection is uneven. The proportion of the population infected in Tonkin and north and central Annam varies from 50 to 68 %. In these parts the long duration of the wet season and the corresponding persistence of moisture in the soil are favourable to the embryos. Cochin-China has a rate of 15–25 %, south Annam 20 %, Laos 29 %, Cambodia 17 %, and parts of north Annam, where there are salt marshes (inimical to the embryos), not more than 7 %. These figures represent the amount of infection discovered; they do not represent the amount of disease, since light infection is compatible with good health.

Infection with *Strongyloides*, another worm whose embryo makes its way through the human skin, is found in Tonkin, 318 cases being reported during 1937. This infection, though not nearly so important as hookworm, should be borne in mind, since it appears to be unusually prevalent. It is generally an infection of dogs and cats, but in Tonkin, for some reason as yet not clear, it is apparently rare in these animals.

Of the other worm infections, that with the common roundworm, *Ascaris lumbricoides*, appears most frequently, but is rarely a serious condition. The oriental liver fluke, *Clonorchis sinensis*, found in the lowlying parts of Tonkin and Annam, may be acquired by the eating of raw or undercooked fresh-water fish in which the worm embryos are encysted; it causes serious destruction of the liver.

Filariasis and its sequel, *elephantiasis*, are found. The mosquito carriers of this infection have not been fully reported for Indo-China, but *Anopheles minimus* and *A. jeyporiensis* are mentioned; doubtless species of *Culex* and *Mansonia* are mainly responsible.

Schistosomiasis has been reported in a few cases, but with reservations.

Sparganosis, an infection of man due to an embryonic worm, is not uncommon in Indo-China. This embryo is normally a parasite of frogs and is acquired by man as a result of the native custom of applying split frogs, or compresses made with frog tissue, to inflamed spots, more particularly the eye. The custom gives evidence of the influence of Chinese medicine. The reasoning underlying the procedure is interesting: inflammation produces heat, the frog is cold-blooded, therefore frog tissue will remove inflammation. Or, alternatively, inflammation of the eye is due to worms, the frog eats worms, therefore frogs applied to the eye will remove the inflammation.

Unfortunately, in actual fact, the worm causing sparganosis is introduced in the process.

Leprosy is well known in Indo-China. In 1937 some 5,000 cases were known to exist, but the full total probably reached about 15,000. This is not a particularly heavy incidence rate in comparison with the figures reported from Burma, India and central Africa, but it is enough to constitute a problem for the health authorities. Special institutions for leprosy have been established at Hanoi, Bac Ninh and Thai Binh in Tonkin, as well as four leprosy villages conducted under native administrations of their own. In Annam there are similar institutions at Thanh Hoa, Kontum, Djiring and Qui Hoa, in Cochin-China at Cho Quan and Culao Rong, in Cambodia at Treong.

Tropical phagadaenic ulcer. The cause of this condition is not definitely known, but it has been thought to have some connexion with yaws, though this is doubtful. Labourers suffer most frequently from this disease, which appears to start from small abrasions or wounds of the legs, and may lead to great destruction of the tissues. During 1937 there were 121,543 cases, chiefly from central Annam.

Yaws is widespread and has been noted particularly in the Indo-Malay peoples of Cambodia, Laos, western Cochin-China and the Annam coast. In Cambodia the incidence is especially high in Kompong Thom, Benglovea and Battambang; in Cochin-China there are endemic centres at Gia Dinh, Thu Dau Mot and Chau Doc. In the whole of Indo-China 97,442 cases were reported during 1937. It is stated that 70 % of infants are affected, that 45 % of adults show late signs of the disease, and that, as so often in the tropics, the natives regard it as inevitable. Fortunately, the disease is rarely a fatal one, though it may lead to conditions which incapacitate the patient for long periods; the disfiguring condition gangosa, which destroys the tissues and bones of the face, occurs fairly frequently and is a sequel of yaws. Transmission is by direct contact, and no insect vector has been definitely proved. Natives treat the lesions on the skin with plant juices; modern treatment with arsenic and bismuth preparations has proved highly successful.

Venereal diseases. Syphilis is perhaps the most important venereal disease, 86,093 cases being reported in 1937, of which more than half were found in Annam. The causative organism of syphilis is indistinguishable from that of yaws, but the manifestations and course of the two diseases are not the same. Yaws is not usually associated with sexual contact, syphilis is typically transmitted in this fashion. The drugs used in treatment are similar, but syphilis is much more difficult to cure than yaws.

In Saigon 60%, in rural districts near Saigon 20%, and in Hanoi 35% of samples of the population have been found to give positive results to blood tests for syphilis. These figures are, however, probably vitiated by the fact that in yaws the same result is obtained with the test. Congenital syphilis in schoolchildren seldom occurs, which may be attributed to the fact that most of the syphilitic children fail to survive, since congenital syphilis is not uncommonly seen in the newborn in maternity homes.

There are in Indo-China a number of institutions for the treatment of syphilis; dispensaries and hospitals also treat this disease. Surveillance of prostitutes is attempted.

Gonorrhoea is probably more widespread than syphilis. In 1937 there were 70,000 known cases, but those undetected probably numbered far more. In Saigon almost all the prostitutes examined suffered from this infection. Gonorrhoea is a major problem; like syphilis it leads to sterility in women, though by different means, and until recently treatment, unless carried out thoroughly over a long period of time, proved ineffective. Newly discovered drugs have, however, revolutionized the position, and in due course it may be expected that these will be available on a scale large enough to influence the spread of the disease.

Soft chancre accounted for about 15,000 cases in 1937, and *Lymphogranuloma inguinale* for about 2,300, being found, in many instances, along with other venereal diseases.

Tuberculosis. This disease is far more widely spread in tropical countries than in many temperate lands where it is more well recognized. In Indo-China the extent of the problem is indicated by the fact that during 1935, 35,014 cases, and during 1937, 48,120 cases were reported. It is not clear, however, whether these represent new cases or include some which had been diagnosed and recorded in previous years. Even should these not all be new cases, there can be little doubt that as the figures stand they understate the position, since in a country like Indo-China, with a low proportion of doctors to population, many cases of tuberculosis will not be reported.

As in other countries tuberculosis is more prevalent in towns and cities than in rural districts. Malnutrition plays an important part in the predisposition to tuberculosis, but overcrowding exercises a more important influence. Tuberculosis is, in fact, an infective disease usually passed from man to man. Sputum, containing the bacilli responsible for the disease, is expelled from the mouth of persons with pulmonary tuberculosis either as a fine droplet spray in the act of coughing or sneezing, or in the act of spitting. The bacilli may be inhaled with the droplets or in dust from contaminated floors. In countries of the Far East there is little tuberculous milk.

The heaviest incidence appears to be in Tonkin and Cochin-China, but the high figures reported from these areas may be the result of the greater facilities for diagnosis which exist in Hanoi and Saigon than in many other places. The point is that where the facilities exist the cases are found.

To deal with tuberculosis the French have created special hospitals at Lalung Bounaire, Thu Dau Mot, Phu Lam, Hanoi, Saigon and Hue, and have reserved pavilions or beds for the disease in many other hospitals. In Cochin-China there is a travelling dispensary with X-ray apparatus, and in many parts there are fixed dispensaries. Preventive vaccination by means of BCG (the bacillus of Calmette and Guérin) has been widely used. This method, introduced in France by the workers named, has been largely accepted as of value by authorities of that nation, though in other countries the results obtained have not been such as to encourage great optimism. The solution of this most difficult problem of tuberculosis seems to lie in the improvement of housing conditions to avoid overcrowding, the improvement of nutrition, the treatment and isolation of infective cases, and the general education of the people in the understanding of the principles of infective disease.

Smallpox. In Indo-China this disease is constantly present in endemic form, and has, from time to time, flared up as widespread epidemics, either from the spread of existing foci or as a result of introduction from abroad. Considerable epidemics were reported from Cochin-China, Tonkin, Laos and Cambodia in 1917–20 and in 1924–5. The latter epidemic followed that which affected India, China, Japan and Siam in 1923. In 1937 there were 3,000 cases with 680 known deaths.

To cope with this disease the usual port health regulations in regard to immigrants are in force, and vaccination is performed on a large scale. In 1904 a vaccine institute for the preparation of lymph was created in Hanoi, and now similar centres exist in Saigon, Hue, Vientiane and Xieng Khouang. Trained natives perform vaccination and millions of people are dealt with each year ($7\frac{1}{2}$ millions in 1928).

Of the diseases which commonly occur in temperate climates *influenza* has been reported, sometimes in epidemics. *Pneumonia* is common, not only during influenza outbreaks, but as a constant and fatal disease. In 1937 there were 6,936 reported cases and the fatality rate in hospitals was 32·6 %. *Cerebrospinal meningitis* not uncommonly occurs in epidemic form in labour camps and, if not treated with modern drugs, may be a highly fatal disease. *Diphtheria* is found, especially in Cambodia, 123 cases being reported from here in 1937. Schick tests in schools of Thanh Hoa showed positive results of only about 4·4 %, and in Dalat and Haut Donnai of 18–20 %, indicating a high level of immunity. The disease was not seen in Laos or Kwang Chow Wan in 1937. *Measles, chickenpox* and *mumps* occur, the two latter especially in Annam. It is important to be able to distinguish between chickenpox and smallpox. *Whooping cough* is relatively common, and a few cases of *scarlet fever* have been reported from Cochin-China. There was an outbreak of *infantile paralysis* in 1935, when 248 cases were reported; in 1937 there were only twelve.

Trachoma, a disease of the eyes, is said to affect 5 million of the inhabitants of Indo-China and to be particularly common among the poor. It is associated with childhood, affecting 43 % of the school-children in Phnom Penh. In Annam the disease occurs very frequently, and although in the majority of cases mild and chronic, tending to spontaneous cure, it may lead to trichiasis and entropion and to complications which eventually produce impairment of vision. These complications are seen in Kwang Chow Wan, though trachoma itself is stated to be rare. Although probably less important than gonorrhoea as a cause of blindness, nevertheless it presents a sufficiently serious problem, and anti-trachoma work forms a specific part of the duties of the rural health services.

Rabies of man and animals is found. In Tonkin during 1937 there were nineteen, in Vientiane three and in Saigon two human deaths from this cause; sixty-two animals suffered from the disease. At the Pasteur institutes of Saigon and Hanoi, and the laboratories at Hue, Phnom Penh and Vientiane, 5,663 treatments were given in that year.

Anthrax has been found in past years and was recorded as an epidemic in 1914. It probably occurs in cattle and may be contracted by man by the eating of undercooked flesh of animals dead of the disease.

Tetanus was responsible for 286 cases in 1937, but probably occurs more frequently than this figure indicates. It causes a high proportion of infant mortality; it is contracted through contamination of the umbilical cord, but the incidence is falling with an improved mid-wifery service.

Alcoholism and Drug Addiction. Alcoholism is widespread in the towns, and among those engaged in certain unusually exhausting occupations; in the rural districts it is virtually non-existent. Of the 1,600 cases reported in 1937 the majority came from Cambodia, Annam and Cochin-China. The annual number of admissions to lunatic asylums, due to alcoholism, is very small. The natives drink rice spirit as a rule only on ritual occasions or at family celebrations. Opium addiction is rare among the vast bulk of the rural population, but habitual among the Chinese, a proportion of the wealthy Annamites, and those town dwellers who frequent the squalid dens.

Cancer is not rare, occurring most frequently in Cochin-China, Annam and Tonkin. The majority of cases involve the external genitalia, only 5 % being growths of the alimentary tract.

Venomous Bites. The most important poisonous snakes are the cobra, *Naja naja*, the king cobra, *Naja hannah*, the krait, *Bungarus fasciatus* and *B. candidus*. These members of the cobra family are all dangerous, having a powerful action on the nervous system. Of the viper family the daboia, *Vipera russelli*, *Ancistrodon rhodostoma* and *Trimeresurus gramineus* (the banana snake) may be classed as dangerous, having a powerful action on the tissues round the bite and on the blood. Pythons may attain enormous size, up to 9 m.; these are never poisonous and are said not to attack man. Poisonous sea snakes are encountered.

Spiders and scorpions are common and their bites or stings may produce severe symptoms. Of the biting insects *Brachinus crepitans* is said to discharge formalin gas with a loud noise, and to attack man.

NUTRITION

The state of nutrition of the agricultural classes of Indo-China is poor. For half the year the diet available for these people is just adequate in quantity though poor in quality, but during the other half they exist on almost a starvation level. In general they know no food except rice taken with salt or preserve. Other classes fare better, vegetables, fish and meat forming part of the diet in Cochin-China, Cambodia and southern Annam, more rarely in Tonkin and northern Annam. Fish is commoner than meat, and fresh-water fish, sea fish and shellfish are used. The commonest meat is pork, and pigs are extensively bred; the natives also use dogs and buffaloes as food, while poultry are frequently kept and their eggs eaten.

Besides rice, the staple food, maize is relatively widely grown, and the soya bean has been recently encouraged, its rich protein and fat content making a valuable addition to the diet. From it are prepared soya milk and soya cheese. In addition, the natives grow manioc, yams, taro, sweet potatoes, beans, sesame seeds, sugar cane as well as a number of vegetables and fruits. Although the wealthier classes and the people in the districts where these foods are available obtain an adequate diet, the fact remains that a vast proportion of the 23,000,000 inhabitants exist on a diet of rice which in quantity is barely adequate.

As a food, prepared rice has certain disadvantages. In the process of removal of the husk by modern mechanical means the germ and certain layers covering the grain are also removed, resulting in a product known as polished rice which, though white and clean to the eye, consists almost solely of starch and is devoid of protein and of vitamins. In particular, the important vitamin B_1 is removed, and it is known that a diet consisting of 66% starch and deficient in this vitamin leads to the serious disease *beriberi*. These conditions are often fulfilled in Indo-China, but fortunately the common native method of milling rice is not so complete as the mechanical method, so that some part of the vitamin-containing layers of the grain is left. Nevertheless, according to one authority, out of 3,000–4,000 cases of beriberi diagnosed each year 10% die of the disease, which ranks eighth in the list of diseases treated in hospitals. Another report (1937) gives a figure of 25,706 cases, with 250 deaths. The disease is widely distributed. In Cochin-China, where the use of polished rice is increasing, there are many grave cases, especially between the ages of 20 and 45, in women after childbirth, and in coolies. Treatment with vitamin B_1 gives excellent results. Few cases of beriberi are known in Laos and Kwang Chow Wan, since polished rice is here not much used.

It is incumbent on those who administer these countries to encourage the cultivation of good crops, to promote the use of animal protein and fats, and to foster, if necessary by legal action, the preparation of rice in such a manner that its essential constituents are not removed by milling.

There is a report to the effect that stone in the bladder is a common condition in young children. This may be evidence of vitamin deficiency, and in India has been associated particularly with lack of vitamin A.

INFANTILE MORTALITY

The mortality rate for children from birth up to the age of fifteen is high, though few statistics are available owing to the incomplete registration of births and deaths. From the following figures, based on statistics furnished by the large towns, it appears that the rate is lower in Cambodia and Laos than in Tonkin, Annam and Cochin-China:

Area	Infantile mortality under 15 years per 1,000 live births
North Annam	421
South Annam	424
Tonkin	453
Cochin-China	424
Laos	375
Cambodia	400

Source: P. Chesneau, 'Natalité et mortalité infantile au Cammon (Laos), en Sud Annam et en Nord Annam' *Congrès International de la Population, Paris, 1937*, vol. VI, p. 96 (Paris, 1938).

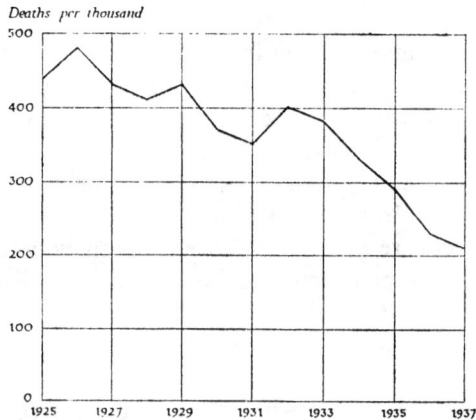

Fig. 51. Infantile mortality among the native population at Hanoi, 1925–37

Source: *Annuaire statistique de l'Indochine, 1936–37*, p. 29 (Hanoi, 1938).

Fig. 51 shows the mortality curve for infants under one year of age during the period 1925–37. Although the rate has fallen rapidly in recent years, it still remains high. The figure of 210 per thousand in 1937 should be compared with that of 65 per thousand in France and 58 per thousand in England and Wales in the same year.

WATER SUPPLIES

The question of water supplies is closely bound up with disease in tropical countries. Not only do water-borne diseases occur in epidemic form, but water is essential for the breeding of the mosquito vectors of malaria, filariasis, dengue and, in countries where it occurs, yellow fever. Irrigation canals provide a difficult problem in anti-malaria work and, since the natives use this water for drinking purposes, in the control of water-borne disease.

The domestic water supplies in cities like Hanoi and Saigon and almost all provincial capitals are good. Deep wells form the chief

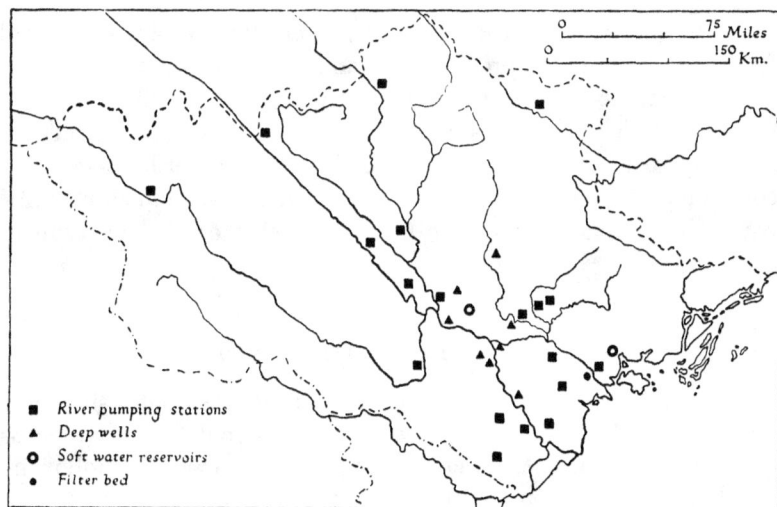

Fig. 52. Water supplies in Tonkin
Source: League of Nations Health Organization. *Inter-governmental Conference of Far Eastern Countries on Rural Hygiene. Preparatory Papers: Report of French Indo-China*, Fig. 24 (Geneva, 1937).

sources of supply, but in Hue and Phnom Penh river water, after full treatment, is used. At Haiphong the local water is brackish, and the city supply is therefore obtained from the river 35 km. distant (Fig. 52, Plate 57).

In the larger rural centres high-level reservoirs, pumping stations and distributing systems are being installed, the water being obtained from rivers, malaria drainage systems and other sources. Small purifying plants are gradually being installed. In the course of time these measures may be expected to be highly successful, and to exert a definitely beneficial effect upon public health, but the matter is not everywhere so straightforward. In the delta of the Mekong and the Dong Nai the land lies almost at sea level and is crossed by innumerable canals and watercourses, largely affected by the tides. The water is in consequence brackish, and the line of demarcation between fresh and brackish water in these watercourses varies with the periods of the year. For drinking purposes, therefore, rain water is largely used, and the natives have formed the habit of using ponds to conserve water. Surface ponds must, under these conditions, inevitably be heavily contaminated. There is a considerable trade in water, and water sellers, whose methods cannot be satisfactory, are common (Fig. 53).

In the more remote rural districts, where the supply is obtained from shallow wells, unprotected streams or canals, contamination is general. Such supplies are used indiscriminately for all purposes—for the watering of animals, the washing of clothes and for drinking. Although tea made with boiling (and therefore sterile) water is a common drink, enough water is taken in the raw state to afford some part of the explanation of the heavy incidence of cholera, typhoid and dysentery.

Hints on the Preservation of Health

The list of diseases given above appears formidable. But it should be remembered that the list refers to the native population. Europeans can avoid most diseases by taking simple precautions. The following simple points are important:

(1) Many diseases are liable to be picked up from the native inhabitant. It is advisable to live as far as possible from villages and labour camps.

(2) Malaria is only conveyed from man to man by certain species of mosquito (*Anopheles*). The mosquito must first bite a man whose blood contains the germ of malaria: the mosquito incubates the germ for a week, and is then prepared to inoculate it into a man if it should bite him. All mosquitoes breed in water; unfortunately many can fly a long way, seeking blood.

(*a*) To avoid malaria, camp as far as possible from swamps, rivers, and irrigated land: half a mile will afford adequate protection. Camp away from villages because the *Anopheles* often picks up the germ from the native.

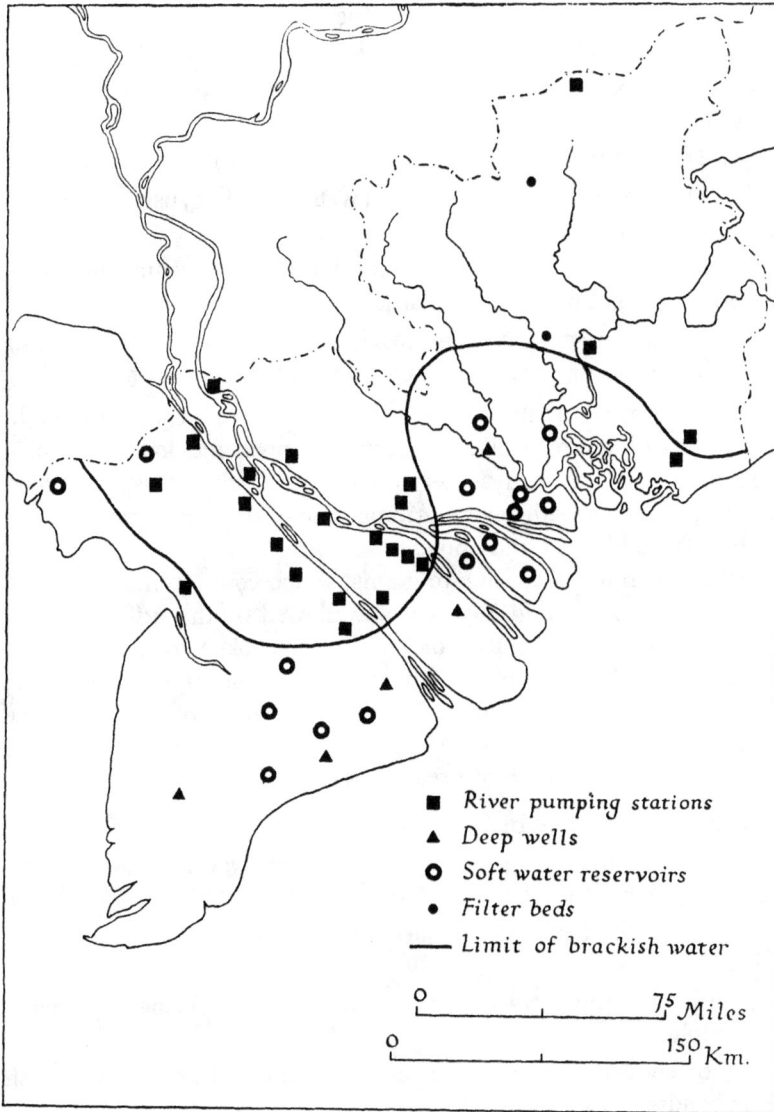

Fig. 53. Water supplies in Cochin-China

Source: League of Nations Health Organization. *Inter-governmental Conference of Far Eastern Countries on Rural Hygiene. Preparatory Papers: Report of French Indo-China*, Fig. 23 (Geneva, 1937).

(*b*) Sleep under a mosquito net carefully used and tucked in and kept in good repair. If sleeping on the ground, tuck the edge of the net under a ground sheet.

(*c*) Avoid being needlessly bitten: no bare legs or arms at or after sundown.

(*d*) If possible kill mosquitoes in tents, etc., with fly spray.

(*e*) Destroy the mosquito larvae in water, by oiling, using poisonous dusts, draining, etc.

(*f*) A dose of 5 grains of quinine taken each evening has some action in preventing attacks of malaria.

(*g*) Treat a case of fever by making the patient lie down, giving 10 grains of quinine and a dose of salts.

(3) In warm climates, intestinal ailments are very common in Europeans. They may take the form of gripes and looseness: or a frequent diarrhoea; or dysentery (which means the passage of blood and mucus, often with severe griping pains); or more serious things such as typhoid fever and cholera.

All these troubles are due to germs, which come from some other person's excrement and have been swallowed by the sufferer. They may be swallowed in water, or milk, or uncooked food (raw fruit, salads, etc.). They are carried about in a variety of ways: for instance, the cook may soil his hands in the latrine and then infect the food he is serving; flies may feed on a deposit of human faeces, and then on a lump of sugar or piece of bread, etc.

These diseases may be avoided

(*a*) by chlorinating or boiling all water (however clean it looks) before drinking it or cleaning teeth in it;

(*b*) by never drinking unboiled fresh milk, or locally prepared mineral waters;

(*c*) by not eating lettuces, etc. (which cannot be cleaned by reason of the folds);

(*d*) by endeavouring to make cooks and those who serve food wash their hands;

(*e*) by providing facilities for hand washing in all latrines;

(*f*) by insisting on the cleanliness of cookhouses, and burning of odd scraps of food;

(*g*) by keeping latrines clean, and as far as possible fly-proof;

(*h*) by insisting that latrines, and no other spots, are used;

(*i*) by keeping one's body warm at night;

(*j*) by being vaccinated against smallpox and inoculated against typhoid, paratyphoid and cholera.

Minor intestinal troubles should be treated by rest (i.e. lying down, taking water only for a day or so), warmth and a dose of salts.

(4) If lice appear in the clothes take immediate steps to get rid of them. In Indo-China there is always some risk of typhus and of relapsing fever, which are transmitted by lice. In some parts fleas carry disease.

(5) The bilharzia disease (urinary schistosomiasis) occurs in many tropical countries. This is an unpleasant condition, leading to the passage of blood in the urine and serious complications. If this risk is known to exist, it is extremely important that water should not come in contact with the skin, in bathing, washing, or in any other way, since the disease is contracted by the worm penetrating the skin; the worm embryo develops in water.

(6) If it is windy and dusty use celluloid eye screens.

(7) In parts of Indo-China great changes of temperature occur, especially in the mountains, where it may be very cold at night. Clothes should give protection from wind and cold. The sun, even in summer, is much less dangerous than people used to think.

(8) Whenever possible wash all over, not only because a man gets so dirty in a hot and dusty place, but also because soreness may easily develop, particularly between the toes and in the crutch: if these parts become inflamed it is not easy to cure them. Do not walk about barefoot.

(9) Venereal diseases are more common than at home, and one particularly unpleasant tropical one exists. Take no risks.

(10) To prevent septic sores and ulcers avoid minor injuries; if they occur treat at once with antiseptic; maintain the general health with local fruit wherever possible.

(11) Discipline in all matters relating to health (e.g. boiling of water, avoidance of raw bazaar foods, use of mosquito nets) is an important factor in the avoidance of disease.

BIBLIOGRAPHICAL NOTE

(1) A general survey of the medical services and health conditions is given in the following publications of the League of Nations: F. Norman White, *The Prevalence of Epidemic Disease and Port Health and Port Procedure in the Far East*, pp. 127–36 (Geneva, 1923); *Inter-governmental Conference of Far Eastern Countries on Rural Hygiene. Preparatory Papers: Report of French Indo-China* (Geneva, 1937).

(2) For an account of the chief diseases in the country see: E. Vogel and M. Riom, 'Les maladies épidemiques, endemiques et sociales dans les colonies françaises pendant l'année 1937', *Annales de Médecine et de Pharmacie coloniales*, vol. XXXVII, pp. 257–552 (Paris, 1939). *Far Eastern Association of Tropical Medicine. Transactions of 8th Congress, Siam 1930*, vol. I, 103–21, 333–43, 350–72, 377–410, vol. II, 373–411, 438–98 (Bangkok, 1930).

(3) A number of recent papers in the *Revue médicale française d'Extrême Orient*, the *Archives des Instituts Pasteur d'Indochine*, the *Bulletin de la Société de Pathologie exotique*, the *Bulletin de l'Office International de l'Hygiène publique* and the *Tropical Diseases Bulletin* have also been used in the preparation of this chapter.

Chapter VII

THE PEOPLE

Introduction: Physical Types: Languages: Cultural Groups: Relations between the
Cultural Groups: Religion and Art: Education and Culture: Bibliographical Note

INTRODUCTION

The population of Indo-China is not a homogeneous one. Differences in physical characteristics, language, religion and mode of life
divide the people into several large groups within which there are
many local differences in physical and cultural development. These
groups include the Annamites, the Cambodians, the Cham, the Moi,
the Laotians (a branch of the Thai), the Thai proper, and a number
of tribes such as the Man, Miao and Lolo in the mountains of Laos
and Tonkin (Fig. 54). Indo-China has been a meeting-place for the
outposts of two great civilizations, the Hindu and the Chinese, and
the impact of these external influences is clearly apparent over a large
part of the country.

Apart from the ethnic groups which are specifically Indo-Chinese
there are also those constituted by recent immigrants, including a
large number of Chinese and small numbers of Europeans, Indians,
Malays, Javanese and Japanese. Unions between such immigrants
and Indo-Chinese, especially between Chinese or French and
Annamites, have produced various hybrid groups such as the Minh-
Huong, a Sino-Annamite cross, the Sino-Cambodians and the
Eurasians of European-Annamite blood. This chapter, however,
deals primarily with the Indo-Chinese and only slight reference is
made to the recent immigrant groups (see pp. 249–55).

PHYSICAL TYPES

The ethnic history of the people of Indo-China is difficult to
reconstruct, but certain views, admittedly little more than speculation, have been put forward. According to these the earliest
identifiable type in Indo-China would seem to be the Negrito, a
dark-skinned, long-headed primitive people using simple, polished
stone tools. Later there arrived people of Caucasoid affinities, perhaps to be distinguished as a Nesiot type, with similarities to a type

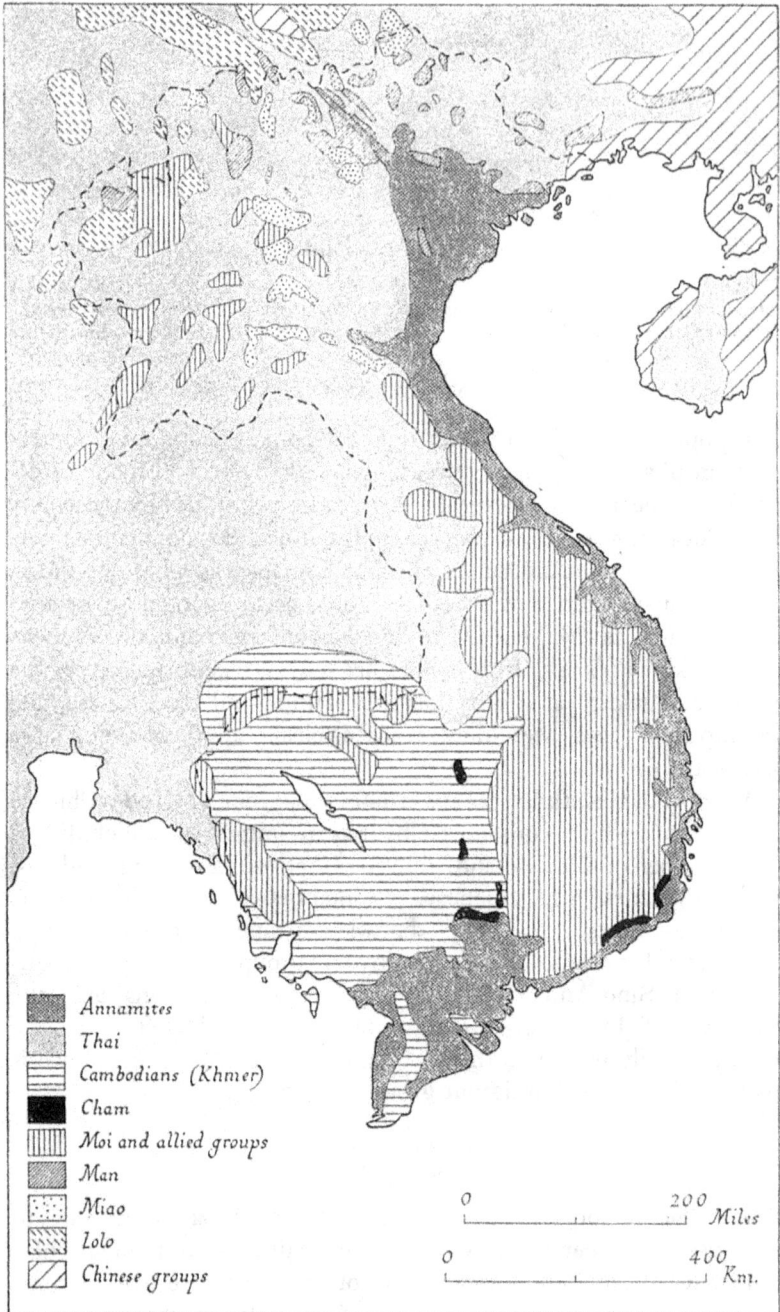

Fig. 54. Peoples of Indo-China and adjacent regions

The precise area occupied by each cultural group is indeterminate; the area of
south China and Hainan shown as inhabited by the Thai peoples probably also
includes groups of Man, Miao and Lolo.

Source: *Atlas de l'Indochine*, plate 18 (Hanoi, 1928).

found today in Indonesia. They came possibly from the islands of the south, driving out or absorbing the Negrito and spreading especially over the lands near the coast. Later again came a succession of Mongoloid invasions from the continent to the north, beginning a movement which has continued without interruption to the present day and which has driven the Nesiots into the southern mountain regions. About the beginning of the Christian era some elements, already racially mixed, entered the south of Indo-China by sea from India.

A classification of the present-day peoples of Indo-China on the basis of physical characters, such as skin shade, proportions of the head, type of hair and stature is difficult, for intersettlement and interbreeding have taken place to a very high degree. But in general terms, two main physical types may be distinguished:

(1) Pareoean or southern Mongoloid type: fairly short in stature, broad-headed, yellow to brown skin, short flattened nose, lank black hair and oblique eyes with the epicanthic or 'Mongolian' fold.

(2) Nesiot type: short in stature, long-headed, light skinned, moderately broad nose, with wavy black hair and straight eyes.*

The Annamites belong essentially to the Pareoean or southern Mongoloid stock, though some authorities hold that they are a cross between an early Nesiot stock in Tonkin and Mongoloid invaders. The average height of the men is about 160 cm. (5 ft. 3 in.) with less than 10 % taller than 168 cm. (5 ft. 6 in.). They are commonly a pale yellow in skin shade, with straight hair, well-marked cheek bones and oblique eyes which have the Mongolian fold at the inner corner. Although of slight build and with slender limbs, the Annamites have a reputation as hard and skilled workers (Plates 11, 12, 13).

The Cambodians have been thought to show traces of Dravidian stock as well as of the Mongoloid elements. They are slightly taller and darker of skin than the Annamites; those who work out of doors have a coffee or even chocolate tint. The head is distinctly broad, but unlike the typical Pareoean stock, the hair is often wavy and the Mongolian fold generally absent from the eye. On the whole, the Cambodian is a better built man than the Annamite, though he is not marked by the same industry and enterprise (Plate 16).

On the mountains and plateaux of Annam, Cambodia and parts of Laos are a number of small groups known collectively as Moi (Plate 14). These people are mainly of a Nesiot type, physically more akin to some Indonesians than to other types in Indo-China, though

* The Nesiot type has been called Indonesian by some authorities, but since this is already a linguistic term the name Nesiot has been adopted for the physical type.

a systematic study of their local variations has still to be made. In general, they are of small stature with a copper-coloured skin, more or less wavy hair and straight eyes. Among them, however, are to be found individuals with broad noses, depressed at the base, crisped hair, and a type of feature akin to the Negrito of the mountain ranges of the Malay peninsula and the Philippines. The small groups of Cham who live along the south coast of Annam and in parts of Cambodia are physically not unlike the Moi, though they are rather taller and more strongly built.

The Thai, who live in Laos and parts of north Tonkin, are closely akin to the inhabitants of Siam. They are primarily of Pareoean stock, but show considerable differences in physical characters according to local grouping. All have fairly brown skins and moderately broad heads, but whereas the people of south Laos have an average height of just under 160 cm. (5 ft. 3 in.), in north-east Tonkin the average height is 165 cm. (5 ft. 5 in.). Such variations indicate that there has probably been considerable intermixture of the Thai with other ethnic groups in the different areas, particularly with the Chinese. The Mongolian fold is usually though not always present among these people. The Thai of Laos has been given a reputation for idleness and lack of energy, but this can be explained by the constant devastation to which his country was subjected in the past; at present, under peaceful conditions which allow of enterprise and co-operative effort, the Laotian has proved himself a satisfactory worker.

In the mountains of Tonkin and Laos live small communities of which the major groups are known as Man, Miao, and Lolo. All these groups originated from China in the last few centuries and are offshoots of the large non-Chinese population living in Yunnan, Kweichow and other provinces of the south-west. Their physical characteristics show some variation, but they are on the whole of middle stature, or somewhat below, and the shape of the head tends to be narrower than that of the other groups described. The men are well built, the women are small. The eye is oblique, usually with the Mongolian fold; the skin colour varies from saffron to pale yellow. They seem to include both Nesiot and Pareoean elements.

Languages

The languages of Indo-China, which show very great variety, are mainly distributed between two great families, the Sino-Tibetan and the south-east Asiatic. In world terms, the latter family extends

Plate 11. Official at the court of the Emperor of Annam
This is typical of the ordinary dress of the upper class.

Plate 12. An Annamite woman from Tonkin

Plate 13. An Annamite peasant from Tonkin

The peasant is carrying a sun hat in his left hand and in his right the long heavy knife which is the common agricultural tool.

Plate 14. Moi youth

The long, wavy hair, bare upper body and loin cloth distinguish these more primitive people from the peasants of the plain.

across southern Asia to the islands of the Pacific, the former through
central and eastern Asia. The languages of the main population
groups in Indo-China have still not been thoroughly studied, and no
classification of them has yet been universally accepted. Annamite,
Cambodian or Khmer and Thai are the three chief languages in the
country.

An important feature of the Annamite language is its tonal character; as in Chinese the same combination of a vowel and a con-
sonant means one thing if uttered in a high tone, and something quite
different in a low tone. Each word has a tone, proper to itself, as real
a part of the word as the vowels and consonants. Thus *ca* spoken
with a high rising tone means 'fish', but spoken with a low rising
tone it means 'all'. There are three main dialects, that of Tonkin
which uses six tones and those of Annam and Cochin-China which
each use five tones. The vocabulary of Annamite is in great part
borrowed from the Chinese as the result of the Chinese conquest of
Tonkin early in the Christian era, but many ordinary words, such
as the names of animals, are Cambodian (Khmer). The tonal structure
on the one hand and the vocabulary on the other have caused Annamite to be classed sometimes with the Sino-Tibetan and sometimes
with the south-east Asiatic family.

The Cambodian or Khmer language is the clearest representative
of the south-east Asiatic family in Indo-China and is closely related
to the Mon speech of Burma and to the Munda of India. Khmer has
recoiled in the west and north before Thai (Siamese) and Laotian
since the thirteenth century when the kings of Cambodia lost their
suzerainty of Siam, and in the south-east before Annamite since the
seventeenth century when the Annamites began to colonize what is
now Cochin-China. It is a monotonal tongue, that is, the tones of
the speaker mark his phrases and convey his expressions of surprise,
questioning, etc. as in English, but do not belong to specific words as
in Chinese. Basically, the words in the Khmer language are monosyllabic, but prefixes and infixes are commonly used to form words
of more than one syllable. Thus from the word *han*, meaning 'to
die', the word *p-han*, meaning 'to kill', is formed by a prefix, and
the word *h-am-an*, 'a grave', by an infix. Otherwise words do not
change their form; there are no declensions, no conjugations, and
meaning depends on the position of the words in the sentence.

The languages of the Moi tribes may also be classed in the south-
east Asiatic family; some such as the Suoy, Mnong, Bahnar, Sedang,
Boloven, and Brao have close affinities with Khmer, others such as

Rade and Jarai are closer to the Malayo-Polynesian group of this family. The language of the Cham is also akin to those in the Malayo-Polynesian group. All these languages are monotonal.

The Thai group of languages is predominant in the mountains of north Indo-China. They include Laotian, Tho, Nung and the speech of the White Thai and Black Thai; a most important member of the group outside Indo-China is the Thai of Siam. These languages, like Chinese, have a system of tones and are monosyllabic, but in some other respects show likeness to the south-east Asiatic (Mon-Khmer) family. Apart from Thai, the mountain peoples of Tonkin and Laos speak languages of which little is known, but which vary considerably from one small group to another. Of these, Lolo belongs to the Sino-Tibetan family with affinities with Burman, while Man and Miao have close connexions with the languages spoken by so-called aboriginal groups in south China, but cannot be attached with certainty as yet to any known linguistic family, though they are most probably related to the Thai group. Each appears to have many Thai, Chinese, or Annamite words in its vocabulary, according to the language spoken by its neighbours.

The external influences perceptible in the vocabulary and structure of some of these languages are seen also in the systems of writing. All the Indo-Chinese scripts derive either from Chinese or Hindu types. The Annamites for centuries used the Chinese system of ideographs, in which each sign represents not a letter but a complete word or idea. About the thirteenth century, however, they invented a new system of their own, using some of the Chinese symbols unchanged, together with others in which the Chinese symbol was made to stand for a sound and not a word. This system, known as the *chu'-nom* or 'vulgar characters', has now largely given place to one introduced in the seventeenth century by European missionaries; this, known as the *qu'oc-ngu*, uses ordinary Roman letters, and is now the official script for Annam, Tonkin and Cochin-China. The Cambodian script, like that used in the once powerful Cham kingdom, is based upon a south Indian alphabet brought by Hindu immigrants about the beginning of the Christian era. The Thai script has close affinities with that of the Cambodian or Khmer language.

CULTURAL GROUPS

The peoples of Indo-China, as in their physical type and speech, show strongly marked differences in their cultural development.

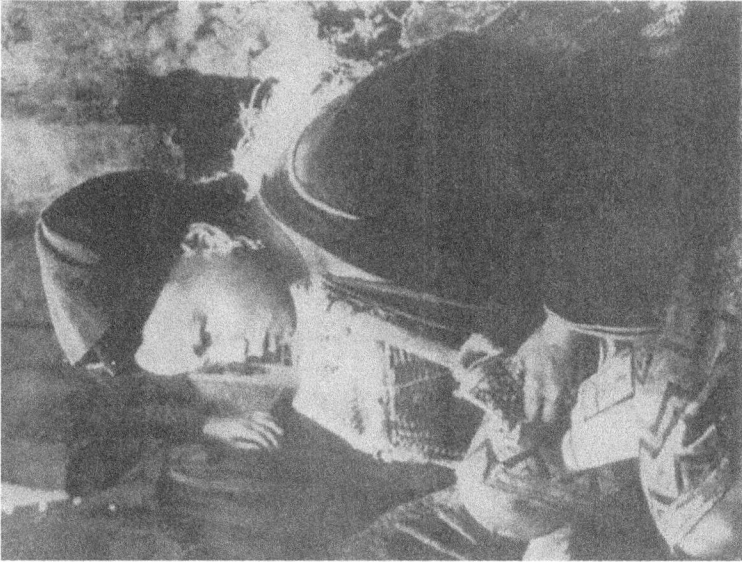

Plate 15. Muong girl

The Muong, who live in the hills of northern Annam and
western Tonkin, are culturally akin to the Annamites.

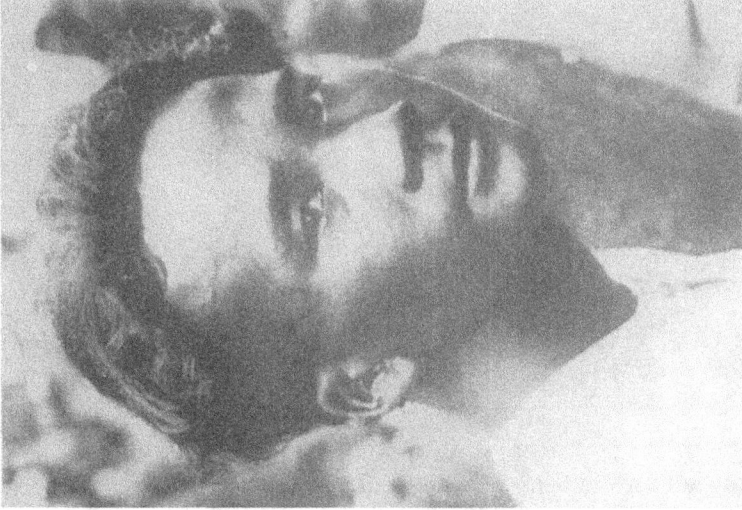

Plate 16. Cambodian youth

Plate 17. An Annamite home

The house has two buildings set at right angles, both standing on the ground. The main building in the centre has a verandah partly closed by bamboo screens. The roofs are thatched with palm leaves.

Plate 18. Annamite women at market

These small traders sell a variety of fruits and vegetables including red and green peppers, cucumbers, sugar cane and pumpkins.

Broadly speaking, however, they are alike in this fundamental respect, that the basis of their existence is a peasant economy of a primarily agricultural type, with their material culture of houses, food, clothing and tools drawn mainly from plant sources. In this economy rice plays a vital role and at times attains ritual significance.

Annamite Culture

The Annamites occupy the plains of Tonkin, Annam and Cochin-China and have also penetrated into Cambodia and Laos. They are skilled rice cultivators and, using Chinese technique, apply human

Fig. 55. Covered bridge at Bac Ninh in the Tonkin delta

It is narrow, cannot be used by vehicles, and contains a small Buddhist shrine.
Source: P. Gourou, *Les Paysans du Delta tonkinois*, plate 44 (Paris, 1936).

labour more intensively and irrigate on a larger scale than does any other cultural group in the country. Apart from farming, the Annamites are skilful fishermen and adept craftsmen in wood-working, textile-making, basketry and lacquering. Their craft-work is done without machinery and on a non-capitalist basis; a marked feature of it is the tendency to specialization from one village to another (see p. 317).

The village is the basic unit of Annamite society. Each village is enclosed within a hedge of bamboo which defines its limits and helps to keep out robbers. Unauthorized cutting of this hedge is an offence; on the other hand, a village may be punished by being obliged to fell its hedge, thus being made to stand naked as it were in the countryside. Within the village, the streets are usually laid out in a plan, often in parallel lines. The houses are built directly on the ground—unusual in Indo-China—with the exception of those of the Muong, a community of Annamite origin in Tonkin, which are built on piles. The houses are ordinarily of bamboo with wooden supports and a thatched roof, though houses with tiled roof and brick walls are now becoming common; most of the houses have an altar where ritual ceremonies are held in celebration of the ancestors of the family (Plate 17).

The Annamite village is an autonomous community, regulating differences among its members. Local government is nominally in the hands of a village council elected by families, but in practice authority is often exercised by a single man of wealth and influence. Various forms of association of village members are common, as of literati, merchants, old men and musicians. Each village has as its focal points a communal house, which serves as a place of assembly for the men, and a Buddhist temple, sometimes outside the village precincts, which serves as a place of resort for the women.

A marked feature of Annamite society is the strong communal system which binds together citizens of a village, or even a larger unit, in a set of fiscal, religious and political obligations. The commune, strong in the cohesion and loyalty of its members, administers public buildings, the partition of communal lands, a co-operative system in irrigation, and communal granaries for holding reserve stocks of rice. The Annamite peasant is thus not an isolated individual, socially or economically; he is sustained by the efforts of his fellows.

Annamite civilization on its material and social side has been deeply influenced by that of the Chinese, by whom they were politically controlled for over 1,000 years. The family organization is very strong, and patriarchal after the Chinese fashion. The father is the priest of the ancestral cult and also enjoys complete authority over his children. The mother holds a privileged position in the family, but one of much less importance than among the Cambodians or the Cham. The Annamite Code of Ceremonial or Book of Rites which regulates marriage also lays down the duties of the family members. In respect of marriage, the rules are intricate and carefully formulated and cover a wide range of matters, such as the kinship of the parties, a clear understanding by both families as to the physical and moral qualities of the pair to be married, the

Plate 19. The procession of the Emperor of Annam to the triennial festival (Nam Giao) at the Temple of Heaven

The Emperor, in a palanquin presented to the court of Annam by Louis XVI in 1789, is proceeding to the Temple of Heaven where, after purification by baths and fasting, a ceremonial sacrifice is made to Heaven, to Earth and to the Imperial ancestors.

Plate 20. The officiating mandarins at the rehearsal of the Nam Giao festival in the Temple of Heaven

In the afternoon before the proper ceremony, which occurs at night, an elaborate rehearsal is held. Musical instruments can be seen in a line on the left with the ritual dancers in the background on the right. The temple is surrounded by a grove of trees which forms the background to the photograph.

marriage contract, the customary presents to be made, penalties for a breach of the contract or for marriage while still in mourning, the marriage ritual itself and grounds for divorce. Polygamy, authorized by law, is practised by men of wealth, though only the first wife has formal authority and dignity as a spouse. The marriage properly so-called, that is, the first union, is arranged by the parents without consultation of the young people and may be the result of their betrothal while still infants. Normally, the wife joins her husband's family and in law ceases to belong to her own, but sometimes provision is made for the 'calling of the son-in-law' to live with his wife's parents in cases where she is required to tend them in their old age. On the conclusion of the engagement presents are given from the man's family to that of the bride. Fruit and cloth are usual, together with symbolic gifts of a black pig in a cage, a bottle of rice spirit and a box of betel materials. Among the richer families the presents include buffaloes, pigs, cloth, women's garments, jewellery and bars of silver. When the man's family are too poor to afford gifts the man goes 'to act the son-in-law' to the girl's family, commonly working for them for three years before the marriage is concluded. This, however, is contrary to the Book of Rites.

The close connexion of the family with the ancestral cult involves great attention to the funeral rites. A rich coffin and a huge red- and gold-lacquered hearse, resembling a house several stories high, are used; the household mourns in shabby white garments of a prescribed cut; and the corpse is accompanied to its burial by a long procession. Several months after the funeral a banquet is given by the heir to all who followed in the procession.

The three official cults of the Annamites are Confucianism, Buddhism of the Chinese type, and Taoism. Although Confucianism is the religion of the Emperor and the high mandarins, in general all three cults are intermingled. The Annamites in addition sacrifice to innumerable good and evil spirits. In the 17th century European missionaries introduced Christianity to the Annamite peoples and there are to-day many thousands of adherents to the Christian faith. Cao-daism, a religious movement which seeks to unite Confucianism, Buddhism, Taoism and Christianity, has existed for fifteen years in Annam and Cochin-China. The subversive political activities of Cao-daism have led the French government to arrest several of its leaders.

Ceremonial festivals, associated with the religious cults, figure prominently in Annamite life. The Têt or festival of the New Year is celebrated in every village and elaborate processions are organized as part of the rejoicings. The most important of the festivals is the triennial festival of the Nam Giao in which the emperor performs the Sacrifice to Heaven. This solemn, colourful ceremony, which usually takes place upon a night in March or April, is performed in the Temple of Heaven, about three kilometres south of Hue. It is of Chinese origin and dates back several thousand years (Plates 19 and 20).

The Chinese cultural influence brought to bear upon the Annamites resulted in the creation of an elaborate political organization of an imperial kind, and in the rise of a highly civilized, educated class. A system of literary examinations instituted on the Chinese model at the beginning of the fourteenth century has been maintained, with some modifications, till the present day, and much of the Annamite literature has followed the Chinese formulae. During the last century, however, a more popular national spirit has manifested itself, stimulated especially by contact with the West; translations, plays, poems, satires and educational works, apart from the vernacular press, display the growing interest in Annamite as distinct from Chinese culture.

Annamite historical literature takes the form of legends, proverbs and epic poems, a large proportion being essentially didactic in purpose. The legends, which cover a wide variety of subjects, abound in supernatural events and usually portray the triumph of the good over the evil spirits. Many of the legends, however, are not written down, but transmitted by word of mouth from generation to generation. The Annamite proverbs are well known for their ironic sense of humour; they allude to agricultural experiences, social affairs in the village, and astronomical phenomena. The medieval epic poems *Kim Van Kieu* and *Luc Van Tien* rank as the masterpieces of Annamite literature, and both have been translated into French. Confucian and Buddhist philosophy underlies their thought: thus, the hero in the *Luc Van Tien*, despite physical and moral trials, upholds the standard of right conduct to which every Annamite tries to conform; and the heroine in the *Kim Van Kieu* is made to suffer many ordeals as expiation for the faults committed in a former existence. Both poems are composed in couplets of six-syllable and eight-syllable lines each, and there is an ingenious system of internal rhyming.

Musical expression among the Annamites is mainly confined to the chanting of songs, with either a guitar or monochord as accompaniment. The people sing refrains which have been handed down through the ages. There are few professional musicians, for the Annamite code does not regard music as an honourable calling; a certain number of professional singers, mostly women, and orchestras entertain the wealthy mandarins and other native functionaries.

The drama is widely appreciated by the Annamites, though the stage profession, like that of music, is held in disrepute. All the important towns have their theatre and travelling troupes of actors perform in the villages. Many of the historical dramas last for two or three days and are based on material in the Chinese Annals; according to Western standards, the plots are weak and artificial, while the characters are thinly drawn and stereotyped. In their allegorical symbolism, the Annamite dramas are reminiscent of those of Greece.

Cambodian Culture

The economy of the Cambodians is primarily an agricultural one. They cultivate rice, maize, cotton, tobacco and many kinds of vegetables. Along the river banks and around the lake of Tonle Sap, fishing is an important occupation, though with the Cambodians it is mainly for subsistence; Annamites and Chinese are the chief producers of fish for export. In general, the Cambodians are a quiet, hospitable folk, not remarkable for their industry, indifferent farmers, and as traders inferior to both Chinese and Annamites who are established in the country in considerable numbers.

The Cambodian house is usually single-storied and constructed on piles, of wood and bamboo, roofed with palm-leaf thatch (Fig. 81). The characteristic costume of both sexes is the 'sampot', a piece of stuff folded round the loins and between the legs to make a kind of baggy trousers; to this the men add a close jacket and the women a tunic or a large coloured scarf which leaves the back and arms bare.

Family life is strictly regulated. Every boy goes at an early age into a monastery, and after his period there he sleeps in a communal house each night until the time comes for him to be married; the girls live with their parents until puberty, and then retire into seclusion. Purity of morals, about which the Cambodian family is very particular, is thus maintained. Selection of a marriage partner is made by the parents, though occasionally the children seem to be able to exercise some choice. On his betrothal the young man gives presents to the parents of the girl, and he goes 'to act the son-in-law' to them for a period. Owing to the great expense involved the marriage ceremony may be postponed indefinitely, and even be omitted altogether.

The funeral rites are elaborate and expensive. A high, gilded, flower-decorated hearse is used, the youngest son of the deceased rides in a palanquin in front as 'conductor of the soul', and the cortege is accompanied by musicians, hired women mourners, monks and the family clad in white with their heads shorn. The ceremony is completed by the cremation of the corpse. So costly is the ceremony that families may give a temporary burial and wait for several months or even years, until they have accumulated several of their dead, before they hold the final cremation rites.

The religion of the Cambodians is Buddhism of the Southern or 'Lesser Vehicle' (Hinayana) type, and the Buddhist monks hold an important position in Cambodian life. The people are much attached to their religious duties and ritual, though they combine the orthodox tenets of their faith with a system of belief in many types of local good and evil spirits. These include tree spirits, spirits of deified ancestors, ghosts of women who died in childbirth and of people who died by violence. The spirits are propitiated by offerings of rice, fruit, fowls and even of goats and buffaloes.

Society in the state is organized on a class basis, with members of the royal house, nobles, monks, freemen and (formerly at least) slaves, in descending order. The court, which resides at Phnom Penh, still keeps up a great deal of ceremony, and every year the 'Water Festival', a regatta of a religious character marked by colourful pageantry, takes place in the capital.

Cambodian literature is largely made up of romances in verse and scholarly poems, based on the *Ramayana* and on Indian legends of Buddha. Almost all the romances and poems have a moral purpose, and the merit of a particular composition lies not so much in its aesthetic beauty or emotional power as in its depth of learning and scholarship. Alliteration and internal rhyming are characteristic features of the prosody. Prose works also form a considerable part of the literature; they include expositions on the tenets of the Buddhist faith and technical treatises on astrology, medicine and ceremonial etiquette.

The chanting of songs and an intricate kind of ballet dancing, performed by highly trained professional dancers, is beloved of all Cambodians. At the time of the New Year festival and on ceremonial occasions groups of singers chant traditional songs in which love is the principal theme. The trials and sufferings of love figure prominently and stress is also laid upon the Buddhist doctrine of the futility of all earthly achievements. Professional singers, together with a

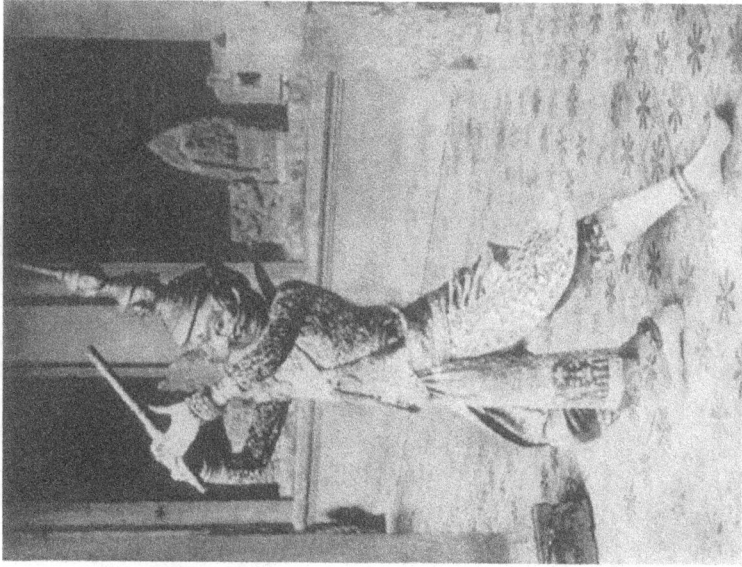

Plate 21. Cambodian female dancer as a demon prince

Plate 22. Cambodian female dancer as the nymph Kinnari

Plate 23. Angkor Wat

A general view showing the five towers of the central building and the tanks which are such a feature of the site of Angkor.

Plate 24. Angkor Wat from the air

This gives a good view of the three terraces and the steps leading up to them.

small orchestra, also accompany the rhythmic pantomimes which are the only form of drama organized by the Cambodians. The performance of plays, so popular among the Annamites, is unknown. The actor-dancers, who are always women, represent special type-characters by a series of extremely graceful postures; they wear ornamental garments and headdresses and their faces are either whitened with chalk or masked (Plates 21 and 22). The theatrical repertory is mainly derived from works of Siamese origin, though Indian legends are also used.

Cham Culture

In scattered parts of Cambodia and south Annam live small groups of people known as the Cham whose culture is now only a pale reflexion of its ancient glory when the kingdom of Champa extended over a large part of south-eastern Indo-China (see p. 172). After the overthrow of the Champa kingdom by the Annamites in the late fifteenth century, the Cham culture rapidly declined. In economic and social affairs, the Cham remain at a distance from their Annamite conquerors, but maintain their ancient close relations with the Moi, with whom they trade and from whom in many respects it is difficult to distinguish them either linguistically or culturally.

The Cham of to-day are primarily agriculturalists, growing rice, maize, tobacco, cotton and groundnuts. They irrigate their fields, though they have allowed large areas of land to revert to brushwood for lack of upkeep. Buffaloes, goats, poultry and a few horses are kept, but no cattle or pigs, as the flesh of these is forbidden by their religion. They manufacture heavy carts and resin torches, and prepare beeswax for export. Many of their settlements lie on the river bank or a lake side, and some are even built on huge floating rafts; the staple industry of these groups is the building of light boats and racing skiffs.

Owing to a belief that the shade of a tree exercises a baneful influence over the house beneath it, the Cham villages are notable for the complete absence of all vegetation, in which respect they contrast strongly with the tree-surrounded Annamite settlements. The social organization is matrilineal: family connexions, property and ancestral cults are all transmitted through females. In marriage the people are very conservative, frowning on unions outside the Cham community. Etiquette and ritual are highly developed. All the Cham groups of Cambodia are Muslims, but most of the groups living in south Annam are Hindu. The followers of Islam are unorthodox in many respects and are strongly influenced by Hinduism.

Moi Culture

The so-called Moi peoples, who inhabit the plateaux and high valleys of south-central Indo-China, are the most primitive groups in the whole country. (The name Moi is the Annamite term for 'savages'.) They are divided into many tribes and sub-tribes, among the most important of which are the Kha Katang, Kha Pakho and Boloven in the north and north-west of the area, inland from Hue; the Reungao, Jarai, Sedang and Bahnar towards the centre and east; the Brao in the west; and the Rade, Mnong, and Stieng in the south. They show many differences of culture, in dress, ornaments, type of house, pottery, weaving and social institutions, but essentially their life is dominated by their upland forest environment.

The Moi cultivate a variety of crops including rice, maize, yams and sweet potatoes. Unlike the agriculturalists of the plains, who grow crops continuously on the same soil by means of irrigation, the Moi practise a form of shifting cultivation (known as *ray*). In the dry season a large area of forest or savanna is cleared by cutting and burning, and rice is sown soon after the first heavy summer rains. This agricultural work is done by communal labour, in which often not only the village people but friends in other villages also participate. The result is a rice field, covering sometimes, as among the Mnong, 80 ha. (200 acres) or more. Among the Mnong and some other tribes the field is abandoned after one crop, and a new clearing made; this process is repeated through a cycle of about twenty years, by which time the forest has reconstituted itself. Among the Rade and the Stieng, who cultivate the richer red soils, the same field can be used for as many as five successive crops of rice. Some of the tribes, however, such as the Katang and the Boloven, have come strongly under Laotian (Thai) influence, and have abandoned shifting cultivation for permanent agriculture.

The Churu, a Moi tribe who have been deeply influenced by the Cham, irrigate their rice lands in the broad valleys of the south of the Plateau de Djiring, and plough them with the aid of buffaloes. On the other hand, most Moi groups, who combine rice cultivation with the raising of buffaloes, use them mainly for feasts and sacrifices, and not as traction animals. Again, the Preh Mnong, living on a poor soil, have turned from agriculture to the more lucrative capture of elephants and to trade with Laos and Cambodia. The Moi keep only small reserve stocks of grain. Their granaries are usually empty by July, and they then live by hunting and collecting till the next harvest in September or October.

Moi crafts include the working of iron in a simple forge equipped with vertical bellows using two bamboo cylinders. Weaving, basketry and pottery-making are also practised. Although matches have been introduced they are still not common, and fire is kindled either by use of flint and iron, or by sawing a dry bamboo with a length of cane until the dust formed begins to glow.

The Moi economy is not entirely a closed one, though communications are poor, and most of the rivers are spanned only by slender bridges of rattan cane (Fig. 56). Elephants' tusks, stag and

Fig. 56. Wooden bridge in the province of Luang Prabang

Source: Georges Maspero, *Un Empire Colonial français: l'Indochine*, vol. I, plate 5 (Paris, 1929).

rhinoceros horn, eagle wood and cinnamon are exported; the principal imports include gongs and pottery jars (superior to the Moi sun-dried ware), both of which have a ritual value.

The dress of most Moi is scanty; the men wear a loin-cloth with a flap in front, and the women a brief skirt. A cape is also sometimes worn, the men often rolling it bandolier-fashion across the chest. The hair is often dressed in a kind of 'bun'; the lobes of the ears are pierced and often greatly distended by wooden rings or other ornaments till they may even touch the shoulders. Some tribes practise tattooing and sawing out of upper incisor and canine teeth.

The houses of a Moi village are generally erected on piles; bamboo is the main material, with a thatch of straw, palm leaves or mats (Fig. 57). Some tribes build large communal houses, those of the Mnong being rarely less than 9 m. long and sometimes reaching a length of 90 m.

In general, the village community is the largest political and social unit of Moi culture; inter-village relations are often confined to war. Government of the village is on a democratic basis, though chiefs, sometimes hereditary, sometimes elected, act as leaders. Differences

Fig. 57. A Moi village

Source: Exposition Coloniale Internationale, Paris, 1931. *La Cochinchine*, facing p. 15 (Saigon, 1931).

of wealth and social status exist, however, in the ownership of elephants, gongs, and jars; and a family with many grown-up daughters may become rich on the proceeds of their weaving and pot-making. Slaves are kept; they are either captives taken in war or debtors who have been unable to repay their obligations. There is no unowned land in the Moi territory. All the land claimed by the village community is collective property, and no person from outside has a right to cultivate any piece of it without the communal authorization. A piece of land used for shifting cultivation is privately held during the time of its exploitation, but reverts to the community once it has been abandoned. Cattle and domestic implements are usually family property, while individuals own jewellery, pipes, weapons and other small articles.

Among the most important items of Moi wealth, at least among the Mnong, the Stieng, the Jarai, the Rade, and other southern tribes, are large pottery jars imported from Cambodia, Cochin-China, Annam or even from China. These are of many colours and often decorated with dragons, ape-faces, or geometrical designs. Each type has its place in an elaborate scale of values. The rarest and most valuable, worth several buffaloes, have each a personal name and a history, and are regarded as the dwelling-place of ancestral spirits. These jars play an impressive role in Moi social and religious life. They are not only a sign of wealth, but are used to hold fermented rice spirit which is drunk at feasts; they are an important accessory to most sacrifices for agriculture or hunting; they are used in funeral rites and may even be broken on the grave of the dead owner.

The ritual life of the Moi is complex, and characterized by feasts and sacrifices. Magicians hold an important position, divination and the healing of the sick being two of their major functions.

The Moi are a fierce and war-like people, adept in the use of the cross-bow and in the stratagems of guerilla fighting. In the past they have given the French administration much trouble, and as late as 1935 a punitive expedition was sent against one group. Road-building, however, and the establishment of military posts has promoted security and the circulation of money, while the colonization of the Plateau du Darlac in the east of their territory has involved some Moi in the dispossession of their lands.

Laotian Culture

The Laotians, a branch of the Thai, have close affinities with the groups in western and northern Tonkin and with the present-day Siamese. They are primarily agriculturalists, with fishing, hunting, boat-building and weaving as important secondary occupations.

The costume of the Laotian men consists of the 'sampot' as in Siam and Cambodia, with a scarf worn over the shoulder, or, in the presence of a superior, rolled round the waist. The women wear a vertically striped petticoat and a bright scarf, with a head-dress varying according to the district, and different for married and unmarried women.

The greater proportion of the population live in hamlets of a few houses. The social organization is of a semi-feudal order, with a number of units akin to principalities, ruled by an oligarchy of

notables, which in their turn owe allegiance to a more powerful
lord.

The predominant religion is Buddhism of the Southern or 'Lesser
Vehicle' (Hinayana) type, but in addition to the monks there are also
magicians, who function as diviners and healers. The Laotians are
a gay and likeable people, musical, and less strict in their moral code
than their fellow-Buddhists of Cambodia. One of their more
picturesque institutions is the formalized courting of the girls by the
young men. In the evenings the marriageable girls, seated on a stage
and wrapped in bright-hued scarves, are serenaded with compli-
mentary verses from the young men. The betrothal and marriage
ceremonies which follow flirtations of this kind are of the same type
as in Cambodia and Siam.

Laotian literature is characterized by long prose works on sacred
subjects and by historical romances in verse, taken from the *Ramayana* and *Mahabharata* legendary cycles of India. The Laotians also
write poetry which provides the lyrical material for their songs. If
the Laotians resemble the Khmers in their literary productions and
in their love of singing they differ from the people of Cambodia in
their lack of attention to miming and dancing. There are few professional dancers, and the technique of dancing is less developed than
in Cambodia.

Communities in the Mountains of Tonkin and Laos

In the mountain regions of Tonkin and Laos, deeply cut by
ravines, partly forested and offering only small space for cultivation,
live the primitive peoples grouped as Thai, Man, Miao, and Lolo
(Fig. 54). The last three all originated from south-west China where
their counterpart groups, often under the same names, still form a
large part of the population. Their movement into Indo-China,
stimulated partly by pressure from the Chinese, and partly by the
need to seek less exhausted lands, began about the thirteenth century,
and was led by the Man. The origin of the Thai is less certain; some
at least were established in Tonkin at an early date, and from there
spread south and east along the rivers, particularly along the Mekong,
where they formed the Laotian states. In the north and east, however, they were blocked by the Annamites and remained within the
valley confines, usually in small communities.

The distribution of these primitive groups can be broadly defined
in terms of altitude. On the floor of the large valleys, at a relatively
low level, are the Thai, normally carrying on permanent rice culti-

vation. Above them, in the zone of the hills between 300 and 900 m. live the Man who practise a shifting cultivation, with rice, maize, cotton and vegetables. Their firing of the brushwood, as in the case of the Moi, threatens the deforestation of the hills, with its accompanying soil erosion. In the high mountains live the Miao, who appear unable to acclimatize themselves to heights much below 900 m. They are assiduous cultivators, growing rice on irrigated terraced mountain slopes, as well as maize and a great variety of vegetables; they also tend cattle, buffaloes, goats, and pigs and possess a hardy race of ponies. The Lolo display no preference for a particular altitude and are found side by side with any of the other groups, though perhaps most frequently in the valleys near the Thai.

The Thai are split up into several sub-groups, including the White and Black Thai, so-called from the colour of their garments, the Tho, Lu, Nung and Nhang. With the exception of the two last, they have all been strongly affected by Annamite culture. They wear tunic and trousers (with skirt as well in the case of the women), buying much of the cotton from the Man; they leave carpentry and ironwork largely to the Annamites and Chinese, and employ both Annamite and Chinese weights and measures in their commerce. The patrilineal family is the basis of their social organization.

The Nung and Nhang have social institutions much like those of the other Thai, but since they arrived from China only about the sixteenth century they bear a much stronger Chinese imprint. The main food of the Nung is maize, and rice is generally reserved as a luxury for feast days, though in recent years it has become more and more important in their diet. The Nhang, on the other hand, live mainly on rice. Both these peoples are specially skilled in trading; many of them work as pedlars and caravan-men. As with the other groups of Thai the patriarchal family is the basic social unit.

The Man, who are of the same stock as the Yao of south-west China, explain their origin by a curious myth, according to which they are descended from a dog, who by killing the enemy of a Chinese emperor, obtained his daughter in marriage as a reward. Half the empire was promised as her dowry, but to lessen his sacrifice the emperor divided the territory, not by area, but vertically, thus handing over only the hills and mountains, which were of little value. This myth accounts for two features of Man sociology: they inhabit the mountain slopes and, unlike the Annamites and Chinese they do not eat the flesh of dogs, since the dog is a totem animal. Although in their economy and social life the Man are similar to the Thai, they manufacture gunpowder, the sulphur for which is bought from the Chinese, and they pay more attention to the cultivation of cotton. They have not an autonomous administrative organization, but draw their chiefs and officials mainly from Thai communities. Their most characteristic institutions are those connected with marriage and funerals.

The Miao are late-comers to Tonkin, and their entry was accompanied by bitter struggles with the Thai and the Man. The costumes of the Miao men are rather plain, in most cases very similar to those of the Chinese, but the women are clad in brightly coloured garments, magnificent with embroidery, and wear elaborate headdresses. Their villages are usually small and the walls of the houses are built of beaten earth. Like the Man, the Miao are manufacturers of firearms and powder. Similarly also their administration is in the hands of Thai officials. Unlike the other groups of this region, however, the patrilineal family system and the ancestral cult are not highly developed; on the death of the father of a family it is the mother and not the eldest son who assumes the leadership and control of the family property; and marriage is often concluded without the consent of the parents. Some Miao practise a kind of 'marriage-fair' which the young people of both sexes attend and use as an avenue to future unions. The cult of the dead is also less rigorously observed by the Miao than by either the Thai or the Man.

Of the Lolo little need be said, since they have tended to adopt the institutions of the Thai, Man or Miao groups among or near whom they live.

RELATIONS BETWEEN THE CULTURAL GROUPS

The most striking factor is the drive to the south of the Annamites. The colonization of Indo-China by the Annamites was not complete on the arrival of the French in 1860, and the process of penetration has continued steadily since then, assisted at times by the efforts of the French administration to promote transfer of population from the overcrowded delta regions of Tonkin (see p. 239).

The penetration of the Annamites has provoked some resistance from the local population. In Cochin-China, Cambodia and also in Laos the local groups are apt to consider the Annamites as too enterprising and grasping, and the hostility is not lessened by memory of territorial disputes. In Cambodia, the Annamites are tolerated as artisans and craftsmen, but efforts are made to exclude them from

Plate 26. Cham dancer at Tra Kieu

Plate 25. Angkor Wat

A near view of the flight of stone steps leading up to the third terrace.

Plate 27. Bas relief, Angkor Wat

The figures are Devatas or semi-goddesses. They have floral crowns, probably originally coloured and gilded, and are carrying lotus flowers and wearing sarongs.

Plate 28. Detail of bas relief, Angkor Wat

Parade of the army of King Surayavarman II, founder of Angkor Wat. The vigorous style conveys a remarkable effect of movement.

administrative posts, the teaching profession and the ownership of land. In Laos the view is expressed that the Annamites should submit to Laotian laws and regulations instead of living in autonomous communities, and here also attempts have been made to prevent them from engaging in rice cultivation. The Annamites deny accusations of wishing to exploit these territories, and claim that they perform a useful economic function which should be recognized by equal facilities with the local groups.

Meanwhile the Annamites themselves are threatened to some extent by Chinese immigration, not by direct competition in the labour market, but by the financial hold which the Chinese tend to obtain over the Annamites, in common with the other peoples of Indo-China. Although comparatively few in number, the Chinese have succeeded in building up a powerful economic position by lending money at high interest and taking the rice crop in default of payment, by greater thrift and frugality, and by greater skill in trading. In Tonkin and Annam the Chinese have tended to form primarily a trading group, often of a floating character, but in Cochin-China and Cambodia they have also devoted themselves to agriculture and fishing. In all the states Chinese penetration has been of a pacific nature; they have adapted themselves easily, speaking the local language, often marrying the native women, and have been granted in the early stages at least the same civil rights as native citizens. In Cambodia, their position has been facilitated by the fact that whereas the Cambodian dislikes the Annamite, he likes and admires the Chinese.

RELIGION AND ART

Religion and art have always been closely associated in Indo-China, and the art of the people, though nowadays of less importance, has left its mark in magnificently decorated temples and finely carved statues. Among the Annamites, Chinese influence has been so strong that it is often difficult to recognize the purely indigenous art. The earliest pagodas in Tonkin date only from about the twelfth century, and few of the original buildings now remain. Annamite art reaches its highest expression in bronze, wood, lacquer and ceramic work.

The civilizations of Cambodia and Champa, which received much of their stimulus from India, early showed Hinduism and Buddhism in association. Hinduism almost certainly appeared first, with the worship of Siva, especially embodied in his phallic form, as predominant. Vishnu was also held in honour, and some of the finest statues in ancient Cambodia represent them both in the form of a single deity, Harihara. By the end of the eighth century, the south of Indo-China shared in the expansion of Buddhism of the Mahayana or 'Great Vehicle' type which had developed a philosophical conception of the Buddha, multiplying his personality into a hierarchy of forms and attributes. This is the type found in China and Japan. In the early fifteenth century, Buddhism of the simpler Hinayana or 'Lesser Vehicle' type began to replace the earlier faiths and is now the religion of Cambodia and Laos. The Hinayana type of Buddhism is also prevalent in Siam, Burma and Ceylon.

The Khmer art of Cambodia flowered in two periods. The first, in the seventh century, was marked by the building of temples in brick, with fine towers either isolated or in groups, decorated with designs in painted stucco, and crowned with a high pyramid symbolizing a sacred mountain. A single door only led into the interior where there was an altar with a statue of a Hindu god, or sometimes a phallus. The designs sculptured on the exterior were borrowed from Indian art and included marine monsters on the lintels, stylized birds on the columns, and the 'Celestial Palace' of gods, genii and fabulous animals on the walls.

The art of the second period was associated with the capital of Angkor, from the time of its founding about the end of the ninth century to the early part of the thirteenth century. The architects of this period used stone instead of brick, and indulged in a great variety of sculpture. The most perfect example of this art is Angkor Wat, the 'Cambodian Parthenon', a vast temple erected to Vishnu, which, standing buried for centuries in the forest, has been uncovered and preserved through the work of French scholars (Plates 23, 24, and 25). The temple has a stone platform, 13 m. high and about 240 m. square, with five towers and numerous galleries. The central tower, over 40 m. high, dominates all the great plain of Angkor. Below the first platform is a second with decorated galleries, and the whole is surrounded by a wall about 1 km. from east to west and 800 m. from north to south. The sculptures of the temple are of an amazing richness. The celebrated galleries of bas-reliefs alone comprise eight panels each between 50 and 65 m. long, covered with carvings of stories from Indian epic poems, representations of the Hindu Last Judgement, and reviews of troops by the king-builder (Plate 28). There are also figures and floral motifs of immense variety, all in stone. On the friezes and gallery walls are divine dancers; Brahmins

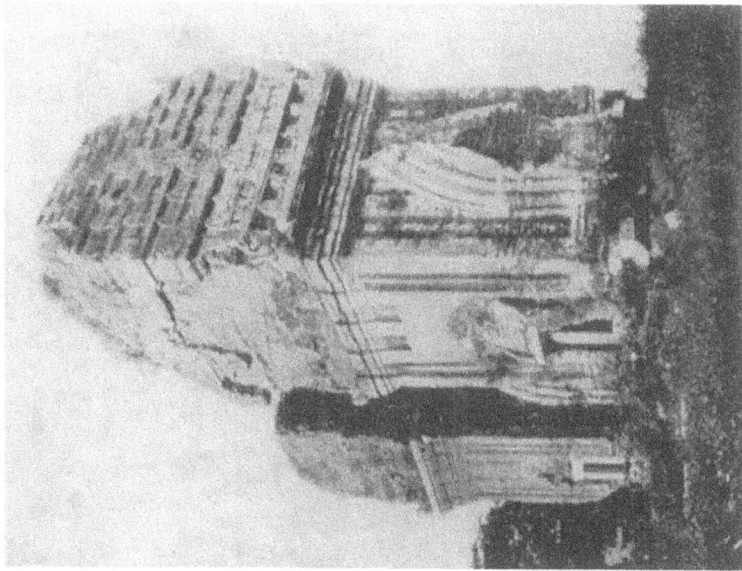

Plate 29. Cham towers at Mi Son near Tourane

These towers, unlike those at Angkor, are built of brick.

Plate 30. Northern gate of Angkor Thom

The gigantic human faces, one on each side of the gateway, have been built up from slabs of stone. They are of the Hindu god, Siva.

Plate 31. Divine dancer, Angkor Wat

Plate 32. Detail of bas relief, Angkor Thom

at prayer are bent at the bases of pillars; lions mount guard at the steps; snakes form balustrades; gods and goddesses richly decked in stone jewels adorn the façades (Plates 27, 28, and 31).

About 1 km. north of Angkor Wat are the magnificent ruins of the royal city of Angkor Thom. The city is surrounded by a moat and by a wall almost eight metres high. It is square in plan and has an area of nearly 9 sq. km. There are five entrances, each with a massive stone gateway, 20 m. in height, crowned by carvings of the four faces of Siva (Plate 30). Straight avenues over 1 km. in length, lead from these gateways to the temple of the Bayon in the centre of the city. The Bayon is perhaps the most striking and most original of the sacred buildings of ancient Cambodia. It consists of fifty-one elaborately carved and finely proportioned stone towers arranged in three terraces in such a way as to give a pyramidal effect to the whole. The towers rise above vast galleries covered with bas-reliefs which are as rich and varied in their sculptures as those of Angkor Wat (Plate 32). North of the Bayon lies another temple, the Baphuon, the great central square or forum and the royal palace.

The art of the Cham is in many respects similar to that of the Khmer, though their temples were built only in brick. The finest surviving example of their work is at the holy city of Mi Son, in central Annam. Here in a deserted valley more than sixty monuments exist, the principal temple being a fine tower dating from the end of the sixth century, and dedicated to a phallic cult of Siva (Plate 29). The exterior is decorated with sculptures in brick, of lions, elephants, mythological birds and animals, divine dancers making the gesture of prayer, and many other motifs. Some magnificent stone figures have been transported to the *Musée Cham* at Tourane. Other fine examples of Cham art are the temples at Tra Kieu and Dong Duong in the province of Quang Nam (Plate 26).

Laotian art is best seen in the temples at Luang Prabang, Vientiane and on the Plateau du Tran Ninh. All these temples, dedicated to Buddhism of the 'Lesser Vehicle' (Hinayana) type, are constructed both in brick and wood, some of modest appearance, some richly elegant in their architecture. The Laotians have also in the past been distinguished for their skill in making bronze statues, finely moulded and skilfully finished.

During the present century, energetic steps have been taken to preserve the historical monuments and works of art in Indo-China. The *Ecole française d'Extrême Orient*, founded in 1900, has performed invaluable renovation work and also fostered the establishment of museums for collections of archaeological and historical interest.

EDUCATION AND CULTURE

In the early years after their occupation of the country, the French sought through the medium of native schools to inculcate Western ideals, paying little attention to the study of native philosophy and customs. This assimilationist system was later recognized as unsuited to the needs of the country, and the present organization seeks to educate the people in the history and traditions of Indo-Chinese life. Although instruction is given in the native language, one of the basic principles of the educational system is that the study of French should be generally encouraged. Another cardinal feature of French policy is that the mass of the population shall receive only simple instruction on subjects associated with their daily life, and that education beyond the primary stage shall be restricted to those who are not likely to abuse such privileges by fomenting political troubles and creating social unrest.

In 1939, there were over 536,000 children attending state schools, of which total only 50,000 were girls. If the number of children of school age is taken as 3,300,000, that is, about one-seventh of the total population, the proportion attending school is only 16 %. A very large number of children thus receive no instruction at all.

Primary Education

Primary schools, which provide free instruction for children up to twelve years of age, are of two kinds, the one using the native tongue, the other French as the language of instruction. The first kind are known as 'Preparatory Schools' in Cochin-China, 'Pagoda Schools' in Cambodia and 'Communal Schools' in Annam and Tonkin. Many of these schools are attached to Buddhist temples. In a three-year course, the children are taught to read and write in their own language, and they also receive instruction in Buddhist and Confucian philosophy as well as in the history and geography of Indo-China. There is also an optional course in the French language. The second kind of primary schools, mainly found in the large towns and more important rural centres, have a similar curriculum, though in addition to the study of French, the Annamites have to learn Chinese characters, and the Cambodians, Pali and Sanskrit. The better students at the end of three years proceed to higher elementary schools, where there is a further weeding-out process designed to select the boys most suited to secondary education. In 1939 there were 7,141 primary or elementary schools for native children with 519,000 pupils and 12,200 teachers. Only about 10 % of the pupils entered the higher elementary schools, and under 1 % proceeded to secondary schools.

An important feature of native primary education is the provision of school books printed in the Annamite, Cambodian and Laotian languages. Nearly five million of these text-books had been printed up to the end of 1930, over 80 % of which were in the Annamite language.

Primary education for French children is given in kindergartens, elementary and higher elementary schools, as in France. These schools have been built in all the towns where there is a large European population. The number of pupils totalled 6,296 in 1939.

Secondary Education

Education beyond the primary stage is provided in *lycées* and *collèges* which resemble those in France. Native secondary schools exist at Hanoi, Haiphong, Nam Dinh, and Lang Son in Tonkin; at Thanh Hoa, Vinh, Hue and Qui Nhon in Annam; at Saigon, My Tho and Can Tho in Cochin-China; at Phnom Penh in Cambodia and at Vientiane in Laos. There are similar schools for French children at Hanoi (*Lycée Albert Sarraut*), Saigon (*Lycée Chasseloup Laubat*) and Dalat. Dalat, however, is the only *lycée* exclusively for Europeans. The teaching staffs are composed of French Masters of Arts or *agrégés* and a small number of native teachers who have been trained either at a university in France or at the University of Hanoi. The course of study is for seven years, and it is a tribute to the high quality of the secondary education that the school-leaving diploma or *baccalauréat* is officially regarded as equal to that of France. In 1937 there were 4,611 students in the secondary schools of Indo-China.

Four large schools carry all courses from the primary through the secondary grades. They are the *Ecole Petrus Ky* at Saigon with 879 students; the *Ecole de Protectorat* at Hanoi with 840 students; the *Ecole Sisowath* at Phnom Penh with 732 students; and the *Ecole Khai Dinh* at Hue with 692 students. Each of these schools is handsomely constructed and well equipped.

The University of Hanoi

The University of Hanoi, founded in 1917, and reorganized by Governor-General Merlin in 1925, includes schools of medicine, law, fine arts, education, agriculture and commerce. In 1937 there were 631 students of whom 87 were French, 541 Annamite and 3 Chinese. If account is taken of the modest number of natives who receive secondary education, the high proportion of native students in the university is a most striking feature. Scholarships are awarded to encourage students in secondary schools to proceed to the university. The medical degree is officially considered of equal standing to that of any French university; but all doctors who qualify for this degree are required to practise in Indo-China.

The lecture rooms, laboratories, libraries, and other buildings of the university form a 'University City'. Nearly 500 of the 631 students are boarders.

Professional and Technical Education

Professional and technical education has made rapid progress during the present century. A school at Phnom Penh in Cambodia provides vocational training in a variety of subjects including scientific farming, public hygiene, and the elements of legal procedure. The courses usually extend over a period of two years. They are open to young men between 18 and 25 years of age who have been recommended as suitable candidates by the French Resident. Other vocational institutions include a school for industrial apprentices at Hue, and a school of applied industry at Haiphong. At Hanoi there is a school of veterinary science and at Saigon a school of handicraft work. Although the number of students in these technical schools totalled only 2,000 in 1931, vocational training of this kind is likely to become more and more important, especially in the towns.

Apart from the technical schools, designed to provide a practical knowledge in agriculture and industry, there are also two schools at Hue and Hanoi for the study of Annamite culture. These schools, which are attended by the native intelligentsia, provide courses in Annamite history and traditions as well as in the teachings of Buddha, Confucius, Lao Tze and Christ.

Private Schools

Private schools, which give education to about 60,000 pupils, are of three kinds. In the first place there are the Roman Catholic mission schools, which number about 650 and provide instruction for more than 36,000 children. The largest of such schools are the *Ecole Taberd* at Saigon, the *Ecole Puginier* at Hanoi, and the *Ecole Pellerin* at Hue. Secondly, Annamite native schools are found in many of the villages of Annam; as in the days before the French conquest, the best students are chosen by the cantonal officials to take part in examinations for entry into the mandarinate. The Chinese schools are the third kind of private teaching establishment. They have been built to serve the Chinese colonies in Tonkin, Cochin-China and Cambodia; the largest of these schools is at Cho Lon in Cochin-China.

Cultural and Scientific Institutions

The *Ecole française d'Extrême Orient*, founded in 1900 by a decree of the Governor-General, promotes historical, archaeological and philological research in Indo-China and in other countries of the Far East. It is under the *Académie des Inscriptions et des Belles Lettres* of France, but the control exercised by this body is slight and the School has virtual autonomy. The direction and organization are modelled on those of the other French Schools in Rome, Athens, Cairo and Morocco. The School is centred at Hanoi. It publishes a tri-monthly bulletin, in which the inventories of historical monuments are among the most important of the contributions.

The *Société des Études indochinoises* was created in 1883 to continue the work undertaken by the Committee of Agriculture and Industry which had been founded in Cochin-China as early as 1865. Economic questions are now no longer discussed, and the work of the society is mainly confined to ethnography, history and fine arts. The results of its researches are published in a bulletin.

The *Société des Amis du vieux Hué*, founded in 1913, initiates and encourages research on the history and traditions of Annam. It publishes a tri-monthly bulletin.

The *Société de Géographie de Hanoi* organizes conferences and archaeological excursions. It is the only geographical society in Indo-China.

The *Institut des Recherches agronomiques*, founded in 1925, is the most important scientific establishment in the country. Chemical, botanical and entomological work is carried on. The main laboratories are at Hanoi and Saigon. Other scientific institutions include the *Bureau de Climatologie et de la Météorologie agricole*, the *Institut océanographique* and the *Institut Pasteur*.

The *Conseil de Recherches scientifiques de l'Indochine* was formed by the decree of 25 March 1928. It is designed to assemble and co-ordinate the results of all scientific research undertaken in the country and also to promote further research. There are forty members on the council, drawn from higher grades of civil servants and from the scientific institutions.

Libraries and Museums

The *Bibliothèque centrale de l'Indochine* in Hanoi, formed in 1917, is the largest library in the country; it contains about 60,000 volumes and is used by nearly 40,000 readers a year, two-thirds of whom are natives. Hanoi also possesses the fine library of the *Ecole française d'Extrême Orient* which has an invaluable collection of printed works and manuscripts.

Outside the capital, libraries are found at Saigon, Phnom Penh (*Bibliothèque centrale de Cambodge*), Hue (*Bibliothèque de la Société des Amis du vieux Hué*) and Luang Prabang.

Indo-China has six museums, each under the supervision of the *Ecole française d'Extrême Orient*. The French School has its own museum at Hanoi, where there is an important archaeological collection as well as a large number of early coins. There are two museums in Annam, the *Musée Khai Dinh* at Hue, which possesses numerous fine specimens of Annamite art, and the *Musée Cham* at Tourane, which houses many inscriptions and monuments of the ancient kingdom of Champa. The *Musée Blanchard de la Brosse* at Saigon and the *Musée Albert Sarraut* at Phnom Penh have valuable collections of Khmer monuments. Finally, in Laos the *Musée de Vientiane* preserves specimens of Laotian art and handicraft work.

Newspapers and Periodicals

At the present day, there are altogether forty newspapers in French, twenty-five in the native language (Annamite or Cambodian) and four in Chinese. The leading newspapers in Tonkin are *L'Avenir du Tonkin, La France-Indochine* and *Le Courrier d'Haiphong*; in Cochin-China the most important ones are *L'Impartial, L'Opinion*, and *La Dépêche*, published in both French and Annamite. The circulation is small, ranging from 2,000 to 5,000 for each paper. All news contained in the papers is subject to a strict censorship.

About fifty periodicals are published in the French language. Apart from the literary and scientific bulletins, the following official periodicals are also published: the *Journal officiel de l'Indochine*, the *Annales des douanes et régies*, the *Bulletin administratif* of each of the five states, the *Bulletin du Service météorologique*, the *Bulletin de l'Instruction publique* and the *Bulletin économique de l'Indochine*.

There are twenty-three periodicals written in Annamite, the most important of which is the *Nam Phong*. The *Svok Khmer* and *Campuchea Saurya* are the only periodicals in the Cambodian language.

BIBLIOGRAPHICAL NOTE

(1) A general account of the peoples and languages of Indo-China is given n the following works: H. Baudesson, *Indo-China and its Primitive Peoples* (Paris, 1919). Sylvain Levi, *Indochine*, vol. I, Exposition Coloniale Internationale, Paris, 1931 (Paris, 1931). Georges Maspero, *Un Empire Colonial français: l'Indochine*, vol. I (Paris, 1929). J. Sion, 'Asie des Moussons', *Géographie Universelle*, vol. IX (Paris, 1929). Interesting and still valuable accounts are found in P. P. Cupet, 'Les populations de l'Indochine', *Bulletin de la Société de Géographie de Lyon*, vol. XXII, pp. 239–305 (Lyon, 1907) and in L. de Lanessan, *L'Indochine française* (Paris, 1889). A number of important articles on this subject appear in the publications of the *Ecole française d'Extrême Orient*.

(2) Annamite culture. The classical description is J. B. Luro, *Le Pays d'Annam* (Paris, 1878). Recent accounts are found in A. Dumarest, *La Formation des Classes sociales en Pays Annamites* (Lyon, 1935), P. Pasquier, *L'Annam d'autrefois* (Paris, 1930) and Virginia Thompson, *French Indo-China* (London, 1937).

(3) Cambodian culture. The most comprehensive survey is E. Aymonier, *Le Cambodge*, 3 vols. (Paris, 1900–04). A more recent work is P. Collard, *Cambodge et Cambodgiens* (Paris, 1925).

(4) Cham culture. See Georges Maspero, *Le Royaume de Champa* (Paris, 1928) and J. Leuba, *Un Royaume disparu: Les Chams et leur art* (Paris, 1923).

(5) Moi Culture. A full treatment is given in H. Maître, *Les Régions Moi du Sud-Indochinois*, 3 vols. (Paris, 1909–12).

(6) Laotian culture. See L. de Reinach, *Le Laos* (Paris, 1911).

(7) Mountain communities of Tonkin and Laos. The following works contain a great deal of information about these peoples: M. Abadie, *Les Races du Haut Tonkin* (Paris, 1924); E. Diguet, *Les Montagnards du Tonkin* (Paris, 1908); R. Demarez, 'Les modes de vie dans les montagnes de l'Indochine française', *Recueil des Travaux de l'Institut de Géographie Alpine*, vol. VII, pp. 453–561 (Grenoble, 1919).

(8) Religion and Art. From the large literature relating to this subject the following works are recommended: J. Commaille, *Guide aux Ruines d'Angkor* (Paris, 1928). A. K. Coomaraswamy, *History of Indian and Indonesian Art* (London, 1927). G. Groslier, *Angkor* (Paris, 1924). G. Groslier, *La Sculpture Khmere ancienne* (Paris, 1925). R. Grousset, *Les Civilisations de l'Orient*, vol. II (Paris, 1929). H. Marchal, *Guide archéologique aux temples d'Angkor* (Paris, 1928). Philippe Stern, *Le Bayon d'Angkor Thom et l'évolution de l'Art khmer* (Paris, 1927).

(9) Education and Culture. A good account is given in Sylvain Levi, *Indochine*, vol. II, Exposition Coloniale Internationale, Paris, 1931 (Paris, 1931), in Virginia Thompson, *French Indo-China* (London, 1937), and in Francisque Vial, *Le Problème humain de l'Indochine* (Paris, 1939).

Chapter VIII

HISTORY

INTRODUCTION

The history of Indo-China is primarily the history of the two native kingdoms of Annam and Cambodia and also of a third—the realm of Champa—which formerly occupied most of what is now Annam. Annam, Cambodia and Champa corresponded to three distinct lowland peoples, namely, the Annamites, Khmers and Cham, and, though the kingdoms were sometimes split up between rival princely families, they never entirely lost their 'national' identities. The mountainous region of Indo-China, which now comprises northern Laos and north-western Tonkin, was, until the nineteenth century, loosely held by a number of small principalities, such as those centred on Luang Prabang and Vientiane, none of which has had an important influence upon the political development of the rest of the country.

The nomenclature of Indo-Chinese history is somewhat confusing, because certain of the names have had a different range of meaning at different times. Cambodia formerly comprised a far larger territory than at the present day; it covered, in addition, not only the modern Cochin-China—the Mekong delta—but also the greater part of the area of modern Laos and Siam. The present Cochin-China, on the other hand, represents a geographical shift of a name originally applied by European voyagers to the coast of Annam farther north; in those days the Mekong delta was still Cambodia, but it became part of Cochin-China later through the Annamite conquest, and then, still later, after the French conquest, the name was restricted to the area which bears it to-day. The name Annam was originally a literary designation bestowed by the Chinese on the kingdom of Dai-co-viet which had been formed by the Annamite people in what is now Tonkin; as this kingdom extended its power southward by stages over a period of centuries, the name of Annam was applied to all its territory, and then in the period of French rule it was restricted again to the territory left under the nominal administration of the emperor of Annam at Hue, i.e. the old Annam minus present-day Cochin-China and Tonkin.

Throughout history, political power in Indo-China has gravitated to the two large, compact and continuous areas of level, cultivable land, namely, the Fleuve Rouge delta of Tonkin in the north and the Mekong delta, together with the Tonle Sap basin, in the south. These areas favoured the growth of strong, unified kingdoms with a sub-stantial revenue from the surplus of agricultural production and easy intercommunication by inland waterways between the various parts of the realm. The primacy of the cities of Hanoi and Saigon, in the north and south respectively, shows how these two areas have re-tained their pre-eminence even in modern times. The intervening coastal belt—the land of the ancient Champa—could never compete in natural wealth or geographical cohesion; though it had coastwise communications by sea, its cultivable lowland was no more than a strip between the mountains and the seashore. Even less capable of becoming the seat of a paramount power was the region of Laos, with its many forested plateaux and almost unnavigable rivers. It was the alluvial plains of the lower reaches of the Mekong and Fleuve Rouge which were destined by nature to become the homelands of the two dominant nations of Indo-China.

Although its peoples, particularly the Khmers, have shown a considerable degree of originality in the adaptation of borrowed culture, Indo-China has never been an independent source of high civilization. As its name implies, it has been the meeting-place of cultural influences coming from India on the west and from China on the north. Indian influence has in fact been the great formative factor in the history of Cambodia and Champa, Chinese in that of Annam. The Hindus reached Indo-China either by the sea route round Malaya or by the way of the Kra isthmus and the Tenasserim coast; their influence prevailed as far as Champa by the second cen-tury A.D., for the oldest Sanskrit inscription yet discovered in Indo-China is in Champa and is considered to date from this period, and the geographical record of Ptolemy (about A.D. 150) gives place names of Sanskrit origin all along the coasts of Indo-China. They came to the country as traders or as bands of military adventurers, identified themselves with the regions where they settled and retained no political connexion with India.

The Chinese entered Tonkin for the first time in the second century B.C. and held it as part of their empire. Chinese dynasties controlled it down to the tenth century A.D., though the great bulk of the population remained Annamite in speech and was often in revolt against the Chinese domination.

The influence of the Europeans in Indo-China was first felt in the sixteenth century, but it did not become important until two hundred years later. With the subsequent conquest and unification of the peninsula by the French in the latter half of the nineteenth century, Indo-China, as we know it to-day, was born.

INDO-CHINA BEFORE THE ENTRY OF THE EUROPEANS

THE KINGDOM OF ANNAM (Figs. 58-61)

Chinese Rule (181 B.C.–A.D. 939)

The earliest dated history of Indo-China is known from Chinese sources and goes back to 181 B.C., when the son of a general sent by the Chinese Ts'in dynasty to subdue the tribes of south China adopted the imperial title and founded a kingdom called Nan Yueh, which included the modern Tonkin, the strip of lowland between Thanh Hoa and Ha Tinh, as well as the provinces of Kwangtung and Kwangsi. Seventy years later Nan Yueh was subdued by the Han dynasty which ruled over all China, so that Tonkin (later known as 'Annam') became the most southerly province of the Chinese empire. Chinese rule endured in this region for over a thousand years.

When the Chinese entered the lands of what is now Tonkin and north Annam they found the inhabitants living under most primitive conditions. The soil was crudely cultivated with hoes of roughly polished stone and little attempt was made to clear the forests or drain the swamps. The social organization was predominantly tribal in character, and primitive customs, such as tattooing, were widely practised. In the course of their long rule, the Chinese demonstrated the use of the plough, brought new grounds under cultivation, founded many schools and introduced Chinese customs and rites. These economic and social changes provided the foundations for a strong, independent Annamite state.

Independence of Annam or Dai-co-viet (A.D. 939–1407)

In A.D. 939 an Annamite revolt brought to an end the long age of Chinese ascendancy in Tonkin. A new kingdom was established

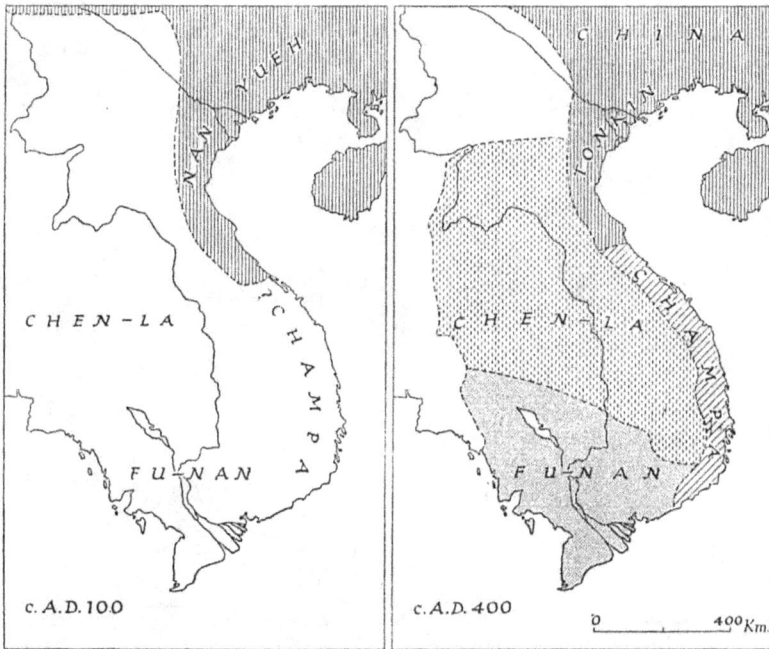

Fig. 58. Indo-China in the second and fifth centuries

Source: A. Hermann, *Historical and Commercial Atlas of China*, pp. 27 and 31 (Cambridge, Mass. 1935).

which gave itself the name of Dai-co-viet, but from 1164 it was known to the Chinese under the name of An-nan meaning 'pacified south'; the former designation will be used here for the period during which the state remained more or less limited to the modern Tonkin, in order to avoid confusion with Annam as extended territorially in modern times.

Dai-co-viet had little difficulty during the three centuries after its creation in maintaining its independence from China. The Sung dynasty made one unsuccessful effort to recover the country in 1076, and when the Mongol forces under Kublai Khan attempted to invade it in 1280 they were compelled to retreat. The mountains which separate the Si Kiang and Fleuve Rouge basins gave Dai-co-viet a good natural frontier, and this region was no longer the jungle border-land which had been conquered by the generals of the Han empire; agriculture in the Fleuve Rouge delta was now highly developed while

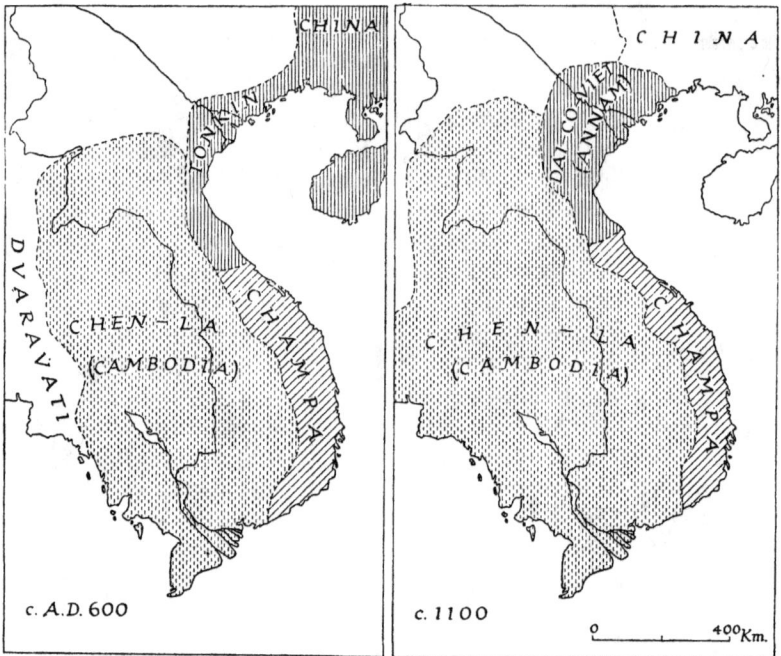

Fig. 59. Indo-China in the late sixth and twelfth centuries

Source: A. Hermann, *Historical and Commercial Atlas of China*, pp. 35 and 47 (Cambridge, Mass. 1935).

the population was politically well organized. The survival of the Annamite language as the speech of the country gave a sense of distinction from the Chinese, a sort of national consciousness; on the other hand, the Annamites retained an indelibile imprint of Chinese civilization, and in their diplomatic relations with China their kings or 'emperors' conformed to the usages of the Chinese court, which assumed a unique status of superiority for the Chinese monarch and treated all presents from foreign embassies as 'tribute'. Such conformity from Annam, as from other minor states in contact with

China, was partly due to the Chinese practice of granting trade licences only to the merchants of nations which brought tribute, but it was partly an expression of real respect from peoples who, though resolved to be free from actual Chinese control, nevertheless looked up to China as the greatest power on earth. In Annam, this sentiment was strengthened by the use of Chinese script for writing and an acquaintance with Chinese literature among the educated.

If the relations of Dai-co-viet with China were generally pacific, those between Annam and Champa were perpetually hostile, and the conflict only ended with the complete overthrow of the neighbouring Cham and the destruction of their culture. The borders of Dai-co-viet were extended southward along the coast in a series of wars, and the provinces lost by Champa were colonized by Annamites, so that there was a permanent ethnographic change and not merely a temporary shift of power.

Renewed Chinese Occupation (1407–28)

Annamite history was interrupted between 1407 and 1428 by a new Chinese occupation (Fig. 60). Champa, after its defeat in 1402 (see p. 172), appealed to China, now under the rule of the Ming dynasty, and the Emperor Ch'eng Tsu sent an army into Tonkin; the resistance of the Annamites was broken and they remained subject to Chinese control until 1428. In this year the Chinese forces were driven out by a revolt under the leadership of Le Loi, who founded a new dynasty destined to retain sovereignty in Annam until 1786.

Annamite Kingdom (1428–1673)

During the early years of the Le dynasty Annam became more powerful than ever before; the emperor Le-Thanh-ton (1460–97) not only obtained decisive victory over Champa, but gave his realm an administrative system, modelled on the Chinese, which enabled the gains in the south to be consolidated. Nevertheless, the elongated shape which Annam now assumed was not favourable to firm central control, and the rivalry of great noble families tended to split the country asunder. In 1527 the Mac family usurped the throne and proclaimed a new dynasty; they held the capital, the modern Hanoi, but the Nguyen family, whose power was established in the province of Thanh Hoa to the south, remained loyal to the deposed Le dynasty and appealed to the emperor of China against the usurpation. The Chinese emperor assembled an army and received the submission of the Mac claimant; he then confirmed the Mac in his rule of Tonkin

as a Chinese governor-general, while recognizing the reign of the
Le heir in the territory from the northern border of Thanh Hoa
southwards (1540). Annam was thus divided into two separate states,
and this arrangement endured for half a century; in 1592, however,
the Le forces captured Hanoi, killed the reigning Mac, and reunited
Annam under the rule of the old dynasty.

Although the Le dynasty managed to regain control of the whole
state at the end of the sixteenth century, it was only a nominal control,

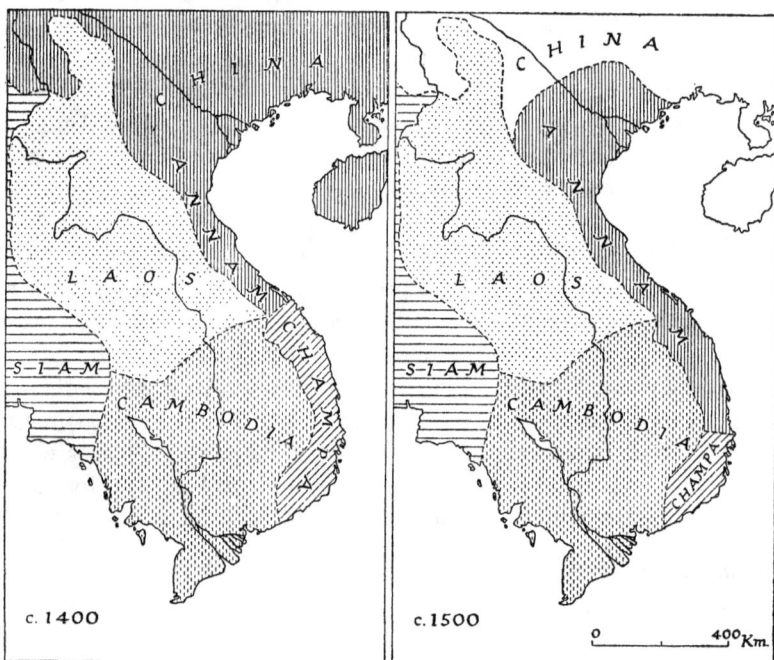

Fig. 60. Indo-China in the early fifteenth and sixteenth centuries
Source: A. Hermann, *Historical and Commercial Atlas of China*, p. 55 (Cambridge,
Mass. 1935).

for its emperors were puppets in the hands of two great baronial
families, the Nguyen and the Trinh, and their quarrels soon led to a
fresh partition of the realm. It was actually a Trinh who brought
back the Le emperor to Hanoi, but the Nguyen remained powerful
in the south, ruling over the neighbourhood of Hue. War broke out
between the two houses in 1627, though neither was able to subdue
the other. From 1673 the Annamite 'empire' was divided into the
two separate kingdoms known to Europeans as Tonkin and Cochin-

China, ruled by the Trinh and Nguyen families respectively; the imperial title remained with the heir of the Le under the protection of the Trinh, but the head of the house of Nguyen assumed the style of a king and claimed complete independence. The frontier between the two realms was marked by a wall at Dong Hoi, north of Hue.

It was towards the close of the seventeenth century that French influence first came to be felt in Annam, and the future history of the Annamite state is bound up with the expansion of French power in the Far East.

THE KINGDOM OF CAMBODIA (Figs. 58–61)

Political History from the Second to the Thirteenth Century A.D.

In the earliest period of its existence as a kingdom, from about the second century A.D., Cambodia, or Fu-nan as the Chinese called it, seems to have consisted of a collection of principalities under a loose suzerainty. Fu-nan, with the vassal state of Chen-la, was certainly a much larger area than the modern Cambodia; it included what is now Cochin-China and also the greater part of present-day Siam (Fig. 58). There were many wars for supremacy, as a result of which Chen-la became predominant during the sixth century (Fig. 59). Between 600 and 800 A.D., periods of confusion alternated with periods of stability and prosperity. Hsuan-tsang, a Chinese Buddhist pilgrim of the seventh century, describes the Cambodia of his day as bounded on the east by Champa and on the west by the Mon kingdom of Dvaravati.

The Cambodian kingdom reached the zenith of its power during the four centuries 800–1200, when it comprised both the Mekong and Menam basins as far north as the neighbourhood of Luang Prabang; its real frontiers were the mountains east of the Mekong and the ranges which separate Siam from Burma. In this period were erected the great buildings for which Cambodia is famous. King Indravarman (877–99) began the building of the city of Angkor, and it was completed by his son Yasovarman. In the centre of it was the temple of Bayon, the ruins of which still remain; outside the walls was Angkor Wat, well known for its three great towers and magnificent approaches. The state cult was the worship of Siva; as present in the Bayon temple, his title was the 'king-god' or 'the god who is the kingdom'. The religion of this 'king-god' was closely bound up with the monarchy, and its high priesthood was hereditary in a family whose power was second only to that of the kings themselves. Sivaism, however, was not an exclusive religion; other Hindu deities were worshipped, as also were gods and spirits of native Khmer origin, and Mahayana Buddhism flourished in addition. Buddhism gradually gained ground at the expense of Sivaism; the caste system and brahmanic ascendancy were weakened in being transplanted from India to a different social environment and failed to take firm hold on the Khmer people (see p. 154).

Towards the end of the thirteenth century, an embassy from the Yuan or Mongol dynasty of China was sent to Cambodia, and we have an account of the country from a certain Chou Ta-kuan, a member of the embassy. Angkor was then still the capital and the reigning king was Srindravarman, who had usurped the throne. Chou Ta-kuan gives a vivid picture of this monarch and of the pomp of Cambodian royalty in his day. The king wore a coat of mail as a precaution against sudden assassination, and when he left his palace he was always escorted, not only by a large force of cavalry and soldiers on elephants, but also by a band of girls of the palace, armed with shields and spears, who formed his personal bodyguard. All the royal princes and ministers went on ahead of the king in these processions; the king himself rode on an elephant holding in his hand a golden sword, the emblem of the royal power. There was an abundance of gold and silver in the trappings of the elephants and horses, and huge parasols embroidered with gold were a principal feature of the *cortège*. Despite all this magnificence, however, the Chinese chronicles make it clear that the Cambodian kingdom was at that time being hard pressed by the Thai and was already in decline.

Relations of Cambodia with the Thai and its Decline as an Independent State

The southward movement of Thai tribes from the highlands of what is now Yunnan had begun in the twelfth century and seems to have been a sequel to the extension of Chinese settlement in the territory of the former kingdom of Nan Chao, which had been a Thai state with its capital at Talifu. The movement was accelerated by the invasion of the Mongols, who captured Talifu in 1254. The Thai stock spread both to the west and south; the three peoples known as Laotians, Siamese and Shans are in reality branches of the same stock and speak dialects of one language. The main difference is that, whereas the Laotians and Shans continued to inhabit highland valleys and remained split up politically into numerous small principalities, the Siamese, having overrun the broad plain of the Menam, formed a large and powerful kingdom, which was soon able to challenge

Cambodia on equal terms. This Siamese kingdom had its first capital at Sukhothai in the upper Menam basin; about 1300 it extended eastward to, and beyond, the Mekong, westward to Pegu in Burma, and southward to the Gulf of Siam. It had thus cut away from Cambodia the latter's loosely held outer belt of territory consisting of petty vassal kingdoms (all probably of Mon-Khmer speech) on the Menam and along the Mekong north of Pakse, and all these lands were settled by Thai and became predominantly Thai-speaking.

The kingdom of Siam was from the beginning in conflict with Cambodia and the latter was irreparably weakened by a long series of wars which began towards the end of the thirteenth century. The Siamese repeatedly invaded Cambodia and captured Angkor in 1313, 1351, 1420 and 1473. They did not succeed in permanently occupying or subduing the country, but the ravages of war changed the whole character of Khmer life and institutions. The great city of Angkor, four times put to the sack, was abandoned to be overgrown by the jungle, and the capital was transferred, first to Lovek and later on to Phnom Penh, where it remains. Great social changes occurred; the old aristocracy and priesthood with their Sanskrit culture and Sivaite state religion lost their power owing to the slaughter and the loss of their revenues, and the Khmer people, who survived the collapse of the Indian superstructure, emerged with a simpler and poorer, but less 'colonial', culture. The kings began to use Khmer instead of Sanskrit names, and the Khmer language, previously consigned to a humble role in official and literary use, came more and more into its own. At the same time Hinayana Buddhism, spreading from Siam, became the national religion, superseding Sivaism and Mahayana Buddhism, whose cults were bound up with the old aristocracy. The reception of this religion in Cambodia did not at all imply a submission to the temporal power of Siam; on the contrary, it seems to have been the new faith which knit the Khmers together and enabled them to maintain their national existence after the ruin of their former empire.

The Cambodian monarchy has had a continuous life down to the present day, though it sank into a condition of vassalage to Siam or Annam (or both) before it finally became a protectorate of France.

THE KINGDOM OF CHAMPA (Figs 58–61)

Champa was a considerable kingdom from about A.D. 200 to 1470, though it could not rival Cambodia either in size or wealth. It had much closer contacts with China than Cambodia had, and Chinese

armies twice successfully invaded it—once in 446 and again in 605—
but did not make any lasting conquest. Champa was often at war
with Cambodia, and there were several Khmer invasions which finally
led to Champa becoming a province of Cambodia for a time early in
the thirteenth century. The real threat to Champa, however, did not
come either from China or Cambodia; what was ultimately fatal to
the Cham was the rise of the independent and aggressive Annamite
kingdom in Tonkin.

In their struggle against the Annamites the Cham in the end
ceased to exist as a separate political entity. After a disastrous war,
Champa had to cede about a third of its territory to Dai-co-viet
in 1402. The pressure on Champa was relieved for a time by a
Chinese intervention in Dai-co-viet and the Cham were able to
recover their lost provinces, but in 1470 they were defeated even
more severely than before and their kingdom was reduced to the
coastline and hinterland between Cap Varella and the Mekong delta,
where it still appears on European maps of the sixteenth and seventeenth centuries. The line of nominal Cham kings continued until
1822, but the monarchy gradually lost all semblance of sovereignty
and its territory was absorbed in the eighteenth century by the
southern Annamite state called Cochin-China. The Cham still exist
as a distinct people (see p. 145), though their numbers are small and
dispersed among Annamites and Khmers in such a way that they can
hardly be counted as a nationality in the modern sense.

EARLY EUROPEAN INFLUENCE

PORTUGUESE INFLUENCE

The merchants and missionaries of Portugal and, to a very much less
extent, of Spain, were the first Europeans to make contact with Indo-
China. At the beginning of the sixteenth century, the Portuguese had
captured Malacca and made it the base for their activities in Far
Eastern seas; in 1517 they sailed along the coast of Annam, and from
about 1540 carried on trade with this region. In 1546 the Portuguese
poet, Camoens, suffered shipwreck off the mouth of the Mekong and
place names of Indo-China figure in the *Lusiads*. In addition to its
traders, Portugal was also soon represented in Indo-China by
Catholic missionaries and by soldiers of fortune, the latter including
Spaniards from the Philippines, as well as Portuguese. Portuguese
Dominicans were established in Cambodia from 1553 and maintained

close relations with the secular adventurers from Europe whose military abilities gave them great influence at the Cambodian court. One of the latter was Diego Belloso, who married a princess of the royal house and, in company with a Spaniard named Blas Ruiz de Hernan Gonzales, persuaded King Sotha I of Cambodia to seek the aid of the Spanish governor of the Philippines against the aggressions of Siam. After long negotiations in which Diego and Blas Ruiz acted as a Cambodian embassy in Manila, a force was sent from the Philippines, but in the meantime the Siamese had captured Lovek, the capital, Sotha I had fled to Laos, and the throne of Cambodia had been seized by a usurper. Diego and Blas Ruiz made an adventurous journey into Laos to look for the exiled king; he died before they could find him, but they brought back his son, Pona Tan, and set him on the throne, subsequently receiving rich rewards for their intervention. Their influence over the new monarch, however, aroused the jealousy of a company of Malay and Japanese mercenaries who had also entered Pona Tan's service and they were both killed in a palace mutiny (1598).

In the seventeenth century, two other European nations, namely, the Dutch and the French, appeared on the scene in Indo-China and challenged the influence of the Portuguese.

DUTCH INFLUENCE

The Dutch arrived to trade in Cambodia in 1602, but the Portuguese stirred up the Khmers against them and they were at first ill received; later, they established a trading post at Phnom Penh and competed with the Portuguese for influence at court. This rivalry resulted in a victory for the Portuguese in 1637, when the Khmers accused the Dutch of espionage on behalf of Siam and seized a Dutch ship by way of reprisal; relations between Cambodia and the Dutch became still worse a few years later when all the Dutch residing in Phnom Penh were massacred or imprisoned on the king's orders. Cambodia was not very vulnerable to Dutch sea power, since its capital lay far inland and the Dutch East India Company did not care to waste men and money on continental conquests. The threat of an alliance with Siam, however, was sufficient to induce Cambodia to make reparation for the outrage and commercial relations were restored. Subsequently, Cambodia receded into the background as a goal of maritime trading enterprise, as the Mekong delta fell into the hands of the Annamites of Cochin-China.

In Annam, trade centred on the port of Tourane, where, as in Cambodia, the Dutch and Portuguese entered into competition, though without the complications which occurred in Cambodia; the Nguyen princes of the seventeenth century knew how to hold the balance between the rival merchant groups and made use of them as suppliers of arms for the struggle with the powerful Trinh family who held sway over the northern part of the Annamite empire.

FRENCH INFLUENCE

The early French influence in the Far East was, for the most part, religious. French missionary activity was from the first directed principally towards Annam and not Cambodia; the pioneers of

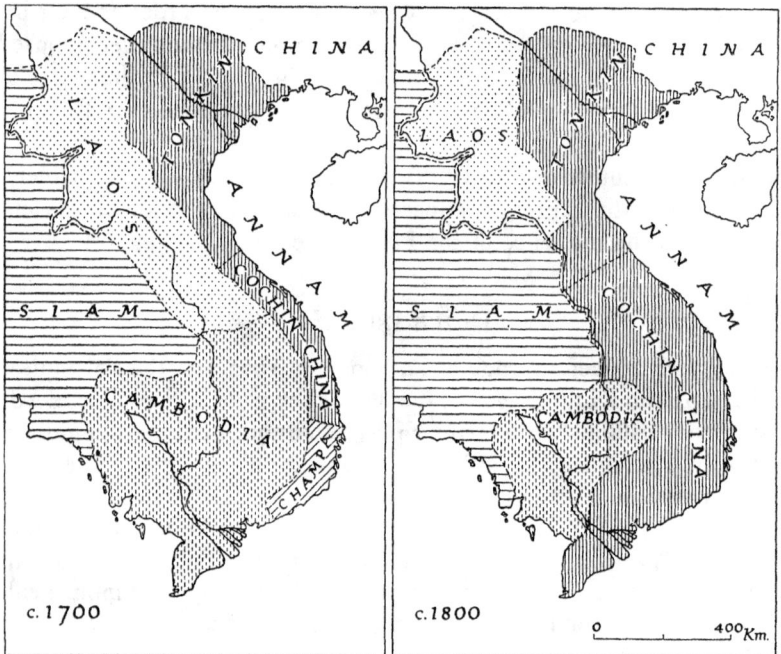

Fig. 61. Indo-China in the late seventeenth century and beginning of the nineteenth century

Source: A. Hermann, *Historical and Commercial Atlas of China*, p. 59 (Cambridge, Mass. 1935).

Catholicism in Annam had been a band of Jesuits, mostly Portuguese and Italians, but including one notable Frenchman, Alexandre de Rhodes, who went to Rome to obtain the appointment of bishops for the new Church. This raised the question of the Portuguese ecclesiastical jurisdiction in the Far East; Portugal held the sees of Malacca and Macao and was opposed to the creation of new bishoprics which would infringe her spiritual monopoly. French interest in the question, however, had now been aroused, and in 1658 the Pope appointed two Frenchmen as bishops *in partibus infidelium* for the Far Eastern mission field; they installed themselves in Siam and French missions, principally organized by the newly founded *Société des Missions étrangères*, were established both in Tonkin and in Cochin-China.

In the latter half of the seventeenth century, the French missionaries in Indo-China combined religion with commercial activities. Trading stations were set up in Tonkin, but, owing to inadequate financial resources and to hostility from the Dutch, they proved abortive. Although further attempts were made to open Indo-China to French commerce, as, for example, the expedition of Pierre Poivre in 1749, all ended in failure. During the course of the eighteenth century, the Annamites became increasingly prejudiced against European traders, while this commercial animosity was paralleled by an increasing hostility against Catholicism. Outbursts of persecution were frequent, particularly in Cochin-China, so that in the third quarter of the eighteenth century no mission work could be carried on, except in the outlying provinces away from the capital. Among the priests of the *Missions étrangères* was one Pigneau de Behaine, who arrived in 1767 in the district of Ha Tien at the farthest south-western extremity of the Annamite kingdom. It was this Pigneau de Behaine who was destined to lay the foundations of the French colonial empire in Indo-China.

FRENCH PENETRATION AND CONQUEST

PIGNEAU DE BEHAINE AND THE ESTABLISHMENT OF THE ANNAMITE EMPIRE UNDER GIA LONG (1777–1820)

Since the partition of the old Dai-co-viet or Annam in 1673 into the two states of Tonkin and Cochin-China, the latter had greatly extended its territory to the south. The remnant of Champa had been absorbed, and in 1701, after a campaign against Cambodia, the forces of Cochin-China remained in possession of the Mekong delta and the area around Saigon (Fig. 61). This was no mere military occupation, for the whole region was quickly settled by Annamites who reclaimed marshland left uncultivated by the Khmers. Thus, the territory which now forms the French colony of Cochin-China became preponderantly Annamite, and Cambodia was cut off from the sea, except for a short seaboard on the Gulf of Siam.

It was in the Ha Tien neighbourhood, which marked the farthest limit of the Annamite expansion, that Nguyen Anh, the legitimate heir to the throne of Cochin-China, took refuge in 1777 after a dynastic quarrel in the course of which most of his near relatives had been massacred. Hiding in the jungle near Ha Tien, the young Nguyen was supplied with food and also with good advice by Pigneau de Behaine. Meanwhile the Tay Son family, who had usurped the power in Cochin-China, accepted the suzerainty of the Trinh over Tonkin in order to get their support in any future hostilities with the Nguyen. After 1782, however, the house of Trinh was itself torn by an internal feud, and the Tay Son, turning their arms northward, captured Hanoi in 1786 and added Tonkin to their territory. The last Le emperor fled to China and died at Peking seven years later.

After the fall of Hanoi and the flight of the emperor, the Tay Son family determined to make an end of Nguyen Anh, who had gathered an army soon after his original flight and had been carrying on war locally ever since. Nguyen Anh soon received a very effective reinforcement, for in 1784 he had confided his son Canh, aged five, to the care of Pigneau de Behaine and had appealed to the latter to seek for him the protection of the king of France. The missionary took back the child prince with him to France and made himself the advocate of the Nguyen cause in the highest social and official circles, arousing sympathy for the forlorn infant while he strove to point out what advantages would accrue to France from a restoration of the legitimate ruler of Cochin-China under French auspices. Opinion at Versailles was divided; one party was in favour of a project which might bring compensation for the defeat of French designs in India, while another considered it foolish and dangerous. Finally, a treaty was signed in the name of Nguyen Anh, and Pigneau de Behaine was appointed French commissioner in Cochin-China; he was further given a letter of instructions to Conway, commander of the French troops in India, but, with an inconsistency appropriate to the government of Louis XVI on the eve of the Revolution, a letter was at the same time sent to Conway giving him full discretion to act as he thought fit. When, therefore, Behaine arrived at Pondicherry, he met with nothing but obstruction from Conway, but by sheer persistence he managed at last to recruit a force under French officers with which he landed in Cochin-China in July 1789. Thus, the same month memorable in French and European history for the fall of the Bastille saw also on the farther side of Asia French soldiers led by a Catholic bishop marching through a tropical jungle to risk their lives in the strife of two Annamite factions.

The war against the Tay Son was long and bitter, and before it was over Behaine, who acted virtually as prime minister to Nguyen Anh, fell ill and died. But victory rested with the Nguyen army; Hue was captured in 1801 and Hanoi in the following year. Nguyen Anh thus united all the Annamite lands under his rule (Fig. 61) and proclaimed himself emperor at Hue, taking the reign title of Gia Long (1802). After twenty-seven years of exile and struggle he had raised the fortunes of his family to a height to which his ancestors had never aspired, and his descendants have ever since reigned in Hue as emperors of Annam.

In order fully to consolidate his position, Gia Long sought and obtained investiture as a tributary ruler from the emperor of China. It was this tributary relation which later on involved complications between China and France when the French tried to establish a protectorate over Annam. It was a relation between states not admitted in modern Western international law, for China repudiated responsibility for the acts of her vassal kingdoms, but claimed a vague right of intervention in their affairs which was incompatible either with their full sovereignty or with the protection of them by European nations. In the early part of the nineteenth century, however, this question did not arise, for Annam had no formal relation of subordination to France, and even French influence virtually disappeared after the death of Gia Long in 1820.

Decline in French Influence (1820–57)

Although Gia Long showed gratitude for the aid he had received, his son and successor, Minh Mang, began to manifest suspicion and dislike both towards the European traders and towards the Catholic missionaries in the country. The Confucian *literati* of Annam—for Confucianism, as part of Chinese civilization, played the part of a state religion—were increasingly resentful at the propagation of Christianity, and in this attitude they were doubtless influenced by the anti-Christian sentiment prevalent in contemporary China. A regular persecution of the missionaries and their converts soon broke out and continued until 1857.

The persecution of religion was used by the French as a pretext for opening up trade by force and for the later occupation of the peninsula. During the reign of Minh Mang's successor (1841–7), the French naval squadron in the China Seas twice appeared off Tourane, the port of Hue, with demands for the release of French missionaries who had been condemned to death. Despite this action, persecution was intensified, and in 1855 and 1857 diplomatic protests were sent to Hue by Napoleon III through M. de Montigny, the French Consul in Siam and Cambodia. Montigny demanded religious liberty for Christians and the opening of Hue to French trade, but these remonstrances had no effect. The refusal of Chinese demands and the turn of events in China led Napoleon III to take coercive action.

CONQUEST OF COCHIN-CHINA (1858–67)

As the Treaty of Tientsin (1858), which ended the two years' war between France and Britain on the one hand, and China on the other, provided among other things for the tolerance of Christianity, it was not likely that Annam would long be allowed a freedom to persecute that had been renounced by China—the less so as part of the expeditionary force which had fought in China was now available for the coercion of Annam. A French naval squadron, under Rear-Admiral Rigault de Genouilly, arrived before Tourane at the end of August 1858. It was accompanied by a Spanish warship, for Spain also was interested in the fate of Catholic missions in Indo-China on account of the share of the Spanish Dominicans of Manila in the evangelization of Tonkin. The European fleet soon reduced the forts of Tourane and troops were landed, but owing to lack of supplies the expedition was unable to advance inland; the attack, therefore, was shifted south to Saigon, which was a rice granary for the whole of Annam.

The French naval forces which had bombarded Tourane, captured Saigon in February 1859 and, after a period of indecisive fighting, in the course of which a Franco-Spanish garrison was besieged in Saigon by an Annamite army, reinforcements under Admiral Charner arrived and overran a large area up to the borders of Cambodia. The emperor of Annam now sued for peace, and Admiral Bonard, who had been left in charge of the French forces, signed a treaty by which the three eastern provinces of Cochin-China—Bien Hoa, Gia Dinh and My Tho—were ceded to France (June 1862). The treaty was sent back to France for Napoleon III to ratify and he gave his consent to it, but there was no lack of opposition both from those who disliked all distant colonial commitments and from those who wished to concentrate the energies of the Second Empire on the expedition to Mexico. Spain made no attempt to acquire territory in Indo-China, and France might have given up the ceded provinces when Annam, soon after the cession, offered to buy them back for a large sum of money, but the Minister of Marine, the Comte de Chasseloup-Laubat, fought for their retention and got his way against the opinion of the majority of his colleagues in the government, the Hue court having meanwhile spoilt its chances of success by haggling over the price.

As a result of the treaty of 1862, the three western provinces of Cochin-China—Ha Tien, Chau Doc and Vinh Long—were virtually cut off from the main body of Annam. These detached provinces became irredentist centres, and in order to prevent trouble, Admiral Lagrandière, the successor to Bonard, annexed them in 1867, thus completing the territorial formation of the French colony of Cochin-China as it exists to-day.

EXTENSION OF FRENCH POWER INTO CAMBODIA (1863–4)

A few years before the annexation of western Cochin-China, French power had been extended into Cambodia. This state had in course of time declined further and further from its ancient grandeur until it had been reduced to a condition of vassalage both to Siam and Annam, who were rivals for suzerainty over it during the first half of the nineteenth century. The defeat of Annam at the hands of the French had more or less eliminated the Annamite ascendancy, but the power of Siam remained unbroken. The Khmers had already at the time of the French campaign in Cochin-China shown themselves friendly to the French, whom they regarded as possible allies against their Siamese and Annamite oppressors. So when in 1863 Admiral Lagrandière went to Oudon, the Cambodian capital, and opened negotiations with the aid of Mgr. Miche, the Vicar Apostolic, he obtained the king's signature to a protectorate treaty which was immediately despatched to Paris for ratification. The ratification, however, was held up by the French Ministry of Foreign Affairs, which was unwilling to offend Siam, so the king of Cambodia, terrified at having incurred the wrath of Bangkok without assurance of French support, hastened to sign a treaty with Siam by which he renounced the title of king and accepted that of Siamese viceroy. Pending the decision in Paris, a French naval detachment then advanced to Oudon; meanwhile, the protectorate treaty was at last ratified in France and Lagrandière took steps to reinforce it. At the coronation of the Cambodian king, Norodom, on 3 June 1864, the representative of Siam claimed the right to place the crown on the king's head, but it was the French representative who did so, and this symbolic act marked the end of Siamese control over Cambodia.

The French encroachment into Cambodia was deeply resented in Siam, and the French Foreign Ministry concluded a treaty with Bangkok, whereby Siam formally renounced her suzerainty over Cambodia, but received in compensation the two Cambodian provinces of Angkor and Battambang which, although still nominally Cambodian territory, had been under Siamese occupation since 1795. Neither the French governor of Cochin-China nor the king of Cambodia were consulted in this arrangement, a procedure typical of the lack of co-ordination at that time between French foreign policy and the local activities of French empire-builders.

EXPLORATION OF THE MEKONG (1866–7)

With the conquest of Cochin-China and Cambodia, the French controlled all the rich lands of the lower Mekong, but the hinterland to the north remained more or less unknown to them; in particular, the flood of the Mekong, flowing out of an unmapped country, presented a challenge to French scientific and commercial enterprise. In June 1866, an expedition to explore the middle and upper reaches of the Mekong was sent out from Saigon under Doudart de Lagrée, with Francis Garnier, a young naval lieutenant, destined to play an important part in the conquest of Tonkin, as second in command; it reached the borders of China, then crossed to the Yangtse, finally returning by way of Shanghai after two years of exploration. Enough information was gained by this effort to show that the rapids of the middle Mekong rendered it useless as an avenue of commercial approach to China, but that there were better prospects of access by the Fleuve Rouge (Red River).

CONQUEST OF TONKIN AND ANNAM (1867–85)

Since the exploration of the Mekong by Lagrée and Garnier in 1866–7 had demonstrated the impracticability of commercial intercourse by this river with the southern provinces of China, French interest now became focused on Tonkin. In 1873, Jean Dupuis, a merchant from Canton, travelled up the Fleuve Rouge and arranged to transport goods, especially arms, to Yunnan. Although the Annamites agreed to this trade, they nevertheless confiscated certain of the French goods and, as internal strife threatened to disrupt commerce altogether, Francis Garnier was sent to Tonkin in November 1873 with an escort of 188 French and 24 Annamite soldiers to negotiate about navigation on the Fleuve Rouge. Meeting with hostility from the Annamites, Garnier attacked and captured the citadel of Hanoi, as well as the other leading cities in the Tonkin delta. A short time after this successful exploit, Garnier was killed in an ambush by the Black Flags, a band of Chinese marauders, and his policy of placing the whole of Tonkin under French administration was delayed for several years.

Opinion in France at this time was not favourable to military adventures, and the governor of Cochin-China was ordered to desist from operations in Tonkin and obtain the right of navigation on the Fleuve Rouge by purely diplomatic means. A treaty with Annam opening the river was signed at Saigon in 1874, but the piracies of the Black Flags nullified the concession in practice, and in 1882 it was decided to make a fresh military advance into Tonkin. The expeditionary force, under Commandant Henri Rivière, occupied Hanoi, and, when the Annamites attempted to retake it in the following year, an expedition under Admiral Courbet threatened to bombard Hue. Under this pressure Annam capitulated, accepted a French protectorate for itself, and undertook to withdraw its troops from Tonkin, which was to be placed under French administration.

The surrender of Annam did not dispose of the Black Flags or the Chinese troops in Tonkin, who declined to acknowledge French authority and continued to resist. Chinese local opposition was involved in a larger diplomatic conflict between France and China. In the treaty of 1874 France had recognized the complete independence of Annam vis-à-vis every foreign power and had promised to defend Annam against any aggression, in return for which the emperor of Annam undertook to 'conform his foreign policy to that of France and to change nothing in his present diplomatic relations'. The French regarded this treaty as terminating Annam's relation of vassalage to China, but the Annamites and the Chinese held that the relation remained unaffected and Annam continued to send envoys with tribute to Peking once every two years. When the French invaded Tonkin for the second time in 1882, the Chinese Minister in

Paris lodged a vigorous protest with the French government and demanded the withdrawal of the expeditionary forces. After protracted negotiations, however, the Chinese government on 11 May 1884, signed the Convention of Tientsin, agreeing to withdraw all Chinese troops from Tonkin and 'to respect in the present and the future the treaties concluded or to be concluded between France and the Court of Hue'.

France had now in fact gained her end as far as suzerainty over Annam was concerned, but the Convention of 11 May did not close the conflict with China. A dispute arose as to the time limit for the evacuation of the Chinese troops from Tonkin and a clash occurred between French and Chinese forces at Lang Son at the end of June. The French government, of which Jules Ferry was Prime Minister, now addressed to China an ultimatum demanding payment of indemnity for the Lang Son incident; this was refused by China on the ground that the French had been the aggressors. The French fleet thereupon began hostilities against China. Ferry, however, avoided a declaration of war and asserted that France remained in a state 'not of declared war, but of reprisals, always ready to reopen negotiations'. The war dragged on for nine months and the French were unable to achieve any decisive result, owing to the weakness of their military forces in the Far East; moreover, the naval operations aroused the resentment of other Western powers because of the interruptions of trade which they caused. The military and diplomatic situation became so unfavourable that Ferry beat a political retreat, abandoned the demand for an indemnity, and tried to end the war by an agreement which, in effect, merely confirmed the Convention of Tientsin. The final treaty with China was signed on 9 June 1885.

By 1885, France held Cochin-China as a colony under full sovereignty and Tonkin and the residue of Annam—to which henceforth the name of Annam was restricted—as protectorates. From the first, however, the French administration of Tonkin was virtually direct, and in 1897 the Annamite viceroyalty there was suppressed. In Annam itself the emperor and his officials continued to govern under the supervision of a French Resident and French advisers.

ACQUISITION OF LAOS (1893)

The French conquest of Indo-China was completed by acquisition of the territory which is now included in the protectorate of Laos. In the valley of the middle Mekong and adjoining plateaux a number of petty principalities had long fluctuated in a loose allegiance between Annam and Siam. Since the defeat of Annam by France had entirely destroyed the prestige of the Annamite monarchy, the Siamese were left with a clear field in Laos, and they even threatened to advance to the sea at Vinh. In 1893, however, France laid claim to the entire left bank of the Mekong and French troops were sent to expel Siamese outposts established east of the river, while warships were despatched to threaten Bangkok. Siam submitted and signed a treaty renouncing all claims to territory east of the Mekong or to islands in the river. Laos was thus added to Cochin-China, Annam, Tonkin and Cambodia as a fifth constituent of the 'Union of Indo-China'; it was organized as a protectorate with a resident-general at Vientiane, but was in fact brought under direct administration, except for the kingdom of Luang Prabang in the extreme north, which had been the largest and strongest of the former states.

POLITICAL HISTORY SINCE THE FRENCH CONQUEST*

INTERNAL POLITICAL DEVELOPMENT

By the close of the nineteenth century the French had completed their conquest in Indo-China and created a unified country (Fig. 62) with a governor-general supreme over the governor of Cochin-China and the residents-general of Tonkin, Annam, Cambodia, and Laos. For the subsequent administrative development of Indo-China, see pp. 189–92; it suffices here to say that Indo-China became one of the battlefields for the contest between rival schools of colonial policy and served to some extent as a laboratory for methods which were afterwards applied in other parts of the French colonial empire.

The Annamites, Khmers and other native peoples have been in the main the passive subjects of their rulers' programmes and experiments. A nationalist movement has, however, developed among the Annamites—to a much lesser extent among the Khmers—with claims for autonomy and even complete independence. This movement did not arise so much among the ruling classes in Annam and Cambodia, who had gradually adjusted themselves to French control, but rather among the new 'westernized' class produced by French education. It was stimulated first by the victory of Japan over Russia

* An account of economic affairs since the French conquest is given in chapters XI (Agriculture), XIII (Industry) and XV (Commerce).

in 1905—which showed that an Asiatic people could prevail over a
European—and secondly, by the Chinese Revolution, especially in
its later 'anti-imperialist' Kuomintang phase from 1920 onwards.
The 'Young Annamite' nationalism inspired by the Chinese example was democratic and republican in outlook, sometimes with

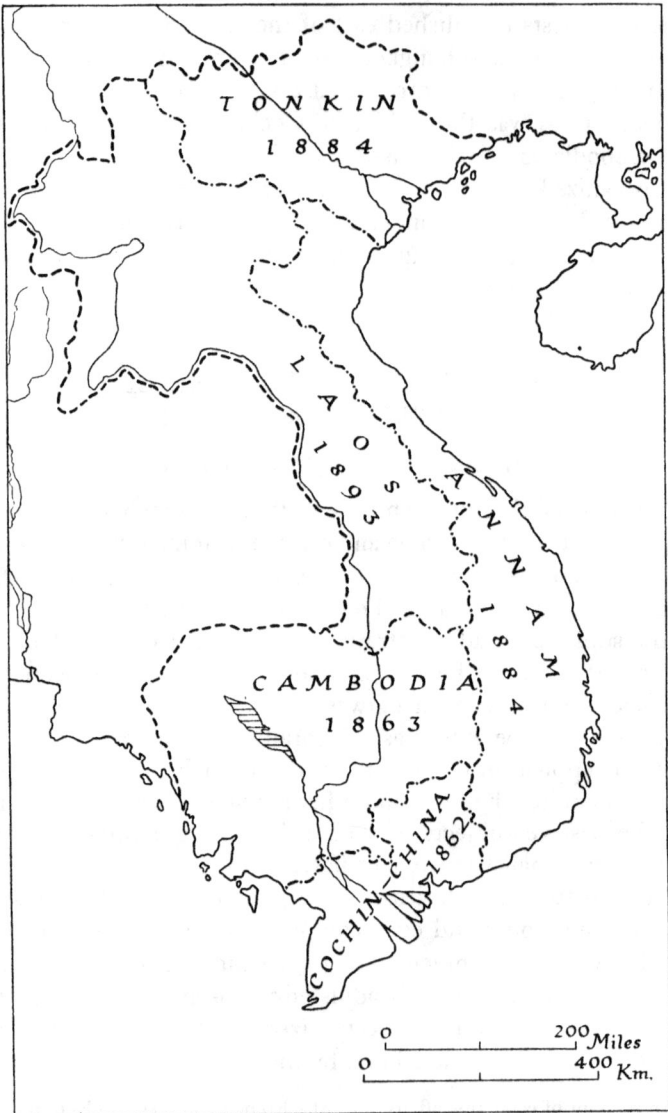

Fig. 62. French acquisition of Indo-China in the nineteenth century

Communist leanings, and was encouraged by 'left' influences emanating from France itself; it took root both in Cochin-China and Tonkin. In Annam national sentiment still tended to centre round the old monarchy, and independent Siam was a more acceptable model for progress. Neither agitation for democratic self-government nor schemes for reviving the imperial power in Hue had had any appreciable effect on the structure of French rule down to the time of the European collapse of France in 1940. A revolutionary outgrowth of the nationalist movement which led to serious disturbances in 1930–1 was rigorously suppressed and French authority was never seriously endangered.

FOREIGN RELATIONS

Relations with Siam and Burma

The external history of Indo-China for a long time turned mainly on its frontier relations with its three continental neighbours—Siam, Burma (in the Shan States) and China. Conflict with Siam was not terminated by the latter's capitulation in 1893. The treaty in this year provided that the French should occupy Chantaboun as a guarantee of execution; they did not evacuate it until 1904 and then occupied the district of Krat instead. Endless wrangles took place over the application of the treaty of 1893, and France used the military occupation of Siamese territory to obtain successive rectifications of the frontier at Siam's expense. Frontier delimitations in 1902 and 1904 both added to the territory of Indo-China areas west of the Mekong, and in 1907, in return for the evacuation of Krat, Siam finally ceded the former Cambodian provinces of Angkor and Battambang which France had relinquished to Siam in 1867. This cession was naturally popular in Cambodia, as it reunited the Cambodian realm as it had existed in the eighteenth century (including the ruins of Angkor Thom), but the exaction provoked the lasting resentment of the Siamese, so that Siamese 'revisionism', after lying dormant for 33 years, suddenly emerged when opportunity beckoned in 1940.

In the disputes of France with Siam, Britain was always concerned as a watchful third party. Although Britain had not obstructed the expansion of French power in Indo-China, it was her policy to check any enlargement of the French sphere westward in the direction of India. Alarm at the strength of French influence in Mandalay, consequent on the French conquest of Tonkin, was one of the principal motives for the undertaking of the Third Burmese War in 1885. Eight years later, the French naval demonstration in front of Bangkok led to considerable tension between France and Britain, as it was suspected in London that France intended to establish some kind of protectorate over Siam. British policy for the security of the Indian Empire required the maintenance of Siam as an independent buffer state in the east, corresponding to Afghanistan in the north-west. France did not in fact directly challenge this British interest, and so Siam remained a sovereign state, while her sister kingdoms of south-eastern Asia, Burma and Annam fell under European rule.

In 1896, France and Britain concluded an agreement defining most of Siam as a neutral zone into which each power undertook not to send any troops or to seek exclusive privileges. The pact was not applicable to the north of Siam, and this wild mountainous area, which had been a wedge of Burmese suzerainty over numerous petty Shan principalities reaching eastward to Laos, became British territory after the annexation of Burma. As the Shan States were too small to stand by themselves as a buffer, it was necessary to fix a frontier between the British and French empires, which proved a matter of some difficulty owing to uncertainties of earlier allegiance and claims advanced by Siam and China as well as by Britain and France; however, the problem was in the end solved by taking the Mekong as the border between British Burma and French Laos. All questions in dispute became easy to deal with after the period of Anglo-French colonial rivalry, which had lasted through the eighties and nineties of the nineteenth century, was succeeded by the Entente of 1904; from then, until the epoch of Vichy 'collaboration' with Japan in Indo-China in 1940, there was no noteworthy clash of British and French policies in the Far East.

Relations with China

By her control of Tonkin and Laos, France had acquired contiguity with the Chinese provinces of Yunnan and Kwangsi and with a corner of Kwangtung. In 1899, the small territory of Kwang Chow Wan, part of Kwangtung, was leased to France by the Chinese for a period of 99 years (see App. X). Apart from minor adjustments, there was no important frontier issue with China after 1885, but questions of some magnitude for French foreign policy arose with respect to communications across the frontier. The idea of tapping the trade of China's hinterland through Tonkin, which had inspired the French empire builders in Indo-China in the days of Lagrée and Garnier, persisted for a long time in spite of many disappointments. There had indeed always been some trade from Tonkin with Yunnan up the Fleuve Rouge and with Kwangsi via Lang Son and Lungchow. The Fleuve Rouge, however, was not navigable except for light craft above Lao Kay and there was no river route into Kwangsi.

Hopes revived for the extension of French trade with Yunnan when the era of railway construction (or, at least, concessions for railway construction) in China suddenly began after the Sino-Japanese war of 1894–5. At the conclusion of hostilities in 1895, China had to borrow money in order to pay her indemnity to Japan, and was at the same time anxious to have railways built as a means of emerging from her economic and military weakness. France took the opportunity of negotiations for a loan to obtain from China an agreement for the continuation on Chinese territory of railways built or projected in Indo-China and for a priority for mining concessions in Yunnan, Kwangsi and Kwangtung. At this time it was widely believed that China was about to disintegrate and might at any time be partitioned by the European Great Powers: France, working diplomatically in close co-operation with Russia, aimed at staking out for herself a 'sphere of influence' in that part of China adjacent to Indo-China. Closely connected with this political design was a scheme for a railway to the Yangtse which would divert the trade, not only of Yunnan and Kwangsi, but also of Kweichow and Szechwan, from Shanghai and Hong Kong. In the end a railway was actually built from Haiphong to Yunnanfou (Kunming); it was completed in 1910 at the cost of a large capital outlay and the death of tens of thousands of labourers from malaria. This line tapped the trade only of the then relatively poor and undeveloped province of Yunnan; engineering difficulties and uncertainty as to the future halted the railway at Kunming, and no attempt was made to prolong it to the Yangtse until 1940, when the Chinese government, having withdrawn to Chungking and lost contact with the outer world through its own ports, was trying to open up new lines of communication from Szechwan to the south. By one of the ironies of history, a Franco-Chinese agreement was about to give reality to this old dream of the French pioneers in the Far East when events in Europe placed Indo-China at the mercy of Japan.

Relations with Japan

From the time when France composed her colonial quarrels with Britain in order to make common cause with her in Europe, she had little reason for concern about the external security of Indo-China. China was too weak to be a threat, the British navy assured protection by sea, and Japan was until 1921 Britain's ally. The war of 1914–18 did not come near Indo-China, except for one or two appearances of German commerce raiders in neighbouring seas. The clouds of a new storm began to gather over the coasts of Annam when in 1938 the the armed forces of Japan, in the course of their undeclared war against China, moved to the south-west from Japan's outpost in Formosa and the Pescadores, first capturing Canton and then landing on the island of Hainan, lying athwart the great bend of the Gulf of Tonkin. This step was a prelude to Japanese aggressive action in Indo-China two years later and to the occupation of the country in 1941.*

BIBLIOGRAPHICAL NOTE

(1) There is no book in English dealing with the early history of Indo-China. Among the most useful French works on this subject are Sylvain Levi, *Indochine*, vol. I, Exposition Coloniale Internationale, Paris, 1931 (Paris, 1931) and Georges Maspero, *Un Empire Colonial français: l'Indochine*, 2 vols. (Paris, 1929 and 1930).

(2) For the history of the separate states the following books are recommended: E. Aymonier, *Le Cambodge*, vol. III (Paris, 1904). Georges Maspero, *L'Empire khmer* (Phnom Penh, 1904). Georges Maspero, *Le Royaume de Champa* (Paris, 1928). C. B. Maybon, *Histoire moderne du Pays d'Annam* (1597–1820) (Paris, 1920). A. Pavie, *Recherches sur l'Histoire du Cambodge, du Laos, et du Siam*, vol. II (Paris, 1898).

(3) For the French conquest of Indo-China and recent political history see: T. E. Ennis, *French Policy and Developments in Indochina* (Chicago, 1936). G. Hanotaux (ed.), *Histoire des Colonies françaises*, vol. v (Paris, 1932). G. Hardy, *Histoire de la Colonisation française* (Paris, 1928). H. B. Morse and H. F. Macnair, *Far Eastern International Relations* (Cambridge, Mass. 1931). S. H. Roberts, *History of French Colonial Policy*, 2 vols. (London, 1927 and 1931). Virginia Thompson, *French Indo-China* (London, 1937). R. Levy, G. Lacam, A. Roth, *French Interests and Policies in the Far East*, Institute of Pacific Relations (New York, 1942).

* For an account of the Japanese invasion and occupation of Indo-China in 1941 see pp. 485–9.

Chapter IX

GOVERNMENT, ADMINISTRATION, AND LAW

Historical Introduction: Federal Government: State Government: Legal System:
Police System: Bibliographical Note

HISTORICAL INTRODUCTION

In Indo-China France has experimented with many different systems
of government. From the conquest of Cochin-China in 1862 to the
formation of the Union of Indo-China in 1887, government policy,
although primarily assimilationist, threatened to destroy the native
administration and to replace it by a wholly French system of
government. This was especially the case under the rule of Admirals
Charner, Bonard and Lagrandière, but when civil governors were
first appointed in 1879 the earlier military regime was modified and
more attention given to indigenous customs. In Cochin-China, Le
Myre de Vilers formed a *Conseil colonial* to serve both French and
native interests; in the dual protectorate of Annam-Tonkin, as it then
was, Paul Bert set up a purely native body known as the *Conseil de
Notables.* Neither of these measures proved successful, because of
opposition from Frenchmen living in the colony and in France itself,
to whom the associative principle or indirect rule was anathema. In
the economic field, an ambitious public works programme could not
be organized, owing partly to lack of co-operation between the newly
acquired territories and partly to inadequate financial support from
the mother country. The first of these difficulties led to the creation
of a political union in 1887 between Annam, Tonkin, Cochin-China
and Cambodia, which, however, in the early years proved to be only a
nominal union since administrative policy remained under the control
of France. Paul Doumer, Governor-General from 1897 to 1902, was
the man destined to form a strongly unified country and at the same
time to give financial stability, hitherto lacking in Indo-China.

During his five years' term of office as Governor-General, Doumer
increased the power of the federal government by curtailing that of
the individual states, particularly Cochin-China, where the over-
riding influence of the *Conseil colonial* was considerably reduced. His
main achievement as an administrator lies in his creation by the decrees of 31 July 1898 and 19 April 1899 of the Indo-Chinese Union as

it exists to-day and in the financial reorganization and economic development of the country. A general budget for the Union and a local budget for each of the states was instituted. Although this progressive fiscal policy placed a heavy burden on the people, it provided the means for economic advancement which gained practical expression in a public works programme, embracing the construction of railways, roads, buildings and irrigation or drainage schemes.

If Doumer's financial policy laid the foundations for economic progress within Indo-China, in the political sphere his adherence to a strict assimilative code injured French authority. This danger was recognized by succeeding administrators, and since 1902 associative rather than assimilative principles have been followed in the government of the country.

Between the departure of Doumer in 1902 and the outbreak of war twelve years later, three men, Beau, Klobukowsky and Sarraut, held the office of Governor-General and each made important administrative changes. As a counter to the over-centralized system of the Doumer regime, Beau (1902–7) partly restored the powers of the mandarinate and created native provincial councils and an advisory chamber in Tonkin. He also improved the facilities for education and extended medical assistance. Klobukowsky (1908–10), though handicapped by disaffection resulting indirectly from the Russian defeat at the hands of the Japanese in 1905, continued the policy of his predecessor, among other things insisting that all government officials should be well versed in a knowledge of the country. The work of Albert Sarraut (1911–14) is outstandingly important in the administrative history of Indo-China, since not only did he greatly extend the principle of indirect rule, but also lightened the strain of heavy taxation imposed by Doumer and carried out a reform of the judicial service. As the number of functionaries was excessively large, in order to economize, Sarraut reduced their number and, following Klobukowsky, sought to enforce a more rigorous training of personnel, while at the same time he admitted natives to certain of the administrative posts previously held only by Frenchmen. In legal matters, the judiciary powers of the native courts were further strengthened and the criminal codes revised.

During the war of 1914–18 there were no important changes in the administrative machine, though the despatch of nearly 140,000 Annamite troops and labourers to Europe had far-reaching repercussions upon political life within the peninsula. The detachment of the natives from their ancestral soil and the events of the war, which tended to dispel the belief in white superiority, gave birth to a feeling of independence and of nationalist ideas. This found expression at a later date in subversive literature and in minor uprisings against French rule.

Since 1918 modifications have been made in the federal and state government on lines projected by Albert Sarraut and in the light of a growing demand for improved native representation. In the early twenties, the native membership of the *Conseil colonial* of Cochin-China was increased from six to ten and the native electorate set on a broader basis; in Tonkin the power of the communes was extended and in Laos provincial assemblies were introduced for the first time. Maurice Long, Governor-General from 1920 to 1922, who carried out these reforms, did little to improve the federal administration. At this period state finance was in a distressing condition because the resources of the federal budget had been drained to subsidize local budgets. Alexander Varenne (1925–8) overcame these fiscal difficulties by rigid economies and fresh taxation. In his tenure of office as head of the state, Varenne also made it possible for Annamites to qualify for administrative posts on equal footing with the French, though there continued to be disparity in the rates of pay.

The associative policy of Long and Varenne was continued by Pierre Pasquier (1928–34) who, unlike all his predecessors in the office of Governor-General, had already spent many years as an official in the colony and had a deep knowledge of its problems. Although Pasquier realized the need to increase the salaries of the Annamite officials, financial economies had to be made to balance a budget hit by the world economic depression of 1930. Competence in the native language was made an essential qualification for all French functionaries, while the *Grand Conseil des Intérêts économiques et financiers* was created to give a wider representation of French and native economic interests. Pasquier's anxiety to help the natives was shown by his support of the 'revolution' which occurred in the Annamite court in 1932–3, on the return of the young emperor, Bao Dai, from a five years' sojourn in France. The emperor of Annam purged the royal cabinet of reactionary elements, modernized various laws and completely separated the administrative and legislative powers.

Administrative changes since the end of the world economic depression in 1935 have been associated with economic rather than political affairs. A public works programme was vigorously pursued despite native discontent which led to an ineffective uprising in parts of north Annam. Labour conditions were improved by a new and comprehensive code promulgated in 1937.

FEDERAL GOVERNMENT

The federal government of Indo-China was organized and given formal shape by the decrees of 17 October 1887, 31 July 1898 and 19 April 1899, which created a political federation, consisting of the colony of Cochin-China, and the protectorates of Annam, Tonkin, Cambodia and Laos.*

Governor-General

The head of the federal administration is the Governor-General, who is appointed by a decree of the Council of Ministers of France. He normally holds office for five years and the seat of residence is at Hanoi. The powers of the French Republic, with certain exceptions, are delegated to the Governor-General; thus, under one man are combined the responsibilities held by the various ministers of state in France. He issues the decrees made by the French Parliament relating to colonial affairs and also has authority to issue decrees of his own motion, subject to the approval of the Ministry of Colonies, a legislative procedure not introduced in British colonial administration. He directs financial matters, supervises the law courts, and all administrative officials are appointed on his recommendation. Not only can he take repressive action against undesirable persons or seditious bodies, but he can also dissolve or suspend the *Conseil colonial* of Cochin-China, the native councils of the protectorates and the municipal councils. Although prohibited from commanding in the field, the Governor-General disposes of the land and sea forces, and is responsible, under the authority of the Ministry of Colonies, for the protection of the country. He represents France in all relations with foreign powers but has no authority to conclude treaties without the sanction of the French parliament.

The Governor-General is assisted by the Secretary-General, the *Cabinet*, the *Conseil de Gouvernement*, the *Grand Conseil des Intérêts économiques et financiers*, and the *Conseil de Défense*. The Secretary-General, who holds the rank of a Chief Resident, acts as direct head of the government. He directs the work of the *Cabinet*, upon which

* The Indo-Chinese Union also includes the small territory of Kwang Chow Wan which was leased from China in 1900 (see Appendix X).

Plate 33. Palace of the Governor-General at Saigon

Plate 34. Royal palace at Phnom Penh

This modern palace, built of concrete, has been the residence of the king of Cambodia since 1919. The style is typically Siamese. It has multiheaded nagas (a snake-cobra capella) at the end of the balustrades in front of the building, pagoda-shaped towers and triangular-shaped roof tops in row formation.

body devolves a large part of the Governor-General's executive functions.

Conseil de Gouvernement

The *Conseil de Gouvernement*, which is a purely consultative body, is formed of thirty-seven high officials, including among its members the administrative heads of Cochin-China, Annam, Tonkin, Cambodia and Laos, the commanders-in-chief of the army and navy, the directors of the various civil establishments and one native functionary from each of the five states. The council meets once a year on the summons of the Governor-General. It must be consulted on all questions relating to the budget and to new taxation. Its advice and authority are also required for the fixing of wages, for the building of roads and railways, and for any proposed frontier modifications between the states or the provinces. A permanent committee, formed of members of the council, facilitates the work of the larger body and enables decisions to be reached during the intervals between the annual sessions. The advisory powers of the *Conseil de Gouvernement* are delegated in full to this committee, except with respect to drawing up of the annual budget.

Grand Conseil des Intérêts économiques et financiers

This council has fifty-six members, half of whom are Frenchmen and half natives, elected either by various local assemblies or nominated by the Governor-General. It must be consulted on all economic and financial questions relating directly or indirectly to the general budget. The Governor-General fixes the dates of the meetings, which usually occur once a year, and lays down the programme of work for each session. When not in session the work and powers of the council are delegated to a permanent committee.

In economic and financial affairs, the *Conseil de Gouvernement* and the *Grand Conseil* work in close collaboration. They meet not only at Hanoi, the capital and seat of government, but also at Saigon, Hue and Phnom Penh.

Conseil de Défense

The *Conseil de Défense* is responsible for the military organization of the country and for the commissioning of such public works as are needed for its defence. There are five permanent members: the Governor-General, the Commander-in-Chief of the Navy, the Commander-in-Chief of the Army, the Officer Commanding the Infantry, and the Officer Commanding the Artillery. In certain circumstances the Chief of Health Services, the Inspector-General of Public Works and other high officials are requested to attend its meetings.

General Services

In addition to the three advisory councils whose functions are outlined above, the federal government comprises a number of departments and general services. The *Direction des Finances* and the *Trésorerie générale* prepare the annual budget; the *Services judiciaires* draft legislative enactments and advise the Governor-General on all legal matters; upon the *Direction de la Police et de la Sûreté générale* devolves the responsibility of maintaining public order; The *Inspection générale de l'Hygiène et de la Santé publique* controls the medical services of the country; the *Inspection générale des Travaux Publics* is responsible for the construction and maintenance of roads and railways; other departments are concerned with the administration of agriculture, industry, education, and scientific research.

Civil Service. The civil service of Indo-China which provides the French personnel of the federal and state government is formed of *administrateurs* and *administrateurs-adjoints*, holding the more important positions, and of *chefs des bureaux*, holding the subordinate positions. Almost all the appointments to the higher offices of state are given to men who have passed through the *Ecole coloniale* in Paris. In 1937, there were 4,654 French civil servants in the country.

STATE GOVERNMENT

The structure of state government in Indo-China mainly consists of a dual control by French and native officials acting in close association and holding supreme administrative powers, subject only to the direct authority of the Governor-General. There are wide differences within this general framework, determined by the history and traditions of each state. The states are discussed in the order in which they became members of the French empire.

Cochin-China

Cochin-China became a colony of the French empire in 1862 and is the only state of Indo-China which is governed directly and almost exclusively by white officials. At the time of the French conquest, the delta of the Mekong was thinly peopled and in process of colonization by Annamites from the north. As there existed no long-established

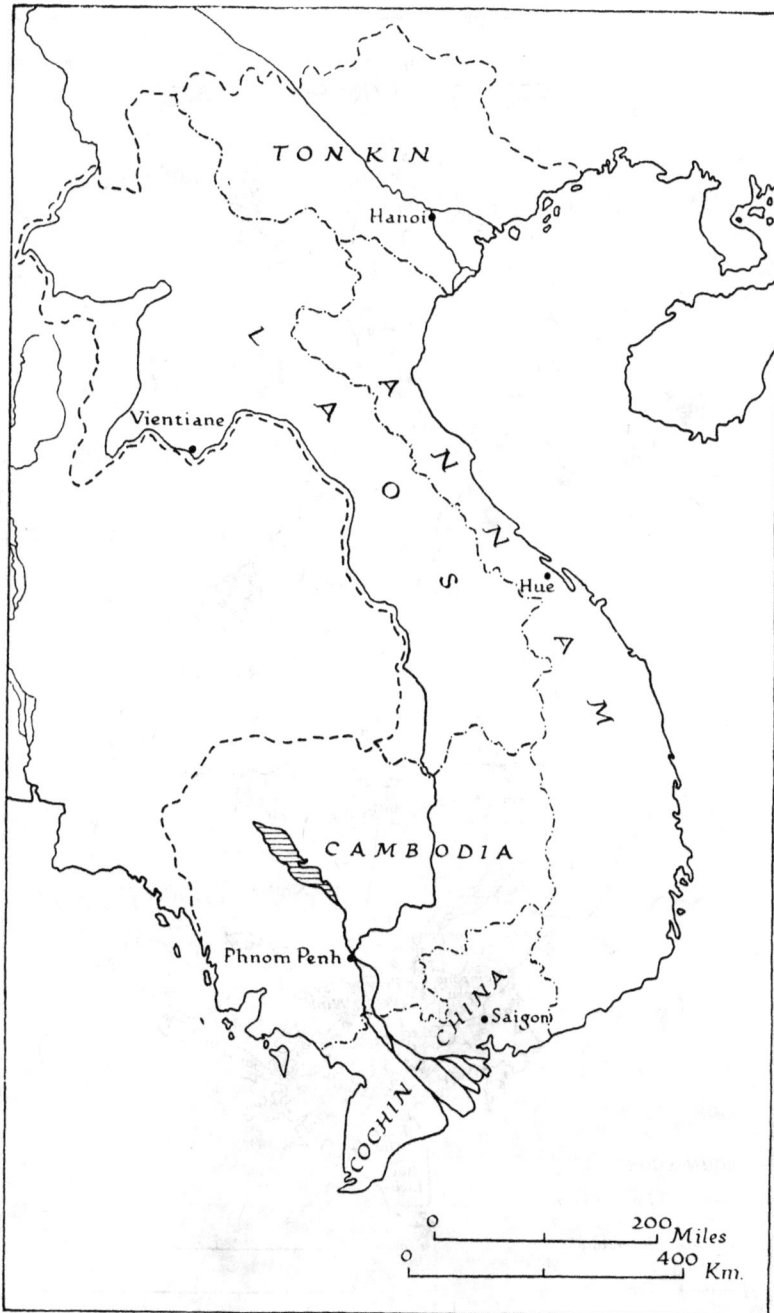

Fig. 63. The states and their capitals
Source: *Atlas de l'Indochine*, plate 10 (Hanoi, 1928).

Fig. 64. The provinces

Source: *Atlas de l'Indochine*, plates 22–7 (Hanoi, 1928).

H.N., Ha Nam; H.Y., Hung Yen; P.Y., Phuc Yen; V.Y., Vinh Yen.

native government and as the Annamite mandarins fled at the approach of the Europeans a system of direct rule was set up which has been maintained, with certain modifications, until the present day.

By virtue of its status as a colony, Cochin-China is represented in the French parliament by a deputy. This official is elected by the resident French citizens.

The head of the administration is the Governor, in whose hands are centred all the activities of the state. He is assisted by the *Conseil privé* and by the *Conseil colonial*. The former has ten members, all nominated by the Governor-General, including the Commander-in-Chief of the Army, the Solicitor-General, the Chief Engineer of Public Works, and two native officials. This council is a consultative assembly which, among other things, deliberates over financial matters and considers claims for the acquisition of property as well as requests for naturalization. In its functions, it resembles the executive councils organized by the British in Kenya and Nigeria.

The *Conseil colonial* is composed of ten members elected by universal suffrage of resident French citizens, ten native members elected by a restricted native suffrage, two delegates from the chamber of agriculture and two from the chamber of commerce. It meets once a year and is consulted on questions concerning the budget, the disposal of property and organization of public works. When not in session, the work of the council is carried out by a small permanent committee of about five members, two of whom must be natives. Although claiming to be representative of French and native interests, the *Conseil colonial* has no legislative power, unlike the representative councils in British colonies, and acts only in an advisory capacity, while any of its decisions can be annulled by the *Conseil privé*.

Cochin-China has two separate chambers of agriculture and commerce, the former with ten and the latter with twenty members, elected to represent the interests of the various economic activities within the state. About one-fifth of the members are natives or Chinese. The chambers in Cochin-China, like those in the other states of the country, have an important influence in matters of trade and general economic development; they advise the government on commercial legislation and on the imposition of customs and excise duties. As they are composed mainly of experienced business men and merchants, with practical knowledge of economic affairs, they are more qualified than the administrative services in the planning of agricultural and industrial enterprises, and this fact has long been recognized by the government authorities. These institutions were founded shortly after the conquest of Cochin-China by the French and the rapid development of the colony has been due in no small measure to their influence.

Although a number of native officials are members of the administrative councils they play a subordinate part in the affairs of state. This is also the case in the provincial administration. At the time of the French occupation, Cochin-China comprised six large provinces, each subdivided into small units, and the structure of government was similar to that found in the provinces of Annam at the present day. This native organization was eliminated and there are now twenty-one provinces or *arrondissements* (Fig. 64) under the control of French officials, whose duties compare with those of a prefect in Metropolitan France. The provinces are divided into communes, each governed by a *Conseil de Notables*, but their administrative powers are very restricted.

The towns of Saigon and Cho Lon form a single administrative division known as the 'Région Saigon-Cho Lon', though they have separate municipal councils. The municipal organization is similar to that existing in the towns of France.

Cambodia

Cambodia was declared a French protectorate in 1863, two years after the conquest of Cochin-China, and was thus the first of the native kingdoms to come under European control. As a monarchical form of government, with a hierarchy of officials and with an elaborate organization of laws and customs had been established for many centuries, the French introduced a system of indirect rule whereby the native administration was retained, but with its powers strictly limited and subordinated to those of the French authorities. The Convention of 1884 forms the basis of the administrative machinery as it exists to-day.

The protectorate of Cambodia is governed by a Chief Resident, in whom are vested the supreme legislative and executive powers, subject only to the control of the Governor-General. His functions and powers are similar to those of the Governor of a British protectorate. A *Conseil du Protectorat*, consisting of the heads of the services and delegates from the chambers of agriculture and commerce, assists the Chief Resident, though, like the *Conseil privé* of Cochin-China, it can act only in an advisory capacity. Another purely advisory body is the *Conseil consultatif indigène* which expresses native views on social and economic questions. The assembly consists of forty-one members, elected for a three-year term by a small electoral college of high Cambodian officials and five other members nominated annually by the native government. A French official attends its meetings.

In Cambodia, there is no separate chamber for agriculture and commerce, as in Cochin-China, but a single chamber concerned with both fields of economic affairs. The government is financed by local revenues, mainly in the form of direct taxation, and with the aid of grants from the federal government.

Cambodia is divided into thirteen provinces or 'residencies' (Fig. 64), each under the control of a Resident, whose duties resemble those of the Provincial Commissioners in Uganda and Kenya. Native councils advise the Resident on economic and financial matters.

A municipal commission is responsible for the administration of Phnom Penh, the capital of Cambodia. It is composed of both French and native members.

The native administration in Cambodia resembles, superficially at least, the form of government established before the European occupation. The king is the head of state, and though he is in fact only a figure head, the French have been careful to maintain the traditional pomp and dignity of his court. At the court in Phnom Penh, there are three special assemblies: a *Conseil de la Famille royale*, composed of eight princes or princesses appointed by the king; a *Tribunal de conciliation*, charged with the solution of disputes between members of the royal household; and a *Commission d'avancement du personnel du palais*, comprising the Secretary-General of the palace and the Ministers of the palace (Plate 34).

The king governs by means of ordinances which have to be agreed to and countersigned by the Chief Resident. All Cambodians are forced to comply with the provisions of these ordinances. A ministerial council, five in number, assists the sovereign: the Minister of the Interior is responsible for land affairs and for public health; the Minister of Justice deals with legal affairs; the Minister of the Palace acts as liaison official with the French authorities and deals also with civil expenditure; the Minister of Marine controls the state barges and is also concerned with river traffic; finally, the Minister of War and Public Instruction is responsible for military affairs, communication and education. These ministers are all appointed by the king, subject to the approval of the Chief Resident, from among native officials who have given faithful and meritorious service to the state.

The ministers of the crown and other high-ranking members of the Cambodian civil service hold honorary titles in addition to their official position. Decorations are widely appreciated and by conferring them liberally the French have created a body of loyal officials who are an important stabilizing influence in native affairs.

The native administrative divisions are, in order of decreasing size, the *khet*, the *srok*, the *khand* and the *khum*. The *khet*, whose boundaries are almost invariably coterminous with those of the French province, is governed by a native civil servant of high rank and dignity who works in close collaboration with the French Resident. Native civil servants are also in charge of the smaller divisions of the *srok* and the *khand*.

The village (*khum*) is the basic unit of native administration in Cambodia, as in the other protectorates of Indo-China. It is recognized that the preservation of the elaborate village system provides an assurance of general peace and good order over the whole country. Each village is under the control of a head-man, assisted by a *Conseil de Notables*. The head-man represents to the provincial authorities the needs and desires of the village community and also performs a large number of varied duties, including the keeping of the village register, the collection of taxes and the upkeep of public buildings. He is unsalaried, but he receives commissions on the collection of revenue. Among the chief duties of the *Conseil de Notables* is the drawing up of the annual budget which must be submitted to the provincial authorities for their approval. Although the head-man and the *Conseil de Notables* are both elected by the householders, the power in the village tends to be in the hands of one or two influential families. The form of village government is thus in practice more oligarchical than democratic.

Annam

Annam has been a protectorate of the French empire since 1884. The country was politically well organized at the time of the European occupation, an autocratic and absolute monarch ruling with the aid of a highly trained civil service. Indirect rather than direct rule was recognized as the system of government most likely to ensure the continued stability of the state, and a dual control by the French on the one hand and by the Annamites on the other was therefore instituted. The treaty of 6 June 1884 settled the relations between Annam and the protecting power.

A Chief Resident, representing the Governor-General, is the administrative head of the country. He supervises and is responsible for the actions of the native government; in addition, he directs those

Plate 35. Gate of the Emperor of Annam's palace at Hue

The architecture is in the rich, modern Chinese style decked with coloured tiles and crowned with dragons as imperial symbols.

Plate 36. Throne room of the Imperial palace at Hue

In this room the great festivals and receptions are held. It is in the traditional Chinese style and was built at the beginning of the nineteenth century. The ceilings and columns are coated with red and gold lacquer. An imperial dragon tapestry hangs behind the throne, in front of which is a table inlaid with mother of pearl. In the foreground is a tripod incense vessel.

public services, such as customs and excise, posts and telegraphs, and medical assistance, which are solely the province of the French administration. A *Conseil du Protectorat*, a *Chambre indigène des Représentants du peuple*, and a council representing French economic and financial interests advise the Chief Resident.

As in Cambodia, agriculture and commerce in Annam are not represented in the government by separate chambers. There are two of these mixed chambers, one at Vinh, with eleven members, two of whom are natives, and another at Tourane, with ten members, three of whom are natives.

Annam is divided into sixteen provinces (Fig. 64), each governed by a Resident. A *Conseil provincial*, formed of native officials, assists the Resident and acts as an intermediary between him and the native administrative organization.

The towns of Thanh Hoa, Vinh, Ben Thuy, Tourane, Qui Nhon and Dalat are administered by a municipal commission, composed of French and Annamite members, nominated and presided over by the head of the province in which they lie.

The Annamite administration, which exists side by side with that of the French, differs little in structure from the time when the country was an independent kingdom. The king or emperor, as the temporal and spiritual sovereign of his people, is the supreme head of native affairs. As in the old Chinese empire, the sovereign calls himself the Son of Heaven and is regarded with deep reverence by all; disobedience to his will is considered a sacrilege. The succession to the throne is by order of primogeniture, applying to the first-born of the emperor's first wife and not to the children of his other wives. The present ruler, Bao Dai, is, however, the son of a concubine of the former emperor, Khai Dinh.

The orders of the king or, during his minority, of the regent, are executed by six ministers who form the ministerial council or *Co Mat*, namely, the Ministers of the Interior, of Finance, of Rites, of War, of Justice and of Public Works. All decisions of the native government must be approved by the Chief Resident. Other administrative organizations at Hue, the seat of government, include the council of the *Ton Nhon*, formed of members of the royal family, which sits as a disciplinary tribunal; the *Noi Vu Phu* or royal treasury, which prepares the annual budget in collaboration with the Minister of Finance; the *Kham Thien Giam* or observatory, charged with the establishment of the annual calendar and with the choice of suitable days for rites and other festive occasions; and the *Quoc Su Quan* or

Bureau of Public Records. There are, in addition, three institutions more closely attached to the person of the emperor: the *Noi Cac*, or royal secretariat, which informs interested parties of the royal decrees and ordinances; the *Thi Ve Xu*, or royal bodyguard, under the direction of a high mandarin bearing the title of Minister of the Palace; and the *Can Tin Ty*, or Intendant of the Palace. Three French functionaries act as liaison officers between the court and the Chief Resident.

The ministers of state, who assist the emperor and execute his orders, as well as the provincial governors, are drawn from the mandarinate, a body of native officials, with civil or military functions. The civil mandarins are imbued with a deep knowledge of Confucian philosophy and with the history and the literature of Annam. All aspirants to the status of a mandarin must first take an examination to demonstrate their proficiency in these subjects. The military mandarins, who, in keeping with Confucian dogma, are regarded as of lower rank than those with civil functions, are generally chosen for their physical prowess rather than for their intellectual attainments. Both the civil and military mandarins are divided into nine degrees, each with two classes. The councillors of the court and provincial governors are mandarins of the first to the third degree and are addressed as 'Votre Eminence'; the lower ranking officials are normally styled 'monsieur le Mandarin'. The mandarins, as officially appointed representatives of the emperor, partake of his religious authority, and are profoundly respected.

Honorary titles and decorations are awarded by the emperor for long and meritorious service to the state. Members of the royal family, mandarins and ordinary citizens may receive these honours. Five degrees of nobility are conferred, none of which is directly related to a particular office. A relatively unimportant official may thus be superior in rank to a highly placed official in the court. Whereas scholarly wisdom and intellectual achievement are necessary before anyone can take part in the higher government of the state, personal merit is the sole criterion for the bestowal of an honorary title. The title conferred is hereditary, but the degree of nobility diminishes with each succeeding generation so that a family holding the highest rank loses its titled position in the sixth generation.

The local administration in Annam is in the hands partly of mandarins and partly of officials appointed by the people. In each of the sixteen provinces created by the French, the authority of the emperor is delegated to a mandarin (*tong doc*) who centralizes the affairs of the province and works in intimate association with the Resident. Other mandarins, subordinate to the provincial mandarins, govern the larger administrative units, *phu, huyen* or *chau*, within the province. The reforms of the reigning emperor (Bao Dai) have led to a separation of administrative and judicial powers, whereas formerly they were both in the hands of the same official.

Representatives of the people rather than royal nominees govern the cantons and communes, into which each *phu, huyen* or *chau* is divided. The canton, which comprises a varying number of communes, is a purely administrative unit like that in France. Its head is elected from among the members of the several communes. His responsibilities include the protection of the interests of the canton, the settlement of disputes, and the maintenance of public order, but his chief function is to provide a link between the commune and the provincial administration.

The commune, comprising a single village or group of villages, is a self-governing body upon which rests the whole pyramid of native administration. It is administered by a *Conseil de Notables* or village council. The notables, whose term of office varies from district to district, themselves nominate their successors so that the village tends to be ruled by a narrow oligarchy. One of the members of the council is elected to the position of mayor. This official does not preside over the council like the mayors in France and England, but acts as their agent in matters connected with external affairs; he represents to the council the wishes of the cantonal and provincial governments, and, through them, of the central government.

Tonkin

As Tonkin was formerly part of the kingdom of Annam, it came under French control as a result of the treaty in 1884 between France and the Court of Hue. At first the native political organization was maintained, but in 1897 the office of viceroy, representing the king of Annam in Tonkin, was abolished, and since then other changes have further weakened the influence of the native government. Although Tonkin is officially a protectorate, its administration is direct rather than indirect, and in some respects resembles that of Cochin-China.

The administration of Tonkin is in the hands of a Chief Resident whose powers are rather greater than those of the corresponding officials in Annam and Cambodia, owing to the absence of a centralized native government such as exists in the other protectorates. The Chief Resident, at his seat in Hanoi, takes all decisions and is assisted, as in Annam, by three councils, the *Conseil du Protectorat*, the *Chambre indigène des Représentants du peuple*, and the council representing French economic and financial interests.

Two separate chambers represent the interests of agriculture and commerce. The chamber of agriculture has twelve members, and the chamber of commerce twenty members. They advise the government on all questions relating to the economic development of the state.

Tonkin is made up of twenty-three provinces (Fig. 64), each divided into *phu* or *huyen*, cantons and communes. In addition to the provinces, there are also four military territories, lying in those parts of Tonkin which adjoin the Chinese frontier. They are governed by an officer of high rank, though he is subordinate to the civil administrator. Both the provinces and the military territories are under the control of a French Resident. As in the kingdom of Annam, the administration of local government, except in the two smallest divisions, is in the hands of mandarins though they are nominated by and directly responsible to the Chief Resident, since in Tonkin the Court of Hue has delegated all its powers to the French authorities. The provincial mandarins (*tong doc*) collaborate more fully with the French Resident than in the provinces of Annam. Like the mandarins who control the *phu* and *huyen*, their chief task is to ensure obedience to the laws and maintenance of public order.

The commune is the smallest administrative unit and, as in Annam, its maintenance is recognized as essential for the continued stability of the state. Its administration, however, differs from that in the other protectorates. Instead of the single *Conseil de Notables* there are two administrative bodies: the council of the *toc bieu*, which is charged with the government of the commune, and the council of the *ky muc*, including ex-cantonal officials and members of the mandarinate, which has the right to pass or annul the decisions made by the council of the *toc bieu*. The commune in Tonkin is thus far less independent and autonomous than that in Annam.

The towns of Hanoi and Haiphong each have a municipal council. A mayor, nominated by the Governor-General, from among the higher ranks of the civil service, presides over the meetings of the council. A municipal commission administers the smaller towns of Nam Dinh and Hai Duong.

Laos

The territory of Laos, acquired by the French in 1893, is ruled partly as a protectorate and partly as a colony. In the kingdom of

Luang Prabang, a system of indirect rule prevails, whereas in Laos proper the French authorities are solely responsible for the social and economic welfare of the natives. Both regions are under the supreme authority of the Chief Resident, whose seat is at Vientiane.

The kingdom of Luang Prabang comprises three of the ten provinces of Laos, namely, Luang Prabang, Houa Phan and Phong Saly (Fig. 64). The king governs the country, assisted by a royal council composed of three members: the Minister of the Interior, the Minister of Justice and Culture, and the Minister of Finance, Public Works, Agriculture and Commerce. No royal decree can become law without the sanction of the Chief Resident.

The provinces in both administrative divisions are governed by a French official with the title of 'Commissioner'. They include smaller administrative units called *muong* when inhabited by Laotians and *kong* when inhabited by other peoples. The native officials who govern these units are responsible for their actions to the French Commissioner. Like the *phu* or *huyen* of Annam, the *muong* or *kong* are further divided into cantons and communes, with a self-governing native administration.

LEGAL SYSTEM

The administration of justice is shared between French tribunals which are concerned with all matters affecting French citizens and assimilated groups, and native tribunals which deal exclusively with native affairs. French citizens are either persons born of French parents or persons who have acquired citizenship by naturalization. Native candidates for citizenship must know the French language, and have served in the army, navy or public service for ten years, or have married a Frenchwoman according to French law. The assimilated groups (*assimilés*) are Europeans, other than Frenchmen, and other aliens, who have the same status as French citizens. All the other inhabitants of the country, those born in Cochin-China being classed as *sujets* and those in the protectorates as *protégés*, are subject to native law. A Director, appointed by the Governor-General, fulfils the role of legal adviser to the federal government and ensures the unity of direction necessary for the smooth working of both French and native law. The judicial organization rests upon the decrees of 19 May 1919 and 16 February 1921, with later modifications.

French Legal System

The *code civil* of France, based on the 'Code Napoléon', applies equally to Indo-China. Justice is administered, in accordance with the articles of these codes, by *cours d'Appel, Cours criminelles, Tribunaux de première instance*, and *Juges de paix*.

Two *cours d'Appel* sit at Hanoi and Saigon respectively, the one including in its province Tonkin, north Annam and that part of Laos adjoining Tonkin; the other covering the rest of the country. Each court is composed of three judges and four counsellors. The Attorney-General and Solicitor-General are also attached to the *parquet* or permanent official staff of the courts of appeal. These courts consider appeals against sentences of the lower tribunals, and only in a few cases, such as the discharge of bankrupts, do they exercise an original jurisdiction. Another form of appeal court is the *Chambre d'annulation* which considers appeals from the tribunals of the justices of the peace.

Altogether there are six *Cours criminelles* corresponding to the *cours d'Assise* in France. They try serious crimes such as murder and arson. Crimes committed by Frenchmen or foreigners are judged by the courts at Hanoi and Saigon, their provinces being the same as those for the courts of appeal. Each is composed of three members of the *cour d'Appel* and four 'assessors' elected annually from a register of French officials. At Hanoi, in addition to the criminal court, there also exists a *Commission criminelle* set up to ensure swift punishment of crimes and misdemeanours directly threatening the security of the state. The other criminal courts at My Tho, Vinh Long, Can Tho and Phnom Penh, pass judgement on crimes committed by Annamites of French citizenship and Asiatics resident in the country. Three magistrates, one of whom is a member of the *cour d'Appel*, and two native 'assessors' preside at these courts.

The form of procedure in the criminal courts is the same as that practised in the *cours d'Assise* of France, and is different from that practised in Britain and British colonies. The accused party is first submitted to a preliminary examination by a *juge d'instruction*, and if he finds there are prima facie proofs of guilt the case is brought before a *Chambre des mises en accusation*. If there is sufficient ground for further proceeding, the tribunal refers the case to the criminal court, where the presiding judge first submits the prisoner to a searching interrogation and then calls the witnesses on both sides. After the counsels for the prosecution and for the defence have spoken, the verdict is given on a majority vote of the jurors. No appeal is allowed against the decisions of these courts.

Minor crimes (*délits*), such as assault, theft, and fraud, are tried by *Tribunaux de première instance* which sit in the larger towns and which consist of a judge, a public magistrate, and a recorder. The procedure resembles that in the criminal courts, except that there is no jury. If the accused party is found guilty an appeal can be made to the courts of appeal.

The *Tribunaux de première instance* also sit as civil courts in which capacity they deal with disputes concerning affairs such as breach of contract and mortgages. The plaintiff is represented by either an *avoué* (solicitor) or *avocat* (barrister). As in criminal cases, the verdicts of the tribunals are subject to revision by the courts of appeal.

In a number of towns of Cochin-China, and in certain provinces of the protectorates, *Juges de paix*, with extended jurisdiction, preside over small tribunals, taking cognizance, without appeal, of cases where small amounts of money are at stake. They inflict fines for minor infringements of the law, but submit all serious cases to the *Tribunal de première instance*. The provinces of the protectorates in which there is neither a *Tribunal de première instance* nor a *Juge de paix* with extended jurisdiction have residency tribunals, presided over by the French Resident. The only *Juge de paix* with ordinary jurisdiction is at Saigon.

Commercial tribunals, composed of non-professional judges elected by business men, sit at Hanoi, Haiphong, Saigon and Phnom Penh. They deal with all litigation relating to commercial affairs.

In addition to the 'civil' law there also exists, as in France, the 'administrative' law (*droit administratif*) which is concerned with litigation involving government officials. Cases of this nature are brought before the *Conseils des contentieux administratifs*, one of which sits at Hanoi and the other at Saigon. These councils consist of a magistrate of the *cour d'Appel* and three civil servants of high rank. They meet twice a month. Appeals can be made against their decisions to the Council of State in France.

Native Legal System

The native judicial organization existing before the French conquest of Indo-China has been in part maintained, though the legal codes have been made more coherent and brought more into line with those of France. Native and French law is fundamentally divergent, for whereas the one is based on respect and protection for the family, the other is based on the freedom and equality of the individual. The introduction of French law has led to the weakening of family ties and to social discontent.

Oriental and Occidental legal systems clash not only in their basic theories of collectivism on the one hand and individualism on the other, but also with respect to the punishment of crime. Corporal punishment and slow deaths, so common in the old native codes, are abhorrent to the western mind. Strangulation or decapitation were decreed for more serious offences such as treason, murder or arson, while adulterers were given to the elephants in the manner as described by a seventeenth-century missionary:

> The offender is conducted out of the Towne into a Plaine; where in the presence of an infinite number of people, he is brought into the midst of the place with his hands and feet tied neere unto the Elephant, unto whom the sentence of the party that is to be put to death is read, that he may execute it from point to point. The order being thus: That first he shall seize on him, take him and straine him with his trunke, and hold him so suspended in the aire, showing him to all the world; then that he cast him up with violence, and receive him againe on the point of his teeth, that by the heavy fall of his weight he may gage himself thereon and that then he dash him against the ground and that in the end he tread him under his feet. All of which the Elephant doth, without failing in one point, to the great astonishment and terror of all that are present. (Christopher Borri, *La nouvelle mission des Pères de la Compagnie de Jésus dans la Cochinchine*, ch. 6, Rennes, 1631.)

This penalty was only abolished in 1875. Other corporal punishments have also been abolished by the French, and though caning is still imposed, terms of imprisonment, with the death sentence or exile in extreme cases, have taken their place. In appraising these changes, the attitude of the native to corporal punishment is frequently forgotten. As self-control is regarded as the consummation of human dignity, and as an individual feels himself important only when constituting part of the community in which he lives, physical pain is accepted as more humane than a term of imprisonment or exile. In the eyes of the Annamites, a sentence of exile is more severe than the death penalty, since absence from the ancestral tombs causes considerable moral suffering, whereas the Annamite belief in a celestial world, inspired by Buddhist teachings, makes him approach death with serenity and fearlessness.

Cochin-China. In judicial as in political affairs the natives of Cochin-China play an insignificant part. They have no tribunals of their own, and all litigation concerning them is handled by the French courts, which, however, act according to Annamite and not French law. Annamite *Juges de paix* have recently been appointed to give advice on all questions relating exclusively to the native population.

Cambodia. The protectorate of Cambodia has an elaborate native judicial organization based upon the royal ordinance of 1922. *Juges de paix* administer legal affairs in the administrative divisions known as the *khand* and the *srok*; they interrogate and pass judgement on delinquents who have been apprehended by the head-men of the village. Tribunals of first instance are found in every provincial capital, while serious penal offenders are brought before a *Cour criminelle* at Phnom Penh. A *cour d'Appel* held in the state capital has the right to annul or modify decisions of the lesser courts. The native judiciary service is placed under the control of a French magistrate appointed by the Chief Resident.

Annam. In Annam the legal code instituted by the Emperor Gia Long (1820) is still nominally in force, though, as already noted, punishments have been alleviated and royal decrees have made further modifications in judicial procedure, notably in the separation of administrative and judicial powers. The village councils refer, through the mayor, all delinquents to the mandarin at the head of the *phu* or *huyen*, who submits all his decisions for approval to the provincial mandarin. Extreme cases are referred to the emperor.

Tonkin. The legal system of Tonkin is administered in accordance with the civil and penal codes promulgated by the French in 1917. The Director of Judicial Administration in Indo-China is the head of native justice in Tonkin, under whom are a hierarchy of mandarins appointed by him to preside over the tribunals in the provinces and smaller administrative units. These mandarins have only judicial powers. There are tribunals of three degrees, that of the third degree which sits at Hanoi considering appeals made against verdicts of the lesser tribunals.

Laos. In both the kingdom of Luang Prabang and Laos proper justice rests upon decrees made by the Governor-General in 1927. The Chief Resident controls the judicial organization, which includes tribunals of the first and second degree and a high court of appeal, with its seat at Vientiane.

POLICE SYSTEM

Public order in Indo-China is assured by a police system under the control of the *Direction de la Police et de la Sûreté générale*. The *garde indigène* of the protectorates and the *garde civile* of Cochin-China are the main police organizations, though there are also a number of auxiliary forces.

The *garde indigène*, commanded by both French and native officers, numbers about 12,000 men, 5,000 of whom are in Tonkin, 3,200 in Annam, 2,200 in Cambodia and 1,650 in Laos. It is formed into brigades, which vary in size according to the importance of the province or military territory in which they operate. In the maintenance of public order this force has powers similar to those of the *gendarmerie* of France.

In Cochin-China, the functions of the *garde indigène* are assumed by the *garde civile*. The officers of the *garde civile* are all natives.

The auxiliary police forces include the *garde impériale* of Annam, the *garde des tombeaux impériaux* at Hue, the *garde royale* of Cambodia, and the *garde du roi* at Luang Prabang. There are also small police forces in the *phu* or *huyen* of Tonkin and Annam and in the *srok* of Cambodia, whilst others, known as the *partisans*, co-operate with the *garde indigène* in the preservation of order in the frontier provinces bordering on China.

Prisons

Criminals condemned to a term of hard labour are sent to the prisons (*pénitenciers*) at Thai Nguyen, Ha Giang, Cao Bang, and Lao Bao, and on the islands of Poulo Condore and Phu Quoc which lie off the coast of Cochin-China. Other criminals with long terms of imprisonment go to the central prisons (*maisons centrales*) at Hanoi, Tourane, Saigon, Phnom Penh and Vientiane. There are also prisons in each of the provinces (*prisons provinciales*) which detain delinquents with sentences of under three years. Reformatories (*maisons de correction*) for boys have been built at Nha Nam in Tonkin and at Thu Dau Mot, in Cochin-China.

BIBLIOGRAPHICAL NOTE

(1) The fullest treatment of Indo-Chinese administration is found in the following works: Sir Hesketh Bell, *Foreign Colonial Administration in the Far East* (London, 1928); J. de Galembert, *Les Administrations et les Services publiques indochinois* (Hanoi, 1930); M. J. Harmand, *L'Indochine française politique et administrative* (Paris, 1930); Sylvain Levi, *Indochine*, vol. II, Exposition Coloniale Internationale, Paris 1931 (Paris, 1931); Georges Maspero, *Un Empire Colonial français: l'Indochine* vol. II (Paris, 1930).

(2) The historical development of the administrative organization since the French conquest is described in: T. E. Ennis, *French Policy and Developments in Indochina* (Chicago, 1936); G. Hanotaux (ed.), *Histoire des Colonies françaises*, vol. V, L'Indochine (Paris, 1932); S. H. Roberts, *History of French Colonial Policy*, 2 vols. (London, 1927 and 1931); Virginia Thompson, *French Indo-China* (London, 1937); R. Emerson, L. A. Mills, Virginia Thompson, *Government and Nationalism in South-East Asia*, Institute of Pacific Relations (New York, 1942).

(3) On particular subjects the following works are recommended:

(a) Annamite administration: A. Dumarest, *Les Formations des Classes Sociales en Pays Annamites* (Lyon, 1935); P. Pasquier, *L'Annam d'autrefois* (Paris, 1930); and R. Petit, *La Monarchie Annamite* (Paris, 1931).

(b) Civil service: J. Suignard, *Les Services civiles de l'Indochine* (Paris, 1931).

(c) Legal System: *L'Organisation de la Justice en Indochine*, Exposition Coloniale Internationale, Paris, 1931 (Paris, 1931).

Chapter X

GROWTH AND DISTRIBUTION OF POPULATION

GENERAL FEATURES

The population of Indo-China in 1936 was 23,030,000, or about half that of Great Britain, rather more than half that of France, and over one-third that of any other French colonial possession. In the following table, the population of Indo-China is compared with that of the neighbouring countries of south-east Asia:

	Population (thousands)	Area sq.km.	Density per sq.km.
Indo-China (1936)	23,030	740	31
China Proper	422,707	7,520	56
Siam (1937)	14,465	518	28
Burma (1931)	14,667	605	24
India (1931)	352,786	4,684	75
Malaya (1931)	4,355	136	32
Netherlands East Indies (1930)	60,727	1,904	32
Philippines (1918)	10,315	296	34

Source: *League of Nations Handbook, 1938–39*, pp. 16–17 (Geneva, 1939).

The mean density of population in Indo-China is thus higher than in Siam and Burma, but lower than in China and India. The figure of 31 inhabitants per sq.km., however, is misleading, since Indo-China, in common with the other countries of south-east Asia, has a large area of thinly settled mountains. Only 8% of the country is under cultivation. On the basis of cultivated area instead of total area the mean density is then 383 inhabitants per sq.km., which gives a truer conception of the pressure of population.

In 1936, over 95 % of the population comprised native groups including the Annamites, the Cambodians, and various mountain tribes, such as the Moi, the Thai and the Man. The Chinese, who live mainly in the towns of Cochin-China and Cambodia, constituted the only other large group (see pp. 253–55). The number of Europeans in this year represented no more than 0·18% of the total population (see pp. 249–53). The numbers and composition of the population groups in each state are shown in the table below.

Population groups	Annam (thou- sands)	Cam- bodia (thou- sands)	Cochin- China (thou- sands)	Laos (thou- sands)	Tonkin (thou- sands)	Total (thou- sands)
French subjects or protected persons:						
Annamites	4,835	191	3,979	27	7,647	16,679
Muong	99	—	—	—	112	211
Cambodians	—	2,597	326	2	—	2,925
Thai: Laotians	0·4	20	0·1	565	3·5	589
Others	17	—	—	100	669	786
Man and Meo	1·4	—	—	47	166	214
Moi groups	664	54	52	247	—	1,017
Minh-Huong (Sino-Annamites)	—	—	62	—	11	73
Malays and Cham	23	73	8	—	—	104
Other groups	—	—	—	20	37	57
Foreign Asiatic sub- jects:						
Chinese	11	106	171	3	35	326
Indians and others	0·2	3	2	0·2	0·5	6
Europeans and assi- milated groups with European status	5	2	16	1	19	43
Total	5,656	3,046	4,616	1,012	8,700	23,030

Source: *Annuaire statistique de l'Indochine, 1936–37*, p. 21 (Hanoi, 1938).

At least three-quarters of the population is dependent upon agriculture for its living and relatively few persons are employed full time in industry and commerce, though no complete occupational statistics are available. As may be gathered from this occupational distribution, the great proportion of the natives live in rural areas. In 1936, the urban population totalled about a million; only four cities—Hanoi, Saigon, Cho Lon and Phnom Penh—had over 100,000 inhabitants.

A quantitative study of the population of Indo-China is handicapped by the inadequacy and unreliability of statistical material. The population of a particular district is evaluated by local officials who use the capitation tax, affecting all persons between the ages of 18 and

60, as the basis for their assessment and multiply the number of adults by an arbitrary coefficient to obtain the total population. This method of assessment is frequently inaccurate, since the coefficient figure is generally too high, while it often happens that after the death of the father, a child under 18 years of age is declared to be an adult in order to ensure the continued allotment of communal land to the family. Vital statistics are equally unreliable, for, though there is compulsory registration of births and deaths in Tonkin and Cochin-China, many of them are not recorded, and in Annam, Cambodia and Laos, this form of registration is almost non-existent.

Unless otherwise stated all the population figures in the following account refer to the year 1936.

DISTRIBUTION OF POPULATION

The population of Indo-China is unequally distributed, over 80% of the population living on 13% of the area. Fig. 65 shows the marked concentration in the alluvial plains and also the large part of the country, comprising mainly the upland regions of the interior, with less than 10 inhabitants per sq.km. There is a considerable area of dense population in the Tonkin delta, and this region of high density further extends in a narrow belt along the shores of the Gulf of Tonkin almost as far south as the Porte d'Annam. Along the greater part of the coastal lowland of Annam, areas of high and low density alternate, the lower densities becoming predominant in the southern stretches of coast from Cap Varella to Cap Saint Jacques.

In the deltas of the Dong Nai and Mekong there are several discontinuous areas with over 200 inhabitants per sq.km., while a belt of medium density extends inland to Phnom Penh and Battambang in Cambodia. With the exception of north-eastern Tonkin and small parts of Laos, all the rest of the country has a low average density of population. The most sparsely populated regions are the Monts des Cardamomes, the basin of the Se San and the limestone plateaux near the Col d'Ai Lao.

The contrasts in population density may be attributed to physical and economic factors, especially the suitability of the lowlands for an intensive rice cultivation, to the virulence of malaria in the mountain regions, and to the political expansion of the Annamite peoples. Rice is the staple food crop, and there is a close coincidence between the main areas of rice production and those of high population density (cf. Figs. 65, 83). The inequality in population as between the uplands

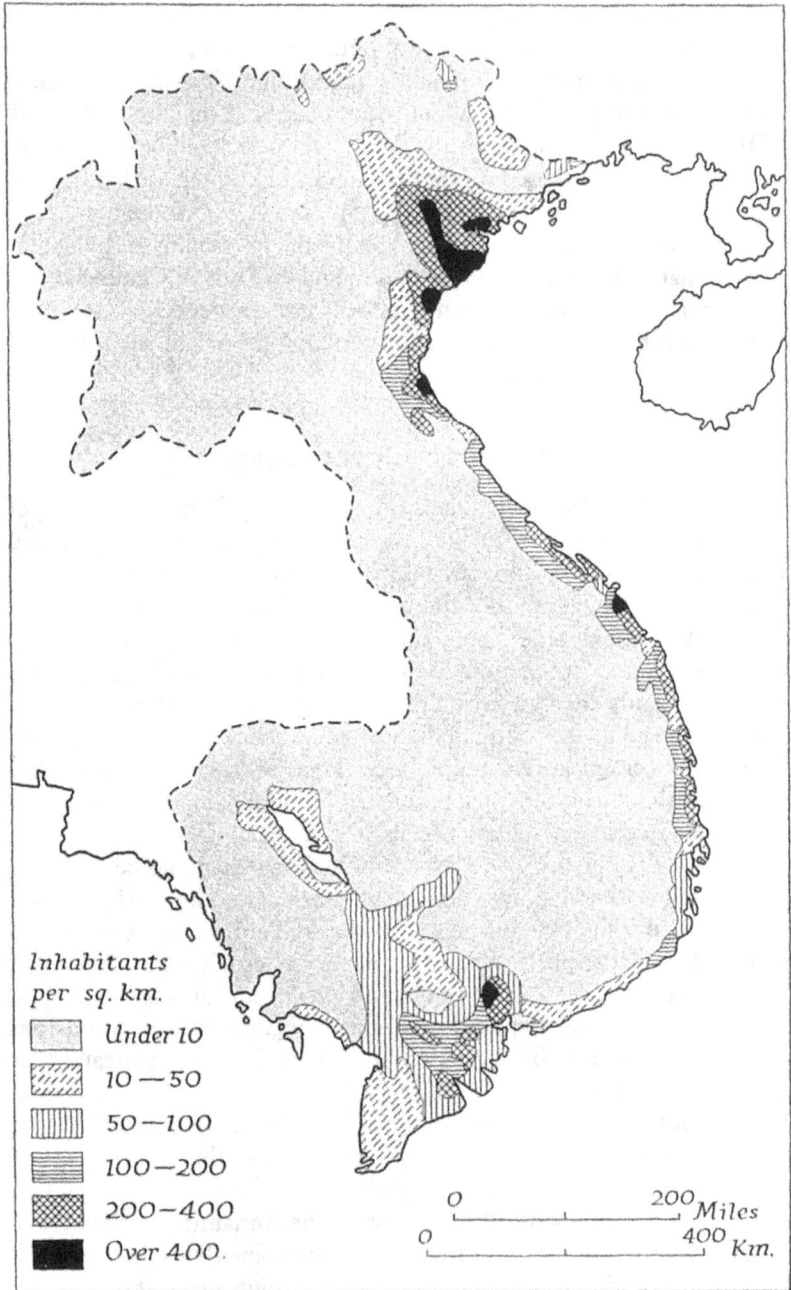

Inhabitants
per sq. km.

Under 10

10 — 50

50 — 100

100 — 200

200 — 400

Over 400

Fig. 65. The distribution of population

Based on J. Sion, 'Asie des Moussons', *Géographie Universelle*, vol. IX, pt. 2, Fig. 83 (Paris, 1929), with additional information from various sources.

and the alluvial plains is to a large extent a measure of the proportionate differences in cultivable area, for whereas in the latter regions from 60 to 80% of the land is classed as cultivable, in the former regions only about 5% is so classified. The alluvial plains and coastal lowlands can thus support a much greater population than the mountains and plateaux of the interior.

A more important factor which has led to the concentration of population in the lowlands is the relative absence of endemic malaria. By contrast, the upland regions are seriously affected by this disease and almost all the inhabitants suffer from it during some period of their life (see p. 110). Malaria is not only one of the primary causes of death among the mountain peoples, but it has also far-reaching social repercussions, since by reducing fertility and increasing infant mortality, it retards natural increase and may even bring about a decline in population. The traditional aversion of the Annamites for the mountains is founded on the knowledge that malaria is virulent in these parts and many of their legends refer to 'l'eau mauvaise' and 'la fièvre des bois'.

If the contrasts in population density between the mountains and lowlands are attributable to physical, economic and health factors, the variations in density between the lowlands of the north and those of the south have in the main resulted from the historical development of Annamite colonization. The Annamites cultivate the soil more intensively and seem to be more prolific than the other peoples of Indo-China. It is not surprising, therefore, that the highest densities of population to-day are found in the deltas of Tonkin and north Annam, which formed the original homeland of the Annamite state during the many centuries of Chinese rule and during the centuries of independence which followed. In the fourteenth century the Annamites began to push southwards along the coast, and by the end of the seventeenth century they had reached the Mekong delta. The lowlands of south Annam and Cochin-China were still in process of colonization at the time of the French conquest. The Annamites who had settled in these regions multiplied rapidly, but though there are several areas of high density, no part of the southern lowlands has densities as high as those which occur in the Tonkin delta.

Distribution of Population in the Tonkin Delta

The Tonkin delta or delta of the Fleuve Rouge is one of the most densely populated regions in the world. Nearly 7 million people live within its area of 15,000 sq.km., and the average density of the rural population approaches 450 per sq.km. In Europe, a rural density of 200 per sq.km. is exceptional. The density in this part of Tonkin may be compared with that in Java where there are 315 rural inhabitants per sq.km. and with that in the Dacca district of Bengal where there

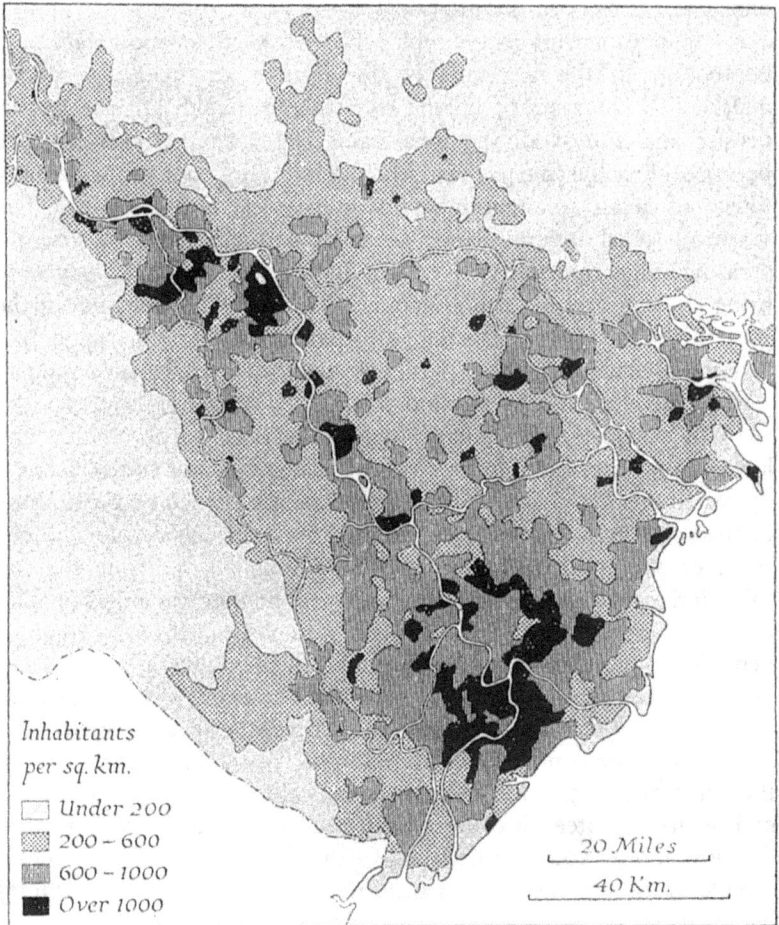

Fig. 66. Density of population in the Tonkin delta
Source: P. Gourou, *Les Paysans du Delta tonkinois*, folding map (Paris, 1936).

are 486 per sq.km. The density in Bengal is very much less over an area equal to that of the Tonkin delta. The figure of 450 inhabitants per sq.km. is also equal to that of the most densely peopled lowlands of China and Japan.

Only 350,000 persons are classed as urban dwellers, which represents rather less than 5% of the total population. The urban population is distributed in numerous small towns, many of which are little more than enlarged villages. Only one centre, Hanoi, the capital and seat of government, has over 100,000 inhabitants, and only three others, Haiphong, Nam Dinh and Dap Cau, have populations of more than 10,000.

A belt of dense population, with an average of over 600 persons per sq.km., lies close to the Fleuve Rouge along almost the whole of its course from Viet Tri to the sea (Fig. 66). In the neighbourhood of Son Tay, the high density is due partly to the establishment of modern irrigation works, which have increased the agricultural productivity of the soil and partly to the large number of industrial handicraft workers in this region. High densities occur in the environs of Hanoi (149,000), the capital of Indo-China, which is situated on the right bank of the Fleuve Rouge, a little below the junction of the main stream with the Canal des Rapides. The city is an important industrial and railway centre. The region of greatest rural density lies below Hung Yen and in the area between the Song Tra Ly and the Song Day, south of Ninh Binh. On an area of 1950 sq.km. there lives 1,625,000 people, which gives a mean density of 833 per sq.km. Many villages in the provinces of Nam Dinh and Thai Binh have densities of more than 2,000 inhabitants per sq.km. and some even exceed 3,000 per sq.km. Although the reasons for such heavy concentrations are not fully known, an important factor is the greater fertility of the soil here relative to the rest of the delta, which allows a more intensive land utilization. Nam Dinh (25,347), in the centre of this thickly peopled region, is not only an important market town, but has also a cotton-spinning mill, which uses imported raw cotton and distributes the thread to local weavers. The belt of high population density does not reach the sea, except where fishing has attracted settlement; the shoreline is constantly changing and the coastal region, which comprises stretches of sand and mud flats, has only recently been settled (Figs. 66, 68).

In the east and north of the delta only a few scattered areas have densities exceeding 600 per sq.km. (Fig. 66). The main concentrations are found near the market towns of Hai Duong and Kien An and near the port of Haiphong. Haiphong (70,000), which is the second port of Indo-China, lies on the right bank of the Cua Cam, a tributary stream of the Song Thai Binh. The town has many industries, among which the manufacture of cement is particularly important. It is the

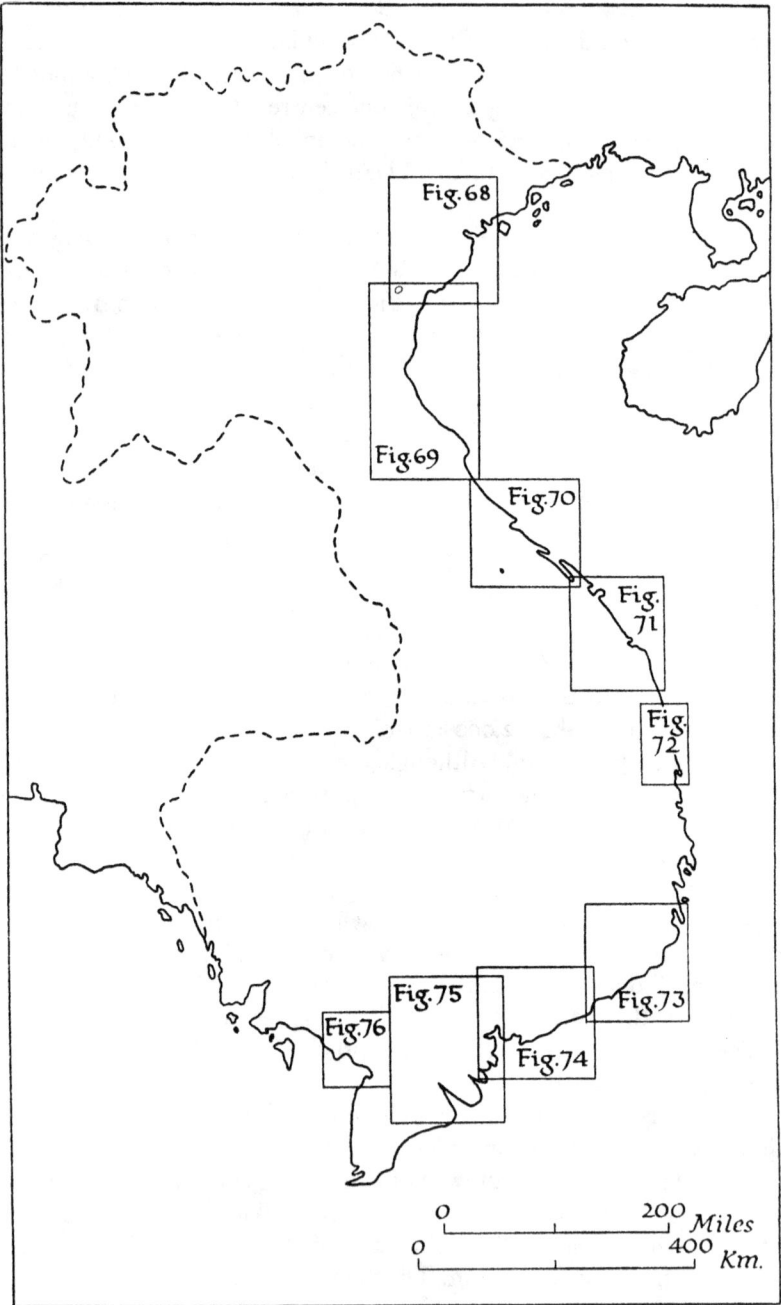

Fig. 67. Key to Rural settlement maps (Figs. 68–76)
It should be noted that these maps are only concerned with rural settlement; urban areas are not shown.

terminus of a railway which runs by way of Hanoi to Lao Kay and Kunming in Yunnan (see pp. 429-32). The poor soils of the high ground along the northern borders of the delta support a small population, and there is a mean density of less than 200 per sq.km. Dap Cau (11,000), the largest town in this part of the delta, is a river port, handling rice, wood, bamboo, pottery and silk, and is also a paper-manufacturing centre.

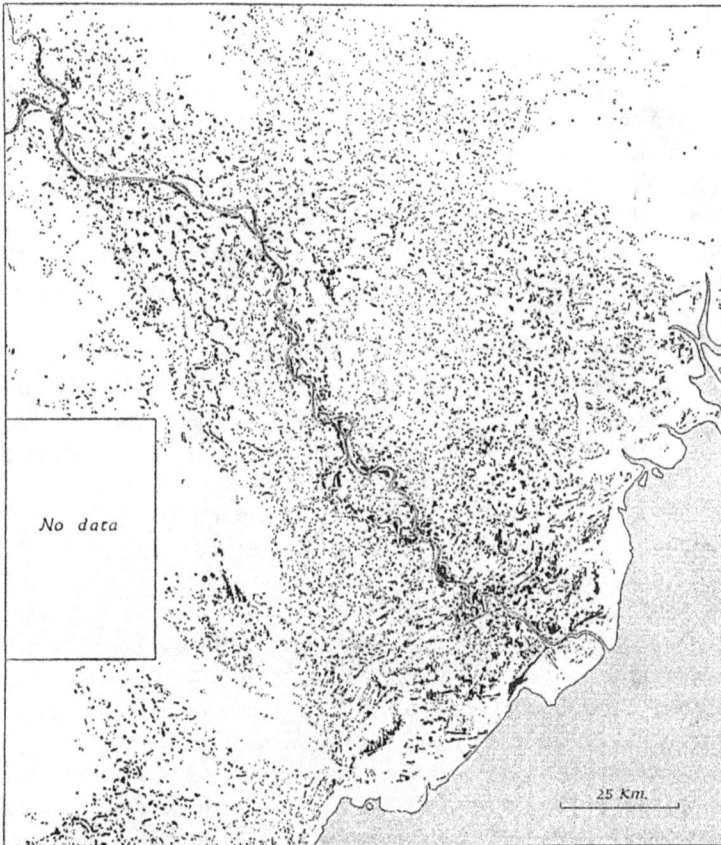

No data

25 Km.

Fig. 68. Rural settlement in the Tonkin delta

Source: P. Gourou, *L'Utilisation du Sol en Indochine française*, folding map (Paris, 1940).

Distribution of Population in the Mountains of Tonkin

A striking contrast exists between the density of population in the Fleuve Rouge delta and that in the upland regions of Tonkin, where the total population is only about 1,200,000 on an area of 100,000 sq.km. or an average of 12 per sq.km. Although the density of 12 per sq.km. is very low compared with that in the delta, it is appreciably higher than the density in the other upland regions of Indo-China. The interior of Tonkin, at least that part east of the Fleuve Rouge, has relatively easy communication with the southern provinces of China, and Chinese immigrants were early attracted by its many fertile valleys and rich mineral resources.

The proportion of the population in urban centres is as low in the mountains of Tonkin as in the delta region. The largest town is Cao Bang, with a population of 8,929. Only three others, Tuyen Quang, Lang Son and Mon Cay, have more than 5,000 inhabitants. The total urban population is given as 46,182. Certain places, however, such as That Khe, Bao Lac, Nguyen Binh, Cho Bo and Dien Bien Phu, are omitted from the official census of towns, though they are no less important than many of the smaller urban centres. If these other centres are included, the urban population probably totals about 60,000.

The mountain country to the east of the Fleuve Rouge supports a much greater population than that to the west of the river. The most densely peopled areas lie on the periphery of the eastern zone (Fig. 65). In the district around Mon Cay, where a belt of alluvial soils in the Song Ca Long valley has permitted the development of an intensive agriculture, the population exceeds 100 per sq.km., and a similar density is found in the plains of Lang Son and Cao Bang. Lang Son (6,458), which lies on the railway from Hanoi to Na Cham and on the main road leading into China, is an important military post and market town. About 150 km. to the north is the garrison town and commercial centre of Cao Bang (8,929), which stands on the right bank of the Song Bang Giang, a tributary stream of the Si Kiang. The relatively thickly peopled area near Cao Bang extends westward over an undulating sandstone plateau, drained by a tributary of the Song Bang Giang, to the range of prominent hills which forms the watershed between streams flowing east to the Si Kiang and west to the Fleuve Rouge. The valuable deposits of tin and zinc ore at Pia Ouac and Cho Dien, first worked by Chinese and later by Europeans, have attracted settlers to this region. Except in their lower courses, the left bank tributaries of the Fleuve Rouge, such as the Rivière Claire and Song Gam, flow through sparsely peopled areas with under 10 per sq.km., for their valleys, in contrast to those of the Song Ki Cong and Song Bang Giang, are narrow and only provide a small area of cultivable land. Tuyen Quang, which lies at the confluence of the Rivière Claire and Song Gam, is the effective head of navigation for all river craft, except canoes and rafts. Below this town, the density of population increases as the delta region is approached.

West of the Fleuve Rouge the average density of population is less than 5 per sq.km. The mountains are higher and more inhospitable than those in the east, while they lack the mineral resources which brought settlers to the Cao Bang region. The only large area with a density of over 20 per sq.km. lies in the valley of the Rivière Noire below Hoa Binh and in the hill country between this town and the Fleuve Rouge delta. Elsewhere, this western part of Tonkin is almost uninhabited, except for the valley of the Fleuve Rouge near Lao Kay, the plain of Nghia Lo, west of Yen Bay, the depression north of Van Yen, and the plain of Lai Chau, in all of which areas irrigated rice cultivation is carried on. Hoa Binh, Van Yen and Lai Chau are small towns serving as market centres for the neighbouring countryside.

Distribution of Population in Annam

In Annam the narrow strip of coastal lowland, broken by spurs of the Chaîne Annamitique, has 4,550,000 inhabitants or 80% of the population of the state. The rural population, which numbers about 4,400,000, has an average density of 300 per sq.km. and, as in the Fleuve Rouge delta, local variations in density are for the most part related to the suitability of the soil for intensive agriculture. The urban population is estimated to total 160,000 or about 3% of the total population. Only seven towns, Hue, Vinh, Tourane, Phan Ri, Phan Thiet, Thanh Hoa, Qui Nhon, have populations of 10,000 and over.

The most northerly plain of Annam, which comprises the delta region of the Song Ma and Song Chu, resembles the Tonkin delta in its distribution of population. There is the same concentration close to the banks of the main rivers and along the parallel lines of sand dunes near the coast. The Song Ma and Song Chu delta region has, however, an area of only 2,864 sq.km. and a density of 253 per sq.km. compared with the 15,000 sq.km. and a density of 450 per sq.km. in the Tonkin delta. Thanh Hoa (10,000), the capital of the province of that name, stands on a small tributary of the Song Ma and is an important market centre for agricultural and forestry products (see p. 476). The town is in the centre of an area with a population density of over 400 per sq.km., partly caused by the great extent of land bearing two rice crops in the year and partly by the rich maritime fisheries of this region. Certain villages north of the Lach Truong have over 700 inhabitants per sq.km. Because of the attraction of fishing, the density remains high in the coastal communes as far south as Phu Tinh Gia, but in general the density in the plain farther inland falls gradually south of the Song Chu (Fig. 69).

In the upland parts of the province of Thanh Hoa the population is estimated to total about 100,000, with a mean density of 10 per sq.km. The distribution of population bears a close relation with altitudinal zones: thus, over 90% of the inhabitants dwell in the zone between 25 and 200 m., which stretches up the valleys of the Song Ma and Song Chu almost to the borders of the province and which has a density approaching 25 per sq.km. Almost all the rest of the population is found at heights between 200 and 400 m.; the mountains about 400 m. in elevation are uninhabited, except for a few nomadic tribes of Man and Meo who practice a shifting cultivation. This altitudinal zonation is connected with the extent of the cultivable land and more especially of land suitable for rice cultivation.

South of the Song Chu an upland zone, formed mainly of steep-sided limestone hills, reaches almost to the coast and forms a thinly peopled area separating the Thanh Hoa region from the plain of the Song Ca. As soon as the plain broadens again in the neighbourhood of Cap Falaise and Phu Dien the population increases to an average of 345 inhabitants per sq.km. and, as in the Thanh Hoa region, many of the villages lie on the parallel lines of sand dunes. The highest densities, however, occur in the valley of the Song Ca, particularly near the provincial capital of Vinh, where the mean density is about 420 per sq.km. Farther south, near Ha Tinh, the rural population is less concentrated, owing to the high proportion of ancient alluvial soils, many of which are infertile and uncultivable, and owing to the absence of large streams which makes irrigation a difficult problem. In this area the density falls to about 200 per sq.km., while between the Song Rac and the spur of the Chaîne Annamitique known as the Porte d'Annam, it is less than 100 per sq.km.

The contrast in population density between the coastal plain and the uplands is not so clearly marked here as in the province of Thanh Hoa and in Tonkin. A narrow band of alluvium follows the banks of the Song Ca nearly as far as the state frontier, and the valley of this river in its middle reaches has a density of over 300 per sq.km., while other concentrations are found in the Song Con valley and in the neighbouring hills near Phu Quy where rich basaltic soils have led to

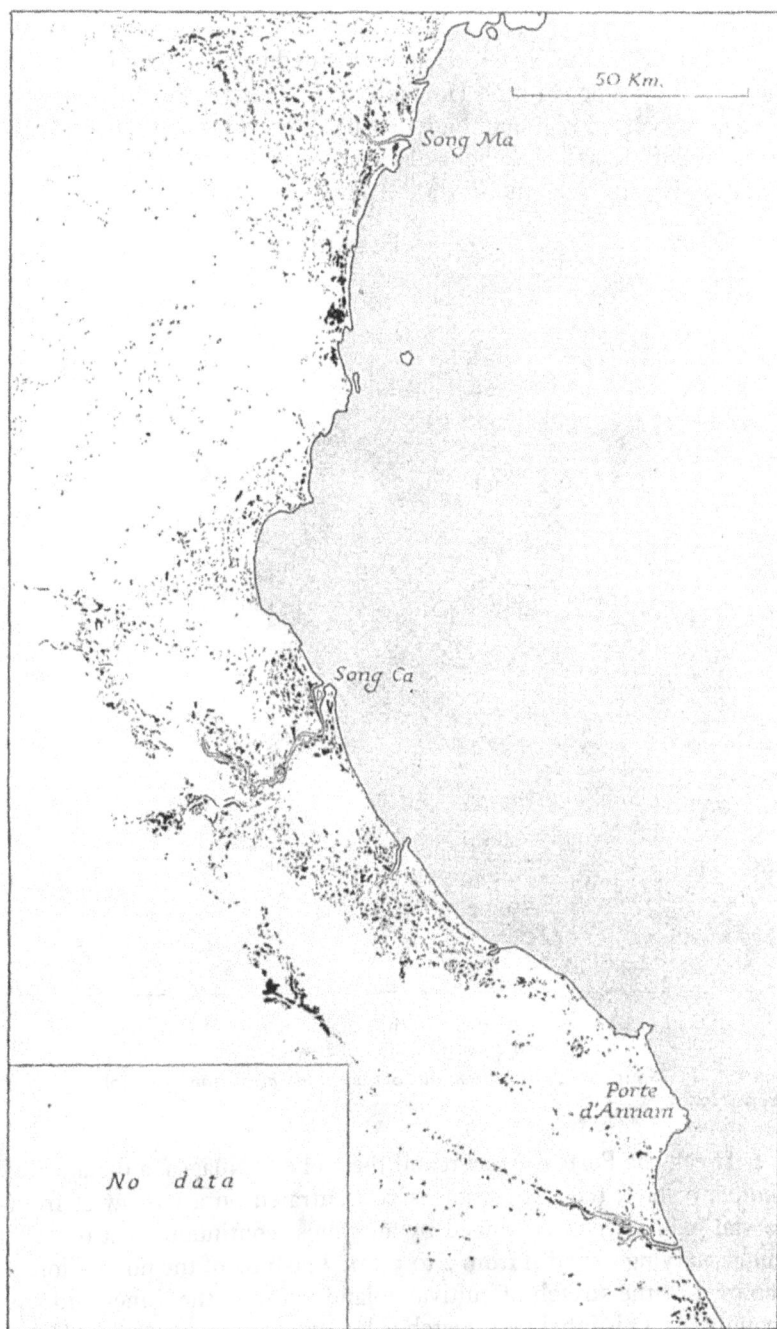

Fig. 69. Rural settlement from the Song Ma to the Porte d'Annam
Source: P. Gourou, *L'Utilisation du Sol en Indochine française*, folding map (Paris, 1940).

the growth of coffee plantations. South of the Song Ca the broad trench carved by the Ngan Sau and separated by a range of hills from the coastal lowlands around Ha Tinh, has a density of 276 per sq.km. This is an isolated region of high density, however, for surrounding it are areas with less than 10 per sq.km. and certain of the limestone and granitic plateaux near the Porte d'Annam are uninhabited.

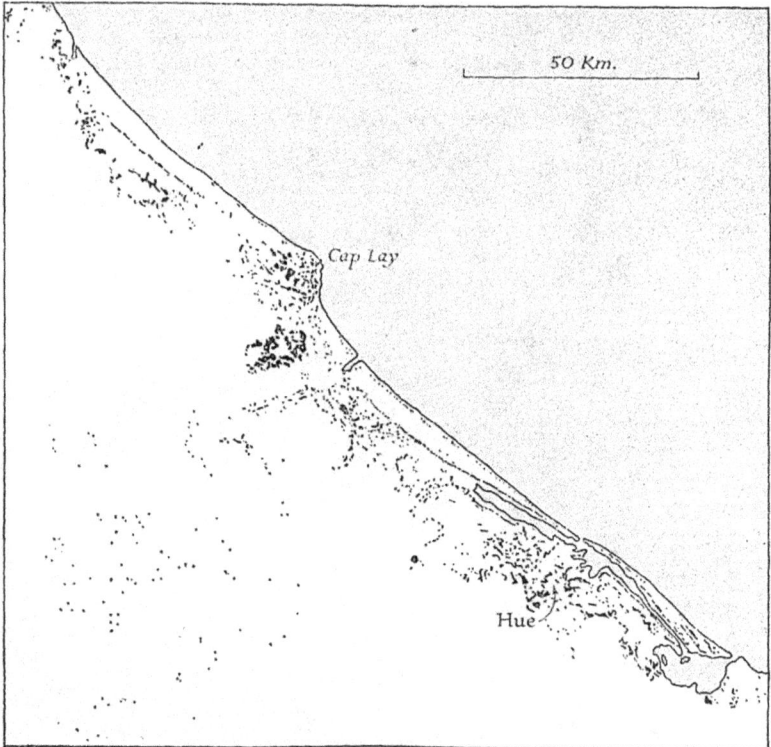

Fig. 70. Rural settlement in the neighbourhood of Hue and the coast to the north-west

Source: P. Gourou, *L'Utilisation du Sol en Indochine française*, folding map (Paris, 1940).

Between the Porte d'Annam and the Col des Nuages, a distance of about 250 km., the population is concentrated on a narrow strip of coastal plain, which is fringed by an almost continuous belt of sand dunes, varying in width from 2 to 5 km. The bulk of the population is confined to the stretch of cultivable land between the dunes and the mountains. This inhabited stretch is less than 10 km. wide near Dong

Hoi and Quang Tri, broadening to about 20 km. in the neighbourhood of Hue. The mean density in the plain is more than 300 per sq.km. The contrast with the upland regions is very striking, though the valley of the Song Giang, which is followed by the railway to Vinh, and that of the Rivière de Quang Tri, which gives access to Savannakhet in Laos, are fairly well settled. Three low basaltic plateaux which lie just north of the Rivière de Quang Tri, form regions of low population, their average density amounting to about 100 per sq.km. Hue (43,000), the capital of Annam, is situated about 12 km. from the sea on the Huong Giang or Rivière des Parfums. Excluding the town and its environs, the surrounding plain has over 350 inhabitants per sq.km. and the villages are more scattered than farther north, extending on to the lowlying strip of land which borders the lagoon at the mouth of the Huong Giang. Sea fishing is an important occupation in this area. The mountains fall sharply to the shores of the Lagune de Cau Hai, and from here to the Col des Nuages the coastal region is thinly populated (Fig. 70).

From the Col des Nuages southwards, the coastal plain of Annam becomes more broken and the population taken as a whole is smaller than in the northern part of the state, though certain favoured areas, restricted in size, have very high densities. The availability of land for irrigated rice cultivation is the main factor determining the concentration of population. Tourane (23,000), the most important town in Annam after Hue, stands on the bay of the same name, a short distance to the south of the Col des Nuages. It has a large coastwise trade in agricultural products. The plain in which the market towns of Quang Nam and Faifoo lie has a density of from 300 to 500 per sq.km., which is equal to the density in the Thanh Hoa region and in parts of the Tonkin delta. The plain of Quang Nam and Faifoo, however, covers only an area of 1,450 sq.km., while that of Thanh Hoa covers nearly 3,000 sq.km. and that of the Tonkin delta nearly 15,000 sq.km. The population remains dense as far south as Tam Ky, but becomes thinly distributed in the upland zone which reaches the coast at Cap Batangan (Fig. 71). In the valley of the Song Tra Bon the density of population again exceeds 300 per sq.km., and the Annamites have pushed their settlements far inland, though the main concentrations occur quite close to the sea. Quang Ngai is a provincial capital and market town in the centre of this thickly peopled area. An upland zone of low density separates the plain of Quang Ngai from that of Binh Dinh, in which the average density is 326 per sq.km. Nowhere in Annam is the contrast between mountains and lowlands so abrupt for the 25 m. contour, which is also the limit of intensive rice cultivation, forms a clear-cut dividing line in population density; below this level the land is thickly peopled, while above it the density is less than 2 per sq.km. On the coast in

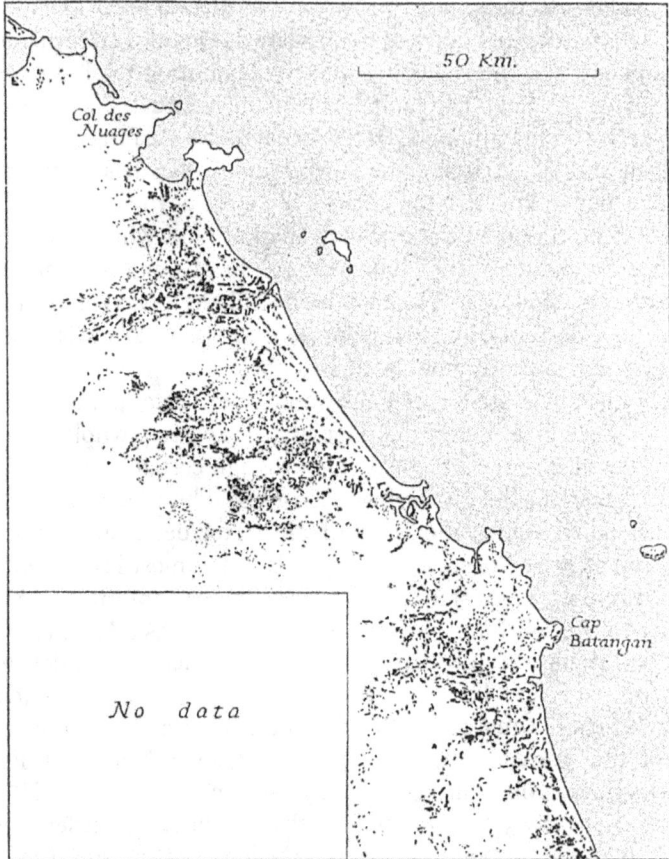

Fig. 71. Rural settlement from the Col des Nuages to Cap Batangan
Source: P. Gourou, *L'Utilisation du Sol en Indochine française*, folding map (Paris, 1940).

this region lies the small town and port of Qui Nhon (10,000), which has an important trade in salt, silk, groundnuts, areca nuts and coconuts (Fig. 72). Unlike the upland regions near Binh Dinh and Qui Nhon those near Phu Yen, a little to the south, have a density in parts exceeding 50 per sq.km., owing to their fertile soils and relatively low altitude. They have been an area of colonization by the Annamites, like the hills to the west of Quang Ngai and Quang Nam. The influence of relief and poverty of soil upon the density of population is well seen in the mountain range of La Mère et L'Enfant, to the south of the Song Ba valley and with its eastern termination in Cap Varella. This range, which has an average elevation of over 1500 m., is composed of infertile crystalline rocks and is uninhabited.

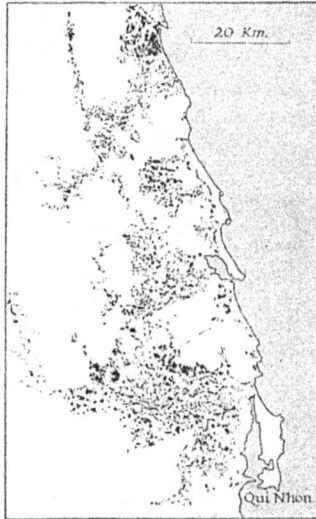

Fig. 72. Rural settlement in the neighbourhood of Qui Nhon and the coast to the north

Source: P. Gourou, *Esquisse d'une étude de l'habitation annamite*, p. 60 (Paris, 1936).

The coastal lowlands of Annam south of Cap Varella are small in size and there are few regions of dense population, owing partly to the restricted cultivable area and partly to the incomplete colonization of this region by the Annamite peoples. The cultivable area is restricted to narrow strips which lie between the shores of the sheltered bays and the steep-sided forested mountains. At the head of the Baie de Binh Cang, the plain in which Ninh Hoa stands has an area of only 100 sq.km. and that surrounding the important market town of Nha Trang only 135 sq.km., while the plain of Ba Ngoi, bordering the Baie de Cam Ranh, has an equally small area. In all these regions the density of population averages about 250 per sq.km (Fig. 73).

An interesting feature in many of the lowlands between Ba Ngoi and the frontier of Cochin-China is the high proportion of fertile soils which remains uncultivated. These lowlands formed part of the ancient kingdom of Champa, and a number of ruined buildings and traces of former irrigation suggest that the Cham cultivated areas at present unproductive. As it is only in comparatively recent times that the Annamite peoples have settled in this region, they have not yet been able to bring under cultivation all the land which had fallen into dis-

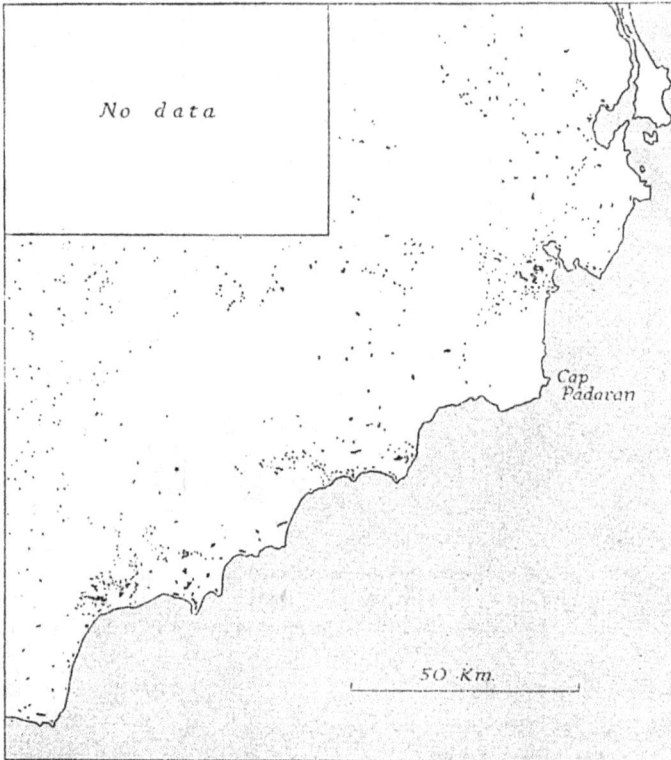

Fig. 73. Rural settlement in the neighbourhood of Cap Padaran
Source: P. Gourou, *L'Utilisation du Sol en Indochine française*, folding map (Paris, 1940).

use after the decline of the Champa kingdom. In the province of Phan Rang, the lowlands cover altogether 520 sq.km., but the area settled does not exceed 220 sq.km.; the density is 115 per sq.km. on the basis of the total area and 272 per sq.km. on the basis of area settled. A similar proportion of the plain of Phan Ri is uncultivated. South-west of Phan Ri is a broad zone of sand dunes, uninhabited except for a few scattered hamlets. Sea fishing is an important occupation, and Phan Thiet (15,500), the largest town in south Annam, owes its importance to the fishing industry.

The mountainous regions of south Annam, including the plateaux of Djiring, Darlac and Lang Bian, have an average density of under 10 inhabitants per sq.km. Many areas are devoid of all settlement. The mountain resort of Dalat and its immediate neighbourhood has a density above the average for the region.

Distribution of Population in Cochin-China

Cochin-China, which mainly comprises the deltas of the Mekong, Vaico and Dong Nai, has a population of 4,616,000, and of this total about 4,200,000 are classed as rural and 416,000 are urban. The average rural density is 66 per sq.km. for the state as a whole, but 100 per sq.km., in the delta regions, a relatively low density when compared with the corresponding figure of nearly 450 inhabitants per sq.km. in the Tonkin delta. The marked disparity in this respect between Cochin-China and Tonkin cannot be attributed to natural conditions, since although the climate of the one is less favourable to continuous cultivation than that of the other, both regions have similar relief and soil characteristics. Differences in historical development provide the true explanation. The Tonkin delta is the cradle of the Annamite people and has been settled for a long period of time; Cochin-China, on the other hand, first received Annamite colonists at the end of the seventeenth century or as late as the mid-nineteenth century in parts west of the Fleuve Postérieur (Bassac). In the Mekong delta the Annamites entered upon land occupied by indolent Cambodians and, as in other areas of Annamite colonization, they improved agricultural technique and increased rapidly in numbers. Despite the swift growth of population during the last fifty years, the density in the Mekong delta still remains less than one-quarter that in the Tonkin delta.

Urban dwellers in Cochin-China form 9% of the total population, which, though still small, is a rather higher proportion than in the other states of Indo-China. The estimated total of 416,000 is certainly too low, since near the large towns there are many villages with very high population densities and with only a small number of their inhabitants engaged in rural occupations. Saigon and Cho Lon are the two principal cities, together forming a single urban centre with over 250,000 inhabitants. Only four other towns, Can Tho, Bac Lieu, My Tho and Vinh Long, have populations of more than 10,000.

Four well-defined population regions can be distinguished in Cochin-China. The first region includes the delta of the Dong Nai and the hill country in the north and east of the state; the delta of the Mekong with the area around Saigon and Cho Lon forms the second region; the third is the region known as the Plaine des Joncs, which lies to the north of the Fleuve Antérieur; and the fourth includes the entire western and southern parts of the state, comprising mainly the provinces of Bac Lieu, Rach Gia and Ha Tien (Figs. 74, 75, 76).

The northern and eastern parts of Cochin-China, which make up the first population region, have a mean density of 15 per sq.km. The delta of the Dong Nai is almost entirely overgrown by mangroves and is uninhabited, except for a few fishing villages. By contrast, there is a zone of high population density to the east of the delta in the low-land region around the small market town of Baria. On an area of 104 sq.km. live 30,000 persons which gives a mean density of 288 per sq.km. A number of the communes have densities exceeding 400 per sq.km., while that of Phuoc Loi has 840 and that of Phuoc Tho 1530 per sq.km. These exceptionally high densities, which recall those of the Tonkin delta, are due partly to the rich agricultural resources of the region, especially its suitability for rice cultivation, and partly to the important development of the salt industry. A narrow belt of thinly forested hills separates this region from the dune coast, where there is another concentration of population near Phuoc Hai. The commune in which this village lies has a density of nearly 550 per sq.km. Sea fishing is the main occupation, and the fishing industry is more highly developed here than in any other part of Cochin-China.

Apart from the densely peopled regions around Baria and Phuoc Hai, the north and east of Cochin-China, in the provinces of Bien Hoa, Thu Dau Mot, and Tay Ninh, has a very small population composed mainly of primitive Moi tribes. A few areas in the Dong Nai and Song Be valleys north of Bien Hoa have about 20 inhabitants per sq.km., but the average density for the whole region is under 5 per sq.km. The virulence of malaria is one of the main factors which has caused the sparse population of these parts. In recent years the development of rubber plantations has led to the settlement of several thousand Annamite workers in regions formerly uninhabited, though many of the workers do not settle permanently (see p. 238).

The region of the Mekong delta, with an extension northwards to include the valleys of the lower Vaico and Rivière de Saigon, is the most densely peopled part of Cochin-China. Nearly 70% of the population dwell here and the average rural density is 160 per sq.km.

The fertile alluvial soils permit an intensive rice cultivation, and the magnificent system of natural and artificial waterways facilitates the drainage or irrigation of the paddy field (see p. 275). An interesting feature in the distribution of population is the relative thinness of settlement in the coastal zone, which may be attributed to the vast

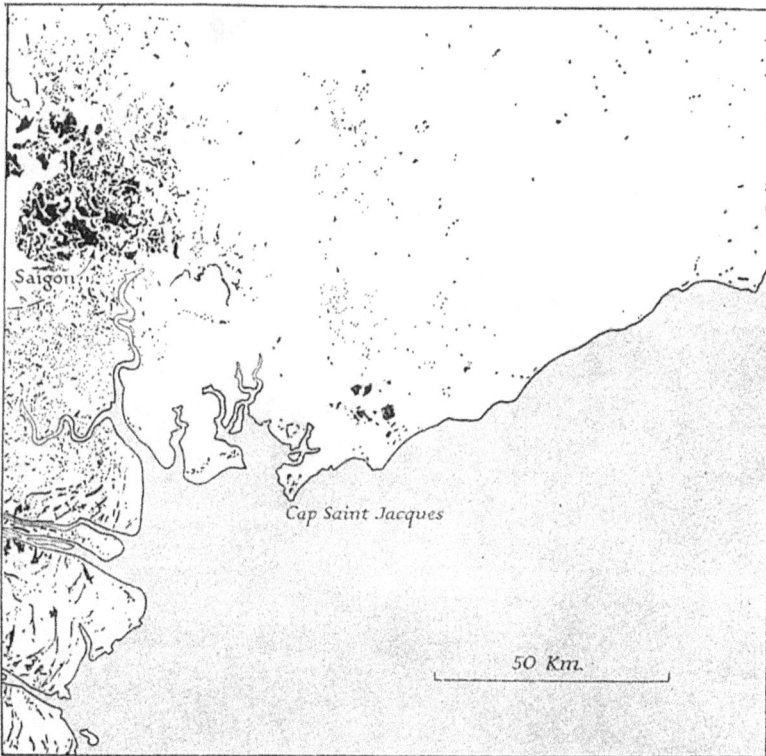

Fig. 74. Rural settlement along the coast eastwards from Cap Saint Jacques and in the neighbourhood of Saigon

Source: P. Gourou, *L'Utilisation du Sol en Indochine française*, folding map (Paris, 1940).

area of sandy or brackish soil, and also to the fact that malaria is more common here than inland. The average density near the coast is about 70 per sq.km. The great bulk of the population in the delta is concentrated along the river banks, particularly those of the Fleuve Antérieur, the Song My Tho, and the Fleuve Postérieur. So strong are the attractions of the rivers that in the mesopotamian region between the two main arms of the Mekong, the density of population is relatively low. Thus, in the provinces of Sa Dec, and Tra Vinh, a number of communes has under 90 inhabitants per sq.km. and some

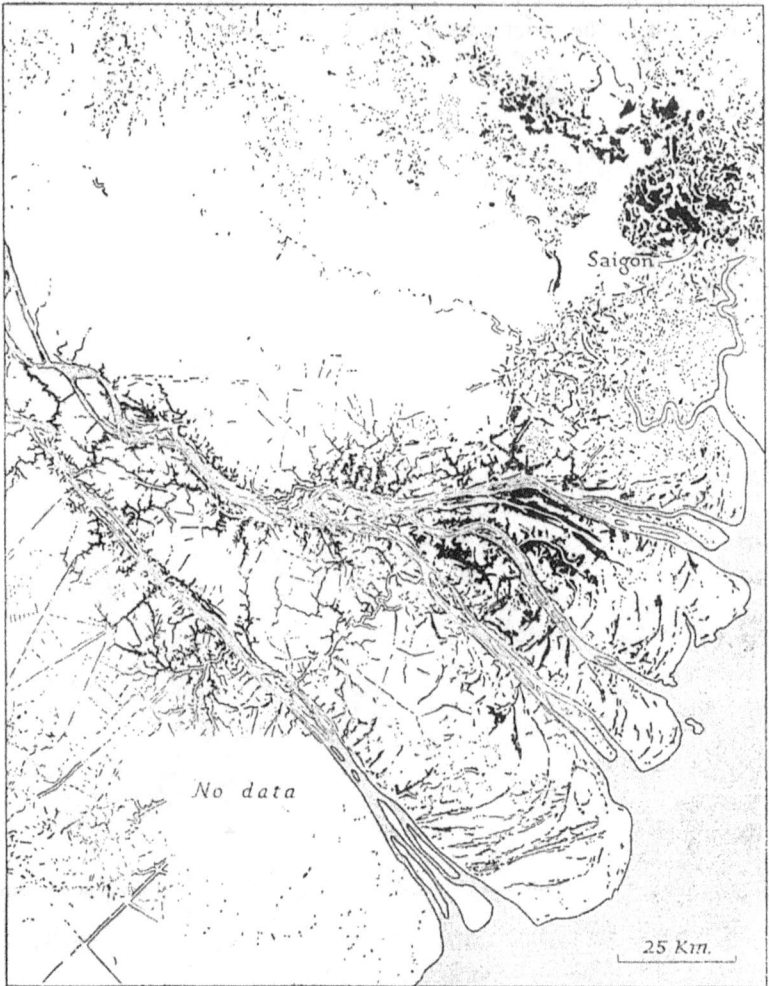

Fig. 75. Rural settlement in the Mekong delta
Source: P. Gourou, *L'Utilisation du Sol en Indochine française*, folding map (Paris, 1940).

less than 50 per sq.km. All the towns of the Mekong delta are situated on river banks. At the point where the Fleuve Antérieur divides into four branches is the market town of Vinh Long (13,000), and on the most northerly of the branches is the small port of My Tho. My Tho (25,000) is the terminus of the Trans-Indo-Chinese railway, and is the most important town of Cochin-China after Saigon and Cho Lon (see p. 407). It handles large quantities of rice as well as a great variety of goods brought by river from Cambodia.

In the valleys of the lower Vaico and Rivière de Saigon the population is again concentrated mainly on the river banks, except in the environs of Saigon and Cho Lon. These two towns together form the largest urban agglomeration in Indo-China. Saigon (111,000), the leading port in the country, stands on the right bank of the Rivière de Saigon, a tributary of the Dong Nai, about 80 km. from the sea (see pp. 373–80). Cho Lon (145,000) has grown up along the banks of the Arroyo Chinois and the Canal de Doublement which flow into the Rivière de Saigon. The town is not only an important river port and commercial centre, but is also the greatest industrial centre in Indo-China (see p. 472). There are over twenty rice mills, three distilleries, several soap works and a match factory.

To the north and east of the crowded banks of the Fleuve Antérieur lies a thinly populated region known as the Plaine des Joncs. The average density is about 11 per sq.km. Bad drainage and a high proportion of alum in the soil makes the region unattractive for settlement, though, with the introduction of modern hydraulic methods of draining, it is believed that large areas could be settled.

The fourth population region is that part of Cochin-China to the south and west of the Fleuve Postérieur (Bassac). It has an average density of about 60 inhabitants per sq.km., but this figure is misleading for the contrasts in density are very great. In general, the population decreases westwards from the Fleuve Postérieur. The country immediately adjacent to the river is thickly peopled, with an average density of over 150 per sq.km. A very high proportion of the cultivated land is under rice. Can Tho (27,108) is an important collecting and distributing centre for rice and has a rice experimental station. Long Xuyen and Chau Doc are other market towns on the banks of the Fleuve Postérieur. About 50 km. west of the river the population becomes rather less dense, though its density is still as high as 70 per sq.km. in a belt reaching to Rach Gia on the north and to Bac Lieu, with an extension to Ca Mau, in the south. The limits of this belt follow closely those of the rice fields and of the canals, upon which all cultivation depends. The extremely lowlying, undrained land, extending inland almost to Ca Mau, has in most parts a density as low as 6 per sq.km. There is a similar region of low density along the coast between the two small ports of Rach Gia and Ha Tien, but the density increases to over 100 per sq. km. along the banks of the canal joining Ha Tien to Chau Doc. About half-way between these two centres are several isolated granitic hills, and at their foot are a number of villages of which the largest is Tri Ton (Fig. 76).

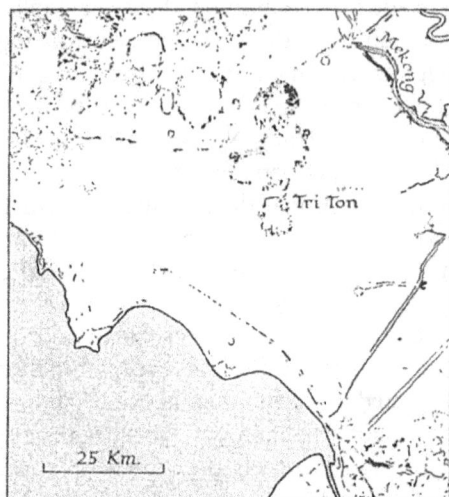

Fig. 76. Rural settlement in the Tri Ton district of Cochin-China

Source: P. Gourou, *L'Utilisation du Sol en Indochine française*, folding map (Paris, 1940).

Distribution of Population in Cambodia

Cambodia is a thinly populated state, for only 3,046,000 people live within its area of 181,000 sq.km., which represents a mean density of 17 per sq.km. The regional variations in density are as great as in the other states; over four-fifths of the population is concentrated on rather less than one-third of the area. The population is predominantly rural; Phnom Penh, Pursat and Battambang are the only large towns.

The bulk of the population is centred in the lowlands extending from the frontier of Cochin-China northwards to Kompong Chhnang and to Kompong Cham. The mean density here is 70 per sq.km. In the extreme south settlement follows the canal linking Ha Tien with Chau Doc, which forms the boundary line between Cambodia and Cochin-China. North of this canal, the plain is thickly peopled and rice and maize are the principal crops grown. Phnom Penh (103,000), which lies in the centre of the plain at the confluence of the Mekong with the river of Tonle Sap, is the capital of Cambodia and an important river port (see pp. 475–6). The area around Kompong Cham, north-east of Phnom Penh, is one of the most densely peopled, and at the same time most intensively cultivated, regions of Cambodia. Many crops are cultivated, including rice, maize, groundnuts, beans, fruits, tobacco and cotton. Fishing is also an important occupation in this area as well as in the densely peopled zone along the banks of the river of Tonle Sap. The inhabitants of Kompong Chhnang depend almost entirely upon fishing for their livelihood.

The population of the lowlands to the north and south of the lake of Tonle Sap is confined to a narrow band, with an average density of under 25 per sq.km., between the marshes bordering the lake and the forested hills. Although most villages lie above the summer flood level of Tonle Sap, a certain number, built on piles, are found along the banks of the lake. Siem Reap, on the northern branch of the Route Coloniale No. 1 from Phnom Penh to the Siamese frontier, is a small town near the famous ruins of Angkor. Battambang, the second largest town in Cambodia, lies in the centre of a well-cultivated lowland.

In the other parts of Cambodia the average density of population is under 5 per sq.km. The Monts des Cardamomes and the Chaîne de l'Eléphant, which rise steeply from the sea, are almost uninhabited, and the narrow coastal plain has only a few scattered villages. The vast area of forest and savanna in the north and the plateaux of the Chaîne Annamitique in the east of the state are also thinly peopled. The only large villages are found along the banks of the Mekong.

Distribution of Population in Laos

Laos has much the smallest population of the states of Indo-China, though in area it is easily the largest. Its population is estimated at about a million, and there is a mean density of under 5 per sq.km. The main settlements lie in the valley of the Mekong. These include the small towns of Pakse, Savannakhet, and Thakhek and the larger towns of Vientiane, the capital, and Luang Prabang. The Mekong is widely used for transport purposes, especially in the stretch between Savannakhet and Vientiane. Away from the river, the mountains and plateaux, for the most part covered with dense forest, offer few attractions to settlement and large areas are uninhabited. Among the more favoured areas, which have a density of from 5 to 10 per sq.km., are the plains around Saravane and Tchepone in the south and the valley of the Nam Hou in the north of the state. The recent development of the tin mining at Nam Patene has led to the growth of mining villages in a region previously occupied only by small scattered groups of Moi tribes.

Growth of Population

The population of Indo-China has increased and is still increasing at a rapid rate, but no detailed survey can be made of the past or present position, owing to incomplete statistical material. Not until 1906 was a general census taken, and only since 1921 have returns been made at regular intervals. The following table shows the growth of the population since the early years of the present century:

Year	Population
1906	15,859,000
1921	18,800,000
1926	20,500,000
1931	21,450,000
1936	23,030,000

Source: T. Smolski, 'Les statistiques de la population indochinoise', *Congrès International de la Population, Paris, 1937*, vol. VI, p. 56 (Paris, 1938).

The population has thus increased by 44% in thirty years or about 1·2% per annum. It cannot be too strongly stressed, however, that these figures are little more than rough estimates, for the methods of assessment lead to frequent inaccuracies. Even allowing for such errors, a considerable increase of population certainly took place between 1906 and 1936. This growth was due principally to a high rate of natural increase among the native peoples, though it also resulted in part from immigration and from territorial changes, since the province of Battambang, with about 300,000 inhabitants at the present day, became part of Indo-China in 1907.*

Natural Increase

The rate of natural increase is high among the native peoples of Indo-China. In Tonkin the birth-rate in 1934 was about 30 per 1,000 and the death-rate stood at 15 per 1,000. Both these figures are almost certainly too low, for in the city of Hanoi, where vital statistics are most carefully recorded, the former was given as 35 per 1,000 and the latter as 25 per 1,000. The natural increase of the population of Tonkin is thus between 10 and 15 per 1,000. A similar balance is

* The province of Battambang was part of the territory ceded by Indo-China to Siam in March 1941 (see p. 485).

found in Cochin-China where the birth-rate in 1934 stood at 39 per 1,000 and the death-rate at 24 per 1,000. Vital statistics are not available for Annam, Cambodia and Laos. The balance of births and deaths is probably not greatly different from that in Tonkin and Cochin-China. Although, in general, births exceed deaths by a considerable margin, the reverse is sometimes the case in certain over-populated regions, where a bad harvest may lead to famine and to a great increase in the number of deaths.

IMMIGRATION, EMIGRATION AND INTERNAL MIGRATION

Statistics relating to immigration, emigration and internal movement of population in Indo-China are more accurately known than those for natural increase, since the various movements fall under rather special categories in which a large measure of control can be exercised. First, the Europeans are small enough in number to allow a careful census of their entries and departures; secondly, all foreign Asiatics are subject to strict regulations and few manage to enter or leave the country without surveillance; finally, the migration of native workers is almost entirely under the direct control of the state authorities.

In recent years there has been a steady increase in the numbers of Europeans entering Indo-China. Between 1919 and 1936 the excess of immigrants over emigrants has averaged from 1,000 to 1,500 per annum. Over 80% of the Europeans settle in the two states of Tonkin and Cochin-China (see p. 250).

During the last two decades, an average of about 45,000 Chinese have yearly entered the country; emigration is on a rather lower scale and there has been a steady excess of entries over departures. The Chinese come principally from Hainan and from Canton and Fukien (see p. 254).

Other Asiatic peoples, including Javanese, Japanese, Filipinos and Indians, have also entered the country, but their numbers are insignificant.

Emigration to countries overseas by the indigenous native population is practically non-existent. A small number have, however, moved as contract labourers to the French colonial possessions in the south-west Pacific (see p. 341).

Internal Migration

The lack of balance in population between the north and south of Indo-China on the one hand and between the coastal lowlands and interior mountains on the other, is a significant factor influencing internal migration. Since the war of 1914–18, natives from Tonkin have been recruited to work on the rubber plantations of Cochin-China and Cambodia. According to figures given by the General Labour Inspectorate about 104,000 Annamite labourers disembarked at Saigon between 1919 and 1934, while 52,000 sought repatriation in the same period, giving an average annual excess of 3,500. These statistics refer only to organized contract labour (see p. 339); an indeterminate number of natives also migrates southwards under no binding contract.

Mineral exploitation has been responsible for another movement of population. As the anthracite mines of Hon Gay and the tin mines of Nam Patene both lie in thinly peopled areas, the labour supply for their working has had to be brought from the coastal lowlands of Tonkin and north Annam.

The number of Annamites who have migrated to the southern plantations and to the chief mining districts is only a small fraction of the total population living in the coastal lowlands. These migrations are, moreover, almost exclusively temporary in character. Permanent settlement of the thinly peopled areas has never been on a large scale, despite the introduction of many organized schemes for its encourage-ment.

RURAL OVER-POPULATION

In the coastal lowlands of northern Indo-China the rural population frequently exceeds the means of subsistence, and in bad years when the rice harvest is a failure, many thousands of peasants suffer under-nourishment. Attempts have been made to allay these conditions by increasing the quantity and quality of production and by encouraging migration to other parts of the country. Irrigation and drainage schemes and a more careful selection of seed grain have led to an increase both in rice output and in the yield per hectare. Even if further increases in rice output are achieved, however, and the areas under supplementary crops extended, the average annual increase of the delta populations is probably too rapid to adjust agricultural pro-duction to human requirements. Moreover, in none of the over-populated areas is industry likely to prove capable of absorbing more than a few thousand of the surplus workers. The only immediate solution lies in the transference of the surplus population to the more thinly settled regions.

As early as 1888 efforts were made to relieve congestion in the Tonkin delta by encouraging settlement in the interior. An Order in this year granted free concessions of land to all natives who made application, while a subsequent Order in 1925 laid down that holdings should not be more than 5 ha. and simplified the procedure whereby a provisional concession could become permanent. Neither of these measures achieved more than a limited success. In November 1937, according to statistics furnished by local officials, only about 1,000 emigrants from the delta were living in the province of Thai Nguyen and about 150 in the province of Yen Bay, while the other thinly settled provinces of Tonkin had an even smaller number of emigrants. The failure of the policy for individual concessions has led since 1936 to the adoption of a scheme for group colonization. Although the establishment of collective concessions is likely to prove more successful than the 'petite colonisation' or colonization by individual families, it may be questioned whether the uplands of the interior can ever absorb the surplus population from the delta. In north and west Tonkin, where inhospitable plateaux and mountain ranges predominate, the fertile zones of small extent along or near the valley bottoms have long been occupied by native groups such as the Thai, Man, Miao and Lolo, so the areas available for settlement are seriously restricted. It is estimated that not more than 80,000 ha. in this region can offer a living to sedentary cultivators; thus, on the basis of 1 inhabitant per ha. (100 per sq.km.) under 100,000 new colonists could settle here, and even assuming a density similar to that of the Tonkin delta is possible the region could not absorb much in excess of 300,000 emigrants.

The schemes for colonization in the interior of Tonkin have been paralleled by attempts to organize migration from the over-populated provinces of the delta to the newly formed alluvial lands along the coast. An Order of July 1930 directed that all such ground should be reserved for the indigenous population, and during the last decade many thousands of peasants have been settled in these areas. The reclaimed coastal regions, however, can be expected to absorb only a small fraction of the surplus population.

Settlement of Tonkinese families on the lowlands of the south offers the real solution to the demographic problem. Excluding the organized movement of contract labourers, whose migration to the southern plantations has for the most part been of a temporary character, few systematic efforts to encourage permanent settlement in Cochin-China and Cambodia took place before 1936. A decree in this year reserved 28,000 ha. for Tonkinese settlement in the provinces of Rach Gia and Ha Tien in Cochin-China; another decree in 1938 extended the area to 70,000 ha. This reserved zone lies north of the canal from Rach Gia to Ha Tien; the soil here is fertile, though canals are needed for purposes of drainage. The transference of families to this region is rather in the nature of an experiment which, if successful, should encourage further settlement in western Cochin-China, where it has been estimated that an area of 500,000 ha. could be set aside for settlement by the Tonkinese population.

Over-population is a serious problem also in the narrow, coastal lowlands of north and central Annam. Attempts have been made to settle colonists on the little-developed lowlands of south Annam and on the plateaux of the interior. From the plains around Binh Dinh and Phu Yen access to the plateau regions is relatively easy, and before the French occupation two Annamite settlements had already been established in the Moi country near An Khe and along the Song Ba valley. Since the beginning of the present century, the French government has sought to increase the number of Annamite colonists in these regions as well as in the Darlac and Lang Bian plateaux and in parts of Laos. The movement has been facilitated by improved road communications. As a means of encouraging further settlements, a decree in 1936 established settlement offices in all the provinces of Annam.

The successful settlement of Tonkinese and Annamites in the interior and in the Mekong delta seems indispensable to the future economic development of Indo-China. By creating in 1937 a *Conseil supérieur de Colonisation*, the government recognized the urgency of the problem caused by a rapidly growing population on limited agricultural land and the need for a comprehensive, efficiently organized scheme covering the whole country. This body selects areas suitable for colonization, sets up experimental farms, arranges for the transportation of migrants, and grants credit loans to the peasants in the early years of their settlement.

RURAL SETTLEMENT

The great majority of the population of Indo-China lives in small nucleated villages and dispersed or scattered settlement is exceptional. In Tonkin, Annam and Cochin-China, where the villages are usually surrounded by a bamboo hedge, the nucleation of settlement may be attributed to the communal organization of Annamite society, to the need for co-operative effort in agricultural activities, to the greater

Plate 37. Levee settlement to the north of Hanoi in the Tonkin delta

The photograph was taken in the dry season and the fields on the left are in the dry bed of the Fleuve Rouge, a channel of which runs diagonally across the picture. Pits from which earth for the embankments has been dug can be seen full of water to the right of the river. The absence of scattered houses is a notable feature.

Plate 38. Hill-foot settlement to the north of Haiphong, bordering the Tonkin delta

Small rounded hills determine the siting of villages in this region. Narrow, terraced fields on the upper slopes of the hills contrast with the larger fields of the flat country.

degree of security which such concentration offered and to the attractions of a particular site. Similar causes lie behind the nucleation of villages in other parts of the country. This type of rural settlement is characteristic of almost all the lowland areas of south-east Asia.

A satisfactory study of the settlement patterns and sites is handicapped by the lack of large-scale maps covering the whole country. Although a considerable stretch of the coastal lowlands is mapped on the scales of 1 : 25,000 and 1 : 100,000, vast areas in the interior have no maps on a scale greater than 1 : 500,000. Figs. 68–76, which have been photographically reduced from the 1 : 25,000 sheets, show accurately the pattern of rural settlement in the coastal plains. A number of distinctive settlement types emerge and these are discussed below, while a brief statement is also made of the types of settlement in the regions not covered by large-scale maps.

Levee Settlements

In the delta regions of Tonkin and Annam the levees developed by the rivers and the man-made embankments designed to prevent the flooding of the rice fields form one of the most important settlement sites. These levees and embankments are favoured because they give security from floods and provide land for dry crops and orchards, but, above all, because they provide a site for buildings which will not restrict the area available for rice cultivation. It is significant that the need for water has in no way influenced this form of settlement; the water supply is obtained not from the rivers or canals, but from natural ponds collecting rain water and from wells which reach down to the water table (Plate 37 and Fig. 77). The villages on the levees are strung out in a roughly rectangular form and sometimes stretch uninterruptedly for many kilometres. They are found along both banks of the Fleuve Rouge, the Song Day and many other rivers in the Tonkin delta, and are also seen in the lower valleys of the Song Ma, Song Ca and Song Tra Khuc in Annam.

In addition to the levee settlements on the river banks, there are also groups of habitations on the levees which appear in the middle of the river and on those which flank an abandoned meander. The villages of Luang Quan, east of Son Tay, and Tu Nhien, south of Hanoi, lie on embankments built up by the Fleuve Rouge; they are entirely surrounded by the waters of the river during the flood season, but at other times are connected with the villages on the main banks by a narrow stretch of sand and mud (Fig. 77). Many fine examples of settlements on the levee of an abandoned meander are found near Vinh Yen in the Tonkin delta and along the lower course of the Song Ma in Annam.

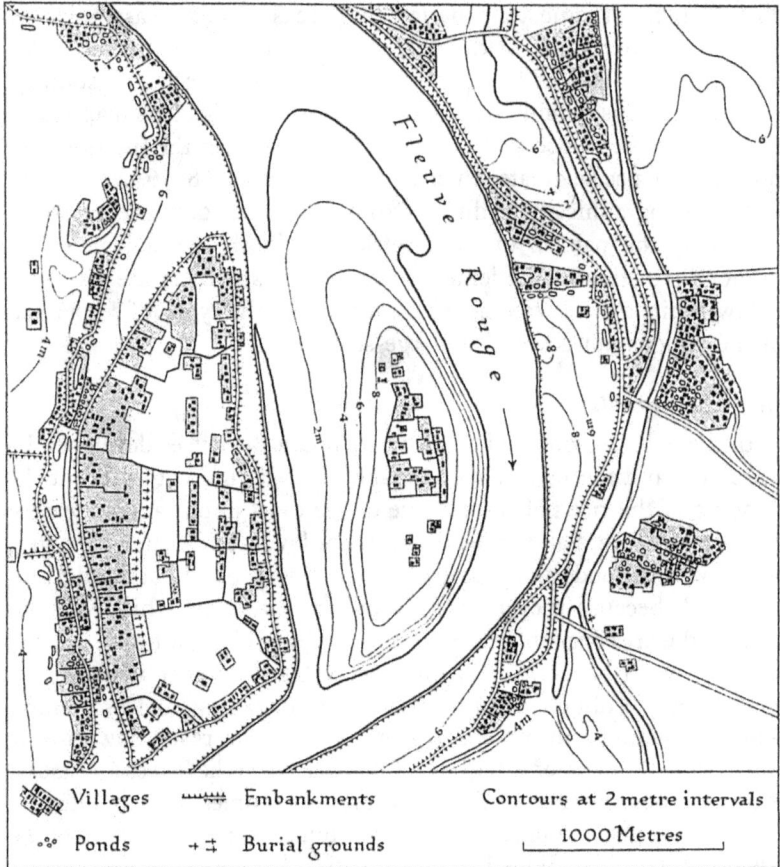

Fig. 77. Village sites: embankment type

Most of the villages are protected from flooding by artificial embankments. The one in the centre of the map is on a sandbank thrown up by the river and is above normal flood level, though it is surrounded by water at such times. The lowest land, even where it is protected by embankments, is reserved for rice growing, and the villages are placed on higher ground which is less valuable agriculturally. Tracks have been omitted except in the villages or where they follow the embankments.

Source: Carte du Delta du Tonkin, 1 : 25,000; sheet no. 27 (1903).

Hill-foot Settlements

A large number of villages are arranged around the foot of hills bordering or rising like islands above the plain. As in the case of levee settlements, these villages form perfect illustrations of the tendency on the part of the peasants to establish themselves on slightly elevated ground, which gives shelter from flooding and at the same time leaves the greatest possible area of lowland available for rice

Fig. 78. Village sites: hillfoot type

The embankments in this area are smaller than those in Fig. 77 and serve to regulate the water supply rather than to protect the villages. Tracks have been omitted except in the villages or where they follow the embankments.

Source: Carte du Delta de Thanh Hoa, 1 : 25,000; sheet no. 73 (1905).

cultivation. In the Song Len and Song Ma valleys, small isolated knolls of crystalline rocks form prominent features of the landscape, and at their base villages are strung out in an elliptical pattern, while the surrounding lowland is almost entirely devoid of settlement (Fig. 78). Further examples of hill-foot villages are seen in the Tonkin delta (Plate 38) and in western Cochin-China, where the granitic hills of Tri Ton have a girdle of settlement (Fig. 76). As in the levee villages, the supply of water is obtained from ponds and wells.

Sand-dune Settlements

Settlements on or at the foot of sand dunes are a common feature along a large part of the coastline. In the Tonkin delta and north Annam, the sand dunes, which extend in a series of parallel bands

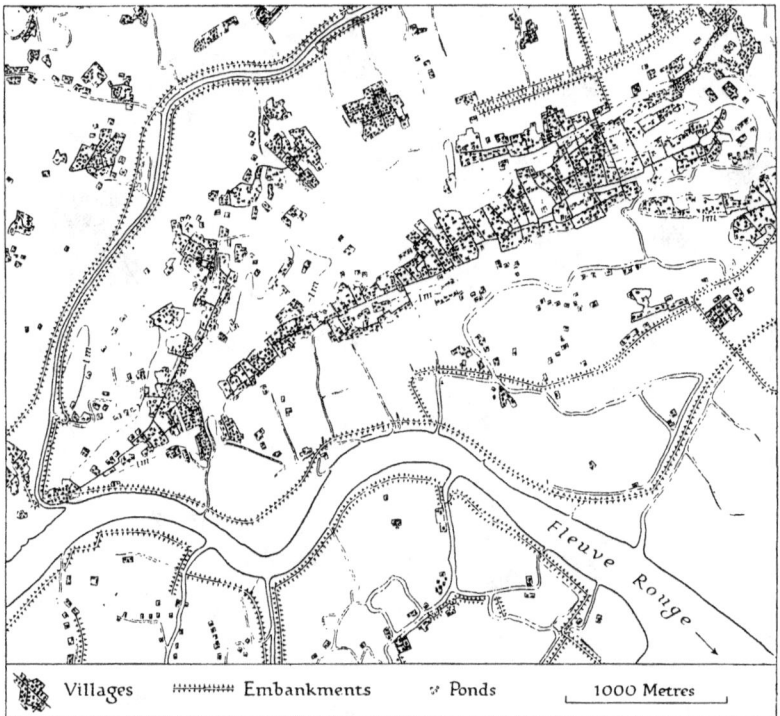

Fig. 79. Village sites: sand-dune type

The old-established villages are confined to the sand dunes which are only slightly higher than the surrounding land. The scattered houses are new settlements, a feature which departs completely from the Annamite tradition. Tracks have been omitted except in the villages or where they follow the embankments.

Source: Carte du Delta du Tonkin, 1 : 25,000; sheet no. 62 (1905).

from the coast, are occupied by long lines of villages, while the low-lying land between the dunes is devoted to rice cultivation (Figs. 69, 79). The height of the dunes above the surrounding land is frequently less than 2 m. In the stretch of coastline between the Porte d'Annam and Hue the sand dunes are much higher, in places attaining an elevation of 10 m., and form a single continuous band (Fig. 70). The settlements here are found in strips at the foot of the seaward and landward slopes and the summits are deserted, whereas villages spread over the whole surface of the low dunes farther north. The welling up of springs at the junction of the permeable sands and impermeable clays has been a factor influencing settlement. Other sand-dune villages are seen in the coastal plains near Quang Ngai, Quang Nam, Phan Rang (Annam) and Tra Vinh (Cochin-China)

River Bank Settlements

Levee, hill-foot and sand-dune settlements predominate in the plains of Tonkin and Annam, while most of the villages in Cochin-China lie along the banks of the rivers (Figs. 75, 80). This striking contrast in settlement sites as between the lowlands of the north and south is closely related to the differing hydrographical conditions. The rivers of the north have, in general, an unstable regime and annually flood their banks restricting settlement, as we have seen, to levees and artificial embankments. The Mekong, on the other hand, does not overflow its banks, since a large part of the summer flood water drains into the lake of Tonle Sap before reaching the delta, while the rest is evenly distributed through a number of broad channels. An almost continuous line of villages runs along both banks of the two main arms of the Mekong; villages are also found in narrow strips along the banks of many other streams and almost all the main canals. Settlement on these sites is advantageous from the commercial viewpoint, owing to the ease of communication by water. The interfluves are devoted to rice cultivation.

Lake Settlements

Two distinct kinds of settlement sites are seen in the Tonle Sap region of Cambodia. Most of the settlements lie on rising ground above the summer level of the lake as, for instance, Pursat, Kompong Thom and Siem Reap, but a certain number have been built on the banks of these lakes at its low-water level. These villages are built on piles, and in summer when the lake overflows they are entirely surrounded by water. Kompong Luong is one of the largest of the villages so situated. The great abundance of fish in the lakes is the chief attraction to settlement (Fig. 81).

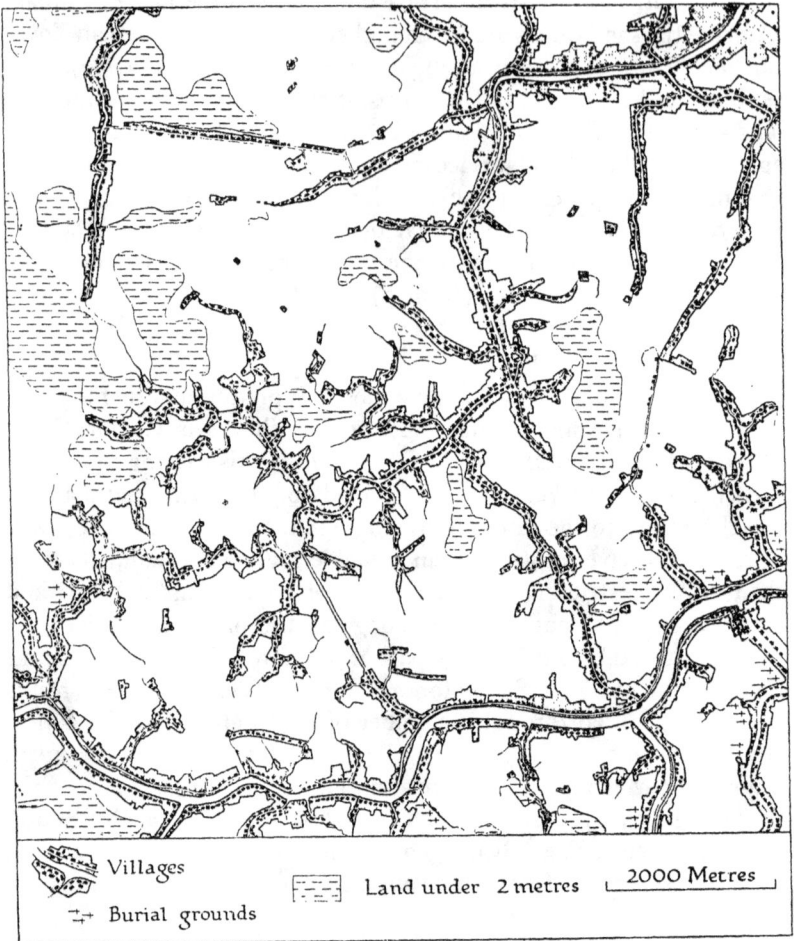

Fig. 80. Village sites: river-bank type

The rivers in the Mekong delta are not liable to floods; consequently there are no embankments and the villages line the river banks. The remainder of the land is used almost exclusively for rice growing.

Source: Carte de Cochinchine, 1 : 25,000; sheet no. 234/12 (1928).

Dispersed Settlements

As already indicated, dispersed settlement is rarely seen in Indo-China, though it is found on the newly colonized mud flats of the

Tonkin delta and southern Cochin-China. In both these regions the coastline is rapidly extending seawards and the new land has attracted a number of settlers (see p. 239) whose houses are widely scattered or grouped along a protecting embankment. This form of settlement is well seen near the mouth of the Fleuve Rouge (Fig. 79).

Fig. 81. Fishing village built on piles, Tonle Sap

Source: P. Chevey and F. Le Poulain, 'La Pêche dans les eaux douces du Cambodge', *Travaux de l'Institut océanographique de l'Indochine*, no. 5, plate 26 (Saigon, 1940).

Mountain Settlements

The absence of large-scale maps precludes any detailed study of settlement in the mountain regions. A few general observations, however, can be made. The Moi group of peoples live in small villages set in forest clearings; though shifting cultivation is practised (see p. 146), the villages normally remain permanently in one place. In the mountains of Tonkin and northern Laos, the valley bottoms are occupied by Thai settlements, while at higher levels there are the settlements of the Man and Miao peoples (see p. 151).

Rubber Plantation Settlements

The development of rubber plantations in eastern Cochin-China and Cambodia has given rise to a special kind of settlement pattern. As the plantations lie in thinly peopled areas, imported Tonkinese labour is largely employed and villages have been built to accommodate the labourers. These groups of habitations are frequently linear in pattern with long, low wooden houses set wide apart (Plate 42). As the labourers work for wages and produce no necessities themselves, each village has a weekly or twice-weekly market where food, clothing and other necessities are obtained from Chinese and Annamite merchants.

Mining Settlements

In the coal-mining region of Hon Gay (Tonkin) and the tin-mining region of Nam Patene (Laos), where imported labour is used, the settlements resemble those on the rubber plantations. There is the same linear arrangement, but the houses are generally more crowded together (Plate 47).

TOWNS AND CITIES

The development of towns and cities on western lines has been one of the most striking transformations carried out by the French in Indo-China. Before the French conquest urban growth was most backward; the towns were of two kinds, namely, administrative centres and commercial centres, but, owing to frequent political changes, both kinds lacked stability, the suppression of the one usually leading to the decline of the other. The towns only began truly to prosper with the unification of the peninsula at the end of the last century and with the long period of economic progress which followed. The growth of agriculture, industry and commerce, and the construction of roads and railways has been paralleled by the rebuilding of old and the creation of new towns. Among the rebuilt towns are Hanoi, Haiphong, Nam Dinh, Bac Ninh and Lang Son in Tonkin; Hue, Tourane, Vinh, Qui Nhon and Nha Trang in Annam; Saigon, My Tho, Can Tho and Bac Lieu in Cochin-China; Phnom Penh, Battambang and Siem Reap in Cambodia; Vientiane and Luang Prabang in Laos. The newly created towns include the health stations of Dalat and Chapa, the agricultural centre of Kontum and the port of Ream.

In 1936 there were forty-five towns in Indo-China with a population exceeding 5,000:

Over 100,000	4
50,000–100,000	1
20,000–50,000	7
10,000–20,000	9
5,000–10,000	24

Source: Recensement de 1936, *Statistique générale de l'Indochine* (Hanoi, 1937).

The four cities of over 100,000 inhabitants were as follows: Hanoi, 149,000; Cho Lon, 145,000; Saigon, 111,000; Phnom Penh, 103,000. Indo-China has thus a greater number of such cities than the neighbouring countries of Siam and Burma, but none of the four approaches in size either Bangkok (886,000 in 1937) or Rangoon (400,000 in 1931). Hanoi is the seat of the central government and an important communications centre; Cho Lon is the leading industrial centre and Saigon the chief port of the country; Phnom Penh is the capital of Cambodia and a large river port. Each of these cities, with the exception of Cho Lon, has been planned on the basis of French models, with well-constructed buildings, broad streets and tree-lined boulevards. Since 1931, from an administrative point of view, Saigon and Cho Lon have formed one single urban agglomeration.

Of the forty-one centres with a population of between 5,000 and 100,000, thirteen are maritime ports, while the remainder are provincial capitals and market towns, some of which, like Nam Dinh, Dap Cau, and Can Tho, have important industries. In this group certain of the towns, such as Haiphong (70,000) and Tourane (23,000), have a building and street pattern which clearly bears the stamp of French influence. On the other hand, there are a number of 'historic' towns—Thanh Hoa, Dong Hoi, Hue, Binh Dinh—with the traditional urban pattern, in which the main buildings are surrounded by a wall and a moat (Plates 83, 86). Although modern buildings have been constructed alongside the old, these towns are still more Annamite than French in character.

The concentration of urban centres in the coastal plains is the most striking feature in the distribution pattern of the towns and cities. The distribution follows naturally from the physical conditions and from the history of both native and European colonization. Out of the forty-five towns of over 5,000 inhabitants, thirty-four are situated along or near the coast, nearly two-thirds of which number lie in the delta regions of the Fleuve Rouge and the Mekong. Of the remaining eleven towns, seven are located either in the inland plains of Cambodia or in the valley of the Mekong. Thus, only four towns with populations exceeding 5,000 are found in the mountainous regions which form the greater part of Indo-China, and all, except one, are in Tonkin.

THE EUROPEAN POPULATION

In Indo-China, as in other tropical colonies, the Europeans form a small minority of the total population. Despite an increase in their numbers from 24,000 in 1913 to 42,345 in 1937, there is still only

1 European, on the average, for 544 inhabitants, taking the country as a whole; the proportion in each state is shown in the table below:

	Total population	Europeans and assimilated groups	No. of inhabitants, per European	% of Europeans in relation to total population
Annam	5,656,000	4,982	1,135	0·09
Cambodia	3,046,000	2,534	1,202	0·08
Cochin-China	4,616,000	16,084	286	0·35
Laos	1,012,000	574	1,763	0·06
Tonkin	8,700,000	18,171	478	0·35
	23,030,000	42,345	544	0·18

Source: *Recensement européen du 28 janvier* 1937.

The term 'Europeans and assimilated groups' includes all persons holding the status of a 'European' in the country, whatever their nationality or colour. The proportion of whites to the total population is thus even lower than the figures indicate.

Almost all the 'Europeans' live in the coastal lowlands and interior plains; more than three-quarters are in the two delta areas of the Fleuve Rouge and the Mekong, more than half in the towns of Saigon, Cho Lon, Hanoi, Haiphong, Hue, Tourane, and Phnom Penh. It is significant that very few live in the mountain regions for, at heights below 1,000 m., the virulence of malaria forbids their settlement, while the high areas have in general the disadvantage of poor communications and inadequate labour resources; the health stations at Chapa, Tam Dao and Dalat attract large numbers of temporary visitors, but only few permanent residents.

In 1937 the occupations of the 'Europeans' were as follows:

Occupation	No.
Army and navy	10,779
'Fonctionnaires'	3,873
Liberal professions	1,795
Commerce, banking and insurance	1,766
Mining and industry	1,097
Agriculture and forestry	705
Transport	419
Domestic and personal service	75
Total gainfully occupied	20,509
No occupation	21,836
	42,345

Source: *Annuaire statistique de l'Indochine, 1936–7*, p. 25 (Hanoi, 1938).

Over two-thirds of the gainfully occupied 'Europeans' are thus either in the army or navy or in official government positions. Many individuals in the military class only stay in the country for one or two years, though some return several years later. The 'fonctionnaire' class includes all those employed in the administrative and civil services as well as in the organization of the police system. Their numbers have fallen by nearly 25% since 1929, owing partly to the repercussions of the world economic crisis and partly to the increasingly common practice of replacing Europeans by native officials. Outside the military and 'fonctionnaire' classes nearly a third of the 'Europeans' are gainfully occupied in the liberal professions, especially law, medicine, and teaching. The small number employed in transport is misleading because, as all the railways, except the Yunnan line, are state-owned, those working in railway services are classed as 'fonctionnaires'. One of the most significant features of the table is the low place of agriculture and forestry in the list of occupations; almost all the 705 'Europeans' engaged in agriculture and forestry are managers or supervisors of plantations, worked by native labour, and only very few cultivate the ground themselves.

The place of birth of the 'European' population in 1937 is given in the following table:

Place of birth	Males	Females	Total
France	13,229	5,816	19,045
Indo-China	7,552	7,886	15,438
French India	674	324	998
Other French colonies	1,752	593	2,345
Japan	108	99	207
Other countries	2,796	699	3,495
Not known	441	376	817
Total	26,552	15,793	42,345

Source: *Annuaire statistique de l'Indochine, 1936–7*, p. 24 (Hanoi, 1938).

The small number of 'Europeans' living in Indo-China, born outside the French empire, is one of the most striking features of this table. This group includes not only whites, mainly Britons and Americans, but also a few Asiatics, of which the Japanese and Filipinos are most numerous. Apart from the foreign 'Europeans' and the 3,343 born in French India and the other French colonies, chiefly Réunion and the Antilles, all the rest have their place of birth either in France or in Indo-China. Those of French birth constitute the largest group; most originate from the departments of the Midi and, above all, from Corsica, though Bretons are fairly numerous. The group of individuals born in Indo-China is very heterogeneous. Over half are of a mother born in Indo-China, over one-quarter of a mother and father both born in Indo-China, while only about one-seventh are of a mother and father born in France. This category also includes many individuals of mixed blood, who have obtained French citizenship through one or other of their parents, and a number of natives who have been naturalized, made up mainly of native women legitimately married to a European. It is this last group which has largely caused the number of females born in Indo-China to be higher than that of males, whereas the reverse is true for those born in all the other countries.

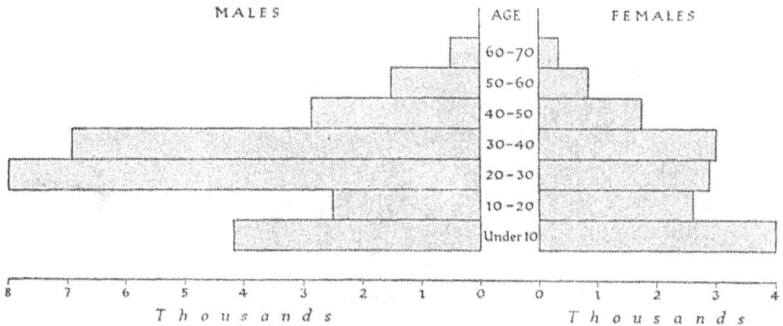

Fig. 82. Age groups of the European population, 1937
Source: C. Robequain, *L'Evolution économique de l'Indochine française*, p. 32 (Paris, 1939).

The relative number of 'Europeans' in the two sexes at various ages is shown in Fig. 82. Although the proportion of females has increased since the beginning of the present century, thanks to the progress made in the combating of disease, in the improvement of domestic hygiene and in the provision of health stations, they are still numerically very much smaller than the males. The small number of 'Europeans' between 10 and 20 years of age living in the country is an indication that most parents still prefer to send their children to France to be educated. Another interesting feature brought out by the age pyramid is the predominance of the 20–40 age group, and the very high proportion of males within the group. Over half of the male 'Europeans' over the age of 15 years are celibate. The unbalanced sex ratio has thus led to an instability in the resident population.

The following table on the length of stay of 'Europeans' in Indo-China is further evidence of their instability:

Length of stay	No.
Under 1 year	5,732
1 to 5 years	11,333
5 to 10 years	7,531
10 to 15 years	5,182
Over 15 years	11,195
Not known	1,372
Total	42,345

Source: C. Robequain, *L'Evolution économique de l'Indochine française*, p. 33 (Paris, 1939).

Nearly 40% had lived in Indo-China for less than 5 years. Of the 26% who had made the country their residence for over 15 years, a high proportion probably comprised 'Europeans' of mixed blood; this percentage would certainly be much lower if calculations were based on pure whites alone.

In view of the mixed nature of the 'European' population and of the impermanency of their sojourn in the country, it is impossible to give satisfactory figures for the natural increase of the pure white element. If detailed vital statistics were available they would throw light on the effects of a tropical climate upon the natural reproduction of a western European. The birth-rate figure of 32 per 1,000 and the death-rate figure of 14 per 1,000 as given in the *Annuaire statistique de l'Indochine* for 1936 relates to the 'European' population as a whole and not specifically to those of pure white blood. The death-rate has fallen rapidly during the present century with the improvement of medical assistance and of hygiene.

THE CHINESE POPULATION

Chinese immigrants have for many centuries played an important part in the economic life of Indo-China. The political domination of China early in the Christian era led to a considerable influx which did not cease with the formation of an independent Annamite kingdom in the ninth century. At the time of the arrival of the Europeans in the sixteenth century the Chinese had established a firm hold over commercial activities in Annam, and in company with the political expansion of the Annamites, their influence later spread into the Mekong delta, or what is now Cochin-China. The French conquest further strengthened their power in the country, not only because it assured peace and order and stimulated economic activity, but also because the Chinese came to be regarded as useful intermediaries between the whites and the natives. As a result of these favourable conditions, the Chinese population in Cochin-China alone increased from 44,000 in 1879 to 56,500 in 1889 and to 120,000 in 1906. In the country as a whole they have increased from 293,000 in 1912 to 400,000 in 1926 and to 419,000 in 1931, declining to 326,000 in 1936, owing to the effects of the world economic crisis. The numbers are now again rapidly increasing under the stimulus of the war in China.

The Chinese population is unequally distributed among the five states. In 1936 their distribution was as follows:

	No. of Chinese	% of total population
Annam	11,000	0·2
Cambodia	106,000	3·5
Cochin-China	171,000	3·7
Laos	3,000	0·3
Tonkin	35,000	0·4
Total	326,000	1·4

Source: *Annuaire statistique de l'Indochine, 1936–7*, p. 21 (Hanoi, 1938).

Over 80% of the Chinese thus live in Cochin-China and Cambodia and they form a higher proportion of the population than in the other states. Large groups are found in Cho Lon, Saigon, and Phnom Penh. As in the other countries of south-east Asia, where they form a much higher percentage of the total population, the Chinese have come mainly from the southern provinces of China, specially Kwang-tung, Fukien and Hainan. They are organized into communities which function as charitable and mutual aid associations.

The figures given in the above table do not include the large numbers of Chinese of mixed blood, the offspring of unions with the native population. Sino-Annamites, who are referred to in the census as 'Minh-Huong', number about 62,000 in Cochin-China and 11,000 in Tonkin; Sino-Cambodians number over 100,000.

Most of the Chinese in Indo-China are traders or commercial middlemen. They own almost all the many thousands of river craft which ply on the rivers and canals of Cochin-China; they buy the bulk of the rice crop grown by the peasant, while gaining a strangle-hold over him by means of loans at high rates of interest; and they prepare the rice for export in their own mills. The export of fresh-water fish from Cambodia is for the most part under their control. They are also found as retailers in many market towns both in the plains and the mountains. Outside these commercial activities there are a number of Chinese who practice market gardening in the neighbourhood of the large towns, while the large-scale cultivation of pepper near Ha Tien and Kampot is largely in their hands. Further, some are employed as artisans in a variety of small industries.

Many of the Chinese immigrants are celibate and many more leave their family on the native soil, to which they return after a period of stay abroad. Since the Revolution of 1911, however, an increasing proportion has elected to remain permanently in Indo-China. Although the proportion of women to men has increased in the same period the sex ratio is still unbalanced. Both the birth-rate and the death-rate are probably high, but detailed vital statistics are not available.

BIBLIOGRAPHICAL NOTE

(1) The census returns for 1936 are published by the *Statistique générale de l'Indochine*, Hanoi. Summarized statements appear in the *Annuaire statistique de l'Indochine, 1936–7* (Hanoi, 1938).

(2) *Distribution of Population.* A good account is given in P. Gourou, *L'Utilisation du Sol en Indochine française* (Paris, 1940).

(3) *Growth of Population.* This section is based on C. Robequain's 'Notes sur les modifications du peuplement de l'Indochine française depuis cinquante ans', *Comptes Rendus du Congrès International de Géographie, Paris, 1931*, vol. III, pp. 491–500 (Paris, 1934) and T. Smolski's 'Les statistiques de la population indochinoise', *Congrès International de la Population, Paris, 1937*, vol. VI, pp. 56–67 (Paris, 1938).

(4) *Rural Over-population.* This subject is treated in the following works: P. Bernard, *Nouveaux aspects du problème économique indochinois* (Paris, 1937); P. Gourou, *L'Utilisation du Sol en Indochine française* (Paris, 1940); 'Conseil supérieur de la Colonisation', *Bulletin économique de l'Indochine*, vol. XLI, pp. 715–56 (Hanoi, 1938); C. Robequain, *L'Evolution économique de l'Indochine française* (Paris, 1939); Tran Van Thong, 'Mémoire sur la colonisation indigène en Indochine', *Bulletin économique de l'Indochine*, vol. XLI, pp. 1117–25 (Hanoi, 1938).

(5) *Rural Settlement.* P. Gourou, 'Les divers types de village du Delta tonkinois et leur répartition', *Comptes Rendus du Congrès International de Géographie, Paris, 1931*, vol. III, pp. 487–90 (Paris, 1934); P. Gourou, *L'Utilisation du Sol en Indochine française* (Paris, 1940); C. Robequain, *Le Thanh Hoa: Etude géographique d'une Province annamite*, vol. II (Paris, 1929).

(6) *Towns and Cities.* C. Briffaut, *La Cité annamite*, 3 vols (Paris, 1909–12); Georges Maspero, *Un Empire Colonial français, L'Indochine:* vol. I, p. 48 (Paris, 1929).

(7) *The European Population.* The fullest treatment is given in C. Robequain's *L'Evolution économique de l'Indochine française* (Paris, 1939) and in Virginia Thompson's *French Indo-China* (London, 1937).

(8) *The Chinese Population.* On this subject see Etienne Dennery's *Foules d'Asie* (Paris, 1930) and C. Robequain's *L'Evolution économique de l'Indochine française* (Paris, 1939).

Chapter XI

AGRICULTURE AND FORESTRY

Introduction
Native Agriculture: Rice; Subsidiary Food Crops; Oleaginous Crops; Fibre Crops;
   Other Agricultural Crops; Livestock; Land System; Agricultural Credit and
   Agricultural Co-operation
Plantation Agriculture: Rubber Plantations; Coffee Plantations; Tea Plantations
Forestry: Forest Exploitation; Forest Conservation and Improvement
Bibliographical Note

INTRODUCTION

Agriculture is the chief means of livelihood for most of the inhabitants
of Indo-China. Food crops form the primary source of wealth and the
rearing of livestock is little developed, though many oxen and buffaloes are kept for work in the fields. The capital, initiative and engineering skill of the French colonists, seen in the establishment of
irrigation schemes and in the setting up of agricultural research
stations, have led to improvements both in the quality and output of
native production. During the last half-century modern plantations,
employing native labour under white supervision, have been organized for the large-scale production of rubber, coffee and tea; their
advanced methods of cultivation and of marketing contrast with the
primitive techniques of native agriculture. Although the development of plantations has opened up large areas hitherto uncultivated
or only partially cultivated, the area under native and European crops,
owing to the existence of vast forested mountains and plateaux, is still
only about 6 million ha. out of a total area for the whole country of
74 million ha.

In a country where agriculture is the predominant occupation a
knowledge of soil types and soil characteristics has special significance.
Climate is the principal factor influencing soil formation in Indo-
China. Over the greater part of the country the annual rainfall greatly
exceeds evaporation and results in a downward movement of water
which leaches out the soluble bases from the soil. The amount of
organic matter (humus) in the soil largely determines the order in
which the bases are removed. Despite the luxuriance of the plant
growth, humus is generally found in small proportions, owing to the
continually high temperatures which rapidly break down the plant

remains, and since water containing little or no humus dissolves silica more easily than alumina and iron oxides, the former is the first to be washed away. This process is termed laterization, and lateritic soils when fully formed as a rule comprise only alumina and iron oxides. When laterization is immature the soil may be very fertile, the fertility depending in part on the parent material, as in the case of the 'terres rouges' which have developed on basaltic lava flows. These red soils lie for the most part in the uplands of south Indo-China (Fig. 83) and cover altogether about 35,000 sq.km. of which 70% may be used for agricultural purposes.

Laterization is retarded by forest cover and when the land is cleared for cultivation good crops may be obtained for a few seasons, but the minerals are rapidly leached out of the soil which soon becomes uneconomic to work. For this reason, many native agriculturalists practise the system of shifting cultivation, in which the land is cropped for a short time and then abandoned. This method of cultivation, however, has destructive effects, for in addition to the loss of mineral matter, the clearing of the forest lays the soil open to surface erosion which is particularly active owing to the intensity of the rainfall. The ill effects of laterization and soil erosion can be avoided by proper methods of cultivation and manuring combined with strict control of forest exploitation.

The Tonkin delta is built up of alluvial soils, comprising sand, loam (*limon*) and clay in varying proportions. The soil is predominantly sandy near Phu Lang Thuong, to the north of the Fleuve Rouge, and west of Hai Duong; loam, the most common soil in the delta, may be red, yellow or grey in colour, and, when very dry, often becomes too hard to be ploughed; clay and humus is generally as low as 40 parts per thousand, with an even lower proportion after heavy rains. All the soils of the delta suffer from impoverishment by leaching, though the flooding of the rice fields slows up the process of laterization. Owing to the great care taken in cultivating the ground, and on account of the increased use of chemical fertilizers the delta soils will probably retain their fertility almost indefinitely.

In Cochin-China the most fertile areas extend along both banks of the Mekong, and consist of recent alluvium, which is rich in nitrogen and potassium, but poor in lime and phosphorus. By contrast, the older alluvial land near Saigon is extremely poor, and consists of about 90% pure silica in the form of fine sand, with only a few traces of lime or potash. These 'terres grises' will probably remain of little value for anything other than forest products.

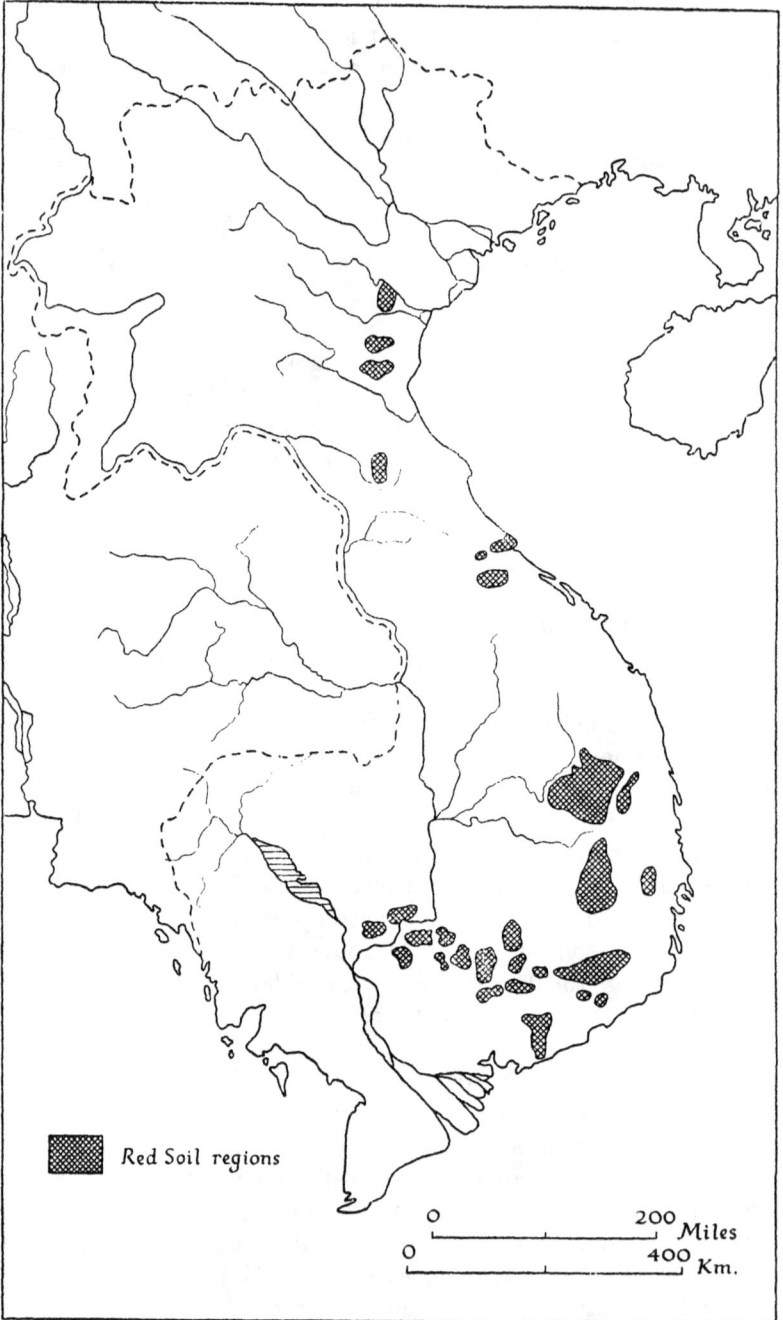

Red Soil regions

Fig. 83. Red soil regions
Source: G. Grandidier, *Atlas des Colonies françaises*, 'Indochine', p. 5 (Paris, 1934).

NATIVE AGRICULTURE

Native agriculture in Indo-China is characterized by a great variety both in the methods and in the intensity of crop production. Three regional types of land utilization can be distinguished. In the coastal plains of Tonkin and Annam as far south as Binh Dinh, the ground is intensively cultivated and two or even three crops are harvested each year; subsistence farming predominates and the exchange of products is insignificant. A second type of agriculture is found in the vast plains of Cochin-China and central Cambodia. Here, land utilization is much less intensive. It is rare for more than one crop to be gathered annually from the same field, while large areas of fertile soil remain uncultivated; the economy is not a closed one and there is a considerable surplus of products for export overseas. Finally, in the forested uplands primitive tribes practise a shifting cultivation, thus following extensive rather than intensive methods. The mountain dwellers are almost entirely self-sufficient and have little commercial dealing with the outside world.*

Farming conditions in the country vary with the regional types of land utilization and are also an index to the great contrasts in social development, especially as between the agricultural lands of the north and those of the south. Although tenant farming is not unknown, direct or family cultivation is the general rule in the coastal plains of Tonkin and Annam where for many centuries the Annamites have tilled the soil and where agriculture is the pivot of the economic system in which the village community is the unit of organization. The peasant lives in a small rudimentary house and generally owns a few poultry and one or two pigs. He grows his crops in the small fields which lie close to the village, and the whole family takes part in the agricultural work; the various families in the village assist one another by sharing an ox or a buffalo and by helping to make up for any shortage of labour at harvest time. The agricultural implements are made of wood and are primitive in design. Rice is the chief crop though maize, legumes, manioc and various fruits are also grown. The peasant is occupied in the production of these crops for the greater part of the year.

The standard of living of the average peasant in Tonkin and Annam is extremely low. According to detailed surveys of family budgets made in the Fleuve Rouge delta by the Chamber of Agricul-

---

* For an account of agriculture in the mountain regions of Indo-China see Chapter VII *passim*.

ture in Tonkin and by independent research workers, the small peasant proprietor, with a family of four and owning about 1 ha. of land, had the following capital resources and annual budget in the year 1934.

Capital Resources

	Piastres
Land	150
Farmhouse	35
Household movables	20
Agricultural implements (including plough, harrow, hoe, five scythes)	12
Buffalo	3
	220

Annual Budget

Expenses:	Piastres	Receipts:	Piastres
Food (other than rice)	22	Sale of poultry and eggs	10
Clothing	9	Sale of piglets	26
Upkeep of house	4	Sale of crops (other than	12
Lighting	3	rice)	
Agricultural implements	2	Hiring out of buffalo	2
Taxes	9	Agricultural wages	5
Miscellaneous (including feasts, marriages, funerals)	12		55
	61		

Source: P. Gourou, *Les Paysans du Delta tonkinois*, pp. 563-4 (Hanoi, 1936). (The figures given are averages computed from several particular cases.)

The balance between expenditure and receipts was principally made up by the sale of what remained of the paddy crop after the required amounts had been set aside for consumption purposes and for seed. In this year the peasant produced about 1,500 kg. (15 quintals) of paddy, with a capital value of 60 piastres, on the basis of the existing selling price of 4 piastres per quintal so that the total annual income of the peasant amounted to 115 piastres. Out of the total paddy production 950 kg. were consumed by the family and 60 kg. set aside for seed, leaving 490 kg. for sale, which brought in a revenue of 19·6 piastres. Although expenses and receipts were satisfactorily balanced in this year, in other years, owing to the great fluctuations in rice production, the peasant has frequently either to cut down his consumption of rice and live at a semi-starvation level or borrow money on usurious terms.

Farming conditions in Cambodia resemble those in the coastal plains of Tonkin and Annam in that the land has long been settled and that peasant proprietorship is the ruling form of agricultural holding (see p. 292). The agriculture, however, is less intensive and there is also not the same mutual assistance of one family by another in the village. Rice is the predominant crop, but secondary crops, such as maize, are more important than in the Annamite countries. The income of the farmer would appear to be slightly higher than that in Tonkin and Annam, but in practice he is no better off, for much of his yearly earnings are taken up with the payment of his debts to Chinese moneylenders.

In Cochin-China conditions differ quite considerably, for, unlike the other lowland regions, the delta of the Mekong has only in comparatively recent times been agriculturally developed. Cochin-China was the first region of Indo-China to be conquered by the French, who were able to parcel out large land holdings for themselves because of the thinness of native land settlement. As a result, the natives settling in the Mekong delta have found it difficult to acquire land, so that to-day indirect cultivation of the soil or tenant farming predominates in this region, while there is also a large 'floating' population of landless agricultural workers (see p. 292). The tenant farmer, or *ta dien*, usually lives in a small roughly constructed house with a vegetable garden and perhaps a few fruit trees adjoining. As in Tonkin, primitive wooden instruments are used. Rice is almost always the most important crop; at harvest time the *ta dien* has frequently to hire additional labour.

The tenant farmer in Cochin-China, with a family of five and a holding of 5–10 ha. of rice fields, has an annual revenue of 150–200 piastres, which is greater than that of the peasant proprietor in Tonkin and Annam, though the higher cost of living in the south tends to equalize these differences. The greater part of the annual revenue is obtained from the disposal of the paddy crop, about 30% (1,250 kg. valued at 50 piastres in 1931) of which is consumed by the family, about 50% is handed over to the proprietor as payment for the land, and the remainder is sold. The sale of paddy on the average brings in rather less than 30 piastres, so that in order to cover his expenses, which amount to about 80 piastres, he either seeks wage-paid employment or receives an advance in money or in paddy from the landowner, whom he repays in kind at the next harvest. Many landowners, however, demand a high interest payment in addition to the payment in kind, and under these conditions the tenant farmers live in perpetual fear of eviction from their land if they fail to return the debts which they have contracted.

RICE

Rice or paddy is the most important crop in Indo-China, covering 5 million ha. out of a total cultivated area of 6 million ha. It forms nearly 90% of the native diet and about 70% of the export trade. Rice straw plays a leading part in the peasant economy as domestic fuel and as fodder for livestock. The rhythm of agricultural life is determined by the needs of rice production, and all other crops give way to its requirements. Fig. 84 shows the chief regions of rice cultivation. Rice is grown by the typical oriental method in which the crop is sown in nursery beds and transplanted in the seedling stage.

Owing to a low average yield of from 12 to 13 quintals per ha., varying according to area and year, the annual production of rice only amounts to about 60 million quintals, which is less than half that of Japan.

A Rice Bureau (*L'Office indochinois du Riz*), two experimental research stations and a number of advisory centres have recently been established to investigate possible improvements in rice production. The Rice Bureau, created in May 1930, includes representatives of the agricultural, industrial and commercial interests; it has attempted to increase the yield and to impose a standard quality for rice entering the factories. The two research stations at Can Tho and Battambang have carried out experimental work on plant selection, hybridization, and the use of fertilizers. Practical help to the farmer is provided by the advisory centres, most of which lie in the Tonkin delta (Fig. 85).

Rice Cultivation in the Tonkin Delta

The cultivation of rice in the Tonkin delta is dependent upon the successful control of river floods. A complex system of waterways, comprising the Fleuve Rouge and its main distributaries, divides the delta into small basins (*casiers*) which appear as one great paddy field interspersed with many small, scattered villages and burial grounds (Fig. 86). The rivers are in flood during the summer, and both natural and artificial embankments protect the land from inundation. Although embankments (*digues*) had been constructed many centuries before the French occupation, the Annamites never succeeded in gaining complete protection against flooding, with the result that famines frequently occurred owing to the destruction of the rice crop. Even after the French had taken over Tonkin, serious ruptures of the embankments continued and widespread flooding occurred in

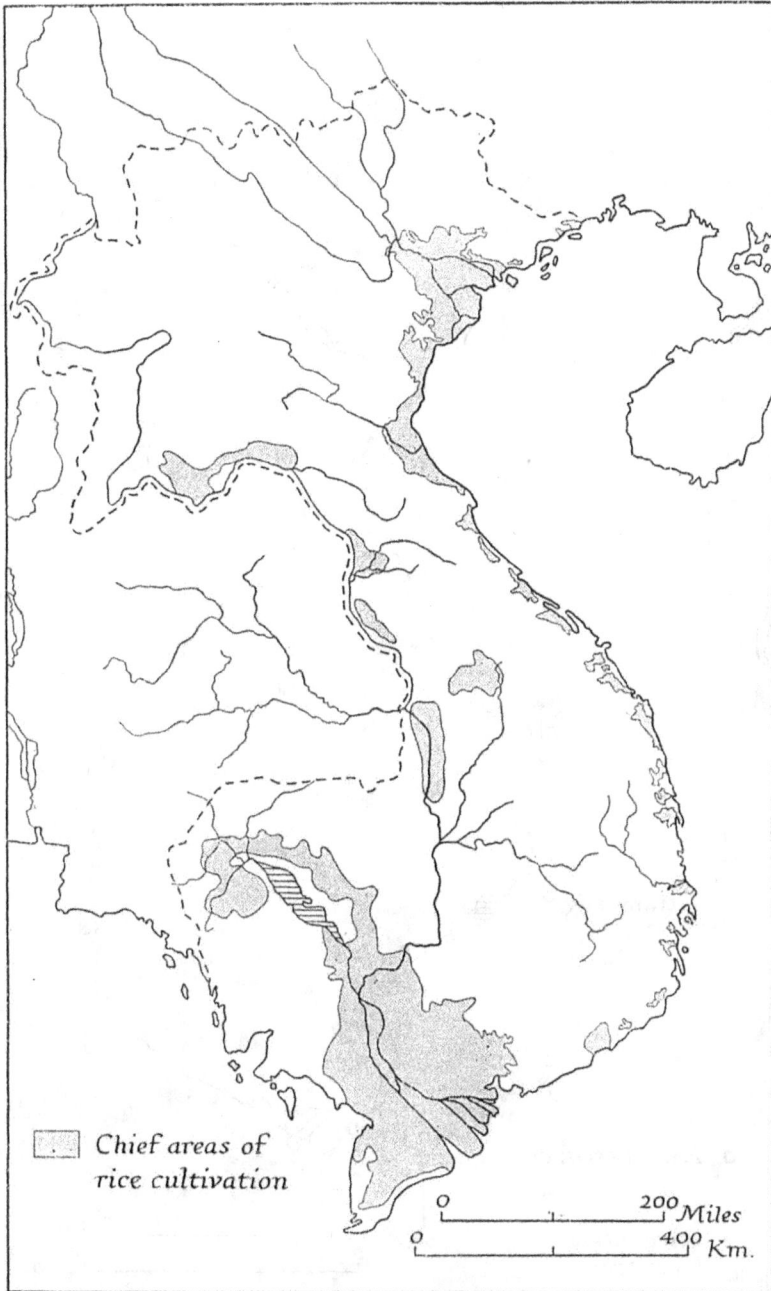

Chief areas of
rice cultivation

0   200 Miles

0   400 Km.

Fig. 84. Chief rice-growing districts
Source: Exposition Coloniale Internationale, Paris, 1931. *Riziculture en Indochine,*
following p. 44 (Hanoi, 1931).

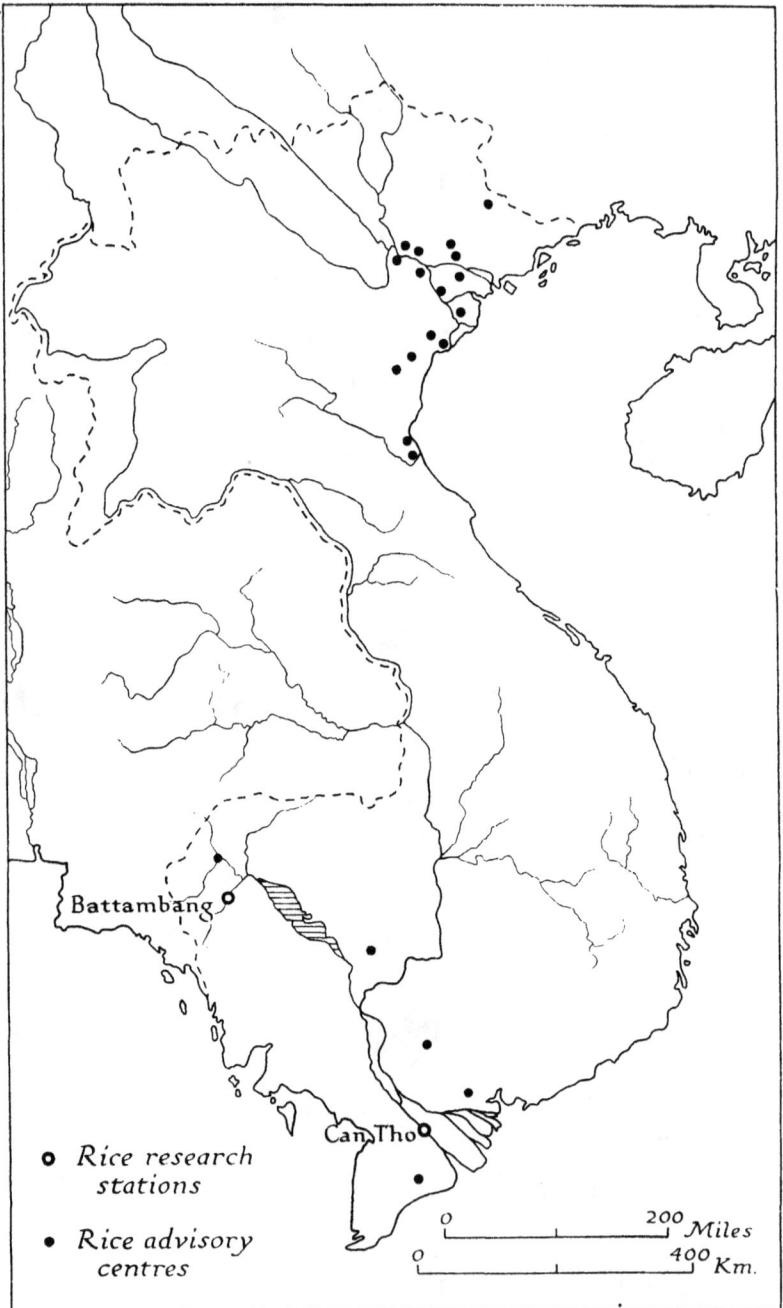

Fig. 85. Rice research stations and advisory centres

Source: Exposition Coloniale Internationale, Paris, 1931. *Riziculture en Indochine*, facing p. 40 (Hanoi, 1931).

thirteen of the years between 1902 and 1926. In the disaster of 1926, flood water covered nearly one-third of the delta. Since then the

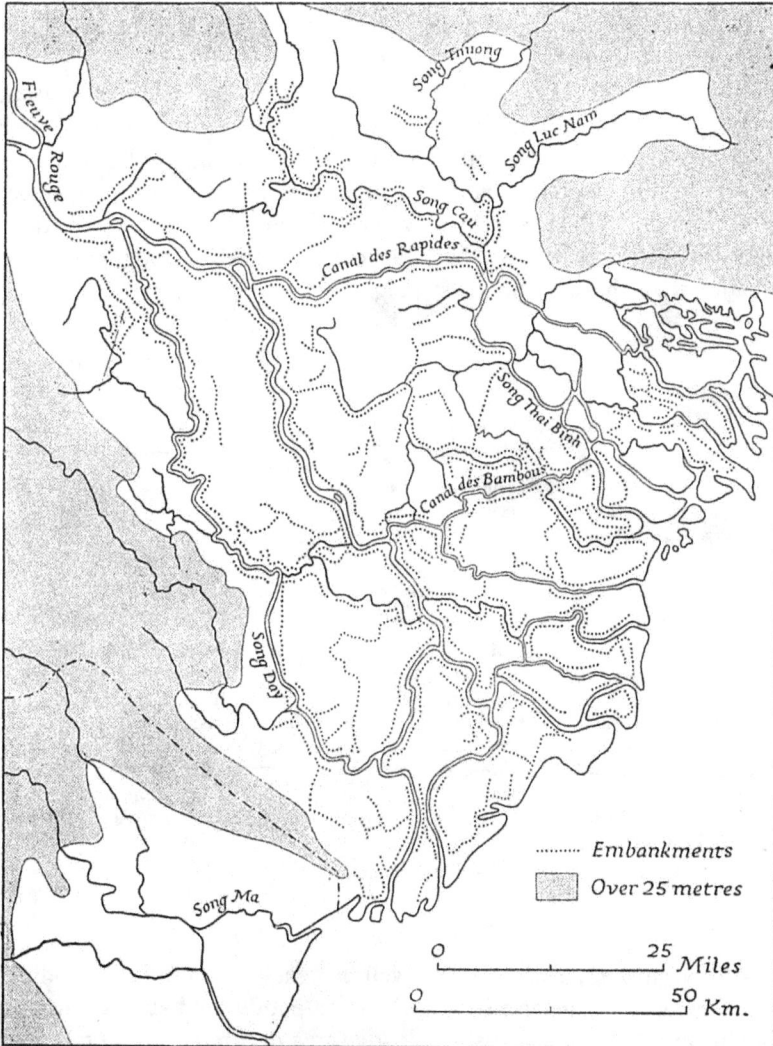

Fig. 86. Embankments in the Tonkin delta
Source: P. Gourou, *Les Paysans du Delta tonkinois*, p. 73 (Paris, 1936).

principal embankments have been enlarged to a thickness of 50 m., whereas in 1885 none exceeded 15 m.; they have also been increased in height to as much as 13 m. near Hanoi, where the river floods attain their maximum level (Fig. 87). The enlargement and strengthening of the embankments proved so successful that no flooding occurred between 1926 and 1936.

In the eastern part of the delta the rice fields have to be protected from tidal immersion, rather than from river floods. The Song Thai Binh receives far less water than the Fleuve Rouge, while it flows at a level slightly below the surrounding land, so that there is not the same need for high and continuous embankments along the course of the river. On the other hand, the tides are here a constant menace, and as highly saline, brackish water is inimical to rice cultivation, many embankments have had to be constructed, though they are smaller than those in the west (Fig. 8).

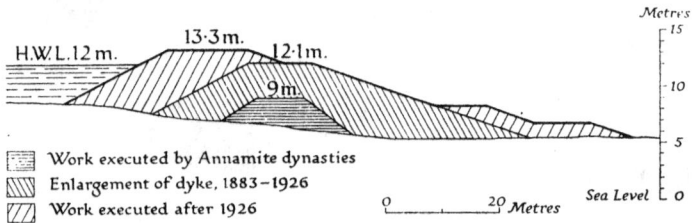

Metres

H.W.L.12 m.   13·3 m.   12·1 m.   9 m.

▦ Work executed by Annamite dynasties
▨ Enlargement of dyke, 1883–1926
▧ Work executed after 1926

0   20 Metres

Sea Level

Fig. 87. Diagrammatic section through the embankment of the
Fleuve Rouge (Red River) at Hanoi

Throughout history the bed of the Fleuve Rouge has slowly been rising above the level of the surrounding plain owing to the deposition of silt. Thus, the dykes executed by the Annamite dynasties, which were originally 1 m. or so above the high-water level of the river, soon failed to safeguard the lowlands from inundation. The people suffered constantly, and it was only in 1883, under French administration, that the embankments were raised above high-water level of the river. But even this measure did not prevent annual flooding, and in 1926 one of the worst floods in history caused the French to raise the embankments above the highest recorded level of the river.

Source: Exposition Coloniale Internationale, Paris, 1931. J. Gauthier, *Digues du Tonkin*, facing p. 96 (Hanoi, 1931).

Although the rice crop is now well protected from serious flooding, the correct drainage and irrigation of the paddy field still remains an urgent problem. Rice must be flooded to a depth of 10–15 cm., or in certain cases up to 30 cm., from the time of planting up to maturity. During the present century several modern hydraulic works have been built for regulating the flow of water into the various *casiers* (Fig. 88). In the extreme north, the system around Kep (7,700 ha.) was completed in the period from 1906 to 1914, that around Vinh Yen (17,000 ha.) between 1914 and 1922, and that in the Song Cau

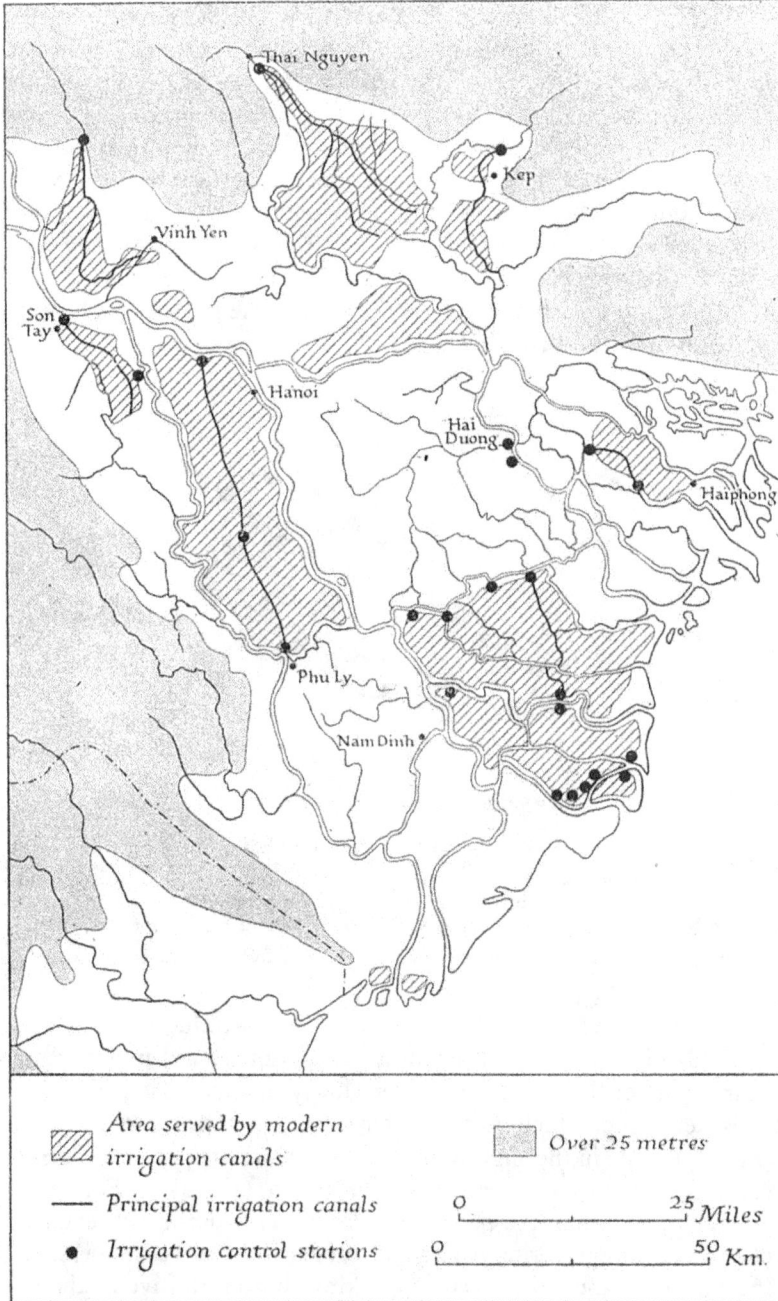

Fig. 88. Irrigation system in the Tonkin delta

Source: C. Robequain, *L'Evolution économique de l'Indochine française*, p. 251 (Paris, 1939).

valley (33,800 ha.) between 1922 and 1938. Each system comprises a river barrage and a series of canals which lead water into the paddy fields by gravity. At Son Tay, west of the Fleuve Rouge, another method has been adopted in which an electrically worked pump raises by 5 m. the water of the Fleuve Rouge; canals then distribute the water over an area of 10,000 ha. The great Song Day barrage, 260 m. wide, controls the flow of water into the Ha Dong-Phu Ly basin (110,000 ha.), while drainage and irrigation of the north and south Thai Binh basins has been effected by the construction of sluice gates at selected places in the encircling embankments; canals bear the water to or from the paddy field.

Fig. 89. Irrigation by means of a sliding scoop

In the lowest lying parts of the Tonkin delta this simple method of irrigation is commonly used. The scoop is filled, pulled up the low bank and emptied on to the land to be irrigated. The rice has just been transplanted from the nursery beds.

Source: P. Gourou, *Les Paysans du Delta tonkinois*, following p. 82 (Paris, 1936).

Despite the recent progress made in the introduction of modern methods of water control, primitive irrigation is still practised over a large part of the delta. In the very lowlying areas, the peasant uses a basket-scoop which raises water up to a maximum of 20 cm. (Fig. 89) while in the slightly higher districts the tripod scoop is more common and raises water as much as 40 cm. (Fig. 90). For heights greater than 40 cm. the pedal noria (Fig. 91) is used. The extension of hydraulic engineering works and canals will relieve the peasant of the toilsome labour involved in working these primitive methods of irrigation.

Fig. 90. Irrigation by means of a scoop and tripod

The scoop is suspended from the tripod and when full is raised by pivoting about the point of suspension. It is then swung across over the land.

Source: P. Gourou, *Les Paysans du Delta tonkinois*, following p. 82 (Paris, 1936).

Fig. 91. Pedal noria

A wooden chain carrying paddles is moved along a sloping trough, the lower end of which is under water. The chain is moved by passing round a wheel turned by two men who stand at the sides and work pedals. The water is carried up the trough by the paddles and runs out into a tank or on to the land.

Source: P. Gourou, *Les Paysans du Delta tonkinois*, following p. 82 (Paris, 1936).

The following table gives the approximate times of the year for the sowing, transplanting and harvesting of rice in the Tonkin delta.

	Sowing in nursery	Transplantation	Harvest
Rice harvested in summer	Mid-October to beginning of May	Mid-November to mid-January	Beginning of May to mid-June
Rice harvested in winter	End of May to beginning of July	End of June to beginning of August	Mid-October to mid-November

About 1,100,000 ha., or over 90% of the total cultivable area, is devoted to rice cultivation. Of this total, about 250,000 ha. put under the crop is gathered in summer and 350,000 ha. in winter, while over 500,000 ha. has harvests at both seasons. Rice is harvested in June in the area west of the Fleuve Rouge and in the *casiers* between the Canal des Rapides and the Song Cau, where difficulties of water evacuation during the summer prevent the planting of rice for a winter harvest. The farmers of the higher, better drained lands in the north only plant rice for harvesting in November, but almost the whole central and eastern parts of the delta have a double harvest (Fig. 92).

The agricultural technique employed in the delta is remarkable for its adaptation to the environment and for its intensive cultivation of the soil. Three hundred varieties of rice are grown and the peasant shows a keen appreciation of their particular qualities such as resistance to dryness, suitability for heavy or light soils and ability to withstand great depths of water. A relatively light soil, if available, is chosen for the seed-bed or nursery, the ground of which is most thoroughly prepared by wet ploughing and harrowing as many as three times. The plough and harrow are made of wood and are usually drawn by oxen or buffaloes (Figs. 93, 94). Many kinds of fertilizer, including human excreta as well as the droppings of swine and water buffalo, are applied; on very acid soils, some lime is spread over the land though very few farmers can afford to use chemical fertilizers. In certain parts of the delta, farmers manure their land with the water plant, Azolla, which dies in early summer and greatly enriches the soil. After sowing, the nursery is watered to ensure moist soil, though care has to be taken not to submerge the ground completely since too much water would soften the seedlings and so make them more liable to damage on transplantation. The seedlings remain in the seed-bed for a month or sometimes $1\frac{1}{2}$ months when they are pulled up, tied in small bundles, and planted in the rice

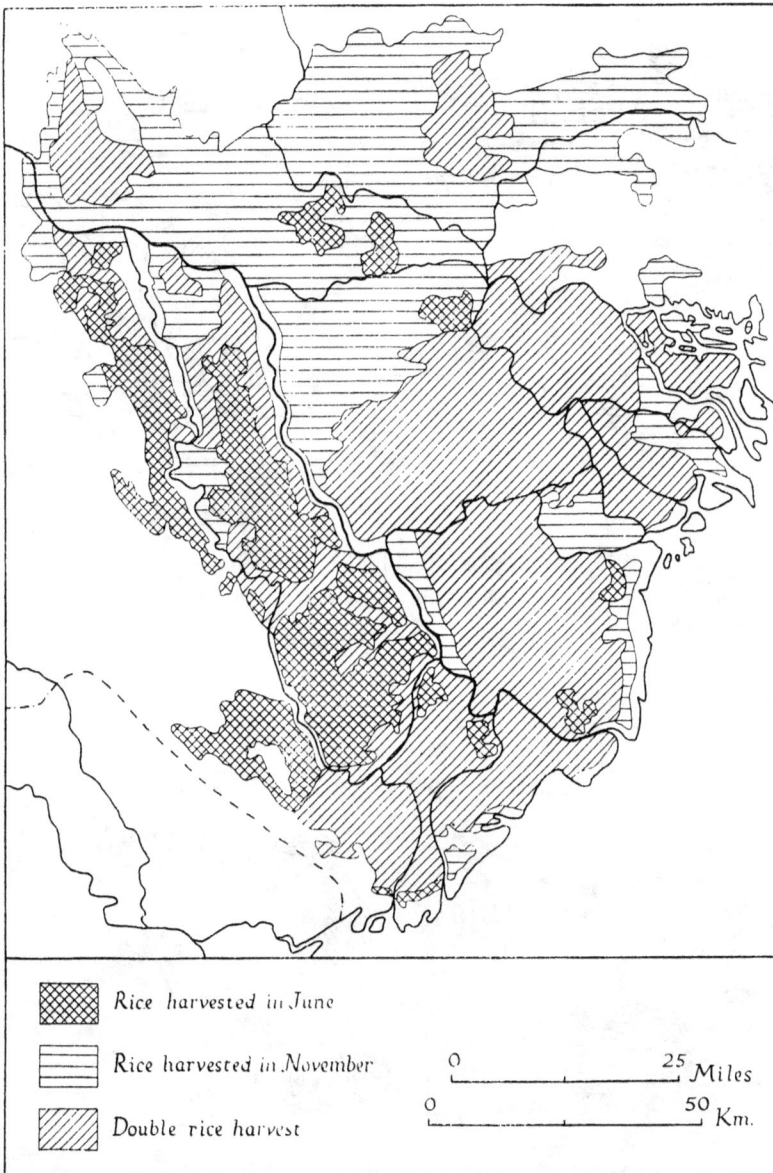

Rice harvested in June

Rice harvested in November

Double rice harvest

0   25 Miles

0   50 Km.

Fig. 92. Times of rice harvests in the Tonkin delta

Source: P. Gourou, *Les Paysans du Delta tonkinois*, p. 396 (Paris, 1936).

Fig. 93. Rice cultivation: ploughing

Source: J. Sion, 'Asie des Moussons', *Géographie Universelle*, vol. IX, plate 7a (Paris, 1929).

Fig. 94. Rice cultivation: harrowing

Source: Exposition Coloniale Internationale, Paris, 1931. *Riziculture en Indochine*, facing p. 7 (Hanoi, 1931).

field which receives the same thorough preparation in the way of ploughing, harrowing and irrigating as the nursery (Figs. 95, 96). The rice is harvested 3½–5½ months after transplantation, but before this takes place the land is carefully drained. Harvesting makes great demands upon the labour supply and, as already noted, the peasant frequently hires additional labour at this time (see p. 259). The grain is cut down with a small sickle, packed in baskets and carried on the back of the peasant to the farmhouse. Here, threshing is carried out either by beating the grain against some hard object or by allowing it to be trampled over by the feet of one or two buffaloes. After threshing, the grain is laid out to dry and then stored in bamboo paniers.

The average yield of rice in the delta is 14 quintals per ha. The yield varies widely from year to year as a result of irregularities in seasonal rainfall. It also varies from region to region, owing to differences in soil fertility; in some parts 20–25 quintals per ha. may be obtained, while in others the yield may be as low as 3–5 quintals per ha., in a bad year.

The annual output of rice in this region amounts to 22 million quintals or approximately one-third of the Indo-Chinese production. In a normal year, about 18 million quintals of paddy are consumed locally, 2 million quintals go to Haiphong for export abroad, 750,000 quintals are required as seed rice, 500,000 quintals enter distilleries and 300,000 quintals move to markets in the interior.

Rice Cultivation on the Coastal Plains of Annam

Although rice is the principal native crop in the coastal plains of Annam it covers only 800,000 ha., or 300,000 ha. less than in the Tonkin delta. The largest areas under rice are in the north of the state, especially around Thanh Hoa and Vinh. As most of the rivers are small in size, there are few embankments to protect the rice fields; only in the Song Ma and Son Ca delta regions do artificial embankments approach those of the Tonkin delta in size. A number of modern irrigation works have been constructed near Thanh Hoa (50,000 ha.), Quang Tri (5,000 ha.), Hue (17,300 ha.), Phu Yen (19,000 ha.) and Phan Rang (6,000 ha.). Most of the rice, however, is still grown with the aid of primitive irrigation, and the methods employed are similar to those already described. In some parts of Annam a giant 'noria' is used to raise water.

The time of the rice harvest varies widely in different parts of the state. North Annam has a double rice harvest, in June and November,

Fig. 95. Rice cultivation: pulling up seedlings for transplanting

Source: Exposition Coloniale Internationale, Paris, 1931. *Riziculture en Indochine*, following p. 8 (Hanoi, 1931).

Fig. 96. Rice cultivation: planting out

Source: J. Sion, 'Asie des Moussons', *Géographie Universelle*, vol. IX, plate 7b (Paris, 1929).

but farther south harvest times change and three crops are sometimes sown and gathered in the year. In the plain around Quang Nam, the June harvest is replaced by one in April; near Quang Ngai, harvests occur in April, September and January, near Binh Dinh in April and September, near Nha Trang in September and January. The frequency of typhoons in October and November precludes a rice harvest at this season in central and south Annam.

The annual production of rice in Annam amounts to some 10 million quintals, with an average yield of 12 quintals per ha. The low yield may be attributed to widespread poverty of soil and to extreme irregularity of rainfall.

Rice Cultivation in Cochin-China

In 1937 rice covered 2,200,000 ha. in Cochin-China, which represents an increase of 1 million ha. since the beginning of the present century and a fourfold increase since 1880. Almost the whole crop is grown on the alluvial soils of the Mekong delta where, even more than in Annam and Tonkin, it holds undisputed possession, occupying over 90% and in some places 100% of the cultivated land. As most of Cochin-China, particularly the regions of the centre and west, has been developed only recently and still has a relatively low density of population (see p. 229) rice cultivation here is far less intensive than in the other lowland areas; the seed-beds and rice fields are less carefully prepared and there is seldom more than one harvest in the year.

Water control in this region is not so difficult a problem as in the Tonkin delta. The summer flood of the Mekong never threatens to submerge the whole plain, since its flood waters are well distributed not only through the five broad mouths of the major stream, but also through tributaries which enter the Gulf of Siam. A large number of canals further facilitates drainage, and rice cultivation has increased correspondingly with the extension of the canal system (Fig. 97). Owing to the even dispersal of flood water through both natural and artificial channels high protecting embankments like those in Tonkin are absent, though many small ones (*diguettes*) have been constructed to regulate the water level in the paddy field. Cochin-China has the great advantage of regular precipitation and the rice crop rarely suffers from dryness or excessive rainfall.

A large proportion of the rice is sown in the nursery beds in June–July, transplanted in August–September and harvested in December–January. The farmers of the Ca Mau region, however, plant an early maturing variety for harvesting in late November in order to save the crop from brackish water which threatens this region at the end of the rainy season. Along the banks of the Mekong near Vinh Long, Sa Dec and Can Tho the seedlings are twice transplanted. River and tidal water is allowed to submerge the land without the interference of embankments, and during the flood period of October the depth of water may be as high as 40 cm. This depth of water necessitates a rice stalk 70 cm. in height which may more easily be achieved by a double transplanting. A tall rice stalk is also essential because the luxuriant growth of weeds in this region would kill a smaller plant. Rice

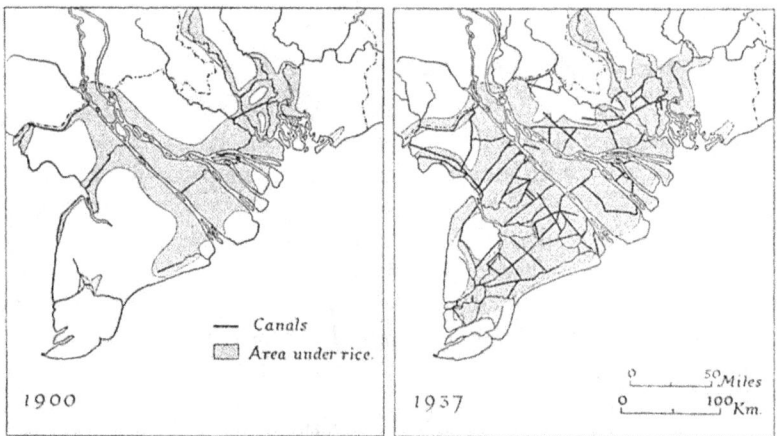

Fig. 97. Areas of rice cultivation in relation to the canal system in Cochin-China, 1900 and 1937

Source: C. Robequain, *L'Evolution économique de l'Indochine française*, p. 244 (Paris, 1939).

cultivated under these conditions has a longer maturing period, being sown in June or July and harvested in February or March (Fig. 98).

In the north of Cochin-China along the banks of the Fleuve Antérieur and Fleuve Postérieur, normal lowland paddy culture cannot be carried on, owing to the depth of the flood waters, and this region was almost completely unproductive until the introduction of 'floating' rice at the end of the nineteenth century. No seed-bed is employed with this method of cultivation. The plant is sown directly on the dry land in the low-water period of March or April after which it requires little attention, though to protect it from submersion care is taken to ensure that the rise of the water does not exceed 12 cm. a day. The rice stalk may be over 6 m. in height. The harvesting takes place in December or January.

A large number of seasonal workers help in harvesting the rice. Many of these workers take part in more than one harvest during the course of the year; in November they move to the region around Ca Mau and between December and March to the main rice-growing areas in the central parts of the delta.

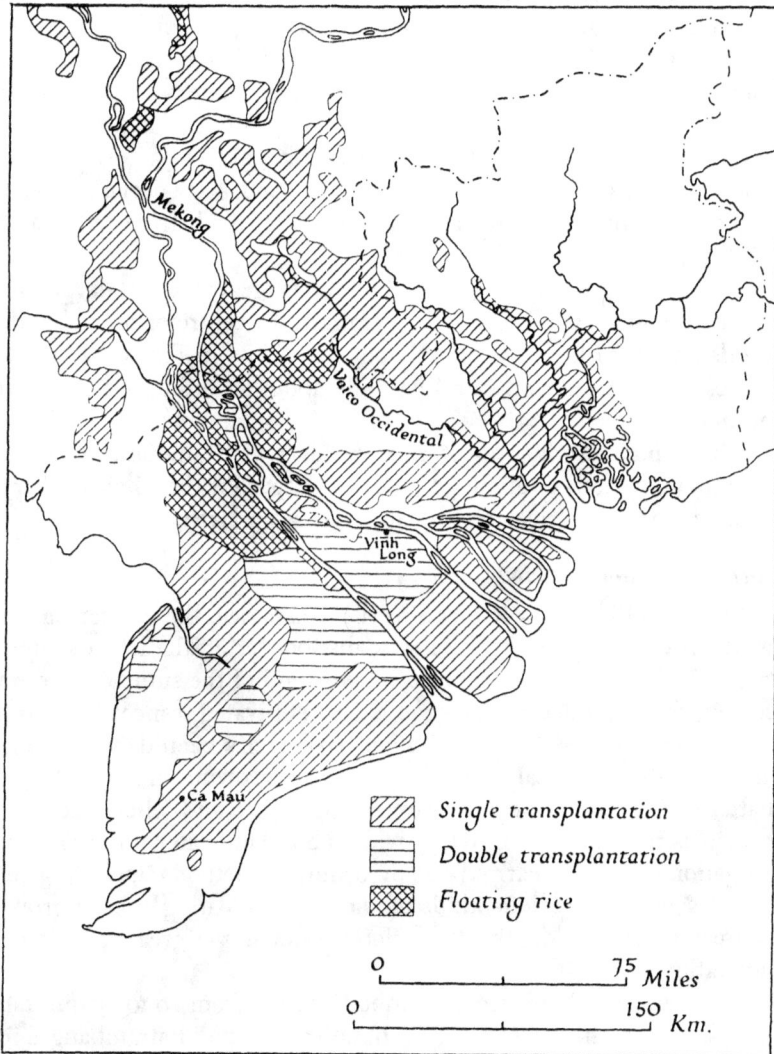

Fig. 98. Types of rice cultivation in south Indo-China

Source: Exposition Coloniale Internationale, Paris, 1931. *Riziculture en Indochine*, following p. 44 (Hanoi, 1931).

As in Tonkin and Annam, the implements used for rice cultivation in the Mekong delta are made of roughly fashioned wood. The plough and harrow are generally drawn by oxen or buffaloes. In harvesting, a small sickle is used, and, when cut down, the grain is laid out in the fields for one or two days so that it may dry in the sun. After drying, the paddy is packed either in baskets, which are carried on the shoulders of two men by means of a bamboo pole, or in small carts drawn by buffaloes. Threshing takes place either in the fields or in one of the farm buildings; it is sometimes done with the aid of buffaloes and sometimes by beating the paddy against a bamboo screen. The small tenant farmer stores his paddy in a corner of his house; the large landowner, on the other hand, has special granaries for storing purposes, some of which can hold from 20,000 to 40,000 kg.

The yield of rice in Cochin-China averages 13 quintals per ha. Near Go Cong, Ben Tre and Tra Vinh, in the centre of the delta, the yields are as high as 18 quintals per ha., while in the western provinces of Rach Gia and Bac Lieu only about 10 quintals per ha. are produced.

The annual production of rice in this region amounts to nearly 30 million quintals or about 50% of the output for the whole country. A large part of the rice crop is exported (see p. 347).

Rice Cultivation in Cambodia

In Cambodia, about 800,000 ha. lie under rice, the greater part of which is concentrated in the low plains bordering the lake of Tonle Sap. Most of the rice is harvested at the end of the summer or rainy season, though a dry season crop is also cultivated, especially in bad years when the yield from the other harvest has been deficient. The most suitable physical conditions for rice growing are found near Battambang, where the soil is extremely fertile and where the river known as the Stung Sang Ke provides abundant water for irrigation. Irrigation is entirely carried out by primitive methods, including the basket-scoop and various kinds of 'norias'. 'Floating' rice is grown in areas where the depth of the flood water is too great for normal cultivation.

The average yield of rice in Cambodia varies from 10 to 15 quintals per ha., the highest yields being obtained around Battambang and Kompong Chhnang. The annual production approaches 9 million quintals.

Subsidiary Food Crops

Maize

Maize covers approximately 500,000 ha. in Indo-China, of which 70% is grown in the Cambodian plain and in the Tonkin delta. It forms part of the diet of the peasant, especially during the years when the rice crop is below normal. In Cambodia, maize is widely grown along the banks of the Mekong and its tributaries; the area under this crop increased very rapidly from 50,000 ha. in 1929 to 300,000 ha. in 1936. In the Tonkin delta about 70,000 ha. lie under maize with the chief centres of production on either side of the Fleuve Rouge and the Canal des Rapides. The natives of Annam, Laos and Cochin-China also grow this cereal, but there are no very large single producing areas.

Until about 1905, maize was cultivated only for a local market. Since then export to France has been encouraged and in 1937 over 500,000 tons or 90% of the annual output was shipped to the mother country. The maize of Indo-China is very poor in quality when it reaches the French market, and, despite its favoured and protected position, it is at a disadvantage against the excellent grain from Argentina and Romania. Intrinsically, the grain of Indo-China is of first quality and the imperfections are caused solely by faulty preparation before it leaves the country.

Sweet potatoes

Sweet potatoes are widely grown in both the mountains and the plains. They are a dry-season crop, normally planted in mid-October and harvested in January or February, though a second harvest is frequently obtained before the beginning of the summer rains in late May. This crop grows on many kinds of soil from coarse sands in parts of the Moi country to heavy clays in the Tonkin delta; nowhere can the yield compare with that in other tropical countries. In parts of Tonkin and Annam, an increase in sweet potato culture has been a factor in countering the danger of famine. The further extended use of the sweet potato as a food will give the peasant a more balanced diet.

Taro, Manioc, Yam, Millet

These crops are cultivated in many parts of the country, but returns have not been made concerning either the area under each crop or the annual production. Near Binh Dinh in Annam the natives use manioc to make a variety of vermicelli.

Vegetables

A great variety of vegetables are grown, including haricot beans, cabbages, tomatoes, cucumbers, marrows, garlic, onions, shallots, and several aromatic plants such as mint and sweet basil. The soya bean is grown in certain areas. Almost every village prepares some legumes for home consumption and sometimes even for export. The country around Dalat is one of the chief producing areas; from here, vegetables are sent to Saigon and Cho Lon by road or rail.

Fruits

The cultivation of fruits on any considerable scale is limited to a few small regions. The main producing areas are found in the alluvial plains of Cochin-China and of Annam. Oranges, mandarines, and citrons predominate in the former area, whereas in Annam the banana is more extensively grown than any other fruit. In Tonkin, fruit production is insufficient for the needs of the population; the best fruit is grown in the foot-hills fringing the Fleuve Rouge delta.

OIL-YIELDING CROPS

Coconuts

The coconut is extensively grown in the coastal plains, though low winter temperatures preclude its cultivation in north Annam and Tonkin. The plains around Bong Son and Binh Dinh in Annam have over 2,000 ha. under coconuts, and there are minor producing areas near Faifoo and Quang Ngai. Typhoons frequently cause widespread damage to the trees. The main coconut-growing areas in Cochin-China lie close to My Tho, Ben Tre and Vinh Long. Oil and copra are obtained, but there is room for considerable improvement in the methods of preparation.

Groundnuts

The groundnut or peanut is cultivated fairly extensively in Annam. It is also the chief oleaginous crop of the Tonkin delta.

Sesame and Aniseed

These plants grow in many scattered parts of the country. Their seed and oil are used for culinary purposes.

Plate 39. Rice fields near Cao Bang in northern Tonkin

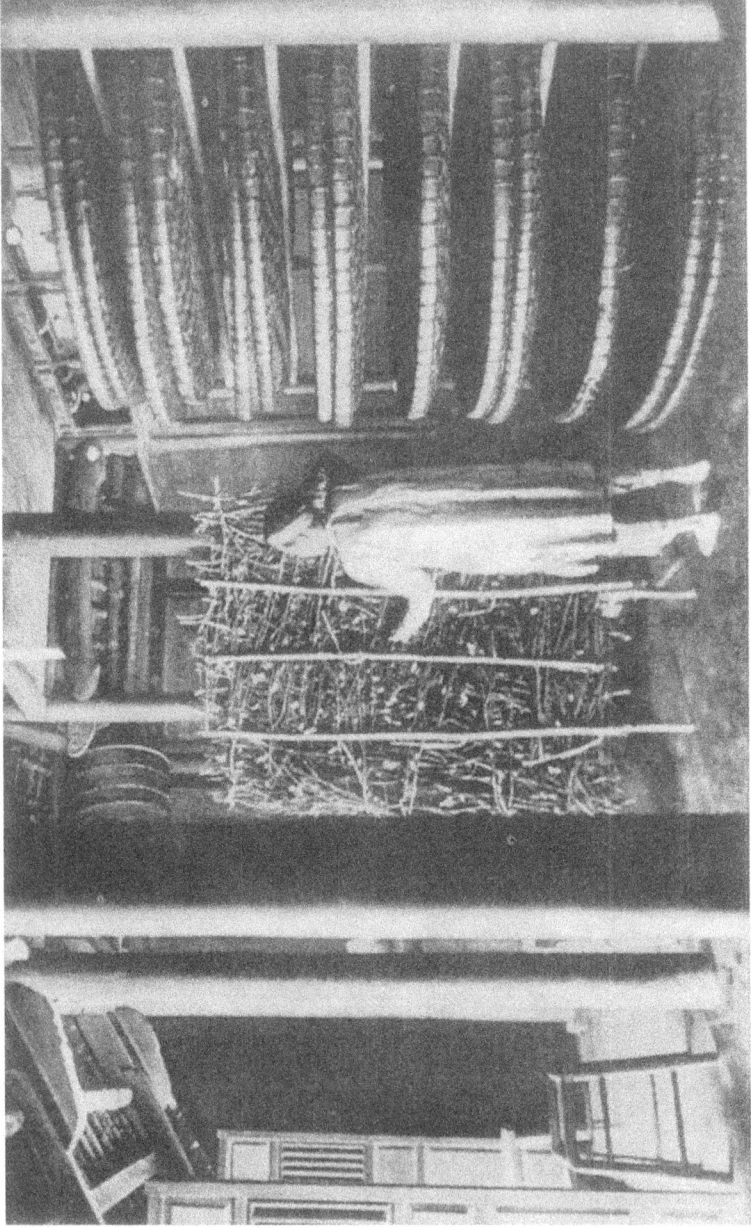

Plate 40. Silkworm rearing in Annam

In the large circular trays, the silkworms are reared during the early stage of their development. The worms make their cocoons on the structure formed of branches, straw and dried leaves seen in the centre of the photograph.

FIBRE CROPS

Sericulture

The lowlands of Indo-China, with their high temperatures and dense population, possess conditions well suited both to mulberry cultivation and to the rearing of silkworms. Sericulture is practised in many parts of the country, but chiefly around Hai Duong in the Tonkin delta and Thanh Hoa, Quang Nam and Binh Dinh in Annam.

Unlike the mulberry of China and Mediterranean Europe, that of Indo-China is principally a tree of dwarf size which has a remarkably rapid growth. After planting in December or January, the first leaves may be collected as early as March and successive gatherings occur every thirty or forty days until the beginning of September. The peasants frequently grow the mulberry in association with rice or maize.

Silkworm rearing generally takes place close to the areas of mulberry cultivation. The silkworm is raised either in the home or in huts made of straw and thatch. Large circular trays carry the worms and their chief food, the mulberry leaf (Plate 40). The period of time between the hatching of the silkworm's eggs and the final cocoon stage varies from twenty-three to twenty-seven days and five or six separate broods a year may often be obtained.

The government has advanced considerable sums of money towards the extension of sericulture in Indo-China. Between 1920 and 1930 over 500,000 piastres were expended in Tonkin alone. Experimental stations have been created and competent officials appointed to supervise research. Despite the wide distribution of improved silkworm's eggs, sericulture still remains in a backward condition, and the silk thread produced cannot compete either with that from China or with rayon imported from Europe. This unsatisfactory development is regrettable, since silk production, through its close association with rural industry, seems to be well adapted to the densely peopled lowlands and to represent an important factor of equilibrium in their economy.

Cotton

Cotton occupies a small area around Thanh Hoa in Annam and along or near the banks of the Mekong in Cambodia. The peasants grow a short stapled fibre of low quality, with a very short growing season, which allows time for gathering the crop before the summer rains and enables the fields to be cleared and used for a summer rice crop. None of the attempts to introduce a long stapled cotton has proved successful.

At first sight the extension of cotton cultivation would seem to present interesting possibilities, since the country annually consumes between 19,000 and 20,000 tons of raw cotton, whereas it produces only between 2,000 and 3,000 tons. This leaves an annual deficit of some 17,000 tons, so that on the basis of 80 kg. of fibre per ha. at least 200,000 more hectares could be planted. Such an expansion, however, appears unlikely because cotton culture gives a poor monetary return to the peasant as compared with that from other products. On the other hand, in view of the acute shortage of cotton in the Far East every effort is likely to be made to increase its production in Indo-China.

Jute

This crop is unimportant in Indo-China, even though the delta region of Cochin-China offers conditions closely comparable with those of Bengal. The jute sacks used in the export of rice and maize are imported from India.

Kapok

Small quantities of kapok are produced in Cochin-China and Cambodia. The natives usually gather the fruits of the kapok when they have fallen to the ground. The preparation of the fibre is very rudimentary and the product obtained is low in quality.

OTHER AGRICULTURAL CROPS

Sugar Cane

In 1937, sugar cane covered about 43,000 ha. in Indo-China (cf. Java, 85,000 ha.) of which 25,000 ha. lay in Annam, 13,000 ha. in Cochin-China, 4,000 ha. in Tonkin, and 1,000 ha. in Cambodia. The chief producing region is found along the strip of lowland between Tourane and Cap Varella and, above all, near Quang Ngai, Binh Dinh, Quang Nam and Phu Yen. In eastern Cochin-China, it has recently extended rapidly in the valleys of the Vaico Oriental, the Rivière de Saigon and the Dong Nai. A large labour supply is a necessary requirement of sugar cultivation, and during the harvest period in Cochin-China 6,000 workers are employed in the fields or in the transport of cane to the factories. In Tonkin, the refining process takes place in rudimentary buildings which shelter a millstone and wooden cylinders worked by oxen. Molasses or syrup is the most common form in which the Tonkinese consume their locally grown sugar.

The yield of sugar is very low, averaging only 2,400 kg. per ha. in Cochin-China and 1,500 kg. per ha. in Annam and Tonkin (cf. Java, 22,000 kg. per ha.). This low yield is due to careless management and, as the per capita consumption is amongst the lowest in the world, the peasants have made few attempts to establish improved methods of cultivation. Although the peasants consume such meagre quantities of sugar, the production (42,700 tons) in 1937 was insufficient to meet requirements and over 1,000 tons had to be imported.

Tobacco

This crop is grown in every state of Indo-China, though there are relatively few important regions of intensive cultivation. The neighbourhood of Nam Dinh in the Tonkin delta, the Tourane-Faifoo region in Annam, and the area around Gia Dinh, Hoc Mon and Kompong Cham in Cochin-China and Cambodia lead in the production of tobacco. Smoking and chewing are almost universally practised, and the peasants favour a dark, strong tobacco, rich in nicotine. Tobacco of this kind demands a heavy, compact soil, well watered and carefully manured, which conditions are best fulfilled in the deltas and coastal lowlands. Only these well-populated regions, moreover, can provide the skilled and unskilled labour required for successful tobacco cultivation.

Tobacco is a dry season crop in Indo-China. It is normally sown in September, October or November and is harvested four to six months later—January in Cochin-China, May in Tonkin and Annam. The plant needs constant care and attention throughout its growth. After planting, human or animal manure is applied to enrich the soil, while the fields are irrigated at frequent intervals until the period of maturity. Picking of the leaves at harvest time is done entirely by hand. The leaves are first stacked together in the shade and, after they have turned yellow, they are cut up for final drying in the sun.

In recent years, attempts have been made to create an export surplus of high-quality tobacco suitable for the French market. The coarse, dark tobacco produced in the lowlands is disliked by the average European who prefers a lighter variety with a low proportion of nicotine. The mountainous regions of Tonkin and Annam, with soils derived from crystalline rocks and basalt, are most suited to the cultivation of light tobacco. Groups of Moi peoples have indeed long grown this crop in parts of central Annam, but the quality of the leaf is extremely low. To-day, the best light tobacco is grown near the Col d'Ai Lao and in the valley of the Song Ba. A considerable amount of research has been carried out on plant selection and proper soil fertilization with a view to an extension of the area under this kind of tobacco. An increase in tobacco cultivation is likely, since it gives a good return and provides the peasant with a valuable secondary cash crop.

Pepper

As a producer of pepper, Indo-China ranks second in the world. Almost all of it is grown in the plains surrounding Kampot in Cambodia; its cultivation is exclusively in the hands of the Chinese. The whole crop is exported to France.

LIVESTOCK

In Indo-China, as in most countries of south-eastern Asia, the rearing of livestock has little importance. Physical, economic, and social factors have contributed towards this backward condition. The alternation of wet and dry seasons with high humidity throughout the year affects the animals adversely, retarding their growth to such an extent that many do not reach physical maturity until they are about six years old. Natural grassland, moreover, is rare, and forest reaches up to the summits of the mountains; even where a clearing has been made constant supervision must be maintained to prevent the forest from re-establishing itself. In the extensive savannas of Laos, Cambodia and south Annam annual burnings are made to restrict tree growth, while the generally tough grasses found here offer poor nourishment. Animal diseases, which are more common and more vicious than in Europe, make the rearing of healthy stock especially difficult. On the economic and social side, the pressure of population in the lowlands and the traditions of cultivation in Eastern Asia have discouraged pastoralism on any large scale. In the over-populated deltas of Tonkin and north Annam almost all the available land is required to produce food crops and livestock play an unimportant part in the economy. Meat and milk seldom figure in the peasant's diet, so that there never has been any great incentive to an expansion or improvement of stock raising. The relatively insignificant position occupied by cattle, swine, sheep, and horses is one of the essential characteristics of Indo-Chinese economy.

Cattle

In 1937, Indo-China had 2,300,000 oxen and 2,250,000 buffaloes, a very small total for a country of 740,000 sq.km. and 23,000,000 inhabitants. The following table gives the number of cattle in each state. The cattle are principally used by the peasant for transport purposes and for work in the rice fields; the small number of animals owned by Europeans, however, are kept only for their manure which proves a valuable fertilizer in coffee and tea cultivation.

	Oxen	Buffaloes
Annam	500,000	400,000
Cambodia	1,200,000	600,000
Cochin-China	150,000	300,000
Laos	250,000	300,000
Tonkin	200,000	650,000
Total	2,300,000	2,250,000

Source: *Annuaire statistique de l'Indochine, 1936-7*, p. 99 (Hanoi, 1938).

The densely peopled plains of Tonkin, Annam and Cochin-China have a large number of cattle per square kilometre, but a small number per head of the population. In the Tonkin delta, there are about 500,000 oxen and buffaloes, which gives an average of 33 per sq.km. and 1 animal for 14 of the inhabitants. Despite their relatively high areal density, cattle have little importance in a region where almost all the cultivated land lies under rice. The animals are seldom used for purposes other than harrowing and ploughing. Stock rearing has never been well developed in the delta, and some 30,000–40,000 head are annually imported from the districts around Lang Son and Thanh Hoa. The number of livestock is also insufficient for the needs of the other densely populated coastal lowlands; both Annam and Cochin-China import cattle from Laos and Cambodia.

In contrast to the coastal plains, the interior of the country has a small number of cattle in relation to its area, but a large number per head of population. Cambodia is the most important state for the rearing of cattle, having 1,200,000 oxen and 600,000 buffaloes, or 2 animals for 3 of the population and 10 per sq.km. The chief stock-raising areas lie near the Mekong and the lake of Tonle Sap. Three types of pastoral activity can be distinguished. First, in the thinly peopled forest regions, the Cambodians confine their attention to the care of buffaloes; the animals are allowed to wander about in search of food since, unlike cows, they can protect themselves against the attacks of wild beasts. In the more settled forest clearings, however, cattle are pastured around the village by day and shut in pens at night. Finally, the villages situated on fertile land close to the rivers and to Tonle Sap have developed a third type of pastoralism; during the dry season the animals graze in fields near the village, then towards the middle of June they are moved in herds, sometimes numbering as many as 200, to the forest clearings on higher land; the cattle return to the lowlands after the paddy harvest.

Although pastoralism is more developed in Cambodia than elsewhere, the natives, as in other parts of Indo-China, pay little regard to the health or improvement of their stock. Cattle often starve from lack of sufficient food and water. The great proportion serve as beasts of transport or draw ploughs in the rice fields, though some of the better breeds move to the slaughterhouse. Cambodian beef has a high reputation in Phnom Penh, Saigon and other large towns.

Many attempts have been made to increase milk production and improve the quality of the meat. The mixture of local stock with various European breeds did not prove successful, and the best results have so far been attained by crossing with Ongole and Sind cattle from India.

Cattle rearing offers most promise on the extensive plateaux of Tran Ninh, Cammon, Kontum and Darlac. Owing to the impoverishment of the soil through natural causes and the effects of shifting cultivation, the grazing areas must be of an extensive character. Experiments have shown that each animal requires at least as much as 5–6 ha. of pasture; the area varies with the length of the dry season. On this basis and on the assumption that herds less than 3,000 in number would be economically unprofitable, concessions of 15,000 to 18,000 ha. will prove necessary. As experience has proved in Northern Rhodesia and the Belgian Congo, farms of this size are essential if cattle rearing is to become a successful industry.

Swine

Swine constitute the principal source of meat and fat for the native and, as each peasant family owns one or more pigs, the greatest number of swine occurs in the chief areas of dense population, such as the delta of the Fleuve Rouge, the coastal plains of Annam and the delta of the Mekong.

State	No. of swine
Annam	950,000
Cambodia	800,000
Cochin-China	700,000
Laos	250,000
Tonkin	1,500,000
Total	4,200,000

Source: *Annuaire statistique de l'Indochine, 1936–7*, p. 99 (Hanoi, 1938).

The swine of Indo-China are most prolific, reach maturity at an early age, and have a small frame. The great proportion of the animals derive from crosses between native races and breeds from China and Europe (Yorkshire, Berkshire, Craonnais). Little care or method is applied to their rearing. They are generally left to find food for themselves either in the farmyard, in the woods, or in the rice fields after the harvest. At night the swine sleep in simple piggeries made of wood and thatched with straw. Indiscriminate breeding has caused decadence in the stock; thus whilst a 'Yorkshire Middle' at 8 months weighs 90 kg., an Indo-Chinese pig at the same age never weighs more than 50 kg. Many of the best animals, moreover, are sold to the butcher and the poorer ones left for breeding purposes. Despite the inferior quality of the swine several hundreds of thousands annually move to slaughterhouses in the large towns; the marketing of swine brings to the small cultivator a valuable monetary return.

Sheep

Sheep were practically unknown in Indo-China before the coming of the French, and even to-day their numbers are extremely small (17,500 in 1937). The chief sheep-rearing area lies near Phan Rang in south Annam where the low rainfall, scanty population and nearness to Saigon and Dalat make conditions particularly suitable. Other centres of sheep production are found near Phu Ly in south Tonkin, and on the Plateau du Tran Ninh in Laos.

Two distinct methods of sheep rearing are practised. In south Tonkin, the animals remain indoors throughout the year, owing to the uniformly high humidity and to the almost complete absence of a dry season. Elsewhere in Indo-China, sheep farming is extensive rather than intensive; the flocks spend the night in folds and wander over the pasture grounds during the day.

As there were no indigenous sheep, the French imported breeds from Europe and other parts of Asia: Solognot, Berrichon, Merino, Southdown, Romney Marsh, Corriedale, Yunnan, Kelantan. The

Romney Marsh is well adapted to the humid climate experienced here, though conditions vary so much that no one breed could possibly suit every area. Sheep rearing in Indo-China is handicapped by the lack of good grazing land and by the susceptibility of the animals to disease. The agricultural and veterinary services have achieved some success, but work on pasture improvement and immunization still remains in its infancy.

Goats

Goats, like sheep, are unimportant in Indo-China, numbering altogether only 58,000 (1937). They are found principally in north-east Tonkin where the rough limestone plateaux offer a meagre subsistence.

Poultry

The rearing of poultry is widely practised, especially amongst the peasants of Tonkin, Annam and Cochin-China. After the rice harvest, the hens, ducks, and geese feed on the stubble; rice chaff is given to them when they return to the farmyard. The poultry are generally of indigenous origin though many European strains have recently been introduced; thus, in Tonkin, the veterinary service is now distributing Leghorns, while an experimental breeding station near Saigon has begun to raise Orpingtons, Plymouth Rocks and Rhode Island Reds. At the present time, ducks are more carefully raised than the other varieties of poultry.

Poultry not only form an important part of the diet of the peasant, but they also supplement his income. The eggs draw a high price in the large towns; in 1937, 4,700 tons of eggs were exported in the form of albumen and yolk for industrial purposes.

Horses

Indo-China has never possessed a large number of horses, and in 1937 they totalled only 100,000, over 60% being in the two states of Tonkin and Cambodia. The motor car and the bicycle have led to decline in their importance as transport animals, but they are employed for this purpose in certain parts of the interior. A small number of horses are also commissioned for use in the army and in the racecourses at Hanoi, Haiphong, Saigon and Phnom Penh.

Since the end of last century the French have made constant, if often ineffective, attempts to improve the native breed which, though hardy and well suited to mountain pathways, was too small and round-backed for European requirements. Breeding stations were established at Nuoc Hai, near Cao Bang, Thanh Hoa, Hue, An Khe and Gia Dinh; they carried out experiments with stock imported from Burma, Java, Africa and Arabia. Much of the experimental work achieved no practical success, but during the last fifteen years the station at Nuoc Hai has produced a cross-breed which, though taller and square-backed, retains all the qualities of the native horse. This result has been obtained by crossing the Arab horse with the indigenous breed. An extension of the rearing of this animal is handicapped by the development of racing, since the wealthy racecourse proprietors can afford to pay large sums for the best imported breeds, and their interests incline towards English rather than Arab stock.

Elephants

Altogether there are some 2,000 domesticated elephants in Indo-China, found mainly in the regions of Kontum and Ban Me Thuot in south Annam. The natives use them for carrying logs and clearing the forest. Elephants cannot be reared in captivity, and hunts have to be organized if more animals are needed.

LAND SYSTEM

In the lowland agricultural regions of Indo-China a certain proportion of the land belonging to each village is communally owned, while the rest is divided up among all those members whose names appear in the *dia bo* or village register.* The subdivision of the land and the methods of land tenure vary widely in the different states. Small holdings with peasant proprietorship predominate in the north, whereas large estates, with plots of land let out to tenants, are a more common feature in the south.

Land System in the Tonkin Delta

An important feature in the Tonkin delta is the extreme subdivision of the cultivated land. Altogether there exists some 16 million parcels or lots; the province of Bac Ninh alone has more parcels than the whole of Cochin-China. The requirements of an intensive rice cultivation have partly led to this subdivision, since small fields are necessary if the crop is to receive satisfactory irrigation. Another cause has been the custom of allotting equal parts of the family inheritance to each child. In this manner, subdivision in-

---

* For the regulations concerning the acquisition of new land see p. 239.

creases progressively with the advance of time. As the northern part
of the delta is more anciently settled than that near the sea it has a

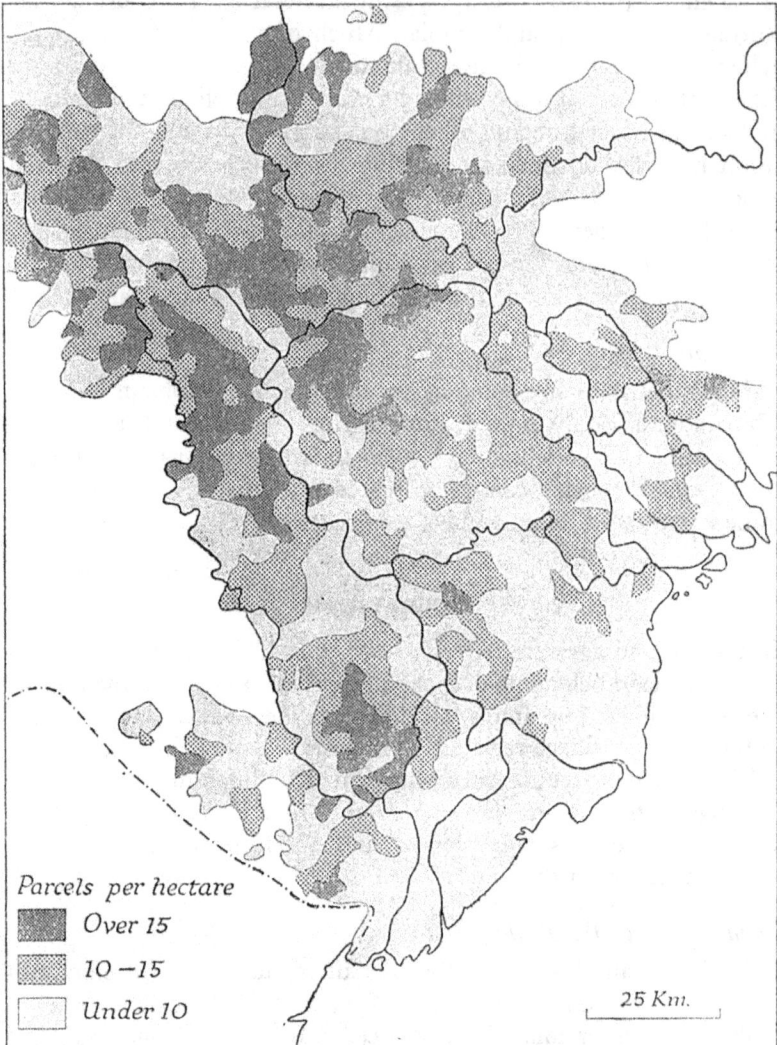

Parcels per hectare

Over 15

10 – 15

Under 10

25 Km.

Fig. 99. Subdivision of the land in the Tonkin delta
Source: P. Gourou, *Les Paysans du Delta tonkinois*, folding map (Paris, 1936).

greater number of parcels per unit area (Fig. 99); thus, the province
of Bac Ninh has an average of 14 parcels to the hectare, while there
are only 8 to the hectare in the province of Thai Binh.

The very small peasant property is the chief form of land holding in this region. Small properties (less than 2 ha.) occupy about 36 % of the cultivated surface, medium-sized properties (2–4 ha.) 27 %, and large properties (over 4 ha.) 17 %. These figures cannot claim to be wholly accurate, for no detailed census has yet been taken. The small proprietors farm their land themselves, but many of the medium-sized ones and almost all the large ones are let out to tenants.

Communal property forms the remaining 20 % of the agricultural land. It is most frequently found near the coast and along the banks of the Fleuve Rouge. Division of the property takes place at varying intervals of from one to three years; few adults receive plots of more than a tenth of a hectare in area. The allotment of communal land is open to much abuse and peculation.

Land System in the Coastal Lowlands of Annam

The existing land system in Annam does not differ materially from that in the Tonkin delta. There is the same subdivision into diminutive parcels and the same predominance of small properties under a system of direct farming. On the larger properties which increase in number from north to south, tenant farming is again the rule. The varying geographical conditions cause certain unusual features in the payment of rent. Thus, near Quang Ngai, owing to the expenses involved in raising irrigation water, the landowner seldom takes more than one-third of the rice crop, whereas in Tonkin the proportion taken is about one-half; and the growers of sugar cane return a similar proportion of their output, since this crop requires large capital expenditure for its successful cultivation. In the south around Phan Rang and Phan Thiet, where conditions are relatively unfavourable for agriculture, many proprietors advance money to their tenants and also provide livestock as well as varieties of seed.

Communal property is more widespread than in the Tonkin delta, for in Annam it covers about 26 % of the land under cultivation. Some districts have the whole of their cultivated land in communal ownership.

Land System in Cochin-China

The subdivision of land in Cochin-China is not so excessive as in Tonkin and Annam, because of its more recent economic exploitation and lower density of population. In no province of the state is the average size of the parcels less than 1 ha. (cf. the average of $\frac{1}{10}$ ha. for the parcels of the Tonkin delta). The parcels increase in size from east to west.

Land holdings are larger here than elsewhere in the country. Cochin-China had 255,000 properties in 1930 with a rural population of slightly over 4 million, and a cultivated area of about 2,400,000 ha. or 1 holding for every 15 inhabitants and an average of 9 ha. per holding (cf. the figures of 6·7 inhabitants and 1·2 ha. per holding in the Tonkin delta). The basis of division into large and small properties cannot be the same as in Tonkin. The small property (under 5 ha.) occupies 12% of the cultivated surface, the medium-sized ones (5–50 ha.) 43%, and the largest (over 50 ha.) 45%. Holdings of less than 10 ha. are usually farmed directly by the owner, but the greater proportion of the medium- and large-sized holdings are let out in plots of 3–10 ha. to tenants, who are known in Cochin-China as *ta dien* (see p. 261). The tenants pay for their own house and for any labour they employ; about 50% of the rice crop is given up as rent for the land.

The early colonized region in the centre and east of the delta has on the average smaller holdings than the more recently settled area in the west, though even in the former area nearly one-third of the surface is occupied by properties over 50 ha. in extent. Most of these large properties are held by wealthy Annamites as 'concessions' from the French government, according to conditions laid down by the decree of 4 November 1928 (see p. 295).

Communal property is much less important in Cochin-China than in either Tonkin or Annam. In 1930 it represented only 2·5% of the cultivated land.

Land System in Cambodia

In Cambodia the average size of the parcels of land is about 1 ha. or roughly the same as that in Cochin-China. The small peasant property is the chief form of holding as is shown in the following table, which relates to five of the provinces and which may be taken as representative of the conditions in the whole state:

	Small properties under 5 ha.	Medium-sized properties		Large properties over 50 ha.
		5–10 ha.	10–50 ha.	
	%	%	%	%
Battambang	76·3	18·3	5·3	0·12
Soai Reng	80·3	16·5	3·0	0·22
Prey Veng	87·0	10·5	2·4	0·14
Kompong Cham	96·8	2·8	0·4	—
Kandal	99·0	0·9	0·1	0·02

Source: P. Gourou, *L'Utilisation du Sol en Indochine française*, p. 306 (Paris, 1940).

Small properties of under 5 ha. thus form on the average more than four-fifths of the holdings, while properties of over 50 ha. are almost non-existent.

AGRICULTURAL CREDIT AND AGRICULTURAL CO-OPERATION

Almost all the native farmers of Indo-China live in varying degrees of indebtedness. The small- and medium-size landholder often requires short-term loans which bring a monthly interest rate of from 15 to 25 %; even the large property owners borrow money, generally on long-term conditions, to cover their high capital expenses. The rates claimed by the usurers are so high that they absorb the greater part of the peasant's resources. Wealthy Annamites and Chinese practise usury, but the Hindu moneylenders or *Chettys* have perhaps the greatest influence.

The schemes for agricultural credit and agricultural co-operation introduced into Indo-China during this century have sought to combat the spread of usury and to raise the living standard of the peasant. As early as 1875 a clause in the decree founding the Bank of Indo-China recognized the necessity for agricultural loans on government security, but the first credit society was not formed until 1913. In this year, there was formed the *Société indigène de Crédit agricole mutuel de Cochinchine*, and by 1929 each province in this state had its own society; since 1932, a central body has co-ordinated the work of the provincial associations. In the other states, except Laos, a decree of 1926 instituted a *Crédit populaire agricole* based on the one which had proved successful in Java. This credit scheme led to the setting up of a number of *Caisses indigènes de Crédit agricole mutuel*. In 1933, the various credit societies throughout the country were centralized under a body entitled *L'Office indochinois du Crédit agricole mutuel*. Despite the growth of these organizations, usury remains a serious problem (see p. 365).

Co-operative associations affiliated to the credit societies have recently been established to promote better conditions in the production and marketing of agricultural commodities. The first modern co-operative association was founded in the Tonkin delta in November 1934, and since then seventeen more have been set up both in the densely populated coastal lowlands and also in parts of the interior (Fig. 100). Already they have improved the production of silk, tobacco, and certain oil-yielding crops. Many more organizations of this kind, which can secure an equitable distribution of public money and disseminate technical knowledge, are sorely needed, for the chief remedy to the wretched condition in which the great mass of the peasantry to-day find themselves lies in a quantitative as well as qualitative increase in agricultural production.

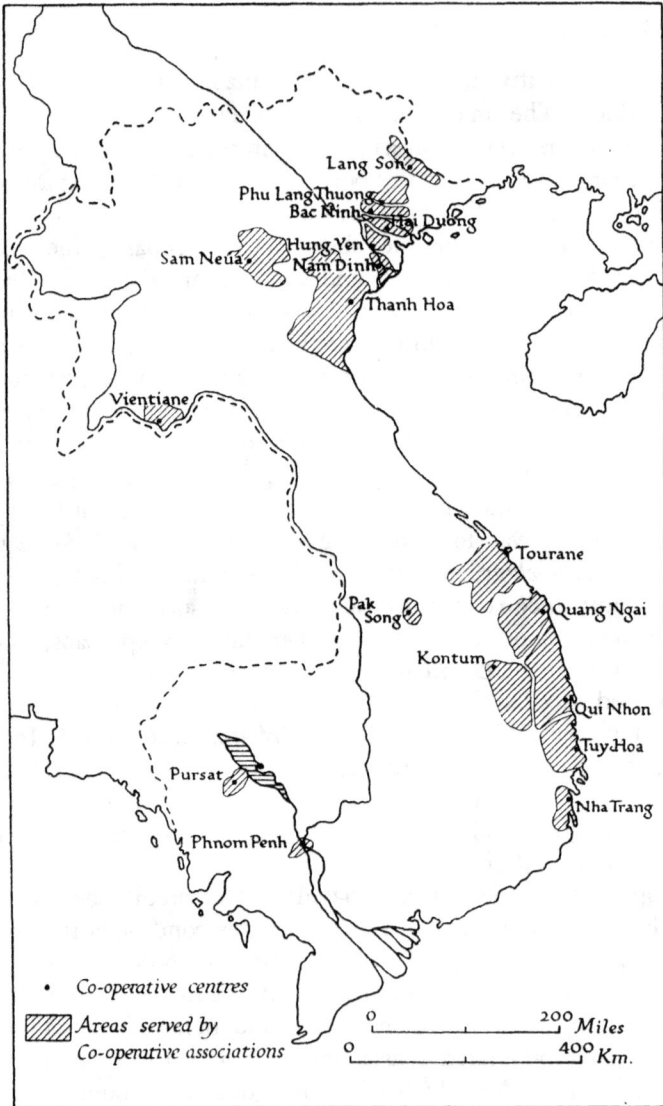

Fig. 100. Areas covered by agricultural co-operative associations

Source: M. Guillaume, 'La Coopération agricole en Indochine', *Bulletin économique de l'Indochine*, vol. XLI, facing p. 50 (Hanoi, 1938).

PLANTATION AGRICULTURE

In Indo-China, as in other tropical countries, the establishment of agricultural enterprises financed by Europeans and employing native labour has been an important feature of white colonization. The chief areas of French colonization lie in the south of the peninsula, more especially in eastern Cochin-China, where large areas of 'terre rouge' (see p. 257 and Fig. 83) provide excellent conditions for agricultural development. Plantations are found along the banks of the Rivière de Saigon and of the Dong Nai in Cochin-China, near Kompong Cham in Cambodia and widely scattered parts of Laos, north Annam and south Tonkin. The decree of 4 November 1928 controls the awarding of all agricultural concessions. In order to encourage small-scale colonization, free concessions are awarded up to a maximum area of 300 ha. Grants of land above this limit, but below 1,000 ha., are adjudicated by the Chief Resident, grants of from 1,000 to 4,000 ha. by the Governor-General, and grants over 4,000 ha. by recommendation from the Ministry of Colonies. The planter does not receive a definitive title to his land until it is officially considered as under proper cultivation, and if there is undue delay in cultivating the ground the property may be confiscated. No foreigners are allowed to receive concessions or to become members of plantation companies.

In 1937, the area of agricultural concessions in French ownership amounted to approximately 1 million ha., of which rather more than 400,000 ha. were under cultivation, representing a threefold increase over the corresponding figures at the beginning of the century. The following table shows the area of agricultural concessions in each state in 1937:

	Provisional concessions ha.	Definitive concessions ha.	Total ha.	Area under cultivation ha.
Annam	80,000	80,000	160,000	25,000
Cambodia	80,000	40,000	120,000	30,000
Cochin-China	190,000	420,000	610,000	300,000
Laos	700	600	1,300	1,000
Tonkin	11,000	97,000	108,000	44,000
Total	361,700	637,600	999,300	400,000

Source: *Annuaire statistique de l'Indochine, 1936–7*, p. 92 (Hanoi, 1938).

Of the 400,000 ha. of concessions under cultivation more than 60% are devoted to rice and are not plantations in the true sense. This land is almost always let out to tenants. The remainder of the concessions is chiefly planted with rubber, coffee or tea; the other plantation crops, including coconuts, kapok and palm oil, are unimportant at the present time, though they have great potentialities in the future.

RUBBER PLANTATIONS

Rubber is to-day the most successful plantation crop in Indo-China, though it held an insignificant position at the beginning of the century. Its success may be attributed to favourable soil and climatic conditions, to the fact that as the plantations developed late they could profit from the experiences of those in other countries, and finally to the preferential treatment in the French market.

Before the development of *Hevea* plantations, rubber was obtained from many varieties of trees, especially lianes, growing in the virgin forest. Production by this means could never be on a large scale and experiments were made with plants imported from Ceylon, Malaya, and the Netherlands East Indies. In the period 1890–1900, the four species, *Castilloa elastica, Manihot Glazowii, Ficus elastica,* and *Hevea brasiliensis*, were tried out, but only the latter proved suitable. The cultivation of *Hevea* in Indo-China dates from 1897 when 2,000 of these trees were planted in the Botanical Gardens at Saigon. The research station at Ong Yem, in the province of Thu Dau Mot, and the *Institut Pasteur* near Nha Trang also established experimental rubber plantations about this time. Although these experiments demonstrated the great potentialities of this product in Cochin-China and south Annam, *Hevea* culture at first made little progress. Not until 1915 did the output of plantation rubber exceed that gathered from other trees.

In Cochin-China, parts of Cambodia and south Annam, the *Hevea brasiliensis* found physical conditions eminently suited to its development. Uniformly high temperatures are experienced throughout the year, while the rainfall, though not so heavy as in Malaya, is adequate. The 'dry' season, which normally lasts for five months, has indeed proved beneficial, since the trees appear to be less subject to certain diseases that affect them in areas of heavier rainfall. Favourable soil conditions have also encouraged the rapid extension of *Hevea* cultivation. Many plantations have been developed on the ancient alluvial soils or 'terres grises' of eastern Cochin-China, though a hard lateritic pan occasionally makes them unsuitable. A large proportion of the rubber is to-day grown on the 'terres rouges', soils derived from the

Plate 41. Irrigation system near Thanh Hoa

A sluice, lock gates and weir have been constructed to control the flow of water in the three channels of the river. In the right of the photograph there is an irrigation canal branching from the river.

Plate 42. Rubber factory and plantations

In the large buildings which form the rubber factory the raw latex is coagulated and then passed through a rolling mill to produce sheets of rubber. The smaller buildings are the houses of the labourers on the plantation.

Plate 43. Rubber plantation, Cochin-China

Latex is obtained by cutting the bark of the rubber tree in the manner shown in the photograph. The latex collects in a small cup which can be clearly seen near the base of the tree in the foreground.

decomposition of basalt and other igneous rocks, which extend in a crescent about 300 km. from south-east to north-west and 20–40 km. in width from the delta of the Mekong to the sandstone plateaux of Cambodia and south Annam. The 'terres rouges' are difficult to exploit, since a dense vegetation covers them and the thin population of Moi tribes cannot provide the necessary labour supply. Exploitation has proceeded hand in hand with the settlement of immigrant labour and with the development of communications.

Rubber plantations in Indo-China covered 126,700 ha. in 1937, of which 98,000 ha. were to be found in Cochin-China, 27,000 ha. in Cambodia and 1,700 ha. in Annam. The plantations numbered 1,005 altogether, of which 304 had more than 40 ha., but only 52 exceeded 500 ha. The 304 large plantations had an area of 119,000 ha. or 94% of the total; three plantations in the Thu Dau Mot province of Cochin-China, and one along the banks of the Mekong in Cambodia were of more than 5,000 ha. (Fig. 101).

The cultivation and preparation of rubber is a complex process demanding large capital resources and an abundant labour supply. Weeding and ploughing of the soil first takes place, then, after a short period in nursery beds, the trees are planted in June or July. Many plantations grow tea, coffee, or sugar in association with the rubber. The first collection of latex occurs when the trees are five or six years old. In the early rubber plantations a daily collection was made, but as this method greatly reduced the yield it is now customary to rest the trees during a part of the dry season. The tapping is made in the early morning, and each labourer has generally from 150 to 200 trees allotted to his care. The bowls containing the latex are emptied into vats for transport to the factories. As the latex ferments very quickly transport must be rapid and the largest plantations are divided into sections, each having a reception post with fleets of lorries. In the factories, which normally lie in the centre of the plantation, they use acetic acid for the process of coagulation, and, after coagulation, the latex passes through a rolling mill which produces the sheets of rubber. When dry, the sheets are ready for the secondary processes of manufacture. The rubber is of high quality (Plates 42, 43).

Many groups of planters have formed companies and pooled their capital resources. This growth of rubber-production companies is more marked in Indo-China than elsewhere; the most powerful of such bodies is the *Société financière de Caoutchoucs*, which controls plantations not only in Indo-China but also in Sumatra and Malaya.

Since the war of 1914–18, rubber production in Indo-China has steadily increased despite the vagaries of world economic conditions (see p. 350). An immediate post-war boom was followed by a slump, and in 1922 the Stevenson Plan sought to raise the price of rubber by giving a limiting export quota to the main producing countries. As

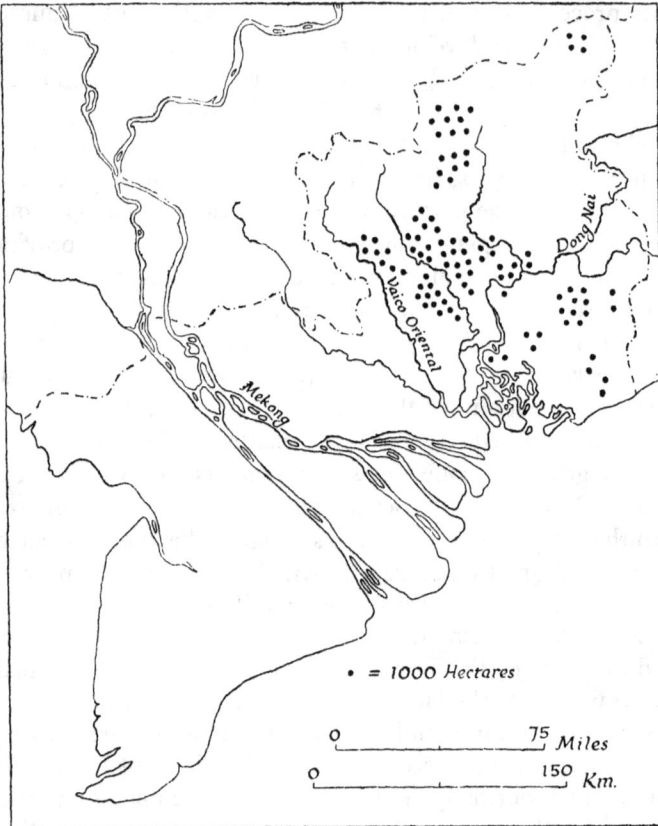

= 1000 Hectares

Fig. 101. Rubber plantations in Cochin-China

Source: based on figures in *Annuaire statistique de l'Indochine, 1936–37*, p. 92 (Hanoi, 1938).

Indo-China was not included in the scheme this led to a local boom and the plantations rapidly expanded. The Stevenson Plan thus proved detrimental to the interests of the large rubber-producing countries which caused it to be abolished in 1928. Prices again fell and they reached a very low level with the onset of the world economic depression of the early thirties. State aid alone saved the Indo-

Chinese rubber industry from disaster; large loans were granted from the General Budget in order to discourage the abandonment of young plantations which had not yet reached maturity. Further, in March 1931, the government created a reserve fund and imposed duties on the import of foreign rubber into France. Three years later an international committee was formed in London for the control of rubber production, and this body recommended that Indo-Chinese planters should increase their output to meet the French demand. This end was accomplished for the first time in 1938 when rubber production in Indo-China reached about 60,000 tons.

COFFEE PLANTATIONS

Although coffee was among the earliest plantation crops to be grown in Indo-China, it has never become important. French colonists established the first coffee plantation in 1888, near Phu Ly in the hilly country surrounding the Tonkin delta. The planters soon encountered serious difficulties since the soil rapidly became exhausted and a shifting cultivation, like that practised in Brazil, proved impossible owing to the unsuitable nature of the soil in the interior. Careful soil fertilization appeared to be the only solution. Animal manure was found most successful, and to-day a characteristic feature of coffee cultivation in Indo-China is its close association with the rearing of livestock.

In recent years coffee cultivation has spread southwards into central and south Annam, where the crop thrives very well in the red soil regions of the interior plateaux. The threat of destruction by typhoons prevents the establishment of coffee plantations on hill slopes facing the sea. The altitude for optimum production increases from 100 m. near Vinh to 300 m. near Quang Tri, 500 m. on the Plateau du Darlac, and 600 m. on the Plateau du Lang Bian. Excessive sunlight harms the coffee plant, and in south Annam a tree called the Lamtoro is specially grown to provide the necessary shade. Since the growth and preparation of coffee requires relatively little capital expenditure, it is usually a 'small-man' concern and the plantations may often be less than 100 ha. in area.

Indo-Chinese coffee is principally obtained from the well-known *Coffea arabica*, though *C. robusta*, *C. excelsa* and *C. chari* predominate in Tonkin. Production is irregular as the trees frequently suffer from parasites; attacks by the 'borer' in 1920–1, 1925–6, and 1928–9 seriously diminished the output in these years. In 1937–8, a normal year, only 1,500 tons of coffee were produced from a plantation area of about 13,000 ha. Despite the large French demand only a very small proportion of the crop is exported.

TEA PLANTATIONS

Unlike rubber and coffee, the tea plant had been cultivated by native farmers long before the European occupation of the country. Even after the French conquest, for a long time little attempt was made to establish modern plantations owing to lack of capital. The government, however, took steps to improve the quality of the native crop; a research station was set up at Phu Tho (Tonkin) in 1917 for the experimental cultivation of selected plants imported from Assam and Ceylon. Only since 1924 have large tea plantations been established under French management. These lie principally between 500 and 1,000 m. on the red soil plateaux of south Annam; the highest one, that of Arbre Broye, on the Plateau du Lang Bian, is nearly 1,500 m. above sea level. The European tea plantations to-day cover about 3,000 ha. of which about 2,500 ha. lie in southern Annam. The plantations vary in size from 100 to 800 ha.

The tea plant requires constant attention at all stages of its growth. It is first cared for in nursery beds, then at the age of 12–16 months it is transplanted. The soil must be well manured and clear of weeds; as in coffee cultivation, trees provide shade from the sun. In Annam, gathering of the leaves first takes place at the end of the third year after planting, but the maximum yield is normally obtained at the age of 7 or 8 years. As the picking has to be done by hand a large labour supply is an important factor in tea cultivation. In certain of the processing methods, however, such as rolling the leaves, machines have partly replaced hand labour.

Tea production on the European plantations was only 812 tons in 1937–8. The greater part is exported to France where Indo-Chinese tea has recently enjoyed special consideration. A future increase in production will probably depend on the continuance of this protected market, which is admittedly small, and also upon the extent to which the tea from Indo-China can vie with that from other French colonies.

FORESTRY

The forests of Indo-China, with their varied character and infinite diversity of species, constitute an invaluable economic resource. Innumerable varieties of wood and wood products are obtained from the dense tropical vegetation which clothes even the highest summits, from the extensive forest clearings, and from the various forest zones along the coast. There are first of all many trees which provide material for high-quality woodwork: these include the rose-wood (*Dalbergia cochinchinensis*), the ebony (*Diospyros mun*), the sandalwood (*Dysoxylon Loureiri*), and the mahogany (*Melanorrhea laccifera* and *Sandoricum indicum*). A large number of other species supply wood for use in agriculture and industry: the most common are the *sao* (*Hopea odorata*), the *lim* (*Erythrophlaeum fordii*), and the *dau* (*Dipterocarpus*). Certain woods such as those from the *bang lang* (*Lagerstroemia*), the *ca chac* (*Shorea obtusa*), and the *cam xe* (*Xylia dolabriformis*), lend themselves particularly to ship construction. The poorer quality woods, including the *bo de* (*Styrax tonkinensis*) and the *vang* (*Mallotus cochinchinensis*), are used for firewood, charcoal and for the manufacture of matches.

A great number of minor forest products are utilized by both native and European. The nut of the *Areca* palm, with the betel leaf, is used in the preparation of a popular form of chewing material. The many species of bamboo serve in the construction of houses, in paper making, in lattice working and in countless other activities. Various rattans are cut down and made into canes, baskets and articles of furniture. Mangroves are an important source of firewood, while tannin is extracted from their bark. Oil from the abrasin tree (*Aleurites montana*), similar to the valuable tung oil of China, is collected in fairly large quantities around Lang Son and Thanh Hoa, for the manufacture of paints and varnishes. Varnish is also manufactured from the lacquer tree and from shellac, which is a coloured resinous substance produced by an insect as an incrustation on the branches of trees. The incrustations are called 'stick-lac'. Other forest products include cinnamon and quinine.

Forest Exploitation

Until the beginning of this century forestry had developed on only a small scale in Indo-China, but since then it has made rapid strides following the colonization of the interior and increased demand for

wood of all kinds. Fig. 102 shows the production trend for firewood
and constructional wood from 1910 to 1936. It will be seen that the
output rose swiftly in the decade after 1918, fell precipitously during

Fig. 102. Production of timber and firewood, 1911-36

Source: P. Maurand, 'L'Indochine forestière', *Bulletin économique de l'Indochine*,
vol. XLI, p. 820 (Hanoi, 1938).

the years of economic depression (1929-33) and recovered again from
1933 to 1936. In 1936, the position was as follows; statistics are
not available for Laos, since no organized forestry service has been
developed as in the other states.

	Constructional timber cu.m.	Firewood cu.m.
Annam	110,100	130,500
Cambodia	210,100	346,300
Cochin-China	175,200	885,800
Tonkin	165,600	175,400
Total	661,000	1,538,000

Source: P. Maurand, 'L'Indochine forestière', *Bulletin économique de l'Indochine*, vol. XLI, p. 819 (Hanoi, 1938).

Thus, the output of wood for commercial or constructional purposes still lags far behind that of firewood.

The production of bamboo is greater than that from any other single group of species. Over 80% of the total comes from Tonkin, as is shown in the following table.

	Production of bamboo (1936) cu.m.
Annam	261,700
Cambodia	99,600
Cochin-China	10,600
Tonkin	869,100
Total	1,241,000

Source: P. Maurand, 'L'Indochine forestière', *Bulletin économique de l'Indochine*, vol. XLI, p. 1352 (Hanoi, 1938).

Production of the other forest crops varies too greatly from year to year for the figures for a single year to have any general significance.

The axe is universally employed for felling operations, and as many of the trees have an exceedingly broad base (Fig. 49) they are normally cut down 1½–2 m. above the ground. The logs vary in length from 2 to 8 m. Special trucks, sometimes drawn by as many as twenty pairs of buffaloes, carry the heavier logs as far as the rivers or metalled roads; elephants are often used for transport of wood on the Plateau du Darlac in south Annam and around Siem Reap in Cambodia. Two-wheeled carts drawn by a single pair of buffaloes or oxen, transport the lighter logs of timber. After this preliminary journey by truck or cart, the logs wherever possible are floated down the main rivers to the principal timber-marketing centres. The foresters make rafts of the felled timber and on smaller streams they are left free to drift with the current, but on the Mekong and the Fleuve Rouge steam-boats tow the rafts to prevent them becoming a hindrance to navigation. Transport of wood in this manner is only possible at certain periods of the year: on the Mekong, from the beginning of the floods in July until December; on the lake of Tonle Sap, only from November until about February; on the Fleuve Rouge, all the year, but especially between September and May. On the tributary streams, flotation can generally be carried out immediately after the season of maximum rainfall. Where no river lies within reach of the forest area, transport is made by railway or motor lorry; in many cases both roads and bridges have been specially constructed to aid in the disposal of timber. The facilities for water, rail and road transport thus control the areas of timber exploitation.

Forest Conservation and Improvement

The conservation and improvement of the forest resources is a pressing problem, owing to the rapidly increasing production of timber and to the vast areas which are annually being denuded of fine stands through the destructive methods of shifting cultivation. Moreover, in most of the forests the lianes and other plants growing in tangled masses close to the ground tend to obstruct natural regeneration and to cause a marked scarcity of desirable species. A recent census taken on 4 ha. of dense woodland in the province of Bien Hoa (Cochin-China) revealed that out of 1,080 trees of more than 10 cm. diameter hardly 250 were at all useful and only nine sufficiently large to be commercially valuable. The commonly adopted methods of exploitation, in which the better trees are cut down without attention to future supply have further aggravated the position. As a result of these conditions many forests to-day are rapidly becoming exhausted: in Cochin-China, the formerly important *sao* species (*Hopea odorata*) has now almost entirely disappeared; other species are approaching exhaustion in parts of Tonkin and Cambodia.

In an effort to solve the problem of forest conservation and improvement, large reserves have been established under direct protection of the government forestry service. These reserves totalled 2,252,000 ha. in 1939, distributed as shown in the following table (Fig. 103):

	Forest reserves ha.
Annam	765,000
Cambodia	670,000
Cochin-China	533,000
Tonkin	284,000
Total	2,252,000

Source: P. Gourou, *L'Utilisation du Sol en Indochine française*, p. 393 (Paris, 1940).

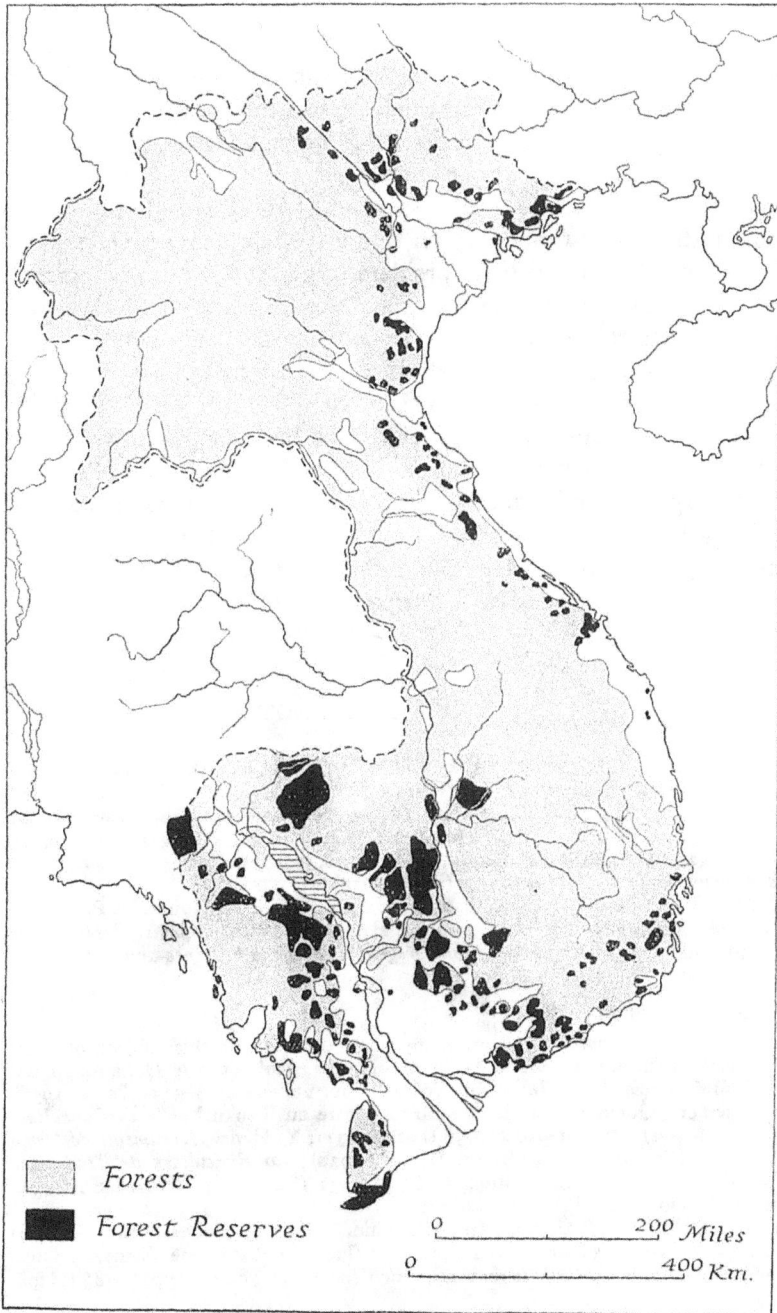

Forests

Forest Reserves

0   200 *Miles*

0   400 *Km.*

Fig. 103. Forest reserves

Source: P. Maurand, 'L'Indochine forestière', *Bulletin économique de l'Indochine*, vol. xli, folding map (Hanoi, 1938).

Careful supervision of these reserves has reduced the number of forest fires, which elsewhere still break out and annually burn down several thousand hectares of valuable woodland.

In both protected and unprotected forest zones, attempts have been made to control exploitation by a strict rotation for tree cropping. The results have proved moderately satisfactory for firewood but negative for constructional timber. Even where the forests are protected and systematically exploited the problem of improvement still remains, for, as already noted, the luxuriant development of undergrowth restricts natural regeneration. To ensure the continuance of fine stands, it is necessary to create plantations free from undergrowth and composed exclusively of trees of good species. During the past few years in Cambodia, a technique has been successfully adopted whereby the natives are authorized to cut down or burn the less desirable species and climbing plants in the traditional manner of shifting cultivation. Since 1936, about 500 ha. have received this treatment, which provides a nice adjustment between the customary procedure of primitive agriculture and the requirements of modern forestry.

BIBLIOGRAPHICAL NOTE

A. GENERAL

(1) The following general works contain much valuable information on the agriculture of Indo-China: P. Bernard, *Le Problème économique indochinois* (Paris, 1934); P. Gourou, *L'Utilisation du Sol en Indochine française* (Paris, 1940); Y. Henry, *Economie agricole de l'Indochine* (Hanoi, 1932); Georges Maspero, *Un Empire Colonial français: l'Indochine*, vol. II (Paris, 1930); C. Robequain, *L'Evolution économique de l'Indochine française* (Paris, 1939).

(2) Detailed studies on the agriculture of special regions are found in: P. Gourou, *Le Tonkin* (Hanoi, 1931); P. Gourou, *Les Paysans du Delta tonkinois* (Hanoi, 1936); C. Robequain, *Le Thanh Hoa: Etude géographique d'une Province annamite*, 2 vols. (Paris, 1929).

B. NATIVE AGRICULTURE

(1) *Rice Cultivation.* There are many works dealing with this subject, of which the most useful are: Bigorgne, 'L'Hydraulique agricole dans le Delta tonkinois', *Bulletin économique de l'Indochine*, vol. XLI, pp. 268–93, 486–515 (Paris, 1938); P. Braemer, 'Quelques aspects de la Riziculture au Tonkin', *Riz et Riziculture*, vol. V (Fasc. 2), pp. 101–16, 215–36 (Paris, 1931); Y. Henry, *Documents de Démographie et Riziculture en Indochine* (Hanoi, 1928); *La Riziculture de l'Indochine*, Exposition Coloniale Internationale, Paris, 1931 (Paris, 1931); P. Mariotte, 'Le Riz de l'Indochine', *Riz et Riziculture*, vol. XII (Fasc. 1), pp. 1–32 (Paris, 1938); Tran Van Huu, 'La Riziculture en Cochinchine', *Riz et Riziculture*, vol. II (Fasc. 4), pp. 255–70; vol. III (Fasc. 1), 1928, pp. 1–15 (Paris, 1928); M. de Visme, 'L'Office Indochinois du Riz', *Bulletin économique de l'Indochine*, vol. XLI, pp. 76–83 (Hanoi, 1938).

(2) *Other Native Crops.* The material on the native cultivation of crops, other than rice, has been obtained from P. Gourou, *L'Utilisation du Sol en Indochine*

française (Paris, 1940) and from the following articles: M. Guillaume, 'Rapport sur le Cocotier en Indochine', *Bulletin économique de l'Indochine*, vol. XXVII, pp. 137–91, 269–323 (Hanoi, 1924); M. Guillaume, 'Situation économique de l'Industrie sucrière en Indochine', *Bulletin économique de l'Indochine*, vol. XXXVI, pp. 387–92 (Hanoi, 1933); F. Herbette, 'La Soie en Indochine', *Annales de Géographie*, vol. XLI, pp. 167–76 (Paris, 1932); R. Jauffret, 'Les Maïs de l'Indochine', *Bulletin économique de l'Indochine*, vol. XXXVII, pp. 643–702 (Hanoi, 1934); M. Lagleyze, 'La Culture du Tabac en Indochine', *Bulletin économique de l'Indochine*, vol. XXX, pp. 1–40 (Hanoi, 1927).

(3) *Livestock.* This section is based on: J. Bernhard, 'Notes sur l'Elevage du Cheval dans le 2e Territoire militaire', *Bulletin économique de l'Indochine*, vol. XXXVI, pp. 714–39 (Hanoi, 1933); B. Havard-Duclos, 'Possibilités d'amélioration et de développement de l'Elevage en Indochine', *Bulletin économique de l'Indochine*, vol. XLII, pp. 1125–70 (Hanoi, 1939); R. Vittoz, 'L'Evolution de l'élevage porcin dans le centre et l'est cochinchinois', *Bulletin économique de l'Indochine*, vol. XXXIX, pp. 487–526 (Hanoi, 1936).

(4) *Agricultural Credit and Agricultural Co-operation.* On this subject see: P. de Feyssal, *L'Endettement agraire en Cochinchine* (Hanoi, 1933); M. Guillaume, 'La Coopération agricole en Indochine', *Bulletin économique de l'Indochine*, vol. XLI, pp. 31–65 (Hanoi, 1938); L. M., 'Les Sociétés de crédit agricole mutuel en Cochinchine (S.I.C.A.M.) de 1913 à 1938', *Bulletin économique de l'Indochine*, vol. XLI, pp. 780–800 (Hanoi, 1938).

(5) *Land System.* The fullest treatment is found in P. Gourou, *L'Utilisation du Sol en Indochine française* (Paris, 1940) and in Y. Henry, *Economie agricole de l'Indochine* (Hanoi, 1932).

C. PLANTATION AGRICULTURE

A wealth of information on plantation agriculture is contained in the following works: C. Bernard, 'La Production du Thé au Tonkin', *Bulletin économique de l'Indochine*, vol. XXXI, pp. 121–34 (Hanoi, 1928); P. Carton, 'Le Caoutchouc en Indochine', *Bulletin économique de l'Indochine*, vol. XXVII, pp. 349–456 (Hanoi, 1924); P. Michaux, *L'Heveaculture en Indochine* (Paris, 1937); D. de Montaigut, *La Colonisation française dans l'est de la Cochinchine* (Limoges, 1929); A. Rome, 'Aperçus sur la culture du Caféier en Indochine française', *Revue de Botanique appliquée et d'Agriculture tropicale*, vol. XV, pp. 525–34, 608–15 (Paris, 1935); J. Trochain, 'La Production du Thé et les améliorations apportées à la culture du Thé en Indochine', *Revue de Botanique appliquée et d'Agriculture tropicale*, vol. XIII, pp. 613–50 (Paris, 1933).

D. FORESTRY

There is a general account in P. Gourou, *L'Utilisation du Sol en Indochine française* (Paris, 1940), but the most detailed treatment is given in P. Maurand, 'L'Indochine forestière', *Bulletin économique de l'Indochine*, vol. XLI, pp. 801–29, 975–1061, 1350–74 (Hanoi, 1938).

Chapter XII

FISHERIES

Introduction: Fresh-water Fisheries: Salt-water Fisheries: Bibliographical Note

INTRODUCTION

The fishing industry holds a leading place in the economy of Indo-China, since fish with its various by-products forms an indispensable item in native diet. Production figures for the whole country cannot be given accurately, as a large proportion of the catch is consumed on the spot, though all authorities agree that the fisheries are second only in importance to rice cultivation and far ahead of other agricultural crops, of forestry products and of all manufacturing industries. Fishing is carried on as a part-time activity by almost the whole population; the number of persons engaged solely in fishing would appear to be relatively small, though no complete statistics are available. The fresh-water catch far exceeds that from salt water, owing partly to the meagre stocks of fish in the tropical sea and partly also to the lack of a maritime tradition.

FRESH-WATER FISHERIES

Almost all the native peoples of Indo-China practise fresh-water fishing. The particular nature of this activity can best be understood by a study of its development in the Tonkin delta and in the Tonle Sap region of Cambodia.

The Tonkin Delta

The many rivers, canals, lakes and flooded rice fields of this region have favoured a large-scale and intensive fresh-water fishing industry. At all times of the year, except during the replanting and harvesting of rice, the peasant and his family may be seen occupied in some kind of fishing operation. They often employ the most simple methods, such as seizing the fish by the hand from the mud of the rice fields; numbers of crabs are also caught in this manner. Other methods of catching include the use of the *nom*, the *giam* and the *dieu tom*. The *nom*, a small bamboo cage of conical shape, is dug into the mud and the fish are picked out by hand when they have entered the trap.

The *giam* is a broad scoop, fixed to a bamboo pole in the ground; the peasant stirs the mud either with his feet or with a bamboo stick and the fish take refuge in the scoop (Fig. 104). Finally, there is the *dieu tom*, a basket which differs from the other two in that it is dragged through the mud and not kept stationary.

The peasants, as distinct from the professional fishermen, consume all the fish they catch. In any case, the small quantities gathered by each individual would bring in only a trifling monetary return.

A small proportion of the natives in the Tonkin delta devote the whole or greater part of their energies to the fishing industry. These professional fishermen live in villages along the banks of the principal

Fig. 104. Fishing in a flooded rice field at the end of the harvest
Source: P. Gourou, *Les Paysans du Delta tonkinois*, plate 39 (Paris, 1936).

rivers and lakes, while some are found among the many 'floating' hamlets, the inhabitants of which possess no land and spend their whole life in boats. The fishermen employ the same instruments as the peasants, except that nets are a more common feature. They frequently use the *carrelet*, a large square net, of from 2 m. to 4 m. square, suspended by a bamboo rod attached to a long pole; the pole is balanced on an axis and the net can be raised or lowered at will. The *carrelet* is sometimes erected on bamboo rafts, but more often worked from the banks of the river or lake (Fig. 105).

Many of the professional fishermen practise an intensive pisciculture in their privately owned lakes. They collect young fish from the Fleuve Rouge in the summer months and transfer them to lake water, enriched by the addition of human and animal manure. At the end of six months the fish are sold fresh; some men, however, sell their catch in a dried state or as *nuoc mam*, a very popular sauce prepared from fish liver. Pisciculture in the lakes could well be improved by more careful selection of species, and in the rice fields there is a great future for its development. The *Institut des Recherches agronomiques et forestières* considers that the carp, by reason of its rapid growth and high quality flesh, would prove the most suitable fish to be reared. Experiments have shown that a yield of 50 kg. of carp per hectare of rice field can reasonably be expected, so that from the 1,100,000 ha. under this crop the total quantity would approximate to 55,000,000 kg., or an annual average of about 8 kg. for every person in the Tonkin delta.

Fig. 105. Fishing with *carrelets*
When the *carrelet* is raised the catch is collected by the men in small boats shown on the right.
Source: Ernest Flammarion, *Les Colonies françaises*, p. 206 (Vincennes, 1931).

The Tonle Sap Region of Cambodia

This region has a more active fishing industry than any other part of Indo-China and in intensity of production it is unique in the world. The lake of Tonle Sap produces 10 tons of fresh fish per sq. km. as compared with only 1 ton per sq. km. from the fishing grounds of the North Atlantic and North Sea. This exceptional productivity may be ascribed to the peculiar hydrographical conditions. In the dry season, from November to June, the lake covers 2,700 sq. km. and flows towards the Mekong; during the summer flood period (June to October), owing to the great height of water at Phnom Penh, the direction of flow is reversed and the lake exceeds 10,000 sq. km. in area. From the beginning of June, the fish spawn freely in the great expanse of flooded forest land which provides inexhaustible nutritious food. The fish which feed on the abundant vegetable matter of the lake increase in size more rapidly than those living in the Mekong, the river of Tonle Sap and other tributary streams.

Plate 44. Fish weir on a Cambodian river near Tonle Sap

A weir is built across the river and in the low-water season fish pass through an opening in the middle of the river into a rectangular wickerwork pound (seen in centre of picture) from which they are removed in sampans.

Plate 45. Floating fish pound near Tonle Sap

The fish pound, constructed of bamboo, is a common method of transporting fish to market. The small building of straw and thatch at one end forms a shelter for the fishermen. The bed of leaves covering the fish pound protects the fish from the heat of the sun. The fish pound is being drawn along the river by a boat seen in the left of the picture.

Plate 46. Fishing fleet at Phan Thiet, south Annam

Phan Thiet is one of the most important sea fishing centres along the coast to Annam. *Nuoc nam*, a sauce prepared from fish liver, is manufactured here. The wooden structures projecting from the front of the boats in the left foreground are used at sea to support large square nets known as *carrelets*.

About 30,000 persons are engaged in the fishing industry as a whole or part-time activity. The permanent population of professional fishermen live in pile dwellings or houses built on bamboo rafts (Fig. 81); the hamlet of Snoc Trou, near Kompong Chhnang, is the most important settlement along the banks of Tonle Sap. In the main fishing season (October to January) the numbers increase considerably, Annamites, Chinese and Malays migrating to the lake region from Cochin-China.

A great variety of machines is employed to catch the fish, some such as the *angruth*, and the *chneang* resembling the *nom* and *dieu tom* already described. In the river of Tonle Sap, between Kompong Luong and Phnom Penh, a large proportion of the fish are caught by the method known as the *day*. Two rafts, with a sampan between them, are moored in the river, and tied to the rafts is a conical shaped net, about 30 m. long and 15 m. in maximum diameter, at the end of which is fastened a long, narrow bamboo basket, held in position by a rope from another sampan close by. As the fish follow the current downstream they enter the net and are trapped in the basket which is raised and lowered at frequent intervals. A number of *day* are usually worked together in order to increase the catch.

In the rivers flowing into the lake of Tonle Sap and in the lake itself the most common method of catching the fish is the formation of 'chambres de capture' or elaborate fish weirs. When the fish seek to return from outlying flooded areas at the end of the high-water season a certain proportion are caught by small wattle-screens set up across each of the rivers entering the lake (Plate 44), but as these have a maximum height of 4 m. many fish escape in the early days of the declining flood. A few of the fish that have succeeded in escaping follow the current and are caught by similar but larger river barrages while many which remain in the lake are accounted for by nets and by the method known as the *samra* (Fig. 106). The *samra* consists of fixed wattle-screens interwoven with tree branches, enclosing a square water surface of 1–100 ha.; an opening at one of the sides gives access to the 'chambre de capture'. Large numbers of fish attracted by the nutritious foliage, enter the *samra* in flood time, only to be trapped as the water falls to a level below the height of the wattle-screens. The natives, standing up to their shoulders in water, drive the fish with the help of nets towards the 'chambre de capture' where other fishermen kill the fish and separate them according to their species.

Out of an estimated annual production of 120,000 tons, less than half enters the market fresh and the remainder in a dried state. The whole catch from Tonle Sap is dried or smoked before export, since the mud sill of Snoc Trou prevents the easy transport of fresh fish. Flat-bottomed junks, which carry the dried fish, have to be pushed by manual labour over the mud to reach the river of Tonle Sap; for a fully loaded junk the journey from Kompong Luong to Phnom Penh takes 15 days. Unlike the lake region proper, the riverine areas export both fresh and dried fish, with the former predominating. The catch is transported on sailing junks, or by means of bamboo rafts floated downstream with the current (Plate 45). From fish offal the natives annually prepare about 1,500 tons of oil, the chief centres of production

Fig. 106. Fishing by means of a trap (*samra*)

Source: P. Chevey and F. Le Poulain, 'La Pêche dans les eaux douces du Cambodge', *Travaux de l'Institut océanographique de l'Indochine*, no. 5, plate 34 (Saigon, 1940).

being at Battambang, Kompong Thom, Snoc Trou, Prek Phnau, Rockakong, and Loeukdeck. Fish and its various by-products form one of the most important commercial and fiscal resources in Cambodia; the trade is entirely in the hands of the Chinese.

Over-exploitation has caused a diminution in the catch during recent years, and to prevent further decline, stricter measures of control over the industry need to be introduced. Many owners of fishing lots use their nets or barrages at all seasons of the year, a pernicious practice which the observation posts established by the *Institut océanographique* seek to restrict; a close period should be effective from 31 May, the beginning of the spawning season, until the end of October. It is also thought necessary to forbid the employment of several methods of catching fish, such as the *day* and the larger *samra*. Finally, more careful conservation should be enforced in the forests surrounding the lake, since when flooded they play a supremely important part in nourishing the fish.

Fresh-water fishing in other parts of the country differs little from that developed in the Tonkin delta, and in the Tonle Sap region of Cambodia. The lowlands of Cochin-China and Annam have a thriving industry, but no production figures are available. In the interior, many Laotian tribes catch large quantities of fish from the Mekong for local consumption; fish are unimportant, however, in the left bank tributaries of the Se Khong, Se San, and Srepok.

SALT-WATER FISHERIES

The physical features of the Indo-Chinese coastline and adjoining seas appear to favour the development of an active salt-water fishing industry (Fig. 107). A broad, shallow continental shelf lies off the whole coast-line, with the exception of the part between Cap Varella and Nha Trang, while numerous bays and rocky inlets provide excellent shelter for fishing craft. Moreover, although the high average temperature of the water is inimical to the growth of an abundant fish population, the sea nevertheless contains good quality stock. Despite these not unfavourable physical conditions, the annual production of salt-water fish in Indo-China does not exceed 150,000 tons. Coastal waters provide almost all the catch; deep-sea fishing is quite insignificant.

Coastal fisheries in Tonkin have relatively small importance. The bays of Fai Tsi Long and Along, which seem to present ideal conditions for the industry, in fact shelter very few fishermen while farther south in the Fleuve Rouge delta, along a coastline 150 km. long, only about 4,500 are engaged in this occupation. Small groups of fishermen live in hamlets bordering the coast, but the one important centre is Do Son, where a rocky promontory gives shelter to sea-going craft.

Along the coast of north Annam the salt-water fishing industry is very active. In the single province of Thanh Hoa there are about 18,000 engaged in this activity, or four times the number in the Tonkin delta. The fishermen, who employ sampans and rafts, seldom sail more than 8 km. out to sea. They use a number of methods for catching the fish: some work a *carrelet* similar to that described above (Plate 46); the great majority, however, prefer the more remunerative trawling net, and the method of seine fishing, in which one end of a large net is fixed on land and the other end tied to a sampan which

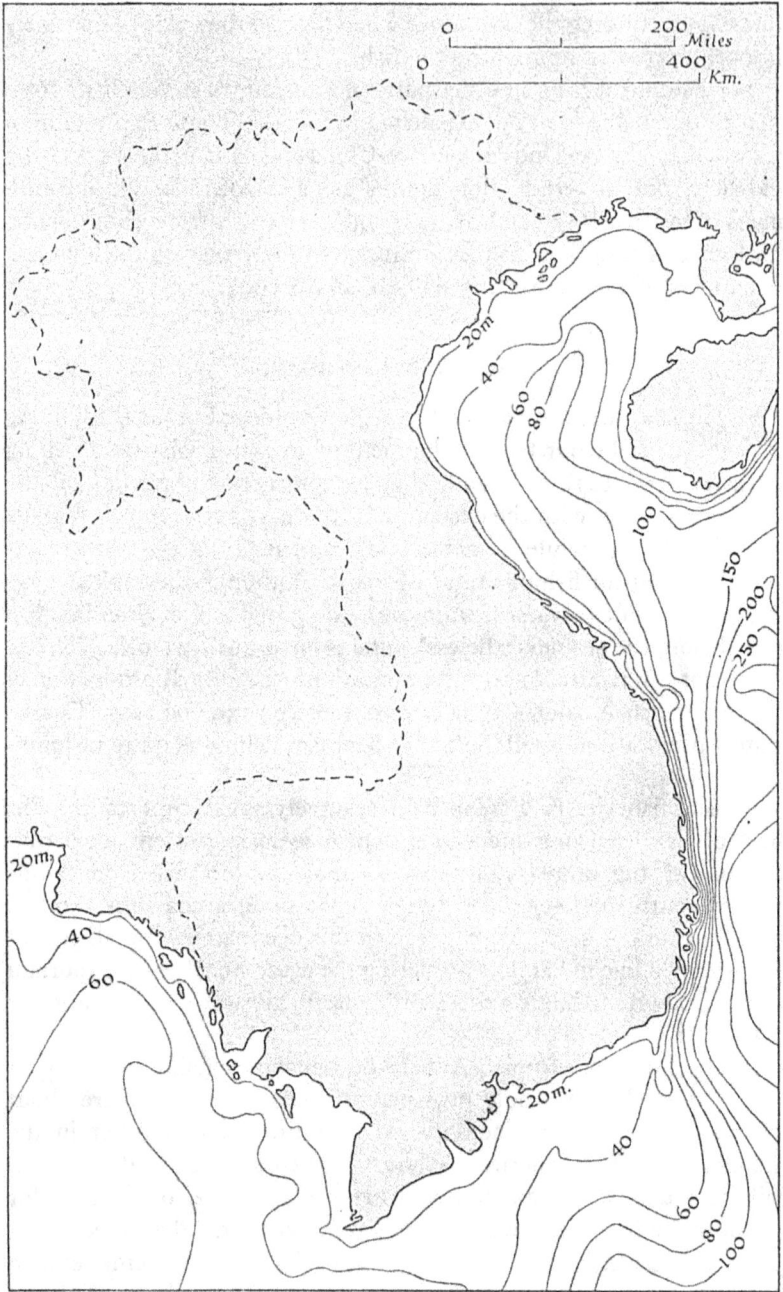

Fig. 107. Submarine contours
Source: *Atlas de L'Indochine*, plate 10 (Hanoi, 1928).

traps the fish by moving round in a circle. A large proportion of the catch is either dried or transformed into *nuoc mam*.

For several hundred kilometres south of the Porte d'Annam maritime fishing is little developed. Scattered settlements near Cap Lay indeed carry on a primitive fishing industry, but only in the extreme south of Annam around Phan Thiet does production again become significant. In this region large quantities of *nuoc mam* are prepared for export to Cochin-China; the fishermen also extract from certain fish an oil used for lighting and industrial purposes (Plate 46).

The sea-fishing industry is highly developed in Cochin-China, partly by reason of especially favourable physical conditions. From October to April, when the waters of Tonle Sap flow seawards, the mouths of the Mekong receive enormous quantities of nutritious vegetable matter on which the fish thrive. The fishermen market the greater part of their catch in Saigon or Cho Lon; cray-fish are caught along the shores of the Presqu'île de Ca Mau and turtles off the Ile de Phu Quoc.

The fish of the Cambodian coast are valued for their great size and weight. Barrages have been erected to capture the fish as they migrate along the coast during winter. From 200 to 300 barrages of this kind are at present in operation, chiefly near Chha Or and between Koh Kong and the Siamese frontier. In the summer, crab-fishing is carried on.

BIBLIOGRAPHICAL NOTE

(1) A useful summary is given in P. Gourou, *L'Utilisation du Sol en Indochine française*, ch. 11 passim (Paris, 1940).

(2) The fisheries of the Tonkin delta are fully dealt with in P. Gourou, *Les Paysans du Delta tonkinois*, pp. 432–45 (Paris, 1936) and in the following two articles: J. Lemasson, 'Possibilités d'amélioration et d'extension de la Pisciculture dans le Delta tonkinois', *Bulletin économique de l'Indochine*, vol. XXXVI, pp. 430–33 (Hanoi, 1933); and J. Lemasson, 'Renseignements sur les methodes de Pisciculture dans le Delta tonkinois', *Bulletin économique de l'Indochine*, vol. XXXVI, pp. 707–13 (Hanoi, 1933).

(3) There is a large literature on the fisheries of Cambodia. The fullest and most recent accounts are: P. Chevey and F. Le Poulain, 'Rapport préliminaire sur la Pêche dans les eaux douces Cambodgiennes', *Bulletin économique de l'Indochine*, vol. XLII, pp. 39–83 (Hanoi, 1939). P. Chevey and F. Le Poulain, *La Pêche dans les eaux douces du Cambodge* (Saigon, 1940). This work contains many maps, plans and photographs. It has also a detailed bibliography. A shorter account of the fishing in this area is given in J. Lebas, 'Les Pêcheries du lac Tonle Sap', *Annales de Géographie*, vol. XXXIV, pp. 69–73 (Paris, 1925).

(4) For an account of the sea fisheries of the Gulf of Tonkin see, L. Guilbert, 'La Pêche dans le Golfe du Tonkin', *Bulletin économique de l'Indochine*, vol. XIX, pp. 133–91 (Hanoi, 1916).

Chapter XIII

INDUSTRY

INTRODUCTION

The characteristic feature of industrial activity in Indo-China is its great variety, whether concerning the materials employed or the stage of development. Natural resources of many kinds, the large population of the lowlands traditionally skilled in handicraft and other work, and the initiative of the European have brought about this diversity in manufacturing effort. A distinction must be drawn between small-scale native craft industries generally carried on within the home of the peasant, and the highly capitalized modern factory industries established by the French during the last half-century. Despite the widely scattered nature of the one and the recent progress of the other, the proportion of the population engaged in handicraft work, mining and processing is extremely small, perhaps no more than 5%. The gross output of individual goods, moreover, has never been large and in the country's foreign trade manufacturing products play a subordinate role.

NATIVE INDUSTRIES

The native industries have a significant place in the economic life of Indo-China, since they provide the essential requirements of food, clothing and shelter. Agricultural and forestry operations supply the materials for these several activities and in most villages there is a close interdependence between agriculture, forestry and the various kinds of manufacture. Few studies of the native industries have been made and detailed knowledge about them is only available for the Tonkin delta and for the province of Thanh Hoa in Annam.

Native Industries in the Tonkin Delta

According to an unofficial census published in 1936 about 250,000 peasants in the Tonkin delta, or rather less than 7% of the adult population are engaged in industrial occupations for the greater part of the year. The following table gives the numbers employed in each major group of manufactures:

Industry	Number employed
Textiles	54,200
Foodstuffs	54,000
Basket-work	42,000
Wood-working	32,000
Masonry and brick-making	14,000
Paper	11,000
Metal	7,600
Ceramic	1,500
Miscellaneous	33,700
(Domestic service, chemists, electricians, musicians, etc.)	
	250,000

Source: P. Gourou, *Les Paysans du Delta tonkinois*, pp. 460–505 (Paris, 1936).

Village specialization is a feature of peasant industry in the Tonkin delta. There exist villages entirely devoted to such industries as weaving, carpentry, or the husking of rice. This specialization even goes so far as to bring about a certain division of labour which exhibits several forms: for example, some villages utilize only a part of the raw materials they buy and resell to other villages their unused goods; again, many villages send semi-finished wares for final processing to workers in the neighbouring district. All the native industries are for the most part family occupations with no wage-earning labour.

Textiles. Cotton weaving is the most important textile industry in the delta, the principal concentrations lying west of Hanoi. The natives use thread prepared by the modern cotton factory at Nam Dinh; spinning within the home has never developed. Cotton fabrics of many kinds are prepared for local use. Other textile industries include silk, lace, and the manufacture of rope.

Foodstuffs. The preparation of paddy for local consumption and for export absorbs nearly 37,000 of the 54,000 workers engaged in this group of industries. Two provinces, Hai Duong and Thai Binh, have the greatest number of workers so occupied, a concentration due mainly to their ease of communication with the large market centres. The dehusking of the rice is done almost entirely by hand, with the aid of only very simple machines.

The distillation of alcohol holds second place amongst the alimentary industries of the Tonkin delta, despite the fact that it has been declared illegal, save when carried on in modern factories under state control. Although the *per capita* consumption of alcohol is not high, the curtailment of its manufacture is a common cause of friction, since alcohol plays an important and essential part in the numerous festive occasions which figure largely in native life. Moreover, owing to its particular quality and much lower price, the native prefers alcohol distilled by traditional methods to that produced in the factory. Contraband traffic from village to village greatly increased after 1930, principally because the collapse of world prices led to a diminution in the export of rice from Tonkin and more of the crop became available for distillation. In 1935, the government sought to reduce the amount of contraband traffic by lowering the price of factory alcohol and by establishing near Bac Ninh a small manufacturing centre where native workers could practise their own methods of distillation.

Basket and wicker-work. An infinite variety of basket and wicker-work is used in the household, in the fields and for purposes of transport. The materials employed include bamboo, latania leaves, and rattan cane. Latania leaves provide the raw material for hats and capes. Three types of hats are manufactured; the most common is of conical shape, worn especially by the men; the women wear another type, slightly larger and less pointed in the middle; finally, in the isolated districts less finely worked hats are made and worn by both men and women. The cape made with latania leaves is a garment universally worn in the delta as a protection against rain and cold.

Wood-working. This industry is especially important west of the Fleuve Rouge, where floods preclude a rice harvest in winter and the inhabitants have consequently been forced to seek another remunerative occupation at this eason. The wood-workers frequently leave their native village to perform work in other parts of the delta and sometimes they migrate even as far afield as Laos and Cochin-China, returning to Tonkin in the summer. Furniture and agricultural implements are among the chief articles of manufacture; boat-building, lacquer and inlaid work are also important.

Miscellaneous industries. These include masonry and brick-making, paper manufacturing, and metallurgical work. The masons use bricks made within the delta region and, like the wood-workers, they move from village to village, and from town to town. Paper manufacturing is concentrated in a few villages near Hanoi. The natives make their paper from the *cay gio*, a tree growing in the hills around Phu Tho. The bark of this tree is subjected to a complex series of operations: they first immerse the bark in clear water and later in water containing lime where it is left to soak for at least three days; a stone mortar then pounds the moistened bark into a soft paste which is afterwards mixed with water in large wooden basins; finally, the paste is pressed under simple stone rollers and dried in an oven. The principal uses for paper are in the manufacture of decorative fans and of images, commonly burnt in religious ceremonies.

Metallurgical work has relatively little importance in the Tonkin delta, though there is very great variety in the type of activity pursued. Primitive forges manufacture iron implements for use in agriculture, while some villages specialize in copper and jewellery work.

Native Industries in the Province of Thanh Hoa

The native industries of the province of Thanh Hoa do not differ greatly from those in the Tonkin delta. There is the same diversity and the same village specialization. Certain industries, however, have particular features which call for comment. Textiles again rank first, but cotton and silk manufacture is more evenly balanced than in Tonkin. The natives here, moreover, both spin and weave the locally grown cotton fibre, though some thread is imported from China and Japan. Of the other industries, ceramics holds a relatively more important place. It is chiefly concentrated in villages to the north-east of Thanh Hoa, where the presence of a high quality clay and the facility for transporting charcoal to the works by navigable waterway provides excellent conditions for pottery manufacture.

Native Industries in other Areas

Little information is available concerning the handicraft industries in Annam south of Thanh Hoa, and in Cochin-China, Cambodia and Laos. They probably exist all along the coast of Annam in forms similar to those developed further north. The neighbourhood of Nghe Tinh has established a reputation for boat-building and basket-work, while several areas in central Annam manufacture silk goods, rope and high quality ceramic ware. Along several stretches of the coast of Annam, especially in the neighbourhood of Ca Na, salt is obtained in large quantities by the evaporation of brine; the marketing of salt is a state monopoly. Near Phan Thiet the preparation of *nuo cmam*, a condiment obtained by the fermentation of certain fish, has given rise to a small isolated centre of industrial activity.

Native industries are on the whole less developed in the south than in the north of Indo-China. Cochin-China has relatively few areas where they remain important: there is cotton weaving at Go Cong near Saigon, basket-working along the borders of the Plaine des Joncs, net manufacturing from the leaves of the water-palm in the Ca Mau district, and pottery work at Bien Hoa. In Cambodia the native industries are more extensively developed, but village specialization is less common than in the lowlands of the north. Finally, little need be said here regarding the various mountain peoples, other than that in most cases every village, sometimes every family, manufactures all the requirements of daily life.

Handicraft industries in all parts of Indo-China have tended to decline with the gradual westernization of indigenous life and with

Fig. 108. Native potters
The man in the foreground is turning the wheel with his foot as he shapes the pot with his hands. The other man is about to remove a pot from the wheel, while the boy apprentices knead fresh clay.
Source: Ernest Flammarion, *Les Colonies françaises*, p. 188 (Vincennes, 1931).

the competition of imported manufactured articles. The example of India shows that the decline of native manufactures is disastrous for the prosperity of the country concerned; the village craftsmen living in close connexion with the rural population are a factor making for stability and calm. The craftsmen need to receive guidance in the improvement of their equipment and technical methods. Efforts to introduce new methods of production are facilitated by the love of gain and general intelligence of the Annamites, but impeded by their thriftlessness and inability to form organizations. Credit societies, on the lines of those already set up for agriculture, are needed to finance the production and marketing of native manufactured products.

MODERN INDUSTRIES

Modern industry in Indo-China has been developed by the capital and initiative of the European. In the early days of French colonization little progress was made in this direction and the chief development has taken place during the present century or more particularly since the war of 1914–18. Monopolistic control by a few large companies is a feature of both mining and manufacturing in Indo-China. Mining has to-day reached a more advanced stage than the various processing industries, but factories for the working up of agricultural and other products are nevertheless slowly increasing in number throughout the country. In 1937, the total number of workers engaged was estimated at about 140,000.

Mining

Indo-China has a great variety of mineral resources, among which coal, tin, zinc, gold and precious stones are the most important (Fig. 109). These minerals were prospected by the Annamites and Chinese long before the French occupation, but only since then has production been at all considerable. The rugged, often impenetrable nature of the interior, the frequency of 'terres de décomposition' which mask the mineral-bearing rocks, and the unhealthy climate make prospecting difficult. Many faults add to the expense of mining, while the small population and inadequate communications further hinder development. Despite these difficulties mineral production by value has steadily increased during the last twenty-five years, except in the periods 1918–20 and 1930–4. The following table shows the relative importance of the principal mineral products in 1937.

Mineral	Production in thousands of piastres (1937)	% of total
Coal	12,105	63
Tin and tungsten	5,689	29
Gold	512	3
Zinc	384	2
Others	580	3
	19,270	100

Source: P. Guillaumat, 'L'Industrie minérale de l'Indochine en 1937', *Bulletin économique de l'Indochine*, vol. XLI, p. 1250 (Hanoi, 1938).

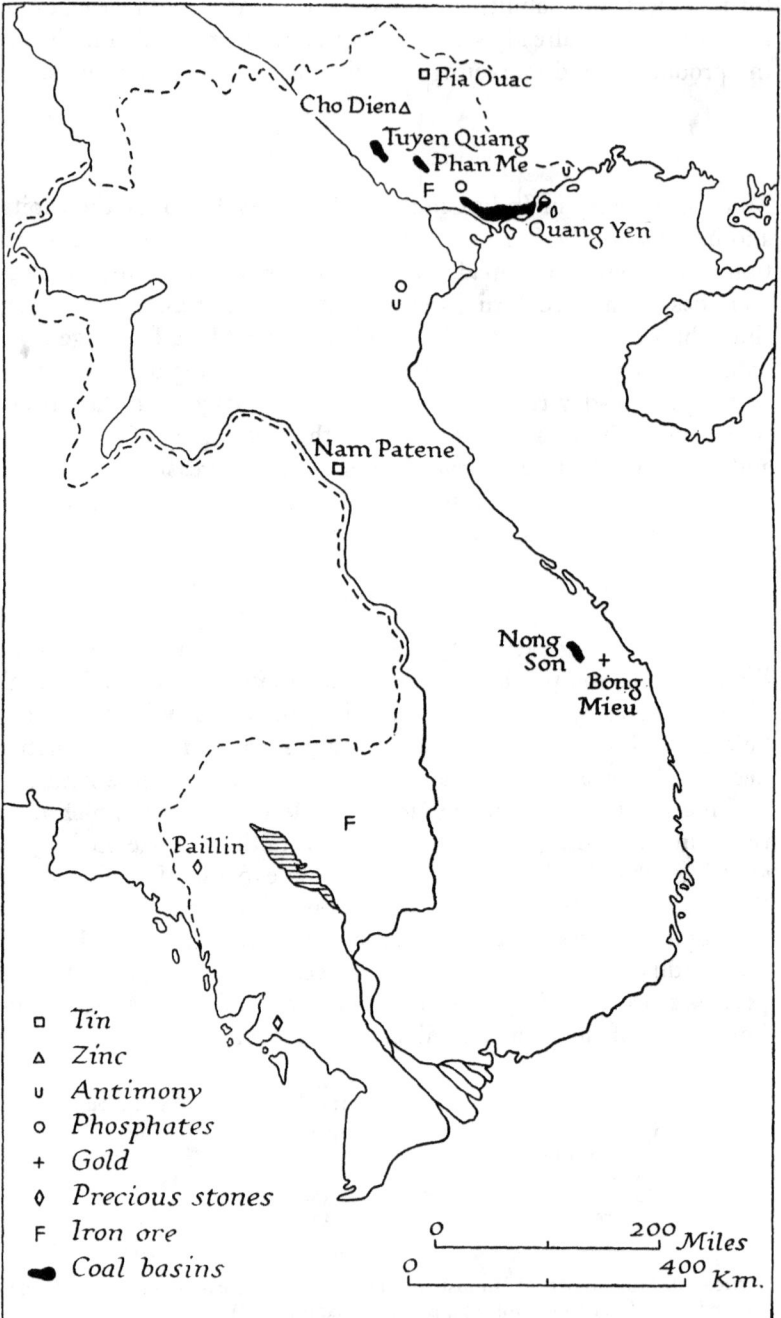

Fig. 109. Distribution of mineral resources
Source: *Atlas de l'Indochine*, plate 12 (Hanoi, 1928).

Coal, tin and tungsten are thus far ahead of the other minerals in value of output. A notable feature of the whole mining industry is its concentration in Tonkin, over 80 % of the total mineral production coming from this state in 1937.

Mineral concessions numbered 355 and covered an area of 252,000 ha. in 1937. The administration of the mining industry is in the hands of the *Service des Mines*, with its centre at Hanoi. This body delegates to local officials its powers of granting concessions. Prospecting cannot be undertaken without a permit from these officials and, if permanent possession is granted, the state takes a small percentage of the profits. Until recently there was no penalization of unworked concessions, but since 1937 a heavy forfeit has been imposed for long-continued inactivity. Foreigners may not own or work the mines; they may, however, invest capital.

In 1937, the mines employed 49,200 native workers and 271 Europeans. Annamites form the great proportion of the labour force.

Coal

The extraction of coal is the most important mining activity in Indo-China. Over 2·3 million tons were mined in 1937, valued at slightly more than 12 million piastres or 63 % of the total mineral production. Apart from a little Tertiary lignite, the coal is of early Mesozoic age and is found principally in the Quang Yen field and in minor fields near Phan Me, Tuyen Quang, and Tourane (Fig. 109).

Quang Yen Field (Tonkin). This coalfield, which was one of the main causes of French intervention in Tonkin, annually produces over 2,250,000 tons of coal, or about 98 % of the output for the whole country. It extends in a mountain arc, convex to the south, from near Phu Lang Thuong and Quang Yen to the Ile de Kebao (Fig. 109). The coal is found in sandy shales of Rhaetic age; a section of barren rocks north of Port Courbet divides the coalfield into two zones, that of Dong Trieu to the west and that of Hon Gay to the east. Although the beds have generally only a slight inclination, severe dips and faulting sometimes hinder exploitation. The coal-bearing seams vary greatly in thickness, from less than 1 m. in the Dong Trieu zone to 60 m. at Ha Tou and as much as 80 m. near Cam Pha. At one time almost all the mines were open-cast, forming vast amphitheatres on the hill-slopes (Fig. 111), but to-day less than 35 % are of this kind, mainly owing to the recent rapid development of deep shafts (100 m. to 200 m.) in the eastern part of the region. In 1937, there were 51,000 m. of underground galleries, of which 35,000 m. had wooden supports,

13,000 m. metal and 3,000 m. concrete. Most of the mining is a hand operation, only about 6 % of the coal in 1937 being cut by mechanical means.

The coal is an anthracite, smokeless, and of high calorific value (7,500 to 8,000 calories), furnishing a good fuel for railways and steamships. It has the disadvantage of often being friable, the friability varying according to the degree of metamorphism to which the coal seams have been subjected. The anthracite of the Dong Trieu zone is harder than that mined near Hon Gay.

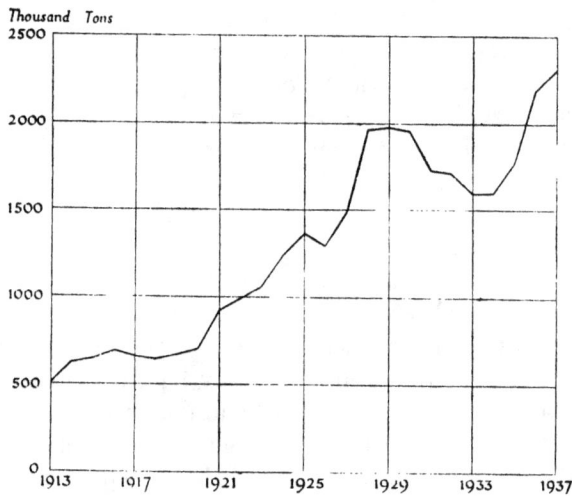

Fig. 110. Coal production, 1913–37

Source: *Annuaire statistique de l'Indochine, 1923–9*, p. 354 (Hanoi, 1931); and *ibid. 1936–7*, p. 254 (Hanoi, 1938).

Coal mining in this region is in the hands of two large companies, the *Société des Charbonnages du Tonkin* and the *Société des Charbonnages du Dong Trieu*. Although founded as early as 1887, the former did not distribute its first dividends until 1900, but since then it has expanded rapidly and has absorbed many of the smaller companies. In 1937, this concern produced 1,638,000 tons or 71 % of the total Indo-Chinese coal output. The *Société des Charbonnages du Dong Trieu* has grown mainly since the war of 1914–18 and to-day handles nearly 500,000 tons a year. The other companies altogether mine annually less than 150,000 tons of coal.

The coalfield has the great advantage of proximity to the coast, to the densely peopled Tonkin delta, and to the shipping route

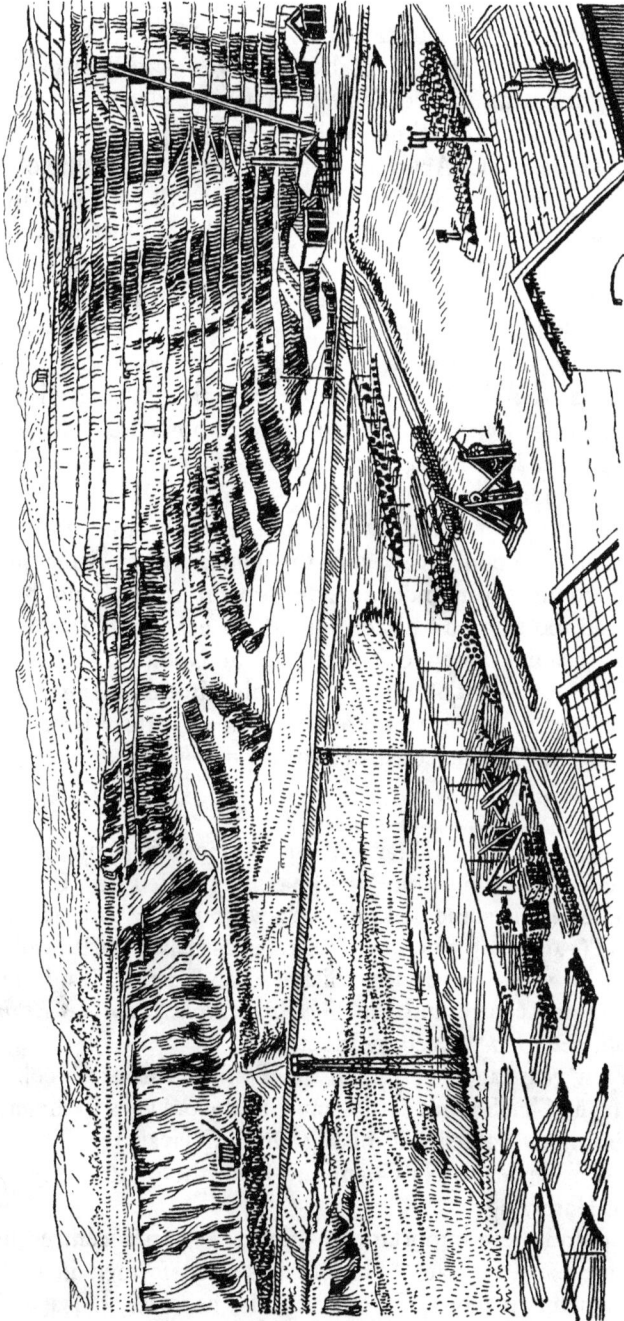

Fig. 111. Open-cast coal mine near Hon Gay

Source: Ernest Flammarion *Les Colonies françaises*, p. 227 (Vincennes, 1931).

from Haiphong to Hong Kong. Railway lines of from 60 cm. to 1 m. gauge run from the mines to the ports of Hon Gay, Cam Pha, and Port Wallut, all of which have coaling wharves as well as buildings with sifting and washing equipment. Thermal electricity stations distribute power over the whole coalfield.

Secondary Coalfields. Apart from the Quang Yen coalfield, only two others, at Phan Me and Tuyen Quang in north-east Tonkin, are in production. Phan Me, near Thai Nguyen, has been exploited since 1910; the coal is mined in pits, reaching almost 100 m. in depth, and transported by rail and by canal to the Tonkin delta. In the Tuyen Quang field, opened in 1915, the coal is a lignite, formed from lacustrine sediments deposited in the synclinal depressions of Mio-pliocene times; the lignite is loaded on to junks and moved down-stream to the large towns of the delta. The combined output of both fields in 1937 was less than 45,000 tons or scarcely 2% of the Indo-Chinese coal production.

A band of coal, at present unexploited, extends from Ninh Binh to Van Yen in the mountains west of the Tonkin delta. After the war of 1914–18 attempts were indeed made to open up this field, but the seams proved too thin and discontinuous for economic exploitation.

The only coalfield outside Tonkin lies at Nong Son in Annam, about 50 km. south-west of Tourane. Mining in this region has now ended temporarily, owing to the exhaustion of surface beds and to the lack of capital for the construction of pits.

Tin

European exploitation of stanniferous ores in Indo-China was first confined to Tonkin; only since 1920 has it extended into Laos. The Tonkin mines all lie some 60 km. south-west of Cao Bang in the Pia Ouac massif (1,930 m.), where cassiterite, in association with wolfram, has formed in veins of varying thickness and depth. Tinh Tuc is the chief mining centre and the *Société d'Exploitation des Etains et Wolfram du Pia Ouac* directs production.

Until a few years ago smelting of the Tonkin cassiterite took place at Cao Bang and Ta Sa, but to-day most of the ore goes to Singapore, where it is highly valued for mixing with Malayan tin. The ore is transported in lorries to Na Cham and from there moved by rail to the port of Haiphong.

A second and more important tin-mining region is centred in the Nam Patene basin of Laos. The ore has been formed in rocks of similar character to those of Tonkin; it is, however, not associated

Plate 47. Mining village in the Quang Yen coalfield

The long, low buildings which form the homes of the workmen are crowded together and linear in arrangement.

Plate 48. Zinc mines near Cho Dien, Tonkin

The open-cast workings are cut in limestone, probably of Devonian age. Zinc blende and calamine are obtained from the mines.

Plate 49. Cement works at Haiphong

This large factory employs 5,000 workers and produces over 200,000 tons of cement annually. In the right of the picture is the Canal de Ha Ly, which flows into the Cua Cam seen in the middle distance.

Plate 50. Alcohol factory at Hai Duong

This is one of five alcohol factories in Indo-China, owned by the *Société française des Distilleries de l'Indochine*. The alcohol is distilled from rice.

with wolfram as in the Pia Ouac region. Before its exploitation by the French, the cassiterite had long been worked by the Laotians who dug shallow pits and smelted the ore in simple charcoal furnaces. Production remained small until after 1920 when the *Société d'Etudes et d'Exploitations minières de l'Indochine* and the *Compagnie fermière de Etains d'Extrême Orient* took over the organization of the mining. To-day the Nam Patene basin produces nearly 60% of the Indo-Chinese tin.

Laotian cassiterite is more difficult to treat than that of Tonkin, owing to the presence of sulphurous and ferruginous compounds.

Fig. 112. Tin production, 1913–37

Source: *Annuaire statistique de l'Indochine, 1923–9*, p. 354 (Hanoi, 1931); and *ibid. 1936–7*, p. 254 (Hanoi, 1938).

Modern plants have been constructed for the washing and sifting processes and for the preparation of concentrates. Little or no smelting is done locally because of the absence of coal, and the concentrates either move south down the Mekong or east by means of the road which connects Thakhek with the coast of Annam. The ore is exported both to France and to Singapore.

The production of tin in Indo-China, calculated as the weight of metal contained in the mineral, rose from only 44 tons in 1913 to 410 tons in 1922 and to 1,600 tons in 1937. Indo-China has benefited from the rise in price which followed the restrictions imposed on world tin output during the last ten years by the Tin Producers' Association. The future of the tin industry seems very promising. The international agreement of 1937 laid down a maximum production of 3,000 tons for Tonkin and Laos, a figure far in excess of the current output (Fig. 112).

Zinc

Zinc is mined in the limestone massif north of Tuyen Quang and Thai Nguyen in Tonkin. Both calamine and zinc blende are found here, though the French have mainly concentrated on the exploitation of the former; the zinc blende was widely used in former times by the Chinese for the manufacture of coinage. The chief mining area lies near Cho Dien and since 1920 production has been in the hands

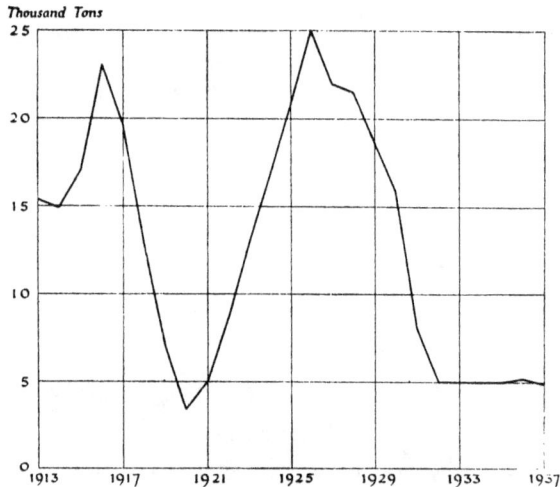

Fig. 113. Zinc production, 1913–37

Source: *Annuaire statistique de l'Indochine, 1923–9*, p. 354 (Hanoi, 1931); and *ibid.*
1936–7, p. 254 (Hanoi, 1938).

of the *Compagnie minière et métallurgique de l'Indochine*. Shortly after taking over this concession, the company erected a smelting plant at Quang Yen which now handles the whole of the present output (5,000 tons in 1937), whereas formerly it all had to be exported. From Cho Dien the mineral is first carried on cable-trucks down the Ban Thi valley, then transported 35 km. by a Decauville railway to the Song Gam, whence it can be moved by water direct to Quang Yen (Plate 48).

After two short boom periods during the years 1914–18 and 1923–9 the production of zinc in Indo-China has rapidly fallen, a decline due not so much to exhaustion of the veins as to the low price of the mineral on the world market (Fig. 113). Prices became low when an increase occurred in the world output following the discovery of a new method of extraction, which permitted the working of mines hitherto believed economically unprofitable. All efforts to raise the price have met with failure. Although the output of zinc continues to decline, a revival may well take place at some future date, since Indo-China is one of the few countries in the Far East possessing workable quantities of this mineral.

Other Minerals

Many other kinds of mineral are found in Indo-China, but none has more than secondary importance. These include wolfram, lead, silver, antimony, iron, graphite, gold and precious stones.

Wolfram, the ore from which tungsten is obtained, occurs in association with the cassiterite of Pia Ouac. Although the war of 1914–18 stimulated production, the Tonkin mines have never seriously rivalled those of China or Burma. The output of wolfram has increased in recent years.

Lead and *silver* veins accompany the zinc blende mines of Tonkin and small quantities were exploited by the Chinese before the French occupation. At the present day, the *Compagnie minière et métallurgique de l'Indochine* produces a little lead and a few dozen kilograms of silver.

Antimony is extracted at Mon Cay in Tonkin and at Co Dinh near Thanh Hoa in north Annam. Chromiferous ores are also found at Co Dinh, though they have not been worked since 1931.

Iron ore mining in Indo-China is chiefly important from the point of view of its potential rather than actual development. Haematite and magnetite occur near Kompong Thom in Cambodia, but the most promising veins seem to be those close to Thai Nguyen and on the Ile de Kebao in Tonkin. Both ferruginous zones contain good quality ore, though their reserves are as yet unknown. In 1937, 12,000 tons of iron ore were mined in the region of Thai Nguyen, and in the same year the *Société des Charbonnages du Tonkin* produced 16,000 tons (45% iron) from the Kebao mines. Other small iron-mining centres are found in north Annam, close to Thanh Hoa, Vinh and Ha Tinh; in these areas, the ore is associated with manganese. Despite the relative wealth of iron ore in Indo-China, the absence of coking coal will handicap the development of a smelting industry within the country.

Gold is obtained from stream beds and alluvium in many parts of the country, particularly in the interior of Tonkin. The great proportion of the output, however, comes from mines. Although several lodes have been worked at Bao Lac and Pac Nam (Tonkin), the only mine at present operating is that of Bong Mieu, near Quang Nam (Annam), where the gold is found in veins of quartz crossing gneiss and mica-schist. The *Société indochinoise d'Exploitations minières et agricoles* controls the mine and has constructed modern processing plants.

Phosphate mining in Indo-China has developed under the stimulus of a rapidly increasing demand for chemical fertilizer in rice cultivation. The mineral is obtained from fissures and cavities in the limestone plateaux of Tonkin and north Annam. In 1937, the production of phosphates amounted to about 20,000 tons.

Graphite occurs in gneiss and other metamorphic rocks near Lao Kay on the left bank of the Fleuve Rouge. Exploitation has now almost entirely ceased, though it was active until a few years ago.

Precious stones, especially sapphires, are extracted from alluvial soils near Paillin and Bokeo in Cambodia. Natives carry out the work of sifting and sorting. In 1937, the production of precious stones was valued at about 100,000 piastres.

The Development of Electric Power

Electric power was first developed in Indo-China as early as the end of last century, though the greatest advances have been made since the war of 1914–18, and more especially during the last ten years. In 1937 the installed capacity of public, as distinct from private enterprises, totalled 61,263 kW., nearly half of which was in Cochin-China, and more than one-third in Tonkin. Of the sixty-four generating centres shown in Fig. 114, only those at Chapa and Ban Me Thuot utilize water power, all the rest making use of thermal energy. The greater part of the thermal electricity is generated with the aid of anthracite mined in Tonkin.

Between 1929 and 1937 the production of electricity increased from 63 million kWh. to 75 million kWh. By far the greater proportion of the power is consumed in the large towns of Hanoi, Haiphong, Saigon, Cho Lon, and Phnom Penh. The table below indicates the importance of the various uses for electric power in Indo-China, expressed as a percentage of the total consumption.

Use	1934 %	1935 %	1936 %	1937 %
Public and domestic lighting	51·8	50·6	49·4	47·4
Industries	40·8	42·9	45·0	47·6
Tramways	7·4	6·5	5·6	5·0
	100·0	100·0	100·0	100·0

Source: 'Production et consommation d'energie électrique en Indochine en 1937' *Bulletin économique de l'Indochine*, vol. XLI, p. 1428 (Hanoi, 1938).

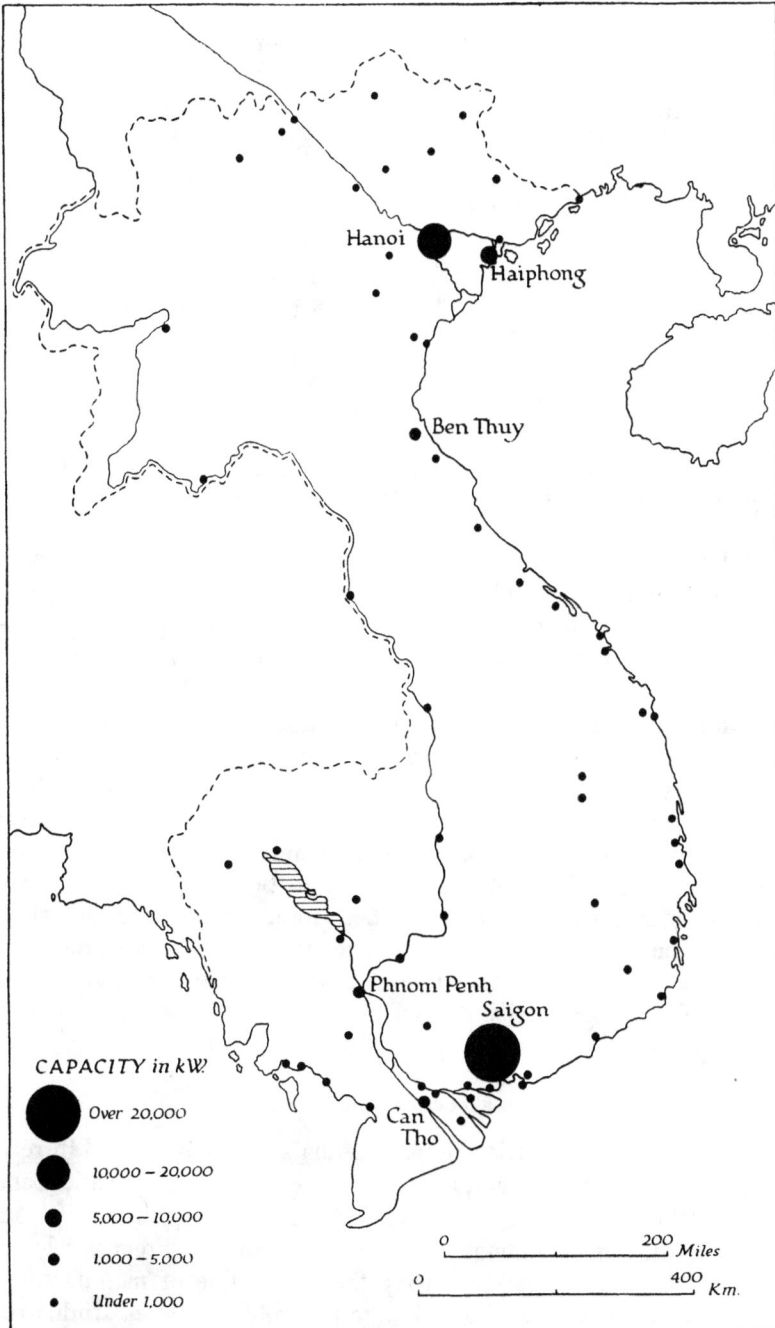

Fig. 114. Electric generating stations, 1937

Source: 'Production et consommation d'energie électrique en Indochine en 1937',
Bulletin économique de l'Indochine, vol. XLI, p. 1433 (Hanoi, 1938).

The proportion of the energy utilized for manufacturing purposes has thus increased, while that for lighting and tramways has declined. The *per capita* consumption of electricity for domestic lighting has increased every year since 1934, although the figure of 1·3 kWh. (1937) is still very small when compared with that of 50 kWh. in France.

A certain number of privately owned industrial concerns, principally in Tonkin, generate electricity for use in their mines and factories.

	No. of generating stations	Installed capacity (kW.)	Production kWh. (000)
Coal mines	9	11,400	23,500
Metal mines	9	4,700	14,500
Miscellaneous	5	16,000	40,000
	23	32,100	78,000

Source: 'Production et consommation d'energie électrique en Indochine en 1937', *Bulletin économique de l'Indochine*, vol. XLI, p. 1432 (Hanoi, 1938).

The installed capacity of plants owned by private firms is thus more than half that developed by public enterprise, while the former exceed the latter in production of electricity. Of the twenty-three generating stations, nineteen are thermo-electric and four hydro-electric plants.

Although electricity in Indo-China has so far been developed only on a relatively small scale, the considerable and partly untapped power resources favour an increased production in the future. The Mekong and Fleuve Rouge, as well as other large streams, offer great possibilities, though they have the disadvantage of irregular regimes. Many more thermo-electric stations could be set up on or near the coalfields and those now established could further increase their production. The extension of electric power will be an important factor in the improvement of rural economic conditions, supplying power for modern irrigation schemes and for all kinds of village industry.

Processing Industries

The processing industries of Indo-China are very backward in relation to mining and agricultural development. Their great variety and general high quality, however, give the country a position of front rank in this field amongst the territories of the French colonial empire. Between 1901 and 1937 the total value of manufactured products increased from 10 million to 180 million piastres. Industrial activity is restricted to the lowlands, owing to the meagre labour supply and difficulties of transport in the mountainous interior. The chief manufacturing centres lie in the Tonkin delta, where the presence of a large population and proximity to the Quang Yen coalfield offer peculiarly favourable conditions.

Processing of Mineral and Forest Products

The *cement* industry at Haiphong, founded in 1899 by the *Société des Ciments Portland Artificiels de l'Indochine*, is the most important manufacturing concern in the country. The factories, which occupy about 400,000 sq. m., stand on a navigable waterway within easy access of the essential raw materials, coal, limestone and clay. Much capital has been expended upon the erection of modern plant; during the past fifteen years productive capacity has greatly increased with the substitution of rotary for vertical ovens. The company has an electric generating station of 12,200 kW. capacity and vast workshops for making wooden and iron barrels as well as paper and jute bags to contain the cement. Altogether 32 Europeans and 5,000 natives are employed in this industry (Plate 49).

Production of cement at the Haiphong factories has steadily increased since the beginning of this century (Fig. 115). Between 1913 and 1929 the output expanded from 50,000 to 184,000 tons and, after a marked decline in the years of economic depression, rose rapidly to the high figure of 235,000 tons in 1937. The cement is considered superior to any other in the Far East and of a quality equal to that of the finest European product. During the last twenty-five years it has been extensively used in Indo-China for the construction of roads, bridges, river barrages, and quays. About 50 % of the cement, however, is exported over a wide area, notably to China, Siam, Malaya, the Netherlands East Indies, the Philippines and Madagascar.

The *Société des Ciments Portland Artificiels de l'Indochine* has a financial liaison with a cement factory at Lang Tho, near Hue.

Brick and *tile* manufacturing is carried on in many small establishments in the deltas of the Fleuve Rouge and Mekong, the soils of which provide inexhaustible raw material for this industry.

Other mineral processing industries include a *glass-bottle* factory at Haiphong and two *porcelain* factories, one at Hanoi and another at Haiphong.

The wealth of timber resources in Indo-China has given rise to several *match* and *paper* factories. There are three match factories in the lowlands of Tonkin and north Annam, one at Hanoi, a second at

Ben Thuy, the port of Vinh, and a third at Ham Rong, near Thanh Hoa. These three concerns in 1937 employed 2,000 workers and produced about 280 million boxes. The paper industry is organized by the *Société des Papeteries de l'Indochine* which owns two mills at Viet Tri and Dap Cau in the Tonkin delta; bamboo is the raw material most commonly used. The firm produced 3,000 tons of paper in 1937.

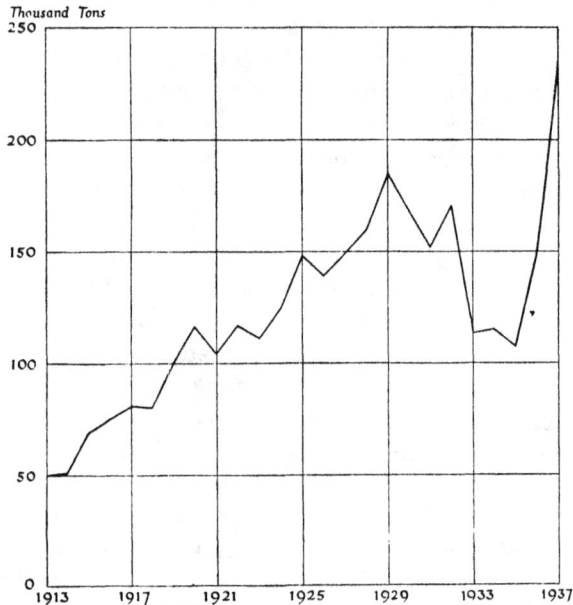

Fig. 115. Cement production, 1913–37

Source: *Annuaire statistique de l'Indochine, 1923–9*, p. 354 (Hanoi, 1931); and *ibid. 1936–7*, p. 255 (Hanoi, 1938).

Processing of Agricultural Products

The *husking and polishing of rice* holds first place in this group of industries. It is principally concentrated at Cho Lon, where there are twenty-seven rice mills situated for the most part on the Arroyo Chinois, the Canal des Poteries and the Canal de Doublement. The mills are ugly buildings, several stories in height and made of corrugated iron; they contain machines usually of American or German origin. During the period of maximum production, from about 15 December to the end of June, the industry gives employment to more than 3,000 workers. In 1937 the value of polished rice exported from the Cho Lon factories totalled 100 million piastres.

A certain proportion of Indo-Chinese rice is used in the *distillation of alcohol*. Shortly after the government imposed restrictions at the beginning of this century on the production and sale of alcohol by the native, the *Société française des Distilleries de l'Indochine* was founded, and, though other small companies have recently been established, it still retains a monopoly. The company owns factories at Hanoi, Nam Dinh and Hai Duong in Tonkin, at Cho Lon in Cochin-China, and at Phnom Penh in Cambodia. Various secondary by-products such as starch and glucose are also prepared in addition to the pure alcohol. In 1937, the distillery industry as a whole used about 90,000 tons of rice and produced 339,000 hectolitres of pure alcohol (Plate 50).

Sugar-refinery on modern lines has only been developed in Indo-China since the war of 1914–18. The largest refinery, belonging to the *Société des Sucreries et Raffineries de l'Indochine*, is that of Hiep Hoa on the Vaico Oriental and close to an important area of cane-sugar cultivation. Others are situated at Tay Ninh, north of Saigon, and near Tuy Hoa, the chief centre of sugar plantations in south Annam. The production of refined sugar rose from 3,000 tons in 1930 to 15,000 tons in 1938.

The recent increase in *tobacco* manufacturing is even more striking than that of sugar refining. Ten years ago the industry scarcely existed, whereas to-day there are four factories, two at Saigon and two at Cho Lon, employing altogether about 1,500 workers. Nearly 3,000 tons of cigarettes were manufactured in 1937.

Textile Industries

Cotton manufacturing in Indo-China received its initial impetus from the desire of the colonial government to make the native weavers independent of foreign thread. Shortly after the French occupation of Tonkin, it became apparent that the native weavers preferred the cheaper cotton thread imported from India and other Far Eastern countries to the kind shipped from the mother country. As these price inequalities could not be satisfactorily smoothed out by the imposition of tariffs, it was decided to establish a spinning industry within the country, at the same time insuring continued protection for the importation of finished cotton goods from France. The first spinning mill was built at Hanoi in 1894, followed by others at Haiphong and Nam Dinh; in 1913, the three mills came under the direction of the *Société cotonnière de l'Indochine*. To-day the Nam Dinh factory has 54,000 spindles and the one at Haiphong,

30,000; the factory at Hanoi is no longer in operation. Almost all the raw cotton is imported from India, China and America, since attempts to grow the crop on a large scale in Indo-China have proved unsuccessful (see p. 282). Each of the works utilizes nearly 15,000 tons of coal annually for heating purposes and for the generation of electricity. Fleets of barges, owned by the company, transport materials to and from the mills.

The factories at Nam Dinh and Haiphong produce about 8,000 tons of cotton thread, the greater part of which goes to the native weavers in the Tonkin delta. Some of the thread, however, is worked up by looms belonging to the company.

The *silk* industry, like that of cotton, has been developed only on a small scale in Indo-China, due partly to the competition of Chinese silk and partly to the desire of silk manufactures in France to maintain Indo-China as a market for their goods. Silk is spun in the home and woven in the factory. There are only two modern silk-weaving factories, the one at Nam Dinh and the other at Phu Phuong in central Annam, on the road between Qui Nhon and Kontum. The native silk proves inadequate both in quantity and quality and both works import the greater proportion of their thread from Shanghai or Canton. The silk fabrics are principally sold to Europeans and natives within the country.

Miscellaneous Industries

In addition to the various processing industries already described, there are a number of minor enterprises which cannot be grouped under any of the above categories. Four factories in the Tonkin delta manufacture explosives, especially petards, which play an important part in the social and religious life of the Annamites and Chinese. There are a number of railway repair shops (see pp. 424, 430) and the port of Haiphong has a small shipbuilding industry.

BIBLIOGRAPHICAL NOTE

(1) A general account of the industries of the country is given in C. Robequain, *L'Evolution économique de l'Indochine française*, pp. 271–340 (Paris, 1939).

(2) There are few modern works which deal in detail with the native industries. P. Gourou, *Les Paysans du Delta tonkinois* (Paris, 1936) and C. Robequain, *Le Thanh Hoa: Etude géographique d'une Province annamite* (Paris, 1929) are recommended. Of the earlier sources the following are most useful: A. Barbotin, 'La Poterie indigène au Tonkin', *Bulletin économique de l'Indochine*, vol. xv, pp. 659–85, 815–41 (Hanoi, 1912). C. Crévost, 'Considérations sommaires sur les Industries indigènes

au Tonkin', *Bulletin économique de l'Indochine*, vol. XII, pp. 298–327 (Hanoi, 1909). V. Demange, 'Les petits métiers du Tonkin', *Bulletin économique de l'Indochine* vol. XXI, pp. 331–62, 591–614 (Hanoi, 1918).

(3) The fullest treatment of the mining industry is found in P. Guillaumat, 'L'Industrie minérale en Indochine en 1937', *Bulletin économique de l'Indochine*, vol. XLI, pp. 1245–1338 (Hanoi, 1938). A short account is given in C. Jacob, *La Géologie et les Mines de France d'Outre-Mer* (Paris, 1932) and in H. Foster Bain, *Ores and Industry in the Far East* (New York, 1933). An account of the history of mining in Indo-China is given in Boris P. Torgasheff, *The Mineral Industry of the Far East* (Shanghai, 1930).

(4) For the development of electric power see, 'Production et consommation d'energie électrique en Indochine en 1937', *Bulletin économique de l'Indochine*, vol. XLI, pp. 1425–40 (Hanoi, 1938).

(5) The cement industry is described in 'L'Industrie du ciment en Indochine', *Bulletin économique de l'Indochine*, vol. XLII, pp. 457–66 (Hanoi, 1939). For an account of the alcohol industry see 'L'Industrie de l'alcool en Indochine', *Bulletin économique de l'Indochine*, vol. XLII, pp. 957–65 (Hanoi, 1939).

Chapter XIV

LABOUR

General Features: Contract Labour: Non-Contract Labour: Forced Labour:
Labour Legislation: Bibliographical Note

GENERAL FEATURES

Labour problems in Indo-China are largely related to inequalities in the distribution of population. In the densely peopled delta regions of Tonkin and north Annam there is a surplus labour supply, whereas in many of the important plantation regions of Cochin-China it is inadequate and for many years a recruiting system has been established to facilitate the transference of workers to regions most in need of additional labour. The movement of Annamites to the southern plantations and to the mining areas of Tonkin and Laos has tended to break up village life and loosen the fetters of patriarchal law. The number of wage-earning workers in agriculture, industry and commerce increased from 55,000 in 1906 to 221,000 in 1931, but the great mass of population still consists of peasants and craftsmen.

The quality of the labour supply is most variable. The Annamites, who form the largest ethnic group, are generally first-class workers, though if they are to perform good work care must be taken to observe as far as possible their customs and traditions (see p. 139). The Cambodians are quiet and hospitable people, indolent and lacking in initiative which lays them open to domination by more enterprising groups such as the Chinese and the Annamites. Although sometimes apathetic and indolent like the Cambodians, the Thai and other mountain peoples, if sympathetically treated, prove willing to work in the service of the European. Finally, there are the Chinese, who specialize in money-lending and act as commercial middlemen between the native farmer and the European.

The great mass of Indo-Chinese workers receives an abnormally low wage. Wages in the north are lower than those paid in the south of the country. In 1933 the average daily wage amounted to 0·29 piastres* for unskilled labourers and 0·38 piastres for skilled workers in Tonkin, and to 0·53 and 1·20 piastres respectively in Cochin-China. Even if the workers earned wages such as these all the year round

* At this time the piastre was stabilized at the rate of 10 French francs.

their total income would be extremely small, but in many cases they are only engaged for a few months out of the twelve. The wage is still further reduced through the extortionate practices of the *cais* or native intermediaries who act as foremen on the European concessions. It has been calculated that the average annual earnings of a worker in 1931 were 44 piastres in Tonkin, 47 in Annam, 55 in Cochin-China and Cambodia, with an average of 49 piastres for the whole country. These figures may be compared with the annual budget of a Frenchman which amounted to 6,200 francs (620 piastres) and with that of a Khammes family, the lowest paid class of agricultural worker in Morocco, which came to about 1,850 francs (185 piastres), or more than four times that of a Tonkinese worker. The trend in the level of wages since 1925 has roughly corresponded with the trend in the cost of living. There was a general rise in the index numbers of both between 1925 and 1930 after which a marked decrease occurred until about 1935, since when there has been a gradual recovery. Although wages and the cost of living have followed a parallel curve in recent years, at no time has the budget of the average worker ever shown a surplus. A substantial increase in the rate of wages to both skilled and unskilled workers is needed to raise the standard of living from its present miserable level.

CONTRACT LABOUR

The recruiting of contract labour from the over-populated lowlands of Tonkin and north Annam for work in the plantations of south Indo-China has been practised since the beginning of the century, though the transference of workers on a large scale did not begin until 1919. Between 1919 and 1934, about 104,000 contract labourers disembarked at Saigon and 52,000 sought repatriation in the same period, or an average annual excess of 3,500 immigrants over emigrants. During the world economic crisis in the early thirties the numbers of workers returning to their native village were greater than those entering Cochin-China, but the rapid development of rubber plantations since 1934 has again brought about an excess of immigrant over emigrant labour.

Elaborate regulations have been introduced to prevent fraudulent recruiting and to improve working conditions. The French official of the district in which recruiting takes place authorizes all recruiting and receives applications through private agencies acting for the plantation owners. The application forms certify the existence of suitable accommodation and of adequate sanitary arrangements. The workers undergo a medical examination before proceeding to the port of embarkation which is usually Haiphong in Tonkin, and Ben Thuy, Tourane, or Qui Nhon in Annam. On arrival at Saigon the workers are again medically examined and then handed over to the employer who undertakes their transport to the plantation. The duration of the contract is three years, with the possibility of renewal for a further term.

The living conditions of contract workers, formerly far from satisfactory, have greatly improved in recent years. Hours of work are now generally limited to ten in the day and minimum wages have been fixed. A deferred pay system enables the workers to return home at the end of their contract with a certain amount of accumulated savings, whereas previously they were often repatriated in a destitute state. The daily food rations have to provide an adult man with not less than 3,200 calories: the minimum quantity of rice is 750 grams, distributed free of charge, and other foods include fish and green vegetables; pure drinking water is obtained from specially constructed tanks and canals. Free housing accommodation is supplied by the employer. Labour supervisors enforce the regulations and they have power to impose ordinary police penalties in the case of breach of contract.

In matters of health and hygiene the workers receive free medical attention and the chief district medical officer carries out periodical visits to all agricultural undertakings. The plantations on the 'terres grises' in eastern Cochin-China are more healthy than those on the 'terres rouges', since in the latter areas malarial carrying mosquitoes are especially common. During the past few years, however, the restriction in the clearing of new land for cultivation has removed the principal cause of fatigue of the workers and consequent reduced resistance to disease. The Pasteur Institute at Nha Trang has also played an important part in the introduction of prophylactic measures against malaria.

The labour force employed on the plantations of southern Indo-China is very unstable, since there is still a powerful bond between the workers and their native soil which leads them to seek repatriation when their contracts expire. This instability means that the workers have insufficient time to become acclimatized to the new conditions, while production necessarily suffers from the fluctuations of successive recruiting. Several plantation owners have endeavoured to induce their workers to settle permanently by recruiting whole families and by building houses and gardens in the Annamite style. Agricultural communities, with their own *Conseil de Notables*, have also been set up (see p. 247). With the further extension of these efforts to provide a congenial environment for the workers, it is believed that an increasing proportion will remain on the plantations and that a spontaneous current of emigration towards the south will develop owing to the incentive of improved living conditions.

Since 1923, contract workers from Tonkin have moved not only to the south of Indo-China but also to the French islands of New Caledonia and New Hebrides in the Pacific. They have been an essential factor in the development of these colonies. The standard contract is for five years.

Non-Contract Labour

This class, which forms the largest proportion of wage-earners in the country, includes about 45,000 agricultural workers and 140,000 workers employed in mining, industrial and commercial undertakings. Non-contract labour is found on some of the plantations in Cochin-China and on all the large concessions in south Annam, as well as in the mining areas of Tonkin and Laos. In general these workers are recruited locally and not from regions far distant. The coal mines near Hon Gay have been able to obtain all the labour they require from the densely populated Tonkin delta; the Annamite generally dislikes to leave his native village, but he does not object to working in these mines since he can normally return home in a single day's journey. About 17,000 workers are at the present day settled in the Hon Gay region. Only in the tin mines of Laos has the question of recruiting presented any real difficulties, for the local population cannot supply all the necessary labour and workers have had to be brought from the coastal lowlands of north Annam. In addition to mine workers, all the employees engaged in factory work come under the category of non-contract labour.

The regulations concerning non-contract labour in Indo-China apply principally to industrial rather than agricultural workers. All industrial wage-earners over 18 years of age are required to possess a work-book which gives details of the successive engagements for which they have contracted. The period of service is usually very much shorter than for contract labour and the interested parties are bound only by the principles of ordinary law rather than by special legislative provisions. Agreements may be either written or verbal. Children under the age of 12 years may not be employed in any undertaking. Hours of work are limited to 8 in the day and minimum rates of wages are fixed, according to the needs of the workers in each industrial region.

Many of the large mining companies have taken steps to improve the health and living conditions of their labour force. The *Société des Charbonnages du Tonkin* and the *Société des Charbonnages du Dong Trieu* have built villages for the workers and each of the principal mining centres has its own infirmary. Monetary compensation is also given to men who suffer from an accident while at work. Similar facilities are provided by the *Société d'Exploitation des Etains et Wolfram du Pia Ouac* and the *Compagnie minière et métallurgique de l'Indochine*.

FORCED LABOUR

The *corvée* system, which required all able-bodied persons to work for a certain number of days in the service of the State, survives to-day only in a few rare cases. In most parts of Indo-China labour dues are exacted in place of the former service contract and since 1937 these dues may always be commuted. Labour requisitioning for transport work and large-scale public enterprises is forbidden, except in isolated areas of the interior. The workers conscripted in these areas, moreover, receive special consideration from the authorities as is shown by the following official document on porterage conditions in Tonkin:

'As a rule, porters are chosen by the chief local European officer or by the local indigenous authority from among able-bodied natives between 18 and 45 years of age. When there is a public medical officer in the district, the workers undergo a medical examination before their departure. In other districts requisitioned workers are employed only if they appear to be in good health and fit for employment as porters. Theoretically, every person liable to be called up for porterage may be employed from 2 to 10 days during each levy, but statistics compiled by the provinces show that the average time worked does not exceed one day a year. The load carried by each man varies from 10 to 15 kg. and they are never called upon to march more than 9 hours in a day. The length of the journey varies from 40 to 100 km. Wages earned by the porters are paid to them either at the end of each day or spell of service, in accordance with rates which vary in the different provinces but are always about 0·40 piastre a day with load and

0·20 piastre without load.' Forced labour also exists among the Mnong and other tribes on the borders of Annam and Laos.

Although various duties and obligations fall to every inhabitant of the native villages, they do not come under the definition of forced labour as laid down by the International Convention (Geneva), 1930. These duties include work for the protection of river embankments and the upkeep of roads.

Labour Legislation

Labour legislation in Indo-China was first introduced between 1896 and 1913, a period of rapid economic development in both agriculture and industry. After several decrees had attempted to regulate working conditions in particular states, the central government in 1910 prepared a labour code for the whole country which brought the recruiting of labour under the control of the local administration and set up a supervising and inspection service. The war of 1914–18, by accelerating economic progress in Indo-China, increased the numbers of the working class population and called for the adoption of more comprehensive labour legislation. In 1918, M. Sarraut, the Governor-General, formulated an Order which displaced the code made eight years previously; its provisions relating to hours of work and living conditions have formed the basis of all recent labour legislation within the country. Labour difficulties became especially acute in the boom period of the early twenties, since the great increase in rubber plantations during these years led to a correspondingly increased demand for workers and much illegal trafficking in coolies took place, while a more clearly defined industrial proletariat sprang into being with the phenomenal growth of mining and manufacturing. This development led to the formulation of new labour laws in 1927 affecting above all the conditions of contract workers, and to the appointment of a General Labour Inspectorate. The world economic depression and opposition from manufacturing interests within the country postponed until 1937 the introduction of improvements in non-contract as distinct from contract labour. The two labour codes of 1927 and 1937 have achieved a considerable measure of success in protecting the worker from unscrupulous exploitation and in improving his standards of life.

With the increasing economic development of Indo-China, the labour legislation at present in force is likely to need constant reform and alteration. Even now it seems inadequate for the working class which is indeed larger in number than would appear from the official statistics. It has been estimated that the figure of 221,000 should be multiplied by four or five, since the statistics only include workers employed in European undertakings at the time of the census, thus taking no account of intermittent wage-paid employment. The continued growth of this wage-earning population will tend further to disintegrate the two traditional pivots of Annamite social life, the village and the family. Future labour legislation must seek to adapt the new social organization to that of the old.

BIBLIOGRAPHICAL NOTE

(1) A detailed study of labour problems is given in J. Goudal, *Labour Conditions in Indo-China*, International Labour Office: Studies and Reports, Series B (Economic Conditions) No. 26 (Geneva, 1938).

(2) There is a short survey of labour conditions in P. Bernard, *Le Problème économique indochinois* (Paris, 1934) and in C. Robequain, *L'Evolution économique de l'Indochine française* (Paris, 1939).

(3) Statistics of wages are given in 'Les salaires des ouvrières en Indochine en 1935', *Bulletin économique de l'Indochine*, vol. xxxvii, pp. 161–76 (Hanoi, 1934).

Chapter XV

COMMERCE

Introduction: Exports: Imports: Direction of Foreign Trade: Commercial Policy:
Bibliographical Note

INTRODUCTION

The foreign trade of Indo-China was on a small scale before
the French occupation and remained relatively unimportant until
the end of last century. Since this time, with the exception of the
periods 1914–18 and 1929–34, it has steadily increased following the

Millions of piastres

Fig. 116. Exports and imports, 1900–38

Source: C. Robequain, L'Evolution économique de l'Indochine française, p. 342
(Paris, 1939).

development of agriculture, industry and means of communication.
Fig. 116 indicates this growth in terms of value. Until 1906, imports
exceeded exports, since vast quantities of materials were required for
the development schemes introduced by Paul Doumer. Although
these imported materials continued to be needed in large quantities
after 1906 they took a relatively less important place and the balance
of trade became favourable. Exports have continued to exceed

imports, apart from the years 1923 and 1931–2, the time of the world economic depression. The variation in trade prosperity during the last twelve years is further demonstrated in the following table giving the index volume of exports and imports, which serves to eliminate the variable factor of price level. The indices of volume, which are based on 1925 (=100), show a rapid fall between 1929 and 1932, followed by an equally swift recovery.

	Exports	Imports		Exports	Imports
1925	100	100	1932	87	91
1926	108	125	1933	101	90
1927	110	139	1934	115	104
1928	117	133	1935	129	108
1929	108	149	1936	142	113
1930	88	130	1937	147	137
1931	77	106			

Source: *Annuaire statistique de l'Indochine, 1936–37*, p. 146 (Hanoi, 1938).

If the total value of Indo-Chinese trade has shown a great increase since the beginning of the present century it still remains small in relation to the population, representing in 1937 only about 18 piastres (180 francs) per capita. This figure is higher than that of India (95 francs) but lower than that of the Netherlands East Indies (310 francs) and the Philippines (470 francs); France in the same year had a per capita value of 1,570 francs.

In addition to the normal foreign commerce there is also a certain amount of transit traffic, valued at 35,400,000 piastres in 1936. Almost all this traffic passes through Haiphong on its way to or from Yunnan.

EXPORTS

Indo-China is essentially an exporter of agricultural commodities and mineral products which have a low value in relation to their weight; the export of finished or semi-finished manufactured goods is insignificant. In 1938, as shown in the table below, rice, rubber, and maize comprised 75·5 % of the total exports by value; of the other exports only coal (4·3 %) and fish (2·5 %) included amounts of more than 2 %.

Rice

Rice is by far the most important product exported from Indo-China. Between 1899 and 1903 the colony annually shipped overseas an average of 809,000 tons of rice; by the period 1919–23 this average

Percentage Values of Principal Goods Exported in 1938

Nature of goods	%	Nature of goods	%
Rice	35·8	Copra	o·6
Rubber	21·8	Live cattle	o·6
Maize	17·9	Hides and skins	o·6
Coal	4·3	Pepper	o·6
Fish	2·5	Lacquer	o·4
Tin (ore)	1·4	Manioc	o·4
Tin (metal)	1·2	Wolfram	o·4
Cement	o·9	Cinnamon	o·3
Eggs	o·9	Zinc (metal)	o·2
Oilseeds	o·8	Coffee	o·1
Kapok	o·8	Sugar	o·1
Tea	o·8	Miscellaneous	5·9
Timber	o·7		
			100·0

Source: *Tableau général du Commerce Extérieur de l'Indochine, 1938,* Table 39 (Hanoi, 1939).

had risen to 1,331,000 tons, and by 1933–7 to about 1,580,000 tons a year. Indo-China provides about 25 % of all the rice which enters the world market, Burma and Siam exporting almost all the remainder. Fig. 117, which covers the period 1928–37, shows the increasing proportion of Indo-Chinese rice sold in France and the fall in the export to China, Japan and the Netherlands East Indies. The bulk of the export comes from Cochin-China, where the area of land under this crop has been rapidly extended and where local consumption is low enough to provide a considerable surplus for export. On the average, only about 300,000–400,000 tons a year are exported from the other states, principally from Cambodia; indeed, the delta regions of Tonkin and north Annam have sometimes to import rice.

The low price of Indo-Chinese rice compared with that of Burma or Siam is due to careless mixing and sorting of the grain. Rice destined for export frequently arrives at the factories with grains of different size, colour and hardness; as a result, the husking, whitening and polishing processes form a heterogeneous product of mediocre quality, containing a high proportion of chaff. A reduction in the number of varieties cultivated and a greater measure of control over sorting would improve the competitive position of Indo-Chinese rice in the world market.

Rice will continue for a long time to play an important part in the economy of Indo-China both as the principal export and as the basic item of native diet. Its export is likely to be limited by an increase in internal consumption, since the population is increasing and even to-day many thousands suffer from under-nourishment. Moreover, although rice still dominates agricultural production, other crops

have become increasingly important, and the proportion of rice to
the total export by value has steadily fallen from about 60 % in
1928 to 45·8 % in 1936 and to 35·8 % in 1938.

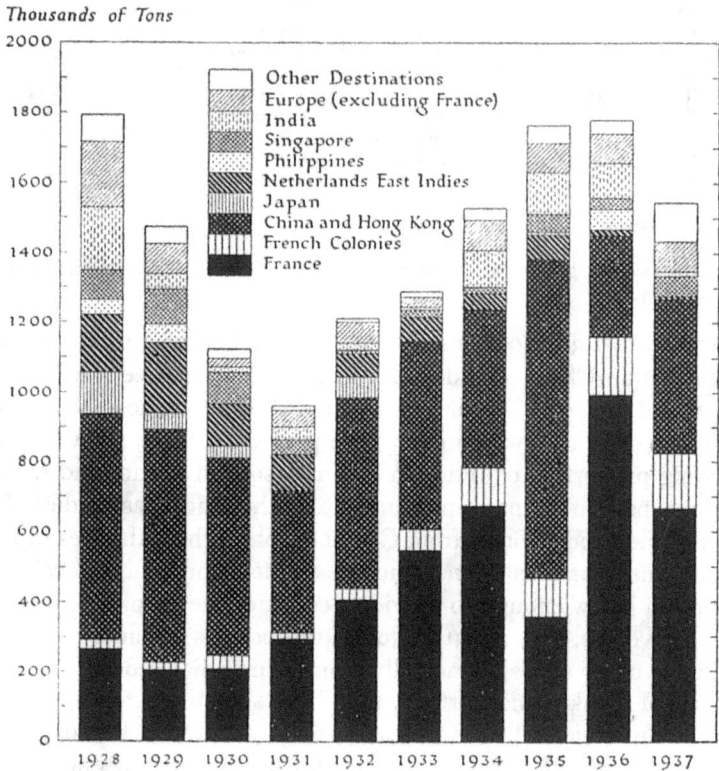

Fig. 117. Rice exports to various countries, 1928–37
Source: *Annuaire statistique de l'Indochine, 1936–7*, p. 259 (Hanoi, 1938).

Other Native Crops

Among the native agricultural crops, maize ranks as the leading
export after rice in terms of value. The quantity shipped overseas
was insignificant at the beginning of this century, but, owing to
French demands, increased to an annual average of 88,000 tons
between 1909 and 1913; after a sharp fall during the years 1914–18
the exports again swiftly increased, reaching 298,000 tons in 1932 and
557,000 tons in 1938. The recent growth in the export of maize has
been more rapid than that of rice (Fig. 118). Almost all of it is sent to
France. Although the intrinsic qualities of Indo-Chinese maize are

not inferior to the best American grades, insufficient care in selecting the grain, as with rice, places it at a disadvantage with that from other countries.

The native crops, apart from rice and maize, form a very low proportion of the total exports. Interesting variations occur in the history of their trade development. The export of pepper rose swiftly from 2,000 tons in 1899 to 6,000 tons ten years later, a total which exceeded the French demand; since 1909, the quantity shipped overseas has been limited to an average of from 3,000 to 4,000 tons a year. Copra exports have increased from 5,600 tons in 1913 to 10,500 tons in 1938, and manioc exports show an even more rapid

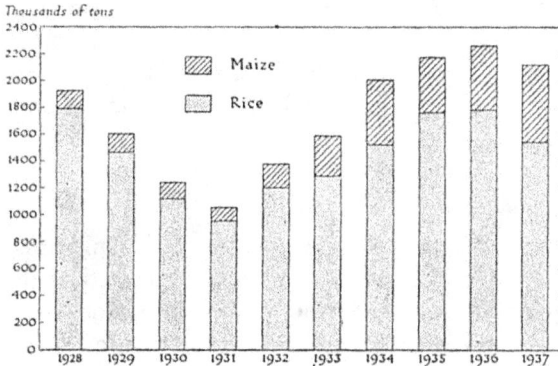

Fig. 118. Export of rice and maize, 1928–37
Source: *Annuaire statistique de l'Indochine, 1936–7*, p. 259 (Hanoi, 1938).

progress (13 tons in 1923, 9,400 tons in 1937). Forest products play a very small part in Indo-Chinese foreign trade: lacquer, wood and various gums are exported in small quantities. The export of industrial crops such as cotton and silk is insignificant.

Livestock and Fish

Livestock hold an unimportant place in native economy, and the export of live animals is small (15,000 cattle, 34,500 swine in 1937). On the other hand, fish and fish products rank fifth among Indo-Chinese exports, though they are valued at only 2·5 % of the total exports. The greater part of the fish is sold in a dried state; shipments overseas, principally to Malaya, averaged 18,700 tons annually from 1899 to 1903, and 27,400 tons in the period 1934–7. Most of the fish exported comes from the Tonle Sap region of Cambodia.

Plantation Crops

The export of plantation rubber from Indo-China has been an important feature of the country's foreign trade only since 1918. Before this date rubber was grown on a very small scale in the country, exports averaging only 160 tons from 1909 to 1913 and 520 tons between 1914 and 1918. The succeeding years saw a rapid extension of the area under rubber and exports correspondingly increased; after the slump which followed the abandonment of the Stevenson Plan in 1928 (see p. 298), rubber exports again rose, reaching 20,000 tons in 1934, 45,100 tons in 1937, 59,000 tons in 1938 and 68,900 tons in 1939. Almost the whole export of rubber comes from plantations in Cochin-China and Cambodia. The principal markets are the United States, France, and Japan.

Apart from rubber, the plantation crops of Indo-China, principally coffee and tea, have achieved only a limited success and shipments overseas are insignificant.

Mineral Products

Mineral exploitation in Indo-China has made rapid progress during the present century, a development clearly reflected by the growth in value of minerals exported from 1·3 % (av. 1899–1903) to 3·5 % (av. 1913–17) and to 7·6 % in 1938 of the total exports. Anthracite occupies first place among the minerals sold abroad, and its export has increased from 200,000 tons at the beginning of the century to 1,581,000 tons in 1938. About half of the anthracite is sent to Japan and nearly one-fifth to France. Almost all the zinc, tin and other minerals produced in the country are shipped either to France or Singapore for refining; the curve of production thus corresponds with that of exportation.

The manufacture and export of cement has shown a remarkable growth in recent years (see p. 333). In 1905, shipments abroad totalled only 400 tons, increasing to about 60,000 tons during the years 1914–18, and to 145,500 tons in 1938. The principal markets are China, Malaya, Siam, the Philippines and the Netherlands East Indies.

IMPORTS

As in other tropical countries where industry is little developed, the imports of Indo-China consist principally of manufactured goods.

The following table gives the percentage value of the principal goods imported in 1938:

Percentage Value of Principal Goods Imported in 1938

Nature of goods	%	Nature of goods	%
Textile fabrics (cotton, silk, rayon, jute)	26·6	Automobiles	3·4
		Paper	2·6
Metals (iron, steel, tin)	9·5	Chemical products	2·5
Machinery	6·4	Tobacco, cigars, cigarettes	2·0
Minerals oils (gasoline, kerosine)	5·3	Wines and spirits	2·0
		Rubber goods	1·7
Dairy products	4·1	Textile thread (cotton, silk)	1·1
Raw cotton	4·0	Miscellaneous	28·8
			100·0

Source: *Tableau général du Commerce Extérieur de l'Indochine, 1938*, Table 38 (Hanoi, 1939).

Textile fabrics thus form the chief class of manufactured articles imported. Long before the French occupation, a certain traffic in European cloths had been carried on with Indo-China through Chinese commercial intermediaries. The development of this trade during the present century may be attributed to the decline of local industries and to the increasing demands of the native population. Cotton occupies first place among the fabrics imported (25 million piastres) followed by silk (10 million piastres) and jute (7 million piastres). The import of cotton thread, which was about 4,000 tons a year between 1925 and 1930, has dropped to less than 2,000 tons since 1931, owing to the activity of Tonkinese mills spinning raw cotton obtained from abroad.

Articles of machinery and metal goods rank next to textiles in the list of Indo-Chinese imports. They comprise in particular the equipment needed for industry and for public works such as iron and steel bars, zinc and copper plates, locomotives, and electrical apparatus. Machinery and machine tools, which represented hardly 2 % of the total value of imports between 1913 and 1920, surpassed 7 % from 1927 to 1931 but dropped to 6·4 % in 1938. The import of automobiles, rubber articles, and petroleum has similarly increased with the extension of the road system since 1918.

A small proportion of the goods entering Indo-China consists of food, drink, and luxury articles in demand by the Europeans. These include dairy products, such as butter and cheese, various fruits, confectionery, chocolates, cigarettes, and French wines. Ready-made clothing is also imported.

Direction of Foreign Trade

Over 80 % of the foreign trade of Indo-China is associated on the one hand with countries in the Far East (28 % in 1938), and on the other with Metropolitan France and the French colonies (53 % in 1938). The country's geographical situation, historical traditions and community of interests, has long favoured a close relationship with China, Japan, and Singapore, while the trade relationship between Indo-China and France has developed from the imperial economic tie

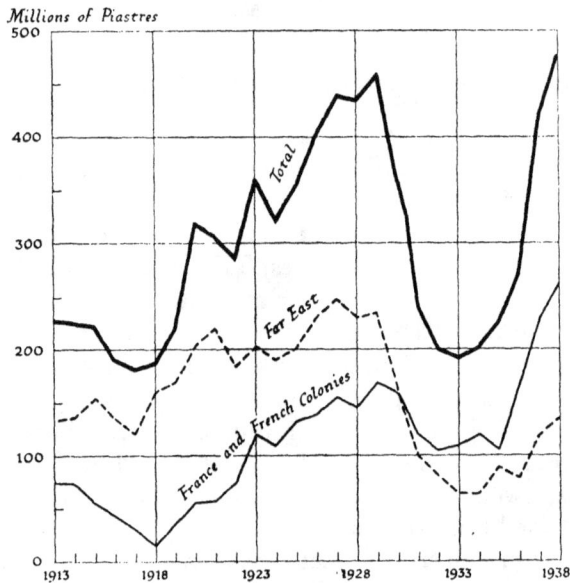

Fig. 119. Direction of foreign trade, 1913–38

Source: C. Robequain, *L'Evolution économique de l'Indochine*, p. 362 (Paris, 1939).

(see p. 357). Until 1930 the Far Eastern countries occupied a more important place than France in Indo-Chinese foreign trade, but since then the position has been reversed owing to the depreciation of Chinese currency and the strengthening of the customs union with France (Fig. 119).

Trade with China and Hong Kong

Indo-China carries on a larger trade with China than with any other country of the Far East. Hong Kong acts as the collecting and distributing centre for most of this traffic; it also handles part of the trade of Indo-China with Japan, the Philippines, the Netherlands East Indies and the United States. Whether by weight or value, rice holds premier place among the exports entering China; the grain is usually in a husked and polished state, though a little unhusked paddy goes to the rice mills of Hong Kong. The quantities of rice exported to this region vary considerably from year to year (Fig. 117) because of the irregular demand, which is conditioned by the success or failure of the Chinese rice harvest and by the fluctuations in purchasing power. The fall in silver prices, which reduced Chinese purchasing power by 40 %, certainly aggravated trade difficulties after 1930 by preventing the sale of rice at a remunerative price. As a result, its export to China and Hong Kong declined from 566,000 tons in 1930 to 292,000 tons in 1936, though it increased to 444,000 tons in the following year.

Indo-China receives from China and Hong Kong in exchange a great variety of goods, none of which has a position as dominating as rice in the export traffic. In point of value, textiles are the principal class of merchandise imported, either as woven silk and cotton fabrics or as silk and cotton thread. There are also various food products such as vermicelli, legumes, and fruits destined for native and European consumption.

Trade with Japan

Industrial raw materials, such as coal and rubber, are the principal articles furnished by Indo-China to Japan. This country is the best client for Tonkinese anthracite, absorbing 28 % of the exports in 1920-4 and 50 % in 1933-7. Shipments of rubber to Japan totalled 5,000 tons in 1937. Other exports include marine salt and fine-grained sand for use in glass manufacture. Food products take a relatively unimportant place among the exports. Between 1913 and 1928 the yearly shipments of rice averaged 109,000 tons, but between 1929 and 1932 the average fell to 36,000 tons annually and to only about 2,000 tons from 1933 to 1937 (Fig. 117). During the past few years, the export of rice from Indo-China to Japan by value has been rather less than one-twentieth that of either coal or rubber.

The imports from Japan chiefly comprise manufactured goods, especially natural silk, woodwork of all kinds, and porcelain. Japan is also the main foreign source for coal tar and pitch, necessary for the manufacture of bitumen and asphalt.

GH (Indo-China)   23

Trade with the Netherlands East Indies

The trade of Indo-China with the Dutch possessions in the East Indies is on a much smaller scale than that with either China or Japan. Rice is the only commodity of any importance in the export trade. From 1913 to 1931 the quantities of rice shipped to this region fluctuated between 30,000 tons (1923) and 377,000 (1931) with an annual average of 136,000 tons, an amount greater than that absorbed by Japan in the same period. Since the world economic crisis, however, the Dutch government has attempted to increase internal rice production, at the same time restricting its import. As a result, rice shipments from Indo-China to the archipelago have fallen to an average annual figure of 40,000 tons between 1933 and 1937 (Fig. 117).

From the Netherlands East Indies, Indo-China receives the greater part of its petroleum and petroleum products. These mineral products form practically the whole import trade, whether in terms of weight or value.

Trade with Singapore

Singapore is a great entrepôt for goods in transit from Indo-China to the Netherlands East Indies, Malaya, India, western Europe and America. It has thus a similar function in Indo-Chinese trade with these countries as Hong Kong has in the trade with China. Some rice and rubber are marketed in Singapore for re-export, but since 1928 there has been a tendency for the Saigon merchants to despatch their goods directly to consumers in Europe and elsewhere. Singapore, however, still remains the principal market for the dried fish of Indo-China. Other exports include livestock, especially swine, cement, and Tonkinese and Laotian tin, almost all of which is refined in Malaya.

Indo-China imports from Singapore large quantities of jute sacks (25,500 in 1935) in transit from India, while second in importance are dried areca nuts, used for the preparation of a form of chewing material (see p. 301). Finally, there are a number of food products imported such as butter, table fruits, vegetables and coffee, for consumption by the European population.

Trade with India

The trade of Indo-China with India is quite meagre even taking into account the transit traffic through Singapore. Burmese rice largely fulfils the Indian demand for this food product, but even so, exports of rice from Saigon often exceed 100,000 tons (Fig. 117). The only other important export commodity, teak, is chiefly a product of the Siamese forests floated down the Mekong to Saigon.

India supplies the French colony with almost all the jute sacks it requires, and as rice production expands the demand for these sacks will correspondingly increase. A high proportion of the goods moves first to Singapore and then is re-exported to Indo-China. Other articles imported from India include cotton goods and coconut fibre.

Trade with the Philippines

Indo-Chinese trade with the Philippines has declined since the early years of the present century. Between 1909 and 1913 the archipelago received 8·4 % of the total exports of Indo-China, but the proportion dropped to 2·7 % in 1924–8 and to under 1 % in 1933–7. This falling off in trade may be attributed to the rapid economic development of the Philippines during the past twenty or thirty years, and also to the high tariffs imposed on foreign goods. Rice, livestock, anthracite, and cement form the greater part of the export trade; tobacco and hemp are received in exchange.

Trade with France

The relative importance of Metropolitan France in Indo-Chinese trade has more than doubled during the past twenty-five years. Although the balance of trade has remained favourable to France, there is a marked tendency towards progressive adjustment or equalization. This growth of a more balanced commercial relationship as between Indo-China and France, which is naturally to be expected in view of the complementary needs of the two countries, has been stimulated by the introduction of imperial preference tariffs and protective duties.

Indo-China sends a great variety of agricultural products and industrial raw materials to France and receives in exchange manufactured articles of many kinds. Rice holds first place by value in the list of exports, and the quantity shipped in the period 1933–7 averaged 647,000 tons a year or about 40 % of the total export of this commodity (Fig. 117). In the period 1909–13 the mother country took only 26 % of the rice exported from Indo-China. The increasing importance of Indo-Chinese rice in the French market, particularly during the last decade, is the result partly of discriminatory trade regulations, and partly of a vast propaganda campaign within France.

The imposition of a quota system, made necessary by the collapse of world prices in 1931, caused larger quantities of rice than formerly to be sent to France, while at the same time Indo-China profited from the barriers imposed on the entrance of foreign cereals into France. For a number of years, moreover, every effort has been made to increase rice consumption and, despite opposition from certain agricultural associations interested in other cereals, the campaign has achieved a considerable measure of success. A large proportion of the rice is used as fodder for livestock.

Maize ranks second in the export trade with France and, as in the case of rice, the quantities shipped overseas have shown a remarkable development in recent years. The total quantity of Indo-Chinese maize entering the Metropolitan market has increased from 128,000 tons in 1929 to over 500,000 tons in 1938; to-day, Indo-China furnishes France with about 80 % of her imports of maize, whereas only a decade ago the proportion was rather less than 10 %. Like rice, the maize is chiefly used for fodder purposes.

The export of rubber comes next in order of value, but unlike rice and maize, France takes a relatively small proportion of the total shipments. Between 1935 and 1937 she received from Indo-China an average of 11,000 tons of rubber a year out of an average annual export of about 38,000 tons.

Other agricultural products exported to France include pepper, tea, coffee, sugar and oilseeds. The export of pepper has long been controlled in order to maintain a satisfactory market price; about 3,000 tons is permitted to enter the country each year.

Mineral products, especially anthracite, form an important part of the export trade with France. Despite the large demand for anthracite in the mother country, the quantities shipped from Indo-China to France remained small until a few years ago, when the depreciation of currency and the introduction of protective measures tended to undermine the colony's trade with countries in the Far East. The quantity of Tonkinese anthracite entering France has increased from 35,000 tons in 1930 to 250,000 tons in 1937. The greater part of the consignment is brought to Europe by the Cape route in order to avoid the heavy canal dues at Suez. In addition to anthracite, France also receives from Indo-China zinc, tin and tungsten in an unrefined state.

Manufactured articles predominate among the French imports into Indo-China, textile and metallurgical products alone representing about two-thirds by value of the total imports from this country.

France supplies the colony with many kinds of cotton fabrics valued at 18 million piastres in 1937; despite foreign competition and the growth of a local textile industry, an average annual import of 7,000 tons has been maintained since the early years of the present century. Rayon (7 million piastres) and garments made from rayon and silk (600,000 piastres) are also imported. Other industrial goods obtained from France include machinery and machine tools, locomotives, automobiles, and chemical fertilizers. Food products, including butter, cheese, wines and spirits, form about one-fifth of the total imports.

Trade with French Colonies

Indo-China sells more to the French colonies than it buys from them. Rice is the principal export, and in 1936 French West Africa and French Equatorial Africa absorbed more than 100,000 tons of this commodity. Tea is exported in small quantities to Algeria and Tunis. Cotton goods, cigarettes and wines form the bulk of the imports.

Trade with other Countries

Indo-China has commercial relations with a large number of countries outside the Far East and the French Empire, though the total volume of this trade is not great. The United States is the principal customer for Indo-Chinese rubber, taking 16,000 tons in 1937 or 5,000 tons more than the export to France in the same year. Small quantities of tin and pepper also form part of the export trade with this country. In exchange the United States sends petroleum products, machinery and machine tools.

Apart from France itself, Great Britain has a larger trade with Indo-China than any other country in Europe. Rice, raw hides and a little rubber form the bulk of the exports; tin plate and a great variety of manufactured goods are the principal imports. Germany, Belgium and the Netherlands also have a small trade with Indo-China.

COMMERCIAL POLICY

The commercial relationship of Indo-China with the outside world has been directed in large part by her obligations as a member of the French Empire. Colonial territories under French rule are regarded as sources of raw materials and markets for Metropolitan goods, and this principle has long governed the trade policy of France with her

Far Eastern possession. Since the natural orientation of Indo-Chinese trade is towards the neighbouring countries of China, Japan and Malaya rather than to Europe, artificial barriers, in the form of tariffs and quotas, have had to be introduced to restrict foreign competition. By the tariff law of 1892 the French home tariff was applied to goods entering Indo-China from foreign countries, and Metropolitan goods were granted free entry into the colony, whilst Indo-Chinese exports to France only gained a reduction in the payment of duty. Although Indo-China enjoyed a high degree of commercial prosperity after the framing of the law, this development occurred independently of the tariff system since foreign imports increased in the same proportion as those from the mother country. The tariff assimilation or unified customs regime proved deterimental to Indo-Chinese interests, for customs duties adapted to the needs of France were clearly unsuited to the different economic conditions prevailing in Indo-China. It had the effect of raising the cost of living, the price of many articles being over 10 % higher than that of similar goods previously imported from nearby markets. The free entry of French goods into Indo-China, moreover, led to higher taxation and to the setting up of monopolies to increase revenue. For many years after 1892 colonial opinion demanded a modification in trade policy, but, with few exceptions, it remained unaltered until the promulgation of the new tariff law in 1928.

The tariff law of 13 April 1928 established a system of reciprocal free trade within the French Empire, whereby products from Indo-China had the same freedom upon entering France as Metropolitan goods enjoyed in the colonial market. The French home tariff continued to be applied to imports from foreign lands, though a long schedule of exceptions was drawn up covering goods which did not compete with the products of the mother country. By its liberal attitude in granting exemptions, France showed its recognition in principle of a separate tariff for Indo-China, but as only the less important products were so affected this change of policy did not bring about any marked reorientation of trade to countries in the Far East. The world economic depression of 1931, indeed, made Indo-China even more isolated from her natural markets, for, with the fall in the price of primary commodities, France had to increase her imports to stave off bankruptcy within the colony. A complicated system of bounties and quotas was also introduced at this time which greatly extended the part played by France in the overseas trade of Indo-China (Fig. 119). Since the depression, the autarchic conception of Indo-China as economically subsidiary to France has become strengthened. The law of 1928 remains the basis of the tariff regulations, and while it must be admitted that the customs union has fostered local industries, the interests of the colony as a whole continue to be sacrificed to those of the mother country.

BIBLIOGRAPHICAL NOTE

(1) A valuable study of the foreign trade of Indo-China is given in C. Robequain, *L'Evolution économique de l'Indochine française*, pp. 341–87 (Paris, 1939).

(2) On special aspects the following articles will be found useful: A. Le Fol, 'Les relations commerciales de l'Indochine avec les pays d'Extrême Orient', *Revue du Pacifique*, vol. XIV, pp. 141–58 (Paris, 1935). F. Leurence, 'Etude statistique sur le développement économique de l'Indochine de 1899 à 1923', *Bulletin économique de l'Indochine*, vol. XXVIII, pp. 127–61 (Hanoi, 1925). A. Nuad, 'L'exportation des grands produits agricoles de l'Indochine', *Annales de Géographie*, vol. XXXVIII, pp. 50–60 (Paris, 1930).

(3) Commercial statistics appear in the *Tableau général du Commerce Extérieur de l'Indochine* and in the *Annuaire statistique de l'Indochine*, both of which are published annually at Hanoi.

Chapter XVI

FINANCE

Currency and the Rate of Exchange: General Budget: State Budgets: Provincial Budgets: Taxation: Banking and Credit: Capital Investment: Bibliographical Note

The financial system of Indo-China is based on the decree issued by Governor-General Paul Doumer in 1898, which created a General Budget for the country and separate budgets for each of the states, together with subsidiary provincial and municipal budgets. The influence of the home government in the financial affairs of the country has been great, for although General Budgets, as instituted by Doumer, were drafted in Hanoi, they received close scrutiny in Paris before instructions were given to make them effective by decree. Further, all capital expenditure required specific authority from Paris, and its cost was covered not by colonial appropriations, but by means of special appropriations from the Metropolitan finances, general contributions to which were periodically made by Indo-China towards imperial developments and defence.

CURRENCY AND THE RATE OF EXCHANGE

The monetary unit of Indo-China is the piastre of 100 cents, which has been stabilized at the rate of 10 French francs since 1930. The value of the franc in relation to sterling stood at about 170 to the £ in 1939. The silver coinage includes the piastre and smaller coins of 50, 20, and 10 cents. Paper notes for 1, 5, 20 and 100 piastres, payable at par, are issued by the Bank of Indo-China.

GENERAL BUDGET

The General Budget is drawn up by the Governor-General on the advice of the *Conseil de Gouvernement* and the *Grand Conseil des Intérêts économiques et financiers*. It is put into force by means of a government decree.

Revenue

The revenue of the General Budget is derived from customs duties, from indirect taxation in the form of government monopolies and taxes on various transactions, and from the returns of the postal, telegraph and telephone services. The following table gives the budgetary receipts in 1938:

					Thousands of piastres	
1.	Customs duties:					
	(i)	Imports	... ...		12,350	
	(ii)	Exports	... ...		509	
	(iii)	Special duty on export of rice	...		5,590	
	(iv)	Special duty on export of rubber	...		2,162	
	(v)	Other duties ...	... ...		7,711	28,322
2.	Indirect taxation:					
	(i)	Monopolies:				
		(a) Opium ...	... ...		12,388	
		(b) Alcohol	... ...		7,450	
		(c) Tobacco	... ...		6,222	
		(d) Salt	... ...		5,858	31,918
	(ii)	Taxes on transactions:				
		(a) Registration of property, contracts, etc.	... ...		4,887	
		(b) Stamp duties ...	... ...		1,514	
		(c) Duties on various transactions			4,780	11,181
	(iii)	Other indirect contributions	...			1,091
3.	Post, telegraphs and telephones	... ...				5,748
4.	Miscellaneous sources	... ...				4,195
		Total revenue	... ...			82,455

Source: *Annuaire statistique de la France, 1938*, p. 291 (Paris, 1938).

Expenditure

The General Budget covers expenditure in the federal government services, in the legal profession, and in secondary and higher education. It also finances public works, makes grants to the local budgets in need of support, and contributes to the annual vote of the Ministry of Colonies in the French budget. The annual vote of the Ministry of Colonies provides for the costs of military defence and certain of the costs of civil administration in the French colonial possessions. In addition to making a contribution to this vote, the General Budget of Indo-China supports the *Agence générale des Colonies* and the *Ecole coloniale* in Paris as well as French consulates and French social workers in China, Japan, Siam, Malaya, the Netherlands East Indies and the Philippines.

In 1938 the total budgeted expenditure amounted to 89 million piastres, as against 35 million piastres in 1914 and 17 millions in

1899. The expenditure of the ordinary budget in 1938 was as follows:

		Thousands of piastres
Debt service	... ...	15,516
Contribution to the French budget	...	4,127
Administrative services	... ...	38,860
Public works and public utilities ...	...	9,841
Loans to local budgets	... ...	12,537
		80,881

Source: *Annuaire de Documentation coloniale comparée, 1938*, p. 91 (Brussels, 1939).

The extraordinary budget accounted for the rest of the expenditure. This budget, which covers among other things the expenditure on national defence, derives its revenue from borrowing and not from taxation.

STATE BUDGETS

Each of the five states of Indo-China has its own budget. In Cochin-China, the state budget is voted by the *Conseil colonial* and approved by the Governor; in the protectorates it is prepared by the Chief Resident after consultation with his advisory councils.

The budget of each state in the year 1936 is given below:

	Revenue millions of piastres	Expenditure millions of piastres
Annam	8·2	8·3
Cambodia	7·4	6·9
Cochin-China	11·3	10·9
Laos	3·1	2·9
Tonkin	11·4	11·4

Source: *Annuaire statistique de l'Indochine, 1936–7*, pp. 224–33 (Hanoi, 1938).

The revenue of the local budgets is derived from direct taxation, comprising a capitation tax and a land tax, and from duties on the registration of property and contracts, together with loans from the General Budget.

The expenses of the royal courts in the protectorates of Annam, Cambodia and Laos are included in the budgetary expenditure. The native rulers, however, prepare their own civil lists and also budget for certain other expenses, such as those involved in the upkeep of the royal tombs in Annam.

PROVINCIAL BUDGETS

The provinces within each state prepare an annual budget which varies greatly in size (50,000–500,000 piastres) according to the wealth and population of the region. Their revenue is obtained from certain direct taxes together with the *centièmes additionnels*, i.e. surtaxes of so many hundredths of these statutory imposts; from the payments in commutation of labour services and from various other sources; they also receive loans from the General and state budgets. The provincial budgets provide money for provincial and cantonal administration, including public health, education, police and transport services.

The village, which is a self-governing administrative unit in a large part of Indo-China, has its own budget drawn up by a *Conseil de Notables*; the towns of Hanoi, Saigon, Phnom Penh, Tourane, Hue and Vientiane also have their own budgets, prepared by municipal councils.

Taxation

An important feature of the financial system of Indo-China is the restriction of indirect taxation to the General Budget and of direct taxation to the local budgets. This rigid separation of the two forms of taxation cannot be regarded as a satisfactory arrangement, since it tends to cause a lack of equilibrium in the financial structure of the country.

Indirect taxation, which forms over 70 % of the revenue of the General Budget, is derived from customs duties and from charges on the sale and consumption of alcohol, opium, salt, mineral oils, and tobacco, all of which are state monopolies. The monopolies, particularly those on salt and alcohol, weigh heavily upon the poorer classes, that is, the great bulk of the population, and have encouraged the growth of a considerable contraband traffic.

Direct taxation, in the form of a capitation and a land tax, provides the main source of revenue of the local budgets. The capitation tax is imposed not only upon all French *sujets*, i.e. upon all the natives, but also upon the Chinese and other foreign Asiatics resident in the country. A large number of natives probably evade this tax, for the lack of a complete registration of births and deaths in many areas makes its imposition difficult. Instead of the capitation tax, the Europeans are taxed on the basis of their income, with a surtax on amounts of over 700 piastres a month (say £400 a year). In the tax on land a distinction is drawn between the 'terrains de rizière' and the 'terrains de cultures diverses'. The rice fields are divided into several classes according to their yield, and the size of the tax varies with this assessment. Land under other crops is also divided into a number of classes for the purpose of taxation: the first class, with the highest tax, usually includes land under tobacco and sugar cane; the second, that devoted to coffee, cotton, rubber, and coconuts; the third, that with aniseed, sesame and peanuts; and the fourth, that under maize, potatoes, beans and fruits. The agricultural concessions granted to Europeans and natives in the mountain regions of Tonkin are free from taxation during the first five years and afterwards are subject to a special tax based on their crop yield. The absence of a cadastral survey for the whole country is a serious handicap to the equitable assessment of the land tax.

BANKING AND CREDIT

The leading bank is the Bank of Indo-China, a joint-stock concern founded by private capital in 1875. It holds a monopoly in the issuing of bank notes. According to the terms of the Convention of 27 February 1921, the bank returns a proportion of its capital to the government if the fiduciary circulation exceeds three times the metallic reserves. Its monopoly of note issue is exercised not only in Indo-China, but also in New Caledonia, French Oceania, Djibouti and the French stations in India. It has further a quasi-monopoly of French banking in China. The capital of the bank amounts to about 15 million piastres. The Bank of Indo-China has its main office at Hanoi with branches at Haiphong, Saigon and Phnom Penh. It has also an office in Paris.

Other private banks in Indo-China include the Franco-Chinese Bank, serving commerce and industry, the *Société financière française et coloniale*, the Hong Kong and Shanghai Banking Corporation, the Chartered Bank of India, Australia and China, and the Yokohama Specie Bank Limited.

A number of credit organizations exist in all the states, except Laos, for the granting of agricultural loans and loans for the purchase of land at low interest rates (see p. 293). Cochin-China has the best developed credit system and in 1936 the standing loans made by the *Sociétés indigènes de Crédit agricole mutuel* and by the *Caisse française de Crédit agricole mutuel* amounted to 9,817,000 piastres, or more than three times the loans made in all the rest of the country. In the other states the *Caisses indigènes de Crédit agricole mutuel* had distributed on standing loan a total of 4,700,000 piastres in 1936 through twenty-six credit banks, twelve of which were in Tonkin, seven in Annam, and seven in Cambodia. The agricultural credit organizations throughout the country are centralized under a body entitled the *Office indochinois de Crédit agricole mutuel*. Credit for the purchase of land is provided by a number of *Sociétés foncières*; their standing loans amount to 9 million piastres. The credit organizations are for the most part supported by funds from the Bank of Indo-China. The rate of interest is usually fixed at about 6 %, of which the bank claims 4 %, the local government 1 % and the credit society 1 %.

The development of these credit organizations has to a certain extent weakened the influence of the native usurers who formerly had a stranglehold over a large part of the agricultural population. As the Agricultural Banks, however, only lend on first-class security, over half the farmers still have recourse to the *Chettys* whose outstanding loans, with inferior security and higher rates of interest, amount to some 9 million piastres.

CAPITAL INVESTMENT

The amount of public and private capital invested in Indo-China up to the end of 1934 has been estimated as equivalent to rather more than 100 million pounds sterling. This is only about one-third of that in the Netherlands East Indies, but roughly the same as that in Malaya, over three times as great as that in the Philippines, and twice as great as that in any single British colonial possession in Africa, except Rhodesia. Private capital has formed nearly 70 % of the investments in Indo-China, whereas in French Equatorial Africa, French West Africa and Madagascar government listed capital has predominated. The distribution of this private capital in the various undertakings, and the extent to which the state has encouraged investments by means of bounties and preferential tariffs, has varied with the economic evolution of the country itself and with world economic conditions.

Before 1918 capital was largely invested in mining and industry, while investments in agriculture took a secondary place. The coal, tin and zinc mines of Tonkin attracted investors in the early years after the French occupation, and a number of companies were formed for their exploitation. Private capital was also sunk in processing industries, such as the mechanical polishing of rice, the distillation of alcohol and the manufacture of matches. Although the tariff law of 1892, by discriminating in favour of Metropolitan rather than colonial industrialists (see p. 358), tended to discourage capital investment, the building of railways with public and private capital provided a stimulus to investment in mining and industry in the decade before the outbreak of war in 1914. Capital was also invested in rubber, tea, and coffee production at this period, but investments in agriculture still remained proportionately inferior to those in other economic undertakings.

In the field of capital investment, the period since 1918 has been marked by a greater attention than formerly to the agricultural resources of the country and by an increased government support of the private investor. The rapid growth in rubber production was the outstanding development of the middle twenties, thanks largely to the 'boom' in the world price of rubber which followed the intro- duction of the Stevenson Plan (see p. 298). Between 1925 and 1929 some 705 million francs were invested in rubber plantations, repre- senting over half of the agricultural investments for the period. The 'boom' in rubber was paralleled by an increased interest not only in other plantation crops, such as tea and coffee, but also in mining, industry and transport. The following table shows the new capital invested in various types of enterprise during the five-yearly period, 1925–9:

New Capital Issues (millions of francs)

	1925	1926	1927	1928	1929
Agriculture	77	276	401	213	136
Mining	19	94	80	184	150
Industries	62	113	62	88	111
Transport	5	5	31	37	47
Commerce	33	60	17	55	42
Total	196	548	591	577	486

Source: C. Robequain, *L'Evolution économique de l'Indochine française*, p. 183 (Paris, 1939).

The above figures relate only to the investment of external capital. If the sums borrowed from the local banks for investment purposes were included the total new capital invested in this period would amount to nearly 3,000 million francs.

Between 1930 and 1935 Indo-China felt the effects of the world economic depression. Many companies suffered large reductions in their capital funds and many more became bankrupt. The threat of bankruptcy caused several companies to pool their resources: thus in 1933, the *Société des Plantations indochinoises de Thé* was formed, with a capital of 26 million francs by the union of three companies; two years later, four rubber companies combined to form the *Société indochinoise de Plantations d'Hévéas*. Only a relatively

Millions of Francs

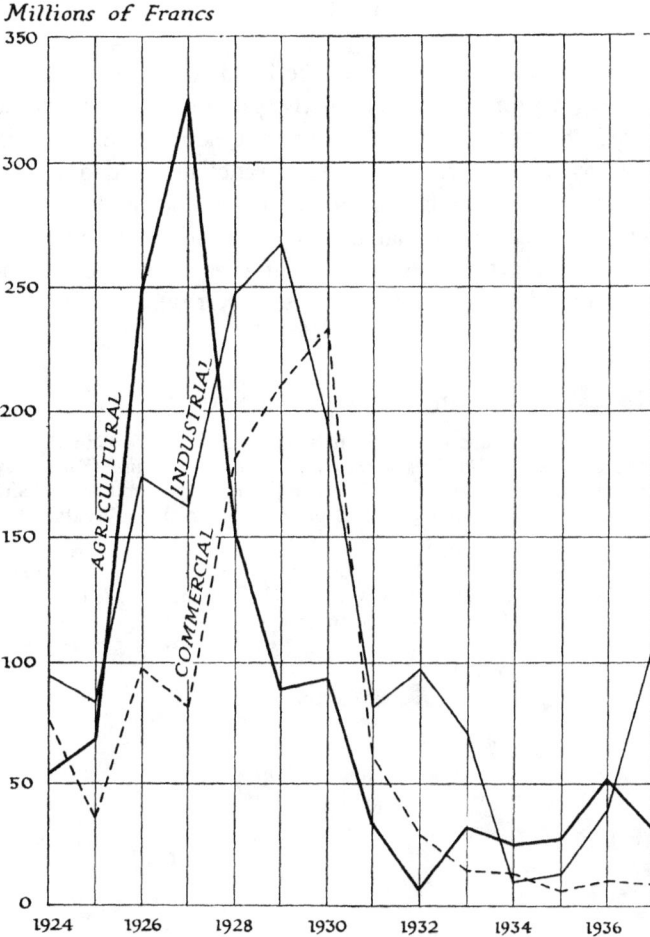

Fig. 120. Capital issues, 1924-37

Source: *Statistique générale de l'Indochine*, 'Les émissions de valeurs mobilières en Indochine en 1937', *Bulletin économique de l'Indochine*, vol. XLI, p. 451 (Hanoi, 1938).

small number of the companies existing in 1930, however, managed to tide over the depression by means of combinations. It has been estimated that the loss of capital in these years amounted to 750 million francs. The loss would have been even more serious but for the action of the French government in causing a budgetary deflation and in introducing a system of bounties and quotas. Moreover, since the tariff law of 1928, Indo-China had enjoyed reciprocal free trade within the French empire and this served the country well in the period of crisis.

The concentration of capital in the hands of powerful companies and active government support of the private investor has enabled the country to recover from the economic depression. New investments of capital rose from 49 million francs in 1934 to 154 million francs in 1937. Although this total of 154 million francs represents a threefold increase over that in 1934, it is still very much smaller than that in the pre-depression year of 1927 when the new investments amounted to 591 million francs (Fig. 120).

BIBLIOGRAPHICAL NOTE

(1)   The fullest account of the financial structure of Indo-China is given in C. Robequain, *L'Evolution économique de l'Indochine française* (Paris, 1939), in A. Touzet, *Le Régime monétaire indochinois* (Paris, 1939), and in Sylvain Levi, *Indochine*, vol. II, *Documents Officiels*, Exposition Coloniale Internationale, Paris, 1931 (Paris, 1931).

(2)   Other works which will be found useful are: A. Duchêne, *Histoire des Finances coloniales de la France* (Paris, 1939); H. Simoni, *Le Rôle du Capital dans le Mise en Valeur de l'Indochine* (Paris, 1929).

Chapter XVII

PORTS

INTRODUCTION

Indo-China has only three ports with a total annual foreign trade of over 1,000,000 tons, though there are several of considerable local importance and many deep-water bays afford good anchorages. Saigon, Haiphong and Hon Gay, which handle 97 % by value of the country's foreign trade, serve as outlets for important agricultural, industrial, and mining regions. The other ports are small by comparison and, apart from simply constructed wharves or jetties, have few modern facilities for handling cargo. These secondary ports show variety in their physical setting, some such as Ben Thuy and Phan Rang lying on a river estuary, others like Tourane, Hone Cohe and Ba Ngoi lying on sheltered inlets. The backwardness of the ports in Annam and Cambodia may be attributed to the mountainous character and meagre economic development of their hinterlands.

Climatic conditions have an important influence upon the use of Indo-Chinese ports as in the case of those of other countries.* The north-east or winter monsoon often creates dangerous seas which complicate the entrance of ships into the ports, particularly those along the coast of Annam. In summer, the south-west monsoon, though generally less violent, occasionally interferes with the use of ports in the Gulf of Siam. The most serious hindrances to shipping in the South China Sea are caused by typhoons, which occur most commonly in the period from July to November (see p. 59). The coastline of Cochin-China and Cambodia rarely experiences this kind of storm. Fog is a common feature in Tonkin during the *crachin* period from February to April; in these months, the coastal regions of Tonkin usually experience fog or mist on about 10–15 days per month. Poor visibility is also common in winter off the coast of Annam; in Cochin-China, fog or mist is rarely encountered.

* For a full account of the climatic conditions in Indo-China see chapter III *passim.*

Port Activities (1938)

Ports	Foreign		Coastal		Total	
	Tonnage shipping	Tonnage merchandise	Tonnage shipping	Tonnage merchandise	Tonnage shipping	Tonnage merchandise
TONKIN:						
Mon Cay	143	—	55,114	16,022	55,257	16,022
Mui Ngoc	4,878	2,886	76,479	4,284	81,357	7,170
Ha Coi	—	—	3,412	2,214	3,412	2,214
Port Wallut	40,808	32,091	80,584	3,154	121,392	35,245
Hon Gay	1,718,992	1,320,107	358,662	158,860	2,120,227	1,478,967
Cat Ba	8,371	75	15,287	2,455	23,658	2,525
Quang Yen	—	—	330,438	23,792	330,438	23,792
Haiphong	2,627,092	1,167,946	2,402,599	528,165	5,158,826	1,696,111
Hanoi	—	—	568,190	123,494	568,190	123,494
Diem Diem	—	—	20,514	14,971	20,514	14,971
Nam Dinh	—	—	12,526	8,655	12,526	8,655
Phat Diem	—	—	45,289	30,357	45,289	30,357
ANNAM:						
Lach Truong	—	—	640	311	640	311
Thanh Hoa	—	—	20,900	15,486	20,900	15,486
Ngoc Giap	—	—	4,166	1,950	4,166	1,950
Do Len	—	—	1,253	995	1,253	995
Du Do	—	—	8,319	3,239	8,319	3,239
Phu Nghia	—	—	9,443	7,862	9,443	7,862
Thanh Son	—	—	2,145	1,472	2,145	1,472
Van Phan	—	—	2,514	2,803	2,514	2,803
Thuong Xa	—	—	4,572	1,392	4,572	1,392
Ben Thuy (Vinh)	18,772	12,041	134,452	86,223	153,224	98,264
Ho Do (Ha Tinh)	—	—	1,612	902	1,612	902
Tien Tri	—	—	612	228	612	228
Quang Khe	—	—	12,168	2,185	12,168	2,185
Dong Hoi	—	—	3,224	2,097	3,224	2,097
Lai An	—	—	20,996	9,492	20,996	9,492
Tourane	91,396	50,231	2,075,684	60,850	2,246,500	111,081
Faifoo	—	—	43,896	22,733	43,896	22,733
Hiep Hoa	—	—	3,666	1,342	3,666	1,342
Son Tra	—	—	4,110	3,752	4,110	3,752
Sa Huynh	—	—	10,407	5,302	10,407	5,302
Tam Quan	—	—	7,434	3,070	7,434	3,070
Co Luy	62	24	23,894	13,158	23,956	13,182
Degi	—	—	20,989	9,592	20,989	9,592
Qui Nhon	39	5,777	719,716	15,613	729,123	21,390
Cu Mong	—	—	3,725	1,101	3,725	1,101
Xuan Day	—	—	4,747	1,886	4,747	1,886
Le Uyen	—	—	12,375	4,105	12,375	4,105
Dong Trach	—	—	13,224	6,682	13,224	6,682
Hone Cohe	23,808	10,040	47,117	21,800	70,425	31,840
Nha Trang	991	453	70,280	5,308	71,271	5,761
Ba Ngoi (Cam Ranh)	171,154	73,053	88,413	20,056	264,922	93,109
Phan Rang	47,596	36,840	14,682	8,369	62,278	45,209
Phan Ri	—	—	12,673	7,903	12,673	7,903
Duong	—	—	15,682	10,531	15,682	10,531
Mui Ne	—	—	45,086	27,286	45,086	27,286
Phan Thiet	—	—	42,489	20,173	42,489	20,173
Lagi	—	—	8,366	4,850	8,366	4,850
COCHIN-CHINA:						
Cu My	—	—	56,354	31,233	56,354	31,233
Saigon	6,157,343	1,935,231	1,549,119	352,621	8,290,688	2,287,852
My Tho	—	—	3,362	1,784	3,362	1,784
Ca Mau	58	33	28,203	2,370	28,261	2,403
Rach Gia	2,728	1,629	9,828	5,075	12,556	6,704
Hon Chong	—	—	1,301	246	1,301	246
Ha Tien	16,702	1,078	15,747	4,513	41,652	5,591
Duong Dong	—	4	46,049	6,036	46,325	6,040
CAMBODIA:						
Kep	365	246	31,632	1,629	38,520	1,875
Kampot	—	—	9,427	3,466	9,427	3,466
Ream	17,890	373	37,823	1,038	73,483	1,411
Snam Crabeu	1,362	437	7,646	50	15,961	487
Ilôt Cône	39	2,203	2,486	796	22,742	2,999
Checko	117	1,866	5,280	670	41,263	2,536
Phnom Penh	—	—	226,930	95,600	226,930	95,600
Grand total	10,950,206	4,654,664	9,515,952	1,836,189	21,413,043	6,490,853

Source: *Tableau général du Commerce Extérieur de l'Indochine, 1938*, Table 79 (Hanoi, 1939).

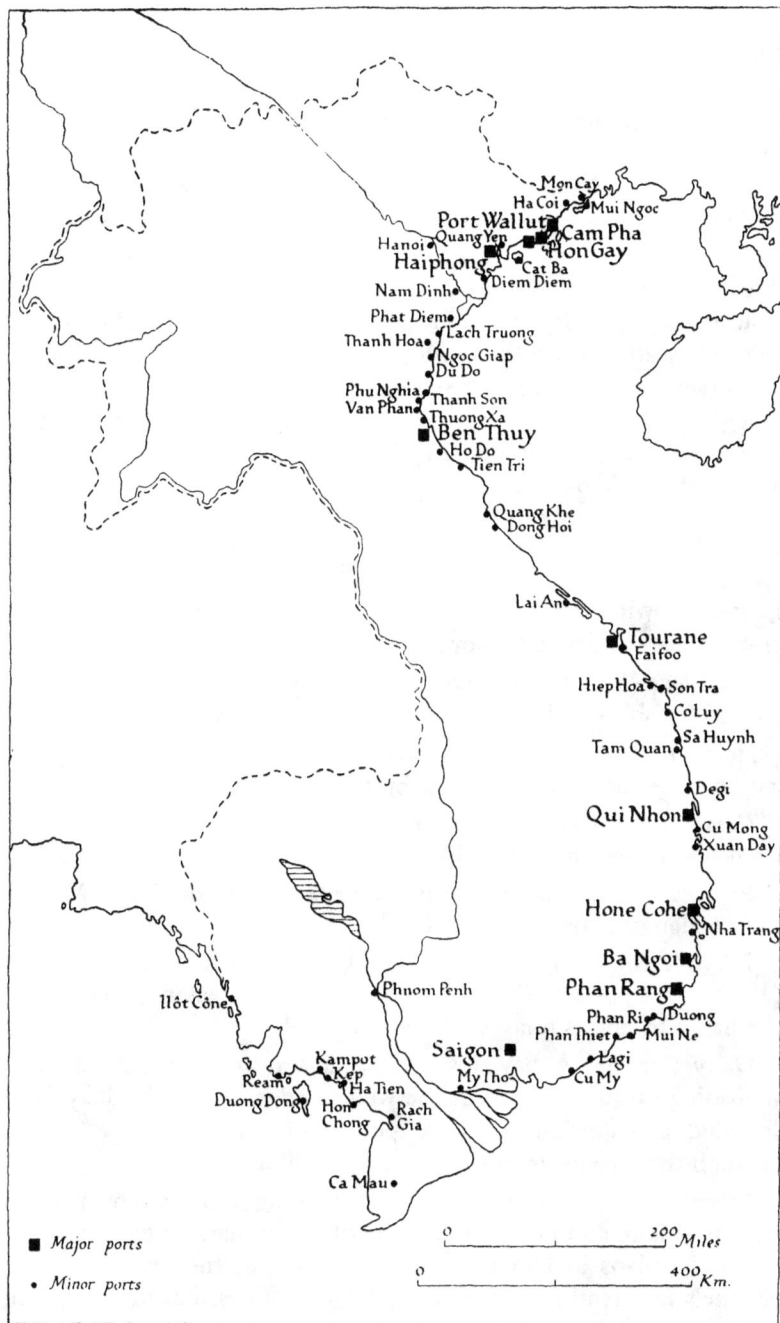

Fig. 121. The ports of Indo-China

Source: *Tableau général du Commerce Extérieur de l'Indochine, 1938*, Table 79 (Hanoi, 1939).

The tides along the northern coasts of Indo-China are predominantly diurnal in character, that is, there is one high and one low water every 24 hr. Along the southern and western shores, however, there are semi-diurnal tides, with two high and two low waters daily. As the tidal range never exceeds 3·9 m. (13 ft.) the need for wet docks does not arise.

The official statistics relating to port traffic in Indo-China name sixty-four separate ports engaging in the foreign and coastal trade (Fig. 121). The traffic of each of these ports in 1938 is given in the table on p. 370. In the following account the ports selected for detailed treatment are those which handle more than 5,000 tons in the foreign trade. There are ten such ports. The port of Cam Pha, though not mentioned in the official statistics, is also regarded as a major port. The remaining fifty-four minor ports are briefly dealt with in the table on pp. 403–8.

Note on terms used

In the following port descriptions a number of terms are employed in the senses as defined below:

Roadstead (Rade).   A stretch of water where there is good holding ground for ships and some protection from heavy seas.

Harbour.   An area of sheltered water or protected anchorage within either natural features or breakwaters.

Breakwater.   A solid structure protecting a harbour or roadstead from heavy seas, and alongside which vessels usually cannot lie.

Pier.   An open-work structure projecting from the shore. Vessels can lie alongside or across the head.

Jetty (Jetée).   (1) A solid structure similar in function to a pier. (2) In some ports the jetty serves as a small breakwater enclosing the harbour, and is quayed on the inner side.

Quay (Quai).   A paved space or area devoted to loading and unloading cargo, bounded at the water's edge by a wall (quay face) founded at sufficient depth to permit of vessels lying alongside (though they may sometimes ground at low water).

Wharf.   An open-work structure of piling and framing parallel with the shore and often connected with it by narrow gangways.

On the plans and in the text the depths of the sea and of the channels are depths at the lowest recorded tides, i.e. the datum of the French marine charts.

SAIGON

Lat. 10° 46′ N, long. 106° 42′ E. Population: 111,000 (1936).
Admiralty Chart 1016. Figs. 122, 123. Plates 51–54, 88–90.

Saigon, the first port in the country, is situated on the right bank of the Rivière de Saigon, about 80 km. from the sea. It handles the bulk of the traffic to and from southern Indo-China and is the main distribution centre for cargoes carried on the Mekong.

Approach and Access

The seaward approach to the estuary of the Rivière de Saigon is well marked by the small island known as Poulo Condore and by the three prominent hills forming Cap Saint Jacques. Ships can anchor in 11–12·8 m. (6–7 fm.) either off this headland or off Pte Can Gio. From the Baie de Ganh Rai inland to Saigon the river follows a circuitous course, but no part is less than 300 m. (984 ft.) in width. The depth of the navigable channel averages from 9 to 12 m. (29–39 ft.), except at the Banc de Corail and along the broad stretch of water (Nha Be) just below the confluence with the Dong Nai, where the least depth falls to 6 m. (19 ft.).

The river at Saigon has a semi-diurnal tidal regime, two high and two low tides occurring every 24 hr. The mean rise varies from 3·2 to 3·8 m. (10½–12½ ft.). Tidal streams run at about 2 knots, though they may sometimes attain 3 or 4 knots; the duration of slack water is seldom more than half an hour. During summer, when the river has its maximum discharge, the tidal currents are less strong than at other seasons of the year. Owing to the powerful scouring action of the tides, the deep-water channel to Saigon is maintained for the most part without dredging operations.

Saigon is accessible to ships of 180 m. (590 ft.) length and 9·3 m. (30 ft.) draught. These turn round by grounding their stems on the river bank and allowing the tidal streams to swing them. The largest ships which visit the port regularly are the *Messageries Maritimes* liners, *Athos II, D'Artagnan* and *Chenonceaux*, with a length of about 153 m. (500 ft.), a draught of 8·4 m. (28 ft.), and a gross tonnage of 15,000. Altogether a total of about forty vessels can be accommodated either at mooring buoys in the river or alongside the quays. The larger ships frequently have to wait for a favourable tide before moving up or down-stream.

Detailed Description

The port of Saigon has a river frontage of about 5 km., extending from the mouth of the Canal de la Dérivation to a little beyond the Arroyo de l'Avalanche (Fig. 123). The quays and wharves which

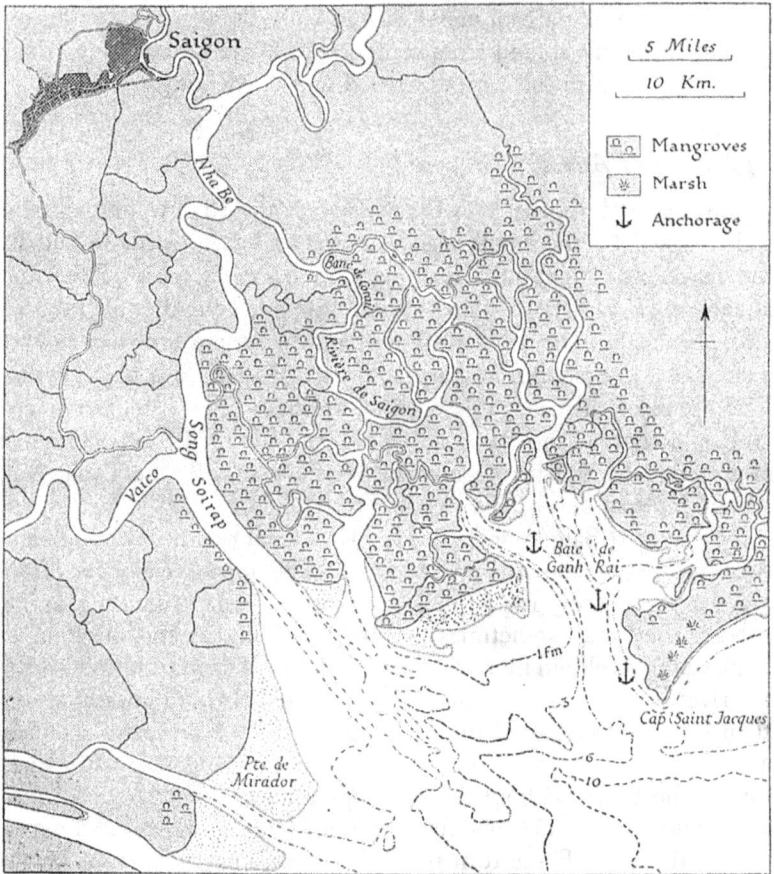

Fig. 122. Approaches to Saigon

Source: (1) Carte de l'Indochine, 1 : 100,000, sheet 239 (1928); (2) Admiralty chart 1016 (1934, corrected to 1939).

handle the commercial traffic lie in the southern section, divided into two parts by the broad Arroyo Chinois, while northwards above the town are the naval dockyards and arsenal. The commercial port consists of three quays, differing in size and function. In the Khanh

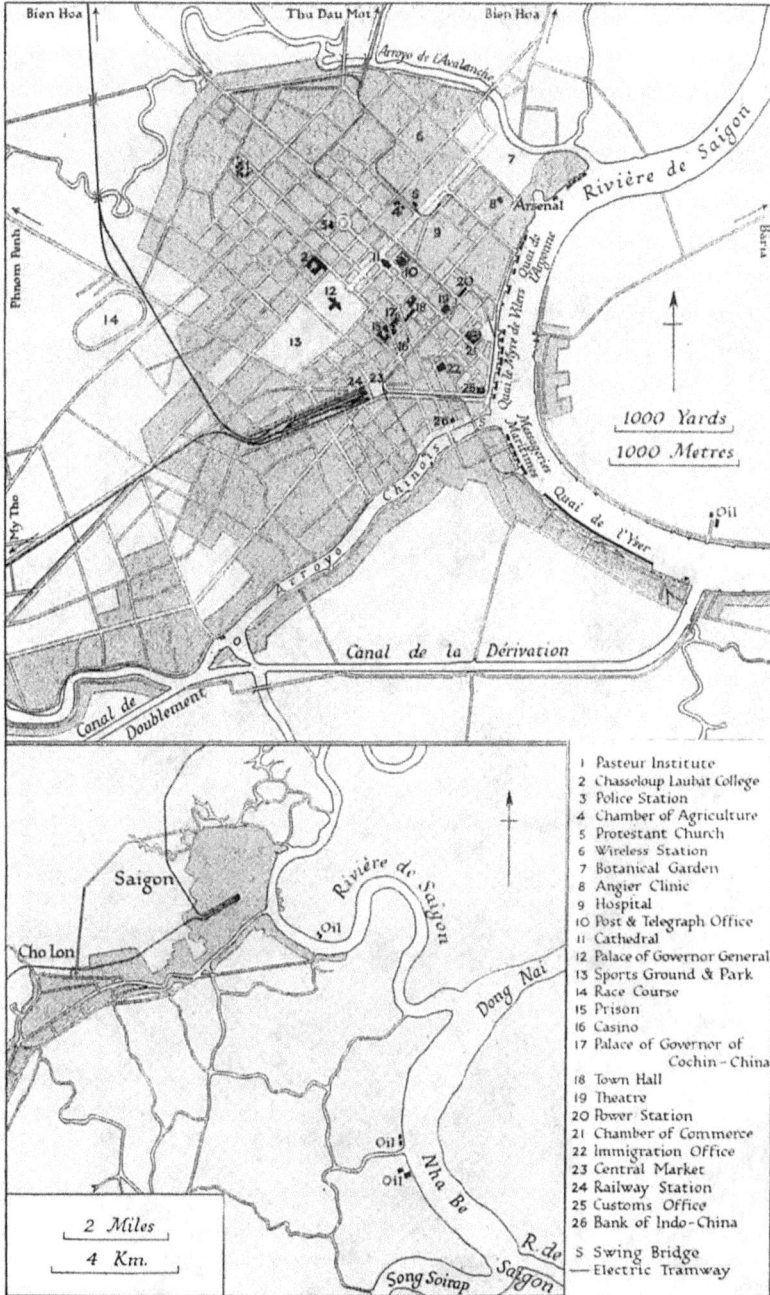

Fig. 123. Saigon

Source: (1) Plan de Saigon-Cho Lon, 1:10,000 (1923 and 1936); (2) Admiralty.

Plate 51. Arroyo Chinois, Saigon

This waterway connects the port of Saigon with Cho Lon. Many hundreds of junks and sampans ply on this stream at all times of the year. Near the confluence with the Rivière de Saigon (seen in the left of the picture) is a swing bridge. Part of the Quai le Myre le Vilers can be seen in the right foreground.

Hoi district is the Quai de l'Yser, 1,029 m. (3,375 ft.) long and from 24·4 to 30·5 m. (80–100 ft.) wide, with depths alongside varying between 5·2 m. (17 ft.) and 7·9 m. (26 ft.). It provides nine berths and handles a large part of the overseas traffic. Passenger ships normally berth alongside this quay. Farther upstream is the Quai des Messageries Maritimes, which has three berths reserved exclusively for vessels belonging to this company; it has a river frontage of 380 m. (1,385 ft.) and a width of 30·5 m. (100 ft.) with depths alongside of from 7·5 to 8·5 m. (24–28 ft.). Finally, above the Arroyo Chinois is the Quai le Myre de Vilers, used by small river tenders and passenger boats. A number of piers, with berthing lengths varying between 38 m. (125 ft.) and 61 m. (200 ft.), extend from this quay. There are also several piers on the left bank of the river opposite the Quai Le Myre de Vilers.

The river frontage of the naval port comprises the Quai de l'Argonne which has a double **T** pier with a berthing length of 76 m. (249 ft.). There are also several small piers.

Over twenty fixed buoys and dolphins provide mooring berths in the roadstead. These have been placed so that vessels can moor parallel to and at a distance of about 80 m. (262 ft.) from the banks, which permits rapid loading and unloading into lighters.

In addition to the berthing facilities for ocean-going vessels along the Rivière de Saigon, there are also a large number of quays for handling local traffic along the canals which link the port with its industrial and commercial suburb, Cho Lon. Two parallel waterways, with intercommunicating channels in three places, form this section of the port; the one is the Canal de la Dérivation continued by the Canal de Doublement, and the other slightly farther north, the Arroyo Chinois (Plate 51).

Port Facilities

The commercial port has nine shore cranes, of which six are 1½-ton electric cranes and three 4–15-ton steam cranes. There are also two floating steam cranes of 16 and 50 tons. All six electric cranes are found on the Quai de l'Yser. There is a 70-ton floating sheerlegs.

Warehouses, constructed of brick, line the waterfront and provide ample storage accommodation. The Quai de l'Yser alone has nine warehouses, with a total extent of 30,000 sq. m.

The port possesses twelve tugs of from 100 to 300 h.p. and 114 steel lighters of from 50 to 200 tons, owned by the port authorities, as well as about 2,000 wooden barges or junks in private ownership. The lighters and barges discharge merchandise from vessels moored in the river.

There are good facilities for fuelling with coal or oil. The main coal depot has a large storage capacity and lies at wharves on the left bank, opposite the naval dockyard. Stocks of oil owned by the three main companies are as follows:

Company	Tankage (tons)			
	Gasoline	Kerosine	Black oils	Total
Shell	11,300	3,800	8,900	24,000
Standard Vacuum	8,600	6,200	6,000	20,800
Texas	7,000	4,800	1,600	13,400
Total	26,900	14,800	16,500	58,200

Based on official sources.

Most of these oil depots are found close to the right bank of the river about 12 km. below the port (Fig. 123 and Plate 53). There are several jetties, at the head of which ships can berth in depths of about 5·8 m. (19 ft.).

Repairs to warships and commercial vessels can be executed in two government dry docks, the one 166 m. (545 ft.) long and 21 m. (67½ ft.) wide, the other 74 m. (241 ft.) long and 10 m. (32·7 ft.) wide, and in a floating dock 50·2 m. (164½ ft.) long and 9·2 m. (30 ft.) wide with a lifting capacity of 344 tons. These three docks are found in the naval section of the port, where facilities are also available for the repair of submarines. There are also four government patent slips, three with a lift of 40 tons and one with a lift of 18 tons (Plate 54). In addition, two private firms, the *Compagnie des Messageries fluviales* and the *Compagnie des Forges, Ateliers, et Chantiers de l'Indochine*, have small repair workshops.

The Town

Saigon has been called the 'Pearl of the Far East'. The city, which lies between the Arroyo Chinois and the Arroyo de l'Avalanche, is well laid out, with broad streets in a rectilinear pattern, imposing buildings and luxuriant gardens (Plates 88–90). Among the main buildings are the palaces of the Governor-General and of the Governor of Cochin-China, the Cathedral, the Town Hall, the Treasury, the Post Office and the Bank of Indo-China. Near the

Plate 52. Vessels moored at buoys in the river at Saigon (looking downstream)

The vessels are between one and six thousand tons. A floating steam crane is seen in the background.

Plate 53. Oil storage depots near Saigon

The depot in the foreground is owned by the *Standard Vacuum Oil Company of New York* and that in the background by the *Compagnie franco-asiatique des Pétroles (Shell)*. They lie about 12 km. below the port of Saigon on the right bank of the Rivière de Saigon, visible in the extreme left of the photograph.

Plate 54. Saigon: Patent slip and dry dock at the Quai de l'Argonne

Cathedral is the library (*Bibliothèque de Saigon*) and the museum (*Musée Blanchard de la Brosse*).

Saigon is the seat of the government of Cochin-China and is also the headquarters of a military and naval command. The town itself is governed by a *Conseil municipal* presided over by a mayor; in addition, there is a *Conseil d'administration* which has control over the urban agglomeration known as the 'Région Saigon-Cho Lon'.

History

The port of Saigon was opened to international commerce in February 1861, two years after its capture by the French expeditionary force under Admiral de Genouilly. Although Saigon had long existed as a commercial centre for river traffic, it was little more than an agglomeration of squalid native villages in the middle of the nineteenth century. On this site the French have built the modern city and port, with its many large buildings, well-kept avenues, and extensive accommodation for ocean-going vessels. The construction of business quarters and quays began as early as 1865, but the principal development took place under the administrations of Doumer and Beau, at the beginning of the present century. The building of the Quai de l'Yser was commenced in 1900 and completed about ten years later. In addition, facilities for native river traffic were considerably improved by the cutting of the Canal de la Dérivation (1906), the Canal de Doublement (1912), and the three channels linking them with the Arroyo Chinois. The improvement of port facilities was rendered necessary by the rapid growth in the production and export of rice which followed upon French settlement in the Mekong delta. The export of rice from Saigon, which averaged 333,000 tons a year in the decade 1874–83, increased to an average annual figure of 877,000 tons between 1904 and 1913. Goods handled at the port also increased with the opening in 1913 of the railway line from Nha Trang. In 1914, Saigon became an autonomous port, controlled by an administrative council, independent of the central state authorities.

Between the outbreak of war in 1914 and the beginning of the world economic crisis in 1930, Saigon maintained its commercial prosperity. The tonnage of ships using the port increased by over 50 %. Quays were extended and many warehouses enlarged. The export of rice increased to an annual average of 1,382,000 tons between 1924 and 1929.

The economic depression of the early thirties caused a temporary decline in the trade of Saigon, but its effects were alleviated by the introduction of bounties and quotas which led to an increase in the trade with France (see p. 358). By 1935, the port had fully recovered its former prosperity. In recent years various improvements have been proposed to cope with the increasing traffic; these include the reinforcement of existing quays, and extension of the buoying and lighting arrangements. A project has also been put forward for the formation of an outport near Ganh Ray, at the mouth of the Rivière de Saigon, which will offer discharging facilities for the largest ships at any state of the tide.

In the present war, Saigon has assumed the role of a garrison town for the Japanese forces. It is also the chief supply base for all Japanese troops stationed in south Indo-China.

Trade

The total quantity of goods entering or leaving Saigon is considerably greater than for any other port in the country. In 1938, its foreign trade amounted to 1,935,231 tons, exports totalling 1,632,630 tons and imports 302,601 tons. Local river and coastal traffic comprised 352,621 tons of merchandise in the same year. Saigon is the outlet for the important rice-exporting region of Cochin-China, and rice forms about 50 % by weight of the shipments overseas. Since the war of 1914–18 rubber exports have steadily increased, and at the present day they average nearly 60,000 tons annually. Other goods exported include maize, livestock, dried fish, copra, pepper and timber. A large proportion of the timber comprises teak which has been floated down the Mekong from forests in Siam. Over 40 % of the exports are marketed in France or in other colonies of the French empire; Hong Kong and Singapore each receive about 20 %, while the remainder finds a market in China, Japan, the Netherlands East Indies, the Philippines, Great Britain and the United States.

Manufactured goods constitute the bulk of the imports entering the port. Two-thirds of the imports come from France and the French empire.

Although Saigon lies off the main steamship route from Singapore to China and Japan, it has a large passenger traffic by reason of its position as capital of Cochin-China, while it also derives importance as the chief point of entry for tourists who want to visit the magnificent ruins of Angkor Wat in Cambodia.

In 1937, a total of 777 vessels entered and 782 cleared the port as shown in the table below:

Nationality of vessels	No. entered	No. cleared	Tonnage entered	Tonnage cleared
French	311	310	1,102,571	1,093,879
British	195	198	497,928	504,033
Dutch	66	67	199,327	201,387
Japanese	50	50	195,899	195,899
Italian	45	45	156,384	156,384
Danish	31	31	97,876	97,876
Norwegian	31	32	86,259	87,937
Greek	15	16	47,183	50,067
German	9	9	44,787	44,787
American	10	10	36,146	36,146
Panamanian	5	5	11,182	11,182
Hungarian	5	5	7,545	7,545
Yugoslavian	2	2	7,165	7,165
Swedish	2	2	3,311	3,311
Total	777	782	2,493,563	2,497,598

Based on official sources.

This table reveals the overwhelmingly important part played by French and British shipping in the overseas trade of Saigon. The *Messageries Maritimes*, the *Chargeurs Réunis*, and the *Société Maritime indochinoise* are the principal shipping companies associated with this trade. In addition to the large vessels engaged in overseas traffic there are nearly 4,000 small river and coastal craft.

Industries

The industries of Saigon, which include a chemical factory, a brick works and several distilleries, manufacture products primarily for use within the country itself. Most of the rice is husked and prepared for export in the mills of Cho Lon (see p. 334).

Communications

Saigon is connected by railway with Hanoi and with My Tho on the Cua Trieu, the northernmost branch of the Mekong. The railway station lies north of the Arroyo Chinois. Tramways lead to Cho Lon, Hoc Mon and Bendongxo, from which town a short railway runs to Loc Ninh; they also run along part of the waterfront. The tramways have the same gauge as the railway; all are electric, except for the section from Thu Dau Mot to Bendongxo in which steam traction is used.

Good roads run from the waterfront into the centre of the town. The Arroyo Chinois is crossed by two bridges near its confluence with the Rivière de Saigon (Fig. 123). A network of metalled roads radiates from Saigon to centres in the Mekong delta, to Phnom Penh and the Siamese frontier, to Dalat and to Hanoi.

Saigon has a regular steamship service providing communication with other parts of Indo-China, as well as with Singapore, Hong Kong and countries in Europe.

There is a civil aerodrome at Tan Son Nhut north of Saigon, and a seaplane anchorage at Cat Lai on the right bank of the Dong Nai about 5 km. east of the town.

HAIPHONG

Lat. 20° 52′ N, long. 106° 40′ E.   Population: 70,000 (1936).
Admiralty Chart 775.   Figs. 124, 125.   Plates 55–57, 79.

Haiphong, the second port of Indo-China, lies about 15 km. from the sea on the right bank of the Cua Cam near the eastern border of the Fleuve Rouge delta. It is the chief commercial outlet for Tonkin and for the Chinese province of Yunnan. Haiphong ranks fifth in size among the towns of Indo-China and is one of the leading industrial centres in the country.

Approach and Access

Owing to frequent silting and to the formation of two bars at the entrance of the Cua Cam, the seaward approach to Haiphong is by the Cua Nam Trieu, a little to the north-east (Fig. 124). A bar also obstructs the entrance to the Cua Nam Trieu, but through it a dredged channel has been made with a depth of 6 m. ($3\frac{1}{3}$ fm.), and a width of 150 m. About 10 km. below Haiphong vessels enter the Canal Maritime or Dinh Vu cut, linking the Cua Nam Trieu to the Cua Cam. This canal is slightly under $1\frac{1}{2}$ km. in length and has a depth of 6 m. ($3\frac{1}{3}$ fm.). Vessels cannot pass one another in the canal. In the final section, from the Dinh Vu cut to the port, a channel has been dredged to 6 m. ($3\frac{1}{3}$ fm.) and is maintained at a constant width by embankments and groynes. The subsidiary port of Port Redon lies on the Cua Nam Trieu about 20 km. above the Canal Maritime.

At Haiphong, there is only one high and one low tide every 24 hr. The highest tides occur once a fortnight, shortly after the moon has reached its greatest declination. The rise is from 3·4 to 4 m. (11–13 ft.); at slack water the level oscillates between 1·6 m. (5 ft.) and 2·2 m. (7 ft.). The time and height of the tides near the entrance to the Cua Nam Trieu is approximately the same. The speed of the tidal current shows considerable variation; in winter the flood stream is from 2 to 3 knots at spring and 1 knot at neap tides, while the ebb stream is about 3 knots and $1\frac{1}{2}$ knots respectively; in summer, the period of high water on the river, the tidal currents become much reduced in speed and the ebb periods are notably longer than in

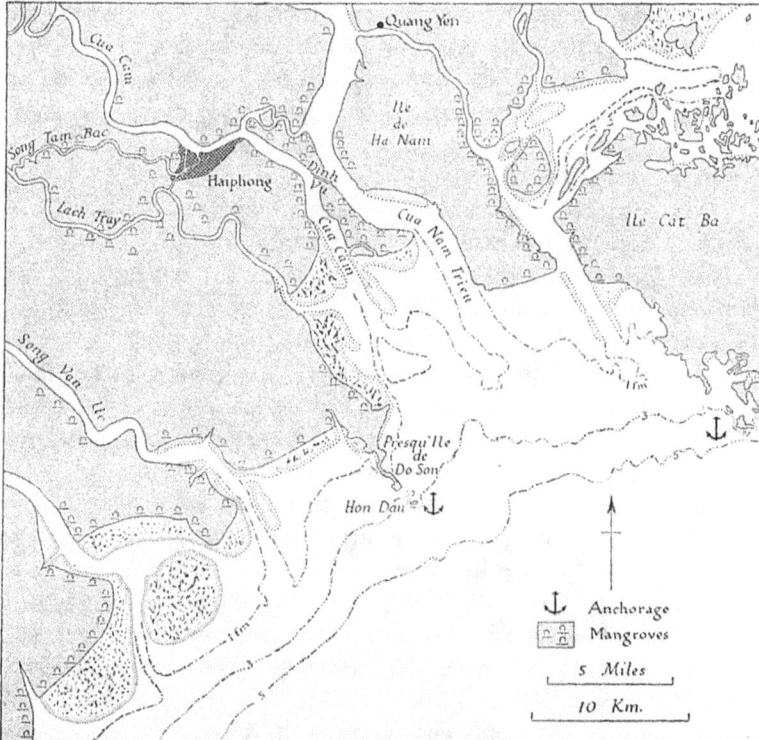

Fig. 124. Approaches to Haiphong
Source: Admiralty chart 775 (1912, corrected to 1936).

winter. At the approaches to Haiphong and at the port itself shipping is endangered, especially in July and August, by typhoons, while further hindrances to the free movement of vessels are caused by bad visibility during the *crachin* period, from the end of January to mid-April.

Vessels drawing 7·9–8·5 m. (26–28 ft.) can reach Haiphong at high water and those of 4·6 m. (15 ft.) at any state of the tide. A chain of beacons makes the port accessible by night as well as by day.

Vessels awaiting the tide anchor either off Hon Dau or off the southern shores of the Ile Cat Ba in depths of about 5·5 m. (3 fm.).

Detailed Description

The port of Haiphong extends along the river for about 5 km. from the bend of the Cua Cam, at its confluence with the Vang Chau channels, to a little way above the Canal de Ha Ly (Fig. 125). Below the town are the commercial wharves, which follow the curve of the river continuously for 912 m. (2992 ft.) with depths alongside of from 7 to 8 m. (23–26 ft.). The wharves, built on iron piles, provide six mooring berths for large vessels, and gangways, averaging 16 m. (52 ft.) long and 7 m. (23 ft.) broad, link them to a quay backed by warehouses (Plate 56).

Vessels occupied in transit trade dock at separate berths built of reinforced concrete, immediately downstream from the commercial wharves. They have a frontage of 130 m. (462 ft.) in length and are connected with the quay by three gangways, 20 m. (66 ft.) long and 6 m. (20 ft.) wide.

Between the filled-in channel of the Song Tam Bac (Canal Bonnal) and its present-day mouth lies the Quai de la Liberté, from which two gangways extend to wharves each 45 m. (148 ft.) long. Shallow-draught barges and small native vessels use this section of the river front, since the depth of water here (5 m.) is not so great as farther east. West of the Song Tam Bac are two berths where ships can take on fuel oil by pipe-line from the shore; and on the left bank of the Cua Cam lie several berths for coaling purposes.

In the Haiphong roadstead there are eleven buoys for mooring purposes in depths of 7 m. (23 ft.), three below and eight above the mouth of the Song Tam Bac.

Along the banks of Song Tam Bac and the Canal de Ha Ly quays have been constructed to handle the considerable river traffic with other parts of the Tonkin delta (Plate 55). Both these channels and the canal linking them with the Lach Tray have a dredged depth of 2·5 m. (8 ft.).

Port Facilities

The wharves and quays of the commercial port are equipped with one 20-ton and six 1½-ton electrically-driven cranes, four steam-driven cranes of 2 tons, and two more of 2 tons worked by hand. On the Quai de la Liberté there is a single crane of 2 tons capacity.

The river front close to the commercial wharves is lined by ware-

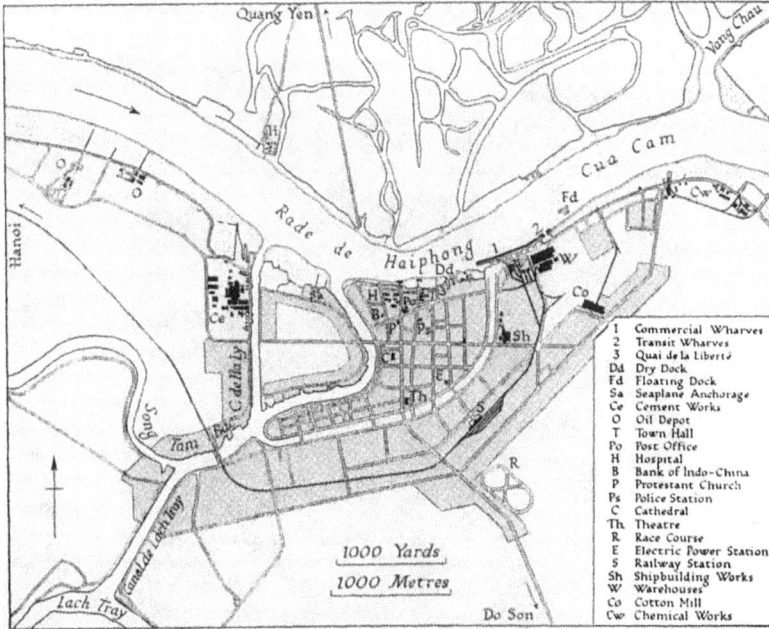

Fig. 125. Haiphong

The commercial port lies east of the mouth of the Tam Bac. A ferry links the Quai de la Liberté with the road leading to Quang Yen. The built-up area is in dark brown; the filled-in channel of the Song Tam Bac can be seen enclosing the main section of the town and running roughly parallel with the railway.

Source: Admiralty.

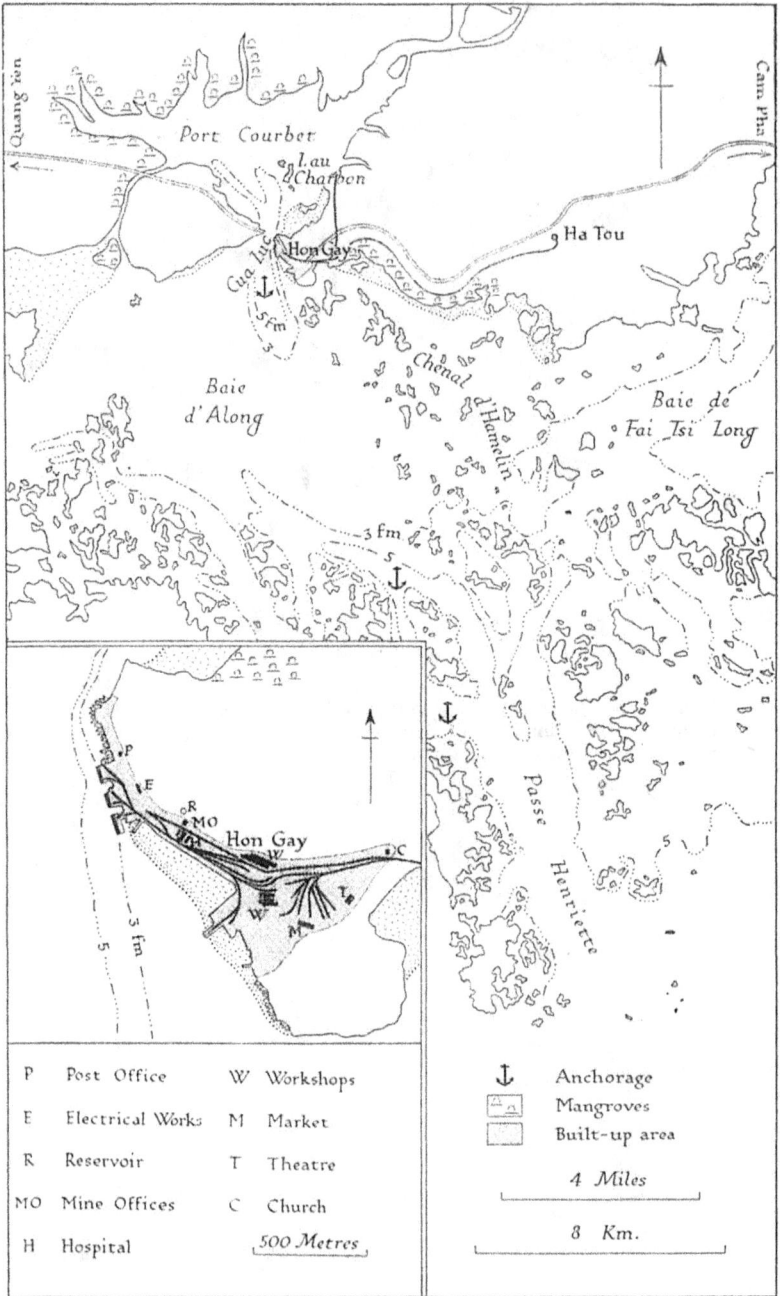

Fig. 126. Hon Gay
Source: (1) Carte de l'Indochine, 1:100,000; sheet 50 (1925); (2) Admiralty.

houses, built of brick with concrete floors, covering 51,850 sq. m. and capable of holding 100,000 tons of merchandise. Most of them belong to the Haiphong Chamber of Commerce. There are also 150,000 sq. m. of storage grounds. A narrow-gauge railway (60 cm.) facilitates movement of cargo from the wharves to the warehouses, while other lines give access to the main railway station in the centre of the town (Plate 56).

Harbour craft of the port includes two dredgers, seven steam barges, three large lighters, four steam launches, three coal barges, three water barges, and many junks up to 100 tons capacity.

As the local water-supply is brackish fresh water is brought to the port from rivers some distance away (see p. 127 and Plate 57). The fuelling of ships is made at coaling wharves, where a considerable stock of coal is normally available. Two important oil depots belonging to the *Compagnie franco-asiatique des Pétroles* (*Shell*) and to the *Standard Vacuum Oil Company of New York* lie above the commercial port. They have the following tankage capacity:

Company	Tankage (tons)			
	Gasoline	Kerosine	Black oils	Total
Shell	4,250	2,325	5,900	12,475
Standard Vacuum	8,700	6,500	1,400	16,600
Total	12,950	8,825	7,300	29,075

Based on official sources.

The careening and repairing of vessels is carried out in the two floating docks, situated a little below the commercial wharves and owned by the *Société anonyme des Constructions mécaniques*. Their dimensions are as follows:

	Length of entrance	Width of entrance	Depth on sill	Lifting power tons
Floating Dock no. 1	60·9 m. (199¾ ft.)	15·0 m. (49 ft.)	2·7 m. (9 ft.)	1,800
Floating Dock no. 2	32·9 m. (108 ft.)	15·0 m. (49 ft.)	2·7 m. (9 ft.)	700

Based on official sources.

The two docks can be coupled together, making a total length of 93·8 m. (307¾ ft.) with a lifting capacity of 2,500 tons. Repairs to ships with a maximum length of 45 m. (148 ft.) and a draught of not more than 3 m. (10 ft.) can be made at two dry docks owned by *Marty et Abbadie* alongside the Quai de la Liberté. There is also a slipway with a lifting power of 400 tons and two building slips. Until recently, Haiphong possessed one of the two naval dockyards in Indo-China. Most of the installations are believed to have been dismantled in 1940, prior to the Japanese invasion.

The Town

The town of Haiphong, which lies for the most part east of the Song Tam Bac, has many modern buildings and tree-lined boulevards. The chief buildings are the Town Hall, the Post Office, the Bank of Indo-China, the Cathedral and the Municipal Theatre. There is a race-course and an extensive sports ground (*Cercle Sportif Haiphonnais*) (Plate 79).

Haiphong is administered by a mayor who presides over a *Conseil municipal*. The mayor is not an elected official as in the towns of France, but is appointed by the Governor-General.

History

The port of Haiphong was founded in the late nineteenth century as a supply base for French explorers and as a disembarkation centre for the expeditionary force despatched to subdue Tonkin. By a treaty in 1874 the French obtained concessions from the Annamite government to develop the site at the confluence of the Song Tam Bac with the Cua Cam, then occupied by a small fishing village. The first quays and warehouses date from 1885 and, after the pacification of Tonkin, Haiphong rapidly became an important commercial port. Its growth was materially aided by various improvements in the approaches from the sea. Until 1895 the Cua Cam had been the sole means of access, but, as shifting bars at its mouth hampered shipping, French engineers in this year proposed that a deep-water channel should be dredged in the Cua Nam Trieu and a passage cut through the Dinh Vu island to join the Cua Cam a little downstream from Haiphong. This new channel was opened to navigation in 1902.

In common with other ports of Indo-China, Haiphong benefited from the vigorous policy of internal economic development pursued by Governor-General Doumer at the beginning of the present century. The ambitious programme of railway and road construction called for considerable quantities of imported raw materials, and this demand in turn led to the extension of port facilities. Between

In the distance are the Cua Nam Trieu and the Canal Maritime or Dinh Vu cut by which sea-going vessels reach the port. The quays and wharves of the commercial port lie on the right bank of the Cua Cam below the confluence of the Song Tam Bac seen in the foreground of the picture.

Plate 56. Haiphong: Commercial wharves and warehouses

Cargo is being discharged from a vessel moored to the wharf. The buildings in the centre are the main warehouses of the port.

Plate 57. Haiphong: the Song Tam Bac

The photograph shows the pumping of fresh water which has been brought from a distance by the vessels moored in the river. The bridge carries the main road from Haiphong to Hanoi.

Plate 58. Tourane (looking east)

The Song Cam Le is in the foreground and the head of the Baie de Tourane, backed by the mountains of the Col des Nuages, in the distance.

1876 and 1912 the wharves were increased from 170 to 280 m. in length, and three cranes were installed, while the introduction of the narrow-gauge railway greatly speeded up the discharging of merchandise. In this period, Haiphong became the terminus of the railway passing through Hanoi and Lao Kay to Yunnanfou (Kunming) which in effect made south-west China as well as Tonkin tributary to the port. The outbreak of war a few years after the completion of this railway brought about an increased commercial activity, which was reflected in the lengthening of wharfage accommodation and in the construction of more warehouses.

The prosperity of Haiphong in the war years, 1914–18, continued for another decade, until the oncome of the world economic depression. During the boom period from 1926 to 1930, it was a thriving centre with eight French and foreign banks, three rice mills, a chemical factory, a large cement works and several well-equipped engineering shops. The slump undermined these various concerns and some have never recovered. Of the eight banks, only one French and two British remain and many firms have had to close down, with the exception of the *Société des Ciments Portland*, which has continued to expand its production in a remarkable manner (see p. 333). Owing to the depreciation of the yen, export of rice from Haiphong to China for a time ceased almost completely, and Chinese business houses were ruined. Although tariff assimilation with France and the imposition of quotas and bounties (see p. 358) probably saved Indo-China as a whole from economic disaster, in the case of Haiphong it threw up an artificial barrier between the port and her main customer, China. Since 1929, the import duty on porcelain from China has increased from 25 to 1,200 francs per 100 kg. and on silk goods from 200 to 1,200 francs per 100 kg. Despite the continuation of this tariff the trade of the port showed a marked recovery in the years 1937 and 1938 (see p. 386).

Haiphong is not likely fully to regain its former prosperity without a further deepening of the main approach channel. As the expense of dredging and maintaining a deeper channel in the Cua Cam would be prohibitive, French engineers consider that the solution to the shipping problem lies in the establishment of an outport immediately below the Dinh Vu cutting on the right bank of the Cua Nam Trieu, where there is a natural depth of at least 10 m. (33 ft.). Cargoes discharged by large vessels at the outport would be despatched by rail or road to Haiphong for further distribution. In addition to this scheme, it is also proposed to cut a canal from the Cua Nam Trieu across the lowlying land south of Quang Yen, which will provide a more direct route for the important barge traffic between Haiphong and the port of Hon Gay.

During the present war, Haiphong has been used by the Japanese as an operational and supply base, just as the French had made use of it for similar reasons in the late nineteenth century. The Japanese troops which occupied Tonkin in 1940 were landed at Haiphong, and from here the subsequent invasion of south Indo-China was partly carried out.

Trade

Haiphong handles the bulk of the goods entering or leaving the state of Tonkin. In 1938, the total foreign traffic amounted to 1,167,946 tons, exports comprising 903,427 tons and imports 264,519 tons, figures in excess of those recorded for the pre-depression year of 1929. Rice, maize and coal are the main exports. The increasing export of maize, principally to France, and the decline in rice shipments, for which China was the main market, reflects the influence of the recent tariff policy (see p. 358). An interesting feature in the shipment of coal overseas during the past decade has been the increasingly greater tonnage taken by Japan. A large quantity of the coal is exported from the subsidiary port of Port Redon. Of the other exports, cement is by far the most important, and large amounts are annually shipped abroad to China, Japan, Malaya, and the Philippines as well as to countries in Europe.

Transit Traffic of Haiphong, 1936 (tons)

	Yunnan		Kwangsi	
	Imports	Exports	Imports	Exports
Hong Kong	5,304	9,230	7	249
China	19,926	646	—	—
Japan	583	—	—	—
Netherlands East Indies	6,073	—	—	—
France	1,831	55	—	36
Other European countries	496	510	—	920
United States	277	309	—	—
Other countries	248	12	—	19
	34,738	10,762	7	1,224

Total transit traffic, 46,731 tons.

Source: *Annuaire statistique de l'Indochine, 1936–7*, p. 175 (Hanoi, 1938).

The imports consist primarily of manufactured articles, iron and steel goods, machinery, metal wares and automobiles, obtained from France, Japan and China. Food products, such as rice, vegetables and fruit are also imported.

The trade figures given in the table above do not take into account the transit traffic which is handled by the port. Haiphong acts as an entrepôt for goods from the Chinese provinces of Yunnan and Kwangsi. The volume of this traffic in 1936 is shown above.

Yunnan exports through Haiphong considerable quantities of unrefined tin ore and tin concentrates as well as hides and skins; in return it imports manufactured goods, especially textiles, and many kinds of fuel oil.

The number of ships entering and clearing the port nearly doubled between 1900 and 1929, while their total tonnage more than trebled during the same period. In 1937, the position was as follows:

Nationality of vessels*	No. entered	No. cleared	Tonnage entered	Tonnage cleared
French	218	218	458,722	462,132
British	170	165	333,194	325,730
Japanese	23	24	81,240	86,325
Norwegian	34	31	59,999	57,421
Dutch	28	27	59,595	54,794
Greek	12	12	36,215	36,215
Panama	4	4	7,407	7,407
Danish	2	2	6,861	6,861
United States	1	1	3,405	3,405
Finnish	1	1	2,889	2,889
Australian	1	1	2,706	2,706
Swedish	1	1	2,611	2,611
	495	487	1,054,844	1,048,496

Based on official sources.

As in the case of Saigon, French and British vessels easily predominate. The chief French shipping lines serving the port are the *Messageries Maritimes*, the *Chargeurs Réunis*, the *Compagnie indochinoise de Navigation*, and the *Société Maritime indochinoise*.

Industries

Haiphong possesses a variety of industrial establishments based on the excellent facilities available for the assembly of raw materials and coal. Cement manufacture is one of its leading industries, the works lying to the west of the town. Other large concerns controlled and managed by Europeans include various shipbuilding and ship-

* A number of Chinese and Italian vessels also call at the port.

repairing yards, a cotton-spinning mill, a glass works, and a chemical works. There are also several rice-polishing mills, owned by Chinese, though, as pointed out above, the number of mills has fallen during the last ten years.

Communications

The commercial port is connected by a branch line with the railway station of Haiphong which lies south-east of the centre of the town. The railway line to Hanoi and Yunnanfou (Kunming) runs south of the town and crosses the Song Tam Bac over a swing bridge.

Several good roads run from the river front to join the main highways linking Haiphong with other parts of Tonkin. The Route Colonial no. 4 links Haiphong to Hanoi, and another important road gives access to the coastal defence area near Do Son. A ferry from the Quai de la Liberté crosses the Cua Cam and communicates with the main road leading to Quang Yen, Hon Gay, and Mon Cay.

Steamships ply between Haiphong and many places in the Fleuve Rouge delta, including Hanoi, Viet Tri, Thai Binh, Nam Dinh, and Phu Ly. There are similar services to Hon Gay, Cam Pha, Port Wallut, Mon Cay, Kwang Chow Wan, and Hong Kong.

On the right bank of the Cua Cam immediately west of the Song Tam Bac is a seaplane station, with two hangars and repair facilities. There is a civil aerodrome on the opposite bank where the Vang Chau channel joins the Cua Cam.

Fig. 127. Panorama of the coast to the east of Hon Gay

HON GAY

Lat. 20° 57′ N, long. 107° 03′ E.   Population: 2,000 (1936).
Admiralty Chart 1169.   Fig. 126.

Hon Gay, an important coal port, lies on the northern shores of the Baie d'Along, 35 km. east-north-east of Haiphong, at the main point of entry to the landlocked bay known as Port Courbet. The port is approached by channels through the western part of the Fai Tsi Long archipelago which consists of innumerable rocky islets; the Chenal d'Hamelin, the deepest channel, has a minimum depth of 3·7 m. (12 ft.), and the bar at its north-western end has been dredged to 4·9 m. (16 ft.). In the Baie d'Along off Hon Gay, ships can anchor in 9·1–18·2 m. (5–10 fm.). The anchorage is sheltered and has good holding ground. Cua Luc, the entrance to Port Courbet, is about 2 cables wide with a depth of 18·2 m. (10 fm.), and the bay itself as far north as the Ile au Charbon has depths of from 7·3–18·2 m. (4–10 fm.), providing secure anchorage; northwards of this island the bay becomes shallow with drying mud banks. There is a tidal rise of 2·1–3·3 m. (7–11 ft.), and only one high and

(drawn from photographs)

one low water normally occurs every 24 hr. The south-moving tidal stream has the stronger flow and after heavy rainfalls attains a rate of 3 knots.

The port has three coaling wharves, one 79·3 m. (260 ft.) long and two 70·2 m. (230 ft.) long; the depths alongside vary from 3·6 to 7·6 m. (12–25 ft.). Each wharf has one travelling crane of up to 7 tons capacity. A 60-ton floating sheerlegs is also available. Close to the centre of the town lies another wharf with a small jetty extending from it, but the depth of water at the head is only 0·7 m. (2½ ft.). The wharves have a light railway serving them, and direct loading and unloading can take place from trucks. There are in addition two short piers, one south of the town wharf and another close to the coal wharves. Two mooring buoys are fixed a short distance within the entrance to Port Courbet.

Cargo is discharged on to the coal wharves and into lighters from ships moored off Hon Gay. Harbour craft includes twenty-five 100-ton lighters and from 10–15 tugs. Large quantities of coal are available for fuelling, and coal can be loaded at a rate of 80 tons an hour. Small repairs to vessels can be undertaken. Storage accommodation is lacking.

Hon Gay ranks third among the ports of Indo-China in total volume of trade, but second in exports alone. In 1936 it exported 1,200,000 tons compared with a total export of 2,100,000 tons from Saigon and 800,000 tons from Haiphong. Coal, which consists mainly of anthracite obtained from mines in the neighbourhood, is by far the most important article of export. France and Japan are the principal markets. The imports, which totalled only 19,000 tons in 1936, generally comprise goods for local consumption.

A metre-gauge railway about 10 km. in length connects Hon Gay with the coal mines of Ha Tou. The port is in communication with Haiphong, Cam Pha and Mon Cay by a metalled road, which passes near the coast and is often in a bad state of repair. Only a few narrow trackways penetrate inland. There is normally frequent communication by boat with Haiphong. A seaplane anchorage is available in Cua Luc.

TOURANE

Lat. 16° 04′ N, long. 108° 13′ E. Population: 23,000 (1936).
Admiralty Chart 1342. Fig. 128. Plate 58.

Tourane, the principal port of Annam, is situated about 100 km. south-east of Hue on the left bank of the Song Cam Le close to where it enters the Baie de Tourane. The bay has forested hills bordering it along the northern side, with a low, sandy shore 16 km. in length,

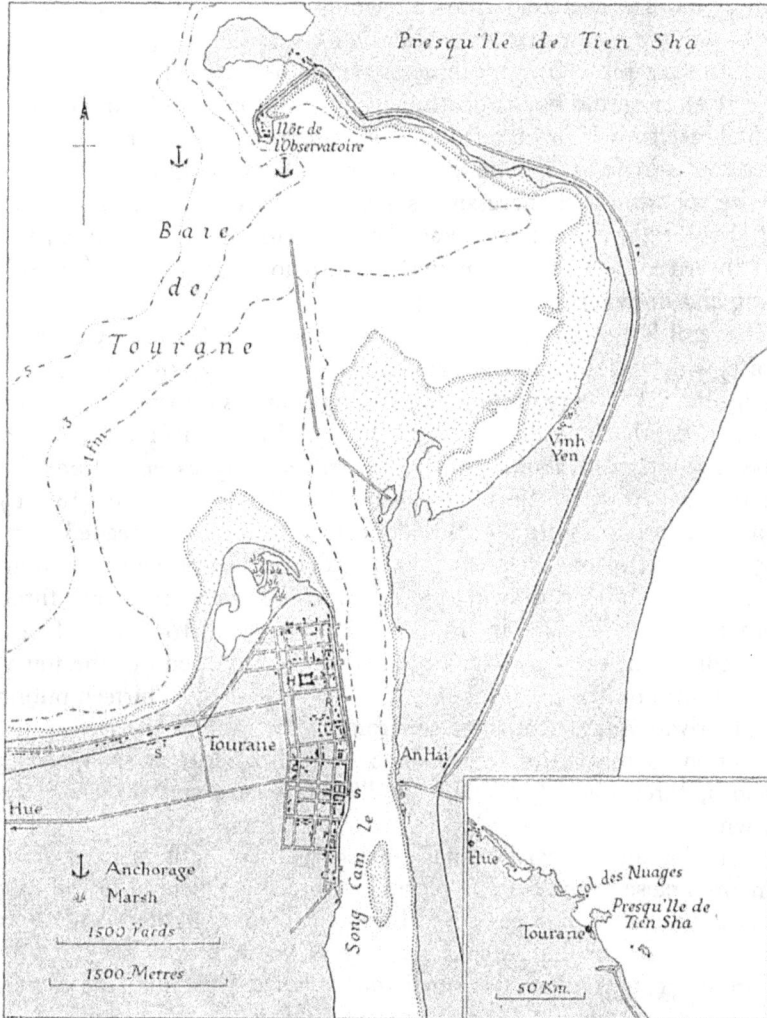

Source: Admiralty.   Fig. 128. Tourane
C. Customs House; H. Hospital; R. Residency; S. Station.

to the west, and with the rocky headland of the Presqu'île de Tien Sha to the east. There is a deep approach from the open sea and large vessels may anchor in the eastern part of the bay in depths from

9 to 18 m. (5–10 fm.). This anchorage, which is about 8 km. by
6 km. in extent, suffers from the disadvantage of being open to
dangerously strong north-east winds during the winter monsoon.
An anchorage sheltered from all winds is available for vessels of
light draught south-east of the Ilôt de l'Observatoire. There are two
breakwaters protecting the inner part of the bay. The entrance to
the river from the bay is obstructed by a shifting sand-bar through
which a channel, protected by breakwaters, has been dredged to a
depth of 4 m. (13 ft.). The river deposits a large quantity of alluvium
at its mouth which necessitates periodical dredging. A tidal rise
of about 1·2 m. (4 ft.) occurs at Tourane with one tide every 24 hr.
In the river port there is swinging room for a ship 76 m. (250 ft.)
long and drawing 3·5 m. (12 ft.).

Several jetties are available for berthing. The Ilôt de l'Observatoire, which is joined to the mainland by a causeway 458 m. (1,500 ft.)
long, has a jetty 137 m. (450 ft.) in length on its north-eastern side,
with a depth alongside of 2·7 m. (9 ft.). In the river port, which
has a frontage of about 3 km., a **T**-headed jetty extends from the
northern part of the town, with a berthing length of 55 m. (180 ft.)
and a depth of 0·3 m. (1 ft.) alongside. Another **T**-headed jetty
49 m. (160 ft.) long, lies near the Residency and provides berthing
facilities for a ship drawing 1·8 m. (6 ft.). Finally, there are three
other small jetties, one in front of the *Messageries Maritimes* offices,
a second near the Customs buildings at the south end of the town,
and a third on the east bank opposite the Residency. Thirteen public
and private quays line the waterfront in the rear of the jetties. In
addition to the jetties, small ships may also berth at six mooring
buoys, three east of the Ilôt de l'Observatoire and three off the
town.

At Tourane, cargo is usually discharged by lighters from ships
moored close to the landing places or from ships moored in the bay.
Harbour craft comprises several wooden or iron lighters and three
tugs, one of 100 h.p., and a number of water boats. Facilities for
handling cargo include two small cranes on the Customs House quay
and a 5-ton crane belonging to the railway. Open stacking space
exists behind many of the quays, but there is very little covered accommodation. A small supply of coal obtained from the Nong Son
field or imported from Tonkin, is normally available for fuelling
purposes, and an oil depot lies on the west bank of the Song Cam
Le about 1 km. south of the Customs House. Small repairs can be
undertaken.

In 1938 goods handled at the port amounted to 111,081 tons, two-thirds of which was purely local river and coastal traffic. The exports include maize, sugar, cinnamon, areca nuts and livestock; the imports are mainly manufactured goods. Owing to the poverty of its hinterland, Tourane will probably long continue to be a small port, though its trade may expand with the further development of the Nong Son coalfield and the tin mines of Nam Patene (see p. 327).

The town of Tourane is well built and extends for nearly 3 km. along the left bank of the river (Fig. 128). It possesses many fine buildings, including the French Residency, the Military Hospital, Post Office and the Customs House.

Tourane lies on the main railway and road between Hanoi and Saigon. The railway runs along the waterfront of the town for about 1 km. A branch railway line and also a metalled road connect An Hai, a small settlement on the right bank of the Song Cam Le, opposite Tourane, with the Ilôt de l'Observatoire. There is a ferry across the river between An Hai and Tourane. The port has regular steamship communication with Hue, Haiphong and Saigon. About 5 km. south of the town there is a seaplane anchorage and a landing ground.

BEN THUY

Lat. 18° 39' N, long. 105° 42' E. Population: no information.
Admiralty Chart 2062. Fig. 129.

Ben Thuy is the port of Vinh, the capital of the province of Nghe An in north Annam. It stands on the left bank of the Song Ca, about 15 km. from its mouth. The entrance to the river is obstructed by a shifting sand bar, through which a channel has been dredged, 5·2 m. (17 ft.) in depth. Above the bar navigation is not difficult, except on the Yen Luu sill where there is a minimum depth of 2·5 m. (8 ft.). The tides, which are here diurnal, rise 1·9 m. (6¼ ft.). At springs the flood stream lasts for 6 hr. and the ebb stream for 18 hr.; the time of slack water at Ben Thuy is about 1¾ hr. after that at the mouth of the river (Cua Hoi). In late summer, typhoons frequently hinder the movement of shipping. While awaiting a favourable tide, ships can anchor off Hon Matt in 20 m. (11 fm.), or off Hon Nieu in 7·6 m. (4¼ fm.).

The port has five short piers with depths of 2–3 m. (7–10 ft.) at their heads, against which vessels can lie on the mud at low water. There is one 5-ton crane. Small repairs can be executed.

In 1938, Ben Thuy handled 98,264 tons of goods, 86,223 tons of which was purely coastal trade. The trade of the port is concerned mainly with the export of timber, amounting to about 25,000 tons a year. The timber is floated downstream from the interior.

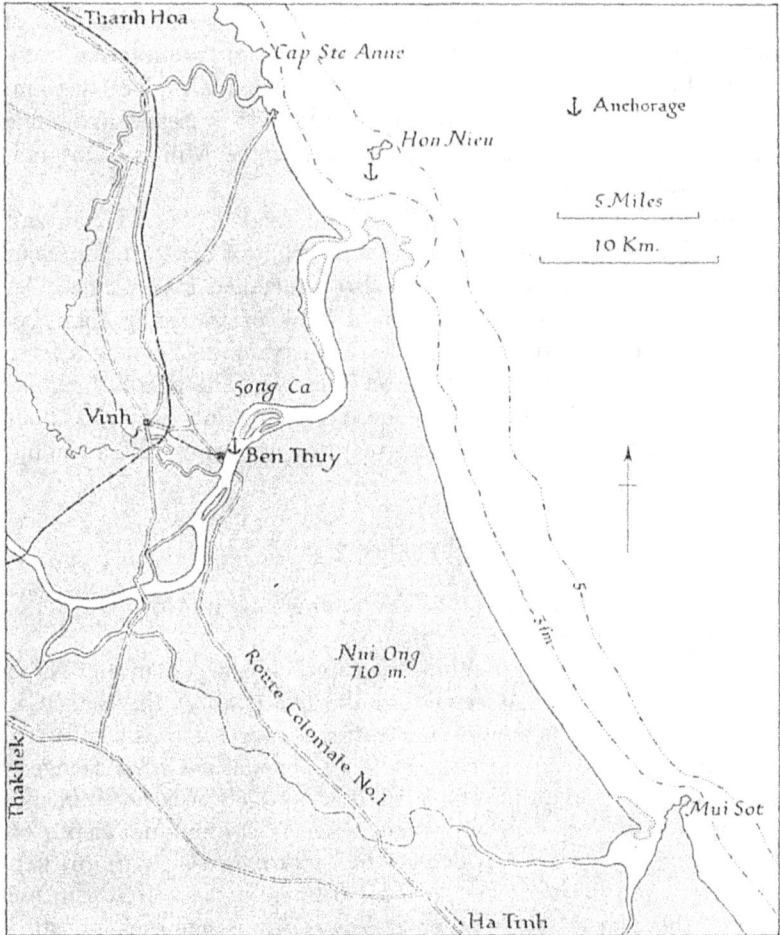

Fig. 129. Ben Thuy
Source: (1) Carte provisoire de l'Annam [Carte de l'Indochine], 1 : 100,000 [sheet 95] (1902); (2) Admiralty chart 2062 (1913, corrected to 1940).

Ben Thuy has rail and road communication with Vinh. The completion of the railway from Tan Ap to Thakhek will make the whole of northern Laos tributary to the port. Steamer services operate from Ben Thuy to Haiphong, Tourane, Qui Nhon, and Saigon. There is a seaplane anchorage and an aerodrome.

BA NGOI (CAM RANH)

Lat. 11° 52' N, long. 109° 11' E. Population: no information. Admiralty Chart 3028. Fig. 130.

Ba Ngoi is a small town and port on the Baie de Cam Ranh. This bay is the finest deep-water anchorage on the coast of Indo-China, and is accessible to the largest ships at all times of the year. It lies 360 km. from Saigon and nearly equidistant from Singapore, Hong Kong and Manila. Mountains surround the bay and provide shelter from the monsoons. The Grande Passe, which forms the entrance to the outer harbour, has a width of 4 km. and a depth of 25 m. (13 fm.), except for the short stretch between Hon Trung and Ba Tien headland where the depth falls to 14 m. (8 fm.). The outer harbour has an area of about 7 sq. km. with depths of from 16·4 to 22 m. (9-12 fm.). There is a good anchorage in the Baie de Binh Ba in 20 m. (11 fm.) and another north of Ile Tagne in 14-18 m. (8-10 fm.). Le Goulet, the entrance to the inner harbour, is slightly over 1 km. wide and 22 m. (12 fm.) deep. This inner section of the bay provides secure anchorages in 11-14·6 m. (6-8 fm.) over an area of about 2 × 5 km.; and in 7·3-11 m. (4-6 fm.) over an area about 3 × 2 km., south of Ba Ngoi. The holding ground is good over these areas. In the south-western part of the bay depths are less than 9 m. (5 fm.), and they gradually decrease inshore.

The port of Ba Ngoi lies on the western shores of the inner harbour. A stone causeway, 732 m. (2,400 ft.) long, has been built to the edge of the coral reef which fringes the shore; at the end of the causeway is a concrete T pier, 92 m. (300 ft.) long with a load capacity estimated at 20 tons and a depth alongside of 5·8 m. (19 ft.). Both causeway and pier carry a railway line. There are two 10 ton cranes at the end of the pier. On the opposite side of the bay near Ping Hai are two more piers about a cable apart; the first is a stone jetty about 92 m. (302 ft.) long, at the head of which is a small wooden landing stage with a depth of 3 m. (10 ft.) alongside; the second is a dilapidated stone jetty and may be more in the nature of a groyne. Four buoys are available for the mooring of ships; one slightly eastwards of Ba Ngoi pier and three about 1½ cables offshore near the settlement of Ping Hai.

In 1938, the trade of Ba Ngoi amounted to 93,109 tons, including 73,053 tons of foreign and 20,056 tons of coastal trade. Exports consist of agricultural products, and imports primarily of heavy constructional materials.

A short branch railway from the Ba Ngoi pier connects with the main Trans-Indo-Chinese railway. This pier also has road con-

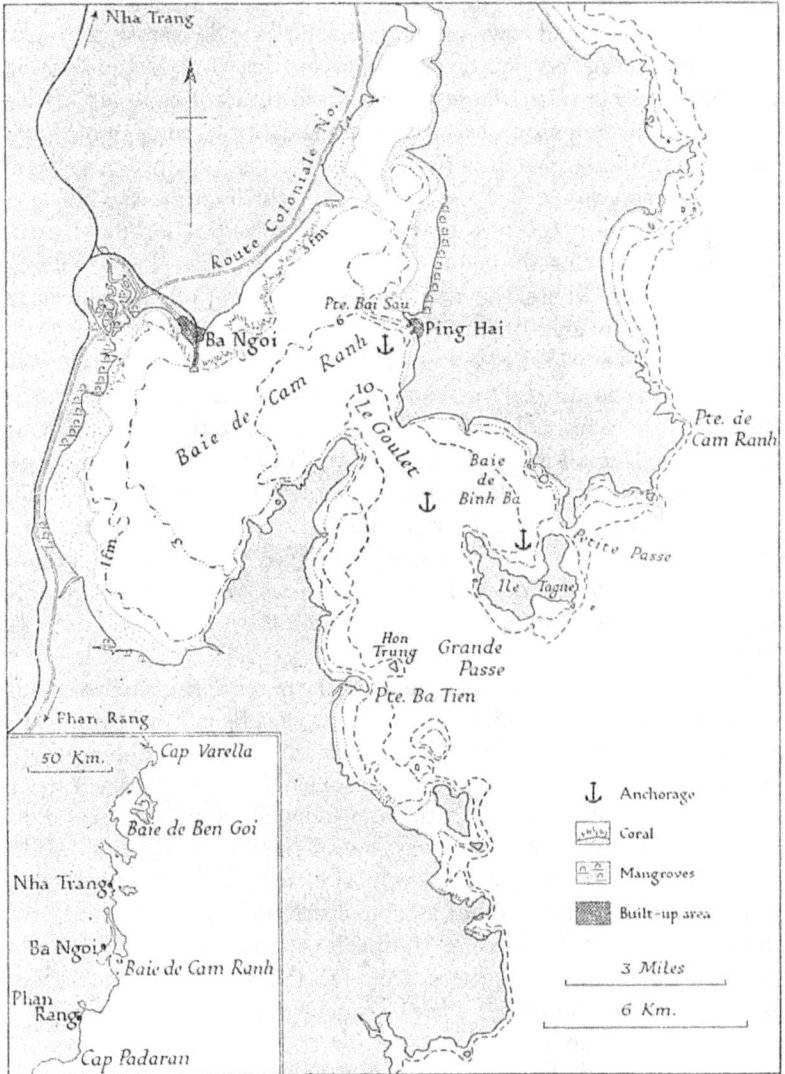

Fig. 130. Ba Ngoi and the Baie de Cam Ranh
Source: Admiralty.

nexions with the Hanoi-Saigon road (Route Coloniale no. 1) which runs round the western shores of the bay and passes through Ba Ngoi. In 1940 a road was under construction between Ba Ngoi and Ping Hai. A landing ground for aircraft is available near the town and there is also an anchorage for seaplanes in the bay.

PHAN RANG

Lat. 11° 32′ N, long. 109° 1′ E.   Population: no information.
Admiralty Chart 1261.   Fig. 131.

The port of Phan Rang in south Annam lies at the head of the bay of the same name, where the Song Kinh Dinh enters the sea. Phan Rang has developed as a port by reason of its proximity to the important health centre of Dalat on the Plateau du Lang Bian, to which

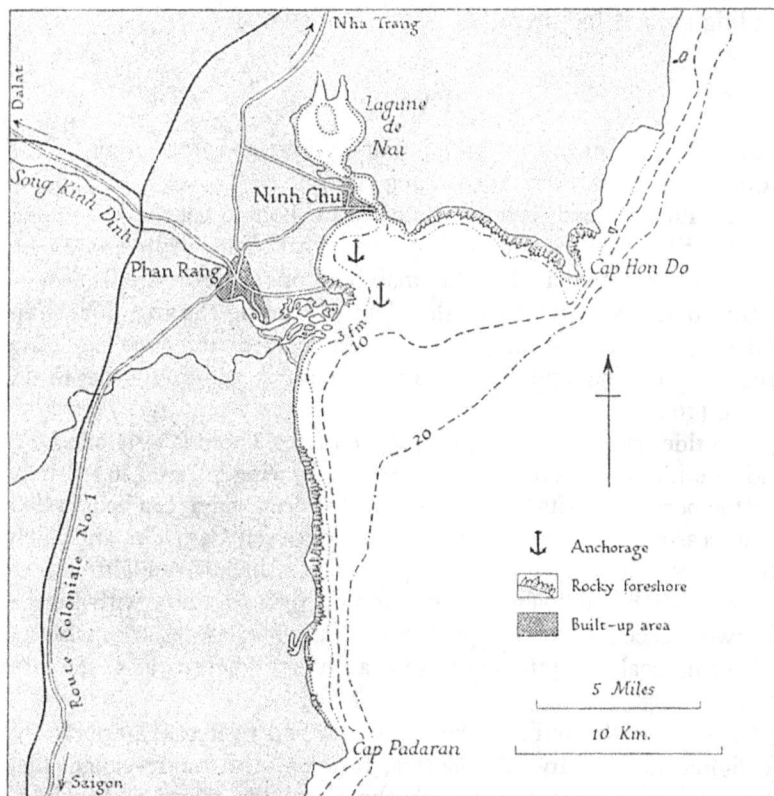

Fig. 131. Phan Rang
Source: (1) [Carte de l'Indochine] 1:100,000 [sheet 214] (1901); (2) Admiralty chart 1261 (1933, corrected to 1939).

it is connected by road and railway. Although the route from the coast is steep and difficult the movement of goods to and from Dalat can be carried out more economically through Phan Rang than by way of Saigon.

In the stretch of water between the mouth of the Song Kinh Dinh and the entrance to the Lagune de Nai there is secure anchorage in a depth of about 7·3 m. (4 fm.). Ninh Chu, at the entrance to the lagoon, has a jetty, but this is the only port construction available along the shores of the bay. Junks and lighters discharge cargo from ships moored in the bay. The total foreign trade of the port in 1938 amounted to 36,840 tons.

Phan Rang is linked by road with Ninh Chu, 7 km. to the north-east. The junction of the Trans-Indo-Chinese railway with the Dalat line lies at Tourcham, a short distance from the port. There is a landing ground for aircraft.

CAM PHA

Lat. 21° 02′ N, long. 107° 21′ E.   Population: no information.
Admiralty Charts 1169, 1965.   Fig. 132.

Cam Pha, a small port on the coast of Tonkin east of Hon Gay, is primarily an outlet for the important coal mines in its immediate hinterland. It is situated on the mainland opposite the Ile de Kebao at the southern extremity of the channel leading towards Tien Yen and is approached through the western part of the Fai Tsi Long archipelago. The approach channels have a minimum depth of 4·8 m. (16 ft.).

The tides rise from 2 to 3 m. (6½–10½ ft.). There is only one high and one low water every 24 hr. Vessels drawing 7·9 m. (26 ft.) may use the port and, as its harbour is well sheltered, cargo can be handled at all seasons of the year. The channel between Cam Pha and Tien Yen is accessible at high water to vessels of shallow draught.

The port has a coaling wharf, 300 m. (984 ft.) long with berths for two vessels. Four transporters on the wharf are each capable of delivering coal at a rate of 125 tons an hour. There is a satisfactory water supply.

Coal forms the bulk of the cargo shipped overseas; imports are negligible in quantity. An electric railway, with metre-gauge line, connects the coaling wharf with the Cam Pha mines, a few kilometres inland. A lightly metalled road runs along the coast from Cam Pha, north to Tien Yen and west to Hon Gay.

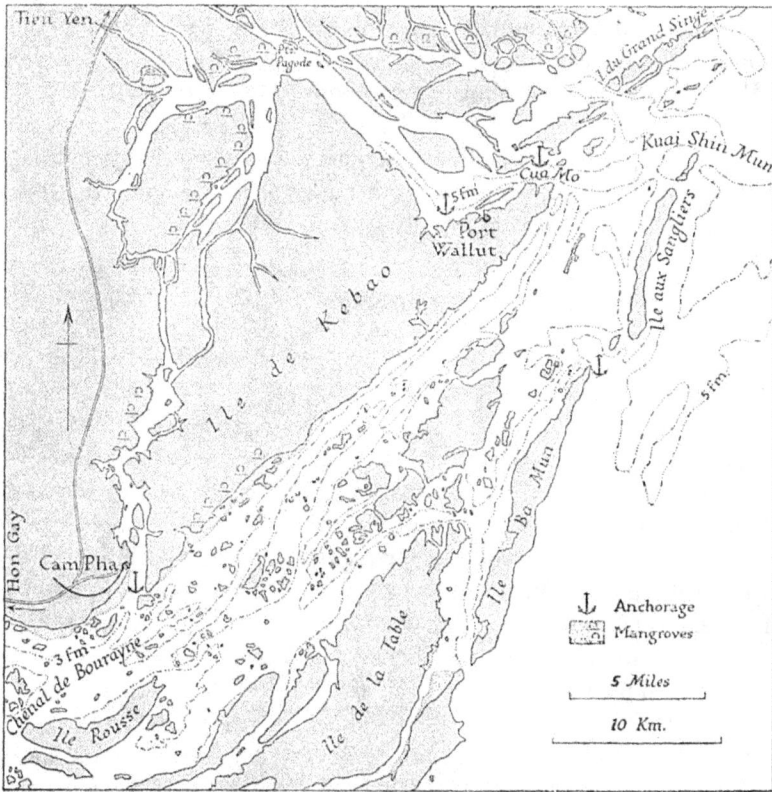

Fig. 132. Cam Pha and Port Wallut

Source: (1) Carte de l'Indochine, 1:100,000; sheets 40 and 51 (1925, 1921);
(2) Admiralty chart 1965 (1912, corrected to 1939).

PORT WALLUT

Lat. 21° 12′ N, long. 107° 33′ E.   Population: no information.
Admiralty Charts 776, 1965.   Fig. 132.

Port Wallut is situated on the north-eastern shores of the Ile de Kebao in Tonkin. It is approached from the sea by the channel known as Kuai Shin Mun, which lies between Ile aux Sangliers and the Ile du Grand Singe and which has a minimum depth of 9 m. (5 fm.). West of the Kuai Shin Mun, vessels proceed through the Cua Mo, then pass north and west of the Ile des Pirates. Near this island there is an anchorage in depths of 7·3–11·9 m. (4–6½ fm.), with good holding ground. There is also an anchorage in the narrow stretch of water between the island and the port, but the strength of the tidal streams and the lack of protection against winds and squalls make it insecure.

Port Wallut has a coaling wharf about 55 m. (180 ft.) in length with a depth of 8 m. (4⅓ fm.) alongside. Small repairs to vessels can be carried out. The trade of the port is almost entirely confined to the export of coal, obtained from mines on the island. In 1938, its foreign trade totalled 32,091 tons.

HONE COHE

Lat. 12° 35′ N, long. 109° 13′ E. Population: no information.
Admiralty Chart 1008. Fig. 133.

Hone Cohe is situated on the north-western shores of the Baie de Ben Goi in the rugged stretch of coast between Cap Varella and Cap Padaran. It owes its importance to the production of salt and of dried fish, while the neighbouring coastal plain, though small, grows agricultural commodities for export. The port is approached through the Baie de Van Fong where there are anchorages in depths of 11–22 m. (6–12 fm.). In the small bay on which Hone Cohe lies there is a secure and sheltered anchorage for small vessels in a depth of about 5·9 m. (3 fm.). The tidal rise varies from 0·5 m. (1·5 ft.) to 1·8 m. (6 ft.).

The port has two jetties, and a dredged channel permits large junks to go alongside the northerly one at all states of the tide. In 1938, the foreign trade of Hone Cohe amounted to 10,040 tons and the coastal trade in the same year to 21,800 tons.

Hone Cohe lies a few kilometres to the east of the Trans-Indo-Chinese railway and of the Route Coloniale no. 1. A lightly metalled road links the port with the main road. There is a seaplane anchorage at the port.

QUI NHON

Lat. 13° 46′ N, long. 109° 15′ E. Population: 10,000 (1936).
Admiralty Charts 264, 3874. Fig. 134. Plate 9.

Qui Nhon is a small port on the coast of Annam about 140 km. north of Cap Varella. It stands at the entrance to a shallow land-locked bay which is approached through a dredged channel having a depth of 5 m. (16½ ft.). Prominent hills flank the bay to the east and west. In the outer approaches there is an anchorage in depths

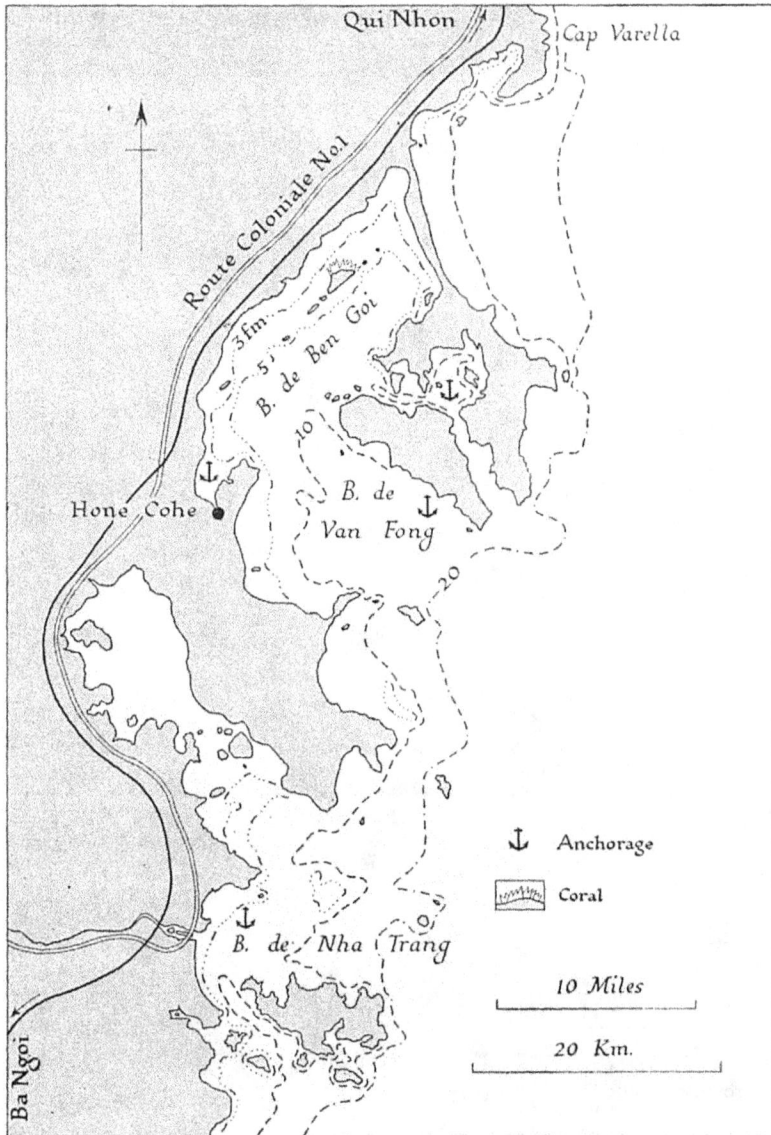

Fig. 133. Hone Cohe
Source: Admiralty chart 1008 (1905, corrected to 1940).

of 5·5–7·3 m. (3–4 fm.), with good holding ground about 7 cables south-east of Pointe Sud; within the bay, the best anchorage is in 11·5 m. (6⅓ fm.) well above the narrow entrance and east of the

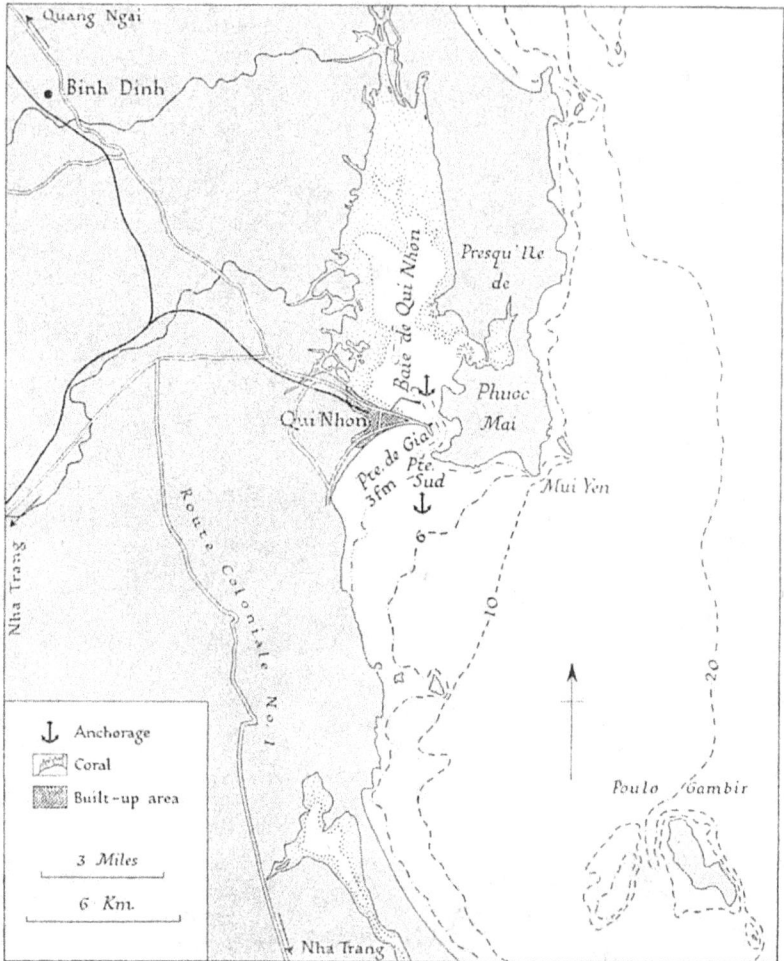

Fig. 134. Qui Nhon
Source: Admiralty chart 3874 (1940).

town. Apart from this deep-water anchorage, the whole of the bay is shallow; the town itself, which lies on a sandspit, is fronted by a shoal with depths of less than 1·8 m. (6 ft.). It is often difficult to enter the bay during the period of the north-east monsoon. There is a tidal rise of about 1·3 m. (4½ ft.) and the tidal streams set east-north-east and west-south-west at 1½–2 knots across the entrance to the bay. Qui Nhon can accommodate six ships of about 1,000 tons.

The port has a wharf, 640 m. (2,100 ft.) offshore and connected with the shore by a causeway. The wharf is 92 m. (300 ft.) long with a depth alongside of less than 1·8 m. (6 ft.). Near the Pointe de Gia is a small jetty with a berthing length of 18·3 m. (60 ft.) and a depth alongside of 3·5 m. (12 ft.). A mooring buoy lies about half a cable north-west of this jetty.

The discharge of cargo is made by lighters from ships anchored in the bay or in the outer anchorage. Harbour craft include a number of lighters and junks, with a total capacity of 1,000 tons, two tugs and a dredger. Some privately owned sheds serve as warehouses, but the accommodation is inadequate. Small repairs to ships can be made.

Qui Nhon serves the plateau regions of Plei Ku and Kontum and the coastal plain from Bong Son to Cap Varella. Its traffic totalled 21,390 tons in 1938, only 5,777 tons of which was foreign trade. The exports include rice, coconut oil, copra, dried fish, and ground-nuts; the imports are mainly goods for local consumption.

Qui Nhon is connected with the main railway and road which passes north-south along the coast of Annam. A branch railway line runs along the wharf and causeway to the north of the town. In the bay there is a seaplane anchorage.

MINOR PORTS

The following table gives short descriptions of the fifty-four minor ports of Indo-China which are mentioned in the *Tableau général du Commerce Extérieur de l'Indochine, 1938*, Table 79 (Hanoi, 1939). They are described in geographical order from north to south. For the trade figures of each port in 1938 see the table on p. 370.

Port	Remarks
TONKIN	
Mon Cay. Lat. 21° 62′ N, long. 107° 55′ E. Population 5,184 (1936)	Near the Chinese frontier on the left bank of the Song Ca Long (Cua Tam) about 10 km. from the sea. Can only be reached at high water. Safe anchorage at mouth of the river where vessels may await the tide. Regular coasting trade with Tien Yen, Port Wallut, Hon Gay, Quang Yen and Haiphong. Connected by road with Tien Yen and Hon Gay. Landing ground. Wireless station
Mui Ngoc (Ngoc San). Lat. 21° 26′ N, long. 107° 57′ E	At southerly extreme of the Ile de Traco, close to the mouth of the Song Ca Long. Vessels anchor near here before proceeding to Mon Cay

Port	Remarks
TONKIN (*contd.*)	
Ha Coi. Lat. 21° 27′ N, long 107° 44′ E	On a small river about 20 km. south-south-west of Mon Cay. Depth of under 2 m. (6½ ft.) in the approach. Population mainly Chinese. Metalled road to Mon Cay and Tien Yen
Cat Ba. Lat. 20° 43′ N, long. 107° 02′ E	Small settlement on the Baie d'Apowan along the southern shores of the rocky and densely wooded Ile Cat Ba. Anchorage in a depth of 7 m. (4 fm.) at entrance to bay, sheltered from the north-east, but open to the south-west monsoon. Stone jetty, available for boats at low water. Wireless station. Bay is frequented by numerous fishing boats
Quang Yen. Lat. 20° 57′ N, long. 106° 46′ E	Lies on the left bank of the Song Chang, a tributary of the Song Bach Dang (Cua Nam Trieu) about 15 km. north-east of Haiphong. Narrow channel with a depth of 2 m. (6½ ft.) has been dredged from the Song Bach Dang to the port. Anchorage in 6·9 m. (3¾ fm.). Jetty. Exports limestone obtained from local quarries. Zinc smelting plant. In communication by road with Hon Gay and Haiphong
Hanoi (see p. 473). Lat. 21° 02′ N, long. 105° 50′ E. Population 149,000 (1936)	On right bank of Fleuve Rouge about 160 km. from the sea (Fig. 144). Approached by way of the Lach Day and Canal de Phu Ly. In high-water season (May to October) vessels drawing 2·7 m. (9 ft.) can reach Hanoi, but at other times they cannot proceed beyond Phu Ly. Depth of 5·9 m. (3¼ fm.) in river off town. Wharves, with frontage of 823 m. (2,700 ft.) and four mooring berths. Handles forest and mineral products brought by boat from interior of Tonkin. Goods for export overseas sent to Haiphong. Large number of industries. Railway and road centre. Airport and seaplane station. Seat of the government of Indo-China
Diem Diem. Lat. 20° 34′ N, long. 106° 33′ E	Lies on shallow river about half-way between the Cua Thai Binh and the Cua Tra Ly. Shifting sandbanks offshore make it impracticable to shipping for the greater part of the year
Nam Dinh (see p. 475). Lat. 20° 26′ N, long 106° 10′ E. Population 25,347 (1936)	On the Canal de Nam Dinh which connects the Fleuve Rouge to the Song Day. Market town. Cotton mill. Railway and road centre. Landing ground
Phat Diem. Lat. 20° 4′ N, long. 106° 5′ E	About 10 km. from sea. On small stream flowing into the Song Day. Market for rice. Manufactures willow mats. Road communication with Ninh Binh, Hanoi and Thanh Hoa
ANNAM	
Lach Truong. Lat. 19° 53′ N, long. 105° 54′ E	On river known as the Lach Truong. Accessible at high water to vessels drawing 3·4 m. (11 ft.). Anchorage in 2·7 m. (9 ft.)
Thanh Hoa (see p. 476). Lat. 19° 48′ N, long. 105° 45′ E. Population 10,000 (1931)	On an arm of the Song Ma about 12 km. above its mouth. In centre of rich agricultural region. Market. Provincial capital. On the Trans-Indo-Chinese railway and the Route Coloniale no. 1. Landing ground

Port	Remarks
ANNAM (*contd.*)	
Ngoc Giap. Lat. 19° 37' N, long. 105° 47' E	On the Song Yen about 20 km. south of the Song Ma. Only accessible to small native boats. On Route Coloniale no. 1
Do Len	No information
Du Do. Lat. 19° 24' N, long. 105° 45' E	On the south bank of the Cua Bang. Accessible only to small boats
Phu Nghia. Lat. 19° 6' N, long. 105° 43' E	On the Lach Quen, a stream entering the sea south-west of Cap Falaise. Sheltered anchorage in depths of about 1 m. (3¼ ft.). Road running inland to join Route Coloniale no. 1
Thanh Son. Lat. 19° 5' N, long. 105° 41' E	On tributary of Lach Quen. Communicates by inland waterway with Thanh Hoa and Vinh
Van Phan. Lat. 19° 2' N, long. 105° 35' E	On same stream as Thanh Son. Approached from the sea either by way of Phu Nghia to the north or the Cua Vann to the south. Large junks can enter by the southern route. Traffic in a great variety of agricultural products
Thuong Xa. Lat. 18° 49' N, long. 105° 42' E	At mouth of shallow, winding river, known as the Song Lo, which enters the sea near Cap Ste Anne. Linked by road with Vinh
Ho Do. Lat. 18° 26' N, long. 105° 54' E	Lies on north bank of the Cua Sot, about 10 km. from the sea. Accessible to boats of 1·8 m. (6 ft.) draught. Port for town of Ha Tinh, with which it is in communication by water and by road
Tien Tri. Lat. 18° 16' N, long. 106° 4' E	On the Cua Nuong. Entrance channel narrow and obstructed by a bar. Accessible only to small boats of very shallow draught. Road inland to join the Route Coloniale no. 1
Quang Khe. Lat. 17° 43' N, long. 106° 38' E	On southern bank of the Song Giang near where it enters the sea. Anchorage in a depth of 11 m. (6 fm.). Traffic in timber and other forest products
Dong Hoi. Lat. 17° 29' N, long. 106° 37' E	Situated near mouth of Kien Giang. Approach difficult owing to tortuous channel. Trade in rice, maize, dried fish, and salt. Provincial capital. Railway and road to Hanoi and Hue. Landing ground
Lai An. Lat. 16° 33' N, long. 107° 34' E	On the Huong Giang or Rivière des Parfums about half-way between Hue and the sea. Accessible only during period of south-west monsoon. Approach channel encumbered with sandbanks and fishing stakes. Port for Hue, the capital of Annam. Trade in rice, groundnuts, fruits, silk and forest products
Faifoo. Lat. 15° 53' N, Long. 108° 18' E. Population 8,000 (1931)	Situated on the Song Thu Bon, 4 km. from the sea. Connected by inland waterways with Tourane. Metalled road to Quang Nam and Tourane. Large traffic in agricultural products of many kinds, and in coal obtained from mines of Nong Son. Provincial capital
Hiep Hoa. Lat. 15° 29' N, long. 107° 41' E	South of Cap An Hoa. Connected by inland water-ways with Tam Ky, Quang Nam and Tourane

Port	Remarks
ANNAM (*contd.*)	
Son Tra. Lat. 15° 24′ N, long. 108° 44′ E	Lies on Song Tra Bon where it enters the Baie de Dung Quat. Anchorage for vessels drawing 1·8 m. (6 ft.). Metalled road to Quang Ngai
Co Luy. Lat. 15° 10′ N, long. 108° 51′ E	On sandspit at mouth of Song Tra Khuc. Port for town of Quang Ngai. Large traffic in rice, sugar-cane, tobacco and cinnamon
Sa Huynh. Lat. 14° 40′ N, long. 109° 6′ E	At entrance to shallow lagoon. Trade in rice, coconuts and dried fish. Metalled road to Quang Ngai and Bong Son
Tam Quan. Lat. 14° 34′ N, long. 109° 3′ E	About 5 km. within entrance to Song Tam Quan. Accessible only to boats of very shallow draught. Trade in coconuts, areca nuts and dried fish
Degi. Lat. 14° 6′ N, long. 109° 11′ E	On southern side of narrow entrance to the Baie de Nuoc Ngot. Road running inland to join Route Coloniale no. 1
Cu Mong. Lat. 13° 32′ N, long. 109° 15′ E	At northern side of entrance to Baie de Cu Mong. Anchorage in a depth of 5 m. (2¾ fm.)
Xuan Day. Lat. 13° 23′ N, long. 109° 11′ E	On southern shore of bay of same name. Sheltered anchorage nearby in depths of from 8–9 m. (4½–5 fm.)
Le Uyen	No information
Dong Trach	No information
Nha Trang. Lat. 12° 16′ N, long. 109° 12′ E. Population 5,500 (1936)	At mouth of Song Cai which flows into the Baie de Nha Trang. Anchorage in a depth of 4¾ fm. (8·7 m.). Traffic in rice, cotton, cattle and swine. Provincial capital. Railway and road centre. Aerodrome
Duong. Lat. 11° 12′ N, long. 108° 39′ E. Population 3,589 (1936)	On Baie de Phan Ri. Small fishing port
Phan Ri Lat. 11° 12′ N, long. 108° 35′ E. Population 10,900 (1936)	Situated near mouth of Song Luy which enters the sea in the Baie de Phan Ri. Anchorage in bay in depths of from 7·3–9·1 m. (4–5 fm.), but the port is only accessible to boats drawing less than 1 m. (3¼ ft.). Trade mainly in dried and salted fish and in fish oil. On Route Coloniale no. 1
Mui Ne. Lat. 10° 55′ N, long. 108° 17′ E. Population 9,000 (1936)	At south extremity of low, wooded peninsula bordering the Baie de Phan Thiet to the north-east. Anchorage during north-east monsoon, in a depth of 6·4 m. (3½ fm.). Fishing port
Phan Thiet Lat. 10° 56′ N, long. 108° 5′ E. Population 15,500 (1936)	Situated at head of bay of same name. Anchorage in bay in a depth of about 7·8 m. (4 fm.). Large trade in dried and salted fish and in fish sauce (*nuoc mam*). Provincial capital. In communication by road and rail with Saigon. Landing ground
Lagi. Lat. 10° 39′ N, long. 107° 46′ E. Population 3,500 (1936)	At mouth of small river. Trade in dried and salted fish

Port	Remarks
COCHIN-CHINA.	
Cu My. Lat. 10° 35′ N, long. 107° 35′ E	Lies on coast about 10 km. north-east of Cap Ba Kiem. Large trade in dried and salted fish
My Tho Lat. 10° 22′ N, long. 106° 22′ E. Population 25,000 (1936)	On Cua Tieu, northernmost branch of the Mekong, about 40 km. above mouth. Entrance to river from sea obstructed by bar with a depth of slightly over 2 m. (6½ ft.). Off port itself there are depths of from 5·5–7·8 m. (3–4 fm.) T pier 45·8 m. (150 ft.) long with depth of 1·8 m. (6 ft.) at head. River is bunded for 457 m. (1,500 ft.). Floating sheerlegs. The *Compagnie des Messageries fluviales* own workshop and small dry dock. Trade in agricultural products, especially rice. Provincial capital. Connected by railway, road and canal with Saigon. Wireless station
Ca Mau. Lat. 9° 12′ N, long. 105° 10′ E	In centre of peninsula of same name. Communicates with sea by the Song Ganh Hao to the east and by the Song Ong Doc to the west. Accessible to small native craft. Trade in dried and salted fish. Road to Bac Lieu
Rach Gia. Lat. 10° 0′ N, long. 105° 4′ E	On bay of same name. Depths are less than 3·7 m. (12 ft.). Large trade in agricultural products, livestock and fish. Canal to Long Xuyen and the Mekong. Provincial capital
Hon Chong. Lat. 10° 9′ N, long. 10° 35′ E	On small bay to north of Cap de la Table. Anchorage in 3·7 m. (12 ft.). Pier. Important trade in pepper and agricultural products. Road to Ha Tien. Steamer service with Ha Tien, Kampot and Ile de Phu Quoc
Ha Tien. Lat. 10° 26′ N, long. 104° 28′ E	At mouth of Rach Giang Thanh. Anchorage. Large trade in agricultural products, especially pepper and dried and salted fish. Canal to Chau Doc on Mekong. Roads to Kampot, Phnom Penh and Rach Gia. Provincial capital
Duong Dong. Lat. 10° 14′ N, long. 103° 57′ E	Main town and port of Ile de Phu Quoc. On western side of island. Trade in dried and salted fish. Wireless station. Steamer communication with Ha Tien
CAMBODIA.	
Kep. Lat. 10° 28′ N, long. 104° 17′ E	On eastern side of prominent headland known as Pte Kep. Anchorage. Accessible only to boats of very shallow draught. Mole. Fishing port
Kampot. Lat. 10° 37′ N, long. 104° 9′ E. Population 5,530 (1936)	On small river entering the Baie de Kampot about 15 km. north-west of Pte Kep. May be approached at any state of tide, but difficult of access during the south-west monsoon. Quay. Important trade in pepper. Provincial capital. Road communication with Ream, Phnom Penh and Ha Tien. Seaplane anchorage
Ream. Lat. 10° 34′ N, long. 103° 37′ E	At entrance to bay of same name. Sheltered anchorage in depth of about 9 m. (5 fm.). Jetty. Roads to Kampot and Kompong Som. Seaplane anchorage
Snam Crabeu	No information
Ilôt Cône. Lat. 11° 20′ N, long. 102° 59′ E	On small island near the Siamese frontier. Anchorage. Two piers. Connected with mainland by stone causeway. Fishing port

Port	Remarks
CAMBODIA (*cont.*)	
Checko Lat. 10° 53′ N, long. 103° 22′ E.	A small fishing port
Phnom Penh (see p. 475). Lat. 11° 35′ N, long. 104° 55′ E. Population 103,000 (1936)	Capital of Cambodia. Situated about 250 km. from mouth of Mekong where the river divides into two branches (Fleuve Antérieur and Fleuve Postérieur) and where it receives the waters of the lake of Tonle Sap. Accessible to ships of from 4,000 to 6,000 tons. Quays and wharves. Trade in great variety of agricultural products, livestock and fish. Railway to Battambang and Sisophon. Roads to Saigon, Kampot, Battambang and Kratie. Aerodrome and seaplane anchorage. Wireless station.

BIBLIOGRAPHICAL NOTE

(1) *China Sea Pilot*, vol. I, 1st ed. 1937 (London, 1938), with Supplement no. 1, 1942. French *Instructions Nautiques: Mers de Chine*, vol. I, 1932 (Paris, 1933), with Supplement, 1940.

(2) A general account of the ports of Indo-China is found in C. Robequain, *L'Evolution économique de l'Indochine française* (Paris, 1939), in Georges Maspero, *Un Empire Colonial français: L'Indochine*, vol. II (Paris, 1929) and in *Les Ports autonomes de l'Indochine*, Exposition Coloniale Internationale, Paris, 1931 (Paris, 1931).

(3) The trade statistics for the ports appear in the *Tableau général du Commerce Extérieur de l'Indochine* which is published annually at Hanoi.

(4) The following articles contain much valuable information on particular ports:

P. Arqué, 'Le Port de Haiphong en 1932', *Revue de Géographie commerciale de Bordeaux*, vol. LVII, pp. 38–53 (Bordeaux, 1933); 'Le Port de Saigon', *Bulletin de la Société de Géographie de Havre*, pp. 37–42 (Havre, 1927); C. Bricka, 'Le Port de Saigon', *Revue du Pacifique*, vol. V, pp. 201–23 (Paris, 1926); M. Gillès, *Le Port d'Escale de Ganh Rai (Saigon)*, Congrès international des Sociétés de Géographie économique (Paris, 1938).

Chapter XVIII

ROADS

Introduction: Geographical Description: Traffic: Bibliographical Note

INTRODUCTION

Road development in Indo-China received little attention before the war of 1914–18. During the late nineteenth century several roads had indeed been constructed from Saigon, and French punitive expeditions in Tonkin had necessitated the driving of tracks across difficult mountains, but over the greater part of the country the railway was the chief means of land communication. As large loans for railway construction were no longer forthcoming with the outbreak of war, it became evident that the unity of Indo-China would be achieved more quickly and more easily by expansion or improvement of the road system. The 1913 loan was the first to allot credits to road building. From that time onwards, particularly after 1918, progress has been rapid and Indo-China now possesses one of the finest road systems in the Far East, comprising in 1939 some 35,636 km. (22,143 mls.).

Constant improvements have been made in road surface, so that to-day over 50% of the roads are well metalled. The metalled roads are from 5 to 6 m. broad except in the mountain regions where, for economical reasons, the width is generally reduced to $4\frac{1}{2}$ m. and sometimes even to 4 m. Most of the bridges measure $2\frac{1}{2}$–3 m. in width and allow only one car to cross at a time. The type of stone used as a road foundation varies according to the region, limestone being employed in south Tonkin, laterite in Cochin-China. As these materials wear away quickly, more resistant stones, granites, quartzites, porphyrites, have been laid down in the neighbourhood of the large cities where traffic is particularly heavy. Unfortunately, the quarries for such igneous rocks seldom lie close to the main centres of population and constructional costs tend to be prohibitive. Tar-macadam is the most common superficial covering, and in parts of Cochin-China, owing to the absence of stone, it forms the actual road foundation. Since the macadamized roads most frequently used by car and lorry require constant repair, the value of an asphalt surface has become more and more widely recognized. The greater proportion of the asphalt roads are to be found near the towns of south Tonkin and Cochin-China. Although more expensive than tar-macadam, there seems every reason to believe that an asphalt surface will be applied to an increasing number of roads in view of its ability to carry heavy traffic for an extended period.

The unmetalled roads in Indo-China are of three types: 'routes terrassées', 'routes non cylindrées', and seasonal tracks. 'Routes terrassées' are highways of rolled and broken stone found principally on steep hill slopes or very flat marshy areas; 'routes non cylindrées', as the name implies, are roads made up of coarse stone which has not been rolled. Finally, many seasonal tracks penetrate the most difficult parts of the country. Very often they have a width of only 3 m., and severe gradients are frequently encountered; the bridges are temporary structures of wood or even bamboo. These tracks give access by motor car, during the dry season, to regions not yet served by the road proper; they are particularly numerous in the plateaux of Tonkin and eastern Cambodia.

The table below gives the total length (in km.) of metalled and unmetalled roads in each state (1939):

	Tonkin	Annam	Cochin-China	Cambodia	Laos	Total
Asphalt roads	1,275	785	1,586	545	22	4,213
Macadamized roads	2,645	3,200	4,565	2,245	1,455	14,110
'Routes terrassées'	1,854	2,961	1,569	377	1,515	8,276
'Routes non cylindrées'	—	452	—	—	196	648
Seasonal tracks	2,519	1,854	1,394	2,440	182	8,389
Total	8,293	9,252	9,114	5,607	3,370	35,636

Based on official sources.

For the purpose of administration the roads of Indo-China are classed into two categories, 'routes coloniales', financed out of the national budget, and 'routes locales', the charge of the local administration. The 'routes coloniales' total twenty-one (c. 9,000 km.) and each has its own road number (Fig. 135).

GEOGRAPHICAL DESCRIPTION

The road pattern is simple. One important line of communication connects Tonkin and Cochin-China, keeping near to the coast the

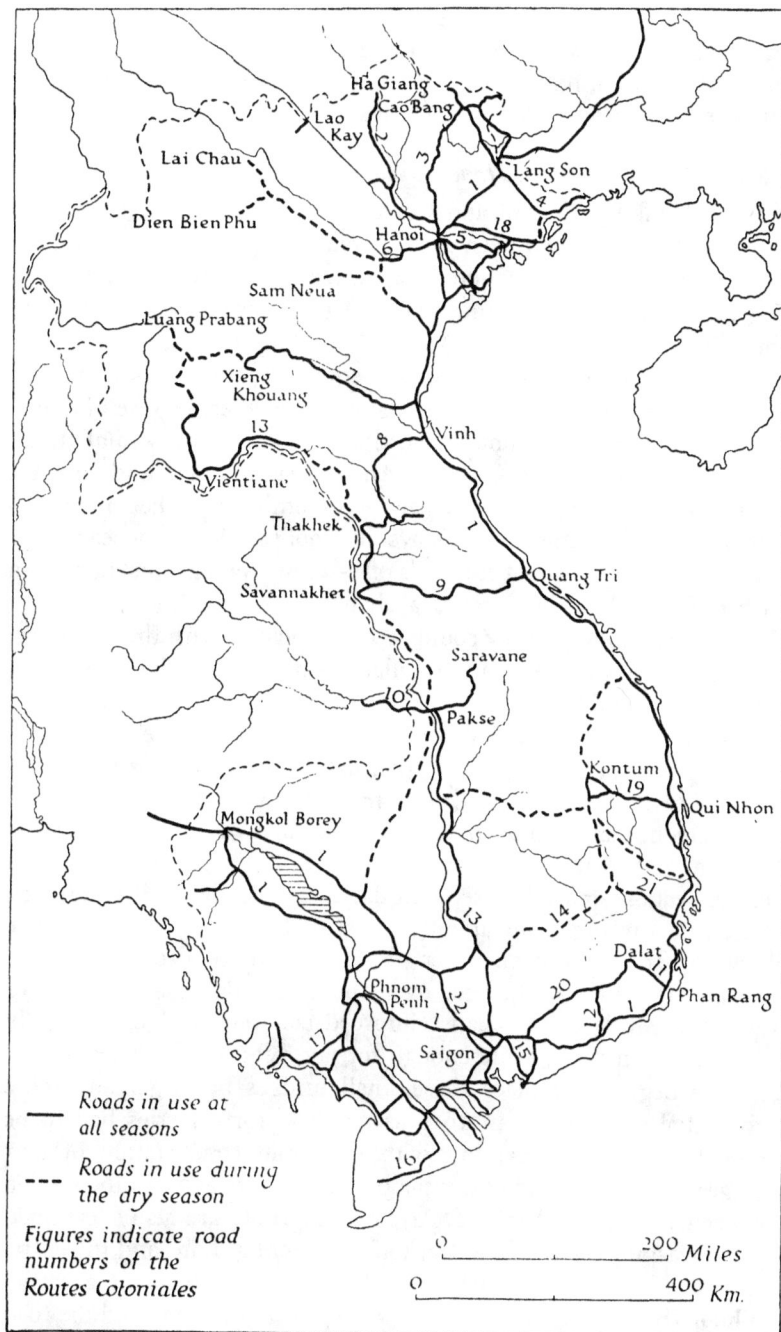

Fig. 135. The Routes Coloniales and other main roads
Source: Réseau routier de l'Indochine, 1 : 2,000,000 (1938).

whole way. A network of other routes spreads fanwise from Hanoi and Saigon, the two chief centres of population in the north and south of Indo-China respectively; and finally, many roads reach far into the little-known plateaux of Laos.

'Route Mandarine' from Hanoi to Saigon

A road linking Tonkin and Cochin-China, commonly called the 'route mandarine', had been constructed by the emperors of Annam before the French occupation. Traffic was, however, very restricted, and few people made journeys beyond their own locality, owing to the generally bad state of the road and the physical difficulties to be overcome. Avalanches of stones frequently blocked the way in certain mountainous areas, while the numerous ferries often became impassable during or immediately after periods of heavy rainfall. In many places along the coast of Annam sand dunes and beaches offered additional obstacles. Wealthy Annamites travelled in palanquins or chairs drawn by relays of coolies. Rest-houses called *trams* were established at intervals of 2–2½ hr. walking distance from each other, and at these *trams* a change in coolies took place. In this manner a long journey could be accomplished with the minimum of delay. This service was particularly well developed between the capital, Hue, and Tourane.

Even as recently as 1913 motor cars could use the 'route mandarine' in only a few sections, but since that date enormous sums have been devoted to its improvement. The modern road which links Hanoi with Saigon, part of the Route Coloniale no. 1 running between the Chinese and Siamese frontiers, is generally well metalled, with certain sections macadamized. In flat coastal lowlands it is terraced at heights varying from about 2 to 5 m. Several bridges measure between 200 and 500 m. in length, and some are also used by the railway; the longest bridge, over the Song Ba, has a length of 1,300 m. Most of the small reinforced concrete bridges are badly constructed and only wide enough for one vehicle; the French have recently begun to replace these small bridges by larger and more substantial structures. In 1918 as many as forty ferries had to be crossed in this journey, but with the rapid construction of new bridges only five ferries now remain. All five ferries lie in the section between Hanoi and Vinh. Delays on this route are also occasioned by the washing away of the track after torrential rain, and in central Annam this frequently happens during the passage of a severe typhoon (September–November). Except when so damaged the road

Plate 59. The Route Coloniale no. 1 near Thanh Hoa

View taken looking east. The broad river in the middle distance is the Song Ma. Thanh Hoa lies off the picture to the right.

Plate 60. Road and railway bridge to the east of Saigon

The bridge is carrying the Route Coloniale no. 1 and Trans-Indo-Chinese railway from Saigon to Hanoi.

Plate 61. Frontier bridge at Mon Cay

This bridge links Mon Cay (on the left) with Tong Hinh in China.

may be used throughout the year. Although many long and straight sections permit a fast motor traffic, the track throughout is narrow, and when passing, vehicles must slow down to a crawl. The journey by road from Hanoi to Saigon can be accomplished in two days, but three is more normal (Plate 59).

The road from Hanoi to Saigon has played an important role in national unification, linking the north and south of the country. It follows a course generally parallel with the railway except in the sections Phu Ly to Ninh Binh, Vinh to Badon (near Dong Hoi), Qui Nhon to a little south of Song Cau, and Phan Thiet to Xuan Loc. Despite the vulnerability from sea attack and the traffic dislocation brought about by typhoons the coastal road seems likely to remain the chief artery of Indo-China. The two largest centres of population are connected by this route which also passes through the intensively cultivated, densely peopled lowland of Annam. The road has greatly reduced the danger of famine.

Roads of North Indo-China

The Fleuve Rouge delta has a well-developed road network centred on Hanoi. Most of the roads keep to the numerous protecting dykes or embankments. Hanoi is connected with Haiphong by the Route Coloniale no. 5; this is terraced to an average height of 2 m. and almost entirely macadamized. By fast driving the distance can be covered in $1\frac{1}{2}$ hr., but owing to the narrowness of the road, accidents occur frequently. A little farther north, Route Coloniale no. 18 links Hanoi with Hon Gay and runs almost parallel to Route Coloniale no. 5. This road is not well maintained, and three ferries delay fast motor traffic.

Apart from these roads and the Route Coloniale no. 1 many others branch from Hanoi to centres in the delta. As in most parts of Indo-China bridges here carry both road and rail. The Pont Doumer, which crosses the Fleuve Rouge near Hanoi, is a traffic bottleneck and sometimes takes up to 10 min. to cross (Plate 64).

Hanoi is also a centre for roads penetrating the mountains and plateaux of Tonkin. The wealthy natural resources, particularly in minerals and forests, stimulated this development, while recent Chinese demands for war supplies have led to many improvements of road surface. Along the littoral the Hanoi to Hon Gay road has been extended to Tien Yen, but some stretches are very muddy and much metalling needs to be done. Another road extends to Lang Son and the Porte de Chine with branches along a north-west to south-

east structural depression to Tien Yen in the south and Cao Bang in
the north. The part between Tien Yen and Lang Son may be used
at all seasons and is well maintained; from Lang Son to Cao Bang
the road, though of good surface, has no great width. This road
running parallel with the Chinese frontier is part of a proposed major
line of communication from Mon Cay on the Tonkin coast to Luang
Prabang in north Laos via Ha Giang, Lao Kay and Lai Chau. Short
sections have been completed to the north-west of Cao Bang and
near Lao Kay. Cao Bang is also linked with Hanoi by a more direct
road which first crosses a broad undulating plateau, then, after passing
over a rugged mountain chain, turns south along a narrow depression to reach the plain of the Fleuve Rouge near Thai Nguyen.
A fourth road, along the valley of the Rivière Claire, connects Hanoi
with Ha Giang; it is in fairly good condition throughout the year,
though occasionally it becomes unserviceable during the rainy season.
Finally, west of the Fleuve Rouge a narrow road, usable for only part
of the year, runs from Hanoi to Son La and Lai Chau with a branch
to the important town of Dien Bien Phu. Beyond Hoa Binh the road
avoids the precipitous Rivière Noire valley and follows a course over
the limestone plateau immediately to the south-west.

Roads of South Indo-China

From Saigon a complex system of roads radiates over the lowlying
lands of the Mekong delta. This network was well established as early
as 1913, and since then has been continually extended farther west.
One road stretches from Saigon to Bien Hoa and Cap Saint Jacques
(Route Coloniale no. 15), another to Can Tho and Rach Gia, another
to Bac Lieu and Ca Mau. The broad arms of the Mekong are rapidly
crossed by large and efficiently handled motor ferries. Owing to
tidal inundations motor traffic cannot proceed south of Ca Mau.

Roads also extend from the Mekong delta far into the interior of
the country. Cochin-China is linked with the level Cambodian plain
surrounding Phnom Penh by way of Kompong Cham in the north
and Chau Doc in the south. The most direct road between Saigon
and Phnom Penh runs through Soai Rieng, north of the ill-drained
Plaine des Joncs. Traffic on this road tends to be heavy, as some of
the produce brought by rail to Phnom Penh is transferred to motor
vehicles for carriage to Saigon. North-west of Phnom Penh there are
two main roads passing respectively to the north and south of the
Tonle Sap lake. The northern branch via Kompong Thom and Siem
Reap has a straight course permitting fast motor traffic; the other

Plate 63. The Route Coloniale no. 13 at Thakhek

The Route Coloniale No. 13 links Saigon with Luang Prabang. It is here n (in the middle di tance) passing through Thakhek a small town on the left bank of the Mekong (in the left foreground).

Plate 62. The Route Coloniale no. 7 in northern Laos

This road runs between Vinh on the coast of Annam and Xieng Khouang on the Plateau du Tran Ninh. The photograph shows the road passing through a mixed oak and pine forest which is a common form of vegetation at heights above 1,000 m. in this part of Indo-China.

route through Kompong Chhnang and Battambang is slower though more heavily metalled. The two roads join at Sisophon, and beyond here to the pre-1941 Siamese frontier the track is rough and inadequately metalled but capable of dealing with the small and unimportant traffic.

Since 1918 large sums have been expended on the construction of roads from Cochin-China across the southern plateaux of Annam. Route Coloniale no. 20, a metalled road suitable for fast motor traffic, runs between Saigon and Dalat. Another route has now been completed (June 1941) from Saigon to Quang Nam, by way of Loc Ninh, Ban Me Thuot and Kontum, which crosses the fertile 'red soil' areas of Annam and provides an alternative means of communication to the route along the coast. This central route branches off Route Coloniale no. 13 (see p. 416) at Loc Ninh and has a good metal surface as far as Sre Khtum, but from here to Ban Me Thuot and Plei Ku it is little more than a track and open for vehicles only in the dry season. The short section between Plei Ku and Kontum 50 km.) has been metalled, but the road again degenerates into a badly kept track in the final mountainous stretch to Quang Nam. Two all-weather routes, Kontum to Qui Nhon and Ban Me Thuot to Ninh Hoa, extend to the Annam coast from this central line of communication; several bus services carrying passengers and merchandise ply on these routes.

Roads of Laos

Road construction has played an important part in the opening up of Laos. Owing to its physical isolation from the chief economic centres of Indo-China, Laos has tended to become orientated towards Siam and roads have been constructed from the east and south as a counter-measure to this natural orientation. Where the mountain chain is narrowest several roads link the China Sea coast with the middle Mekong valley. The easiest route (Route Coloniale no. 9), metalled and practicable throughout the year, links Quang Tri with Savannakhet across the Col d'Ai Lao (410 m.) and the basin of the upper Se Bang Hieng. A second road runs from Vinh to Thakhek by way of Nape following a more difficult though slightly shorter course than Route Coloniale no. 9. After leaving Vinh, it passes along the Ngan Pho valley, then climbs steeply to the major watershed (715 m.), descending almost equally rapidly into the broad Nam Ca Dinh basin where the track turns south-south-east to the Se Bang Fay. In the Se Bang Fay valley the track from Vinh joins a third east-west road which has been constructed between Ban Na Phao and Thakhek.

In north Laos, development of communications proved more difficult than farther south owing to the greater breadth and higher average elevation of the mountain chains. However, the French have constructed roads linking the three important towns of Xieng Khouang, Luang Prabang and Vientiane to the lowlands of Annam and Tonkin. Route Coloniale no. 7 branches from the 'route mandarine' near Vinh and passes north-north-west along the Song Ca valley to reach Xieng Khouang on the Plateau du Tran Ninh by a somewhat circuitous and difficult route. This road is well metalled (Plate 62) and serviceable at all seasons. Beyond Xieng Khouang, tracks extend over rather inhospitable country to join the section of Route Coloniale no. 13 running between Vientiane and Luang Prabang.

Route Coloniale no. 13 or Route René Robin, completed in March 1942, is the most important of all the roads entering Laos. It has a length of about 1,500 km. (932 miles) and extends from Saigon to Luang Prabang by way of Loc Ninh, Kratie, Pakse, Thakhek and Vientiane. The sections Pakse to Savannakhet, Thakhek to Pak Sane, and Vang Vieng to Luang Prabang are practicable only in the dry season. The construction of this new highway was encouraged by the poor navigability of the Mekong; the journey from Saigon to Pakse takes 6 days by water, but only about 12 hr. by road. Critics of the Route Coloniale no. 13 alleged that freight costs from north Laos would be prohibitive except for the richest merchandise and so compel the Laotian producer to use the Siamese railways to the detriment of French commercial houses in Saigon. Whether or not this view is justified there seems little doubt that the Route Coloniale no. 13 will contribute largely to the settlement and economic development of Laos. (Plate 63.)

TRAFFIC

The phenomenal expansion of the road system since 1913 has been accompanied by a corresponding expansion in the number of motor vehicles. Motor vehicles in Indo-China have increased from a little more than 350 in 1913 to 5,663 in 1923 and to about 20,000 in 1936. Traffic is greatest in Tonkin and Cochin-China, particularly in the neighbourhood of Hanoi and Saigon. A recent census reports a daily average of 700 motor vehicles in both directions across the Pont Doumer, 2 km. to the east of Hanoi. Most of the private cars belong to Europeans, Chinese, and the more well-to-do Annamites. Omnibus services operate in the principal towns, and natives use this method of conveyance to an ever-increasing extent. Some services combine with the railways. Thus the traveller from Saigon to Bangkok first goes by bus to Phnom Penh, then takes the train to Mongkol Borey from which station another omnibus service completes the journey to the Siamese railhead at Muong Aran Pradhet. Other bus services run from Na Cham to Cao Bang, from Xom Cuc to Thakhek, from Ban Na Phao to Thakhek, and from Dong Ha to Savannakhet. In addition to motor vehicles, the bicycle has also become increasingly popular in the towns, particularly those of Cochin-China and Cambodia.

Other means of transport still remain important despite the advent of the motor car, lorry, omnibus and bicycle. The elephant continues to be used in the mountains of west Cambodia, in the Plateau du Darlac and in south Laos, but the number of domesticated elephants in the whole country does not exceed 2,000. Over the greater part of Indo-China, more especially in the south, carts drawn by oxen or horses are commonly seen; in Cochin-China, the bullock carts only carry merchandise, whilst the natives themselves crowd into the small horse-drawn vehicles picturesquely called 'boîtes d'allumettes'. In north Tonkin horses and mules are frequently employed as beasts of burden. Finally, along many difficult mountain pathways natives carry goods either on their back or tied to bamboo sticks resting on the shoulders of two men. In the towns a large number of natives draw hand-chairs and push rickshaws as part of their livelihood. These primitive means of transport are becoming progressively less important with road development in the interior and with the increase of motor vehicles in the towns.

BIBLIOGRAPHICAL NOTE

(1) There is no detailed account either in French or English of the roads of Indo-China. The best short survey is A. Pouyanne, 'Les Travaux publics en Indochine', *Bulletin économique de l'Indochine*, vol. XXIX, pp. 463–500 (Hanoi, 1926).

(2) For an account of certain of the roads in Annam and Laos see J. Brunhes, 'Les routes nouvelles de l'Annam au Laos', *Annales de Géographie*, vol. XXXII, pp. 426–50 (Paris, 1923).

(3) The most useful map is the *Carte du Réseau routier de l'Indochine* (Hanoi, 1938).

Chapter XIX

RAILWAYS

Indo-China has only 2,908 km.* (1,817 miles) of railways, representing 0·4 km. of track for 100 sq. km. of surface (cf. Malaya 1·4 km., British India 1·8 km.) or 1·3 km. to 10,000 inhabitants (cf. Malaya 7·6 km., British India 2·0 km.). There is no complex line network, a notable feature being the scarcity of branch and inter-connecting lines.

HISTORY

Until the close of the nineteenth century the government had no extensive plan for railway organization. The first railway in Indo-China was built between 1881 and 1885 to connect the port of Saigon with My Tho on an arm of the Mekong (Fig. 136). This line was to be part of a system extending to Vinh Long, Soc Trang and Phnom Penh; but the extensions have never been completed. In 1890 work began on a second line from Phu Lang Thuong in the north of the Tonkin delta to Lang Son near the Chinese frontier. It was designed to facilitate the provisioning of troops during the French conquest of north Tonkin. Labour proved hard to obtain and bandits regularly carried off Europeans for ransom. The line, only 101 km. long, took 5 years to build and cost 20,000,000 francs.

1898–1914. The year 1898 opened an important new stage in the history of the railway. During this year the French Parliament made a loan of 200 million francs towards the improvement of communications in Indo-China, and Governor-General Doumer formulated a programme of railway construction. Doumer's programme envisaged the creation of four major routes: a line from Haiphong to Lao Kay and Yunnanfou (Kunming); another along the coast to connect Hanoi with Saigon; a third linking the Mekong with the coast of Annam, to give Laos an outlet to the sea; and, finally, Saigon was to be joined through Phnom Penh to the Siamese network. When finished, the length of these lines would total about 3,300 km. Although over 40 years have elapsed since the inauguration of this scheme, the Laotian and Cambodian lines still remain to be completed.

* 3,372 km. if the Chinese section of the Yunnan railway is included.

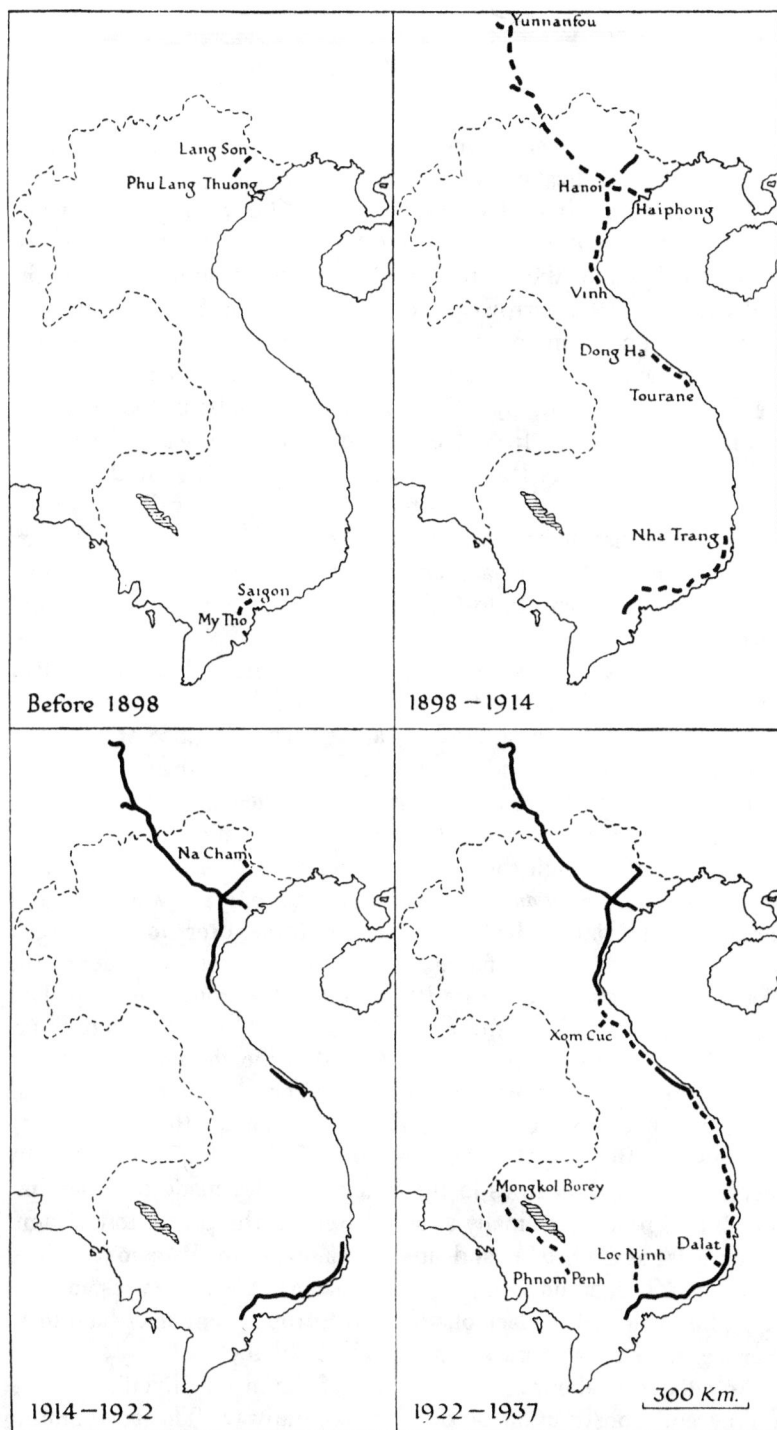

Fig. 136. The historical development of the railway system

The broken lines indicate railways under construction in each period. The continuous lines represent railways completed by the beginning of each period.

27-2

Of all the railway lines projected by Paul Doumer, the Trans-Indo-Chinese line from Hanoi to Saigon was considered the most essential. Its realization would strengthen the political unity of Indo-China, permit exchange of products between geographically diverse zones, and facilitate emigration from Tonkin to the less populated lands of the south. The first work accomplished was the replacement of the narrow-gauge line from Lang Son to Phu Lang Thuong by one of metre gauge and its prolongation as far as Hanoi following the construction (1902) of the famous Doumer bridge over the Fleuve Rouge. In 1905 the line reached Vinh; in the next year another section north from Hue to Tourane was opened for traffic, and extended 3 years later to Quang Tri, at the foot of the Col d' Ai Lao, the easiest routeway to the middle Mekong valley. Finally, the French constructed a third section of the railway round the coast from Saigon, reaching Nha Trang in 1913 (Fig. 136). The remaining sections of the Trans-Indo-Chinese line were not completed until 1936.

The Haiphong-Yunnanfou (Kunming) line, which took over 10 years to build, is one of the most remarkable feats of railway engineering. On Chinese territory alone there are 3,628 engineering works, including 107 bridges or viaducts of more than 20 m. span and 172 tunnels. In 1897 the French obtained a concession from the Chinese government to construct this line, and a company was formed to put through the project (*Compagnie française des Chemins de fer de l'Indochine et du Yunnan*). A private company was necessary, for part of the railway had to be built on foreign territory. By 1903 the line had been built as far as Viet Tri, at the western border of the Tonkin delta; and three years later reached the frontier town of Lao Kay. Beyond Lao Kay, the engineering difficulties were enormous. The Chinese concession provided that the line should run through or near the rich tin-mining centre of Mengtsz. At first a course was surveyed along the upper Fleuve Rouge to Manhao, thence following a tributary valley to Mengtsz and so to Yunnanfou. Exceptionally severe physical difficulties in the Sinchien valley made this plan impossible. The course finally adopted follows the precipitous Namti valley as far as Chih-ts'un and later the valleys of the Pata ho (Si Kiang basin) and Tachan ho (Yangtze Kiang basin). The survey lasted until 1905, but owing to the lack of sufficient European engineers and foremen constructional work did not begin until 1906.

An adequate labour supply was one of the major difficulties in the survey and construction of the Yunnan railway. The surrounding country had few inhabitants, and coolies had to be imported from Tonkin, Annam, and several provinces of China. Many hundreds of coolies deserted either on the journey or shortly after beginning work. A former engineer of the Peking-Hankow railway suggested that 12,000 coolies who were accustomed to railway construction should be brought from Tientsin. About 6,000 of these arrived, but a large number went on strike when it was decided to blast tunnels in the Namti valley; they had deep-rooted superstitions and feared the anger of the 'rock demons'. In March 1905 only 2,500 were left; a serious epidemic carried off 800 of their total, and the remainder started to walk home through China to Tientsin. Cantonese and Annamites were then tried but with little success. The total number of coolies hired was 80,000. It has been estimated that as many as 30 % of the coolies died; while forty out of the 300 Europeans engaged also lost their lives. Despite chronic labour difficulties and severe physical obstacles the line was completed to Yunnanfou in April 1910.

Thus at the outbreak of the war of 1914–18, with three completed sections of the Trans-Indo-Chinese line and with the Yunnan line open for traffic, 2,012 km. had been constructed of Paul Doumer's original programme.

1914–1922. During the war, and until 1922, little progress was made; Indo-China found it almost impossible to obtain either the necessary materials or financial support. The only line built in these years was that from Lang Son to Na Cham near the Chinese frontier, a distance of only 52 km.

1922–1937. After 1922, new loans from the French Government brought about a revival in railway construction. Post-war economic prosperity gave an added impetus to this revival. In 1927 the northern and central sections of the Trans-Indo-Chinese line were linked with the opening of the route from Vinh to Dong Ha. There remained the difficult 534 km. between Tourane and Nha Trang; French engineers successfully overcame the many physical obstacles and completed the section in 1936. A railway connexion between Hanoi and Saigon was thus finally achieved 38 years after the formulation of the Doumer programme. The course followed by this line has been frequently criticized. Its route along the coast invites competition from both road and sea communications. Moreover, it passes through regions greatly exposed to floods and typhoons. During summer, the line in central Annam is frequently cut by flood waters, while in early winter a succession of typhoons often causes extensive damage. A line from Saigon to Hue farther inland would avoid these inconveniences, but its construction would be extremely costly and economically unprofitable at the present stage of development.

The penetration of the interior did not progress very rapidly during the post-war period. In 1933 a branch line from Tourcham (Phan Rang) reached Dalat, a health and residential centre on the Plateau du Lang Bian. Fear lest Siam would tap the resources of Cambodia and Laos encouraged the French to construct new lines. Phnom Penh was linked with Mongkol Borey (1935), a town near the pre-1941 frontier; the line from Phnom Penh to Saigon still remains to be accomplished. Another short line has been built (1933) from Bendongxo* to Loc Ninh, in the centre of a rich forest zone, as part of a projected route north to Kontum. Finally, the French have surveyed the whole course of a proposed line between Tanap and Thakhek which, when completed, will give Laos an outlet to the sea. Only 20 km., Tanap to Xom Cuc, have so far been opened for traffic; monetary difficulties have effectively prevented any further extension of the line (Fig. 137).

Government control of the Indo-Chinese railways has enabled them to be built when no private company would run the risk of a serious financial loss. Receipts now slightly exceed expenditure, but the profits still cannot compare with those earned by the railways of Siam, Java, and Malaya. Indo-Chinese railways, with the exception of the Yunnan line, suffer from the lack of a profitable freight traffic, while all the lines have very high running expenses. Competition from other means of transport has further hindered the success of the railway. Road development in the post-1918 period and the ever-increasing use made of the roads encouraged a reduction in railway rates; fourth class passengers to-day pay about a third of what fares cost in 1925, and approximately half of the 1931 prices. By an agreement in 1935 the two transport systems agreed to enter into co-operation as the only means to end a cut-throat rivalry harmful to the national interests. Economic considerations must play a far larger part in any future railway network than has hitherto been the case. Indo-China is in urgent need of a well-planned series of branch lines to the more populous centres; and in the interior railway expansion should proceed hand in hand with economic development.

---

* Bendongxo is linked to Saigon by a tramway.

Fig. 137. The railway system in 1937

Source: C. Robequain, *L'Evolution économique de l'Indochine française*, folding map (Paris, 1939).

STATE RAILWAYS

The state railways of Indo-China include all the lines constructed in
the country with the exception of the line from Haiphong to Yunnanfou. All lines of the state railway system are of metre gauge with rails
20–30 kg. per metre in weight, and 8–12 m. in length. Sleepers are
sometimes metal and sometimes wood. The metal sleepers, almost
invariably of French or German manufacture, usually weigh about
40 kg.; wooden sleepers (impregnated against white ants) are most
frequently used where the line runs along the sea coast, for a saline
atmosphere is believed to injure those made of metal. Few curves
have a radius less than 400 m., the minimum radius on the Na Cham -
My Tho line being 300 m. The steepest gradient is 1 : 100. The lines
are single track throughout, but all stations have double track or
sidings designed to hold 7, 10, 12, 15 or more wagons varying in size
and number according to the importance of the station. Most of the
stations can accommodate trains 280–300 m. in length.

In December 1937, rolling stock in operation on this system comprised the following units: 53 tank locomotives, 195 tender locomotives, 6 self-propelled cars, 2,059 goods wagons (including 191 tank
wagons) and 438 passenger coaches. The new locomotives (15) which
have arrived in Indo-China for the Hanoi - Saigon route are of the
Pacific (4–6–2) type and can draw a passenger train of 250 tons at the
maximum speed allowed on the line (90 km. per hr.). During 1938
orders were placed for 22 sleeping and dining cars all of which were
to be air-conditioned. The locomotives burn locally mined coal, but
in the south some wood is used. Railway workshops have been set
up at Truong Thi, Hanoi, Vinh, Tourane, Nha Trang and Saigon.

The journey from Hanoi to Saigon takes 42 hr. and express trains
run daily between these two centres. These express trains cover the
distance at an average speed of 43 km. per hr.; over the newly opened
and difficult section from Quang Ngai to Nha Trang the trains average
less than 30 km. per hr. The capacity of the line is only 6 trains in
each direction every 24 hr. Micheline Diesel rail cars, holding 36
passengers, are widely used for local services; they run between Saigon
and My Tho, Saigon and Bien Hoa, Hanoi and Phu Lang Thuong,
Hanoi and Nam Dinh.

Hanoi to Na Cham (179 km.)

After leaving Hanoi, the line as far as Kep (67 km.) crosses an almost
completely level plain, densely peopled and intensively cultivated

Plate 64. Hanoi: the Pont Doumer

The Pont Doumer, which spans the Fleuve Rouge at Hanoi, is the longest bridge in the Far East, with a length of 1,700 m. It carries both railway and road traffic converging on Hanoi from the north and east. The photograph was taken during the low-water season of the Fleuve Rouge.

Plate 65. Hanoi: the railway station

From Hanoi, railway lines run to Yunnanfou (Kunming), to the Chinese frontier near Lang Son, to Haiphong and to Saigon.

Plate 66. The railway station at Qui Nhon

Qui Nhon, a small port on the coast of Annam, is connected by a short branch line with the main Trans-Indo-Chinese line from Hanoi to Saigon.

with rice. In this section the railway and the Route Coloniale no. 1 run parallel with each other, but beyond Kep they diverge, railway and road being separated by the valley of the Song Thuong. North-east of Kep the line enters a region of very different aspect from that of the delta. The countryside becomes undulating, forested, and scantily peopled; military fortifications in the form of blockhouses overlook the track, especially near Cau Son and Phu Vi stations. Further, the course followed is more winding and of more severe gradient than in the plain. Between Bac Le and Lang Giai (125 km.) the track continues to follow the Song Thuong valley, here slightly broader than in its lower course. To the north-west rises the rocky massif of Bac Son, and to the south-east a range of low rounded hills. Military fortifications are again frequently encountered. From Lang Giai a difficult section follows where the line crosses the water-shed between the Fleuve Rouge and Si Kiang basins. Lang Son, 23 km. from Lang Giai, lies in a level basin surrounded on all sides by mountains. The line runs northwards through the centre of the basin, then crosses hilly country to reach Dong Dang and Na Cham.

Hanoi to Saigon (1,745 km.)

Hanoi to Tourane (802 km.). The railway runs southwards from Hanoi across the Fleuve Rouge delta through Phu Ly, Nam Dinh, and Ninh Binh to the hills on the Tonkin-Annam frontier. As far as Cho Ganh station (128 km.) the line is almost level, but from here to the Col de Dong Giao (135 km.) there is a gradual rise to 54 m. The Col de Dong Giao is a gap in the much-broken limestone range alined in a north-north-west to south-south-east direction and separating the Fleuve Rouge and the Song Ma. A fairly steep descent follows to Thanh Hoa from which town the railway proceeds to Vinh over the level plains of the Song Ma, Song Chu, and Song Ca. A short branch line joins Vinh to the river port of Ben Thuy. The whole region from Hanoi to Vinh, apart from the section between Ninh Binh and Thanh Hoa, is densely populated and devoted to rice cultivation. The profile of the line shows few irregularities.

South of Vinh, the lowland becomes restricted and the railway turns inland up the Ngan Sau valley. The line follows a course slightly above the level bottom of the valley. It is from the upper part of this valley that a route has been projected to connect Annam with Laos. The line, which branches from the main Trans-Indo-Chinese line at Tanap, has been completed as far as Xom Cuc, a distance of only

18 km. An aerial ropeway has been constructed between Xom Cuc
and Ban Na Phao to carry materials and food for the workmen. French
engineers have surveyed the remaining section to Thakhek on the
Mekong, but the work of construction has been held up by financial
difficulties and scarcity of labour.

After 150 km. of hilly country the railway enters the long, narrow,
coastal plain which extends from the Porte d'Annam to the Col des
Nuages. The central part of the plain is thickly peopled and intensively
cultivated with rice; sand dunes, sometimes 30 m. in height, fringe
the coast. As far as Dong Hoi the line runs closely parallel with the
main road (Route Coloniale no. 1), but beyond the town rail and road
separate only to come together again north of Quang Tri. The railway
follows a course beneath the hills bordering the plain and at a distance
of 10–15 km. from the sea. Gradients here are very slight and some
sections are level. Thirty-five kilometres south of Hue the line enters
a more difficult section where the mountain range extends eastwards
to reach the coast in the Col des Nuages. The steepest gradients
(1 : 100) negotiated by the railway over the whole distance from Hanoi
to Saigon are found in this area immediately north of the Baie de
Tourane. The railway climbs from Lang Co station at sea level to a
height of 175 m., then passes through a tunnel under the Col des
Nuages. Beyond here the line is cut into the side of boulder-strewn
hills which fall sharply to the sea. The final stage to Tourane is across
a flat plain of sand dunes.

Tourane to Nha Trang (534 km.). In this section, which was completed only in 1936, the railway passes sometimes along the narrow
coastal fringe of lowland and sometimes across low mountain ranges
bordering the sea. It first crosses the deltas of the Song Buong and
Song Thu Bon several kilometres west of the Route Coloniale no. 1,
but a little farther south rail and road run closely parallel with
one another. Between Tourane and Quang Ngai the maximum
gradient is 1 : 180, and many stretches of the line are level. No curve
has a radius less than 300 m., and this radius is only encountered
in two places, the one immediately after leaving Tourane, the other
on the south side of the bridge over the Song Buong. While all the
leading stations on the Trans-Indo-Chinese railway are provided with
double lines the stations of Tam Ky and Quang Ngai in addition have
a third main line as well as an unloading line, a turning triangle, and
lines to a neighbouring machine repair depot.

From Quang Ngai to Dieutri, a distance of 161 km., the railway
continues to run parallel with the main road. The line keeps to within

10 km. of the sea as far as Bong Son, crossing a range of low rounded hills in the neighbourhood of Deo Tach Tanh. After leaving Bong Son the track turns inland up a valley separated from the sea by the massif of Chop Chai, but approaches the coast again 40 km. farther south. The varied gradients and little-developed character of this upland section contrasts with the levelness and intensively cultivated plains around Binh Dinh and Dieutri. A branch line, 10 km. in length, connects Dieutri with the port of Qui Nhon (Plate 66).

The 236 km. from Dieutri to Nha Trang offered special engineering problems, for here the Chaîne Annamitique overlooks the coast except where it is cut through by the Song Ba. Moreover, the great width of the Song Ba near to its mouth entailed the construction of a bridge 1,300 m. long in total span. The Song Ba opens a fairly easy route to Cambodia by way of the Ayounh valley. South of this valley a high mountain spur reaches the coast at Cape Varella, and the railway passes over this obstacle through a tunnel, 1,180 m. in length (Col de Babonneau). The line emerges from the Babonneau tunnel to run along the narrow plain bordering the sheltered Baie de Ben Goi. The massif of La Mère et l'Enfant rises steeply above the line to a height of over 2,000 m. Despite the difficulties imposed by the nature of the relief, Nha Trang is reached without recourse to gradients steeper than 1 : 100.

Nha Trang to Saigon (409 km.). The country crossed by the railway in the neighbourhood of Nha Trang and south to Cap Padaran consists of a narrow coastal plain skirting the high crystalline Plateau du Lang Bian. Nga Ca (1,397 km.) is the junction for Ba Ngoi, a port on the shores of the Baie de Cam Ranh. From Tourcham, the station for Phan Rang, there is a branch line to Dalat which is situated at an altitude of 1,475 m. The suitability of the plateau climate for Europeans led the French to establish a health centre here; the demand for easy transport encouraged the construction of a railway from the coast despite the physical difficulties to be overcome. Two sections of this branch line (Krong Pha to Kabo; Drang to Arbre Broye) are laid as a rack railway with a gradient of 1 : 8. Beyond Cap Padaran the main Trans-Indo-Chinese line moves away from the sea as the coastal plain becomes wider. West of the branch line to the port of Phan Thiet the railway passes through an undulating, densely wooded region near Bien Hoa and reaches the vast deltaic lowlands of Cochin-China. The train enters Saigon station (1,745 km.) after crossing the Rivière de Saigon.

Saigon to My Tho (71 km.)

The line from Saigon to My Tho was the first railway to be constructed in Indo-China. It runs across an almost level plain drained by the Vaico river and the Mekong.

Bendongxo to Loc Ninh (69 km.)

The Bendongxo to Loc Ninh line, which has only recently been completed (1933), connects the intensively cultivated delta with the luxuriant forest zone of the interior. Bendongxq is linked to Saigon, 66 km. away, by a tramway which has the same gauge (metre) as the railway (Plate 67).

Phnom Penh to Mongkol Borey (330 km.)

From Phnom Penh, the capital of Cambodia, a line 330 km. in length runs to Mongkol Borey, a town some 50 km. east of the pre-1941 Siamese frontier. The whole journey is over the Tonle Sap alluvial plain, the railway keeping at a height above the limits of the summer flood waters. An extension of the Phnom Penh to Mongkol Borey line is being built to the former Siamese frontier at Muong Aran Pradhet, and when this connexion is made railway travel will be established between Singapore and Phnom Penh via Bangkok.

Traffic

Passenger traffic on the Indo-China State Railways in 1936, the latest year for which a complete series of statistics is available, amounted to 8,765,000. Of this total 98·9% travelled fourth class, and only 1·1% first, second and third class. The exceptionally high proportion travelling fourth class is due to the very large number of natives who use the trains over short distances. Over 60% of the total receipts are derived from passenger traffic. The following table shows the average distance travelled by passengers:

	1st, 2nd, 3rd class km.	4th class km.
Hanoi - Na Cham	63	29
Hanoi - Saigon (and branches)	271	52
Saigon - My Tho	69	29
Bendongxo - Loc Ninh	32	29
Phnom Penh - Mongkol Borey	199	85

Source: *Annuaire statistique de l'Indochine, 1936–7*, p. 117 (Hanoi, 1938).

Plate 67. Electric tramway at Saigon

Saigon is connected by electric tramway with the important industrial centre of Cho Lon and the small towns of Bendongxo and Hoc Mon.

Plate 68. Railway bridge at Lao Kay

This bridge, which crosses the Namti river at the frontier town of Lao Kay, carries the Yunnan railway. It was destroyed by the Chinese in September 1940 in view of the threat of a Japanese invasion of China through Tonkin.

Plate 69. Railway bridge on the Yunnan line north of Lao Kay

This multiple girder steel bridge spans a gorge in the upper Namti valley, connecting two tunnels cut in the limestone precipices. It is a remarkable example of railway engineering.

Plate 70. The Yunnan railway in the Namti valley

The railway from Lao Kay can be seen following a tortuous course along the slopes of the valley, about 100 km. within Chinese territory.

It will be seen that the small percentage of people using the better class compartments made on the average far longer journeys than the fourth class passengers. Long-distance passenger traffic from Hanoi to Saigon comprises French residents or administrative officials and native emigrants from the overpopulated lowlands of Tonkin. The recently constructed line from Phnom Penh has a fairly large through traffic, for its rail-head, Mongkol Borey, lies only 50 km. from the Siamese railway terminus from which there is access to Bangkok and Singapore.

Freight traffic on this system totalled 693,000 metric tons in 1936 divided among the lines as shown in the following table:

	Tons transported
Hanoi - Na Cham	133,000
Hanoi - Saigon (and branches)	342,000
Saigon - My Tho	6,000
Bendongxo - Loc Ninh	48,000
Phnom Penh - Mongkol Borey	164,000
	693,000

Source: *Annuaire statistique de l'Indochine, 1936–7*, p. 117 (Hanoi, 1938).

All the state railway lines pass through rich agricultural areas or luxuriant forest zones, and the freight carried usually consists of tropical food crops and wood products. The rice harvest for the most part determines the seasonal variations in traffic receipts: in the north freight traffic is greatest after the two annual rice harvests of November and June; on the Cambodian line receipts rise sharply in March, maintaining a high level during April and May when the paddy has been cleared from the fields and is ready for transportation. Other consignments include maize, fruit, sugar, oil, fish, tea, cattle, salt, and tobacco.

YUNNAN RAILWAY

The Haiphong-Yunnanfou railway is a metre-gauge line; the rails, 9·58 m. long and weighing 30 kg. per m., are laid on metal sleepers. Curves of 300 m. and under are encountered, particularly in the section beyond the Indo-Chinese frontier; the minimum curve radius is 100 m. The line is single track over its whole course, but plans are being seriously considered for doubling the section between Haiphong and Hanoi. Between Haiphong and the terminus at Yunnanfou the railway climbs from sea level to a height of 2,025 m. Gradients greater than 1 : 150 are frequent in the mountain section; the steepest gradient is 1 : 40.

According to recent statistics (1937) rolling stock on the Yunnan railway includes 31 tank locomotives (wheel types 0–4–0: 2–4–2), 51 tender locomotives (wheel types 4–4–0: 4–6–0), 207 passenger coaches and 958 goods wagons. There are also six self-propelled cars comprising one Micheline Diesel coach and five Decauville coaches. Railway worshops are found at Gia Lam, Pho Moi, and Amitschou.

A weekly express train covers the 762 km. from Hanoi to Yunnan-fou in 22 hr., at an average speed of 35 km. per hr.; this speed is made possible by the use of a Micheline petrol rail car (pneumatic tyres) in the difficult section through Chinese territory. The line conveys daily between the two termini (turn round takes 15 days), four goods trains each 75 tons, i.e. 300 tons daily, 9,000 tons monthly. The capacity of the line could be greatly increased by the construction of more passing loops.

The Haiphong-Yunnanfou railway is 862 km. long, 398 of which are on Tonkin territory and 464 on Chinese territory. From Haiphong to Hanoi the line runs north-north-west across the flat alluvial lowland of the Fleuve Rouge, where numerous bridges and embankments have been constructed on account of the many waterways and the possibility of flooding. The Yunnan railway passes to the east of Hanoi joining the Trans-Indo-Chinese line at Gia Lam. Gia Lam is the chief repairing centre of the *Compagnie française des Chemins de fer de l'Indochine et du Yunnan* and lies on the main line from Hanoi to Lang Son. The Lang Son and Yunnan lines run side by side for 6 km. after leaving Gia Lam, but at Yen Vien the latter branches off in a north-westerly direction to the northern extremity of the Fleuve Rouge delta. For the next 200 km. the railway follows the course of the Fleuve Rouge here closely encompassed by mountains. Numerous sharp curves down to 100 m. radius are encountered, but the gradient never exceeds 1 : 71.

At the frontier town of Lao Kay the line bears sharply to the north-east up the Namti valley, the most difficult section in the whole journey from Haiphong to Yunnanfou. The Namti valley offered several obstacles to the passage of a railway, numerous trestle viaducts and steel bridges having been built to carry the line across its wild gorges and precipitous slopes. The most important trestle viaduct (at 378 km.) has a length of nearly 153 m. and is approached at one end by a curve of 100 m. radius. About 100 km. from Lao Kay the Namti drops some 600 m. in less than 3,200 km., and the line runs along both sides of the river in a loop having a depth of 8,000 km. At the lower end of the loop the line crosses the river by means of a steel bridge connecting two tunnels. This is a multiple girder bridge supported by a three-hinged arch; two additional supports subdivide the length of the bridge girder into spans not exceeding 22 m. in length (Plate 69). The upper end of the loop is 305 m. higher than the starting point, only 1,000 m. away across the valley.

From Lao Kay to Yunnanfou the profile of the line shows considerable variation. Lao Kay is 80 m. above sea level, and at Lahati (367 km.) the altitude is only 201 m., but near Loshiutung, where the line crosses the watershed between the Fleuve Rouge and Si Kiang, 1,707 m. is reached. From here to Ami (517 km.) it descends to the Si Kiang (1,063 m.), then follows the valley in an upward direction for 177 km. (Iliang), reaching a height of 1,555 m. Near Iliang the railway turns sharply to the west and climbs to the watershed (2,050 m.) between the Si Kiang and Yangtse Kiang. The journey ends with a gradual descent to the town of Yunnanfou (Kunming).*

Traffic

In 1936, passenger traffic on the Haiphong-Yunnanfou railway totalled 3,428,000. As on the state railway system, over 95% of the passengers travelled fourth class. Natives use the line frequently to visit a nearby village or market town; while the average distance travelled by a native is only 42 km., the corresponding figure for persons using the first three classes is 107 km.

Freight traffic is relatively more important on the Haiphong-Yunnanfou line than on the state railway system. Over 70% of the receipts are from goods traffic compared with 37·9% for the Hanoi-Saigon route. This high proportion of goods traffic may be attributed to the absence of serious competition from other means of transport as well as to the position of the line as an outlet for south-west China. In 1936, the Yunnan railway carried 302,000 tons of freight; and this traffic has rapidly expanded with the increase in demand following the establishment of the Chinese government in Chungking. Freight on this line usually comprises highly priced goods such as tin and

* In September 1940, in view of the threat of a Japanese invasion of Yunnan through Tonkin, the Chinese destroyed the frontier bridge at Lao Kay and dismantled the track for a considerable distance northwards from the frontier.

cotton thread. Flooding very frequently causes a hold-up in traffic during the months of August and September.

BIBLIOGRAPHICAL NOTE

(1) The best general sources are: H. J. von Lochow, 'Verkehrswege Französisch-Indochinas', *Zeitschrift des Vereins Mitteleuropäischer Eisenbahnverwaltungen*, no. 7, pp. 79–88 (Berlin, 1940). P. Kandaouroff, 'Les Chemins de Fer de l'Indochine', *Mémoires de la Société des Ingénieurs de France, 1933*, pp. 1061–79 (Paris, 1933). A. Pouyanne, 'Les Travaux publics de l'Indochine', *Bulletin économique de l'Indochine*, vol. XXIX, pp. 361–428 (Hanoi, 1926).

(2) Useful short accounts are found in the following articles: 'Railway Progress in Indo-China', *Railway Gazette*, vol. LXV, p. 214 (London, 1936). 'The Indo-China-Yunnan Railway', *Railway Gazette*, vol. LXXIII, pp. 734–5 (London, 1940). 'The Railways of Indo-China', *Railway Gazette*, vol. LXXVII, pp. 204–5 (London, 1942).

Chapter XX

WATERWAYS

INTRODUCTION

Indo-China has over 13,000 km. of navigable waterways, distributed among each of the states as follows:

	Length of navigable waterways km.
Tonkin	3,280
Annam	3,000
Cochin-China	3,900
Cambodia	1,400
Laos	1,612
	13,192

Source: *Didot-Bottin, Annuaire de Commerce, 1938* (Paris, 1938).

A considerable proportion of the waterways are useable only by shallow-draught vessels for limited periods of the year, and would in France be classified as 'flottable' rather than as 'navigable'.

The waterways were the principal means of transport before the French occupation and even to-day, despite the development of roads and railways, they still play an important part in the economic life of the country. Water transport on a large scale, however, is restricted to the two delta regions of Tonkin and Cochin-China. In the interior, the Fleuve Rouge, the Mekong and many other streams, provide only limited navigational facilities, owing to the extreme variability of their regime and to the existence of rapids and waterfalls a short distance from the sea (Fig. 138).

THE FLEUVE ROUGE (RED RIVER)

The Fleuve Rouge and its chief tributaries, the Rivière Noire, the Song Chay and the Rivière Claire, drain a large part of the state of Tonkin. In its course from Lao Kay, on the Tonkin-Yunnan frontier, to the sea the physical character and navigational possibilities of the main stream exhibits considerable variety.

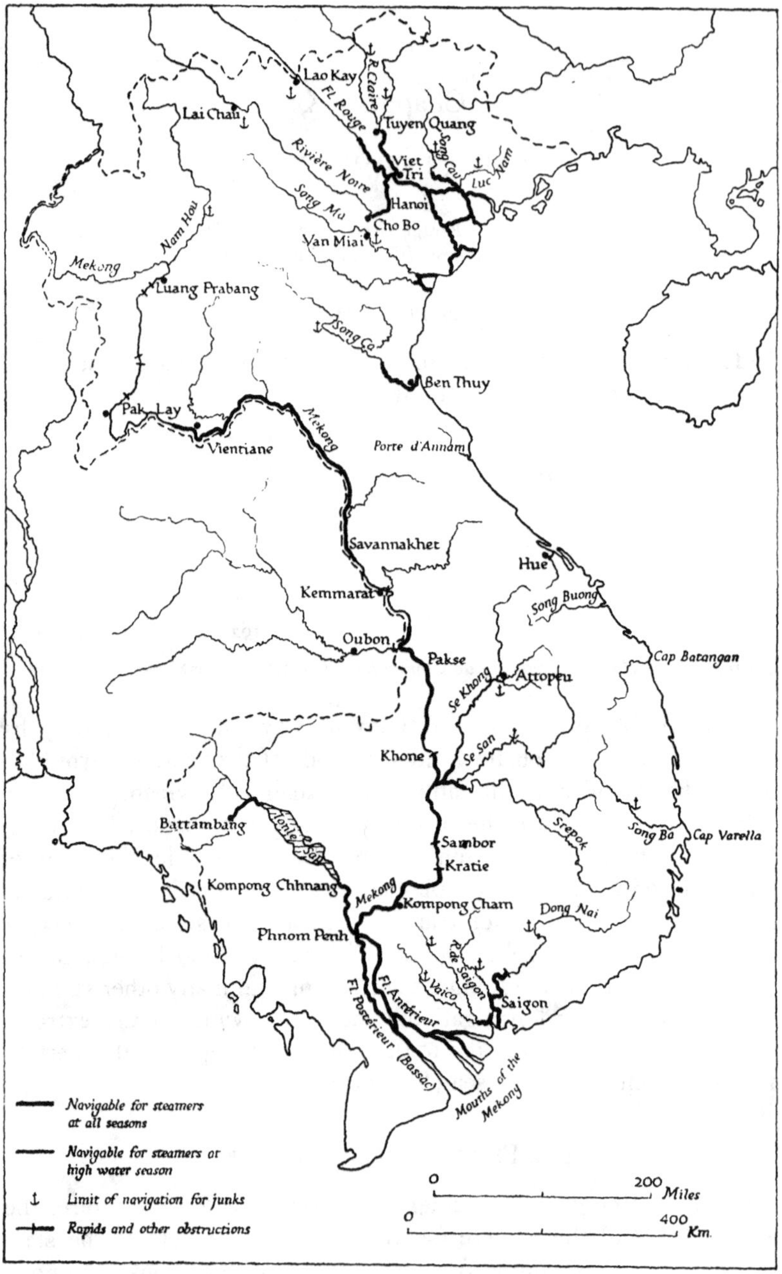

Fig. 138. Navigable waterways
Source: 'The Madrolle Guides', *Indochina*, folding map (Paris and London, 1930).

Lower Reaches (from the sea to Viet Tri)

The Fleuve Rouge has several mouths, the chief of which are the Cua Ba Lat, the Lach Giang, and the Cua Tra Ly. South-west of the main channel of the Fleuve Rouge, the Song Day follows a winding course through the delta and debouches into the sea near the frontier between Tonkin and Annam. In the north of the delta, the dominating stream is the Song Thai Binh which, after receiving the waters of the Song Cau, Song Thuong and Song Luc Nam, divides near Hai Duong into numerous channels and enters the Gulf of Tonkin by the Cua Thai Binh, Cua Van Uc and Cua Cam. Above their mouths the rivers of the delta are interconnected by innumer-

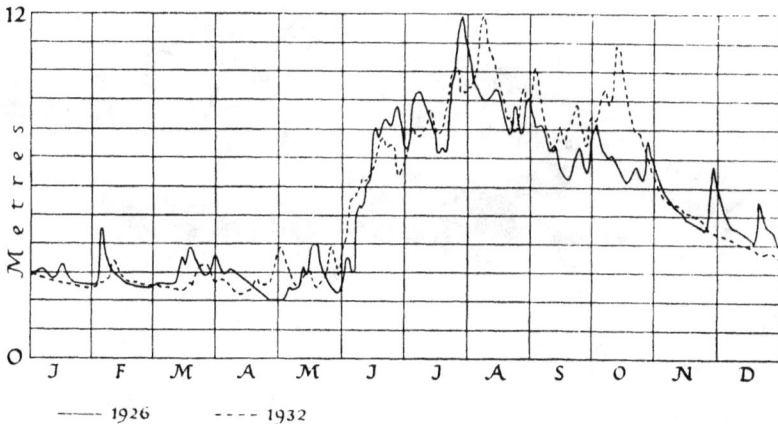

Fig. 139. Water levels in the Fleuve Rouge (Red River) at Hanoi
P. Gourou, Les Paysans du Delta tonkinois, p. 75 (Paris, 1936).

able waterways like the Canal des Rapides, the Canal de Phu Ly and the Canal des Bambous; although these waterways are termed 'canals' by the French they are nevertheless all of natural origin.

The rivers of the delta have very great seasonal variations of water level which affect their navigability. During the period of low water, from March to May, the water level of the Fleuve Rouge at Hanoi is about 2 m. above mean sea level, and the flow is nearly 700 cu.m. per sec.; but at high water, from June to October, the level is frequently about 11 m. with a flow of 23,000 cu.m. per sec. This flow of water is equal to the maximum discharge of the Danube and double that of either the Nile or the Indus. The high-water level during the five months, June to October, fluctuates widely: thus, in 1932, the flood period was marked by eleven successive high-water periods separated by depressions (Fig. 139). In times of flood the speed of the river attains 2 or 3 m. per sec. Embankments have been built to control the flood waters, and whilst primarily designed to prevent inundation of the rice fields (see p. 262), they favour navigation by contributing towards fixation of the river beds.

In addition to the irregularity of the river regime, navigation in the delta is further hindered by constantly shifting banks of mud and sand which obstruct the mouths of the rivers. Vessels drawing 2·7 m. (9 ft.) can enter Cua Day during the high-water season, but sea-going vessels cannot enter any of the mouths farther north,

Fig. 140. Cargo junks at Hanoi

These craft are used for carrying heavy materials such as coal.

Source: P. Gourou, *Les Paysans du Delta tonkinois*, plate 48 (Paris, 1936).

excepting that of the Cua Nam Trieu, where a channel has been dredged to a depth of 6 m. (3½ fm.) which gives access to the port of Haiphong (see p. 380).

All the main waterways of the delta, such as the Fleuve Rouge itself, the Canal des Rapides and the Song Thai Binh, carry a heavy traffic over the greater part of the year. Regular steamship services, mainly organized by Europeans or Chinese, operate between Haiphong, Hanoi, Nam Dinh and other towns. Large numbers of junks and sampans also ply on the rivers of the delta (Fig. 140). Bulky goods, such as building materials, pottery and rice, form the greater part of the traffic, though the steamships carry many passengers in

Plate 71. The Rivière Claire at Tuyen Quang (looking upstream)

The Rivière Claire, a left-bank tributary of the Fleuve Rouge, is one of the chief rivers of Tonkin. Tuyen Quang is the limit of navigation for steamers.

Plate 72. The Rivière Noire near Lai Chau

The river is seen flowing through a deep gorge carved in limestone.

Plate 73. The Huong Giang or Rivière des Parfums at Hue

The river at Hue is about 12 km. from the sea. The sampans seen in the picture are a common form of native craft.

addition to their general cargo; more than 300,000 passengers embark and disembark at Hanoi every year.

Middle and Upper Reaches (from Viet Tri to Lao Kay)

Above Viet Tri the Fleuve Rouge flows for the most part in a narrow entrenched valley surrounded by forested mountains to the north-east and south-west. It is navigable for steamers as far as Yen Bay and for junks and other light craft to Lao Kay.

Two important tributaries enter the main stream near Viet Tri. The Rivière Claire, a left bank tributary which rises in Yunnan, is passable for steamers to Tuyen Quang (Plate 71). The Rivière Noire, which enters the Fleuve Rouge on its right bank, is broad and deep as far as Cho Bo and steamers can reach this village. Rapids interrupt navigation at Cho Bo where the river is no more than from 60–80 m. across. For 60 km. above these rapids steamers may again use the river while junks and sampans can reach Lai Chau 150 km. upstream.

In the forested mountain country of Tonkin, through which the Fleuve Rouge and its tributaries flow, the rivers are frequently the only easy means of communication. This is particularly the case in the western part of the state, where there are vast plateaux of high elevation and where roads are almost completely absent. Although the traffic on the rivers is locally important, few goods are moved over long distances. The Rivière Claire is used for the transport of forest and mineral products to the industrial centres of the delta.

THE RIVERS OF ANNAM

In general, the rivers of Annam are short, swiftly flowing and of little use for navigation. Like the streams in other parts of the country, they also have an unstable regime conditioned by the incidence of the rain-bearing monsoon and by the occurrence of typhoons. Shifting sand bars at the mouths of the rivers are a further hindrance to navigation. Steamers can navigate about 1,000 km. of waterways during the period of high water, but at other seasons they are limited to only 300 km. Sampans and other small native craft can use the waterways at any time of the year.

North of the Porte d'Annam the principal watershed lies in the high plateaux of Laos, and the rivers are much longer than else-where in Annam. The Song Ma, which has built up a delta near Thanh Hoa, is navigable by junks to Van Miai nearly 200 km. upstream. Steamboats of 4 m. draught can sail up the Song Ca as far as the port of Ben Thuy, about 15 km. inland, though farther upstream its winding course and varying depths make navigation difficult. Numerous canals have been built in the coastal lowlands, and it is possible to sail by river and canal from Vinh on the Song Ca, via Thanh Hoa, to Ninh Binh in the Tonkin delta.

In central Annam, from the Porte d'Annam to Cap Batangan, all the main rivers, such as the Song Giang, Huong Giang and Song Thu Bon, pass through lagoons before entering the sea by shallow mouths cut through the sandhills which line the greater part of the coast in this region. In late summer, when the Huong Giang is at its highest, vessels drawing 1·5 m. (5 ft.) can ascend to Hue, the capital of Annam. Canals link the rivers of the plain and native craft ply between Hue and Quang Tri and between Faifoo and Quang Ngai.

South of Cap Batangan, where the mountains and plateaux of Annam rise sharply above the coast, the Song Ba is the only river of considerable length flowing into the South China Sea. It enters the sea north of Cap Varella, but though a broad stream in the lower reaches it is seldom used for navigation owing to shifting channels and variable depths. The other streams, such as the Song Cai and the Song Kinh Dinh, are mainly very short with steep longitudinal profiles; they are for the most part unnavigable, except for a short distance above their mouths.

THE MEKONG

The Mekong, which rises in the high plateaux of western China, is over 4,000 km. in length and flows through Indo-China over the greater part of its course. It is the principal waterway of the states of Laos, Cambodia, and Cochin-China. In the early days of French colonization it was hoped that the Mekong would give easy access to the plateaux of Laos and even to China, but exploratory surveys soon demonstrated the difficulty of navigation along certain stretches of the river. The alternation of rapids with stretches of navigable water renders movement up and down the Mekong slow and difficult. In 1937, during the low-water season, a vessel leaving Saigon took 37 days to reach Luang Prabang, on the upper reaches of the river, and 27 days for the return journey; during the high-water season the length of time taken was 27 and 22 days respectively. Although these times are considerably less than at the beginning of the present century it still takes longer to go from Saigon to Luang Prabang than from Saigon to Marseilles.

Plate 74. The Rivière de Saigon below Saigon

Plate 75. Rice barge on a canal at Cho Lon

Heavy barges of this kind are commonly used to carry unhusked rice or paddy to the mills at Cho Lon. They are moved along the canals by means of long poles.

Lower Reaches (from the sea to Kratie in Cambodia)

The Mekong, which divides into two arms below Phnom Penh, enters the sea in five mouths; the Fleuve Antérieur, the northerly and principal arm of the river, has four mouths and the Fleuve Postérieur (Bassac) a single outlet. In the extreme north of the delta are the mouths of the Vaico, Saigon and Dong Nai rivers. As in Tonkin, mud banks prevent large vessels from entering the rivers, with the exception of the Rivière de Saigon which provides the main seaward approach to the port of Saigon (see p. 373 and Plate 74).

The delta of the Mekong has a more highly developed system of natural and artificial waterways than any other part of Indo-China. The river regime, though irregular, does not interfere with navigation to the same extent as in Tonkin. Shallow basins (*beng*), which lie on either side of the Mekong downstream from Vientiane, take a proportion of the summer flood waters, while there is also a considerable overflow into the lake of Tonle Sap (see p. 22). Below Phnom Penh in the delta itself, large depressions, such as the Plaine des Joncs, receive more of the excess water. As a result of these circumstances, the principal streams, the Fleuve Antérieur and the Fleuve Postérieur (Bassac), maintain a summer high-water level which neither threatens inundation of the surrounding land nor impedes navigation. On the other hand, during the winter dry-season navigation in the Mekong delta would frequently be interrupted were it not for the strong tidal currents at this period of the year. The tide here has greater power than in the Gulf of Tonkin and is felt a long distance inland, its influence extending to Phnom Penh on the Mekong and almost to the source of the Vaico and Saigon rivers.

Navigation in the delta region of Cochin-China has been improved and extended by the dredging of river beds and the cutting of numerous canals. Until 1893 the improvements were made without any mechanical assistance, but since then work has been speeded up by the use of a powerful dredging machine. The annual volume of dredged material which totalled 140,000 cu.m. in 1893, fluctuated between 6 and 10 million cu.m. in the period from 1913 to 1930. To-day there are more than 1,300 km. of primary canals, that is, those having a width of over 22 m. and a depth of over 2 m. at the period of lowest water level. Canals of this kind include the one connecting the Vaico and Saigon rivers near Thu Dau Mot, that from Rach Gia to Ha Tien, and that running NE-SW through the centre of the Presqu'île de Ca Mau. 'Secondary' and 'tertiary' canals, extending altogether for over 1,000 km., vary greatly in breadth and depth. The whole canal system, with the rivers included, forms a close network of navigable waterways, covering a large part of Cochin-China (Fig. 141).

The waterways of the Mekong delta carry heavy traffic and are widely employed for transporting the principal cash products, such as rice and maize. About 3,000 junks, most of them over 16 tons displacement, ply on the rivers and canals; some are man hauled, while others take advantage of tidal movements or of the prevailing wind. In addition to the junks, there are also 191 steamboats of more than 30 tons and 21 motor barges with displacements varying from 50 to 350 tons. The following figures reveal the enormous quantity of materials carried on the most frequented waterways by either junk, steamboat or barge: in 1937, the Lop Vo canal, connecting the Fleuve Postérieur to the Fleuve Antérieur near Sa Dec, bore 4 million tons of goods, and in the same year the Dupré canal, linking My Tho with the Vaico Oriental, bore 4,200,000 tons. The greater part of the traffic converges on Cho Lon which has long been the chief industrial and commercial centre in the delta region (Plate 75).

Beyond the limits of the delta, navigation on the Mekong continues to be very active at least as far north as Kompong Cham. Small sea-going vessels transport livestock and agricultural products from this important marketing centre to Saigon or Cho Lon, by way of Phnom Penh, the capital of Cambodia and a river port of considerable size. Communication between the Mekong and Tonle Sap is easy only in the summer when the river overflows into the lake basin. At this period, boats with a draught of 4 m. sail from Phnom Penh to Kompong Thom, Siem Reap, Battambang, and Pursat. In the low-water season, December to May, Kompong Chhnang is the effective head of navigation, owing to the existence of mud banks above the town. The difficulty of transporting dried fish and paddy by water during these months, especially as the rice harvest around Battambang ends in February, has been an important factor leading to the construction of the railway from Mongkol Borey to Phnom Penh.

Middle and Upper Reaches

From Kratie to its source on the borders of China and Tibet, the Mekong consists of several navigable reaches interrupted by numerous rapids or waterfalls which necessitate frequent transhipment.

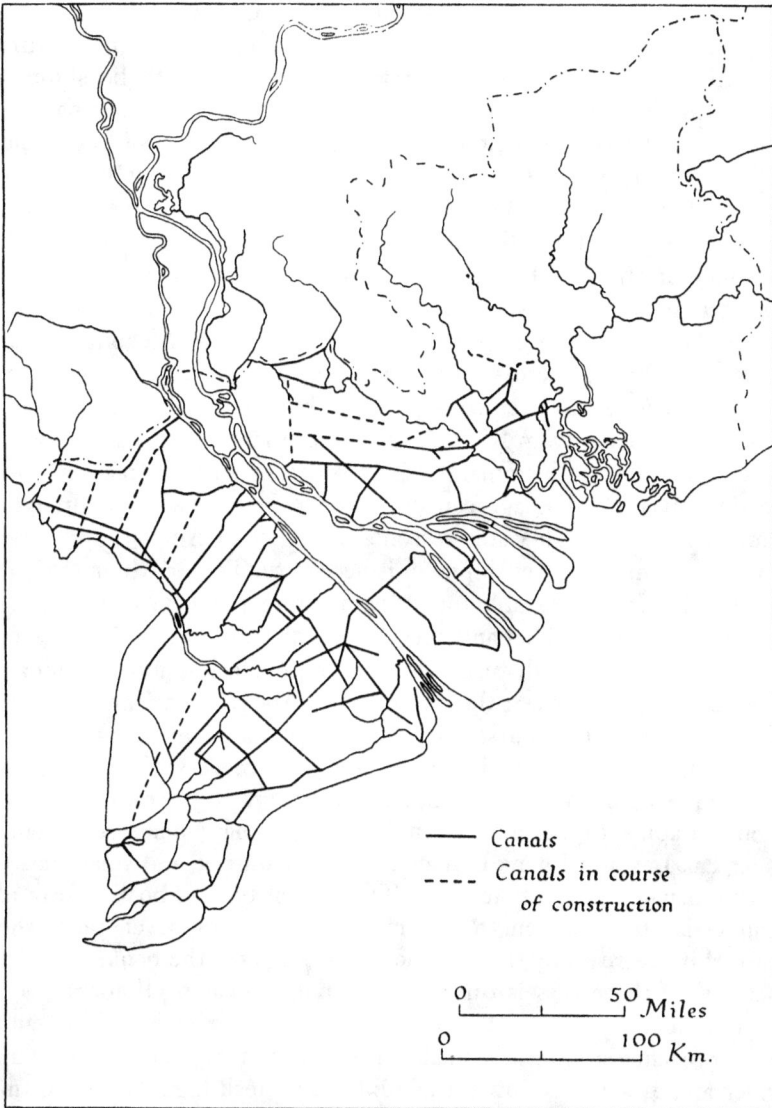

Fig. 141. Canals in the Mekong delta

Source: (1) Georges Maspero, *Un Empire Colonial français: l'Indochine*, vol. II, folding map (Paris, 1930); (2) C. Robequain, *L'Evolution économique de l'Indochine française*, p. 244 (Paris, 1939).

The principal obstacles to navigation are found between Kratie and Savannakhet. The rapids at Sambor and Preapatang upstream from Kratie are passable to small steamers of 50 tons burden only during the high-water season; at other times, goods have to be shipped across in small lighters. A great deal has been done to assist navigation in the low-water period by erecting large numbers of buoys and other guiding signs to mark the most suitable channels. A little above Preapatang the Se Khong and Se San enter the main stream along its left bank; in the rainy season, small native craft can reach Attopeu on the Se Khong, the journey from the confluence with the Mekong taking 18 days, but only 3 days in the reverse direction. The most dangerous and impracticable rapids on the Mekong are at Khone; no boat can cross them at any time of the year, and a railway, 7 km. in length, has been constructed to by-pass them. The Mekong is navigable again from Khone to Pakse, but above here navigation is interrupted by the Kemmarat rapids which extend upstream almost to Savannakhet. Passage can only be effected by shallow-draught launches in the high-water season from May to August, and even then more than one transhipment is necessary. The Se Moun, a right bank tributary, is passable for boats in summer as far as Oubon.

Between Savannakhet and Vientiane, a distance of nearly 500 km., the Mekong flows undisturbed by physical obstacles, and steamboats are able to ply between the two centres. Above Vientiane the river follows a winding course through mountainous territory. As far upstream as Xieng Sen it is over 300 m. broad, with a depth of 1–1½ m. even in the dry season, and an average of 3–4 m. in times of flood. Rapids impede navigation, however, at many places, especially near Pak Lay and Luang Prabang, though launches and small native boats manage to negotiate them. The largest type of boat, a form of canoe, is 16 m. in length and manned by six or seven men who propel it upstream by thrusting long poles against the bank. Regular services of these vessels run from Vientiane to Luang Prabang.

The quantity of goods carried by the Mekong in its middle and upper reaches is extremely small. In 1936, about 5,300 tons moved up river and 4,600 tons down, excluding some teak logs floated downstream from forests in Siamese territory. A small number of passengers are also carried on the river. The traffic is mainly controlled by the *Compagnie saigonnaise de Navigation* formerly known as the *Messageries fluviales*. Even when various schemes for the projected improvement of the waterway have been carried out, French engineers estimate that an average annual traffic of 25,000 tons is likely to be

Plate 76. The Mekong at Phnom Penh (looking upstream)

At Phnom Penh, about 250 km. from the sea, the Mekong (in the right background) divides into two branches—the Fleuve Postérieur (Bassac) seen in the foreground and the Fleuve Antérieur flowing to the right and not visible on this photograph. The winding stream which enters the Mekong in the centre of the picture is the outlet of Tonle Sap.

Plate 77. Steamer alongside the quays at the river port of Phnom Penh

The river is the outlet of Tonle Sap. It joins the Mekong a short distance to the right of the picture. Steamers ply regularly between Phnom Penh and the towns of the Mekong delta.

Plate 78. Rapids on the Mekong near Luang Prabang

the maximum attainable. The future of Laos would thus seem to be more dependent upon the development of roads and railways than upon the navigation of the Mekong.

BIBLIOGRAPHICAL NOTE

(1) A brief survey is found in A. Pouyanne, 'Les Travaux publics de l'Indochine', *Bulletin économique de l'Indochine*, vol. XXIX, pp. 265–85 (Hanoi, 1926).

(2) The regime of the Fleuve Rouge and its influence on navigation is described in M. Pardé, 'Les crues du Fleuve Rouge', *Revue de Géographie Alpine*, vol. XIV, pp. 787–802 (Grenoble, 1926) and in M. Pardé, 'Le régime du Fleuve Rouge', *Annales de Géographie*, vol. XLVII, pp. 191–95 (Paris, 1938).

(3) The following articles also provide useful information on river navigation: F. Le Dantec, 'La Rivière Noire', *Annales de Géographie*, vol. I, pp. 176–85, 249–59 (Paris, 1891). G. Simon, 'Navigation du Mekong de son embouchure à Xieng-kong', *Comptes Rendus de la Société de Géographie de Paris, 1896*, pp. 202–24 (Paris, 1896).

GENERAL BIBLIOGRAPHY

The following short bibliography includes the most valuable general works which have been used in the preparation of this handbook. It is intended to supplement the bibliographical notes which appear at the end of each chapter.

P. BERNARD, *Le Problème économique indochinois* (Paris, 1934).

A clear account of economic and social problems in Indo-China and the attempts made by the French to overcome them. A constructive programme for the future economic life of the country is discussed in detail.

P. BERNARD, *Nouveaux aspects du Problème économique indochinois* (Paris, 1937).

A work similar in scope to that published by P. Bernard in 1934.

T. E. ENNIS, *French Policy and Developments in Indochina* (Chicago, 1936).

This book gives an account of the French conquest of the country and also deals with modern political and economic conditions. There is a good bibliography.

P. GOUROU, *L'Utilisation du Sol en Indochine française* (Paris, 1936).

The fullest and most up-to-date account of land utilization in Indo-China. Thirty-four figures are included in the text and at the end there are five folding maps which show rural settlement in certain parts of the country.

L. DE LANESSAN, *L'Indochine française* (Paris, 1889).

This work, though now out of date, contains much useful information, especially on social customs, not easily found elsewhere.

SYLVAIN LEVI, *Indochine*, 2 vols., Exposition Coloniale Internationale, Paris, 1931 (Paris, 1931).

In vol. 1 there is a comprehensive survey of the history, peoples and architecture of Indo-China. Vol. 2 deals fully with the French and native administration.

C. MADROLLE, *Les Guides Madrolles*, 'L'Indochine du Nord', 'L'Indochine du Sud', 'Indochina'.

These three guides provide a wealth of information for the traveller, especially on historical and architectural subjects. They are well illustrated with maps and photographs.

GEORGES MASPERO, *Un Empire Colonial français: l'Indochine*. 2 vols. (Paris, 1929 and 1930).

A detailed study of the history, administration and economy of Indo-China. There is also a full account of art and architecture. Illustrated with numerous photographs and folding maps.

C. ROBEQUAIN, *L'Indochine française* (Paris, 1935).

One of the best short accounts of the country. There is a useful bibliography.

C. ROBEQUAIN, *L'Evolution économique de l'Indochine française* (Paris, 1939).

The fullest and most recent account of the influence of France in Indo-China. Illustrated with a number of maps and diagrams.

H. RUSSIER and H. BRENIER, *L'Indochine française* (Paris, 1911).

Although now out of date this book contains one of the most useful short surveys of the geography of Indo-China.

A. SARRAUT, *La Mise en Valeur des Colonies françaises* (Paris, 1923).

This work, written by a former Governor-General of Indo-China, outlines the character and objects of French colonial policy. Much information is given on political and economic problems in Indo-China.

J. SION, 'Asie des Moussons', *Géographie Universelle*, vol. IX, pt 2, pp. 394–467 (Paris, 1929).

Contains a good short survey of the physical features, people and economy of Indo-China. Well illustrated with maps and photographs. There is a valuable bibliography.

VIRGINIA THOMPSON, *French Indo-China* (London, 1937).

The only large work in English on Indo-China. Deals fully with the history, administration and economy of the country as well as with the reaction of the native people to European influences. It has a good bibliography.

Travel Books.

A large number of travel books have been written on Indo-China, of which the following are the most useful and interesting:

ALAN HOUGHTON BRODRICK, *Little China: the Annamese Lands* (Oxford, 1942).

Contains a vivid and colourful account of the social customs of the peoples of Annam, Tonkin and Cochin-China. Illustrated with a number of fine photographs.

H. J. COOLIDGE and T. ROOSEVELT, *Three Kingdoms of Indo-China* (New York, 1933).

An account of the expedition organized by the Field Museum of Natural History, Chicago, to make a collection of animals, birds and reptiles in northern Indo-China.

HERMANN NORDEN, *A Wanderer in Indo-China* (London, 1931).

Contains an interesting collection of stories and legends about the native peoples.

H. W. PONDER, *Cambodian Glory* (London, 1936).

A good account of life in Cambodia and of the ruins of Angkor.

GABRIELLE M. VASSAL, *On and Off Duty in Annam* (London, 1910).

The experiences of a French army doctor in Annam.

Bibliographies.

P. BOUDET and R. BOURGEOIS, *Bibliographie de l'Indochine française*, vol. I, 1913–26 (Hanoi, 1929), vol. II, 1927–29 (Hanoi, 1932), vol. III, 1930 (Hanoi, 1933).

H. CORDIER, *Bibliotheca Indosinica*, 4 vols. (Hanoi, 1912–15).

This is the standard bibliography for works on Indo-China published before 1913.

Appendix I

THE PLACE-NAMES OF INDO-CHINA

INTRODUCTION

There are three main groups of native languages in Indo-China, namely, Annamite, Khmer and Thai. Although French is the official language, all three of these groups also have some status: European missionaries who visited the country in the seventeenth and eighteenth centuries were the first to transcribe the Annamite, Khmer and Thai scripts into the Roman alphabet. They used a phonetic system, with diacritical marks to indicate tone, aspiration and unpronounced letters. The work of the missionaries has formed the basis of the *qu'oc ng'u* or romanized Annamite script which is officially used to-day in Annam, Tonkin and Cochin-China. Their work has also been the basis of the romanized script for the Khmer and Thai languages.

In order to facilitate the pronunciation of place-names by Europeans a simpler system in which all or most of the diacritical marks are omitted from the Annamite script has been adopted on certain official French maps. This simpler treatment is also used in the new transliteration of the Thai script, prepared in 1941 by the Royal Institute of Siam in consultation with the *Ecole française d'Extrême Orient*. Khmer script has also been dealt with in this way.

Many of the place-names of Indo-China have two or three parts. The first letter of each part is written in capitals, e.g. Dong Hoi, Ban Me Thuot.

OFFICIAL SYSTEMS OF SPELLING AND TRANSLITERATION

The principles followed by certain official bodies in the spelling of Indo-Chinese place-names are given below:

(1) *French Sailing Directions and Charts*

Place-names in the French Sailing Directions (*Mers de Chine*, vol. I, 1932, Paris, 1933) are written in simple Roman characters with no diacritical marks, except over the 'e' in names such as Cua Bé and over the 'i' in names like Haï Dong and Thaï Binh. Hyphens are occasionally used where there are two parts to the place-name, e.g. Qui-Nhon, Do-Son. The names of geographical features are given either in the native language or in French, e.g. Cua Tra Ly (Cua = mouth of river), Song Ma (Song = river), Hon Mat (Hon = island), but Baie de Tourane, Cap Varella, Rivière de Saigon. Charts follow the same system.

(2) *Service géographique de l'Indochine, Hanoi*

The place-names of the series of maps published by this official body on the scales of 1:25,000, 1:100,000 and 1:500,000 are based on the official French transliteration and use full diacritical marks. No hyphens are used to link the two parts of the place-names. As in the French Sailing Directions and Charts the geographical names, such as river, mountain, cape, are written either in the transliterated native language or in French.

The official *Atlas de l'Indochine* (Hanoi, 1928) of the *Service géographique de l'Indochine* follows closely the orthography of the 1:25,000, 1:100,000 and 1:500,000 sheets, except that all diacritical marks are omitted.

(3) *Permanent Committee on Geographical Names (P.C.G.N.)*

The P.C.G.N. has up to date issued no set of instructions relating specifically to any of the languages of Indo-China. The use of the French form of transliteration, without diacritical marks, as given in the *Atlas de l'Indochine*, has been recommended by the present Committee.

(4) *British Admiralty Pilot and Charts*

The place-names in the *China Sea Pilot*, vol. I, 1st ed. 1937, and on Admiralty Charts are transliterated from French official publications by the R.G.S. II system as laid down on pp. 30–3 of *Alphabets of Foreign Languages*, R.G.S. Technical Series No. 2 published by the R.G.S. in 1933. The system of orthography, however, differs in several particulars from that adopted in French official publications. Thus, 'Qui Nhon' is rendered as 'Ki Nhon' and 'Vung Chao' as 'Vung Shao', while such native names as 'Cua Ron' and 'Binh Cang' become 'Kua Ron' and 'Binh Kang'. No diacritical marks are used. In place names with a geographical term, the geographical part has been translated into English, e.g. Cape Varella, Van Fong Bay. In the *Pilot*, however, English forms are not used throughout, for the French instead of the English term is occasionally used, e.g. 'Cap St Jacques', 'Rade du Crapaud', 'Chenal d'Hamelin'. *Charts* give these names in the English form.

Both *Pilot* and *Charts* are now in process of correction in order to conform with the latest Hydrographic Department rulings (1941), which lay down that the orthography appearing on the official charts and maps of the country concerned is to be accepted both for names and for geographical terms. Corrections made up to September 1942 on both *Pilot* and *Charts* relate only to names along a section of the coast from a little north of Qui Nhon to Cap Varella.

(5) *Geographical Section General Staff* (G.S.G.S.)

G.S.G.S. have issued two series of maps covering Indo-China, no. 2957 on a scale of 1:4,000,000 and no. 2555 on a scale of 1:1,000,000. In the no. 2957 series there are many divergencies from the French system of transliteration: the town of Ha Giang appears as 'Ha Zhiang', Tourane as 'Turan' and Faifoo as 'Feifu'; the geographical terms are written both in French, e.g. Baie de Ben Goi, Cap Saint Jacques, and also in the native language, e.g. Se San, Song Ma. The no. 2555 series follows more closely the French system of transliteration without diacritical marks, but also renders many of the geographical terms in English, e.g. Dung Quat Bay, Cape Hirondelles.

In 1941, G.S.G.S. agreed to adopt the orthography as used on the official maps of the country, and future maps issued by them are expected to conform to this ruling.

THE SPELLING OF PLACE-NAMES IN THIS HANDBOOK

The following principles have been adopted:

(a) The spelling of all place-names, both specific and geographical, follows that used in the *Atlas de l'Indochine* (Hanoi, 1928).

(b) Geographical terms are therefore given either in the native language, e.g. Song Gam, Pou Den Dinh, Nui Ong (see glossary on p. 449), or in French, e.g. Baie d'Along, Lagune de Nai, Plateau du Tran Ninh.

(c) In certain place-names both parts of the name are written in French, e.g. Fleuve Rouge, Rivière Noire, Rivière Claire. This has been adopted as it seemed necessary to follow the *Atlas de l'Indochine* in its spelling, even though anomalous in this respect.

(d) The seas surrounding Indo-China are regarded as 'International' and their names are therefore spelt in English: thus, Gulf of Tonkin, South China Sea, Gulf of Siam. This practice conforms with the rulings of both the Hydrographic Department and G.S.G.S.

Appendix II

SHORT GLOSSARY OF WORDS APPEARING IN PLACE-NAMES

Transliterated form	Language	French equivalent	English equivalent
Cua	Annamite	Bouche	Mouth of river
Hon	Annamite	Ile	Island
Koh (or Goh)	Thai	Ile	Island
Kompong	Malay	Village	Village
Lach	Annamite	Chenal	Channel
Lem	Thai	Cap or Pointe	Cape or Point
Me	Thai	Rivière or Fleuve	River
Mui	Annamite	Cap or Pointe	Cape or Point
Muong	Thai	Ville	Town
Nam	Annamite	Rivière or Fleuve	River
Ngan	Annamite	Rivière or Fleuve	River
Nguon	Annamite	Rivière or Fleuve	River
Nui	Annamite	Montagne or Colline	Mountain or Hill
Phnom	Khmer	Colline	Hill
Pou	Thai	Pic	Peak
Poulo (or Pulau)	Malay	Ile	Island
Rach	Annamite	Rivière or Chenal	River
Se	Annamite	Rivière or Fleuve	River
Song	Annamite	Rivière or Fleuve	River
Stung	Khmer	Rivière or Fleuve	River
Wat	Khmer	Temple or Pagode	Temple or Pagoda

Appendix III

MAPS OF INDO-CHINA

HISTORICAL INTRODUCTION

The first accurate mapping of Indo-China dates from the French occupation of the country in the late nineteenth century. Before this time a number of small-scale general maps had been constructed by missionaries and adventurers, but none laid claim to accuracy. Among the early maps were *La Carte du Royaume d'Annam, comprenant le Tuonkin et la Cochinchine* by P. Alexandre de Rhodes (1654) and *Le Royaume de Siam et pays circonvoisins* by P. Du Val (1686). Between 1861 and 1874, reconnaissance surveys were made of the greater part of the peninsula and these formed the basis of the maps of eastern Indo-China published by Dutreuil de Rhins in 1881 (1:900,000 and 1:1,800,000). In 1893 the Mission Pavie published the first map of the whole country (1:1,000,000); a reduction of this (1:2,000,000) was published two years later.

Triangulation surveys were slow to develop. In 1874, a primary base was measured on the beach at Do Son, but only the coastline of Tonkin and part of the Fleuve Rouge delta had been triangulated by 1886. The *Bureau topographique de l'Etat-Major*, founded in this year, lacked adequate funds and personnel to carry out detailed surveys, though it produced a series of 'cartes provisoires' of the lowlands of Tonkin, Annam and Cochin-China on a scale of 1:100,000. In 1899 it was replaced by the *Service géographique de l'Indochine* which has remained to this day the official body responsible for the mapping of the country. Soon after its foundation, this body began extensive triangulation work producing maps on the scale of 1:25,000 for the delta regions and on the scale of 1:100,000 for the whole of Indo-China. The 1:100,000 series, though still incomplete, has been used for the production of maps on a scale of 1:500,000, 1:1,000,000 and 1:2,000,000.

DESCRIPTION OF MAPS

The maps of Indo-China are described in the following order:

A. French government topographical maps.
B. Maps issued by the Geographical Section of the British General Staff.
C. French Admiralty charts.
D. British Admiralty charts.
E. Geological maps.
F. Miscellaneous maps.
G. Atlases.

In each group the maps are listed as far as possible in order of scale, those on a large scale coming first. The following particulars are given where possible for each series:

(1) Authority responsible for its production.
(2) Date of production, with subsequent revisions.
(3) Number of sheets in the series.
(4) Size of sheets, measured to the margin of the area mapped.
(5) Projection.
(6) Meridian of origin and grid or graticule.
(7) Scale.

(8) Marginal information.

(9) Whether coloured or in black.

(10) Method of representation of relief.

(11) Details of roads, railways, and other information.

A short note is sometimes added on the value of the map, its legibility and accuracy.

A. French Government Topographical Maps

The department primarily responsible for the production of official maps is the *Service géographique de l'Indochine* founded in July 1899.

(1) 1:25,000. Delta regions of Tonkin, Annam and Cochin-China

Sheets covering the delta regions of Tonkin and Annam were produced between 1900 and 1937. Cochin-China is still incompletely covered. 554 sheets have been published. The series is attractively produced and provides a wealth of detailed information. Sheets measure 75 × 51·5 cm. and are printed in colours. Margin divided into 1 min. intervals (centesimal from Paris). Graticule drawn at 5 min. intervals. Scale in metres. Contours at 1 m. intervals up to 15 m. and then at every 5 m. Spot heights in black. Special symbols for embankments, stone, iron and wooden bridges, ferries and river barrages. Rivers and lakes in blue, canals in black. Villages in green, with groups of houses in black. Rice fields, orchards, woodland and mangroves are also shown.

(2) 1:25,000. Kouang Tcheou Wan

Twelve sheets in colour. Sheets 6 and 8–10, 1901; 1–3 revised 1931; 4, 5 and 7 revised 1937; 12 revised 1938.

(3) 1:50,000. Environs of Hanoi and Saigon

Each two half sheets in colour. 1935–36.

(4) 1:50,000. Cambodia

Ten sheets published, size of sheet 50 × 75 cm.

(5) 1:50,000. Frontier region of Lang Son and Cao Bang

Fourteen sheets in colour. This is a photographic enlargement from the 1:100,000 series (No. 6).

(6) 1:100,000. *Carte de l'Indochine*

Produced at intervals since 1899. Sheets already published for the greater part of Tonkin, Annam, Cochin-China and Cambodia, but only a small area of Laos. 160 sheets out of a proposed total of 244 have been published. Size of sheet 75 × 50 cm. Bonne's projection. Margin divided into 2 min. intervals (centesimal from Paris). Graticule drawn at 20 min. intervals. Scale in kilometres.

Sheets published between 1899 and 1904 are variable in colour and are frequently incomplete. They give no indication of the type of forest cover and there is no key to symbols.

Sheets published between 1910 and 1928 are in a different style and contain more information than the earlier ones. There is a full key to symbols; diagrams, which are also given on the earlier sheets, indicate the sources used in compiling the map.

Relief shown by thick contours every 25 m. and interpolated thin contours every 5 m.; the contours are only approximate on the sheets covering the little explored plateau regions. Grey or brown shading is used to indicate steep slopes and rocky ground. Spot heights in black. Rivers and canals in blue. Special symbols for sand dunes, marshes, rice fields, mangroves, bridges in stone, iron and wood, ferries and river barrages. Three types of woodland are indicated by layer tints on some sheets. Railways and tramways shown with symbols for station, tunnel, viaduct, embankment, etc. Metalled roads in double red or black line, other roads and tracks in black.

(7) 1:100,000. *Carte économique de l'Annam*
Forty-three sheets in colour.

(8) 1:200,000. Topographical map
1907–11. Fourteen sheets published, mostly 41 × 25 cm. Graticule drawn every 20 min. (centesimal from Paris). Scale in kilometres. Coloured. Relief shown by form lines, unnumbered and interval not stated, with shading in brown or grey. Spot heights in black.

(9) 1:500,000. *Carte de l'Indochine*
The most recent edition was produced between 1923 and 1937. Previous edition 1899–1903. Twenty-one sheets. Sheets 90 × 50 cm. Conical projection. Margin divided into grades and minutes (centesimal from Paris). Graticule drawn at intervals of one grade. Scale in kilometres. Relief is represented by oblique hill shading in grey and by spot heights in black. Rock exposures in brown. Rivers, showing limit of navigation for steamers and sampans, in blue. Special symbols for provincial capitals, military centres and villages. Railways and tracks in black, roads in red.

(10) 1:1,000,000. *Carte internationale du Monde. Edition provisoire* (1930)
Nine sheets, all published. Sheets 54 × 45 cm. Polyconic projection with two standard parallels. Margin divided into 5 min. intervals (from Greenwich). Graticule drawn every degree. Scale in kilometres and international nautical miles. Coloured. Relief shown by layer tints and contours at 100, 200, 500 m., and then every 500 to 3,000 m. Spot heights in black. Symbols for single track and narrow-gauge railways (in black), three classes of roads (in red). Rivers of constant and intermittent flow are separately distinguished, with limit of navigation and rapids. Navigable canals and irrigation canals are also shown.

(11) 1:1,000,000. *Edition locale* (1928)
Details as for no. 10 but margin divided into minutes (centesimal from Paris). Graticule drawn at intervals of one grade. Scale in kilometres.

(12) 1:1,000,000. *Carte économique du Tonkin et Nord Annam* (1925)

(13) 1:2,000,000. *Carte de l'Indochine*
Prepared by the Mission Pavie and first published in 1895. Latest edition 1936. One sheet 120 × 90 cm. in 5 colours. Scale in kilometres.

(14) 1:2,000,000. *Carte économique* (1937)

(15) 1:2,000,000. *Carte d'étude de l'Indochine* (1929)

(16) 1:3,000,000. *Carte de l'Indochine* (1936)
In six colours.

(17) 1:4,000,000. *Carte d'étude de l'Indochine*
In three colours.

French Government large-scale plans

(18) 1:5,000. *Haiphong*
Published 1934. Four sheets in colour.

(19) 1:10,000. *Haiphong*
Published 1926, revised 1929 and 1937. 47 × 60 cm. Coloured.

(20) 1:10,000. *Hanoi*
Published 1929, revised 1936. In colour.

(21) 1:10,000. *Saigon-Cho Lon*
Published 1923, revised 1936. Four sheets, 50 × 60 cm. Graticule drawn every 5 min. (centesimal from Paris).

(22) 1:10,000. *Vinh-Ben Thuy* (1936)
In colour.

(23) 1:20,000. *Lang Son (environs)* (1931)
In colour.

(24) 1:20,000. *Cao Bang (environs)* (1936)
In colour.

(25) 1:20,000. *Saigon-Cho Lon* (1928)
In colour.

(26) 1:40,000. *Cartes des Ruines d'Angkor*
In colour.

French Government Communication Maps

(27) 1:400,000. *Carte routière de l'Indochine* (1939)
Sheets published covering the greater part of Cochin-China, Cambodia and south Annam. Number of sheets in series not known. 124 × 62 cm. Margin divided into grades (centesimal from Paris). Scale in kilometres. Contours in brown at 100 m. intervals. Rivers, canals and marsh in blue. Four classes of roads, in red, blue, green and brown. Railways in black.

(28) 1:500,000. Railway from Lao Kay to Yunnanfu
In colour.

(29) 1:1,000,000. *Carte routière de Cambodge* (1932)

(30) 1:1,000,000. *Carte routière des Deltas de Tonkin et Cochinchine* (1929)

(31) 1:1,000,000. *Carte aéronautique de l'Indochine* (1935)
Two sheets.

(32) 1:2,000,000. *Infrastructure aérienne de l'Indochine* (1936)

(33) 1:2,000,000. *Carte routière de l'Indochine*
Published 1929. Revised in 1936 and 1938. 60 × 87 cm. Graticule drawn at 5 grade intervals (centesimal from Paris). Relief shown by layer tinting in brown. Roads in red (three grades), railways in black.

(34) 1:200,000. *Carte routière de Laos* (1932)

B. Maps issued by the Geographical Section of the British General Staff

(1) 1:253,440. G.S.G.S. Series 4218, Malaya, Thailand and Indo-China
Compiled and published originally under the direction of the Surveyor-General of India, 1917–41 and revised to 1942. Altogether 123 maps in the series, 59 of which relate to Indo-China; 53 maps have so far been published, mostly of Siam (Thailand). Size of sheet is 42 × 44 cm. Margins divided into 15 min. intervals, latitude and longitude. The grid on the sheets is Lambert Zone III B with grid north, a stated variable number of degrees west of true north. Scale in miles and yards.
Relief is shown by brown contours with a 100 m. interval, but contour values and spot heights are in feet. Rivers in black, forests represented by small tree symbols. Railways in black, showing broad gauge and other gauges, single and double track and milestones. Roads (two grades) and tracks in black.

(2) 1:500,000. G.S.G.S. Series 4221, Indo-China
Photolithographed and printed 1941, from a series of French maps on this scale. Of the intended total of about thirty sheets only two (Saigon and Phnom Penh) have been published. Size of sheets is 45 × 50 cm. Scale in miles and kilometres. Graticule drawn at intervals of 1 grade (centesimal from Paris). Latitude and longitude in degrees given in margin. Other details as for the *Carte de l'Indochine* except that this series is uncoloured (see A. 9).

(3) 1:1,000,000. G.S.G.S. Series 2555, Asia, first edition
Sheets are available in this series for part of Indo-China. They have been copied from a map of the Survey of India and heliographed at the Ordnance Survey Office 1942. International sheet numbers NF. 47, NF. 48, NF. 49, NE. 47, NE. 48, ND. 48, ND. 49, NC. 48, NC. 49. Grid drawn every 1 degree, divisions indicated every 5 min. of latitude and longitude. Sheet size 45 × 63–66 cm. Scale given in kilometres, statute miles and nautical miles. Conversion table (metres to feet) on some sheets.
Relief is shown by contours at an interval of 150 m. up to 600 m. and at 300 m. above this height. Spot heights are given both in metres and feet. Sea, rivers, and lakes coloured blue. Railways in black and roads (three grades) in red. Six symbols to represent towns of different size.

(4) 1:1,000,000. G.S.G.S. Series 2555, Asia, second edition, ground air
Two sheets (NC. 48, NF. 48) were published in 1942. Magnetic declination superimposed in blue. Relief shown by contours and layer-tinting in purple and brown. Conversion table (metres to feet) in margin. Other detail as on B. 3.

(5) 1:4,000,000. G.S.G.S. Series 2957, Asia and Europe
Sheets 34 (2nd edition, 1939) and 46 cover Indo-China. Conical orthomorphic projection, with two standard parallels. Grid divisions drawn every 2 degrees of latitude and longitude. Scale in miles and kilometres.
Brown contours with layer colouring in shades of green and brown, are employed to represent the relief; the heights are given in metres. Symbols for rivers, lakes, canals and marshes in blue. Railways and minor roads are shown by black lines. Main roads in red. Five different symbols are used to indicate the size of towns.

C. French Admiralty Charts

The most recent list of these charts, which are produced by the 'Service hydrographique de la Marine', is to be found in the *Catalogue des Cartes, Plans et Ouvrages* (Paris, 1939).

D. British Admiralty Charts

A key to the charts of Indo-China published by the British Admiralty will be found at the beginning of the *China Sea Pilot*, vol. 1 (London, 1938). These charts are based upon the French Admiralty Charts. A full list of these is given in the *Catalogue of Admiralty Charts and other Hydrographic publications, 1943* (London, 1943).

E. Geological Maps

(1) 1:100,000. *Carte géologique détaillée de l'Indochine* (1923)
Sheets 54 × 66 cm. Geological detail in colour on topographical map, see A. 6.

(2) 1:500,000. *Carte géologique de l'Indochine*
Published by the *Service géographique de l'Indochine (Hanoi)*, 1927–39. Geological detail superimposed in colour on topographical map (see A. 9).

(3) 1:2,000,000. *Carte géologique de l'Indochine*
Two editions in 1931 and 1937.

(4) 1:4,000,000. *Carte géologique de l'Indochine*

F. Miscellaneous Maps

General and Topographical Maps

(1) 1:200,000. *Carte de la Mission Montgiers*
Cambodia-Siam boundary, 1908–9. Five sheets in colour.

(2) 1:200,000. *Carte de la Mission Maître*
1906–8. Five sheets in colour. Covers part of the plateau regions of south Annam.

(3) 1:4,000,000. Malaya and Indo-China
Produced by J. Bartholomew (Edinburgh, no date). Single sheet, 40 × 67 cm. Graticule drawn at degree intervals. Relief shown by contours in fine, black lines at 500, 1,000, 1,500, 2,000, 3,000, 6,000, and 10,000 feet, layer-tinted in shades of green, brown, violet and white. Railways in black. International and state boundaries in red.

(4) 1:4,000,000. Burma, Malaya and Indo-China
Produced by J. Bartholomew (Edinburgh, 1942). Single sheet 52 × 82 cm. Graticule drawn every two degrees of latitude and longitude.
Relief shown by contours at 200, 500, 1,000, 1,500, 2,000, 3,000, 4,000 and 5,000 m. with layer-tinting in green, brown, violet and white. Railways in black and roads (two grades) in red. This forms the folding map at the end of this handbook.

Maps in Guide Books

(5) *Les Guides Madrolles:* 'L'Indochine du Nord'; 'L'Indochine du Sud'; 'Indochina'
Published by Librairie Hachette (Paris and London, 1930). Later edition, 1939. There are three inset folding maps each on a scale of 1:2,500,000 and 44 × 30 cm. in size. Latitudes and longitudes at 2 min. intervals. Relief shown by contours in brown. Main roads in red, railways and rivers in black. There is also an inset folding map of the waterways of the country on a scale of 1:5,500,000.

G. Atlases

(1) *Atlas de l'Indochine*
Printed and published at Hanoi in 1928 by the *Service géographique de l'Indochine*. There are 51 plates, 52 × 33 cm. or 24 × 32 cm. in size. Includes maps of the relief, geology, climate, agriculture, mining, means of communication and administrative units of Indo-China. They have a wide range of colours. The sheets covering the whole country are on a scale of 1:4,000,000. Eighteen relief maps are on the 1:1,000,000 scale, for details of which see A. 11. There are also town plans of Hanoi, Haiphong, Hue, Tourane, Saigon, Cho Lon and Phnom Penh.

(2) *Atlas des Colonies françaises*
Produced under the direction of G. Grandidier and published by the *Société d'Editions géographiques, maritimes et coloniales* (Paris, 1934). In the section on Indo-China there are six maps (60 × 40 cm.) in colour, representing relief, geology and climate and 14 figures in black and white.

Appendix IV

CLIMATE STATISTICS

(1) Mean Monthly Temperatures: Hanoi, Luang, Prabang, Vinh, Hue, Nha Trang, Dalat, Saigon.

(2) Relative Humidity: Hanoi, Chapa, Dalat, Saigon.

(3) Monthly Visibility: Phu Lien, Cap Saint Jacques.

(4) Mean Monthly Cloud Amount: Lao Kay, Hanoi, Hue, Qui Nhon, Cap Padaran, Saigon.

(5) Mean Annual Rainfall: Hanoi, Luang Prabang, Hue, Kontum, Nha Trang, Cap Padaran, Saigon, Val d'Emeraude.

Table 1. *Mean Monthly Temperatures* (° F.)

	Jan.	Feb.	Mar.	Apr.	May	June	July	Aug.	Sept.	Oct.	Nov.	Dec.
Hanoi	63	63	68	75	82	84	84	84	82	77	72	66
Luang Prabang	70	73	79	82	84	84	82	82	82	81	75	70
Vinh	66	66	70	77	82	86	86	86	82	77	72	66
Hue	70	70	73	79	82	84	84	84	81	77	73	70
Kontum	69	72	76	79	80	78	77	77	77	74	72	70
Nha Trang	75	77	79	81	82	84	84	84	82	81	79	77
Cap Padaran	74	75	78	81	82	81	79	79	80	78	76	77
Dalat	63	64	66	68	70	68	66	68	68	66	64	63
Saigon	79	81	84	86	84	82	81	82	82	81	81	79

Source: E. Bruzon and P. Carton, *Le Climat de l'Indochine et les Typhons de la Mer de Chine*, pp. 229–54 (Hanoi, 1930).

Table 2. *Mean Annual Rainfall* (*mm.*)

	Jan.	Feb.	Mar.	Apr.	May	June	July	Aug.	Sept.	Oct.	Nov.	Dec.	Total
Hanoi	24	36	47	90	218	268	321	355	269	105	48	28	1,809 (72 in.)
Luang Prabang	20	14	33	112	150	161	229	308	166	82	31	8	1,314 (53 in.)
Vinh	56	42	51	65	136	122	132	158	382	354	211	79	1,788 (72 in.)
Hue	173	78	105	52	110	80	82	116	357	649	729	372	2,903 (116 in.)
Kontum	1	7	31	122	189	289	358	367	294	155	73	11	1,897 (75 in.)
Nha Trang	64	27	55	22	48	50	46	47	170	348	380	203	1,460 (58 in.)
Cap Padaran	14	4	18	23	77	64	58	29	105	145	151	69	757 (30 in.)
Dalat	9	28	55	180	205	162	254	215	313	222	89	23	1,755 (70 in.)
Saigon	17	3	16	41	212	339	309	284	345	280	113	63	2,022 (81 in.)
Val d'Emeraude	39	42	169	209	525	729	1,049	1,028	781	467	235	67	5,340 (221 in.)

Source: E. Bruzon and P. Carton, *Le Climat de l'Indochine et les Typhons de la Mer de Chine*, pp. 80–159 (Hanoi, 1930).

Table 3. *Relative Humidity*

Alt.	Jan.	Feb.	Mar.	Apr.	May	June	July	Aug.	Sept.	Oct.	Nov.	Dec.
Hanoi (14 m.)	74	79	80	79	73	74	76	78	76	72	71	72
Chapa (1,640 m.)	78	84	86	80	79	87	86	87	90	89	87	83
Dalat (1,500 m.)	67	63	62	68	74	78	82	82	81	78	75	71
Saigon (11 m.)	65	61	60	62	71	78	80	78	80	78	74	70

Source: E. Bruzon and P. Carton, *Le Climat de l'Indochine et les Typhons de la Mer de Chine, pp.* 229–54 (Hanoi, 1930).

Table 4. *Cloud Cover (tenths)*

	Jan.	Feb.	Mar.	Apr.	May	June	July	Aug.	Sept.	Oct.	Nov.	Dec.
Lao Kay	8·2	8·0	7·5	6·7	6·2	7·0	7·0	6·7	6·5	7·2	7·5	7·2
Hanoi	7·2	8·2	8·7	8·2	7·2	7·5	7·5	7·5	6·5	6·0	6·5	6·7
Hue	6·7	6·7	7·2	6·7	6·2	6·5	6·5	6·5	6·5	7·0	7·7	7·7
Qui Nhon	7·2	5·7	5·2	4·9	5·0	5·7	6·4	6·0	6·6	7·4	7·8	8·0
Cap Padaran	6·0	5·5	5·5	5·2	6·2	6·7	7·2	6·7	7·2	7·2	7·2	6·7
Saigon	5·5	4·7	5·2	5·7	7·2	8·0	8·2	8·0	8·0	7·2	6·7	6·2

Source: E. Bruzon and P. Carton, *Le Climat de l'Indochine et les Typhons de la Mer de Chine*, p. 220 (Hanoi, 1930).

Table 5. *Visibility. Number of days per 100 on which the visibility may be expected to be within the limits specified. Period 1931–2*

Phu Lien

Month	0700 local time					1300 local time				
	0–1 km.	1–3 km.	3–8 km.	8–16 km.	Over 16 km.	0–1 km.	1–3 km.	3–8 km.	8–16 km.	Over 16 km.
Jan.	12	18	60	2	8	0	0	42	11	47
Feb.	38	26	27	4	5	21	5	30	9	35
Mar.	34	20	30	8	8	15	3	43	8	31
Apr.	32	10	48	7	3	5	3	44	5	43
May	0	6	41	20	33	1	0	5	16	78
June	0	5	25	25	45	2	0	0	12	86
July	1	5	29	24	41	0	1	5	6	88
Aug.	3	16	21	10	50	0	0	6	0	94
Sept.	5	13	24	17	41	3	4	8	7	78
Oct.	2	5	29	25	39	0	0	19	16	65
Nov.	5	2	56	27	10	0	3	22	18	57
Dec.	10	16	58	3	13	0	0	26	7	71

Cap Saint Jacques

Month	0700 local time					1300 local time				
	0–1 km.	1–3 km.	3–8 km.	8–16 km.	Over 16 km.	0–1 km.	1–3 km.	3–8 km.	8–16 km.	Over 16 km.
Jan.	0	9	82	2	7	0	7	78	0	15
Feb.	0	23	69	8	0	0	2	75	7	16
Mar.	0	7	39	17	37	0	5	43	7	45
Apr.	0	0	21	28	51	0	1	19	3	77
May	4	2	9	24	61	4	0	7	0	89
June	0	2	28	14	56	0	5	27	8	60
July	5	7	32	25	31	2	9	25	3	61
Aug.	1	2	34	14	49	0	2	20	8	70
Sept.	5	9	43	24	19	2	14	30	29	37
Oct.	5	13	40	30	12	4	14	26	22	34
Nov.	0	4	50	38	8	0	5	24	20	51
Dec.	0	0	53	36	11	0	5	43	19	33

Source: *Weather in the China Seas and in the western part of the North Pacific Ocean*, vol. II, p. 151, (London, 1937).

Appendix V

TRADE STATISTICS

Exports from Indo-China by Commodities, 1934–8

(Values in millions of francs)

	1934	1935	1936	1937	1938
Rice	466·3	665·7	781·7	1093·8	1019·8
Rubber	94·1	136·8	244·3	456·6	620·7
Maize	197·4	149·0	303·0	466·6	511·4
Coal	55·9	68·7	80·2	91·1	122·9
Fish and fish products	64·1	59·0	63·0	75·5	81·5
Tin (ore)	20·4	22·9	18·3	30·2	40·2
Tin (metal)	15·0	17·3	23·8	34·0	33·1
Cement	6·1	5·3	9·5	19·5	25·6
Eggs	6·8	10·9	7·5	12·9	25·1
Oilseeds	4·2	10·2	12·8	26·9	24·1
Kapok	3·8	5·0	7·2	15·2	21·9
Tea	7·4	7·9	9·2	16·5	21·6
Timber	12·3	13·6	11·8	17·8	20·4
Raw hides	6·5	10·4	11·5	21·9	17·9
Livestock	2·6	11·0	4·7	14·2	17·7
Copra	3·4	9·0	10·0	19·1	17·1
Pepper	18·0	13·4	11·7	12·1	17·1
Lacquer	11·8	8·2	8·9	10·4	12·7
Tungsten (wolfram)	1·8	3·1	3·5	9·9	12·0
Badiane oil	1·7	0·5	1·3	7·8	11·5
Manioc	—	0·2	2·4	13·8	10·5
Cinnamon	3·8	3·5	5·8	6·7	8·5
Zinc (metal)	3·4	4·2	5·6	3·4	4·6
Castor oil	0·4	0·5	0·6	2·7	3·8
Coffee	2·9	5·7	2·6	3·2	3·8
Sugar	—	1·2	2·0	8·3	2·4
Zinc (ore)	0·3	—	0·2	0·2	—
Other goods	50·2	55·1	44·2	94·8	135·9
Total	1060·6	1298·3	1708·1	2594·1	2843·8

Source: *Tableau général du Commerce Extérieur de l'Indochine, 1938*, Table 39 (Hanoi, 1939).

Imports into Indo-China by Commodities, 1934-8

(Values in millions of francs)

	1934	1935	1936	1937	1938
Cotton tissues	119·2	150·2	133·4	206·5	245·5
Machines and machinery	32·2	39·2	45·5	69·3	124·8
Petroleum and petroleum products	78·7	44·9	69·9	81·6	103·5
Silk tissues	21·9	27·8	33·7	84·8	100·4
Iron and steel	46·4	36·2	38·1	81·0	94·2
Metal goods	48·9	42·9	42·2	86·4	89·4
Dairy products	30·3	33·1	34·8	51·0	79·8
Raw cotton	25·8	27·6	35·0	52·9	79·0
Motor cars	21·1	26·0	34·8	48·6	66·6
Jute tissues	49·5	59·9	46·0	60·0	65·5
Paper	24·2	22·7	24·5	48·5	49·5
Chemical products	13·6	18·2	24·5	45·9	48·4
Tobacco and cigarettes	9·1	13·6	20·6	29·8	40·2
Wines and spirits	30·5	24·5	20·4	35·3	38·9
Cotton yarn	11·6	11·6	8·3	21·3	38·1
Rubber goods	11·7	14·2	16·2	23·5	34·2
Medicinal products	19·0	17·1	22·9	32·2	28·8
Vegetables	12·6	13·3	12·4	18·6	21·1
Cycles	4·7	6·0	7·5	13·8	19·0
Areca nuts	7·6	8·9	9·4	14·2	16·0
Clothing	3·2	5·6	9·8	9·1	15·5
Printing materials	7·1	8·6	10·0	14·4	15·0
Table fruits	7·7	10·2	9·6	12·8	14·3
Perfume and perfumed soaps	6·2	6·0	8·3	11·7	12·1
Dyestuffs	4·8	5·8	5·7	7·5	11·0
Wool tissues	4·9	4·9	8·2	13·8	9·9
Tea	6·9	4·1	5·7	9·1	9·0
Clocks and jewellery	2·1	2·5	3·2	6·1	8·8
Hides and skins	4·0	3·9	0·5	9·2	8·1
Copper	2·9	3·0	2·7	5·0	6·8
Arms and ammunition	4·2	4·3	4·7	5·5	6·4
Jute thread	2·0	2·0	1·9	3·4	4·1
Zinc	2·3	2·8	2·5	4·9	3·8
Other goods	238·4	196·8	215·9	344·7	439·5
Total	914·3	901·4	974·7	1562·4	1947·2

Source: *Tableau général du Commerce Extérieur de l'Indochine, 1938*, Table 38 (Hanoi, 1939).

Exports from Indo-China by Countries, 1929, 1930–4, 1935–8

(Values in millions of francs)

	1929	1930-4*	1935	1936	1937	1938
France and French colonies	606·0	462·9	486·4	1047·5	1349·9	1513·1
China	187·0	114·4	197·3	51·1	139·9	75·7
Hong Kong	839·0	298·5	225·1	145·6	294·8	274·2
Netherlands East Indies	255·0	60·3	28·5	8·5	12·8	28·2
Singapore	271·0	115·6	102·0	108·9	195·9	277·2
Japan	150·0	59·2	54·1	78·3	108·6	87·6
Philippines	90·0	0·8	4·9	29·0	0·9	20·0
India	19·0	16·6	38·9	29·9	4·3	5·2
Ceylon	36·0	5·9	3·4	3·3	7·1	9·8
Siam	11·0	9·7	6·9	6·1	11·9	14·7
United States	31·0	16·5	55·8	107·1	180·1	249·3
Cuba	—	—	7·4	2·1	38·6	8·8
Great Britain	64·0	15·2	17·9	14·4	34·7	59·5
Belgium	21·0	8·7	13·7	8·5	24·4	40·5
Germany	10·0	6·5	13·2	23·7	64·3	37·9
Netherlands	—	—	7·3	13·0	22·6	32·0
Other countries	22·0	19·8	35·5	44·1	103·3	110·1
Total	2612·0	1210·6	1298·3	1708·1	2594·1	2843·8

Percentage of total value

	1929	1930-4*	1935	1936	1937	1938
France and French colonies	23·2	38·2	37·4	61·3	52·0	53·2
China	7·2	9·4	15·2	2·9	5·4	2·7
Hong Kong	32·1	24·7	17·3	8·5	11·4	9·6
Netherlands East Indies	9·8	5·0	2·2	0·5	0·5	1·0
Singapore	10·4	9·6	7·8	6·4	7·5	9·7
Japan	5·7	4·9	4·2	4·6	4·2	3·1
Philippines	3·4	—	0·4	1·6	—	0·8
India	0·7	1·3	3·0	1·6	0·2	0·2
Ceylon	1·4	0·5	0·4	0·2	0·3	0·4
Siam	0·4	0·8	0·5	0·4	0·5	0·5
United States	1·2	1·4	4·3	6·3	6·9	8·8
Cuba	—	—	0·6	0·1	1·5	—
Great Britain	2·5	1·3	1·4	0·8	1·3	2·1
Belgium	0·8	0·7	1·0	0·3	1·0	1·5
Germany	0·4	0·5	1·0	1·3	2·5	1·4
Netherlands	—	—	0·6	0·7	0·9	1·1
Other countries	0·8	1·7	2·7	2·5	3·9	3·9
Total	100·0	100·0	100·0	100·0	100·0	100·0

Source: *Tableau général du Commerce Extérieur de l'Indochine, 1938*, Table 16 (Hanoi, 1939).

* The figures in this column are the average for the period 1930–4.

Imports to Indo-China by Countries, 1929, 1930–4, 1935–8

(Values in millions of francs)

	1929	1930–4*	1935	1936	1937	1938
France and French colonies	1267·0	679·0	527·4	549·9	889·9	1095·3
China	170·0	32·4	70·7	90·3	114·5	143·0
Hong Kong	377·0	124·2	72·0	71·7	135·4	143·4
Netherlands East Indies	186·0	82·0	54·4	58·3	68·6	84·6
Singapore	92·0	36·6	61·4	38·9	58·0	57·8
Japan	41·0	17·3	26·3	34·7	48·3	55·5
India	73·0	39·9	7·3	29·2	43·7	55·4
Siam	13·0	4·3	13·6	15·0	33·1	36·0
United States	137·0	46·3	21·1	23·5	52·0	97·9
Great Britain	52·0	22·7	14·6	24·0	33·4	62·4
Belgium	9·0	8·9	10·9	10·0	25·8	23·2
Germany	83·0	39·1	3·5	4·9	12·1	16·6
Netherlands	11·0	8·7	5·3	7·6	10·1	18·3
Switzerland	22·0	11·9	1·8	2·1	6·0	15·5
Other countries	17·0	17·1	11·1	14·6	31·5	42·3
Total	2550·0	1170·4	901·4	974·7	1562·4	1947·2

Percentage of total value

	1929	1930–4*	1935	1936	1937	1938
France and French colonies	49·7	58·0	58·6	56·3	56·9	56·3
China	6·7	2·8	7·9	9·3	7·3	7·3
Hong Kong	14·8	10·6	8·0	7·4	8·7	7·4
Netherlands East Indies	7·3	7·0	6·0	6·0	4·4	4·3
Singapore	3·6	3·2	6·8	4·0	3·7	3·1
Japan	1·6	1·5	2·9	3·6	3·1	2·9
India	2·9	3·4	0·8	3·0	2·8	2·8
Siam	0·6	0·4	1·5	1·5	2·1	1·8
United States	5·4	4·0	2·3	2·4	3·3	5·0
Great Britain	2·0	1·9	1·6	2·5	2·1	3·1
Belgium	0·3	0·8	1·2	1·0	1·7	1·2
Germany	3·3	3·3	0·4	0·5	0·8	0·9
Netherlands	0·4	0·7	0·6	0·8	0·7	0·9
Switzerland	0·8	1·0	0·2	0·2	0·4	0·8
Other countries	0·6	1·4	1·2	1·5	2·0	2·2
Total	100·0	100·0	100·0	100·0	100·0	100·0

Source: *Tableau général du Commerce Extérieur de l'Indochine, 1938*, Table 16 (Hanoi, 1939).

* The figures in this column are the average for the period 1930–4.

Appendix VI

CAMPING IN RAIN FOREST

Camping in tropical rain forest presents certain difficulties not met with in other places, though the abundance of building material and firewood go some way to offset the disadvantages of climate. These notes are intended as a guide to the methods which have been found in practice to be the simplest for Europeans to adopt when they have little or no assistance from natives. Whenever possible, however, it is very desirable to employ native assistants, and local camping methods, with which the assistants will be familiar, should then be employed.

STORES

The most essential stores are an axe, a large knife (cutlass or machete) with at least a 9 in. blade, matches, a hammock and food, according to availability and needs. A blanket, a lamp and various other articles of furniture and equipment will also be found useful.

A short list of the most generally needed medicines is given below, though many more which might be useful could be added:

> Antiseptic (Eusol is very good for septic sores).
> Atebrin or quinine (for malaria).
> A laxative.
> Aspirin.
> Ferric chloride (for leech bites).
> Chlorodyne (for diarrhœa).
> Lint and sticking plaster.
> Potassium permanganate (for remote risk of snake bite).

SHELTERS

Temporary Shelters

As the frequent heavy rain storms usually last only for a short time, it may be worth while to shelter from them, thus avoiding discomfort and the risk of a chill. If palm leaves are obtainable half a dozen or more should be cut, laid on top of each other and tied or wedged in the fork of a small tree. These make a good shelter from the rain, which usually falls vertically in dense forest. Other large leaves, such as those of wild bananas, can be substituted for palm. If neither shelter nor a change of clothing is obtainable, it is advisable to remove some or all of the clothes and keep them as dry as possible until the rain is over, as severe chilling results from wearing wet clothes, even at tropical temperatures.

Sleeping Places

The type of shelter to be constructed for a night or two depends on whether hammocks or beds are to be used. For hammocks a strong framework is constructed as shown in Fig. 142, using lianes for the lashings. Lianes vary in their suitability for use as rope; this can only be determined by experience unless there are local inhabitants who can be questioned. The strength and pliability of a

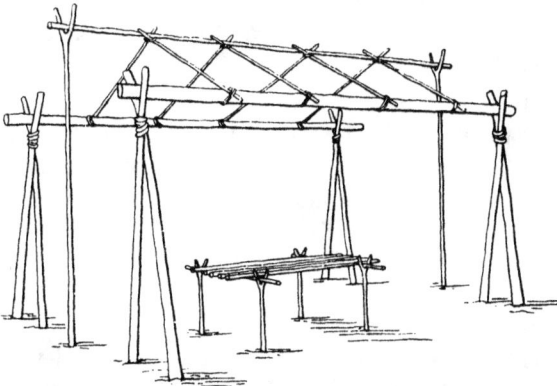

Fig. 142. Construction of a shelter (drawn from photographs)

liane can be improved by twisting, and this is also some test of suitability, as the worst ones will break. A ridge pole is erected (Fig. 142) and the roof thatched with palm or other large leaves, secured with liane. If tarpaulins are available, these can be used instead of leaves for roofing; they should be secured by tying to stakes driven in at intervals along the sides. In exposed situations or very wet weather it may be desirable to cover one or more sides of the hut with palm leaves held in place by lacing between slender stakes. Alternatively the split stems of very soft wooded trees or bamboo can be used. It is usually easier to make several huts for a large party, each with room for about four hammocks, rather than one large one.

If beds are used a light framework to support the thatch is all that is necessary. Beds are in general less convenient than hammocks as they are awkward to carry about and are more accessible to ants and other pests.

A single blanket is adequate covering for the night.

FIRES

Dry wood can be obtained on the wettest day by splitting a dead, but not rotten, log. Many of the trees have very hard wood, but soft wood can always be found with a little searching; this burns better and saves a great deal of time. Thin shavings cut from the split surface of the log are an effective substitute for paper for kindling; dry leaves are seldom satisfactory.

FOOD

Mammals and Birds

Local sources of animal foods are nearly always poor. Game is very difficult to see in the forest, and unless it can be approached quietly and shot before it moves, it nearly invariably gets away. Local inhabitants can often obtain a certain amount of meat where a European, even though a good shot, will get none.

Chickens are general in villages and settlements.

Fish

Fish provide the most generally obtainable animal food. Any of the usual means of catching fish can be tried, though angling is extremely inefficient. It is best to use local fishing methods, where these are known and the apparatus is available (see pp. 308–15). The commonest are nets, various types of trap and fish poisons. Fish poisons are made from a variety of plants and are in use in most tropical countries. When put in a stream or small river they stupefy or kill the fish, which can then be picked out as they float to the surface. Poisoned fish are quite wholesome to eat.

Other Animals

Tortoises, turtles and many large grubs may be eaten, the latter with caution as some are very unpleasant.

Vegetables, Fruits and Nuts

These are generally scarce, and it is unwise to eat even the most tempting looking fruits without certain knowledge or the guidance of local inhabitants. The young shoots of palms, raw or cooked, are a safe and easily recognized food which can usually be obtained.

Yams are generally to be found in villages or cultivation patches in the forest. There are many varieties known by a number of local names, the chief of which are: Taro, Tannia, Eddoe, Yuca and Sweet Cassava. These may all be boiled or roasted, and thorough cooking is desirable, particularly with cassava which is poisonous when raw. If palm oil or other fat is available a kind of 'potato cake' may be made from any of these by boiling, mashing and frying. Sweet potatoes, another commonly grown tuber, are eaten boiled and have a flavour reminiscent of Spanish chestnuts.

Sago, made from the pith of a palm, is much used. Young fern fronds are boiled and eaten in some districts.

Drink

Water should always be well boiled, except when obtained from mountain streams in uninhabited districts.

Certain lianes contain a large quantity of sap which pours out when a piece of stem is cut off. This sap can often be drunk, but the guidance of natives is desirable as some lianes are poisonous.

Bread Making

In all warm damp climates spores of yeast float in the atmosphere and grow rapidly when they settle on any suitable substance. This yeast can be caught and used for bread making by exposing a small quantity of dough to the air in a shady place for a few days. This lump of dough is then kneaded in with the main mass and the bread allowed to rise. When the loaves have risen they are put in an empty gasoline can, or other suitable tin, cut open at one end to serve as an oven. The fire is then built on the top and round the sides of the oven, but not underneath it. The addition of a small quantity of sugar to the dough makes it rise better.

FINDING THE WAY

Visibility in rain forest seldom exceeds 20 m. and it is very easy to get lost. A compass is almost essential for a cross-country journey, though blazing the trunks of the larger trees and cutting through saplings at every few steps is all that is necessary for finding the way back to the starting point. To begin with, it is essential to concentrate on following the blazed trail when returning, but this becomes automatic with practice.

Whistles and guns are of very little use for attracting the attention of people who are lost, as sound only carries a short distance in the forest.

Paths are scarce, and away from villages usually absent. Rivers are everywhere the chief travel routes. If a European boat with an outboard motor is used, paddles or oars should always be carried, as few outboards survive for long on tropical rivers. Native people are familiar with paddles, but have rarely used oars; paddles are therefore preferable if there is a prospect of employing natives. Paddles can be fairly easily made from the thin buttresses of certain trees.

Rafts can be constructed with tree trunks and lianes, but care is necessary in selecting the trees as many tropical hardwoods are heavier than water. No other type of craft can be easily made by the inexpert.

With a little practice it is easy to tell the time by the sun with considerable accuracy.

PESTS

Large dangerous animals are rare and often entirely absent in rain forests; snakes too are much scarcer than is generally believed, and very few kinds will attack man if not molested (see p. 99).

Insects

Ants are ubiquitous and frequently unpleasant, being specially in evidence when trees are felled. They are very difficult to avoid altogether.

Mosquitoes, certain kinds of which may carry malaria, are mostly active after dark. Mosquito nets are desirable for sleeping under; these can be used for hammocks as well as beds, though a rather different type is necessary. Two layers of thin clothing are a more effective protection than one layer of thicker material. Sandflies are often very local and found only near rivers. They are so small that protection from them is almost impossible.

Other Invertebrates

Leeches are particularly active after rain. They may be removed by applying salt or a hot cigarette end and the bleeding stopped by painting the wound with ferric chloride solution.

Ticks are ubiquitous. They may be removed in the same way as leeches. The annoyance of ticks can be minimized by avoiding contact with the undergrowth as far as possible.

Scorpions are rare and easily avoided by the observant.

It is particularly desirable to avoid scratching an itching bite, as septic sores, very difficult to cure, nearly always result. For the same reason any wound, however slight, should be immediately treated with antiseptic.

CLOTHING

There has in the past been much discussion about the advantages of shorts compared with knee breeches. Breeches provide some protection against mosquitoes and ticks but fail to keep out leeches. Shorts are cooler and more comfortable and make the detection and removal of parasites much easier.

Gym shoes are the most satisfactory footwear, and it is important never to go barefoot, even in a hut. Socks or stockings can be worn if desired; they are of little use as protection and very unpleasant when wet.

Very few raincoats are effective in a tropical storm, and any additional garment causes the wearer to sweat so much that he gets just as wet with it as without it.

Hats may not be needed as a protection against the sun within the forest, but are very useful when it rains.

CARE OF PERSONAL PROPERTY

Keeping clothing and stores dry is very difficult, and many things rapidly go mouldy in the warm damp atmosphere of the forest. Leather suffers in this way more rapidly than any other material and should be avoided as far as possible. A waterproof haversack is invaluable for small objects such as matches and watches, which suffer as much from sweat as from rain if carried in the pockets.

In camp stores, clothes and all other objects which might be damaged by wet should be kept on low 'tables' which can be rapidly constructed from saplings as shown in Fig. 142.

Appendix VII

CHIEF TOWNS AND CITIES

In 1936 there were in Indo-China thirteen towns with a population of 20,000 and over, and eight towns with a population ranging from 10,000 to 20,000. Excluding the seaports, which are described elsewhere (see chapter XVII *passim*), fourteen inland towns are dealt with in the following account (Fig. 143).

BAC LIEU (pop. 15,000)

Bac Lieu is one of the chief towns of southern Cochin-China. It lies on the Canal de Bac Lieu about 10 km. from the sea in the well-watered and low-lying plain west of the Fleuve Postérieur (Bassac). The town has been partly rebuilt by the French during the past thirty years and is attractive in appearance.

Rice, salt, and fish are marketed in large quantities at Bac Lieu. It is also a market for the sale of opium and alcohol.

Bac Lieu is connected by metalled roads and by waterways with most parts of Cochin-China. There is a steamboat service to Saigon.

BATTAMBANG (pop. 20,000)

Battambang, capital of the province of the same name, is situated on the banks of the Stung Sang Ke, one of the rivers flowing into the lake of Tonle Sap. The town has grown rapidly since 1907, when it was detached from Siam and became part of the protectorate of Cambodia. In the town there is an agricultural credit bank, a prison, a theatre and a cinema.

The town owes its importance to its central position in one of the most agriculturally productive regions of Cambodia. It is a collecting and distributing centre for rice and has a rice experimental station. It has also a considerable trade in salted fish and a number of forest products. There is a large production of oil from fish offal.

Battambang is on the Phnom Penh-Bangkok railway and is in communication by road (Route Coloniale no. 1) with Sisophon, Pursat and Phnom Penh. During the high-water season, from June to October, boats of 4 m. draught ply between Battambang and the Mekong.

Plate 79. Haiphong

The main part of the town lies between the Song Tam Bac (in the foreground) and the filled-in river channel (in the middle distance). The Cua Cam is seen in the background.

Plate 80. Hanoi

The native quarter is in the foreground and the European quarter in the background. The Fleuve Rouge is on the left of the picture.

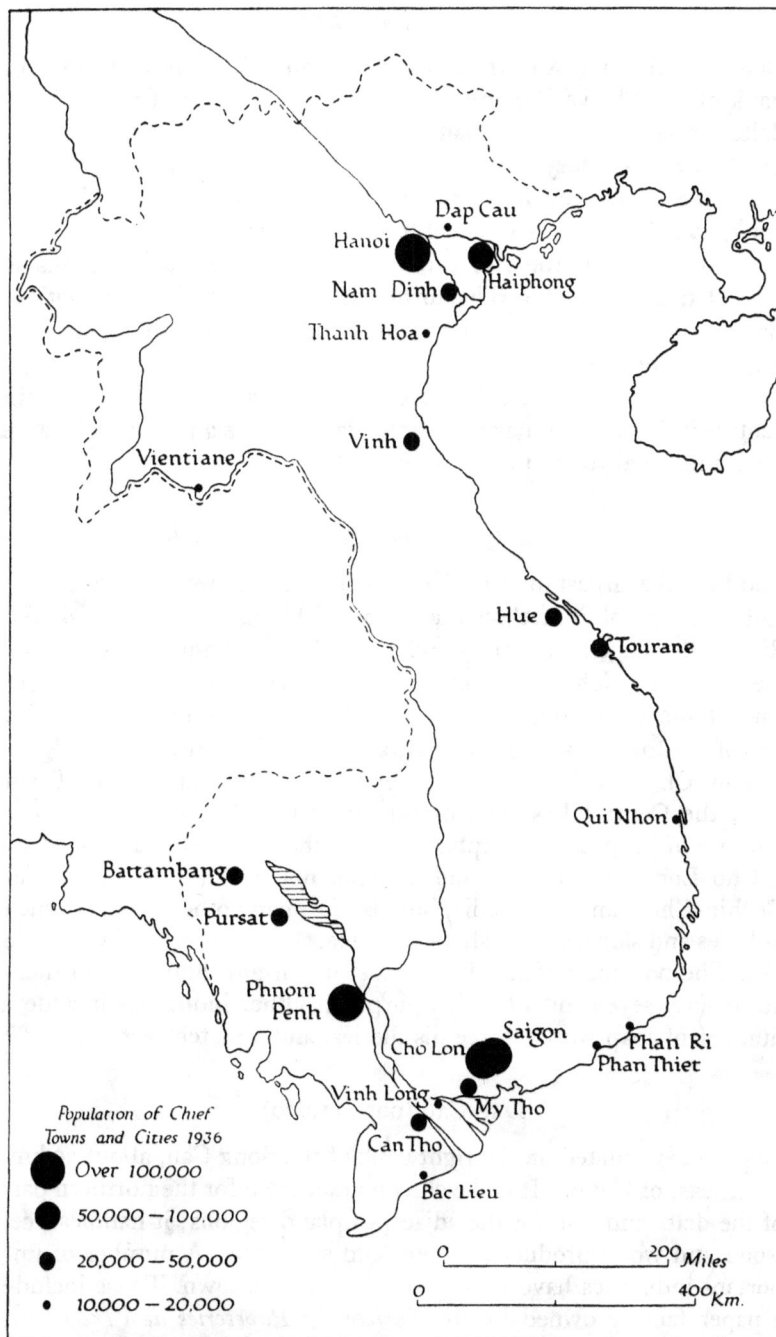

Fig. 143. Population of chief towns and cities
Source: (1) *Annuaire statistique de l'Indochine, 1936–37*, pp. 19–20 (Hanoi, 1938);
(2) *Didot-Bottin, Annuaire de Commerce* (Paris, 1938).

CAN THO (pop. 27,108)

Can Tho, the largest town in central Cochin-China, lies on the right bank of the Fleuve Postérieur (Bassac) in the centre of the Mekong delta. It has risen from a small native village to a modern town during the last half-century. Its population is partly formed of Chinese immigrants. Among its main buildings are the agricultural credit bank, and the secondary school (*collège*) for natives.

A large part of the rice production of central Cochin-China is marketed at Can Tho. The town has a rice experimental station. Brick and tile manufacturing and wood-working are among the leading industries.

Can Tho is connected by road and waterway with all the main centres in Cochin-China and Cambodia. There is a particularly large river and canal traffic to and from the town.

CHO LON (pop. 145,000)

Cho Lon, the largest town in Cochin-China, is an important river port and commercial centre on the Arroyo Chinois, a tributary of the Rivière de Saigon. It was founded by Chinese immigrants towards the end of the eighteenth century and Chinese to-day form the larger part of the population. Since 1932 the town has been fused with Saigon to form a single administrative unit known as the 'Région Saigon-Cho Lon'. Among the principal buildings are the Town Hall, the Central Post Office and the Police Station. There are a number of hospitals, an orphanage, two theatres and a casino.

Cho Lon is the market and entrepôt not only for all the rice of Cochin-China and Cambodia, but also for many other products such as hides and skins, dried fish, pepper, tea, sugar, coffee, and vegetable oils. The polishing of rice is the most important industry and there are twenty-seven mills for this purpose. Other industries include a number of soap works, three distilleries, and a match factory.

DAP CAU (pop. 11,000)

Dap Cau is situated on the right bank of the Song Cau, about 30 km. north-east of Hanoi. It is the chief market town for the northern part of the delta and also for the adjacent upland regions; it handles rice, wood and wood products, pottery and silk ware. A number of important industries have been established in the town. These include a paper factory owned by the *Société des Papeteries de l'Indochine*,

Plate 81. Hanoi: the University

This is one of the many handsome buildings which the French have built in Hanoi.

Plate 82. Hanoi: Rue des Caisses

In the native quarter of Hanoi the streets are usually named after a particular trade. Most of the shops are open to the street.

Plate 83. Hue (aerial view, looking west)

The fortified royal city can be seen in the centre and the commercial suburbs in the right of the picture. The bridge in the left foreground crosses the Huong Giang or Rivière des Parfums, linking the royal city with the European several brick and tile works owned by the *Société des Briqueteries du Tonkin* and by the *Société des Tuileries de l'Indochine*, and an electric power-generating plant.

The town lies on the railway and road leading from Hanoi to the Chinese frontier. It is also connected by road with Thai Nguyen, Haiphong and Hon Gay. There is commmunication by water with all parts of the Fleuve Rouge delta.

HAIPHONG (pop. 70,000); see p. 384 and Plate 79

HANOI (pop. 149,000)

Hanoi, the capital of Indo-China, is situated on the right bank of the Fleuve Rouge, about 160 km. from the sea. A high embankment protects the town from the summer floods of the river. It was an important town in the days of Chinese suzerainty over Tonkin, and when Tonkin became independent in the tenth century the Annamite dynasties chose it for their capital. Hanoi remained the chief town of Annam until the seventeenth century when it gave place to Hue in importance. The French occupied the town in 1873 and set up the central government of Indo-China here in 1900. The selection of Hanoi as the capital of the country reflects the greater importance attached by the French to Tonkin than to the other states at the beginning of the present century, when the rich mineral wealth of Tonkin was being developed and when France was making strong efforts to increase her influence in the southern states of China. The linking of the north and south of the country by railway and road has strengthened the position of Hanoi as the capital city. Hanoi is administered by an autonomous municipal council.

With its shady boulevards, numerous squares and imposing public buildings, Hanoi resembles the towns of France (Fig. 144, Plates 80–82). There are three distinct parts or 'quarters' to the town: the citadel, the native town and the European quarter. The citadel was formerly the seat of the Annamite government, and to-day mainly comprises military barracks and various administrative buildings. Among the many fine buildings of the European quarter are the palace of the Governor-General, which stands at the entrance to the Botanical Gardens, the cathedral, the law courts, the university, the library and museum of the *Ecole française d'Extrême Orient*, and the theatre. In a temple near the Grand Lac to the north of the town is a large bronze statue of Buddha, dating from the eleventh century.

Hanoi is an important industrial and commercial centre. Its industries include a match factory, a paper works, a furniture factory and a number of distilleries. The town has a large transit trade in goods from Yunnan.

The railways and roads of Tonkin converge on Hanoi. It has railway connexion with Haiphong, Yunnanfou (Kunming), Na Cham, and Saigon. There is a good road communication with towns in the delta, with the Chinese frontier and with the south of Indo-China. Hanoi is in communication by water with Haiphong and other centres in the delta. The airport of Gia Lam lies a little way east of Hanoi, and there is a seaplane base on the Grand Lac north of the town.

HUE (pop. 43,000)

Hue, the capital of Annam, lies on the Huong Giang or Rivière des Parfums, about 12 km. from the sea. The town has had a long and varied history. It was an important centre of the Champa kingdom from about A.D. 250 until the beginning of the fifteenth century, when it became part of the Annamite state. In the middle of the seventeenth century it was the seat of government of the powerful Nguyen family (see p. 168), and became capital of the whole of Annam, with the accession of Gia Long, in 1802. It is to-day the seat of the protectorate government.

Hue is one of the most picturesque and interesting towns in Indo-China. It consists of two distinct parts: the fortified city, with its commercial suburbs on the left bank, and the European quarter on the opposite bank, both parts being linked by a bridge 400 m. long (Fig. 145). Like the old Chinese cities, the fortified city or citadel is made up of three concentric wards, separated by walls: the *Kinh-thanh* or 'Capital City', with the main administrative buildings of the Annamite government, enclosing the *Hoang-thanh* or 'Royal City', where audiences and official ceremonies are held, and the *Tu-cam-thanh* or 'Forbidden Purple City', for the exclusive use of the Emperor of Annam and his family (Plate 83). The citadel was mainly built during the reign of Gia Long at the beginning of the nineteenth century.

In the vicinity of the town are a number of royal tombs, renowned for their magnificence of design. Each comprises the tomb proper, surrounded by a 'precious wall' and containing the mortal remains of the sovereign; a funeral avenue, lined with statues, with a pavilion containing a record of the sovereign's qualities and achievements; a

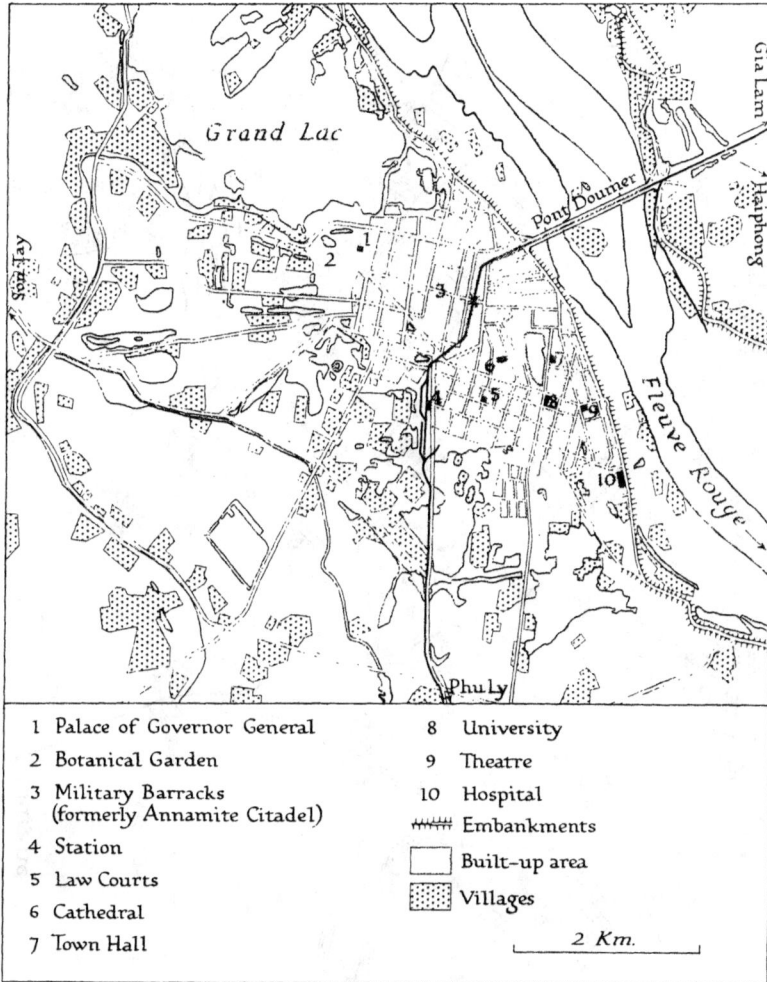

1 Palace of Governor General	8 University
2 Botanical Garden	9 Theatre
3 Military Barracks (formerly Annamite Citadel)	10 Hospital
4 Station	⊞⊞⊞ Embankments
5 Law Courts	☐ Built-up area
6 Cathedral	▓ Villages
7 Town Hall	2 Km.

Fig. 144. Plan of Hanoi
Source: *Atlas de l'Indochine*, plate 47 (Hanoi, 1928).

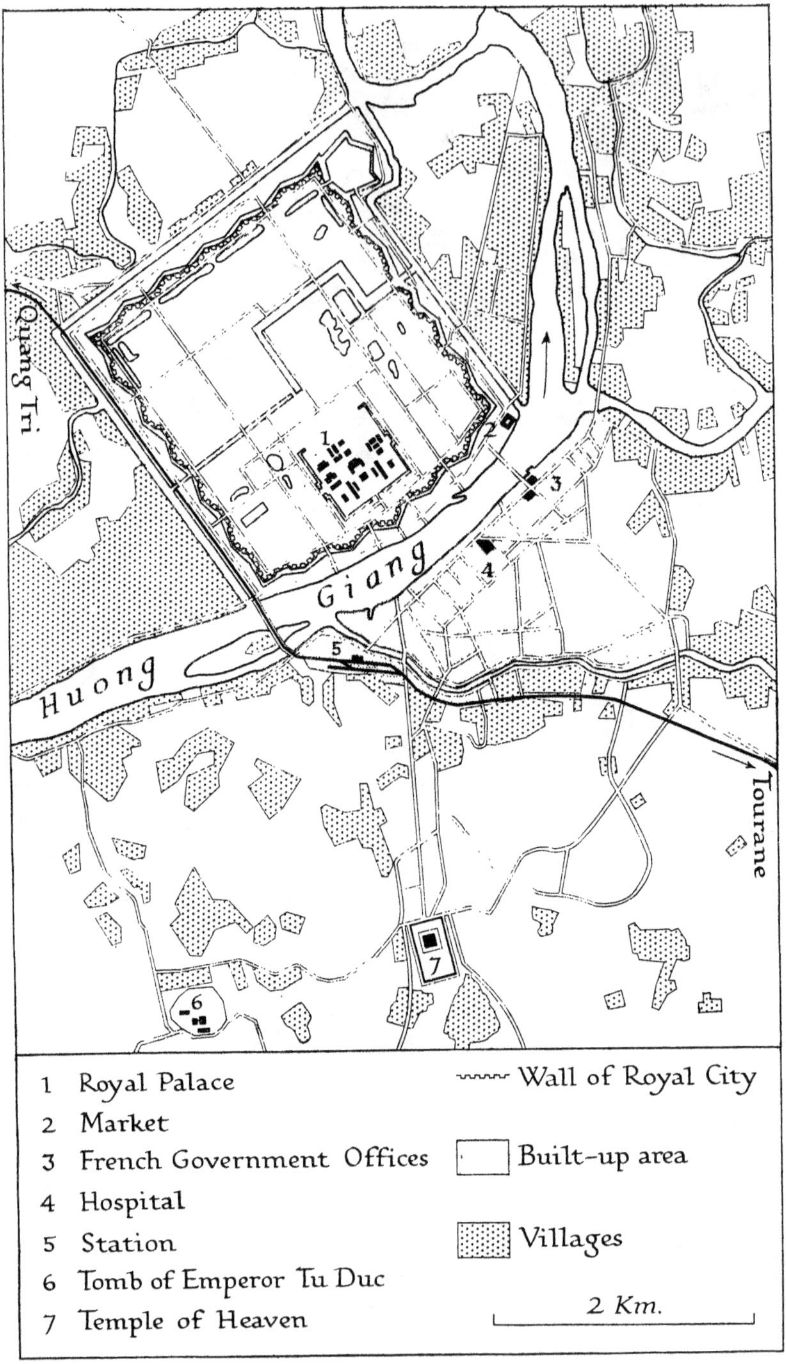
Quang Tri
Huong Giang
Tourane
1 Royal Palace
2 Market
3 French Government Offices
4 Hospital
5 Station
6 Tomb of Emperor Tu Duc
7 Temple of Heaven
Wall of Royal City
Built-up area
Villages
2 Km.

Fig. 145. Plan of Hue

Source: *Atlas de l'Indochine*, plate 49 (Hanoi, 1928).

temple where periodical sacrifices are offered up; and a terrace laid out in tiers for the holding of the ritual ceremonies (Plate 20). In addition to the royal tombs there are also many pagodas and temples near the city, of which that known as 'The Temple of Heaven', south of the European quarter, is the most famous.

The town is primarily an administrative centre and has no large industries. It is in communication by road and rail with Hanoi and Saigon. There is an aerodrome and a seaplane anchorage.

MY THO (pop. 25,000), see p. 407

NAM DINH (pop. 25,347)

Nam Dinh, the third largest town in the Tonkin delta, after Hanoi and Haiphong, stands close to the right bank of the Fleuve Rouge about 40 km. above its mouth (Plate 87). The town has been largely built since the French conquest of Tonkin. In 1922 it was made a municipality with autonomous rights of government; a municipal commission with French and native members controls the affairs of the town.

The industries of Nam Dinh are many and varied. They include a cotton-spinning mill, a sawmill, a distillery and the preparation of lacquer work. Some of the most skilful Annamite handicraft workers are found in this town.

Nam Dinh is on the Trans-Indo-Chinese railway and on one of the many branch roads of the Route Coloniale no. 1.

PHAN RI (pop. 10,900); see p. 406

PHAN THIET (pop. 15,500); see p. 406

PHNOM PENH (pop. 103,000)

Phnom Penh, the capital of Cambodia, has an attractive site on the right bank of the Mekong where the main stream divides into two branches near the confluence with the river of Tonle Sap (Fig. 147). The town first became the seat of government in 1434 when the King of Cambodia moved there from Angkor. It was later abandoned as the royal residence, but again became the capital in 1867, under King Norodom, after the French occupation of the country. Phnom Penh is administered by a municipal commission.

The town has been largely rebuilt by the French and presents a modern appearance. It consists of three parts: to the north, the

European quarter round the *Phnom* or hill; in the centre, the Chinese quarter, where most of the commercial houses are situated; to the south, the Cambodian quarter. The principal buildings are the royal palace, the cathedral, the town hall, and the *Musée Albert Sarraut* (Plates 84, 85).

For the trade and communications of Phnom Penh see p. 408.

PURSAT (pop. 20,000)

Pursat lies on the river of the same name at a level above the summer floods of the lake of Tonle Sap. It is a market town handling a great variety of agricultural and forest products. The town is on the main railway and road between Phnom Penh and the Siamese frontier.

QUI NHON (pop. 10,000); see p. 400

SAIGON (pop. 111,000); see p. 376 and Plates 88–90

THANH HOA (pop. 10,000)

Thanh Hoa, a provincial capital and market town, is situated on a small tributary of the Song Ma in the centre of a densely peopled and well-cultivated plain. The town has been an important administrative and commercial centre for many centuries. The Annamite citadel with its fortifications and palatial buildings, now occupied by Europeans, is well preserved. To the east and north of the citadel are the Annamite and Chinese quarters (Plate 86).

The town lies on the Trans-Indo-Chinese railway and on the Route Coloniale no. 1. The canal from Vinh to Ninh Binh also passes close to Thanh Hoa.

TOURANE (pop. 23,000); see p. 393 and Plate 58

VIENTIANE (pop. 15,878)

Vientiane, the capital of Laos, extends for nearly 5 km. along a bend of the left bank of the Mekong, 1584 km. from the sea. The town was a royal residence of the former Laotian kingdom of Lan Xang, but the invasion of the Siamese in the early nineteenth century led to its abandonment. Its importance was restored when the French took over the administration of Laos in 1893. The government buildings have been built on the site of the ancient royal palace. In the centre of the town are the remains of many beautiful pagodas.

Plate 84. Phnom Penh: the Cambodian quarter
The royal palace is in the left of the picture and the Mekong in the background.

Plate 85. Phnom Penh: Buddhist temple

This temple is built on the *Phnom* or hill overlooking the European quarter of the town. The slopes of the *Phnom* and its immediate surroundings are laid out as ornamental gardens.

The completion of the Route Coloniale no. 13 in 1942 links Vientiane by road with Phnom Penh and Saigon. It also has road communication with the coast of Annam by way of either Xieng Khouang or Savannakhet. The Mekong is widely used as a means of communication in its relatively placid reach between Vientiane and Savannakhet. There is an aerodrome and a seaplane anchorage near the town.

VINH (pop. 25,000)

The provincial capital and market town of Vinh is situated close to the Song Ca, about 15 km. above its mouth. As in Hue, Thanh Hoa and other Annamite towns, there is a fortified part or citadel, where the administrative buildings and larger houses are found, and a native quarter built around it.

Vinh is the market for the agricultural and forest products of the Song Ca valley. Its port lies at Ben Thuy, 4 km. distant (see p. 393).

VINH LONG (pop. 13,000)

Vinh Long stands on the right bank of the most westerly branch of the Fleuve Antérieur (Mekong). It is the capital of the province of the same name. This province has been called the 'garden of Cochin-China' because of the high proportion of its area under cultivation. Vinh Long has a market for rice and garden produce.

The town is well served by roads and is in communication by water with all the main centres of Cochin-China.

Appendix VIII

POSTS, TELEGRAPHS AND TELEPHONES

The postal, telephone and telegraph services are operated by the state, their revenue and expenditure forming part of the General Budget. In most years they run at a loss owing to the numerous post offices with a small turnover, to the enforced use of motor cars on certain postal routes, and to the length and high constructional costs of the telegraph lines.

POSTAL SERVICES

All the towns and larger rural centres in Indo-China are provided with postal facilities. In 1936, there were 338 post offices, two-thirds of which were in the states of Tonkin and Cochin-China. Inland mail is forwarded by railway, river craft and motor car, and in the regions difficult of access, by horse or native courier. Air postal services are little developed, though mails are sometimes carried by air between Hanoi and Saigon.

Overseas mail is handled by the post offices at the ports of Haiphong, Tourane, Qui Nhon, and Saigon. The number of letters and parcels despatched to and received from France by sea amounted to 1,760,000 and 2,243,000 respectively in 1936. Over three-quarters of a million letters were also carried by air in the same year.

Postal Cheques. As in France, the postal cheque system is widely used for the settlement of accounts. In 1936 there were 790,000 transactions effected, amounting to nearly 24 million piastres.

TELEGRAPHS AND TELEPHONES

Indo-China has a well-developed telegraph service with a network of lines, over 20,000 km. in length, extending over a large part of the country. The lines follow the sides of the roads and railways. Almost all the post offices are provided with telegraph facilities.

The development of the telephone services lags far behind that of the telegraph. In 1936 there were 10,438 km. of telephone lines and the number of subscribers was 7,293. The telephone system in Haiphong is fairly efficient and there is connection with Hanoi and Tourane. Saigon has a dial telephone system and it is possible to communicate by telephone with Phnom Penh.

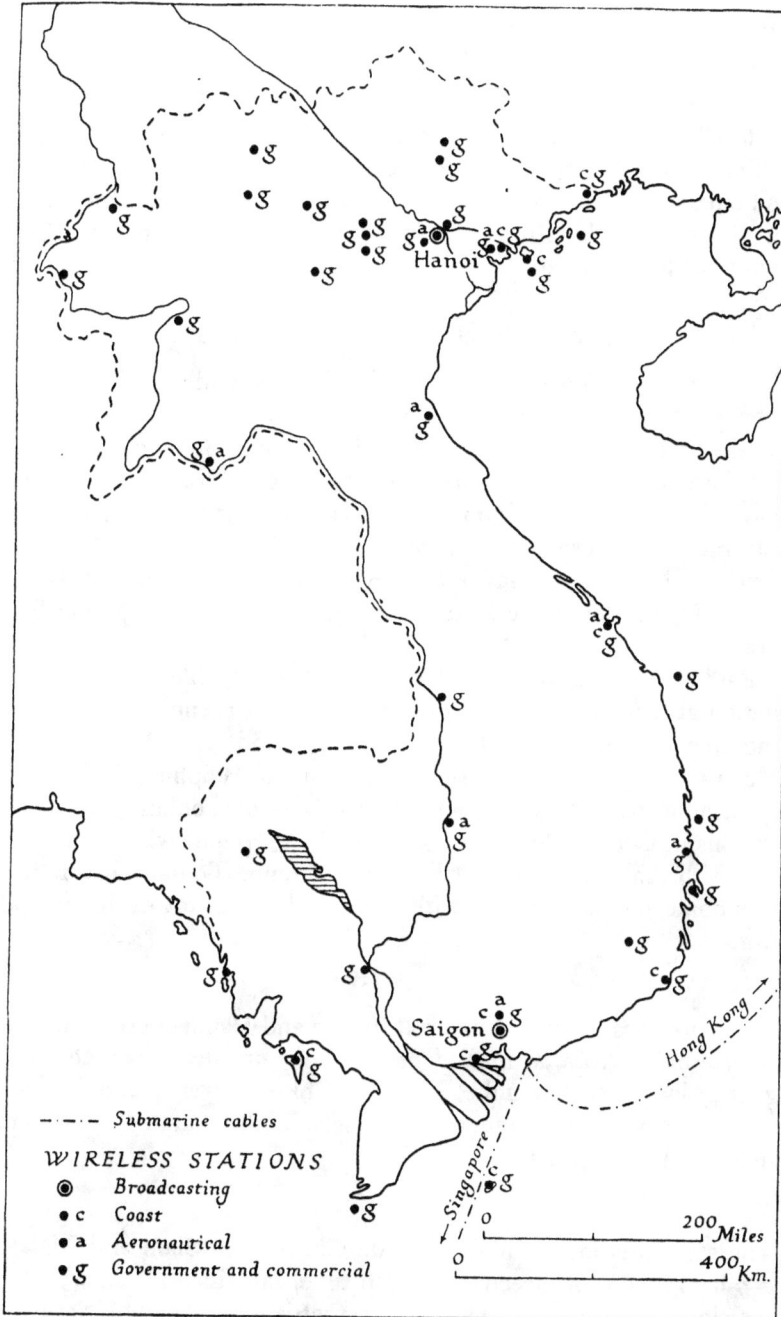

Fig. 146. Wireless stations and submarine cables

Source: (1) *Nomenclature des Stations fixes* (Berne, 1942); (2) *Nomenclature des Stations aéronautiques* (Berne, 1942); (3) *Cartes schématiques des voies de communication télégraphiques internationale* (Berne, 1942); (4) *Admiralty List of Radio Signals*, vol. 1, pp. 49–50 (London, 1942).

SUBMARINE CABLES

Indo-China is dependent upon British cables for communication with countries overseas, as the two French cables from Poulo Condore to Pontianak (N.E.I.) and from Tourane to Haiphong and Amoy have not been in working order for many years. Cables run from Cap Saint Jacques to Hong Kong and Singapore.

WIRELESS TELEGRAPHS AND TELEPHONES

The *Service radiotélégraphique de l'Indochine*, under the management of the P.T.T. (Postes, Télégraphes, Téléphones) operated forty wireless stations in 1942 (Fig. 146). All radiotelegraphic communication between Indo-China and countries abroad is made through the stations at Saigon and Hanoi. Both these stations have direct radiotelegraphic connexion with Paris, Beyrouth, Djibouti, Madagascar, Réunion, New Caledonia, and Tahiti; and with Siam, China, Hong Kong, Japan, the Netherlands East Indies, the Philippines and San Francisco.

Radiotelephonic communication abroad is available only from the station at Saigon. It has direct connexion with French North Africa and many countries of the New World; and with Japan, Siam, Malaya, Java, and the Philippines. Hanoi and Haiphong have communication by radiotelephone with all parts of Tonkin. The radio stations in Cochin-China are connected by telephone with Cambodia and with Annam as far north as Nha Trang. Tourane has radiotelephonic communication with Hue and other towns in central Annam.

BROADCASTING

There are broadcasting stations at Saigon and Hanoi operated by the *Société indochinoise de Radiodiffusion*. They broadcast in many languages, including Annamite, Japanese, Chinese, French and English.

In 1940 there were about 9,000 sets in the country. All were short-wave receivers.

NOTE ON TIME

The standard time adopted in Indo-China as in Siam and Malaya is 7 hr. in front of Greenwich mean time, but since 1 January 1943 the clocks have been set 1 hr. ahead, that is 8 hr. ahead of G.M.T.

The times of sunrise and sunset, duration of twilight and times of moonrise and moonset are given in the *Nautical Almanac*.

Plate 86. Thanh Hoa

A perfect example of an Annamite citadel with the buildings of the native quarters clustered close around it. The Trans-Indo-Chinese railway is seen near the left-hand margin of the photograph.

Plate 87. Nam Dinh (aerial view, looking south-west)

The river on the left flows between the Fleuve Rouge and the Song Day. The confluence with the Fleuve Rouge is about 5 km. above the town.

Appendix IX

CIVIL AVIATION

Indo-China is, by reason of its geographical position, a necessary stage for commercial air lines on the route from Europe to China and Japan, but the advantages of position are to some extent counterbalanced by physical difficulties in the country itself. Except in the lower Mekong basin and Fleuve Rouge delta, level stretches of ground are rare; and even in the two main lowland areas floods often cover the fields, here almost universally cultivated with rice. The heavy summer rains, winter mists, and typhoons further hinder air navigation. Despite these handicaps civil aviation in Indo-China developed rapidly in the period after 1918.

Since 1918, ground facilities for aircraft in Indo-China have been constantly improved. In 1939 there were four fully equipped airports —Hanoi, Saigon, Vientiane, and Vinh—and more than 100 landing grounds scattered widely over the whole country. Landing grounds show particular concentration in Cambodia, north of Saigon, along the coast of Annam, and in Tonkin. Radio and meteorological protection is now well assured, at least in the northern part of Indo-China. Wireless directional posts are functioning regularly at Hanoi, Kien An, Fort Bayard, Vientiane and Vinh; they give bearings and position to aircraft in flight.

In 1938, the passenger planes calling at Gia Lam, the airport of Hanoi, included the Dewoitines of Air France, the de Havillands of Imperial Airways, the Junkers of Eurasia, and the Douglases of the China National Aviation Company. Traffic at Hanoi airport has recently shown an impressive increase. Arrivals and departures of aircraft were $2\frac{1}{2}$ times more numerous in 1938 than in 1937 and over the same period the number of passengers increased five times. Hanoi may well become the leading international airport of the Far East. It is possible for aircraft connexion to be made between Yunnan and Hong Kong via the south of China; there is, further, the possibility of a direct air route between Yunnanfou (Kunming) and Rangoon. But these routes do not offer the same safety for air navigation as the routes passing through Hanoi.

Saigon and Hanoi were connected by a weekly air service from 1931. The planes reached Saigon by way of the Mediterranean, Syria, the north shore of the Persian Gulf, the Indogangetic plain, and Bangkok. They covered the last part of the journey from Saigon to Hanoi by way of the coast of Annam or the Mekong valley, according to weather conditions. The time taken for the air journey from Marseilles to Hanoi was only a week, while the sea journey took about a month. In 1938 this airline was extended to Hong Kong, and in the same year Imperial Airways opened a service from Penang to Hanoi and Hong Kong. On 16 March 1939, Imperial Airways announced that Hanoi would become a regular commercial port of call for their aircraft, whereas formerly permission had only been given for the use of the airport as an optional landing place. The official sanction provided that no passengers were to be taken for internal traffic in Indo-China, and French imperial mail could not be carried. Saigon airport was connected with Singapore, Palembang and Batavia by the Dutch airline company (K.N.I.L.M.).

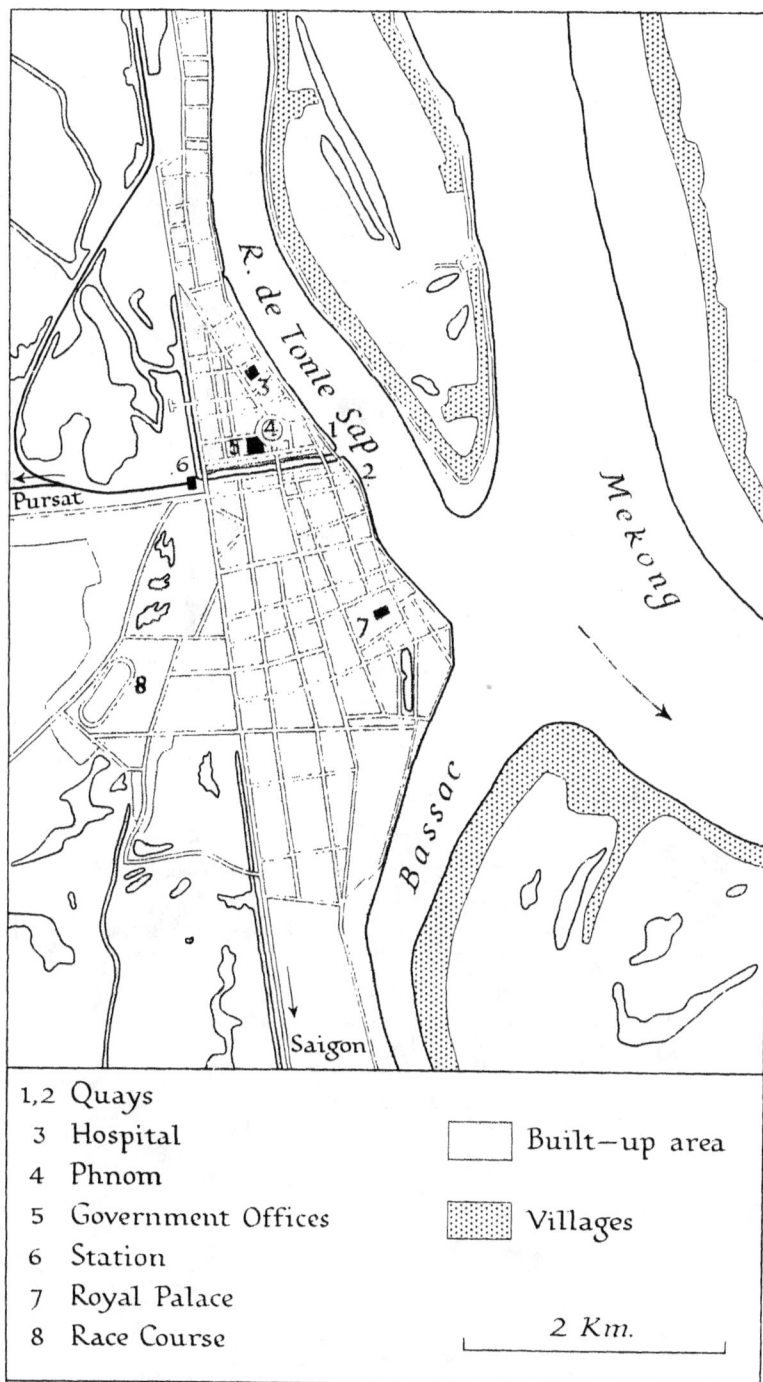

Fig. 147. Plan of Phnom Penh
Source: *Atlas de l'Indochine*, plate 49 (Hanoi, 1928).

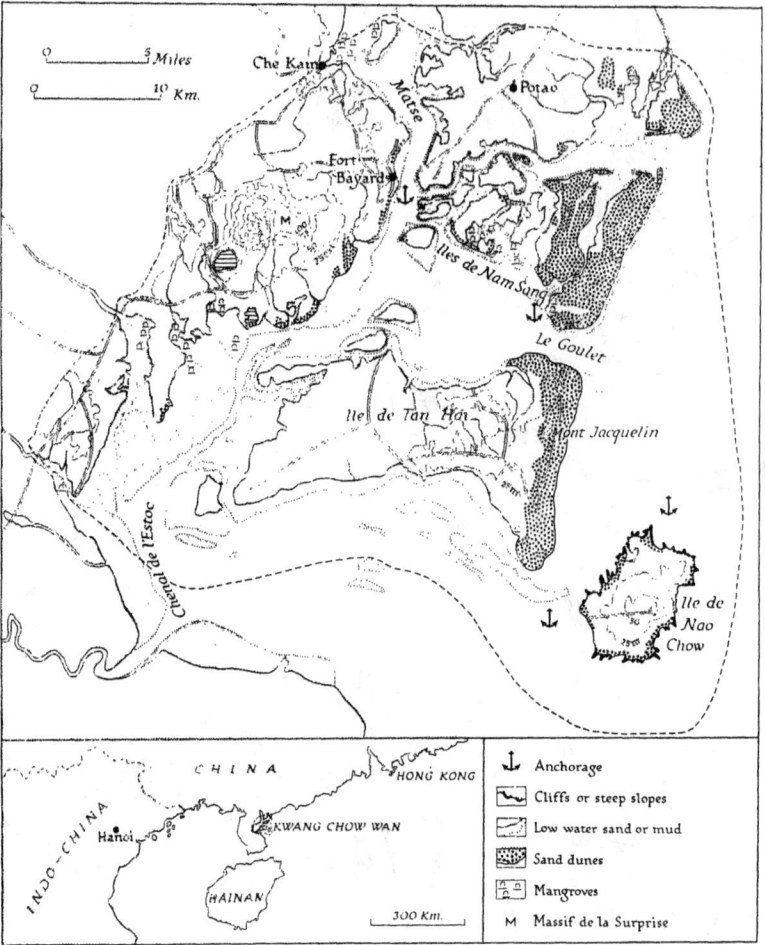

Fig. 148. Kwang Chow Wan

Source: (1) Admiralty; (2) Carte de l'Indochine 1:100,000. Sheet Kouang-Tcheou-Wan (1908).

Appendix X
KWANG CHOW WAN

General Description. The territory of Kwang Chow Wan, which lies to the north-east of the Leitcheou peninsula and forms part of the Chinese province of Kwangtung, was leased to France by China, in 1900, for a period of 99 years as a naval station and coaling depot.* It has an area of 1,200 sq. km. and consists of a narrow, lowlying strip of land enclosing the Matse estuary, with a group of islands (Nam Sang, Tan Hai, and Nao Chow) close offshore. There are two prominent hills, the Massif de la Surprise (155 m.) on the right bank of the Matse near Fort Bayard, and the Mont Jacquelin (108 m.) on the eastern side of Tan Hai. The coasts are for the most part flat and muddy though Tan Hai and Nam Sang have stretches of sand and the shores of Nao Chow are rocky (Fig. 148).

Administration. Kwang Chow Wan is under the control of a Chief Administrator, representing the Governor-General of Indo-China. This official is assisted in his duties by the heads of the three administrative districts into which the territory is divided. As in Annam, the districts are split up into communes, each under a *Conseil de Notables.* The judicial organization, for the Chinese population, is directed by a judge of the court of first instance and by a mixed Franco-Chinese tribunal; a *Juge de paix* with extended jurisdiction handles cases affecting French subjects. Education is provided at numerous Chinese schools and at the *Collège Albert Sarraut,* a large institution with more than 500 pupils. There are native hospitals at Fort Bayard and Che Kam.

Population. The population of Kwang Chow Wan in 1936 was 219,151, made up almost entirely of Chinese, as is shown in the following table:

	French	Foreigners	Chinese	French subjects	Total
Fort Bayard and environs	71	2	9,000	510	9,583
Che Kam and district	7	–	99,000	47	99,054
Potao	4	–	61,500	3	61,507
Tan Hai-Nao Chow	4	–	49,000	3	49,007
Total	86	2	218,500	563	219,151

Che Kam, the commercial centre, and Fort Bayard, the seat of the local administration, are the only towns.

* Kwang Chow Wan was occupied by the Japanese in February 1943.

Products. Kwang Chow Wan produces small quantities of rice, maize, potatoes, groundnuts and sugar cane. Poultry and livestock, especially swine, are reared, and salt-water fishing is also carried on. Sugar refining, sack making, dyeing and the preparation of salt are the principal industries.

Ports. Fort Bayard, the chief port of the territory, is situated on the right bank of the Matse estuary. The main approach to the estuary is made by the narrow channel known as 'Le Goulet' between the Tan Hai and Nam Sang islands (Fig. 148). Vessels may anchor in this channel in a depth of about 12·8 m. (7 fm.), sheltered from northerly and north-easterly winds and with good holding ground. Another anchorage is available in 11·9 m. (6½ fm.) off the port itself. West of the Ile de Tan Hai shoals obstruct the passage to the estuary, and the Chenal de l'Estoc can only be used by small vessels.

The port of Fort Bayard has a pier about 200 m. (660 ft.) long, extending to the outer edge of the drying shore bank. Fuel, oil and water can be obtained. The exports include livestock and various agricultural products; manufactured articles comprise the great bulk of the imports. Fort Bayard is a free port.

Che Kam (pop. 40,000) lies on the right bank of the Matse about 12 km. above Fort Bayard. It is accessible to boats of shallow draught.

Trade. The trade of Kwang Chow Wan is mainly with Hong Kong and only to a small extent with Indo-China. The total exports, including straw sacks, swine, cattle, sugar and groundnuts, were valued at 2,100,000 piastres in 1937; the imports, chiefly cotton yarn, petroleum, matches and refined sugar, were valued at 2,860,000 piastres in the same year. About two-thirds of the ships calling at the territory are of foreign origin, principally British, Portuguese and Norwegian.

Finance. Although the currency of the territory is the same as that used in Kwangtung (dollars and sapeques), the budget is expressed in Indo-Chinese piastres. The budget has increased in amount from about 40,000 piastres in 1913 to 400,000 piastres in 1929 and to nearly 900,000 piastres in 1940.

Communications. Kwang Chow Wan has nearly 300 km. of roads which serve the larger centres (Fig. 148). There is a seaplane base on the Ile de Nam Sang and an aerodrome near Fort Bayard. Telephone and telegraph lines connect Fort Bayard with Che Kam. Fort Bayard and Nao Chow have wireless stations for radio-communication with Indo-China.

Plate 88. Saigon (aerial view, looking north-west)

In the centre of the picture is the Boulevard Charner with the Town Hall at its far end. On the left of the Town Hall is the palace of the Governor of Cochin-China. The cathedral, with its twin spires, can be seen in the background.

Plate 89. Saigon: the Boulevard Norodom

This is one of the main boulevards in Saigon. The palace of the Governor-General is seen in the distance.

Plate 90. Saigon: the Rue Catinat

This street leads from the waterfront to the cathedral.

Appendix XI

POLITICAL AND ECONOMIC CONDITIONS IN INDO-CHINA SINCE 1939

POLITICAL CONDITIONS

From the outbreak of the European war in September 1939 until the fall of France in July 1940 the French government in Indo-China, under Governor-General Catroux, strongly supported the cause of the Allies. Political alinement changed with the appointment of Admiral Decoux as Governor-General in July 1940. He adhered to the Vichy government of Marshal Pétain and gave no support to the Free French movement which won over New Caledonia and the other French colonies in the Pacific. In October 1940, Vichy suppressed the *Conseil de Gouvernement* and the *Conseil des Intérêts économiques et financiers* and all the local advisory councils in the country. The Governor of Cochin-China and the Chief Residents of the protectorate were held responsible to the Vichy government through the Governor-General who was given extraordinary powers; Japan seized the opportunity of the new regime to obtain permission to station 5,000 troops in Tonkin. The passage through Tonkin of a Japanese division in Kwangsi was further requested. Owing to delay in the negotiations, the Japanese precipitated the situation by advancing into Indo-China from Kwangsi and there was some desultory fighting around Lang Son. The French then agreed to the entry of Japanese troops, and Japanese transports, escorted by naval units, arrived off Do Son to occupy Tonkin. The Japanese occupation of Tonkin, though primarily for the purpose of blockading and bombing China, was also the first stage in the conquest of the whole of Indo-China.

Soon after their occupation of Tonkin the Japanese encouraged Siam to attack Indo-China and again there was some desultory fighting. Eventually Japan acted as arbitrator in this dispute, as a result of which Siam in March 1941 reacquired territory in Cambodia and Laos (Fig. 149). In the north, the Japanese in occupation increased from 5,000 to 13,000, and the number of their aircraft varied from 40 to nearly 400. In July 1941, the Japanese moved south and occupied the whole country. Submission to the Japanese was considered

by the French authorities in Indo-China to be the only prudent
course in view of the weakness of the French forces in the country
and the improbability of any quick relief from Britain or the United

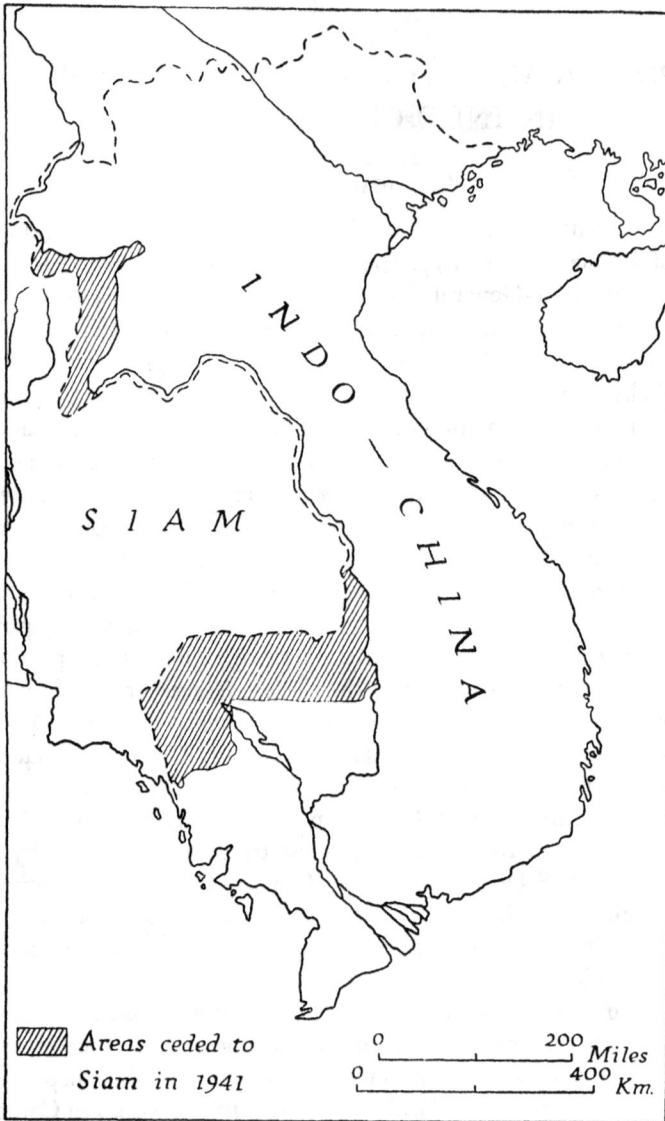

Fig. 149. Boundary changes, 1941

Source: 1:4,000,000 sheet, 'Burma, Malaya and Indo-China', published by
J. Bartholomew (Edinburgh, 1942).

States. Nevertheless, the Japanese occupation was bitterly resented by most Frenchmen in Indo-China, the more so because it involved a public humiliation of the ruling European nation in the eyes of the native Indo-Chinese, who knew that it was a surrender to the superior force of an Asiatic people.

The submission of Indo-China to Japan was accompanied by no major political changes. The Japanese, who wished to make the maximum use of a country efficiently administered and well provided with railways, roads and port facilities, had no wish to cause confusion and breakdown by using violence or removing the French officials; on the contrary, they tried to keep all the machinery of government and commerce running as smoothly as possible, and were at pains to respect the forms of French sovereignty. In spite of this, French prestige was deeply undermined and the Japanese made clear in their declarations that they regarded Indo-China as part of the 'Greater East Asia Co-Prosperity Sphere' in which Japan as the 'stabilizing Power' had a right to leadership. Indo-China, even though it might continue to be administered by French officials, was to become in effect a part of the Japanese, rather than of the French, empire. In accordance with this idea, Vichy left Indo-China to get the best terms it could in negotiations with Japan; the latter dealt with the French Governor-General through a full diplomatic mission, which, although flattering to the dignity of the Governor-General, emphasized the almost complete separation of Indo-China from Metropolitan France. The system of indirect rule, applied by the French to the monarchs of Annam and Cambodia, was now being applied by a stronger Asiatic nation to the French themselves, who participated willy-nilly in the effort of Japan's 'holy war' for the domination of the Far East.

ECONOMIC CONDITIONS

At the beginning of hostilities in Europe in September 1939 the economic situation in Indo-China was more favourable than it had been since before the world economic depression of the early thirties. In most agricultural and industrial enterprises production was increasing and, despite the difficulties of freight transport imposed by war conditions, a large trade was carried on with overseas territories, particularly with France. The orientation of Indo-Chinese trade to the mother country, which had always been a cardinal feature of French commercial policy, perforce changed with the collapse of France in the summer of 1940. The advance of Japanese troops into Tonkin in September 1940 and the arbitration of Japan in the dispute with Siam were more than just military and political manœuvres, for at the same time they enabled Japan to obtain a firmer hold on the economic life of Indo-China. When, in January 1941, Vichy abrogated the tariff law of 13 April 1928 (see p. 358) and granted Indo-China tariff autonomy, it was henceforward possible for Japan to conclude a trade agreement with Indo-China independently of France. After a series of negotiations, an Economic Agreement was concluded between the two countries in May 1941, under the terms of which Japanese manufactured goods were to be granted special terms for entering Indo-China and in return Japan promised to buy increased quantities of Indo-Chinese commodities.

The Economic Agreement of May 1941 was the first important stage in Japan's design for economic domination in Indo-China. Although it appeared to benefit both countries equally, Japan sought to cripple French business by failing to deliver the full quota of goods specified in the agreement. Thus, the quota for cotton goods of all kinds was 1,850 tons per quarter, but the actual delivery amounted to 32 tons. In addition, the Japanese demanded exorbitantly high prices for their own goods, while maintaining the prices of rice, rubber and minerals, the chief items supplied by Indo-China, at a minimum. The policy followed by Japan in applying the economic agreement created financial difficulties for the Indo-Chinese government, since with the growing export surpluses from Indo-China to Japan there was an ever-increasing credit balance. The government was also forced to provide cash for the maintenance of Japanese armies in the country, in return for which they only received more yen credits. 'Co-prosperity', the declared aim of the 1941 agreement, thus reacted unfairly against Indo-China, and conditions were to become even less favourable in the following year.

In 1942 and the early months of 1943, the Japanese greatly strengthened their economic grip on Indo-China. They caused the French to impose a rigid control over the production, sale and marketing of the main resources of the colony, e.g. rice, maize, rubber, coal. They also acquired the right to hold land and industrial concerns, and bought control in a few industries important to them. In the past, concessions were granted only to those whose capital and management were French.

With the acquisition of the Malayan and Netherlands East Indies' supplies of rubber and tin, the Japanese in Indo-China concentrated upon the production of rice and maize and upon the development of mining. Although rice is grown in many other countries under Japanese control, the Indo-Chinese crop is wanted because it is more economical to bring it from Indo-China than from, say, Burma or Siam. Over one million tons of rice were shipped from Indo-China to Japan in 1942, whereas in the years before the collapse of France the shipments to this country amounted to less than 5,000 tons. Similarly, the pre-war exports of maize to Japan were negligible, but in 1942 they totalled 130,000 tons. This total is indeed small when compared with the pre-1940 export to France of over 500,000 tons (see p. 355). An increased local consumption of maize may account for the decline in shipments overseas, though the production may also have fallen. Among other crops in the country which Japan has sought to develop are cotton, kapok and jute.

The production of coal in Indo-China has fallen since the Japanese occupation. In 1942, about 1,200,000 tons were mined compared with 2,300,000 tons in 1937. The decline in output may be attributed to the fact that Japan is now almost the only customer, and production has fallen to an amount which Japan is able to transport plus that required for local industrial purposes. Other minerals exploited include zinc, tin, apatite, antimony and manganese.

Japanese control over the economic life of Indo-China has been facilitated by a Financial Agreement concluded in January 1943 which stipulated that all payment for goods from Indo-China should be settled in 'special yen', which can neither be converted into neutral currency nor serve to increase the controlled import of goods from Japan. Under these artificial conditions, Japanese trade with Indo-China should increase at the expense of French interests.

LIST OF CONVERSION TABLES

METRIC AND BRITISH UNITS

It is customary to think of the 'metre' and the 'yard' as representing unalterable units of length. This is not so. The metre was originally intended to be the 10,000,000th part of the earth's meridional quadrant. But the accurate determination of this length proved to be extremely difficult—partly for technical reasons, and partly because of different conceptions of the 'figure of the earth'. In view of these difficulties it became necessary to define the length of the metre in terms of suitable metal bars measured under specified conditions of temperature, pressure, humidity, etc. Similar standard bars were also used to define the length of other units such as the yard. As all these metallic standards are subject to change, conversion tables differ according to the date of comparison between different bars. The tables that follow are based on the comparison between the yard and the metre made in 1895. This made 1 metre equivalent to 39·370113 inches.

The first five tables provide the ratios between units of the same kind, e.g. length, area, etc. For convenience in printing, negative powers of 10 have been used to indicate very small fractions, instead of the decimal system. Thus the figure 0·00000032 becomes $3·2 \times 10^{-7}$; the first significant figure is the *seventh* after the decimal point. Conversely, $7·34 \times 10^{-5}$ becomes 0·0000734.

Tables 6–18 give more fully the ratios between metric units and their equivalent British units. Metric digits (*0* to *9*) are printed in italics at the top of each table, reading horizontally from left to right. Metric tens, likewise in italics, read vertically from top to bottom on the left of the table. Thus, in Table 6, to convert *87* centimetres into inches, read *8* down on the left, then move horizontally to the right to the *7* digit column, where the answer 34·252 is read.

Metric System. List of Prefixes

Deca means ten times.
Hecto means a hundred times.
Kilo means a thousand times.

Deci means a tenth part of.
Centi means a hundredth part of.
Milli means a thousandth part of.

In abbreviations the Decametre, etc., is Dm., and the decimetre, etc., dm.

Note on 'Nautical', 'Geographical' and 'Statute' miles

A British 'nautical mile' is the length of the minute of the meridian at any given latitude, and is therefore a variable unit. It is given in feet for Clarke's 1880 spheroid by the formula

$$6077 \cdot 1 - 30 \cdot 7 \cos 2 \text{ Lat.}$$

This is the sea mile of the scale of latitude and distance of the Admiralty Charts. From the above formula it will be found to vary from 6,046·4 ft. at the equator to 6,107·8 ft. at the poles, being 6,077·1 ft. at latitude 45°.

The so-called 'international nautical mile' of 1,852 m. or 6,076 ft. is the length of the minute of the meridian at latitude 45° on the International Spheroid. This corresponds to the 6,077 ft. for Clarke's spheroid.

A 'geographical mile' is a fixed unit, being defined by some as the length of a minute of the equator and by others as that of the minute of the meridian at latitude 45°. According to the former definition its value on Clarke's spheroid is 6,087 ft. and according to the latter 6,077 ft. The round figure 6,080 is usually adopted for the purposes of ordinary navigation.

The British 'statute mile' measures 5,280 ft.

Table 1. *Length*

Nautical mile	Statute mile	Kilometre	Metre	Yard	Foot	Inch	Centimetre
1	1·152	1·853	1853	2027	6080•	72,960	185,300
$8·684 \times 10^{-1}$	1	1·60934	1609·34	1760	5280	63,360	160,934
$5·396 \times 10^{-1}$	$6·21372 \times 10^{-1}$	1	1000	1093·61	3280·84	39,370·1	100,000
$5·396 \times 10^{-4}$	$6·21372 \times 10^{-4}$	$1·0 \times 10^{-3}$	1	1·09361	3·28084	39·3701	100
$4·934 \times 10^{-4}$	$5·68182 \times 10^{-4}$	$9·14399 \times 10^{-4}$	$9·14399 \times 10^{-1}$	1	3	36	91·4399
$1·645 \times 10^{-4}$	$1·89394 \times 10^{-4}$	$3·048 \times 10^{-4}$	$3·048 \times 10^{-1}$	$3·33333 \times 10^{-1}$	1	12	30·48
$1·371 \times 10^{-5}$	$1·57828 \times 10^{-5}$	$2·54 \times 10^{-5}$	$2·54 \times 10^{-2}$	$2·77778 \times 10^{-2}$	$8·33333 \times 10^{-2}$	1	2·54
$5·390 \times 10^{-6}$	$6·21372 \times 10^{-6}$	$1·0 \times 10^{-5}$	$1·0 \times 10^{-2}$	$1·09361 \times 10^{-2}$	$3·28084 \times 10^{-2}$	$3·93701 \times 10^{-1}$	1

• This is the customary British practice, and not the 'international nautical mile,' which Great Britain has not adopted.

Table 2. *Area*

Square mile	Square kilometre	Hectare	Acre	Square metre	Square yard
1	2·58998	258·998	640	$258,998 \times 10$	$30,976 \times 10^{3}$
$3·86103 \times 10^{-1}$	1	100	247·106	1,000,000	$119,599 \times 10$
$3·86103 \times 10^{-3}$	$1·0 \times 10^{-2}$	1	2·47106	10,000	11,959·9
$1·5625 \times 10^{-3}$	$4·04685 \times 10^{-3}$	$4·04685 \times 10^{-1}$	1	4046·85	4840
$3·86103 \times 10^{-7}$	$1·0 \times 10^{-6}$	$1·0 \times 10^{-4}$	$2·47106 \times 10^{-4}$	1	1·19599
$3·22831 \times 10^{-7}$	$8·36126 \times 10^{-7}$	$8·36126 \times 10^{-5}$	$2·06612 \times 10^{-4}$	$8·36126 \times 10^{-1}$	1

Table 3. *Yield per Unit Area*

Tons per acre	Metric tons per hectare	Quintals per hectare
1	2·51071	25·1071
$3·98294 \times 10^{-1}$	1	10
$3·98294 \times 10^{-2}$	$1·0 \times 10^{-1}$	1

Table 4. *Volume and Capacity*

Kilolitre	Cubic metre	Cubic yard	Bushel	Cubic feet	Imp. gall.	Litre	Pint
1	$1 \cdot 000027$	$1 \cdot 30799$	$27 \cdot 4969$	$35 \cdot 3157$	$219 \cdot 976$	1000	$1759 \cdot 80$
$9 \cdot 99973 \times 10^{-1}$	1	$1 \cdot 30795$	$27 \cdot 4962$	$35 \cdot 3148$	$219 \cdot 970$	$999 \cdot 973$	$1759 \cdot 75$
$7 \cdot 64532 \times 10^{-1}$	$7 \cdot 64553 \times 10^{-1}$	1	$21 \cdot 0223$	27	$168 \cdot 178$	$764 \cdot 532$	$1345 \cdot 43$
$3 \cdot 63677 \times 10^{-2}$	$3 \cdot 63687 \times 10^{-2}$	$4 \cdot 75685 \times 10^{-2}$	1	$1 \cdot 28435$	8	$36 \cdot 3677$	64
$2 \cdot 83160 \times 10^{-2}$	$2 \cdot 83167 \times 10^{-2}$	$3 \cdot 70370 \times 10^{-2}$	$7 \cdot 78602 \times 10^{-1}$	1	$6 \cdot 22882$	$28 \cdot 3160$	$49 \cdot 8306$
$4 \cdot 54596 \times 10^{-3}$	$4 \cdot 54608 \times 10^{-3}$	$5 \cdot 94607 \times 10^{-3}$	$1 \cdot 25 \times 10^{-1}$	$1 \cdot 60544 \times 10^{-1}$	1	$4 \cdot 54596$	8
$1 \cdot 0 \times 10^{-3}$	$1 \cdot 000027 \times 10^{-3}$	$1 \cdot 30799 \times 10^{-3}$	$2 \cdot 74969 \times 10^{-2}$	$3 \cdot 53157 \times 10^{-2}$	$2 \cdot 19976 \times 10^{-1}$	1	$1 \cdot 75980$
$5 \cdot 68245 \times 10^{-4}$	$5 \cdot 68260 \times 10^{-4}$	$7 \cdot 43258 \times 10^{-4}$	$1 \cdot 5625 \times 10^{-2}$	$2 \cdot 00680 \times 10^{-2}$	$1 \cdot 25 \times 10^{-1}$	$5 \cdot 68245 \times 10^{-1}$	1

Table 5. *Weight*

Ton	Metric ton or Millier	Quintal	Kilogram	lb.
1	$1 \cdot 01605$	$10 \cdot 1605$	$1016 \cdot 05$	2240
$9 \cdot 84207 \times 10^{-1}$	1	10	1000	$2204 \cdot 62$
$9 \cdot 84207 \times 10^{-2}$	$1 \cdot 0 \times 10^{-1}$	1	100	$220 \cdot 462$
$9 \cdot 84207 \times 10^{-4}$	$1 \cdot 0 \times 10^{-3}$	$1 \cdot 0 \times 10^{-2}$	1	$2 \cdot 20462$
$4 \cdot 46429 \times 10^{-4}$	$4 \cdot 53592 \times 10^{-4}$	$4 \cdot 53592 \times 10^{-3}$	$4 \cdot 53592 \times 10^{-1}$	1

Table 6. *Centimetres to Inches*

1 cm. = 0·39370 in.

	0	1	2	3	4	5	6	7	8	9
	—	0·394	0·787	1·181	1·575	1·969	2·362	2·756	3·150	3·543
1	3·937	4·331	4·724	5·118	5·512	5·906	6·299	6·693	7·087	7·480
2	7·874	8·268	8·661	9·055	9·449	9·843	10·236	10·630	11·024	11·417
3	11·811	12·205	12·598	12·992	13·386	13·780	14·173	14·567	14·961	15·354
4	15·748	16·142	16·535	16·929	17·323	17·717	18·110	18·504	18·898	19·291
5	19·685	20·079	20·472	20·866	21·260	21·654	22·047	22·441	22·835	23·228
6	23·622	24·016	24·409	24·803	25·197	25·591	25·984	26·378	26·772	27·165
7	27·559	27·953	28·346	28·740	29·134	29·528	29·921	30·315	30·709	31·102
8	31·496	31·890	32·283	32·677	33·071	33·465	33·858	34·252	34·646	35·039
9	35·433	35·827	36·220	36·614	37·008	37·402	37·795	38·189	38·583	38·976
10	39·370									

Table 7. *Metres to Feet*

1 m. = 3·28084 ft.

	0	1	2	3	4	5	6	7	8	9
	—	3·3	6·6	9·8	13·1	16·4	19·7	23·0	26·3	29·5
1	32·8	36·1	39·4	42·7	45·9	49·2	52·5	55·8	59·1	62·3
2	65·6	68·9	72·2	75·5	78·7	82·0	85·3	88·6	91·9	95·1
3	98·4	101·7	105·0	108·3	111·6	114·8	118·1	121·4	124·7	128·0
4	131·2	134·5	137·8	141·1	144·4	147·6	150·9	154·2	157·5	160·8
5	164·0	167·3	170·6	173·9	177·2	180·5	183·7	187·0	190·3	193·6
6	196·9	200·1	203·4	206·7	210·0	213·3	216·5	219·8	223·1	226·4
7	229·7	232·9	236·2	239·5	242·8	246·1	249·3	252·6	255·9	259·2
8	262·5	265·8	269·0	272·3	275·6	278·9	282·2	285·4	288·7	292·0
9	295·3	298·6	301·8	305·1	308·4	311·7	315·0	318·2	321·5	324·8
10	328·1	331·4	334·6	337·9	341·2	344·5	347·8	351·0	354·3	357·6

Table 7 (continued). Metres to Feet

	0	1	2	3	4	5	6	7	8	9
11	360·9	364·2	367·5	370·7	374·0	377·3	380·6	383·9	387·1	390·4
12	393·7	397·0	400·3	403·5	406·8	410·1	413·4	416·7	419·9	423·2
13	426·5	429·8	433·1	436·4	439·6	442·9	446·2	449·5	452·8	456·0
14	459·3	462·6	465·9	469·2	472·4	475·7	479·0	482·3	485·6	488·8
15	492·1	495·4	498·7	502·0	505·2	508·5	511·8	515·1	518·4	521·7
16	524·9	528·2	531·5	534·8	538·1	541·3	544·6	547·9	551·2	554·5
17	557·7	561·0	564·3	567·6	570·9	574·1	577·4	580·7	584·0	587·3
18	590·6	593·8	597·1	600·4	603·7	607·0	610·2	613·5	616·8	620·1
19	623·4	626·6	629·9	633·2	636·5	639·8	643·0	646·3	649·6	652·9
20	656·2	659·4	662·7	666·0	669·3	672·6	675·9	679·1	682·4	685·7
21	689·0	692·3	695·5	698·8	702·1	705·4	708·7	711·9	715·2	718·5
22	721·8	725·1	728·3	731·6	734·9	738·2	741·5	744·8	748·0	751·3
23	754·6	757·9	761·2	764·4	767·7	771·0	774·3	777·6	780·8	784·1
24	787·4	790·7	794·0	797·2	800·5	803·8	807·1	810·4	813·7	816·9
25	820·2	823·5	826·8	830·1	833·3	836·6	839·9	843·2	846·5	849·7
26	853·0	856·3	859·6	862·9	866·1	869·4	872·7	876·0	879·3	882·5
27	885·8	889·1	892·4	895·7	899·0	902·2	905·5	908·8	912·1	915·4
28	918·6	921·9	925·2	928·5	931·8	935·0	938·3	941·6	944·9	948·2
29	951·4	954·7	958·0	961·3	964·6	967·8	971·1	974·4	977·7	981·0
30	984·3	987·5	990·8	994·1	997·4	1000·7	1003·9	1007·2	1010·5	1013·8
31	1017·1	1020·3	1023·6	1026·9	1030·2	1033·5	1036·7	1040·0	1043·3	1046·6
32	1049·9	1053·1	1056·4	1059·7	1063·0	1066·3	1069·6	1072·8	1076·1	1079·4
33	1082·7	1086·0	1089·2	1092·5	1095·8	1099·1	1102·4	1105·6	1108·9	1112·2
34	1115·5	1118·8	1122·0	1125·3	1128·6	1131·9	1135·2	1138·5	1141·7	1145·0
35	1148·3	1151·6	1154·9	1158·1	1161·4	1164·7	1168·0	1171·3	1174·5	1177·8
36	1181·1	1184·4	1187·7	1190·9	1194·2	1197·5	1200·8	1204·1	1207·3	1210·6
37	1213·9	1217·2	1220·5	1223·8	1227·0	1230·3	1233·6	1236·9	1240·2	1243·4
38	1246·7	1250·0	1253·3	1256·6	1259·8	1263·1	1266·4	1269·7	1273·0	1276·2
39	1279·5	1282·8	1286·1	1289·4	1292·7	1295·9	1299·2	1302·5	1305·8	1309·1
40	1312·3	1315·6	1318·9	1322·2	1325·5	1328·7	1332·0	1335·3	1338·6	1341·9

Table 7 (continued). Metres to Feet

	0	1	2	3	4	5	6	7	8	9
41	1345·1	1348·4	1351·7	1355·0	1358·3	1361·5	1364·8	1368·1	1371·4	1374·7
42	1378·0	1381·2	1384·5	1387·8	1391·1	1394·4	1397·6	1400·9	1404·2	1407·5
43	1410·8	1414·0	1417·3	1420·6	1423·9	1427·2	1430·4	1433·7	1437·0	1440·3
44	1443·6	1446·9	1450·1	1453·4	1456·7	1460·0	1463·3	1466·5	1469·8	1473·1
45	1476·4	1479·7	1482·9	1486·2	1489·5	1492·8	1496·1	1499·3	1502·6	1505·9
46	1509·2	1512·5	1515·7	1519·0	1522·3	1525·6	1528·9	1532·2	1535·4	1538·7
47	1542·0	1545·3	1548·6	1551·8	1555·1	1558·4	1561·7	1565·0	1568·2	1571·5
48	1574·8	1578·1	1581·4	1584·6	1587·9	1591·2	1594·5	1597·8	1601·0	1604·3
49	1607·6	1610·9	1614·2	1617·5	1620·7	1624·0	1627·3	1630·6	1633·9	1637·1
50	1640·4	1643·7	1647·0	1650·3	1653·6	1656·8	1660·1	1663·4	1666·7	1669·9
51	1673·2	1676·5	1679·8	1683·1	1686·4	1689·6	1692·9	1696·2	1699·5	1702·8
52	1706·0	1709·3	1712·6	1715·9	1719·2	1722·4	1725·7	1729·0	1732·3	1735·6
53	1738·8	1742·1	1745·4	1748·7	1752·0	1755·2	1758·5	1761·8	1765·1	1768·4
54	1771·7	1774·9	1778·2	1781·5	1784·8	1788·1	1791·3	1794·6	1797·9	1801·2
55	1804·5	1807·8	1811·0	1814·3	1817·6	1820·9	1824·1	1827·4	1830·7	1834·0
56	1837·3	1840·6	1843·8	1847·1	1850·4	1853·7	1857·0	1860·2	1863·5	1866·8
57	1870·1	1873·4	1876·6	1879·9	1883·2	1886·5	1889·8	1893·0	1896·3	1899·6
58	1902·9	1906·2	1909·4	1912·7	1916·0	1919·3	1922·6	1925·9	1929·1	1932·4
59	1935·7	1939·0	1942·3	1945·5	1948·8	1952·1	1955·4	1958·7	1961·9	1965·2
60	1968·5	1971·8	1975·1	1978·3	1981·6	1984·9	1988·2	1991·5	1994·8	1998·0
61	2001·3	2004·6	2007·9	2011·1	2014·4	2017·7	2021·0	2024·3	2027·6	2030·8
62	2034·1	2037·4	2040·7	2044·0	2047·2	2050·5	2053·8	2057·1	2060·4	2063·6
63	2066·9	2070·2	2073·5	2076·8	2080·1	2083·3	2086·6	2089·9	2093·2	2096·5
64	2099·7	2103·0	2106·3	2109·6	2112·9	2116·1	2119·4	2122·7	2126·0	2129·3
65	2132·5	2135·8	2139·1	2142·4	2145·7	2149·0	2152·3	2155·5	2158·8	2162·1
66	2165·4	2168·6	2171·9	2175·2	2178·5	2181·8	2185·1	2188·3	2191·6	2194·9
67	2198·2	2201·5	2204·7	2208·0	2211·3	2214·6	2217·9	2221·1	2224·4	2227·7
68	2231·0	2234·3	2237·5	2240·8	2244·1	2247·4	2250·7	2253·9	2257·2	2260·5
69	2263·8	2267·1	2270·4	2273·6	2276·9	2280·2	2283·5	2286·8	2290·0	2293·3
70	2296·6	2299·9	2303·2	2306·4	2309·7	2313·0	2316·3	2319·6	2322·8	2326·1

497

Table 7 (continued). Metres to Feet

	0	1	2	3	4	5	6	7	8	9
71	2329·4	2332·7	2336·0	2339·2	2342·5	2345·8	2349·1	2352·4	2355·6	2358·9
72	2362·2	2365·5	2368·8	2372·0	2375·3	2378·6	2381·9	2385·2	2388·5	2391·7
73	2395·0	2398·3	2401·6	2404·9	2408·1	2411·4	2414·7	2418·0	2421·3	2424·5
74	2427·8	2431·1	2434·4	2437·7	2440·9	2444·2	2447·5	2450·8	2454·1	2457·3
75	2460·6	2463·9	2467·2	2470·5	2473·8	2477·0	2480·3	2483·6	2486·9	2490·2
76	2493·4	2496·7	2500·0	2503·3	2506·6	2509·8	2513·1	2516·4	2519·7	2523·0
77	2526·2	2529·5	2532·8	2536·1	2539·4	2542·7	2545·9	2549·2	2552·5	2555·8
78	2559·1	2562·3	2565·6	2568·9	2572·2	2575·5	2578·7	2582·0	2585·3	2588·6
79	2591·9	2595·1	2598·4	2601·7	2605·0	2608·3	2611·5	2614·8	2618·1	2621·4
80	2624·7	2628·0	2631·2	2634·5	2637·8	2641·1	2644·4	2647·6	2650·9	2654·2
81	2657·5	2660·8	2664·0	2667·3	2670·6	2673·9	2677·2	2680·4	2683·7	2687·0
82	2690·3	2693·6	2696·9	2700·1	2703·4	2706·7	2710·0	2713·3	2716·5	2719·8
83	2723·1	2726·4	2729·7	2732·9	2736·2	2739·5	2742·8	2746·1	2749·3	2752·6
84	2755·9	2759·2	2762·5	2765·7	2769·0	2772·3	2775·6	2778·9	2782·2	2785·4
85	2788·7	2792·0	2795·3	2798·6	2801·8	2805·1	2808·4	2811·7	2815·0	2818·2
86	2821·5	2824·8	2828·1	2831·4	2834·6	2837·9	2841·2	2844·5	2847·8	2851·0
87	2854·3	2857·6	2860·9	2864·2	2867·5	2870·7	2874·0	2877·3	2880·6	2883·9
88	2887·1	2890·4	2893·7	2897·0	2900·3	2903·5	2906·8	2910·1	2913·4	2916·7
89	2919·9	2923·2	2926·5	2929·8	2933·1	2936·4	2939·6	2942·9	2946·2	2949·5
90	2952·8	2956·0	2959·3	2962·6	2965·9	2969·2	2972·4	2975·7	2979·0	2982·3
91	2985·6	2988·8	2992·1	2995·4	2998·7	3002·0	3005·2	3008·5	3011·8	3015·1
92	3018·4	3021·7	3024·9	3028·2	3031·5	3034·8	3038·1	3041·3	3044·6	3047·9
93	3051·2	3054·5	3057·7	3061·0	3064·3	3067·6	3070·9	3074·1	3077·4	3080·7
94	3084·0	3087·3	3090·6	3093·8	3097·1	3100·4	3103·7	3107·0	3110·2	3113·5
95	3116·8	3120·1	3123·4	3126·6	3129·9	3133·2	3136·5	3139·8	3143·0	3146·3
96	3149·6	3152·9	3156·2	3159·4	3162·7	3166·0	3169·3	3172·6	3175·9	3179·1
97	3182·4	3185·7	3189·0	3192·3	3195·5	3198·8	3202·1	3205·4	3208·7	3211·9
98	3215·2	3218·5	3221·8	3225·1	3228·3	3231·6	3234·9	3238·2	3241·5	3244·8
99	3248·0	3251·3	3254·6	3257·9	3261·2	3264·4	3267·7	3271·0	3274·3	3277·6
100	3280·8									

Table 8. Kilometres to British Statute Miles

1 km.=0·621372 mile

	0	1	2	3	4	5	6	7	8	9
—	—	0·621	1·243	1·864	2·485	3·107	3·728	4·350	4·971	5·592
1	6·214	6·835	7·456	8·078	8·699	9·321	9·942	10·563	11·185	11·806
2	12·427	13·049	13·670	14·292	14·913	15·534	16·156	16·777	17·398	18·020
3	18·641	19·263	19·884	20·505	21·127	21·748	22·369	22·991	23·612	24·234
4	24·855	25·476	26·098	26·719	27·340	27·962	28·583	29·204	29·826	30·447
5	31·069	31·690	32·311	32·933	33·554	34·175	34·797	35·418	36·040	36·661
6	37·282	37·904	38·525	39·146	39·768	40·389	41·011	41·632	42·253	42·875
7	43·496	44·117	44·739	45·360	45·982	46·603	47·224	47·846	48·467	49·088
8	49·710	50·331	50·952	51·574	52·195	52·817	53·438	54·059	54·681	55·302
9	55·923	56·545	57·166	57·788	58·409	59·030	59·652	60·273	60·894	61·516
10	62·137									

Table 9. Kilometres to British Nautical Miles

1 km.=0·5396 nautical mile

	0	1	2	3	4	5	6	7	8	9
—	—	0·54	1·08	1·62	2·16	2·70	3·24	3·78	4·32	4·86
1	5·40	5·94	6·48	7·01	7·55	8·09	8·63	9·17	9·71	10·25
2	10·79	11·33	11·87	12·41	12·95	13·49	14·03	14·57	15·11	15·65
3	16·19	16·73	17·27	17·81	18·35	18·89	19·43	19·97	20·50	21·04
4	21·58	22·12	22·66	23·20	23·74	24·28	24·82	25·36	25·90	26·44
5	26·98	27·52	28·06	28·60	29·14	29·68	30·22	30·76	31·30	31·84
6	32·38	32·92	33·46	33·99	34·53	35·07	35·61	36·15	36·69	37·23
7	37·77	38·31	38·85	39·39	39·93	40·47	41·01	41·55	42·09	42·63
8	43·17	43·71	44·25	44·79	45·33	45·87	46·41	46·95	47·48	48·02
9	48·56	49·10	49·64	50·18	50·72	51·26	51·80	52·34	52·88	53·42
10	53·96									

Table 10. *Square Metres to Square Feet*

1 sq. m. = 10·76911 sq. ft.

	0	1	2	3	4	5	6	7	8	9
1	—	10·764	21·528	32·292	43·056	53·820	64·583	75·347	86·111	96·875
2	107·639	118·403	129·167	139·931	150·695	161·459	172·222	182·986	193·750	204·514
3	215·278	226·042	236·806	247·570	258·334	269·098	279·861	290·625	301·389	312·153
4	322·917	333·681	344·445	355·209	365·973	376·737	387·501	398·265	409·029	419·792
5	430·556	441·320	452·084	462·848	473·612	484·376	495·140	505·904	516·668	527·432
6	538·196	548·959	559·723	570·487	581·251	592·015	602·779	613·543	624·307	635·071
7	645·835	656·599	667·363	678·126	688·890	699·654	710·418	721·182	731·946	742·710
8	753·474	764·238	775·002	785·765	796·529	807·293	818·057	828·821	839·585	850·349
9	861·113	871·877	882·641	893·405	904·169	914·932	925·696	936·460	947·224	957·988
10	968·752	979·516	990·280	1001·044	1011·808	1022·572	1033·335	1044·099	1054·863	1065·627

Table 11. *Hectares to Acres*

1 ha. = 2·47106 acres

	0	1	2	3	4	5	6	7	8	9
1	—	2·47	4·94	7·41	9·88	12·36	14·83	17·30	19·77	22·24
2	24·71	27·18	29·65	32·12	34·59	37·07	39·54	42·01	44·48	46·95
3	49·42	51·89	54·36	56·83	59·31	61·78	64·25	66·72	69·19	71·66
4	74·13	76·60	79·07	81·54	84·02	86·49	88·96	91·43	93·90	96·37
5	98·84	101·31	103·78	106·26	108·73	111·20	113·67	116·14	118·61	121·08
6	123·55	126·02	128·50	130·97	133·44	135·91	138·38	140·85	143·32	145·79
7	148·26	150·73	153·21	155·68	158·15	160·62	163·09	165·56	168·03	170·50
8	172·97	175·45	177·92	180·39	182·86	185·33	187·80	190·27	192·74	195·21
9	197·68	200·16	202·63	205·10	207·57	210·04	212·51	214·98	217·45	219·92
10	222·40	224·87	227·34	229·81	232·28	234·75	237·22	239·69	242·16	244·63

Table 12. Square Kilometres to Square Miles

1 sq. km.=0·386103 sq. mile

	0	1	2	3	4	5	6	7	8	9
	—	0·386	0·772	1·158	1·544	1·931	2·317	2·703	3·089	3·475
1	3·861	4·247	4·633	5·019	5·405	5·792	6·178	6·564	6·950	7·336
2	7·722	8·108	8·494	8·880	9·266	9·653	10·039	10·425	10·811	11·197
3	11·583	11·969	12·355	12·741	13·128	13·514	13·900	14·286	14·672	15·058
4	15·444	15·830	16·216	16·602	16·989	17·375	17·761	18·147	18·533	18·919
5	19·305	19·691	20·077	20·463	20·850	21·236	21·622	22·008	22·394	22·780
6	23·166	23·552	23·938	24·324	24·711	25·097	25·483	25·869	26·255	26·641
7	27·027	27·413	27·799	28·186	28·572	28·958	29·344	29·730	30·116	30·502
8	30·888	31·274	31·660	32·047	32·433	32·819	33·205	33·591	33·977	34·363
9	34·749	35·135	35·521	35·908	36·294	36·680	37·066	37·452	37·838	38·224
10	38·610									

Table 13. Numbers per Square Kilometre to Numbers per Square Mile
(or square miles to square kilometres)

1 sq. mile=2·58998 sq. km.

	0	1	2	3	4	5	6	7	8	9
	—	2·59	5·18	7·77	10·36	12·95	15·54	18·13	20·72	23·31
1	25·90	28·49	31·08	33·67	36·26	38·85	41·44	44·03	46·62	49·21
2	51·80	54·39	56·98	59·57	62·16	64·75	67·34	69·93	72·52	75·11
3	77·70	80·29	82·88	85·47	88·06	90·65	93·24	95·83	98·42	101·01
4	103·60	106·19	108·78	111·37	113·96	116·55	119·14	121·73	124·32	126·91
5	129·50	132·09	134·68	137·27	139·86	142·45	145·04	147·63	150·22	152·81
6	155·40	157·99	160·58	163·17	165·76	168·35	170·94	173·53	176·12	178·71
7	181·30	183·89	186·48	189·07	191·66	194·25	196·84	199·43	202·02	204·61
8	207·20	209·79	212·38	214·97	217·56	220·15	222·74	225·33	227·92	230·51
9	233·10	235·69	238·28	240·87	243·46	246·05	248·64	251·23	253·82	256·41
10	259·00									

Table 14. Quintals per Hectare to Tons per Acre

1 quintal per hectare = 0·039294 ton per acre

	0	1	2	3	4	5	6	7	8	9
	—	0·03983	0·07966	0·11949	0·15932	0·19915	0·23898	0·27881	0·31864	0·35846
1	0·39829	0·43812	0·47795	0·51778	0·55761	0·59744	0·63727	0·67710	0·71693	0·75676
2	0·79659	0·83642	0·87625	0·91608	0·95591	0·99574	1·03556	1·07539	1·11522	1·15505
3	1·19488	1·23471	1·27454	1·31437	1·35420	1·39401	1·43386	1·47369	1·51352	1·55335
4	1·59318	1·63305	1·67283	1·71266	1·75249	1·79232	1·83215	1·87198	1·91181	1·95164
5	1·99147	2·03130	2·07113	2·11096	2·15079	2·19062	2·23045	2·27028	2·31011	2·34993
6	2·38976	2·42959	2·46942	2·50925	2·54908	2·58891	2·62874	2·66857	2·70840	2·74823
7	2·78806	2·82789	2·86772	2·90755	2·94737	2·98721	3·02703	3·06686	3·10669	3·14652
8	3·18635	3·22618	3·26601	3·30584	3·34567	3·38550	3·42533	3·46516	3·50499	3·54482
9	3·58465	3·62448	3·66430	3·70413	3·74396	3·78379	3·82362	3·86345	3·90328	3·94311
10	3·98294									

Table 15. Cubic Metres to Cubic Feet

1 cu. m. = 35·3148 cu. ft.

	0	1	2	3	4	5	6	7	8	9
	—	35·315	70·630	105·944	141·260	176·574	211·889	247·204	282·518	317·833
1	353·148	388·463	423·778	459·092	494·407	529·722	565·037	600·352	635·666	670·981
2	706·296	741·611	776·926	812·240	847·555	882·870	918·185	953·500	988·814	1024·129
3	1059·444	1094·759	1130·074	1165·388	1200·703	1236·018	1271·333	1306·648	1341·962	1377·277
4	1412·592	1447·907	1483·222	1518·536	1553·851	1589·166	1624·481	1659·796	1695·110	1730·425
5	1765·740	1801·055	1836·370	1871·684	1906·999	1942·314	1977·629	2012·944	2048·258	2083·573
6	2118·888	2154·203	2189·518	2224·832	2260·147	2295·462	2330·777	2366·092	2401·406	2436·721
7	2472·036	2507·351	2542·666	2577·980	2613·295	2648·610	2683·925	2719·240	2754·554	2789·869
8	2825·184	2860·499	2895·814	2931·128	2966·443	3001·758	3037·073	3072·388	3107·702	3143·017
9	3178·332	3213·647	3248·962	3284·276	3319·591	3354·906	3390·221	3425·536	3460·850	3496·165
10	3531·480									

Table 16. *Litres to Gallons*

1 l. = 0·219976 gal.

	0	1	2	3	4	5	6	7	8	9
	—	0·220	0·440	0·660	0·880	1·100	1·320	1·540	1·760	1·980
1	2·200	2·420	2·640	2·860	3·080	3·300	3·520	3·740	3·960	4·180
2	4·400	4·619	4·839	5·059	5·279	5·499	5·719	5·939	6·159	6·379
3	6·599	6·819	7·039	7·259	7·479	7·699	7·919	8·139	8·359	8·579
4	8·799	9·019	9·239	9·459	9·679	9·899	10·119	10·339	10·559	10·779
5	10·999	11·219	11·439	11·659	11·879	12·099	12·319	12·539	12·759	12·979
6	13·199	13·419	13·639	13·858	14·078	14·298	14·518	14·738	14·958	15·178
7	15·398	15·618	15·838	16·058	16·278	16·498	16·718	16·938	17·158	17·378
8	17·598	17·818	18·038	18·258	18·478	18·698	18·918	19·138	19·358	19·578
9	19·798	20·018	20·238	20·458	20·678	20·898	21·118	21·338	21·558	21·778
10	21·998									

Table 17. *Kilogrammes to Pounds*

1 kg. = 2·20462 lb.

	0	1	2	3	4	5	6	7	8	9
	—	2·205	4·409	6·614	8·818	11·023	13·228	15·432	17·637	19·842
1	22·046	24·251	26·455	28·660	30·865	33·069	35·274	37·478	39·683	41·888
2	44·092	46·297	48·502	50·706	52·911	55·115	57·320	59·525	61·729	63·934
3	66·139	68·343	70·548	72·752	74·957	77·162	79·366	81·571	83·776	85·980
4	88·185	90·389	92·594	94·799	97·003	99·208	101·413	103·617	105·822	108·026
5	110·231	112·436	114·640	116·845	119·049	121·254	123·459	125·663	127·868	130·073
6	132·277	134·482	136·686	138·891	141·096	143·300	145·505	147·710	149·914	152·119
7	154·323	156·528	158·733	160·937	163·142	165·346	167·551	169·756	171·960	174·165
8	176·370	178·574	180·779	182·983	185·188	187·393	189·597	191·802	194·007	196·211
9	198·416	200·620	202·825	205·030	207·234	209·439	211·644	213·848	216·053	218·257
10	220·462									

Table 18. Temperature: Equivalents of Fahrenheit and Centigrade Scales

°F.	°C.	°F.	°C.	°F.	°C.	°F.	°C.	°F.	°C.	°F.	°C.
212	100	192	88·8	172·4	78	153	67·2	133·25	56·25	114	45·5
211	99·4	191·75	88·75	172	77·7	152·6	67	133	56·1	113	45
210·2	99	191	88·3	171·5	77·5	152	66·6	132·8	56	112	44·4
210	98·8	190·4	88	171	77·2	151·25	66·25	132	55·5	111·2	44
209·75	98·75	190	87·7	170·6	77	151	66·1	131	55	111	43·8
209	98·3	189·5	87·5	170	76·6	150·8	66	130	54·4	110·75	43·75
208·4	98	189	87·2	169·25	76·25	150	65·5	129·2	54	110	43·3
208	97·7	188·6	87	169	76·1	149	65	129	53·8	109·4	43
207·5	97·5	188	86·6	168·8	76	148	64·4	128·75	53·75	109	42·7
207	97·2	187·25	86·25	168	75·5	147·2	64	128	53·3	108·5	42·5
206·6	97	187	86·1	167	75	147	63·8	127·4	53	108	42·2
206	96·6	186·8	86	166	74·4	146·75	63·75	127	52·7	107·6	42
205·25	96·25	186	85·5	165·2	74	146	63·3	126·5	52·5	107	41·6
205	96·1	185	85	165	73·8	145·4	63	126	52·2	106·25	41·25
204·8	96	184	84·4	164·75	73·75	145	62·7	125·6	52	106	41·1
204	95·5	183·2	84	164	73·3	144·5	62·5	125	51·6	105·8	41
203	95	183	83·8	163·4	73	144	62·2	124·25	51·25	105	40·5
202	94·4	182·75	83·75	163	72·7	143·6	62	124	51·1	104	40
201·2	94	182	83·3	162·5	72·5	143	61·6	123·8	51	103	39·4
201	93·8	181·4	83	162	72·2	142·25	61·25	123	50·5	102·2	39
200·75	93·75	181	82·7	161·6	72	142	61·1	122	50	102	38·8
200	93·3	180·5	82·5	161	71·6	141·8	61	121	49·4	101·75	38·75
199·4	93	180	82·2	160·25	71·25	141	60·5	120·2	49	101	38·3
199	92·7	179·6	82	160	71·1	140	60	120	48·8	100·4	38
198·5	92·5	179	81·6	159·8	71	139	59·4	119·75	48·75	100	37·7
198	92·2	178·25	81·25	159	70·5	138·2	59	119	48·3	99·5	37·5
197·6	92	178	81·1	158	70	138	58·8	118·4	48	99	37·2
197	91·6	177·8	81	157	69·4	137·75	58·75	118	47·7	98·6	37
196·25	91·25	177	80·5	156·2	69	137	58·3	117·5	47·5	98	36·6
196	91·1	176	80	156	68·8	136·4	58	117	47·2	97·25	36·25
195·8	91	175	79·4	155·75	68·75	136	57·7	116·6	47	97	36·1
195	90·5	174·2	79	155	68·3	135·5	57·5	116	46·6	96·8	36
194	90	174	78·8	154·4	68	135	57·2	115·25	46·25	96	35·5
193	89·4	173·75	78·75	154	67·7	134·6	57	115	46·1	95	35
192·2	89	173	78·3	153·5	67·5	134	56·6	114·8	46	94	34·4

Table 18 (continued). Temperature: Equivalents of Fahrenheit and Centigrade Scales

°F.	°C.	°F.	°C.	°F.	°C.	°F.	°C.	°F.	°C.	°F.	°C.
93·2	34	73	22·7	52·25	11·25	31	-0·5	10·4	-12	-10	-23·3
93	33·8	72·5	22·5	52	11·1	30·2	-1	10	-12·2	-10·75	-23·75
92·75	33·75	72	22·2	51·8	11	30	-1·1	9·5	-12·5	-11	-23·8
92	33·3	71·6	22	51	10·5	29·75	-1·25	9	-12·7	-11·2	-24
91·4	33	71	21·6	50	10	29	-1·6	8·6	-13	-12	-24·4
91	32·7	70·25	21·25	49	9·4	28·4	-2	8	-13·3	-13	-25
90·5	32·5	70	21·1	48·2	9	28	-2·2	7·25	-13·75	-14	-25·5
90	32·2	69·8	21	48	8·8	27·5	-2·5	7	-13·8	-14·8	-26
89·6	32	69	20·5	47·75	8·75	27	-2·7	6·8	-14	-15	-26·1
89	31·6	68	20	47	8·3	26·6	-3	6	-14·4	-15·25	-26·25
88·25	31·25	67	19·4	46·4	8	26	-3·3	5	-15	-16	-26·6
88	31·1	66·2	19	46	7·7	25·25	-3·75	4	-15·5	-16·6	-27
87·8	31	66	18·8	45·5	7·5	25	-3·8	3·2	-16	-17	-27·2
87	30·5	65·75	18·75	45	7·2	24·8	-4	3	-16·1	-17·5	-27·5
86	30	65	18·3	44·6	7	24	-4·4	2·75	-16·25	-18	-27·7
85	29·4	64·4	18	44	6·6	23	-5	2	-16·6	-18·4	-28
84·2	29	64	17·7	43·25	6·25	22	-5·5	1·4	-17	-19	-28·3
84	28·8	63·5	17·5	43	6·1	21·2	-6	1	-17·2	-19·75	-28·75
83·75	28·75	63	17·2	42·8	6	21	-6·1	0·5	-17·5	-20	-28·8
83	28·3	62·6	17	42	5·5	20·75	-6·25	0	-17·7	-20·2	-29
82·4	28	62	16·6	41	5	20	-6·6	-0·4	-18	-21	-29·4
82	27·7	61·25	16·25	40	4·4	19·4	-7	-1	-18·3	-22	-30
81·5	27·5	61	16·1	39·2	4	19	-7·2	-1·75	-18·75	-23	-30·5
81	27·2	60·8	16	39	3·8	18·5	-7·5	-2	-18·8	-23·8	-31
80·6	27	60	15·5	38·75	3·75	18	-7·7	-2·2	-19	-24	-31·1
80	26·6	59	15	38	3·3	17·6	-8	-3	-19·4	-24·25	-31·25
79·25	26·25	58	14·4	37·4	3	17	-8·3	-4	-20	-25	-31·6
79	26·1	57·2	14	37	2·7	16·25	-8·75	-5	-20·5	-25·6	-32
78·8	26	57	13·8	36·5	2·5	16	-8·8	-5·8	-21	-26	-32·2
78	25·5	56·75	13·75	36	2·2	15·8	-9	-6	-21·1	-26·5	-32·5
77	25	56	13·3	35·6	2	15	-9·4	-6·25	-21·25	-27	-32·7
76	24·4	55·4	13	35	1·6	14	-10	-7	-21·6	-27·4	-33
75·2	24	55	12·7	34·25	1·25	13	-10·5	-7·6	-22	-28	-33·3
75	23·8	54·5	12·5	34	1·1	12·2	-11	-8	-22·2	-28·75	-33·75
74·75	23·75	54	12·2	33·8	1	12	-11·1	-8·5	-22·5	-29	-33·8
74	23·3	53·6	12	33	0·5	11·75	-11·25	-9	-22·7	-29·2	-34
73·4	23	53	11·6	32	0	11	-11·6	-9·4	-23	-30	-34·4

Table 19. *Pressure: Equivalents of Millibars, Millimetres of Mercury, and Inches of Mercury at 32° F. in Latitude 45°*

Mercury in.	Milli-bars	Mercury mm.	Mercury in.	Milli-bars	Mercury mm.	Mercury in.	Milli-bars	Mercury mm.	Mercury in.	Milli-bars	Mercury mm.	Mercury in.	Milli-bars	Mercury mm.
27·02	915	686·3	27·82	942	706·6	28·62	969	726·8	29·41	996	747·1	30·21	1,023	767·3
27·05	916	687·1	27·85	943	707·3	28·65	970	727·6	29·44	997	747·8	30·24	1,024	768·1
27·08	917	687·8	27·88	944	708·1	28·67	971	728·3	29·47	998	748·6	30·27	1,025	768·8
27·11	918	688·6	27·91	945	708·8	28·70	972	729·1	29·50	999	749·3	30·30	1,026	769·6
27·14	919	689·3	27·94	946	709·6	28·73	973	729·8	29·53	1,000	750·1	30·33	1,027	770·3
27·17	920	690·1	27·97	947	710·3	28·76	974	730·6	29·56	1,001	750·8	30·36	1,028	771·1
27·20	921	690·8	28·00	948	711·1	28·79	975	731·3	29·59	1,002	751·6	30·39	1,029	771·8
27·23	922	691·6	28·03	949	711·8	28·82	976	732·1	29·62	1,003	752·3	30·42	1,030	772·6
27·26	923	692·3	28·05	950	712·6	28·85	977	732·8	29·65	1,004	753·1	30·45	1,031	773·3
27·29	924	693·1	28·08	951	713·3	28·88	978	733·6	29·68	1,005	753·8	30·48	1,032	774·1
27·32	925	693·8	28·11	952	714·1	28·91	979	734·3	29·71	1,006	754·6	30·51	1,033	774·8
27·35	926	694·6	28·14	953	714·8	28·94	980	735·1	29·74	1,007	755·3	30·53	1,034	775·6
27·38	927	695·3	28·17	954	715·6	28·97	981	735·8	29·77	1,008	756·1	30·56	1,035	776·3
27·41	928	696·1	28·20	955	716·3	29·00	982	736·6	29·80	1,009	756·8	30·59	1,036	777·1
27·44	929	696·8	28·23	956	717·1	29·03	983	737·3	29·83	1,010	757·6	30·62	1,037	777·8
27·46	930	697·6	28·26	957	717·8	29·06	984	738·1	29·86	1,011	758·3	30·65	1,038	778·6
27·49	931	698·3	28·29	958	718·6	29·09	985	738·8	29·89	1,012	759·1	30·68	1,039	779·3
27·52	932	699·1	28·32	959	719·3	29·12	986	739·6	29·92	1,013	759·8	30·71	1,040	780·1
27·55	933	699·8	28·35	960	720·1	29·15	987	740·3	29·94	1,014	760·6	30·74	1,041	780·8
27·58	934	700·6	28·38	961	720·8	29·18	988	741·1	29·97	1,015	761·3	30·77	1,042	781·6
27·61	935	701·3	28·41	962	721·6	29·21	989	741·8	30·00	1,016	762·1	30·80	1,043	782·3
27·64	936	702·1	28·44	963	722·3	29·24	990	742·6	30·03	1,017	762·8	30·83	1,044	783·1
27·67	937	702·8	28·47	964	723·1	29·26	991	743·3	30·06	1,018	763·6	30·86	1,045	783·8
27·70	938	703·6	28·50	965	723·8	29·29	992	744·1	30·09	1,019	764·3	30·89	1,046	784·6
27·73	939	704·3	28·53	966	724·6	29·32	993	744·8	30·12	1,020	765·1	30·92	1,047	785·3
27·76	940	705·1	28·56	967	725·3	29·35	994	745·6	30·15	1,021	765·8	30·95	1,048	786·1
27·79	941	705·8	28·59	968	726·1	29·38	995	746·3	30·18	1,022	766·6	30·98	1,049	786·8

Table 20. *Conversion Table for Petroleum Products. Volume per unit weight and weight per unit volume of liquid**

Sp. gravity	Volume per long ton† in				Weight in long tons‡ per			
	Cu.m.§	Imp. gal.	Amer. gal.	Amer. barrels	Cu.m.	Imp. gal.	Amer. gal.	Amer. barrels
0·650	1·57	345	414	9·9	0·638	0·00290	0·00242	0·101
0·700	1·46	320	384	9·2	0·687	0·00312	0·00260	0·109
0·750	1·36	299	359	8·5	0·736	0·00335	0·00279	0·117
0·800	1·27	280	336	8·0	0·786	0·00357	0·00297	0·125
0·850	1·20	264	317	7·5	0·835	0·00379	0·00316	0·133
0·900	1·13	249	299	7·1	0·884	0·00402	0·00335	0·141
0·950	1·07	236	283	6·7	0·933	0·00424	0·00353	0·148
1·000	1·02	224	269	6·4	0·982	0·00447	0·00372	0·156

* The figures in this table are only approximate.
† To obtain volume per metric ton multiply figures in table by 0·98421.
‡ To obtain weights in metric tons multiply figures in table by 1·01605.
§ 1 cu.m. = 10 hectolitres (approximate).

The specific gravity of a product must be known in order to calculate accurately equivalent weights and volumes from the above table. The following table shows how widely the specific gravities of crude oils and commercial petroleum products may vary, and will indicate the degree of error involved in assumption of approximate specific gravity figures.

Product	Specific gravity range
Crude oils	0·800–0·970
Aviation gasolines	0·700–0·780
Motor gasolines	0·710–0·790
Kerosines	0·780–0·840
Gas oils	0·820–0·900

Product	Specific gravity range
Diesel oils	0·820–0·920
Lubricating oils	0·850–0·950
Fuel oils	0·920–0·990
Asphaltic bitumens	1·000–1·100

Thus, if the specific gravity of a crude oil is assumed to be 0·850, a production of 10,000 long tons is equivalent to

7·5 × 10,000 = 75,000 American barrels;

whereas, if its true specific gravity is 0·950, the production is only 67,000 American barrels.

INDEX

For Product Safety Concerns and Information please contact our EU
representative GPSR@taylorandfrancis.com
Taylor & Francis Verlag GmbH, Kaufingerstraße 24, 80331 München, Germany

www.ingramcontent.com/pod-product-compliance
Lightning Source LLC
Chambersburg PA
CBHW070613270326
41926CB00011B/1684